THE ARCHITECTURE OF COMPUTER HARDWARE AND SYSTEMS SOFTWARE

AN INFORMATION TECHNOLOGY APPROACH

Irv Englander

Bentley College

www.wiley.com/college/englander

Acquisitions Editor   *Beth Lang Golub*
Assistant Editor   *Lorraina Raccuia*
Marketing Manager   *Gitti Lindner*
Managing Editor   *Lari Bishop*
Associate Production Manager   *Kelly Tavares*
Production Editor   *Sarah Wolfman-Robichaud*
Illustration Editor   *Jennifer Fisher*
Cover Design   *Jennifer Fisher*

This book was set in 10/12 Minion by Leyh Publishing LLC and printed and bound by Malloy, Inc. The cover was printed by Lehigh Press.

This book is printed on acid free paper.

Screen shots reprinted by permission from Microsoft Corporation.

ISBN: 0-471-07325-3

Printed in the United States of America

10 9 8 7 6 5 4 3 2 1

To four outstanding teachers and great human beings:

With your guidance, inspiration, and patience, you showed me
that everything is possible

Dr. Sidney H. Englander, in memoriam
Mildred K. Englander
my father and mother

Albert L. Daugherty, in memoriam
teacher of science in Cleveland Heights, Ohio
from 1927 to 1970

Edith B. Malin, in memoriam
teacher of English in Cleveland Heights, Ohio
from 1924 to 1958

BRIEF CONTENTS

CONTENTS

■ **CHAPTER 3**   **Data Formats**   54

PART THREE
COMPUTER ARCHITECTURE AND HARDWARE OPERATION   130

■ **CHAPTER 6**   **The Little Man Computer   132**

■ **CHAPTER 7**   **The CPU and Memory   148**

■ **CHAPTER 11**   Modern Computer Systems, Clusters, and Networks   **304**

■ **CHAPTER 12**   **Three System Examples   338**

■ **CHAPTER 15** The Internal Operating System 460

■ SUPPLEMENTARY CHAPTER 1   An Introduction to Digital Computer Logic   648

■ SUPPLEMENTARY CHAPTER 2   Instruction Addressing Modes   660

■ SUPPLEMENTARY CHAPTER 3   Communication Channel Technology   680

PREFACE

I love to read! When I open a new book, in *any* subject, the first thing I want to know is what the book has to offer that makes it worth my while to read it. I would like to try to help you answer that question for the book that you're holding in your hand.

The information systems and technology fields are wonderfully exciting places to be! It seems as though every day brings new developments that alter the ways we create and work with information. Of course, with this excitement comes a challenge. To be a successful player in IS or IT we have to be adaptable and flexible.

Much of the change occurs around computer technology. The computer is, after all, at the foundation of information systems. A deep understanding of computer systems is, therefore, an essential element of success. We must be able to understand each new development, assess its value, and place it in the context of our knowledge of computer systems.

The subject of this book is the architecture of computer systems. Computer architecture is about the structure and operation of digital computers. Computer architecture is concerned with the operational methods of the hardware; with the services provided by operating system software; with the acquisition, processing, storage, and output of data; and with the interaction between computers.

There is a tendency for people in information systems and technology to neglect a study of computer architecture. After all, the technology changes so rapidly—is it really worth trying to understand something that may be out of date by the time I finish this book? There is no question that computer technology has evolved rapidly. Today's personal computer is far more powerful than the mainframe computer of twenty-five years ago, with memory, disk storage capacity, display and multimedia capability, and ease of use that would have been unthinkable just a few years ago.

Interestingly enough, however, as profound as advances in the technology have been, the concepts of computer architecture that really matter have changed only nominally over the last fifty-five years. The new technologies are based on a foundation of architectural concepts that were developed many years ago. The architecture of a modern computer system was developed in the 1940s. The instruction set in a modern personal computer is nearly identical to that of computers built in the 1950s and 1960s. Modern operating system techniques were developed in the 1960s. The graphical user interface is based on a 1960s project. The Internet is more than thirty years old.

So you see that an understanding of computer architecture makes it possible to "ride the wave" of technological change, secure in the feeling that you are equipped to deal with new developments as they occur, and to have fun doing so. When you are done reading this book you will have substantial knowledge about how a computer works and a good understanding of the operating concepts, the hardware, and system software that make up a computer.

You will see the interaction between computers and between data and the computer. Plus, you will have learned lots of jargon that you can show off at parties and job interviews.

This textbook is designed for a wide range of readers, both undergraduate and graduate. The material is specifically directed toward IS and IT majors. There are no explicit prerequisites, although the book assumes that the student is familiar with a personal computer. It also assumes basic programming skills: although there is no programming in the book, program code is occasionally used as an example to clarify an idea, and a knowledge of programming is helpful at understanding instruction set design and program execution concepts. The material in this textbook meets the criteria for IS2002.4, Computer Hardware and System Software Concepts, of the joint IS2002 curriculum. Although the material in this book may be useful as background for other courses, particularly data communications, the course can be placed anywhere in the curriculum.

Most instructors will not cover the entire textbook in a single semester. The organization of the book is designed to allow an instructor to cover the major topic areas in different levels of depth, depending on the experience and needs of the students. On the other hand, it is my intention that this book will serve a student as a useful reference long after the formal course is completed. It is designed for use as a book where a professional can look up the basic concepts that clarify new developments as they occur.

This text is the outgrowth of courses that I have taught to IS majors and minors at Bentley College at both the undergraduate and graduate level for more than twenty years. Student responses to the material and the approach have generally been very enthusiastic. Many students have returned after graduation to tell me that their knowledge in this area has directly contributed to their career development. Along the way, student comments have also been extremely helpful to me in the book's continuing development.

Those familiar with previous editions will notice that the organization of the third edition has been modified somewhat to reflect current technological practices and trends. In particular, computer interconnection concepts are introduced earlier in the book, and there is an increased emphasis on the integration and synergy of the various components of the computer system. Still, the basic philosophy, approach, and coverage remain essentially similar to those of the first edition, reflecting the unchanging nature of the underlying principles.

ORGANIZATION OF THE THIRD EDITION OF THE BOOK

This book seems to have taken on a life of its own. What started as a minor update seems to have blossomed into a new, more substantial revision, with many clarifications and an integrated organization that focuses on the system as a whole. The book is now organized into four parts totaling eighteen chapters, plus three supplementary chapters. The first section serves as an introduction and overview of the role of the computer in information systems; it also provides a brief introduction to each of the components that make up the computer system. Each of the remaining three parts deals with a single architectural aspect of the computer system. Part II discusses the role and representation of data in the computer. Here we consider numbers, text, sound, images, video, and other data forms. Part III presents the hardware architecture and operational concepts. It introduces the components of a computer and shows how they collaborate to execute computer instructions, discusses the nature of a computer instruction set, and explores the interaction between the CPU, memory, and I/O peripheral devices. It also presents the basics of computer interconnectivity, taken from the specific perspective of communication between computers. Part IV discusses the system software, the programs that function to make the resources of the computer system, and other interconnected computer systems and components, accessible to the user and to application programs.

The approach within each group of chapters is layered. Each new layer builds upon the previous material to add depth and understanding to the reader's knowledge. Each topic section consists of a short introduction that places the topic to be discussed into the context of the computer system as a whole and then lays out in detail the organization of the chapters within the section. Each topic area is introduced as gently as possible, using ideas and examples that are already familiar to the student. Successive material is progressive and accumulative. In addition to the numerous examples that are used throughout the text, the hardware and software sections each conclude with substantial case studies that show application of the section material to current examples of importance. Overall, the approach is gentle, progressive, and accumulative. As much as possible, each section is self-contained.

An overview of the organization of each part follows. More details can be found in the introductions to each section.

Part I consists of a single chapter that presents a short overview of computing, placing architectural concepts into the context of information technology. It briefly introduces the components of a computer system and the relationships among the components. The chapter concludes with a short history of computers from the architectural point of view.

Chapters 2 through 5 comprise Part II. Chapter 2 introduces number systems and basic number system operations; it then explores the relationships between numbers in different number bases and the conversion techniques between the different representations. Chapter 3 investigates different types of data formats, including alphanumeric, image, video, and sound formats. It considers the relationship between numerical and character-based representations and briefly introduces various devices and data formats used for data input and output. Chapter 4 studies integer representations and calculations. Chapter 5 does the same for floating point formats.

Part III discusses the hardware architecture and operational aspects of the computer. Chapter 6 begins the study with the introduction of the Little Man Computer, a simple model that provides a surprisingly accurate representation of the CPU and memory. The model is used to develop the concept of an instruction set and to explain the basic principles of the von Neumann architecture. Chapter 7 extends the discussion to a real computer. It introduces the components of the CPU and shows their relationship to the Little Man Computer model. It introduces the bus concept, explains the operation of memory, presents the instruction fetch-execute cycle, and discusses the instruction set. It identifies important classes of instructions and discusses the ways in which instructions can be categorized.

Chapter 8 expands the material in Chapter 7 to consider more advanced features of the CPU and memory. It offers an analysis and comparison of four CPU architectures: CISC, RISC, VLIW, and EPIC. It continues with an introduction to paging, a discussion of techniques for improving memory access, particularly cache memory, and an introduction to current CPU organization, design, and implementation techniques, including pipelining and superscalar processing.

Chapter 9 presents the principles of I/O operation, and Chapter 10 illustrates how I/O is performed in various I/O devices. There is a brief discussion of network communication in the context of I/O concepts. Chapter 11 discusses system integration and system interconnection, focusing on multiprocessing, clusters, and the hardware aspects of network connectivity and high performance systems. Chapter 12 concludes the section with three detailed case studies of important architectures: the Intel x86 family, including the Pentium IV architecture and Itanium extensions, the PowerPC, and the IBM zSystem.

Three supplementary chapters serve as adjuncts to the material in part III. Supplementary Chapter 1 offers an introduction to Boolean algebra, combinatorial logic, and sequential logic for those readers that would like a deeper understanding of the computer in its simplest and most elegant form. Supplementary Chapter 2 considers instruction addressing techniques in depth. Supplementary Chapter 3 discusses communication technology, including the characteristics of different types of communication channels and basic signaling technology.

Part IV is dedicated to a discussion of system software. Chapter 13 provides an overview of the operating system. It explains the different roles played by the operating system and introduces the facilities and services provided. Chapter 14 presents the role of the operating system from the viewpoint of the user of a system. Chapter 15 discusses the operating system as a resource manager, with an in-depth discussion of memory management, scheduling, process control, network services, and other basic operating system services. Chapter 16 discusses the all-important topic of file systems. Chapter 17 provides an introduction to the system development software that is used for the preparation and execution of programs. Chapter 18 concludes Part IV with Windows 2000/XP, UNIX/Linux, and z/OS case studies.

A detailed list of the changes between the second and third editions of the book can be found at the book Web site, www.wiley.com/college/englander.

This book has been a continuing labor of love. My primary goal has been to create and maintain a textbook that explains computer architecture in a way that conveys to you, the reader, the sense of excitement and fun that makes a career in information systems and technology so satisfying. I hope that I have succeeded to some extent.

ADDITIONAL RESOURCES

Additional resources for students and instructors may be found at the textbook Web site, www.wiley.com/college/englander. I can also be reached directly by e-mail at ienglander@bentley.edu.

ACKNOWLEDGMENTS

I've discovered that a major, ongoing textbook project is a formidable task. Many individuals helped me to make the task manageable—and kept me going when, from time to time, I became convinced that textbooks really *do* appear by magic and are *not* written by humans. It is impossible to thank people adequately for all their help and support.

First and foremost, a special thank you to my nearest and dearest friends, Jan Harrington, Wilson Wong, and Ray Brackett. Their continuing backup through three editions has been amazing! I couldn't have asked for a better support team. The champagne is on ice. *Yet* again! Also to the crew at the Café Zin, for getting me started in the morning.

And to my brother and sister-in-law, Jon and Marlene Englander, for their helpful contributions to my work.

My continuing thanks, too, to Stuart Madnick. Your technical inspiration and personal encouragement was invaluable to me. You helped me to believe that this project was actually possible and worthwhile.

Next, I thank the many colleagues at Bentley College who shared their ideas, experiences, and encouragement. Colleagues Wong, Lynn Senne, Jim Linderman, Kay Green, and Peggy Beranek have all offered contributions that have substantially improved the book over three editions. Wong also served as a technical reviewer for the third edition, providing many comments, rewrites, and suggestions for clarification. Ellen Manning, our departmental secretary, went out of her way to make sure things got finished on time.

Thanks to the editors and marketing personnel at John Wiley & Sons and the editors and production people at Leyh Publishing. You hassled me when I needed to be hassled and left me alone when I needed to be left alone. Incredible intuition, that! I consider myself fortunate to have worked with such wonderful people. Particular thanks to Beth Golub, Lorraina Raccuia, Ailsa Manny, Gitti Lindner, Lisa Gee, Lari Bishop, Jennifer Fisher, and Benjamin Reece. I'd work with you people again in a minute!

I would like to acknowledge the reviewers who gave of their time and effort to assure that this book was as good as it could be: Dr. Stu Westin, The University of Rhode Island; Alan Pinck, Algonquin College; Mark Jacobi, Programme Director for Undergrad Computing at Sheffield Hallam University; Dr. Dave Protheroe, South Bank University, London; Julius ilinskas, Kaunas University of Technology; Anthony Richardson; Renee A. Weather; Jack Claff. Your comments, suggestions, and constructive criticism made a real difference in the quality of the book. Thank you.

Many colleagues offered corrections to previous editions that have had important impact on the quality of the current edition. To each and everyone, your assistance in eliminating errors has been much appreciated. Among these, I especially wish to acknowledge David Feinstein and his crew at the University of South Alabama, Gordon Grimsey of AIT in Auckland, New Zealand, and Stu Westin of University of Rhode Island for efforts well above and beyond the call of duty. Stu has also generously made his excellent Little Man Simulator publicly available, for which I am truly grateful. Thanks for everything, Stu.

Numerous students, too many to name you all, also offered corrections, made suggestions, and provided ideas. Please accept my deepest appreciation and thanks.

I hope that I have not forgotten anyone. If I have, I apologize.

I have strived to make this book as technically accurate as is humanly possible. Nonetheless, I know that errors have a way of creeping in when one least expects them. I would greatly appreciate hearing from readers who find errors that need correction. Your comments and suggestions about the book are also welcome.

ABOUT THE AUTHOR

Dr. Irv Englander has been involved in many different aspects of the computing field for more than forty years. He has designed logic circuits, developed integrated circuits, developed computer architectures, designed computer-controlled systems, designed operating systems, developed application software, created the initial system design for a large water monitoring system, performed software auditing and verification of critical control software, and developed and specified hardware components and application software as a consultant for business systems large and small.

As an educator he has contributed papers and given workshops on end-user computing, e-commerce, and on computer architecture education in the IS curriculum. He was an invited contributor and reviewer for the IS-97 information systems curriculum. He is actively involved in the application of new technology to information systems.

Dr. Englander has a Ph.D. from MIT in Computer Science. His doctoral thesis was based on the design of a large image processing software laboratory. At MIT he won the Supervised Investors Award for outstanding teaching. He holds the rank of Professor of Computer Information Systems at Bentley College, where he has taught full-time for nearly twenty-five years.

THE ARCHITECTURE OF COMPUTER HARDWARE AND SYSTEMS SOFTWARE

PART ONE

A computer-based information system is made up of a number of different elements:

- The *data* element. Data is the fundamental representation of facts and observations. Data is processed by a computer system to provide the information that is the very reason for the computer's existence. As you will see, data can take on a number of different forms.

- The *hardware* element. Computer hardware processes the data by executing instructions, storing data, and moving data and information between the various input and output devices that make the system and the information accessible to the users.

- The *software* element. Software consists of the system and application programs that define the instructions that are executed by the hardware. The software determines the work to be performed and controls operation of the system.

- The *communication* element. Modern computer information systems depend on the ability to share processing operations and data among different computers and users, located both locally and remotely. Data communication provides this capability.

The combination of hardware, software, communication, and data make up the *architecture* of a computer system. The architecture of computer systems is remarkably similar whether the system is a personal computer that sits on your lap while you work

AN OVERVIEW OF COMPUTER SYSTEMS

or a large mainframe system that is never actually seen by the hundreds of users who access it every day.

Even more remarkably, the basic architecture of computer systems has changed surprisingly little over the last fifty-five years. The latest IBM mainframe computer executes essentially the same instruction set as the mainframe computer of 1965. The basic communication techniques used in today's systems were developed in the 1970s. As new as it might seem, the Internet celebrated its thirtieth anniversary in 2000. All of this is surprising considering the growth of computing, the rapid change of technology, and the increased performance, functionality, and ease of use of today's systems. This makes the study of computer architecture extremely valuable as a foundation upon which to understand new developments in computing as they occur.

Computer system architecture is the subject of this textbook. Each element of the system is addressed in its own section of the text, always with an eye to the system as a whole.

Part I is made up of a single chapter that presents an overview of the computer system. The chapter addresses a number of issues, including

- The ways in which a knowledge of computer architecture enhances our abilities as computer users and professionals
- The input-output-process model of computing
- The basic components of a computer system

Chapter 1 concludes with a brief architectural history of the computer.

CHAPTER 1

COMPUTER SYSTEMS

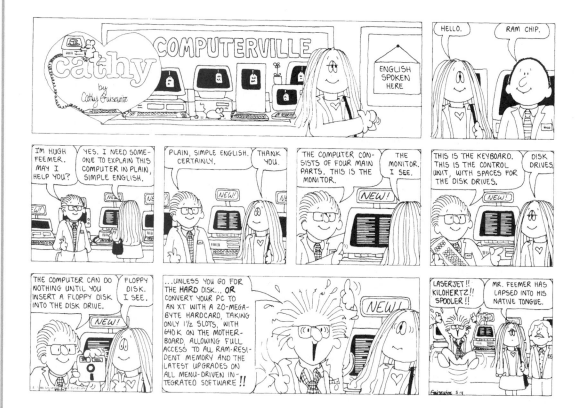

1.0 INTRODUCTION

What do the insides of a computer "look like," and why do we care?

As users, we do not have to know the answer to this question, any more than we have to understand the workings of a car engine in order to drive the car.

We can run standard software packages without understanding exactly how they work; we can program a computer in a high-level language without understanding how the machine executes the individual instructions; we can create Web pages without understanding how the Web browser gets its pages from a Web server or how the Web server creates those pages; we can purchase a computer system from a salesperson without understanding the specifications of the system.

And yet, there is something missing. Perhaps the package doesn't do exactly what we want, and we don't understand the machine well enough to risk fooling around with the package's options. Perhaps if we understood the system we might have written the program to be faster and more efficient. Perhaps we could create Web pages that load faster and work better. Perhaps the salesperson did not sell us the optimum system for our job. Or perhaps it's nothing more than a sense of excitement that's missing. But that's important, too!

The jargon of computers has become a part of the English language. You can open any daily newspaper and find references to "1GB DDRAM" or "XGA TFT display" or "512K level 2 cache" or "56K V.90 modem" in articles and advertisements. (In a way, it's scary!) The ad in Figure 1.1 is typical.

You'll notice that this computer features a 2.7 gigahertz (GHz) Pentium 4 CPU, 1 GB of RAM memory, and an 120 GB hard drive, among other things. But how good a system is this? Are these features important to the user? Is this the right combination of features that you need in your computer to have the computer perform the work that you wish to get done? Is a 2.7 GHz Pentium 4 the best choice of a CPU? Perhaps we are paying too much for the performance that we need. Or maybe we need more. What does the presence of a Firewire port imply in the context of a long-term investment of computers for your organization? Is DVD-RAM the most useful format for your work? What other information about this system would allow you to make a more informed decision?

Some of the expressions used in these articles and ads are obvious from the context. Other references may be more obscure. Presumably, everyone today knows what a "monitor" is. But how many people know what the terms "cache memory" or "multi-tasking" or "PCI bus" mean or understand what their importance is? Yet all these expressions have appeared recently in daily newspaper advertisements with the assumption that people would understand the meaning of the ad.

Perhaps you are a student studying to become a computer professional, or perhaps you are simply a user wanting a deeper understanding of what the computer is all about. In either case, you will probably be interacting with computers for the rest

5

FIGURE 1.1

A Typical Computer Ad

FASTCAT™ Desktop

Top Performance, Great Value!

◊ Intel© 2.7 GHz Pentium© 4 Processor
◊ 1 GB up to 2 GB DDRAM
◊ 120 GB Ultra ATA 7200 RPM HD 16 MB cache
◊ 10/100 PCI Ethernet card
◊ 64 MB GeForce 4x AGP Video
◊ DVD-ROM/RAM + CD-R/RW
◊ 2 USB-2, 1IEEE-1394 Firewire©
◊ 17" Non-Interlaced Full Flat Screen Monitor
   .26dp (1024 x 768) Add $300 for
   17" TFT LCD (1280 x 1024)

ONLY $999

of your life. It's nice (as well as useful) to know something about the tools of the trade. More important, understanding the computer system's operations has an immediate benefit: it will allow you to use the machine more effectively.

As a user, you will be aware of the capabilities, strengths, and limitations of the computer system. You will have a better understanding of the commands that you use. You will understand what is taking place during the operation of the programs that you use. You will be able to make informed decisions about your computer equipment and application programs. You will understand more clearly what an operating system is, and how to use it effectively and to your advantage. You will know when it is preferable to do a job manually, and when the computer should be used. You will understand the most efficient way to "go online," and what benefits might be gained from a home network. You will improve your ability to communicate with system analysts, programmers, and other computer specialists.

As a programmer, it will allow you to write better programs. You will be able to use the characteristics of the machine to make your programs operate more effectively. For example, choosing the appropriate data type for a variable can result in significantly faster performance. Soon you will know why this is so, and how to make the appropriate choices.

Many computers perform integer calculations incorrectly if the integers exceed a certain size, but they do not warn the user of the error. You will learn how this can occur, and what can be done to assure that your programs generate correct results.

You will discover that some computers will process nested loops much more quickly if the index variables are reversed. A rather surprising idea, perhaps, and you'll understand why this is true.

You will understand why programs written in a compiled language like C++ usually run much faster than those written in interpreted program languages like BASIC or scripting languages like Perl or JavaScript.

As a system analyst, you will be expected to specify computer systems for purchase, for yourself and for your organization. You would like to purchase the computer that best meets the needs of the application. You must be able to read and understand the technical specifications in order to compare different alternatives and to match the system to the users' needs. This book will teach you what you need to know to specify and purchase a system intelligently. You'll know the differences between various CPU technologies and the advantages and disadvantages of each. You will learn what peripheral hardware is appropriate for your organization's files and the trade-offs between different file system formats, what is required to build an intranet, and what the speed and size limitations of a particular system are. You'll be able to compare the features of Windows and UNIX knowledgeably and decide which ones are important to you. You'll learn to understand the jargon used by computer salespeople and judge the validity of their sales claims.

You'll be in a better position to determine whether your computer is the right system for a particular job, or whether a different system would be more appropriate. Perhaps a workstation with an Alpha CPU is better suited to your application than a personal computer with a Pentium 4 chip. You'll be able to assist management in making intelligent decisions about system strategy: should the company adopt a large mainframe/"thin client" system approach for its Web servers or would a system consisting of off-the-shelf blade servers provide better performance at lower cost? You'll be better prepared to analyze the best way to provide appropriate facilities to meet the needs of your users. In an era of fast-changing technology, you'll be more able to differentiate between simple technological obsolescence that does not affect your work significantly and major advances that suggest a real need to replace older equipment.

As a system administrator or manager, your job is to maximize the availability and efficiency of your systems. You will need to understand the reports generated by your systems and be able to use the information in those reports to make changes in the systems that will optimize system performance. You will need to know when additional resources are required, and be able to specify appropriate choices. You will need to specify and configure operating system parameters, set up file systems, manage system and user PC upgrades in a fast-changing environment, provide and assure the robustness of system security, and perform many other system management tasks. The configuration of large systems can be very challenging. This text will give you an understanding of operating system tools that is essential to the effective management of systems.

As a Web services designer, you will be able to make intelligent decisions to optimize your Web system configurations, page designs, data formatting and scripting language choices, and operating systems to optimize customer accessibility to your Web services.

In brief, when you complete this book, you will understand what computer hardware and software are and how programs and data interact with the computer system. You will understand the computer hardware, software, and communication components that are required to make up a computer system and what the role of each component in the system is.

You will have a better understanding of what is happening inside the computer when you interact with the computer as a user. You will be able to write programs that are more efficient. You will be able to understand the function of the different components of the computer system and to specify the computer system you need in a meaningful way. You will understand the options that you have as a system administrator or Web services designer.

In an era in which technology changes extremely rapidly, the architecture of the computer rests on a solid foundation that has changed only slightly and gradually over the last sixty years. Understanding the foundations of computer architecture makes it possible to flow with the technological change and to understand these changes in the context of the improvements that they make and the needs that they meet. In fact, interviews with former students and with IT executives and other IT professionals clearly indicate that a deep understanding of the basic concepts presented here is fundamental to long-term survival and growth in the field of information technology and IT management.

This type of understanding is at the very foundation of being a competent and successful system analyst, system administrator, or programmer. It may not be necessary to understand the workings of an automobile engine in order to drive a car, but you can bet that a top-notch race car driver knows his or her engine thoroughly and can use it to win races. Like the professional race car driver, it is our intention to help you to use your computer engine effectively to succeed in using your computer in a winning way.

…These are the goals of this book. So let's get started!

1.1 THE USER'S POINT OF VIEW

Before we begin our detailed study of the architecture of the computer system, let us briefly review some of the fundamental principles that guide computer system design and operation.

From the user's point of view, the purpose of the computer, obviously, is to perform some useful work, whether that work be word processing, retrieval and manipulation of data, simple bookkeeping, solving a difficult mathematical problem, Web browsing, or the graphical display and internal calculation associated with a video game or desktop presentation program.

Consider, for example, a simple online credit card purchasing system for a department store. When a customer makes a purchase, the clerk keys or scans the transaction into a terminal that is used as input to the department store computer. The computer communicates with a bank computer that checks the customer's credit and okays the transaction. It prints a receipt at the terminal for the customer to sign and records the transaction in the customer's account.

Customer accounts are stored permanently on one or more hard disks that are part of the computer system. The program that controls these transactions is also stored on hard disk. The program searches for the matching customer account and reads it into memory, checks the credit, updates the account to reflect the new transactions, and returns the updated account to hard disk storage.

During processing, the processor compares the input data with the customer accounts and with built-in rules and makes decisions so that obvious errors are detected. As an example, a miscoded account number in a transaction will result in a nonmatch with the master customer account file. A customer who has exceeded his or her credit limit will be denied credit. These errors can be printed on the terminal screen so that corrections can be made. At the end of the day, the program also prints out various reports and summaries that are needed by the store.

Figure 1.2 is a representative simplified flow diagram for the credit card update program. The primary processing operations that take place include searching for data, merging of data, and simple calculation. On this system, input is provided via terminal keyboard. Output occurs on the screen and on a printer. Hard disks provide long-term storage.

A seemingly very different operation occurs when you sit at your personal computer working with a word processor. But is it really that different? The text file is probably stored on either a floppy disk or a hard disk. The word processor program itself is also stored on

FIGURE 1.2

A Simplified Credit Card Transaction

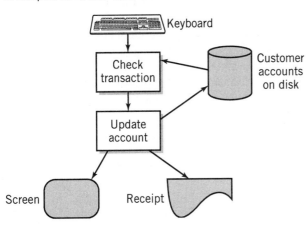

hard disk. The text file being processed is initially loaded into the main memory of the computer as data, just as the customer's credit file was in the previous example.

The word processor accepts commands and input from the mouse and keyboard. As an example of a word processing operation, consider the operation to insert new text. The word processor searches for the correct location in which to perform the insert operation. The insert operation consists of merging the new text input from the keyboard with the text already stored in memory. Output text is filed on the disk, and probably printed as output on the printer. Word processors also perform comparisons and make decisions, just as the credit card program does.

The Input-Process-Output Model

The critical idea here is that regardless of the type of work to be performed, the work of a computer can be characterized by an **input-process-output model (IPO)**; that is, a program receives input from a disk file, mouse, keyboard, or some other input device, performs some processing on the input, and produces output to a disk file, a printer, a video screen, or some other output device. A diagram that describes virtually any computer process is shown in Figure 1.3. The operations performed during processing are limited to simple calculations, sorting, merging, comparisons, simple decisions, and a few other operations. Of course, many of these operations are repetitive, so the ability to repeat an operation and test for a completion condition must be built into the process. The input-process-output model should be familiar to you from your courses in programming language.

FIGURE 1.3

A Computer Process

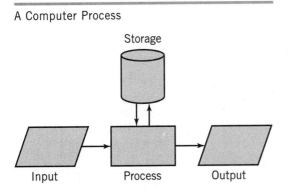

Modern programming technique often adopts an alternative paradigm in which various aspects of a problem are modeled as objects. Objects are entities that are described by their properties and the actions that they can perform. The properties take the form of data; the actions are procedures that are performed on the data. The object model reshapes the input-process-output model, but does not invalidate it. Internal to the object, the same processing must take place. If the previous example is represented by a credit card transaction object, for example, the customer account is still stored on disk, the transaction must still be entered, the same checking takes place, and the same output is produced.

Figure 1.4 summarizes the basic operations that are performed during computer data processing. These operations, in turn, can be reduced to the primitive operations that are also familiar to you from your understanding of programming languages. The primitive processing operations common to high-level programming languages are shown in Figure 1.5.

Although we have not explicitly mentioned storage, you should note that the ability to store programs and data on a temporary, short-term, or long-term basis is fundamental to the system. Computer systems provide a hierarchy of storage for this purpose, including memory for fast short-term access and secondary storage in the form of hard disks, tape, CD-ROM, and other devices for long-term storage.

1.2 COMPONENTS OF THE COMPUTER SYSTEM

There are three components required for the implementation of a computerized input-processing-output model:

1. The computer hardware, which provides the physical mechanisms to input and output data, for manipulating data, and for electronically controlling the various input, output, and storage components.

2. The software, both application and system, which provides instructions that tell the hardware exactly what tasks are to be performed and in what order.

FIGURE 1.4

Basic Data Processing Operations

- Input/output
- Basic arithmetic and logical calculations
- Data transformation or translation (e.g., program compilation, foreign language translation, file updating)
- Data sorting
- Searching for data matches
- Data storage and retrieval
- Data movement (e.g., movement of text or file data to make room for insertion of additional data)

FIGURE 1.5

Basic High-Level Language Constructs

- Input/output (including file storage and retrieval)
- Arithmetic and logical assignment statements
- True/false decision branching (IF-THEN-ELSE or IF-GOTO)
- Loops and/or unconditional branching (WHILE-DO, REPEAT-UNTIL, FOR, GOTO)

3. The data that is being manipulated. This data may be numeric, it may be alphanumeric, it may be graphic, or it may take some other form, but in all cases it must be representable in a form that the computer can manipulate.

In modern systems, input entry, output display, and storage of the data and software used for processing often take place at a location different from the computer where the actual processing occurs. In many installations, actual processing is distributed among computer systems, with particular results passed to the individual systems that require them. Therefore, we must also consider a fourth component:

4. The communication component, which consists of hardware and software that transport programs and data between interconnected computer systems.

The hardware and system software components make up the architecture of the computer system. The communication component connects individual computer systems together. The data component, and also the application software, while fundamental to the operation of the computer system, are supplied to the computer system by the user, rather than being a part of the architecture of the system itself.

The Hardware Component

The most visible part of the computer system is obviously the hardware that makes up the system. Consider the computer system upon which you write and execute your programs. You use a keyboard and mouse to provide input of your program text and data, as well as for commands to the computer. A display screen is commonly used to observe **output.** A printer is frequently available as an alternative output to the screen. These are all physical components.

Calculations and other operations in your program are performed by a **central processing unit (CPU)** inside the computer. **Memory** is provided to hold your programs and data while processing is taking place. Other input and output devices, such as disk and tape, are used to provide long-term storage of your program and data files. Data and programs are transferred between the various input/output devices and memory for the CPU to use.

The CPU, memory, and all the input, output, and storage devices form the **hardware** part of a computer system. The hardware forms the tangible part of the system. It is physical—you can touch it, which is what the word "tangible" means. A typical hardware block diagram for a computer is seen in Figure 1.6. In addition to the input and output devices shown in this diagram, Figure 1.7 lists some other input and output devices that are frequently seen as part of computer systems. The diagram in Figure 1.6 actually applies equally well to large mainframe computers and small personal computers. Large and small computers differ primarily in speed, capacity, and the selection of peripheral devices provided. The basic hardware components and design are very similar.

Conceptually, the CPU itself may be viewed as a composition of three primary subunits:

1. The **arithmetic/logic unit,** or **ALU,** where arithmetic and Boolean logical calculations are performed.
2. The **control unit,** or **CU,** which controls the processing of instructions and the movement of internal CPU data from one part of the CPU to another.
3. The **interface unit,** which moves program instructions and data between the CPU and other hardware components.

FIGURE 1.6

A Typical Personal Computer System

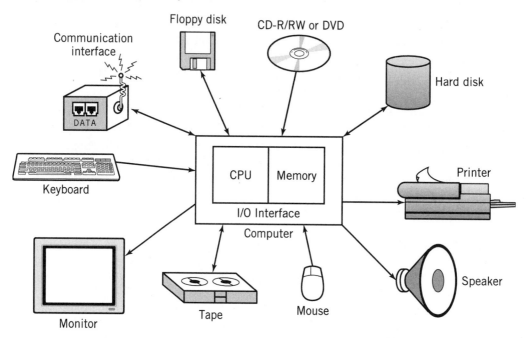

FIGURE 1.7

Other Common Input/Output Devices

- Bar code scanners
- Optical character recognition scanners
- Image scanners
- Video and audio capture devices
- Electronic instrumentation devices
- Light pens
- Graphics tablets
- Plotters

(In modern CPUs, the actual organization is usually modified somewhat to achieve higher performance. More about that later, in Chapter 8.)

The interface unit interconnects the CPU with memory and also with the various I/O modules. It can also be used to connect multiple CPUs together. In many computer systems, a bus interconnects the CPU, memory, and all of the I/O components. A **bus** is simply a bundle of wires that carry signals and power between different components. In other systems, the I/O modules are connected to the CPU through one or more separate processors known as **channels.**

The main memory, often known as primary storage, working storage, or **RAM** (for **r**andom **a**ccess **m**emory), holds programs and data for access by the CPU. **Primary storage** is made up of a large number of cells, each numbered and individually addressable. Each cell holds a single binary number representing data or an instruction. The basic size of the cell in most current computers is 8 bits, known as a **byte** of memory. Eight bits of memory can only hold 256 different patterns, so neighboring cells in memory are nearly always combined to form groupings with a larger number of bits. In many systems, for example, 4 bytes of memory combine to form a **word.**

The amount of primary storage determines the maximum number of instructions and data words that can be loaded at one time. For example, a computer with 524,288 bytes (512 K or 1/2 MB)[1] of memory would not be able to execute a program that requires 790,000 bytes for its instructions and data unless some means is provided within the computer to load the program in sections as each section of the program is needed.

The amount of primary storage provided in a typical computer has increased rapidly as computer technology improves. Whereas 64K bytes of memory was considered a large amount of memory in 1980, most personal computers today have 256 megabytes (MB) of memory or more. Large computers may provide several gigabytes of primary storage. There are programs on the market that require hundreds of megabytes of memory to execute. Increased amounts of memory have allowed the design of very sophisticated programs that would not have been possible just a few years ago.

The same is true for secondary storage. Even small personal computers provide hard disks with storage measured in tens or hundreds of gigabytes. The storage of images and video, in particular, requires tremendous amounts of storage capacity. It is not uncommon to see arrays of hard disks on large computers, providing trillions of bytes of long-term storage.

The instructions that form a particular program are stored within the primary storage, then brought into the central processing unit and executed. Conceptually, instructions are brought in and executed one at a time, although modern systems overlap the execution of instructions to some extent. Instructions must be in primary storage in order to be executed. The control unit interprets each instruction and determines the appropriate course of action.

Each instruction is designed to perform a simple task. Instructions exist to perform basic arithmetic, to move data from one place in the computer to another, to perform I/O, and to accomplish many other tasks. As you are already aware, it is necessary to translate high-level language programs into the language of the machine for execution of the program to take place. It may require tens or even hundreds of individual machine instructions to form the machine language equivalent of a single high-level language statement. Program instructions are normally executed sequentially, unless an instruction itself tells the computer to change the order of processing. The instruction set used with a particular CPU is part of the design of the CPU and cannot normally be executed on a different type of CPU unless the different CPU was designed to be instruction set compatible. However, as you shall see, most instruction sets perform similar types of operations.

The data that is manipulated by these instructions is also stored in memory while being processed. The idea that the program instructions and data are both stored in memory while being processed is known as the **stored program concept.** This important concept is attributed primarily to John von Neumann, a famous computer scientist. It forms the basis for the computer architecture that is standard to nearly every existing computer.

The Software Component

In addition to the hardware requirement, your computer system also requires **software.** Software consists of the programs that tell the computer what to do. To do useful work, your system must execute instructions from some program.

---

[1] 1K = 1024 bytes. Thus, 512 K = 512 × 1024 or 524,288 bytes.

There are two major categories of software: system software and application software. System software helps you to manage your files, to load and execute programs, and to accept your commands from the mouse and keyboard. The system software programs that manage the computer are collectively known as an **operating system,** and differ from the application programs, such as Microsoft Word, or Netscape, or the programs that you write, that you normally run to get your work done. Windows and Linux are the best known examples of an operating system. Others include Unix, Mac OS X, Sun Solaris, and IBM z/OS.

The operating system is an essential part of the computer system. Like the hardware, it is made up of many components. A simplified representation of an operating system is shown in Figure 1.8. The most obvious element is the user interface that allows you to execute programs, enter commands, and manipulate files. The user interface accepts input from a keyboard and, in most modern systems, a mouse or other pointing device. The user interface also does output presentation on the display. On some systems, the output display might be simple text, but more likely the display includes a windowing system, with various gadgets for manipulating the windows.

The **application program interface,** or **API,** acts as an interface for application programs and utilities to access the internal services provided by the operating system. These include file services, I/O services, data communication services, user interface services, program execution services, and more.[2]

Many of the internal services are provided by the kernel module. The remaining services are provided by other modules that are controlled by the kernel. The kernel manages memory by locating and allocating space to programs that need it, schedules time for each application to execute, provides communication between programs that are being executed, manages and arranges services and resources that are provided by other modules, and provides security.

The file management system allocates and manages secondary storage space and translates file requests from their name-based form into specific I/O requests. The actual storage and retrieval of the files is performed by the I/O drivers that comprise the I/O component. Each I/O driver controls one or more hardware devices of similar type.

The network module controls interactions between the computer system and the network(s) to which it is attached.

The operating system software is nearly always stored on a hard disk, but on a few systems the operating system is actually provided as a network service when the system is turned on. In either case, the bootstrap or IPL (Initial Program Load) program in the operating system is stored within the computer using a type of memory known as **ROM,** or **Read Only Memory.** The bootstrap program provides the tools to test the system and to load the remainder of the

FIGURE 1.8

Simplified Operating System Block Diagram

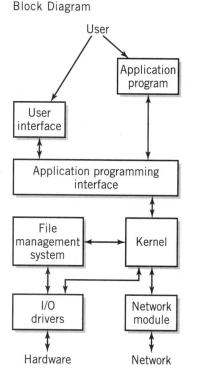

---

[2] The same term (API) is also sometimes used to describe the services provided by one application to another.

operating system from the disk or network. Although the physical medium where the software is stored can be touched, the software itself is considered intangible.

Together, the hardware and system software provide a working computer system environment. Application software, communication support, and user data complete the picture.

As an aside, although we all have an intuitive feel for the difference between hardware and software, it is useful to provide a simple analogy to clarify the difference. Like the computer, your stereo system can also be considered a combination of hardware and software. Again, the hardware is the tangible part of the system: your receiver (equivalent to the CPU) and speakers, record player, tape deck, and so on (all I/O devices). The software is the music that you listen to. Note that, like computer software, the music is actually stored on hardware media (disks and tape cassettes), but the music itself is intangible.

It is interesting that, with the proliferation of computers, the music recording industry has actually adopted the word "software" to refer to DVDs, CDs, audio cassette tapes, and video cassettes.

The Communication Component

Most modern computers do not operate alone. Instead, they are tied to other computers directly, by modem, or through a network. The computers may be located physically close to each other, or they may be separated, even by thousands of miles. To work together, computers must have means to communicate with each other. The communication component requires both hardware and software to achieve this goal. Additional hardware components physically connect computers together into multiprocessing systems, or clusters, or networks, or, via telephone, satellite, or microwave, to computers at other remote locations. A **communication channel** provides the connection between computers. The channel may be a wire cable, a fiber optic cable, a telephone line, or a wireless technology, such as infrared light, cellular phone, or radio. Special I/O hardware, consisting of a **modem** or **network interface card** (**NIC**) within the computer, serves as an interface between the computer and the communication channel. There may be additional hardware within the channel itself.

The communication component also requires additional software within the operating system of each computer to make it possible for each computer to understand what the other computers that they are connected with are saying. This software establishes the connections, controls the flow of data, and directs the data to the proper applications for use.

The Computer System

Our general description of the computer is valid for all general-purpose computer systems, regardless of brand name or size. In more general terms, every computer system consists of a CPU, or central processing unit, where all the processing takes place; memory to hold the programs and data while they are being processed; and some form of input and output, usually one or more keyboards and cathode ray tube (CRT) monitors plus one or more forms of long-term storage, usually disks and tapes. Sometimes more than one CPU is provided within the computer system. A single CPU can process only one instruction at a time; the use of multiple CPUs can increase processing speed by allowing instructions that do not affect each other to be executed in parallel.

The validity of our general description is true regardless of how complex or simple the computer system may seem.

As a specific example, the large zSeries IBM mainframe shown in Figure 1.9 can provide complex Web services to thousands of users at a time. IBM mainframes can have dozens of CPUs working together, with up to 64 billion bytes of primary storage. They are capable of executing instructions at a rate of tens of billions of instructions per second! The powerful z/OS operating system can keep track of hundreds or thousands of simultaneous users and divides the time among them to satisfy their differing requirements. Even in its smallest configuration, the z900 Model 216 system, which is the largest current model at this writing, provides 10 GB of memory and processes instructions at the rate of more than a billion instructions per second.

In addition to the CPU, there are many, large I/O devices—including tape drives and high-speed printers—and disks that store many billions or trillions of characters.

In contrast, the notebook PC shown in Figure 1.10 is designed for personal use. Everything is self-contained in one package. This system only has 128 MB of primary RAM storage and operates at a rate of around 200 MIPS. The built-in hard drive holds 30 GB. The entire system, complete with a color screen and battery, weighs less than seven pounds.

Although these two systems seem very different, the difference is actually one of magnitude, not of concept. The large system operates much faster, can support much more memory, and handles more input and output much faster. It has operating system software that allows many users to share this larger resource.

Nonetheless, the fundamental system architecture is remarkably similar in both cases. Even the actual processing performed by the CPU is similar. In fact, today's CPU operates in the same fundamental way as its CPU counterpart of fifty years ago, even though the construction is very different.

Since computers all operate so similarly, regardless of size or type, it is not difficult today to transfer data between these different systems, allowing each system to do part of the processing for higher overall efficiency. This concept is known as **distributed computing.** The fact that

FIGURE 1.9

IBM Mainframe System

FIGURE 1.10

A Notebook Computer

different types of computers can work together, share files, and communicate successfully is known as **open computing.** Communication technology fulfills the requirements that make open and distributed computing possible.

Computers are sometimes divided into categories: mainframe computers, minicomputers, workstations, and personal computers, but these categories are less significant than they once were. The capability of today's personal computer far exceeds the capabilities of a mainframe computer of just a few years ago. The HP Alpha computer is an example of a workstation that is frequently used as though it were a minicomputer, or even a mainframe. Rather than attempting to categorize a particular computer, it is usually more productive to describe its capabilities in comparison to other systems being discussed or considered.

1.3 STANDARDS AND PROTOCOLS

Except for special applications, most computers perform their operations under common sets of ground rules that make it possible for each hardware or software computer unit to understand what other computer units that they are connected with are saying. The ground rules of communication are known as **protocols.** Protocols exist for communications between computers, for the communications between various I/O devices and a computer, and for communications between many software programs. International **standards** are often created to ensure that the protocols are universally compatible. As an example, HTTP, the HyperText Transmission Protocol, guides communication between Web servers and Web browsers on the Internet. The movement of data through the Internet is controlled by a suite of protocols called TCP/IP, (Transmission Control Protocol/Internet Protocol). CD-ROMs communicate with a computer CPU using a less well-known protocol called ATAPI. There are thousands of such protocols.

In addition to protocols, there are many other standards that govern various aspects of computer operation. Computer language standards, such as Java and SQL, allow programs written on one type of computer to execute properly and consistently on another, and also make it possible for programmers to work together to create and maintain programs. Similarly, data format and data presentation standards, such as the GIF and JPEG image format standard, the Unicode text format standard, and the HTML Web presentation standard allow different systems to manipulate and display data in a consistent manner.

Standards can arise in many different ways. Many standards occur naturally: a proprietary data format belonging to a single vendor becomes a de facto standard due to the popularity of the product. The **PostScript** print description language is an example of such a standard. The format was designed by Adobe Corporation to provide a way of communicating high-quality printed output between computers and printers. Other standards are created because of a perceived need in an area where no standard exists. Often a committee will form to investigate the requirements and create the standard. The **MPEG-2** standard, which sets a standard for the transmission and processing of digital video images, occurred in this way. The committee that designed the standard, made up primarily of motion picture engineers and video researchers, continues to develop the standard as improved techniques evolve. The **JPEG** photographic standard and **MP3** sound standard were also developed formally.

Similarly, each version of HTTP has been formalized after many years of discussion by parties interested in Web communication. A non-standard protocol is limited in use to its supporters and may or may not become a standard, depending on its general acceptance. New protocols are proposed and created and standardized as the need arises.

Satellite telecasting, near-universal telephone communication, wireless communications, and the Internet all demonstrate powerful and useful technologies made possible by protocols and standards. Indeed, the Internet is a measure of the success to which protocols that govern intercommunication between computer hardware and software have been standardized throughout the world. Discussions of various protocols and standards will occur regularly throughout this book.

1.4 OVERVIEW OF THIS BOOK

The focus of this book is upon the internal architecture and organization of the computer. Technically, there is a slight difference in definition between the terms "computer architecture" and "computer organization." In this book we will usually not attempt to differentiate these terms and will use them interchangeably.

In this book, we will be concerned with all three components of a computer system, hardware, software, and data, and the interactions between each component.

We will look at the different forms the input data may take, and we will consider the translation processes required to convert data into forms that the computer hardware and software can process. You will see how the various data types that are familiar to you from programming languages are stored and manipulated inside the computer. You'll learn the many different ways in which math calculations can be performed, and the advantages and disadvantages of each. You will see the difference between a number and the alphanumeric representation of a number, and why that difference can be critical in whether a program works or not. You will be able to relate the size of a word processing text to the storage capability of the computer's disk.

We will take a detailed look at the various components of the hardware and how they fit together. You will learn how the CPU works, how different I/O devices work, and even how text and graphics manage to appear, seemingly by magic, on the CRT screen. You will learn what makes some computers faster and more powerful than others, and what that means. You will learn about different ways of connecting I/O devices to the computer and see why you get a fast response from some devices, a slow response from others. You'll learn the difference between a serial port, a USB port, and a parallel port. We'll even tell you what "no wait states" means.

Most important, you will have the opportunity to see what a simple, program-obedient machine the computer really is. You will learn about the limitations of a computer. We all tend to think of the computer as a resource of infinite capacity, speed, and perhaps even intelligence, but of course that's not true. We will consider how these limitations affect your work as a user, and as a means of specifying a system that will your meet your needs and requirements.

The remainder of this book is divided into four major sections, consisting of discussions of number systems and the representation of data in the computer, the hardware that makes up the computer, the networks that interconnect computers, and the software that the computer uses. Although the communication section consists of only a single chapter, there is additional communication material integrated into the hardware and software sections, as well. There are also two supplementary chapters covering topics that are somewhat outside the scope of the text, but important and interesting nonetheless. The first supplementary chapter introduces the fundamental logic that makes up a computer. The second supplementary chapter provides an introduction to the technology of a communication channel.

Additional related topics of current interest may also be found on the book's Web site, www.wiley.com/college/englander. The Web site also contains numerous links to reference materials, both general to computing, as well as specific to individual topics discussed within the book.

1.5 A BRIEF ARCHITECTURAL HISTORY OF THE COMPUTER

It is not possible, nor particularly useful, to identify the date of the "invention" of the computer. Indeed it has always been the aspiration of humankind to create devices that would simplify people's work. Thus, it is not surprising that people were envisioning mechanical devices to simplify the jobs of routine data processing and calculation even in ancient times. Instead, this discussion covers just a few of the major developments related to computer architecture.

In this context, one could consider the abacus, already in use as early as 500 B.C. by the ancient Greeks and Romans, to be an early predecessor of the computer. Certainly, the abacus was capable of performing calculations and storing data. Actually, if one were to build a binary numbered abacus, its calculations would very closely resemble those of the computer.

The abacus remained in common use until the 1500s and, in fact, is still considered an effective calculating tool in some cultures today. In the late 1500s, though, European inventors again began to put their minds to the problem of automatic calculation. Blaise Pascal, a noted French mathematician of the 1600s, invented a calculating machine in 1642 at the age of nineteen, although he was never able to construct the machine.

In 1801, Joseph Marie Jacquard invented a loom that used punched cards to control the patterns woven into cloth. The program provided by the punched cards controlled rods that raised and lowered different threads in the correct sequence to print a particular pattern. This is the first documented application of the use of punched cards to hold a program for the use of a semi-automated, programmable machine.

Charles Babbage, an English mathematician who lived in the early 1800s, spent much of his own personal fortune attempting to build a mechanical calculating machine that he called an "analytical engine." The analytical engine resembles the modern computer in many conceptual ways. A photo of an early version of the analytical engine is shown in Figure 1.11. Babbage's machine envisioned the use of Jacquard's punched cards for input data and for the program, provided memory for internal storage, performed calculations as specified by the program using a central processing unit known as a "mill," and printed output. Augusta Ada Byron, Countess of Lovelace and the daughter of the poet Lord Byron, worked closely with Babbage and developed many of the fundamental ideas of programming and program design, including the concepts of branches and loops.

A block diagram of the Babbage analytical engine is shown in Figure 1.12. The mill was capable of selecting one of four arithmetic operations, and of testing the sign of a number with a different program branch specified for each result. The sequence of operation was specified by instructions on the operation cards. The operation cards could be

FIGURE 1.11

Babbage's Analytical Engine

FIGURE 1.12

Block Diagram of Babbage's Analytical Engine

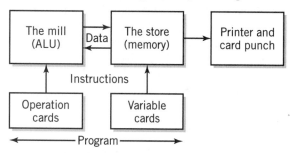

Source: From *Computer Architecture and Organization*, 2nd ed., J. Hayes, Copyright © 1988, by McGraw-Hill Companies, pg. 14 Reprinted by permission.

advanced or reversed as a means of implementing a sort of "goto" instruction. The second set of cards, known as variable cards, were to be used to specify particular memory locations for the data involved in the calculations. Babbage envisioned a memory of one thousand fifty-digit decimal numbers. Each digit was to be stored using a ten-toothed gear known as a counter wheel. Although the analytical engine was never completed, it should be apparent to you that it contains all the essential elements of today's computers.

At approximately the same time, another English mathematician, George Boole, developed the binary theory of logic that bears his name, Boolean logic. He also recognized the relationship between binary arithmetic and Boolean logic that makes possible the circuitry that implements the modern electronic computer.

In the late 1930s and early 1940s, several different groups of researchers independently developed versions of the modern electronic computer. The Mark I, built in 1937 by Howard H. Aiken and associates at Harvard University with help and funding from IBM, used thousands of relays; relays are mechanical binary switches controlled by electrical currents, familiar to you perhaps as the clicking devices that control operations in tape cassette players and telephone answering machines. Although binary relays were used for computation, the fundamental design was decimal. Storage consisted of seventy-two 23-digit decimal numbers, stored on counter wheels. An additional counter wheel digit held the sign, using the digit "0" for plus and "9" for minus.

The design appears to be based directly on Babbage's original concepts and use of mechanical calculator parts from IBM accounting machines. A similar electromechanical computer was designed and built by Conrad Zuse in Germany at about the same time.

The first totally electronic digital computer was apparently devised by John V. Atanasoff, a physicist at Iowa State College, in 1937. The machine was built in 1939 by Atanasoff and a graduate student, Clifford Berry, using electronic vacuum tubes as the switching components. The machine was known as ABC, for Atanasoff-Berry Computer. It is claimed that Atanasoff worked out the original details as he drove restlessly late one winter night from his house in Iowa to a bar in neighboring Illinois. The machine was not intended as a general-purpose computer, but was built to solve physics equations that Atanasoff was working on at the time. There is some doubt as to whether the machine ever worked completely.

ABC was a binary-based machine. It consisted of an arithmetic/logic unit with thirty units that could do addition and subtraction, a rotating drum memory that held thirty binary numbers of fifty digits each, and punched card input. Each punched card held five fifteen-digit decimal numbers. These numbers were converted to binary as they entered the machine.

Despite its limitations, ABC was an important pathmark that led to later significant advances in computer design. It is only recently that Atanasoff has begun to receive recognition for his achievement.

Much of the effort that culminated in a successful general-purpose computer architecture resulted from a wartime need for the solution to difficult mathematical formulas related to ballistic missile trajectories and other World War II research. The ENIAC (for Electronic Numerical Integrator and Computer, believe it or not) is generally considered to be the first all-electronic digital computer. It was designed and built between 1943 and 1946 by John W. Mauchly and J. Presper Eckert at the University of Pennsylvania, using the concepts that Mauchly had seen in Atanasoff's machine, although this was not publicly known at the time.

ENIAC had very limited storage capability, with only twenty locations each capable of holding a ten-digit decimal number. An additional one hundred numbers could be stored in read-only memory. Calculations were performed using decimal arithmetic. Ten electronic vacuum tube binary switches were used for each digit, with only one switch in the "ON" position to represent the value of the digit. Input and output used punched cards. The system could also provide printed output.

Programs could not be stored internally, but were hard wired with external "patch panels" and toggle switches. It took many hours to change programs, and, of course, debugging was a nightmare. Nonetheless, ENIAC was an important machine, some say the most important machine, especially since it led directly to the development of the UNI-VAC I, the first commercially available computer in 1951.

ENIAC contained eighteen thousand vacuum tubes, occupied a floor space of more than fifteen thousand square feet, and weighed more than thirty tons. A photograph of ENIAC, taken from *The New York Times* of February 15, 1946, is shown in Figure 1.13. Even in its day, ENIAC was recognized as an important achievement.

ENIAC operated successfully until 1955, when it was dismantled, but not destroyed. Parts of the computer can be seen at the Smithsonian Institute, at the U.S. Military Academy at West Point, at the Moore School of the University of Pennsylvania, and at the University of Michigan.

In 1945, John von Neumann, a consultant on the ENIAC project, proposed a computer that included a number of significant improvements over the ENIAC design. The most important of these were

1. A memory that would hold both programs and data, the so-called stored program concept. This solved the difficult problem of rewiring the control panels for changing programs on the ENIAC.

2. Binary processing of data. This simplified the design of the computer and allowed the use of binary memory for both instructions and data. It also recognized the natural relationship between the ON/OFF nature of switches and calculation in the binary number system, using Boolean logic.

FIGURE 1.13

The ENIAC

The CPU was to include ALU, memory, and CU components. The control unit read instructions from memory and executed them. A method of handling I/O through the control unit was also established. The instruction set contained instructions representing all the essential features of a modern computer. In other words, von Neumann's machine contained every major feature considered essential to modern computer architecture.

Due to political intrigue and controversy, two different versions of von Neumann's architecture were designed and built, EDVAC at the University of Pennsylvania and IAS at the Princeton University Institute for Advanced Studies (hence the unusual name). Both machines were completed in 1951–1952. The success of EDVAC and IAS led to the development of many offspring, mostly with odd names, and to several commercial computers, including the first IBM computers.

At this point, von Neumann's architecture was firmly established. It remains the prevalent standard to this day and provides the foundation for the remainder of the material in this book. What is obviously most important about this history, then, is the fact that the essential hardware concepts that make up today's digital computers were all developed by 1951. There have been significant advances in technology, and improvements in design that have resulted. Nonetheless, today's designs still reflect the work done on ABC, ENIAC, EDVAC, and IAS.

All of these early electronic computers relied on the electronic vacuum tube for their operation. Vacuum tubes were bulky, made of glass, fragile, short-lived, and required large amounts of power to operate. Vacuum tubes require an internal electric heater to function, and the heaters tend to fail quickly, resulting in what was known as a "burned-out" tube. Furthermore, the heat generated by the large number of tubes used in a computer required a massive forced-air or water-cooling system. A report reprinted by computer historian James Cortada [CORT87] states that the average error-free operating time for ENIAC was only 5.6 hours.

Such bulky, maintenance-requiring systems could not have attained the prevalence that computers have in our society. There have been many major technological developments since the 1940s. The technological breakthrough that made possible today's small, sophisticated computers was the invention of the transistor and, subsequently, the integration of transistors and other electronic components with the development of the integrated circuit.

Companies have developed better ways of moving data between different parts of the computer, better ways of handling memory, and methods for increasing the speed of instruction execution. There is a lot more processing power in today's personal computer than there was in the largest mainframe computer in the 1970s. Nonetheless, the basic architecture of today's machines is remarkably similar to that developed in the 1940s.

The history of system software, particularly operating systems, is much less well defined. According to Cortada,

> Without more sophisticated operating systems, scientists would not have been able to take full advantage of the power of the transistor and later of the [microprocessor] chip in building the computers known today. Yet their contribution to the overall evolution of digital computers has been overlooked by historians of data processing.

Part of the reason, undoubtedly, is that software evolved gradually, rather than as a series of important individually identifiable steps. The first operating systems and high-level programming languages appeared in the early 1950s, particularly associated with IBM and MIT, but, with only a few exceptions, these efforts have not been associated with individual people or projects.

The need for operating system software came from the increasing computer power that resulted from the rapid development of new computers in the 1950s. Although the hardware architecture has not changed substantially since that time, improved technology has resulted in a continuum of ever-increasing computer capability that continues to this day. It has been necessary to continually modify and improve operating system architecture to take advantage of that power and make it available to the user. Computing has changed from single-user batch processing (where only a single user, with a single program, could access the machine at one time), to multiple-user batch job submission (where each user's "job" was submitted to the computer by an operator for sequential runs), to multiuser batch job execution (where the computer executed several jobs simultaneously, thereby keeping the CPU busy while I/O took place on another user's job), to multiuser online computing (where each user had direct access to the computer), to single-user interactive personal computing, to today's powerful interactive networked systems, with multitasking, easy-to-use graphical interfaces, the ability to move data between applications, and near-instant access to other computers all over the world.

Each of these developments, plus various hardware developments—minicomputers, PCs, new I/O devices, multimedia—have required additional operating system sophistication; in each case, designers have responded to the need.

Other historical notes that you might find interesting appear from time to time in this book, where relevant to the particular material being discussed. A more detailed history of operating systems appears in Chapter 14.

A Note on the Terms "Computer Architecture" and "Organization"

As has already been noted, there is a slight technical difference between the terms "computer architecture" and "computer organization."

Computer architecture refers to the way the system and its resources appear to the user, especially to the programmer.

Computer organization describes how the system's components are organized internally and interconnected to realize the computer's architecture.

Even with these definitions, there is disagreement among different writers and theoreticians. Some authors would claim that a description of the instruction set is an architectural issue; other authors describe the instruction set as a part of computer organization.

The difficulty arises because a family of computers may have a common architecture, but each member of the family may be organized in a different way internally to achieve that architecture. Yet some internal factors may have a profound, although hidden, effect on the behavior of the system as seen by a programmer.

For the most part, our discussion will center on what most authors consider to be architectural functions. Occasionally, we will divert our attention to important organizational issues. Although the difference may be important to a computer engineer, this book will make no attempt to differentiate computer architecture and organization, nor will we attempt to identify which is which. The category for some of the discussion will be obvious to you when you read it; the rest won't matter.

SUMMARY AND REVIEW

This chapter has presented a brief review of the basics of computing. We began by recalling the input-process-output model for computing. Next we demonstrated the connection between that model and the components of the computer system. We noted that implementation of the model requires four components: hardware, software, communication, and data. The architecture of the computer system is made up of the hardware and system software. In addition, a communication component exists to enable interconnecting systems. We discussed the general architecture of a computer and noted that the same description applies to CPUs both modern and ancient, both large and small.

KEY CONCEPTS AND TERMS

application programming interface (API)
arithmetic/logic unit (ALU)
bus
byte
central processing unit (CPU)
channel
control unit (CU)

distributed computing
hardware
input-process-output model (IPO)
interface unit
memory
modem
network interface card (NIC)
open computing

operating system
primary storage
protocol
random access memory (RAM)
read-only memory (ROM)
software
standards
stored program concept

FOR FURTHER READING

There are many good general introductory computer texts available for review if you feel you need one. New books appear so rapidly that we are reluctant to recommend any particular one. The same is true of Web sites. The book by Rochester and Gantz [ROCH83] is a fun way to explore the history of computing. Historical facts are blended with other facts, anecdotes, humor, and miscellany about computers. One learns in this book about von Neumann's party habits, about movies that became video games, about computer scams and ripoffs, and lots of other interesting stuff. Perhaps the most thorough discussion of computer history is found in the three-volume dictionary by Cortada [CORT87]. Although Cortada is not really designed for casual reading, it provides ready access and solid information on particular topics of interest. Most of the historical discussion in this chapter was obtained from the Cortada volumes.

If you live or vacation in a city with a computer museum, you can enjoy another approach to computer history. Computer museums even allow you to play with some of the older computers. Well-known museums can be found in Washington, D.C., and within the Science Museum in Boston.

EXERCISES

1.1   Look at the computer ads on the business pages of a large daily newspaper, and make a list of all the terms used that you don't understand. Save this list, and check it from time to time during the semester. Cross out the items that you now understand, and look up the items that have been covered, but which you still don't understand.

1.2   For the computer that you normally use, identify which pieces constitute the hardware and which pieces constitute the system software. Now think about the file system of your computer. What part of the file system is hardware, what part software, and what part data?

1.3   Suppose you would like to buy a computer for your own needs. What are the major considerations and factors that would be important in your decision? What technical factors would influence your decision? Now try to lay out a specification for your machine. Consider and justify the features and options that you would like your machine to have.

1.4   Write a small program in your favorite high-level language. Compile your program. What is the ratio of high-level language statements to machine language statements? As a rough estimate, assume that each machine language statement requires approximately four bytes of file storage. Add various statements one at a time to your program, and note the change in size of the corresponding machine language program.

1.5   Locate a current reference that lists the important protocols that are members of the TCP/IP protocol suite. Explain how each protocol contributes to the operation and use of the Internet.

PART TWO

You are probably aware that all data in a computer is stored in the form of binary numbers, using only 1s and 0s. The situation is more complicated than this, however, because those binary numbers represent both program instructions and data, and they may represent the data in many different forms. Programming languages such as Java, for example, allow a programmer to specify data in primitive form as integer numbers, real numbers, characters, or Booleans. In addition, the files on your computer probably include representations of graphical images, sounds, photo images and video, and who knows what all else!

Each of the myriad different data types and objects uses its own format or formats for storage in the computer. Manipulating data requires keeping track of which format is in use for a particular set of data. Each numerical data format requires a different method for doing arithmetic calculations, and there are a number of different formats for representations of images and the like with different capabilities and manipulation requirements, which complicates data handling even further. Naturally, the computer must be able to perform format conversions between equivalent but different types. Most of this data-type record keeping must be handled within programs; to the computer, the bits all look the same. Only the programs know what the bits actually represent.

Each data type and format has its own uses, advantages, and disadvantages, determined by the context in which it is being used. There is no single "ideal" data type. Knowing when to use each type involves understanding what happens to the data within the computer. When you understand the effect of your data-type choices upon the processing that will be required you can write better, more efficient programs.

Each of the chapters in this section deals with a different aspect of data. We begin in Chapter 2 by reviewing the basics of number systems, to offer you a better understanding

DATA IN THE COMPUTER

of how numbers work, the nature of counting, and how calculations are performed. You will learn how to convert from one number base to another. Although the binary number system is used within computers, we must be able to convert between the system the computer uses and the more familiar decimal system that we use. You will also have a chance to work with the octal and hexadecimal number systems, which are closely related to the binary system. These are frequently used for representing computer data and programs in machine form because they are easy to read and easy to convert to and from binary form.

In Chapter 3 we will explore the ways in which data gets into the computer in the first place and the different forms that it can take inside the computer. We will consider text, sound, and images. You will study the difference between characters and other symbols stored as text and the same symbols stored as images. You will see the different binary codes that are used to represent symbols in text form. We will also consider the difference between numbers stored as groups of numeric characters and those stored in actual numerical form. The chapter also looks at the representations of graphics, photo images, and sound. We present several different formats that are used for the manipulation and storage of image and sound data.

In Chapter 4 we will look at various ways in which integer numbers are stored and manipulated in computers, and in Chapter 5 we will consider real, or "floating point," number representations and calculations. We will discuss the conversion process between real and integer number representations. We will look at the strengths and shortcomings of each type from the perspectives of data storage requirements and calculation considerations. The discussion will conclude by considering when the use of each of the different numerical types is appropriate.

CHAPTER 2

NUMBER SYSTEMS

"I call them numbers, you can add them, subtract them, multiply them, divide them ... find their square root..."

Courtesy of David Ahl, Creative Computing

2.0 INTRODUCTION

As humans, we generally count and perform arithmetic using the decimal, or base 10, number system. The **base** of a number system is simply the number of different digits, including zero, that exist in the number system.

Computers perform all of their operations using the **binary,** or base 2, **number** system. All program code and data are stored and manipulated in binary form. Calculations are performed using **binary arithmetic.** Each digit in a binary number is known as a **bit** (for binary digit) and can have only one of two values, **0** or **1.** Bits are commonly stored and manipulated in groups of 8 (known as a byte), 16 (usually known as a halfword), 32 (a word), or 64 bits (a doubleword). Sometimes other groupings are used.

The number of bits used in calculations affects the accuracy and size limitations of numbers manipulated by the computer. And, in fact, in some programming languages, the number of bits used can actually be specified by the programmer in declaration statements. In the programming language Java, for example, the programmer can declare a signed integer variable to be **short** (16 bits), int (32 bits), or **long** (64 bits) depending on the anticipated size of the number being used and the required accuracy in calculations.

The knowledge of the size limits for calculations in a particular language is sometimes extremely important, since some calculations can cause a numerical result that falls outside the range provided for the number of bits used. In some cases this will produce erroneous results, without warning to the end user of the program.

It is useful to understand how the binary number system is used within the computer. Often, it is necessary to read numbers in the computer in their binary or equivalent hexadecimal form. For example, colors in Visual Basic can be specified as a six-digit hexadecimal number, which represents a 24-bit binary number.

This chapter looks informally at number systems in general and explores the relationship between our commonplace decimal number system and number systems of other bases. Our emphasis, of course, is upon base 2, the binary number system. The discussion is kept more general, however, since it is also possible, and in fact common, to represent computer numbers in base 8 (**octal**) or base 16 (**hexadecimal**). Occasionally we even consider numbers in other bases, just for fun, and also, perhaps, to emphasize the idea that these techniques are completely general.

2.1 NUMBERS AS A PHYSICAL REPRESENTATION

As we embark upon our investigation of number systems, it is important to note that numbers usually represent some physical meaning, for example, the number of dollars in our paycheck or the number of stars in the universe. The different number systems that we use are equivalent. The physical objects can be represented equivalently in any of them. Of course, it is possible to convert between them.

In Figure 2.1, for example, there are a number of oranges, a number that you recognize as 5. In ancient cultures, the number might have been represented as

$$IIIII$$

or, when in Rome,

$$V$$

Similarly, in base 2, the number of oranges in Figure 2.1 is represented as

$$101_2$$

And in base 3, the representation looks like this:

$$12_3$$

The point we are making is that each of the foregoing examples is simply a different way of *representing* the same number of oranges. You probably already have experience at converting between the standard decimal number system and Roman numerals. (Maybe you even wrote a program to do so!) Once you understand the methods, it is just about as easy to convert between base 10 and the other number bases that we shall use.

2.2 COUNTING IN DIFFERENT BASES

Let's consider how we count in base 10, and what each digit means. We begin with single digits,

$$0$$
$$1$$
$$2$$
$$3$$
$$.$$
$$.$$
$$.$$
$$9$$

When we reach 9, we have exhausted all possible single digits in the decimal number system; to proceed further, we extend the numbers to the 10's place:

$$10$$
$$11$$
$$12$$
$$.$$
$$.$$
$$.$$

It is productive to consider what "the 10's place" really means.

The 10's place simply represents a count of the number of times that we have cycled through the entire group of 10 possible digits. Thus, continuing to count, we have

FIGURE 2.1

A Number of Oranges

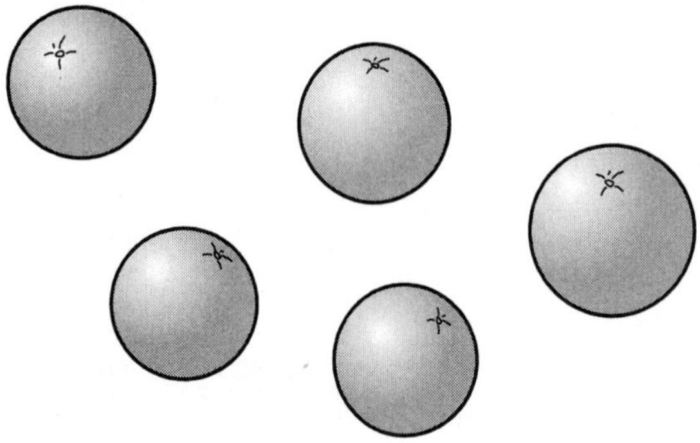

```
1 group of 10 + 0 more
1 group of 10 + 1 more
1 group of 10 + 2
         .
         .
         .
1 group of 10 + 9
2 groups of 10 + 0
         .
         .
         .
9 groups of 10 + 9
```

At this point, we have used all combinations of two digits, and we need to move left another digit. Before we do so, however, we should note that each group shown here represents a count of 10, since there are 10 digits in the group. Thus, the number

$$43$$

really refers to

$$4 \times 10 + 3$$

As we move leftward to the next digit, that is, the hundreds place, we are now counting cycles of the rightmost two digits or, in other words, groups of 10×10, or 10^2, or hundreds. Thus, the number

$$527$$

really represents

```
five groups of (10 × 10) +
two groups of 10 + 7
```

This is also represented as

$$5 \times 10^2 + 2 \times 10^1 + 7 \times 10^0$$

This method can, of course, be continued indefinitely.

The same method, exactly, applies to any number base. The only change is the size of each grouping. For example, in base 8, there are only eight different digits available (0, 1, 2, 3, 4, 5, 6, 7). Thus, each move left represents eight of the next rightmost grouping. The number

$$624_8$$

corresponds to

$$6 \times 8^2 + 2 \times 8^1 + 4 \times 8^0$$

Since $8^2 = 64_{10}$, $8^1 = 8_{10}$, and $8^0 = 1$,

$$624_8 = 6 \times 64 + 2 \times 8 + 4 = 404_{10}$$

Figure 2.2 shows the corresponding method of counting in base 2. Note that each digit has twice the weight of its next rightmost neighbor, just as in base 10 each digit had ten times the weight of its right neighbor. This is what you would expect if you consider that there are only two different values for digits in the binary cycle. You should spend enough time studying this table until you understand every detail thoroughly.

FIGURE 2.2

Counting in Base 2

NUMBER	EQUIVALENT	DECIMAL EQUIVALENT
0	0×2^0	0
1	1×2^0	1
10	$1 \times 2^1 + 0 \times 2^0$	2
11	$1 \times 2^1 + 1 \times 2^0$	3
100	1×2^2	4
101	$1 \times 2^2 \qquad + 1 \times 2^0$	5
110	$1 \times 2^2 + 1 \times 2^1$	6
111	$1 \times 2^2 + 1 \times 2^1 + 1 \times 2^0$	7
1000	1×2^3	8
1001	$1 \times 2^3 \qquad + 1 \times 2^0$	9
1010	$1 \times 2^3 \qquad + 1 \times 2^1$	10

Note, too, that the steps that we have followed do not really depend on the number base that we are using. We simply go through a complete cycle, exhausting all possible different digits in the base set, and then move to the left one place and count the cycles. We repeat this process as necessary to represent the entire number.

In general, for any number base B, each digit position represents B to a power, where the power is numbered from the rightmost digit, starting with B^0. B^0, of course, is one (known as the units place) for any number base.

Thus, a simple way to determine the decimal equivalent for a number in any number base is to multiply each digit by the weight in the given base that corresponds to the position of the digit for that number.

EXAMPLE

As an example,

$$142305_6 =$$
$$1 \times 6^5 + 4 \times 6^4 + 2 \times 6^3 + 3 \times 6^2 + 0 \times 6 + 5 =$$
$$7776 + 5184 + 432 + 108 + 0 + 5 = 13505_{10}$$

■ ■ ■

Similarly,

$$110010100_2 =$$
$$1 \times 2^8 + 1 \times 2^7 + 0 \times 2^6 + 0 \times 2^5 + 1 \times 2^4 + 0 \times 2^3 + 1 \times 2^2 +$$
$$0 \times 2 + 0 =$$
$$256 + 128 + 16 + 4 = 404_{10}$$

You should probably work out these two examples and check your results against ours.

Often it is useful to be able to estimate quickly the value of a binary number. Since the weight of each place in a binary number doubles as we move to the left, we can generate a rough order-of-magnitude by considering only the left-most bit or two. Starting from 1, and doubling for each bit in the number to get the weight, you can see that the most significant bit in the previous example has a value of 256. We can improve the estimate by adding half that again for the next most significant bit, which gives the value of the number in the neighborhood of 384, plus a little more for the additional bits. With a little practice, it is easy to estimate the magnitudes of binary numbers almost instantly. This technique is often sufficient for checking the results of calculations when debugging programs. (You might also want to consider it as a way of doing quick checks on your solutions to exam problems!)

We will discuss number conversion between different bases more carefully later in the chapter.

From the preceding discussion, it is fairly easy to determine the total range of possible numbers—or, equivalently, the smallest and largest integer—for a given number of digits in a particular number base. Since each digit represents a count of the entire group to its right, the value of the power of that digit represents the *range* of the group to its right. Remember that the exponent of the right-most digit is 0, so that the exponent for a given place is exactly equivalent to the number of digits to its right.

Thus, if we want to know how many different numbers can be represented by two decimal digits, the answer is found either in the exponent of the third digit or in the number of digits, which is 2. Thus, we can represent one hundred different numbers (0...99) with two decimal digits.

(It's obviously easier to simply memorize the result; that is, if you have two decimal digits, you can represent 10^2 different numbers, but at least you have seen why this is so.) In general, the range for K digits in base B is

$$R = B^K$$

Just as a pocket calculator stores, manipulates, and displays numbers as a group of digits, so computers store and manipulate numbers as groups of bits. Most computers work with numbers 16 bits, 32 bits, or 64 bits at a time. Applying the preceding formula to a "16-bit" PC, you can represent $2^{16} = 65,536$ different number values in each 16-bit location. If you wish to extend this range, it is necessary to use some technique for increasing the number of bits used to hold your numbers, such as using two 16-bit storage locations together to hold 32 bits. There are other methods used, which are discussed in Chapters 4 and 5, but note that there is *no* way to store more than 65,336 different number values using 16 bits.

A table of base 10 equivalent ranges for several common computer "word lengths" is shown in Figure 2.3. There is a simple way to calculate the approximate range for a given number of bits, since 2^{10} is approximately 1000. To do so, we break up the total number of bits into a sum that consists of values where the range is easily figured out. The overall range is equal to the product of the subranges for each value. This method is best seen with examples.

For example, if you need to know the range for 18 bits, you would break up the number 18 into the sum of 10 and 8, then multiply the range for 10 bits to that for 8 bits. Since the range for 10 bits is approximately 1K (1024, actually) and 8 bits is 256, the range for 18 bits is approximately 256K. Similarly, the range for 32 bits would be (10-bit range) × (10-bit range) × (10-bit range) × (2-bit range) = 1K × 1K × 1K × 4 = 4 gigabytes. This technique becomes easy with a bit of practice.

Notice that it takes 18 bits to represent a little more than five decimal digits. In general, approximately 3.3 bits are required for each equivalent decimal digit. This is true because $2^{3.3}$ is approximately equal to 10.

FIGURE 2.3

Decimal Range for Selected Bit Widths

BITS	DIGITS	RANGE
1	0+	2 (0 and 1)
4	1+	16 (0 to 15)
8	2+	256
10	3	1,024
16	4+	65,536 (64K)
20	6	1,048,576 (1M)
32	9+	4,294,967,296 (4G)
64	19+	approx. 1.6×10^{19}
128	38+	approx. 2.6×10^{38}

2.3 PERFORMING ARITHMETIC IN DIFFERENT NUMBER BASES

Next, we consider simple arithmetic operations in various number bases. Let us begin by looking at the simple base 10 addition table shown in Figure 2.4.

We add two numbers by finding one in the row and the other in the column. The table entry at the intersection is the result. For example, we have used the table to demonstrate that the sum of 3 and 6 is 9. Note that the extra digit sometimes required becomes a carry that gets added into the next left column during the addition process.

More fundamentally, we are interested in how the addition table is actually created. Each column (or row) represents an increase of 1 from the previous column (or row), which is equivalent to counting. Thus, starting from the leftmost column in the table, it is only necessary to count up 1 to find the next value. Since $3 + 6 = 9$, the next column will have to carry to the next place, or 10, just as occurred when we demonstrated counting in base 10, earlier. This knowledge should make it easy for you to create a base 8 addition table. Try to create your own table before looking at the one in Figure 2.5.

Of special interest is the base 2 addition table:

+	0	1
0	0	1
1	1	10

Clearly, addition in base 2 is going to be easy!

Addition in base 2 (or any other base, for that matter) then follows the usual methods of addition that you are familiar with, including the handling of carries that you already know. The *only* difference is the particular addition table being used. There are practice problems representing multidigit binary arithmetic and column arithmetic (Exercise 2.8) at the end of the chapter.

EXAMPLE

Add 11100001_2 and 101011_2 (superscripts are carried amounts).

$$\begin{array}{cccccccccc} {}^1 1 & {}^1 1 {}^1 1 & 0 & 0 & 0 & 0^1 & 0^1 & 1 \\ + & & 1 & 0 & 1 & 0 & 1 & 1 \\ \hline 1 & 0 & 0 & 0 & 0 & 1 & 1 & 0 & 0 \end{array}$$

Let's use the estimation technique to see if our result is approximately correct. 11100001 is approximately $128 + 64 + 32$, or 224. 101011 is approximately 32. Thus, the sum should be about 256; 100001100 is indeed approximately 256, so at least we know that our calculation is in the ballpark.

As an aside, it may be of interest to some readers to consider how this addition table can be implemented in the computer using only Boolean logic, without performing any actual arithmetic: the result bit (the bit in the column that corresponds to the inputs) can be represented by the EXCLUSIVE-OR function of the two input bits. The EXCLUSIVE-OR function has a "1" as output only if either input, but not both inputs, is a "1." Similarly, the carry bit is represented as an AND function on the two input bits. ("1" as output if and only if both inputs are a "1.") This approach is discussed in more detail in Supplementary Chapter 1.

FIGURE 2.4

The Base 10 Addition Table

+	0	1	2	3	4	5	6	7	8	9
0	0	1	2	3	4	5	6	7	8	9
1	1	2	3	4	5	6	7	8	9	10
2	2	3	4	5	6	7	8	9	10	11
3	3	4	5	6	7	8	9	10	11	12
4	4	5	6	7	8	9	10	11	12	13

etc.

FIGURE 2.5

The Base 8 Addition Table

+	0	1	2	3	4	5	6	7	
0	0	1	2	3	4	5	6	7	
1	1	2	3	4	5	6	7	10	
2	2	3	4	5	6	7	10	11	
3	3	4	5	6	7	10	11	12	**(no 8 or 9, of course)**
4	4	5	6	7	10	11	12	13	
5	5	6	7	10	11	12	13	14	
6	6	7	10	11	12	13	14	15	
7	7	10	11	12	13	14	15	16	

The process of multiplication can be reduced conceptually to multiple addition, so it should not surprise you that multiplication tables in different number bases are also reasonably straightforward. The major difference in appearance results from the fact that the carry occurs at different places.

The easiest way to create a multiplication table is to treat multiplication as multiple addition: each column (or row) represents the addition of the value in the row (or column) being created. Thus, in the following table, you can see that 5×8 is equivalent to $5 \times 7 + 5 = 40$. The familiar decimal multiplication table appears in Figure 2.6, with the example just given indicated.

The same technique can be applied to the base 8 multiplication table (Figure 2.7).

FIGURE 2.6

The Base 10 Multiplication Table

×	0	1	2	3	4	5	6	7	8	9
0				← 0 →						
1		1	2	3	4	5	6	7	8	9
2		2	4	6	8	10	12	14	16	18
3		3	6	9	12	15	18	21	24	27
4	0	4	8	12	16	20	24	28	32	36
5		5	10	15	20	25	30	35	40	45
6		6	12	18	24	30	36	42	48	54
7		7	14	21	28	35	42	49	56	63
8		8	16	24	32	40	48	56	64	72
9		9	18	27	36	45	54	63	72	81

FIGURE 2.7

The Base 8 Multiplication Table

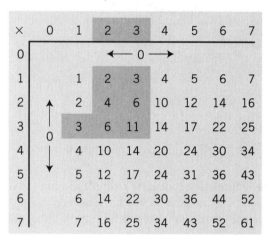

×	0	1	2	3	4	5	6	7
0				← 0 →				
1		1	2	3	4	5	6	7
2		2	4	6	10	12	14	16
3	0	3	6	11	14	17	22	25
4		4	10	14	20	24	30	34
5		5	12	17	24	31	36	43
6		6	14	22	30	36	44	52
7		7	16	25	34	43	52	61

Note in the foregoing table that $3 \times 3 = 3 \times 2 + 3$. Note, though, that counting up 3 from 6 (or adding 3 to 6) results in a carry after 7 is reached: $6 \to 7 \to 10 \to 11$.

The base 2 multiplication table is almost trivial, since 0 times anything is 0 and 1 times 1 is itself:

×	0	1
0	0	0
1	0	1

Because the binary multiplication table is so simple, it turns out that multiplication can be implemented in a computer fairly easily. There are only two possible results: if the multiplier is 0, the answer is 0, even if the multiplicand is a nonzero multidigit number. If the multiplier is 1, the multiplicand is brought down as the result. You might recognize the multiplication table as a Boolean AND function.

If you recall that decimal multidigit multiplication is performed by multiplying the multiplicand by each digit of the multiplier, shifting the result of each multiplication to line up with the multiplier, and adding up the results, then you realize that multidigit binary multiplication can be performed by simply shifting the multiplicand into whatever positions in the multiplier are "1" bits and adding to the result. This is easily illustrated with an example:

EXAMPLE

Multiply

$$
\begin{array}{r}
1101101 \\
\times\ 100110 \\
\hline
\end{array}
$$

1101101	bits shifted to line up with 2's place of multiplier
1101101	4's place
1101101	32's place

1000000101110 result (note the 0 at the end, since the 1's place is
not brought down)

We note in passing that shifting a binary number one position to the left has the effect of doubling its value. This is a result you would expect, since the shift is equivalent to multiplying the value by a 1 in the 2's place of the multiplier. This result is consistent with the fact that shifting a decimal number to the left by one position will multiply its value by 10. In general, **shifting** a number in any base **left** one digit multiplies its value by the base, and, conversely, **shifting** a number **right** one digit divides its value by the base.

Although we have not mentioned subtraction or division, the methods are similar to those that we have already discussed. In fact, the addition and multiplication tables can be directly used for subtraction and division, respectively.

2.4 NUMERIC CONVERSION BETWEEN NUMBER BASES

Conversions between whole numbers in decimal (base 10) and any other number base are relatively straightforward. With the exception of one special case discussed in Section 2.6, it is impractical to convert directly between two nondecimal number bases. Instead, base 10 would be used as an intermediary conversion base.

The easiest intuitive way to convert between base 10 and another number base is to recognize the weight of each digit in the alternative number base and to multiply that weight by the value of the digit in that position. The sum taken over all digits represents the base 10 value of the number. This is easily seen in an example:

EXAMPLE

Convert the number

$$13754_8$$

to base 10.

From the following diagram we can see the result easily:

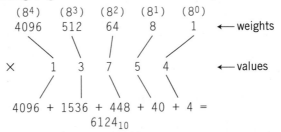

(8^4) (8^3) (8^2) (8^1) (8^0)
4096   512   64   8   1   ← weights

$\times$ 1   3   7   5   4   ← values

$4096 + 1536 + 448 + 40 + 4 =$
6124_{10}

We can use the same method in reverse to convert from base 10 to another base, although the technique is not quite as simple. In this case, it is just a question of finding the value corresponding to the weight of each digit such that the total will add up to the base 10 number that we are trying to convert.

Note that the value for each digit must be the largest value that will not exceed the number being converted. If this were not true, then there would be more than a full grouping of the next less significant digit. This idea is best clarified by example:

EXAMPLE

Suppose that we are reverse converting the preceding example, and we assume that there are six groups of 64 instead of seven. In this case, the 8's place and 1's place combined must add up to more than 64, and we've already seen that is impossible.

This provides a simple methodology for the conversion. Start with the digit whose weight is the largest possible without exceeding the number to be converted. Determine the largest value for that weight that does not exceed the number to be converted. Then, do the same for each successive digit, working from left to right.

EXAMPLE

As an example, let us convert 6124_{10} to base 5. The weights of each digit in base 5 are as follows:

$$15625 \quad 3125 \quad 625 \quad 125 \quad 25 \quad 5 \quad 1$$

Clearly the 15625 digit is too large, so the result will be a six-digit base 5 number. The number 3125 fits into 6124 only once; thus, the first digit is a 1, and the remainder to be converted is 2999. Proceeding to the next digit, 625 goes into 2999 four times with a remainder of 499, 125 into 499 three times with a remainder of 124, 25 into 124 four times, and so on. We get a final result of

$$143444_5$$

It would be useful for you to confirm the answer by converting the result back to base 10.

This method is particularly simple if you are converting from decimal to binary, since the value that corresponds to a particular bit either fits (1) or it doesn't (0). Consider the following example:

EXAMPLE

Convert 3193_{10} to binary. The weights in binary are 4096, 2048, 1024, 512, 256, 128, 64, 32, 16, 8, 4, 2, and 1.

Proceeding as before, the largest bit value in this conversion is the 2048 weight. Subtracting 2048 from 3193 leaves 1145 yet to be converted; thus, there is also a 1 in the 1024 place. Now the remainder is $1145 - 1024 = 121$. This means that there are 0's in the 512, 256, and 128 places. Continuing, you should confirm that the final result is

$$110001111001_2$$

An Alternative Conversion Method

Although the preceding methods are easy to understand, they are computationally difficult and prone to mistakes. In this section we will consider methods that are usually simpler to compute but are less intuitive. It is helpful to understand the reasons that these methods work, since the reasoning adds insight to the entire concept of number manipulation.

BASE 10 TO ANOTHER BASE   Suppose we divide the number to be converted successively by the base, B, that we are converting to, and look at the remainders of each division. We will do this until there is nothing left to divide. Each successive remainder represents the value of a digit in the new base, reading the new value from right to left. Again, let us convert 6124_{10} to base 5:

EXAMPLE

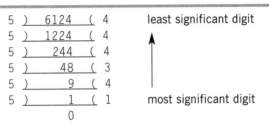

The answer is 143444_5, which agrees with our earlier result.

The first time that we perform the division, we are, in effect, determining how many groups of 5 (or, in the general case, B) fit into the original number. The remainder is the number of single units left over, which is, in other words, the units place of the converted number.

The original number has now been divided by 5, so the second division by 5 determines how many groups of 5^2, or 25, fit into the number. The remainder in this case is the number of 5-groups that are left over, which is the second digit from the right.

Each time we divide by the base, we are increasing the power of the group being tested by one, and we do this until there is no group left. Since the remainders correspond to the part of the number that does not exactly fit the group, we can read the converted number easily by reading the remainders from the bottom up.

Here's another example:

EXAMPLE

Convert 8151_{10} to base 16, also known as hexadecimal:

```
16 )   8151   ( 7
16 )    509   (13    in base 16, this is represented by the letter "D"
16 )     31   (15    in base 16, this is represented by the letter "F"
              1
```

The answer is $1FD7_{16}$. We suggest that you verify this answer by using the technique of digit weight multiplication to convert this answer back to decimal form.

ANOTHER NUMBER BASE TO BASE 10   An alternative method can be used to convert from other number bases to base 10. The technique is also computationally simple: starting from the most significant digit, we multiply by the base, B, and add the next digit to the right. We repeat this process until the least significant digit has been added.

EXAMPLE

Convert 13754_8 to base 10:

$$1$$
$$\underline{\times\ 8}$$
$$8 + 3\ =\ 11$$
$$\underline{\times\ 8}$$
$$88 + 7\ =\ 95$$
$$\underline{\times\ 8}$$
$$760 + 5\ =\ 765$$
$$\underline{\times\ 8}$$
$$6120 + 4\ =\ 6124_{10}$$

If you count the number of times that each digit in the example is multiplied by the base number, in this case 8, you discover that the leftmost digit is multiplied by 8 four times, or 8^4, and that each successive digit is multiplied by 8 one less time, until you arrive at the rightmost digit, which is not multiplied by the base number at all. Thus, each digit is multiplied by its proper weight, and the result is what we would expect. In the next chapter, you will see that this method is also useful for converting a sequence of digits in alphanumeric form to an actual number.

You have now been introduced to two different methods for performing conversions in each direction. You should practice all four methods; then you can use whichever two methods are easiest for you to remember.

2.5 HEXADECIMAL NUMBERS AND ARITHMETIC

The **hexadecimal,** or base 16, **number** representation system is important because it is commonly used as a shorthand notation for binary numbers. The conversion technique between hexadecimal and binary notations is particularly simple because there is a direct relationship between the two. Each hexadecimal number represents exactly 4 binary bits. Most computers store and manipulate instructions and data using word sizes that are multiples of 4 bits. Therefore, the hexadecimal notation is a convenient way to represent computer words. Of course, it is also much easier to read and write than binary notation. The technique for converting between binary and hexadecimal is shown later in this chapter.

Although hexadecimal numbers are represented and manipulated in the same way as those of other bases, we must first provide symbols to represent the additional digits beyond 9 that we require to represent sixteen different quantities with a single integer.

By convention, we use the digits 0–9, followed by the first six alphabetical characters A–F. Thus, the digits 0–9 have their familiar meaning; the letters A–F correspond to what in a decimal base would be quantities of 10–15, respectively. To count in hexadecimal we count from 0 to 9, then A to F, and then move left to the next digit. Since there are sixteen digits, each place represents a power of 16. Thus, the number

$$2A4F_{16}$$

is equivalent to

$$2 \times 16^3 + 10 \times 16^2 + 4 \times 16 + 15, \text{ or}$$
$$10831_{10}$$

Addition and multiplication tables can be created for the hexadecimal number system. These tables each have sixteen rows and sixteen columns, as you would expect. The addition table is shown in Figure 2.8. Before you look at the figure, you should try to work the hexadecimal addition and multiplication tables out for yourself (see Exercise 2.7).

2.6 A SPECIAL CONVERSION CASE—NUMBER BASES THAT ARE RELATED

A special possibility for conversion exists when one number base is an integer power of another. In this case, a direct conversion can easily be made. In fact, with a bit of practice, the conversion can be done mentally and the answer written down directly. These conversions work because a grouping of several digits in the smaller number base corresponds, or maps, exactly to a single digit in the larger number base.

FIGURE 2.8

Hexadecimal Addition Table

+	0	1	2	3	4	5	6	7	8	9	A	B	C	D	E	F
0	0	1	2	3	4	5	6	7	8	9	A	B	C	D	E	F
1	1	2	3	4	5	6	7	8	9	A	B	C	D	E	F	10
2	2	3	4	5	6	7	8	9	A	B	C	D	E	F	10	11
3	3	4	5	6	7	8	9	A	B	C	D	E	F	10	11	12
4	4	5	6	7	8	9	A	B	C	D	E	F	10	11	12	13
5	5	6	7	8	9	A	B	C	D	E	F	10	11	12	13	14
6	6	7	8	9	A	B	C	D	E	F	10	11	12	13	14	15
7	7	8	9	A	B	C	D	E	F	10	11	12	13	14	15	16
8	8	9	A	B	C	D	E	F	10	11	12	13	14	15	16	17
9	9	A	B	C	D	E	F	10	11	12	13	14	15	16	17	18
A	A	B	C	D	E	F	10	11	12	13	14	15	16	17	18	19
B	B	C	D	E	F	10	11	12	13	14	15	16	17	18	19	1A
C	C	D	E	F	10	11	12	13	14	15	16	17	18	19	1A	1B
D	D	E	F	10	11	12	13	14	15	16	17	18	19	1A	1B	1C
E	E	F	10	11	12	13	14	15	16	17	18	19	1A	1B	1C	1D
F	F	10	11	12	13	14	15	16	17	18	19	1A	1B	1C	1D	1E

Two particularly useful examples for computer work are the cases of conversion between base 2 and base 8 and conversion between base 2 and base 16. Since $8 = 2^3$, we can represent binary numbers directly in base 8 using one octal digit to correspond to each three binary digits. Similarly, it takes one hexadecimal digit to exactly represent 4 bits.

The advantage of representing binary numbers in hexadecimal or octal is obvious: it is clearly much easier to read and manipulate four-digit hexadecimal numbers than 16-bit binary numbers. Since the conversion between binary and octal and hexadecimal is so simple, it is common to use hexadecimal or octal representation as a shorthand notation for binary. (Note that base 8 and base 16 are not directly related to each other by power, but conversion could be performed easily by using base 2 as an intermediary.)

Since the correspondence of binary and octal or hexadecimal is exact, the conversion process simply consists of breaking the binary number into groups of three or four, starting from the least significant bit (the unit bit), and converting each group independently. It may be necessary to mentally add 0's to the left end of the number to convert the most significant digit. This is most easily illustrated with an example:

EXAMPLE

Let us convert

$$11010111011000$$

to hexadecimal.

Grouping the binary number by fours, we have

$$0011 \quad 0101 \quad 1101 \quad 1000$$

or

$$35D8_{16}$$

The conversion in the other direction works identically. Thus,

$$275331_8$$

becomes

$$10 \quad 111 \quad 101 \quad 011 \quad 011 \quad 001_2$$

For practice, now convert this value to hexadecimal.

Most computer manufacturers today prefer to use hexadecimal, since a 16-bit or 32-bit number can be represented exactly by a four- or eight-digit hexadecimal number. (How many octal digits would be required?) A few manufacturers still use octal representation for some applications.

You might ask why it is necessary to represent data in binary form at all. After all, the binary form is used within the computer, where it is usually invisible to the user. There are many occasions, however, where the ability to read the binary data is very useful. Remember that the computer stores both instructions and data in binary form. When debugging a program, it may be desirable to be able to read the program's instructions and to determine intermediate data steps that the computer is using. Older computers used to provide binary dumps for this purpose. Binary dumps were complete octal listings of everything stored in memory at the time the dump was requested. Even today it is sometimes important, for example, to be able to read the binary data from a floppy disk to recover a lost or damaged file. Modern computer operating systems and networks present a variety of troubleshooting data in hexadecimal form.

Conversions between binary and hexadecimal notation are used frequently. We strongly recommend that you practice to become proficient at working with hexadecimal notation.

2.7 FRACTIONS

Up to this point we have limited our discussion to whole numbers, or, if you prefer, integers. The representation and conversion of fractional numbers are somewhat more difficult because there is not necessarily an exact relationship between fractional numbers in different number bases. More specifically, fractional numbers that can be represented exactly in one number base may be impossible to represent exactly in another. Thus, exact conversion may be impossible. A couple of simple examples will suffice:

EXAMPLE

The decimal fraction

$$0.1_{10} \text{ or } 1/10$$

cannot be represented exactly in binary form. There is no combination of bits that will add up exactly to this fraction. The binary equivalent begins

$$0.0001100110011_2 ...$$

This binary fraction repeats endlessly with a repeat cycle of four. Similarly, the fraction

$$1/3$$

is not representable as a decimal value in base 10. In fact, we represent this fraction decimally as

$$0.3333333 ...$$

As you will realize shortly, this fraction can be represented exactly in base 3 as

$$0.1_3$$

Recall that the value of each digit to the left of a **decimal point** in base 10 has a strength ten times that of its next right neighbor. This is obvious to you, since you already know that each digit represents a group of ten objects in the next right neighbor. As you have already seen, the same basic relationship holds for any number base: the strength of each digit is B times the strength of its right neighbor. This fact has two important implications:

1. If we move the number point one place to the right in a number, the value of the number will be multiplied by the base. A specific example will make this obvious:

    $$1390_{10} \text{ is ten times as large as } 139.0_{10}$$

    $$139_{\times}0.$$

Moving the point right one space, therefore, multiplies the number by ten. Only a bit less obvious (pun intended),

$$100_2 \text{ is twice as big as } 10_2$$

(Note: We have used the phrase "number point" because the word "decimal" specifically implies base 10. More generally, the number point is known by the name of its base, for example, **binary point** or *hexadecimal point*. It is sometimes also called a **radix point**.)

2. The opposite is also true: if we move the number point to the left one place, the value is divided by the base. Thus, each digit has strength $1/B$ of its left neighbor. This is true on both sides of the number point.

$$246.8_x$$

Moving the point to the left one space divides the value by ten.

Thus, for numbers to the right of the number point, successive digits have values $1/B$, $1/B^2$, $1/B^3$, and so on. In base 10, the digits then have value

$$.D_1 \quad D_2 \quad D_3 \quad D_4$$
$$10^{-1} \quad 10^{-2} \quad 10^{-3} \quad 10^{-4}$$

which is equivalent to

$$1/10 \quad 1/100 \quad 1/1000 \quad 1/10,000$$

This should come as no surprise to you, since $1/10 = 0.1$, $1/100 = 0.01$, and so forth. (Remember from algebra that $B^{-k} = 1/B^k$.)

Then, a decimal number such as

$$0.2589$$

has value

$$2 \times (1/10) + 5 \times (1/100) + 8 \times (1/1000) + 9 \times (1/10,000)$$

Similarly in base 2, each place to the right of the binary point is 1/2 the weight of its left-hand neighbor. Thus, we have

$$.B_1 \quad B_2 \quad B_3 \quad B_4$$
$$1/2 \quad 1/4 \quad 1/8 \quad 1/16 \quad \text{etc.}$$

As an example,

$$0.101011$$

is equivalent to

$$1/2 + 1/8 + 1/32 + 1/64$$

which has decimal value

$$0.5 + 0.125 + 0.03125 + 0.015625 = 0.671875_{10}$$

Since there is no general relationship between fractions of types $1/10^k$ and $1/2^k$, there is no reason to assume that a number that is representable in base 10 will also be representable in base 2. Commonly, it isn't so. (The converse is not the case; since all fractions of the form $1/2^k$ can be represented in base 10, and since each bit represents a fraction of this form, fractions in base 2 can always be converted exactly to fractions in base 10.) As we have already shown with the value 0.1_{10}, many base 10 fractions result in endless base 2 fractions.

Incidentally, as review, consider the hexadecimal representation of the binary fraction representing 0.1_{10}. Starting from the numeric point, which is the common element of all number bases ($B^0 = 1$ in all bases), you group the bits into groups of four:

$$0.0001\ 1001\ 1001\ 1001 =$$
$$0.19999_{16}$$

In this particular case, the repeat cycle of four happens to be the same as the hexadecimal grouping of four, so the digit "9" repeats forever.

When fractional conversions from one base to another are performed, they are simply stopped when the desired accuracy is attained (unless, of course, a rational solution exists).

Fractional Conversion Methods

The intuitive conversion methods previously discussed can be used with fractional numbers. The computational methods have to be modified somewhat to work with fractional numbers.

Consider the intuitive methods first. The easiest way to convert a fractional number from some base B to base 10 is to determine the appropriate weights for each digit, multiply each digit by its weight, and add the values. You will note that this is identical to the method that we introduced previously for integer conversion.

EXAMPLE

Convert 0.12201_3 to base 10.

The weights for base 3 fractions (we remind you that the rules work the same for *any* number base!) are:

$$\frac{1}{3} \qquad \frac{1}{9} \qquad \frac{1}{27} \qquad \frac{1}{81} \qquad \frac{1}{243}$$

Then, the result is

$$1 \times 1/3 + 2 \times 1/9 + 2 \times 1/27 + 1 \times 1/243$$

Two different approaches could be taken at this point. Either we can convert each value to decimal base, multiply, and add,

$$\text{value} = 0.33333 + 0.22222 + 0.07407 + 0.00412 = 0.63374_{10}$$

or, more easily, we can find a common denominator, convert each fraction to the common denominator, add, and then divide by the common denominator. Most easily, we can pick the denominator of the least significant digit, in this case 243:

$$\text{value} = \frac{81 + 2 \times 27 + 2 \times 9 + 1}{243} = \frac{154}{243} = 0.63374$$

If you look at the numerator of the last equation carefully, you might notice that the numerator consists of weighted digits, where the digits correspond to the weights of the fraction as if the ternary point had been shifted five places right to make the fraction into a whole number. (The base 3 number point is called a *ternary* point.) A shift five places to the right multiplies the number by $3 \rightarrow 9 \rightarrow 27 \rightarrow 81 \rightarrow 243$; therefore, we have to divide by 243 to restore the original fraction.

Repeating this exercise with another, perhaps more practical, example should help to solidify this method for you:

EXAMPLE

Convert 0.110011_2 to base 10.
Shifting the binary point six places to the right and converting, we have

$$\texttt{numerator value} = 32 + 16 + 2 + 1 = 51$$

Shifting the binary back is equivalent to dividing by 2^6, or 64. Dividing the numerator 51 by 64 yields

$$\texttt{value} = 0.796875$$

The intuitive method for converting numbers from base 10 to another base can also be used. This is the method shown earlier where you fit the largest product of weights for each digit without exceeding the original number. In the case of fractions, however, you are working with fractional decimal numbers, and the actual calculation may be time consuming and difficult except in simple cases.

EXAMPLE

Convert the number 0.1_{10} to binary representation. The weights for binary fractions are

$$\frac{1}{2} \qquad \frac{1}{4} \qquad \frac{1}{8} \qquad \frac{1}{16} \qquad \frac{1}{32} \qquad \texttt{etc.}$$

These are easier to use when converted into decimal form: 0.5, 0.25, 0.125, 0.0625, and 0.03125, respectively. The largest value that fits into 0.1_{10} is 0.0625, which corresponds to a value of 0.0001_2. The remainder to be converted is $0.1 - 0.0625 = 0.0375$. Since 0.03125 fits into this remainder, the next bit is also a $1:0.00011_2$, and so on. As an exercise, you may want to carry this conversion out a few more places.

To convert fractional numbers from base 10 to another base, it is usually easier to use a variation on the division method shown earlier. Recall that for an integer, this involved dividing the number repeatedly by the base value and retaining the remainders. Effectively, this method works by shifting the radix point to the left one place each time we divide by the base value and noticing what drops over the radix point, which is the remainder. The number point is initially assumed to be to the right of the number.

When the value being converted is to the right of the number point, the procedure must work exactly the opposite. We *multiply* the fraction by the base value repeatedly, and record, then drop, the values that move to the left of the radix point. We repeat this procedure until the desired number of digits of accuracy is attained or until the value being multiplied is zero. Each time we multiply, we effectively expose the next digit.

For example, if the value in base 10 is 0.5, multiplying that by 2 would yield 1.0, which says that in base 2 there would have been a 1 in the 1/2-bit location. Similarly, 0.25 would be multiplied by 2, twice, to reach a value of 1.0, indicating a 1 in the 1/4-bit location. An example of the procedure should clarify this explanation:

EXAMPLE

Convert 0.828125_{10} to base 2. Multiplying by 2, we get

$$
\begin{array}{r}
.828125 \\
\times \qquad 2 \\
\hline
1.656250 \\
\times \qquad 2 \\
\hline
1.312500 \\
\times \qquad 2 \\
\hline
0.625000 \\
\times \qquad 2 \\
\hline
1.250000 \\
\times \qquad 2 \\
\hline
0.500000 \\
\times \qquad 2 \\
\hline
1.000000
\end{array}
$$

The 1 is saved as result, then dropped, and the process repeated

The final result, reading the overflow values downward, is 0.110101_2. This is an example of a conversion that reaches closure. You will recall that we stated earlier that 0.1_{10} is an example of a number that does not convert exactly into base 2. The procedure for that case follows.

$$
\begin{array}{r}
.100000 \\
\times \qquad 2 \\
\hline
0.200000 \\
\times \qquad 2 \\
\hline
0.400000 \\
\times \qquad 2 \\
\hline
0.800000 \\
\times \qquad 2 \\
\hline
1.600000 \\
\times \qquad 2 \\
\hline
1.200000 \\
\times \qquad 2 \\
\hline
0.400000
\end{array}
$$

The repeating nature of this conversion is clear at this point.

Finally, we note that conversion between bases where one base is an integer power of the other can be performed for fractions by grouping the digits in the smaller base as before. For fractions, the grouping must be done from left to right; the method is otherwise identical.

EXAMPLE

To convert 0.1011_2 to base 8, group the digits by threes (since $2^3 = 8$) and convert each group as usual. Note that it is necessary to supplement the second group with 0's. As you would expect, fractional zeros are appended to the right of the fraction.

Therefore,

$$0.101\_100_2 = 0.54_8$$

2.8 MIXED NUMBER CONVERSIONS

The usual arithmetic rules apply to fractional and mixed numbers. When adding and subtracting these numbers, the radix points must line up. During multiplication and division, the radix point is determined in exactly the same way as it would be in base 10. For multiplication in base 8, for example, you would add the number of digits to the right of the radix in the multiplier and the multiplicand; the total would be the number of digits to the right of the radix point in the result.

Extra caution is required when performing base conversions on numbers that contain both integer and fractional parts. The two parts must be converted separately.

The radix point is the fixed reference in a conversion. It does not move, since the digit to its left is a unit digit in every base; that is, B^0 is always 1, regardless of B.

It is possible to shift a mixed number in order to make it an integer. Unfortunately, there is a tendency to forget that the shift takes place in a particular base. A number shifted in base 2, say, cannot be converted and then shifted back in base 10 because the factor used in the shift is 2^k, which obviously has a different value than 10^k. Of course, it is possible to perform the shift and then divide the converted number by the original shift value, but this is usually more trouble than it's worth.

Instead, it's usually easier to remember that each part is converted separately, with the radix point remaining fixed at its original location.

SUMMARY AND REVIEW

Counting in bases other than 10 is essentially similar to the familiar way of counting. Each digit place represents a count of a group of digits from the next less significant digit place. The group is of size B, where B is the base of the number system being used. The least significant digit, of course, represents single units. Addition, subtraction, multiplication, and division for any number base work similarly to base 10, although the arithmetic tables look different.

There are several different methods that can be used to convert whole numbers from base B to base 10. The informal method is to recognize the base 10 values for each digit place and simply to add the weighted values for each digit together. A more formal method converts from base B to base 10 using successive multiplication by the present base and addition of the next digit. The final total represents the base 10 solution to the conversion. Similar methods exist for converting from base 10 to a different number base.

The conversion of number bases in which one base is an integer power of the other may be performed by recognizing that multiple digit places in the smaller base represent a single-digit place in the larger. Conversion is then done by grouping and converting each multiple set of digits individually.

Fractional and mixed numbers must be handled more carefully. The integer and fractional parts must be treated independently of each other. Although the conversion method is the same, the choice of the multiplication or division operation is reversed for the fractional part. Again, directly related bases can be converted by grouping digits in one base and converting each group independently.

KEY CONCEPTS AND TERMS

base	binary-octal conversion	hexadecimal number
binary arithmetic	bit	left shift
binary number	decimal point	mixed number conversion
binary point	decimal-binary conversion	octal number
binary-decimal conversion	fractional conversion	radix point
binary-hexadecimal conversion	hexadecimal-binary conversion	right shift

FOR FURTHER READING

Working in different number bases was part of a trend in the teaching of mathematics in the 1960s and 1970s known as "the new math." The material is still taught in many elementary schools.

Many libraries carry texts with such titles as "Elementary Math." A good, brief review of arithmetic as it applies to the computer can be found in the Schaum outline series book *Essential Computer Mathematics* [LIPS82]. A funny introduction to "new math" can be found on the recording "That Was the Year That Was" by Tom Lehrer [LEHR65]. In addition, most books on computer arithmetic contain substantial discussions of the topics covered in this chapter. Typical computer arithmetic books include those by Spaniol [SPAN81] and Kulisch and Maranker [KUL81]. A clear and thorough discussion of this material can be found in the computer architecture book by Hennessy, Patterson, and Goldberg [HENN02].

EXERCISES

2.1 **a.** Determine the power of each digit for five-digit numbers in base 6.

     b. Use your results from part (a) to convert the base 6 number 24531_6 to decimal.

2.2 Determine the power of each digit for four-digit numbers in base 16. Which place digits in base 2 have the same power?

2.3 Convert the following hexadecimal numbers to decimal:

     a. 4E

     b. 3D7

     c. 3D70

2.4 Some older computers used an 18-bit word to store numbers. What is the decimal range for this word size?

2.5 How many bits will it take to represent the decimal number 3,175,000? How many bytes will it take to store this number?

2.6 **a.** Create addition and multiplication tables for base 12 arithmetic. Use alphabetic characters to represent digits 10 and larger.

     b. Using your tables from part (a), perform the following addition:

$$
\begin{array}{r}
25A84_{12} \\
+\ 70396_{12} \\
\hline
\end{array}
$$

     c. Multiply the following numbers together:

$$2A6_{12}$$
$$\times\ B1_{12}$$

2.7   **a.** Create the hexadecimal multiplication table.

     b. Use the hexadecimal table in Figure 2.8 to perform the following addition:

$$2AB3$$
$$+\ 35DC$$

     c. Add the following numbers:

$$1FF9$$
$$+\ \ \ F7$$

     d. Multiply the following numbers:

$$2E26$$
$$\times\ \ \ 4A$$

2.8 Add the following binary numbers:

  a.

$$101101101$$
$$+\ 10011011$$

  b.

$$110111111$$
$$+\ \ \ \ \ \ \ \ \ \ 1$$

  c.

$$11010011$$
$$+\ 10001010$$

  d.

$$1101$$
$$1010$$
$$111$$
$$+\ \ 101$$

     e. Repeat the previous additions by converting each number to hexadecimal, adding, and converting the result back to binary.

2.9 Multiply the following binary numbers together:

  a.

$$1101$$
$$\times\ \ 101$$

  b.

$$11011$$
$$\times\ \ 1011$$

2.10 Perform the following binary divisions:

   a.

$$110 \overline{\smash{\big)}1010001001}$$

   b.

$$1011 \overline{\smash{\big)}11000000000}$$

2.11 Using the powers of each digit in base 8, convert the decimal number 6026 to octal.

2.12 Using the powers of each digit in hexadecimal, convert the decimal number 6026 to hexadecimal.

2.13 Using the division method, convert the following decimal numbers:

   a. 13750 to base 12

   b. 6026 to hexadecimal

   c. 3175 to base 5

2.14 Using the division method, convert the following decimal numbers to binary:

   a. 4098

   b. 71269

   c. 37

   In each case, check your work by using the power of each digit to convert back to decimal.

2.15 Using the multiplication method, convert the following numbers to decimal:

   a. $110001010010000 1_2$

   b. $C521_{16}$

   c. $3ADF_{16}$

   d. 24556_7

2.16 Convert the following binary numbers directly to hexadecimal:

   a. 101101110111010

   b. 1111111111110001

   c. 1111111101111

   d. 110001100011001

2.17 Convert the following hexadecimal numbers to binary:

   a. 4F6A

   b. 9902

   c. A3AB

   d. 1000

2.18 Select a number base that would be suitable for direct conversion from base 3, and convert the number 22011210_3 to that base.

2.19 **a.** Convert the base 4 number 13023031_4 directly to hexadecimal. Check your result by converting both the original number and your answer to decimal.

    b.   Convert the hexadecimal number $9B62_{16}$ directly to base 4; then convert both the original number and your answer to binary to check your result.

2.20   Convert the base 3 number 210102_3 to octal. What process did you use to do this conversion?

2.21   Convert the octal number 27745_8 to hexadecimal. Do *not* use decimal as an intermediary for your conversion. Why does a direct conversion not work in this case?

2.22   Using whatever programming language is appropriate for you, write a program that converts a whole number input by the user from base 8 to base 10. Your program should flag as an error any input that contains the digits 8 or 9.

2.23   Using whatever programming language is appropriate for you, write a program that converts a whole number input from decimal to hexadecimal.

2.24   Using whatever programming language is appropriate for you, write a program that converts whole numbers in either direction between binary and hexadecimal.

2.25   Convert the following numbers from decimal to hexadecimal. If the answer is irrational, stop at four hexadecimal digits:

    a.   0.6640625

    b.   0.3333

    c.   69/256

2.26   Convert the following numbers from their given base to decimal:

    a. 0.1001001_2

    b. $0.3A2_{16}$

    c. $0.2A1_{12}$

2.27   Convert the following numbers from decimal to binary and then to hexadecimal:

    a.   27.625

    b.   4192.37761

2.28   What is the decimal value of the following binary numbers?

    a.   1100101.1

    b.   1110010.11

    c.   11100101.1

2.29   Draw a flow diagram that shows step by step the process for converting a mixed number in a base other than 10 to decimal.

2.30   Write a computer program in a language appropriate for you that converts mixed numbers between decimal and binary in both directions.

CHAPTER 3

DATA FORMATS

Thomas Sperling, adapted by Benjamin Reece

3.0 INTRODUCTION

In Chapter 2 you had a chance to explore some of the properties of the binary number system. You are already aware that within the computer the binary number system is the system of choice, both for all forms of data storage and for all internal processing of operations. As human beings, we normally don't choose to do our work in binary form. Our communications are made up of language, images, and sounds. For written communications, and for our own data storage, we most frequently use alphanumeric characters and symbols, representing English or some other language. Sometimes we communicate with a photograph, or a chart or diagram, or some other image. Images may be black and white or color; they may be still frames or moving. Sounds often represent a different, spoken, form of written language, but they may also represent other possibilities, such as music, the roar of an engine, or a purr of satisfaction. We perform calculations using numbers made up of a set of numeric characters.

In the past, most business data processing took the form of text and numbers. Today, the multimedia concept, consisting of images and sounds, is of increasing importance. Since data within the computer is limited to binary numbers, it is almost always necessary to convert our words, numbers, images, and sounds into a different form in order to store and process them in the computer.

In this chapter, we consider what it takes to get different types of data into computer-usable form and the different ways in which the data may be represented, stored, and processed.

3.1 GENERAL CONSIDERATIONS

At some point, original data, whether character, image, sound, or some other form, must be brought initially into the computer and converted into an appropriate computer representation so that it can be processed, stored, and used within the computer system. The fundamental process is shown in Figure 3.1.

Different input devices are used for this purpose. The particular choice of input device reflects the original form of the data, and also the desired data representation within the computer. Some devices perform the conversion from external form to internal representation within the input device. At other times, the input device merely serves to transform the data into a raw binary form that the computer can manipulate. Further conversion is then performed by software within the computer.

There are varying degrees of difficulty associated with the input task. Normal keyboard input, for example, is relatively straightforward. Since there are a discrete number of keys on the keyboard, it is only necessary for the keyboard to generate a binary number code for each key, which can then be identified as a simple representation of the desired character. On the other hand, input from a device that presents a continuous range of data (i.e., analog data) presents a more formidable task, particularly if the data

FIGURE 3.1

Data Conversion and Representation

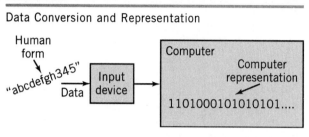

is continuously changing with time, which is the case with a video camera or microphone.

Adequate representation of the sound input from a microphone, for example, will require hardware designed to convert the sound into binary numbers and may require hundreds or even thousands of separate pieces of data, each representing a sample of the sound at a single instant in time. If the sound is to be used within the computer to represent the characters in a word, the task becomes even more challenging, since the translation of sounds into character form is very complex and difficult, requiring sophisticated, specialized software.

The internal representation of data within the computer reflects the complexity of the input source, and also the type of processing that is to take place. There is no need to preserve all the individual points that make up a photographic image, for example, if the goal is only to extract and process the characters that are present on the page; it is only necessary to input and represent the entire set of data long enough to extract the actual data that is to be used or kept. On the other hand, if the image is to be used as a figure in an art book, it will be necessary to represent the image, with all its details, as accurately as possible. For input forms that represent a continuum of values, such as images and sound, the quantity of binary numbers and the number of bits in each that are required to represent the input data accurately will grow quite rapidly with increasing accuracy and resolution. In fact, some form of algorithmic data compression will sometimes be necessary to reduce the amount of data to a manageable level, particularly if the data is to be downloaded or streamed over a low-speed transmission device, such as a telephone modem.

Of course, once the input data is in computer form it can be stored for future use, or it can be moved between computers through networks or by using portable computer media such as CD-ROM or floppy disks. Images and sounds can be downloaded from a Web site or attached to email, for example. Provided that the receiving computer has the appropriate software, it can store, display, and process a downloaded image just as though the picture had been produced by an image scanner connected directly to its own input.

For storage and transmission of data, a representation different from that used for internal processing is often necessary. In addition to the actual data representing points in an image or characters being displayed, the system must store and pass along information that *describes* or *interprets the meaning* of the data. Such information is known as **metadata.** In some cases, the description is simple: to read a pure text file may require only a single piece of information that indicates the number of characters in the text or marks the end of the text. A graphic image or sound requires a much more detailed description of the data. To reproduce the image, a system must know the type of graphical image, the number of colors represented by each data point, the method used to represent each color, the number of horizontal and vertical data points, the order in which data points are stored, the relative scaling of each axis, the location of the image on the screen, and much more. For a sound, the system must know how long a time period each sample represents, the number of bits in each sample, and even, perhaps, how the sound is to be used and coordinated with other sounds.

Individual programs can store and process data in any format that they want. The format used to process and store text in WordPerfect is different from that used by Microsoft Word, for example. The formats used by individual programs are known as **proprietary formats.** Proprietary formats are often suitable for an individual user or a group of users working on similar computer systems. As noted in Chapter 1, proprietary standards sometimes become de facto standards due to general user acceptance.

Note that it is important to distinguish between the data representation used within an individual piece of software and the data representation used for the input, output, storage, and exchange of data, however. Modern computer systems and networks interconnect many different types of computers, input and output devices, and computer programs. A Web page viewed on a Macintosh computer might contain an image scanned on a Hewlett-Packard image scanner, with HTML created on a Dell PC, and be served by an IBM mainframe, for example.

Thus, it is critical throughout this discussion that *standard* data representations exist to be used as interfaces between different programs, between a program and the I/O devices used by the program, between interconnected hardware, and between systems that share data, using network interconnections or transportable media such as CD-ROMs. These data representations must be recognized by a wide variety of hardware and software so that they can be used by users working within different computer environments.

A well-designed data representation will reflect and simplify the ways in which the data is to be processed and will encompass the widest possible user community. For example, the order of the letters in the alphabet is commonly used for the sorting and selection of alphanumeric business data. It makes sense, then, to choose a computer representation of alphabetic characters that will simplify these operations within the computer. Furthermore, the representation of alphanumeric characters will encompass as many of the world's languages as possible to aid in international communication.

There are many different standards in use for different types of data. A few of the common ones are shown in Figure 3.2. We have not included the standard representations for numerical data; those are discussed in the next two chapters.

This section described the general principles that govern the input and representation of data. Next, we consider some of the most important data forms individually.

3.2 ALPHANUMERIC CHARACTER DATA

Much of the data that will be used in a computer are originally provided in human-readable form, specifically in the form of letters of the alphabet, numbers, and punctuation, whether English or some other language. The text of a word processing document, the numbers that we use as input to a calculation, the names and addresses in a data base, the transaction data that constitutes a credit card purchase, the keywords, variable names, and formulas that make up a computer program, all are examples of data input that is made up of letters, numbers, and punctuation.

Most of this data is initially input to the computer through a keyboard, although alternative means, such as magnetic card stripes, document image scanning, voice-to-text translation, and bar code scanning are also used. The keyboard may be connected directly to a computer, or it may be part of a separate device, such as a video terminal, an online

FIGURE 3.2

Some Common Data Representations

Type of data	Standard(s)
Alphanumeric	Unicode, ASCII, EBCDIC
Image (bitmap)	GIF (graphical image format), TIFF (tagged image file format), PNG (portable network graphics)
Image (object)	PostScript, JPEG, SWF (Macromedia Flash), SVG
Outline graphics and fonts	PostScript, TrueType
Sound	WAV, AVI, MP3, MIDI, WMA
Page description	pdf (Adobe Portable Document Format), HTML, XML
Video	Quicktime, MPEG-2, RealVideo, WMV

cash register, or even a bank ATM. The data entered as characters, number digits, and punctuation are known as **alphanumeric data.**

It is tempting to think of **numeric characters** as somehow different from other characters, since **numbers** are often processed differently from text. Also, a number may consist of more than a single digit, and you know from your programming courses that you can store and process a number in numerical form within the computer. There is no processing capability in the keyboard itself, however. Therefore, numbers must be entered into the computer just like other characters, one digit at a time. At the time of entry, the number 1234.5 consists of the alphanumeric characters "1," "2," "3," "4," ".," and "5." Any conversion to numeric form will take place within the computer itself, using software written for this purpose. For display, the number will be converted back to character form.

The conversion between character and number is also not "automatic" within the computer. There are times when we would prefer to keep the data in character form, for example, when the numbers represent a phone number or an address to be stored and processed according to text criteria. Since this choice is dependent on usage within a program, the decision is made by the programmer using rules specified within the program language being used. In simple forms of BASIC, for example, the programmer makes the choice by placing a $ character at the end of a variable name that is to be used to keep data in alphanumeric form. In C++ or Java, the type of variable must be declared before the variable is used. When the data variable being read is numerical, the compiler will build into the program a conversion routine that accepts numerical characters and converts them into the appropriate numerical variable value. In general, numerical characters must be converted into number form when calculations are to be performed.

Since alphanumeric data must be stored and processed within the computer in binary form, each character must be translated to a corresponding binary code representation as it enters the computer. The choice of code used is arbitrary. Since the computer does not "recognize" letters, but only binary numbers, it does not matter to the computer what code is selected.

What *does* matter is consistency. Most data output, including numbers, also exits the computer in alphanumeric form, either through printed output or as output on a video screen. Therefore, the output device must perform the same conversion in reverse. It is obviously important that the input device and the output device recognize the same code. Although it would be theoretically possible to write a program to change the input code so that a different output code would result in the desired alphanumeric output, this is rarely done in practice. Since data is frequently shared between different computers in networks, the use of a code that is standardized among many different types of computers is highly desirable.

The data is also stored using the same alphanumeric code form. Consistent use of the same code is required to allow later retrieval of the data, as well as for operations using data entered into the computer at different times, such as during merge operations.

It also matters that the programs within the computer know something about the particular data code that was used as input so that conversion of the characters that make up numbers into the numbers themselves can be done correctly, and also so that such operations as sorting can be done. It would not make a lot of sense to pick a code in which the letters of the alphabet are scrambled, for example. By choosing a code in which the value of the binary number representing a character corresponds to the placement of the character within the alphabet, we can provide programs that sort data without even knowing what the data is, just by numerically sorting the codes that correspond to each character.

Three alphanumeric codes are in common use. The three codes are known as **Unicode, ASCII** (which stands for American Standard Code for Information Interchange, pronounced "as-key" with a soft "s"), and **EBCDIC** (Extended Binary Coded Decimal Interchange Code, pronounced "ebb-see-dick"). EBCDIC was developed by IBM. Its use is restricted mostly to older IBM and IBM-compatible mainframe computers and terminals. Nearly all other computer and terminal manufacturers have agreed upon Unicode or ASCII for current use.

The translation table for ASCII code is shown in Figure 3.3. The EBCDIC code is somewhat less standardized; the punctuation symbols have changed over the years. A recent EBCDIC code table is shown in Figure 3.4. The codes for each symbol are given in hexadecimal, with the most significant digit across the top and the least significant digit down the side. Both ASCII and EBCDIC codes can be stored in a byte. For example, the ASCII value for "G" is 47_{16}. When comparing the two tables, note that the standard ASCII code is actually defined as a 7-bit code, so there are only 128 entries in the ASCII table. EBCDIC is defined as an 8-bit code. The additional special characters in both tables are used as process and communication control characters.

The ASCII code was originally developed as a standard by the American National Standards Institute (**ANSI**). ANSI also has defined 8-bit extensions to the original ASCII codes that provide various symbols, line shapes, and accented foreign letters for the additional 128 entries not shown in the figure. Together, the 8-bit code is known as Latin-I. Latin-I is an ISO (International Standards Organization) standard.

Both ASCII and EBCDIC have limitations that reflect their origins. The 256 code values that are available in an 8-bit word limit the number of possible characters severely. Both codes provide only the Latin alphabet, Arabic numerals, and standard punctuation characters that are used in English; Latin-I ASCII also includes a small set of accents and other special characters that extend the set to major western European cultures. EBCDIC omits certain characters, in particular, the "[" and "]" characters that are used to represent

FIGURE 3.3

ASCII Code Table

LSD\MSD	0	1	2	3	4	5	6	7
0	NUL	DLE	space	0	@	P	`	p
1	SOH	DC1	!	1	A	Q	a	q
2	STX	DC2	"	2	B	R	b	r
3	ETX	DC3	#	3	C	S	c	s
4	EOT	DC4	$	4	D	T	d	t
5	ENQ	NAK	%	5	E	U	e	u
6	ACK	SYN	&	6	F	V	f	v
7	BEL	ETB	'	7	G	W	g	w
8	BS	CAN	(	8	H	X	h	x
9	HT	EM	)	9	I	Y	i	y
A	LF	SUB	*	:	J	Z	j	z
B	VT	ESC	+	;	K	[	k	{
C	FF	FS	,	<	L	\	l	l
D	CR	GS	-	=	M	]	m	}
E	SO	RS	.	>	N	^	n	~
F	SI	US	/	?	O	_	o	DEL

subscripts in the C and Java programming languages, the "^" character, used as a mathematical operator in a number of languages, "{" and "}," used to enclose code blocks in many languages, and the "~" character, used for UNIX system commands and Internet and Internet URLs. These shortcomings led to the development of a new 16-bit international standard, Unicode, which is quickly supplanting ASCII and EBCDIC for alphanumeric representation in most modern systems. The ASCII Latin-I code set is a subset of Unicode, occupying the values 0–256 in the Unicode table, therefore conversion from ASCII to Unicode is particularly simple: it is only necessary to extend the 8-bit code to 16 bits by setting the eight most significant bits to zero. Unicode to ASCII conversion is also simple, provided that the characters used are limited to the ASCII subset.

The most common form of Unicode can represent 65,536 characters, of which approximately forty-nine thousand have been defined. An additional 6,400 codes are reserved permanently for private use. A more recent standard, Unicode 3.1, allows for multiple code pages that can support millions of different characters. Unicode is multilingual in the most global sense. It defines codes for the characters of nearly every character-based alphabet of the world in modern use, as well as codes for a large set of ideographs for the Chinese, Japanese, and Korean languages, codes for a wide range of punctuation and symbols, and various control characters. It supports composite characters and syllabic clusters. Composite

FIGURE 3.4

The EBCDIC Code Table

	0	1	2	3	4	5	6	7
0	NUL	DLE	DS		space	&	-	
1	SOH	DC1	SOS		RSP		/	
2	STX	DC2	FS	SYN				
3	ETX	DC3	WU5	IR				
4	SEL	ENP	BYP/INP	PP				
5	HT	NL	LF	TRN				
6	RNL	BS	ETB	NBS				
7	DEL	POC	ESC	EOT				
8	GE	CAN	SA	SBS				
9	SPS	EM	SFE	IT				
A	RPT	UB5	SM/SW	RFF	¢	!	|	:
B	VT	CU1	CSP	CU3	.	$	,	#
C	FF	IFS	MFA	DC4	<	*	%	@
D	CR	IGS	ENQ	NAK	(	)	~	'
E	SO	IRS	ACK		+	;	>	=
F	SI	IUS	BEL	SUB	|	¬	?	"

	8	9	A	B	C	D	E	F
0					{	}	\	0
1	a	j	_		A	J	NSP	1
2	b	k	s		B	K	S	2
3	c	l	t		C	L	T	3
4	d	m	u		D	M	U	4
5	e	n	v		E	N	V	5
6	f	o	w		F	O	W	6
7	g	p	x		G	P	X	7
8	h	q	y		H	Q	Y	8
9	i	r	z		I	R	Z	9
A					5HY			
B								
C								
D								
E								
F								EO

characters are those made up of two or more different components, only one of which causes spacing to occur. For example, some vowels in Hebrew appear beneath a corresponding consonant. Syllabic clusters in certain languages are single characters, sometimes made up of composite components, that make up an entire syllable. The private space is intended for user-defined and software-specific characters, control characters, and symbols. Figure 3.5 shows the general code table layout for the common, two-byte, form of Unicode.

Reflecting the pervasiveness of international communications, Unicode is gradually replacing ASCII as the alphanumeric code of choice for most systems and applications. Even IBM uses ASCII or Unicode on its smaller computers, and provides two-way Unicode-EBCDIC conversion tables for its mainframes. Unicode is the standard for use in current Windows and Linux operating systems. However, the vast amount of archival data in storage and use assures that ASCII and EBCDIC will continue to exist for some time to come.

Returning to the ASCII and EBCDIC tables, there are several interesting ideas to be gathered by looking at the tables together. First, note, not surprisingly, that the codes for particular alphanumeric characters are different in the two tables. This simply reemphasizes that, if we use an ASCII terminal for the input, the output will also be in ASCII form

FIGURE 3.5

Two-byte Unicode Assignment Table

Code range (in hexadecimal)	
0000–	} 0000–00FF Latin-I (ASCII)
1000–	} General character alphabets: Latin, Cyrillic, Greek, Hebrew, Arabic, Thai, etc.
2000–	} Symbols and dingbats: punctuation, math, technical, geometric shapes, etc.
3000–	} 3000–33FF Miscellaneous punctuations, symbols, and phonetics for Chinese, Japanese, and Korean
4000–	} Unassigned
5000–	
•	
•	} 4E00–9FFF Chinese, Japanese, Korean ideographs
•	
A000–	} Unassigned
B000–	
C000–	} AC00–D7AF Korean Hangui syllables
D000–	
E000–	} Space for surrogates
F000–	} E000–F8FF Private use
FFFF –	} Various special characters

unless some translation took place within the computer. In other words, printing ASCII characters on an EBCDIC terminal would produce garbage.

More important, note that both ASCII and EBCDIC are designed so that the order of the letters is such that a simple numerical sort on the codes can be used within the computer to perform alphabetization, provided that the software converts mixed upper- and lowercase codes to one form or the other. The order of the codes in the representation table is known as its **collating sequence.** The collating sequence is of great importance in routine character processing, since much character processing centers on the sorting and selection of data.

Uppercase and lowercase letters, and letters and numbers, have different collating sequences in ASCII and EBCDIC. Therefore, a computer program designed to sort ASCII-generated characters will produce a different, and perhaps not desired, result when run with EBCDIC input. Particularly note that small letters *precede* capitals in EBCDIC, but the reverse is true in ASCII. The same situation arises for strings that are a mix of alphabetical characters and numbers. In ASCII the numbers collate first, in EBCDIC, last.

Both tables are divided into two classes of codes, specifically *printing* characters and *control* characters. Printing characters actually produce output on the screen or on a printer. Control characters are used to control the position of the output on the screen or paper, to cause some action to occur, such as ringing a bell or deleting a character, or to communicate status between the computer and an I/O device, such as the Control–"C" key combination, which is used on many computers to interrupt execution of a program. Except for position control characters, the control characters in the ASCII table are struck by holding down the Control key and striking a character. The code executed corresponds in table position to the position of the same alphabetic character. Thus, the code for SOH is generated by the Control–"A" key combination and SUB by the Control–"Z" key combination. Looking at the ASCII and EBCDIC tables can you determine what **control codes** are generated by the tab key? An explanation of each control character in the ASCII table is shown in Figure 3.6. Many of the names and descriptions of codes in this table reflect the use of these codes for data communications. There are also additional control codes in EBCDIC that are specific to IBM mainframes, but we won't define them here.

Unless the application program that is processing the text reformats or modifies the data in some way, textual data is normally stored as a string of characters, including alphanumeric characters, spaces, tabs, carriage returns, plus other control characters and escape sequences that are relevant to the text. Some application programs, particularly word processors, add their own special character sequences for formatting the text.

In Unicode, each alphanumeric character can be stored in two bytes, thus, half the number of bytes in a pure text file (one with no images) is a good approximation of the number of characters in the text. Similarly, the number of available bytes also defines the capacity of a device to store textual and numerical data. Only a small percentage of the storage space is needed to keep track of information about the various files; almost all the space is thus available for the text itself. Thus, a 1.4MB floppy disk will hold about 700,000 characters (note that spaces are also characters, of course!). If you assume that a page has about fifty rows of sixty characters, then a 1.4MB floppy disk can hold almost 230 pages of text or numbers.

In reality, the floppy disk will probably hold less because most modern word processors can combine text with graphics, page layout, font selection, and other features.

FIGURE 3.6

Control Code Definitions [STAL96]

NUL	(Null) No character; used to fill space	**DLE**	(Data Link Escape) Similar to escape, but used to change meaning of data control characters; used to permit sending of data characters with any bit combination
SOH	(Start of Heading) Indicates start of a header used during transmission		
STX	(Start of Text) Indicates start of text during transmission	**DC1,DC2,** **DC3, DC4**	(Device Controls) Used for the control of devices or special terminal features
ETX	(End of Text) Similar to above	**NAK**	(Negative Acknowledgment) Opposite of ACK
EOT	(End of Transmission)		
ENQ	(Enquiry) A request for response from a remote station; the response is usually an identification	**SYN**	(Synchronous) Used to synchronize a synchronous transmission system
ACK	(Acknowledge) A character sent by a receiving device as an affirmative response to a query by a sender	**STB**	(End of Transmission Block) Indicates end of a block of transmitted data
		CAN	(Cancel) Cancel previous data
BEL	(Bell) Rings a bell	**EM**	(End of Medium) Indicates the physical end of a medium such as tape
BS	(Backspace)		
HT	(Horizontal Tab)	**SUB**	(Substitute) Substitute a character for one sent in error
LF	(Line Feed)		
VT	(Vertical Tab)	**ESC**	(Escape) Provides extensions to the code by changing the meaning of a specified number of contiguous following characters
FF	(Form Feed) Moves cursor to the starting position of the next page, form, or screen		
CR	(Carriage return)	**FS, GS,** **RS, US**	(File, group, record, and united separators) Used in optional way by systems to provide separations within a data set
SO	(Shift Out) Shift to an alternative character set until SI is encountered		
SI	(Shift In) see above	**DEL**	(Delete) Delete current character

Graphics, in particular, consume a lot of disk space. Nonetheless, several chapters of this book, graphics and all, fit on a single floppy disk.

Keyboard Input

Most alphanumeric data in the computer results from keyboard input, although alternative forms of data input can be used. Operation of a keyboard is quite simple and straightforward: when a key is struck on the keyboard, the circuitry in the keyboard generates a binary code, called a **scan code.** When the key is released, a different scan code is generated. There are two different scan codes for every key on the keyboard. The scan codes are converted to the appropriate Unicode, ASCII, or EBCDIC codes by software within the terminal or personal computer to which the keyboard is connected. The advantage of software conversion is that the use of the keyboard can be easily changed to correspond to different languages or keyboard layouts. The use of separate scan codes for key press and release functions allows the system to detect and process multiple key combinations, such as those used by the shift and control keys.

The keyboard operation is shown in Figure 3.7. In the figure, the user has typed the three letters "D," "I," "R," followed by the carriage return character. The computer translates the four scancodes to ASCII binary codes 1000100, 1001001, 1010010, 0001101, or their Unicode equivalents. Nonprinting characters, such as Control characters, are treated identically to Printing characters. To the computer, keyboard input is treated simply as a **stream** of text and other characters, one character after another, in the sequence typed. Note that the carriage return character is part of the stream.

The software in most computer systems echoes printable keyboard input characters directly back to the display screen, to allow the user to verify that the input has been typed correctly. Since the display circuitry and software recognizes the same character code set as the input, the characters are correctly echoed on the screen. In theory, a system could accept Unicode input from a keyboard and produce EBCDIC output to a display screen, using software to convert from one code set to the other. In practice, this is almost never done.

Alternative Sources of Alphanumeric Input

OPTICAL CHARACTER RECOGNITION   Alphanumeric data may also be entered into a computer using other forms of input. One popular alternative is to scan a page of text with an image scanner and to convert the image into alphanumeric data form using **optical character recognition,** or **OCR,** software. Early OCR software required the use of special typefaces for the scanned image and produced a lot of errors. The amount of proofreading required often nullified any advantage to using the scanner. As OCR software continues to improve, the use of scanners to read typed text directly from the page will undoubtedly increase as a source of alphanumeric data input.

A variation on OCR is also used to read specially encoded characters, such as those printed magnetically on checks. Attempts have also been made to recognize hand-written input, both from scanned input and from input to a pad or tablet device. This technology continues to improve, but is still limited to small quantities of data, carefully printed.

BAR CODE READERS   Another alternative form of data input is the bar code reader. Bar code input is practical and efficient for many business applications that require fast, accurate, and repetitive input with minimum employee training. You are probably most familiar with its use at grocery checkout counters, but many organizations use bar codes, particularly for inventory control and order filling.

Bar codes represent alphanumeric data. The UPC bar code in Figure 3.8, for example, translates to the alphanumeric value 780471 108801 90000. Bar codes are read optically using a device called a wand that converts a visual scan of the code into electrical binary signals that a bar code translation module can read. The module translates the binary input into

FIGURE 3.7	**FIGURE 3.8**
Keyboard Operation	UPC Bar Code

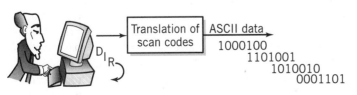

a sequence of number codes, one code per digit, that can then be input into the computer. The process is essentially similar to those already discussed. The code is usually then translated to Unicode or ASCII.

MAGNETIC STRIPE READERS Magnetic stripe readers are used to read alphanumeric data from credit cards and other similar devices. The technology used is very similar to that used for magnetic tape.

VOICE INPUT It is currently possible and practical to digitize audio for use as input data. As we discuss in Section 3.4, most digitized audio data is simply stored for later output or is processed in ways that modify the sound of the data. The technology necessary to interpret audio data as voice input and to translate the data into alphanumeric form is still relatively primitive. The translation process requires the conversion of voice data into sound patterns known as **phonemes.** Each phoneme in a particular language represents one or more possible groupings of letters in that language. The groupings must then be matched and manipulated and combined to form words and sentences. Pronunciation rules, grammar rules, and a dictionary aid in the process. The understanding of sentence context is also necessary to correctly identify words such as to, too, or two. As you can see, the task is a daunting one! Progress is being made, however, and it is expected that voice input will be a major source of alphanumeric input in the foreseeable future.

3.3 IMAGE DATA

Although alphanumeric data has been the traditional medium of business, improved computer technology and the growth of the Web have elevated the importance of images in the business computing environment. Photographs can be stored within the computer to provide rapid identification of employees. Drawings can be generated rapidly and accurately using CAD/CAM systems. Charts and graphs provide easily understood representations of business data and trends. Presentations and reports contain images for impact. Images are central to the success of the Web.

Images come in many different shapes, sizes, textures, colors, and shadings. Different processing requirements require different forms for image data. All these differences make it difficult to define a single universal format that can be used for images in the way that the standard alphanumeric codes are used for text. Instead, the image will be formatted according to processing, display, application, and storage requirements.

Images used within the computer fall into two distinct categories. Different computer representations and processing techniques are used for each category:

- Images such as photographs and paintings that are characterized by continuous variations in shading, color, shape, and texture. Images within this category may be entered into the computer using an image scanner or video camera frame grabber. They may also be produced within the computer using a paint program. To maintain and reproduce the detail of these images, it is necessary to represent and store each individual point within the image. We will refer to such images as **bitmap images.** Occasionally, they are called **raster images.** The GIF and JPEG formats commonly used on the Web are both examples of bitmap image formats.

- Images that are made up of graphical shapes such as lines and curves that can be defined geometrically. The shapes themselves may be quite complex. Many computer experts refer to these shapes as **graphical objects.** For these images, it is sufficient to store geometrical information about each object and the relative position of each object in the image. We will refer to these images as **object images.** They are also known, somewhat incorrectly, as **vector images,** because the image is often (but not always) made up of straight-line segments called vectors. Object images are normally produced within the computer using some sort of drawing or design package. They may also result from other types of processing, for example, as data plots or graphs representing the data in a spreadsheet. More rarely, they may occur as the result of the translation by special software of scanned bitmap images that are simple enough to reduce to object form.

- Most object image formats are proprietary. However, W3C, the international consortium that oversees the Web, has defined a new standard, SVG (scalable vector graphics), based on XML Web description language tags. Macromedia Flash is also in popular use.

Looking at a computer-displayed image, it can sometimes be difficult to distinguish between bitmap images and object images. It is possible, for example, to describe subtle gradations of color within an image geometrically. The processing required to create movement in computer-animated images may dictate the use of object images, even if the objects themselves are very complex. The type of image representation is often chosen on the basis of the computer processing to be performed on the image. The movies *Shrek* and *Toy Story* are amazing examples of the possibilities of object images.

Sometimes, both types of image data occur within the same image. It is always possible to store graphical objects in a bitmap format, but it is often desirable in such cases to maintain each type of image separately. Most object image representations provide for the inclusion of bitmap images within the representation.

Image Input

IMAGE SCANNING   One common way to input image data is with an image scanner. Data from an image scanner takes the form of a bitmap that represents some sort of image—a graphic drawing, a photograph, magnetically inked numbers on a check, perhaps even a document of printed text.

The scanner electronically moves over the image, converting the image dot by dot, line by line into a stream of binary numbers, each representing a single point (actually a small area) in the image, known as a **pixel,** for *pi(x)cture element.* The binary numbers may represent black or white, or they may represent a level of gray or of color. In the illustration in Figure 3.9, for example, each point in the picture is represented by a 4-bit code corresponding to one of sixteen gray levels. Hexadecimal F represents black, and hexadecimal 0 represents white. It should be noted that each pixel also has a coordinate location consisting of a row and column number associated with it, but it is usually not necessary to store the coordinate, because the data is read and stored in a particular order, as defined by the particular format being used.

FIGURE 3.9

Image Pixel Data

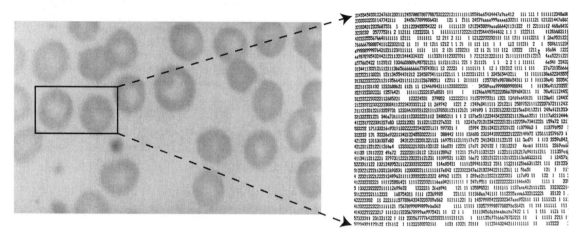

DIGITAL CAMERAS AND VIDEO CAPTURE DEVICES Digital cameras and video cameras can be used to capture bitmap images. The technology of video cameras and digital cameras is described in Chapter 10.

GRAPHICAL INPUT USING POINTING DEVICES Mice, pens, and other pointing devices can be used in conjunction with drawing or painting programs to input graphical data. The input from most of these devices is a pair of binary numbers representing either X and Y coordinates on the screen or relative movements in X and Y directions. Some drawing tablets also provide a measure of the pressure applied to the drawing pen. The pointing device is an input device. The appearance of a cursor on the output screen results from a calculation within the program that detects the current set of coordinates. The program then outputs a cursor as part of the screen image bitmap at the appropriate location on the screen. Internally, the image drawn will depend on the application program being used. Paint packages provide tools that use the pointing device to create "paintings" in a bitmap image form. Drawing packages provide tools that create and manipulate objects. In this case, the result is an object image.

Bitmap Images

As noted previously, bitmap images are made up of pixels representing individual points on the image. The storage and processing of bitmap images frequently requires a large amount of memory, and the processing of large arrays of data. A single color picture containing 600 rows of 800 pixels, with a separate byte to store each of three colors for each pixel, would require 1,440,000 bytes, or nearly 1.5 megabytes of storage. An alternative representation method that is useful for display purposes reduces memory requirements by storing a code for each pixel, rather than the actual color values. The code for each pixel is translated into actual color values using a color translation table known as a **palette** that is stored as part of the display program. This method is discussed in Chapter 10. Data compression may also be used to reduce storage and data transmission requirements.

The image represented within the computer is really only an approximation to the original image, since the original image presents a continual range of intensity, and perhaps also of color. The faithfulness of the computer representation depends on the size of the pixels and the number of levels representing each pixel. Reducing the pixel size improves the **resolution,** or detail level, of the representation by increasing the number of pixels per inch used to represent a given area of the image. It also reduces the "stepping" effects seen on diagonal lines. Increasing the number of levels per pixel increases the number of different gray levels or colors available to describe each pixel and improves the overall accuracy of the colors or gray tone in the image. The trade-off, of course, is in storage requirements and processing and transmission time.

Bitmap representations are particularly useful when there is a great amount of detail within an image, and for which the processing requirements are fairly simple. Typical processing on bitmap images includes storage and display, cutting and pasting of pieces of the image, and simple transformations of the image such as brightness and contrast changes, changing a dimension, or color alterations. Most bitmap image processing involves little or no direct processing of the objects illustrated within the image.

For processing within the computer, the format of the image depends on the software being used. At its simplest, the image could be stored in memory as a simple two-dimensional array. Each member of the array would contain the gray-level intensity of one pixel. The addition of a third dimension would allow for the use of multiple colors. Storage and transmission of bitmap images requires the maintenance of additional information about the picture. The dimensions of the image in pixels, the number of intensity levels for each pixel, the definition of the color palette, the resolution of the image, and identification of the image are some of the parameters that may be required or desirable. A pixel aspect ratio may be included so that display of the image can be adjusted if the pixel is rectangular rather than square. Some bitmap image formats also include data compression to minimize the number of bytes of data that must be stored and transmitted.

EXAMPLE

As an example of a bitmap image storage format, consider the popular **Graphics Interchange Format,** or **GIF,** method of storing images. GIF was first developed by CompuServe in 1987 as a proprietary format that would allow users of the online service to store and exchange bitmap images on a variety of different computing platforms. A second, more flexible, form of GIF was released in 1989. The later version, GIF89a, also allows a series of GIF images to be displayed sequentially at fixed time intervals to created "animated GIF images." The GIF format is used extensively on the Web.

GIF assumes the existence of a rectangular "screen" upon which is located one or more rectangular images of possibly different sizes. Areas not covered with images are painted with a background color. Figure 3.10 illustrates the layout of the screen and its images. The format divides the picture information and data into a number of blocks, each of which describes different aspects of the image. The first block, called the header block, identifies the file as a GIF file and specifies the version of GIF that is being used.

Following the header block is a logical screen-descriptor block, which identifies the width and height of the screen, describes an optional color table for the images on the screen (the palette), indicates the number of bits per color available, identifies the background screen color, and specifies the pixel aspect ratio.

Each image within the screen is then stored in its own block, headed by an image-descriptor block. The image-descriptor block identifies the size and position of the image on the screen, and also allows for a palette specific to the particular image, if desired. The block also contains information that makes it possible to display individual images at different resolutions. The actual pixel data for the image follows. The pixel data is compressed, using an algorithm called LZW. The basic GIF file format layout is shown in Figure 3.11.

Even though we have simplified the description, you can see that a graphical data format can be quite complex. The complexity is required to provide all the information that will allow the use of the image on a variety of different equipment.

FIGURE 3.10

GIF Screen Layout

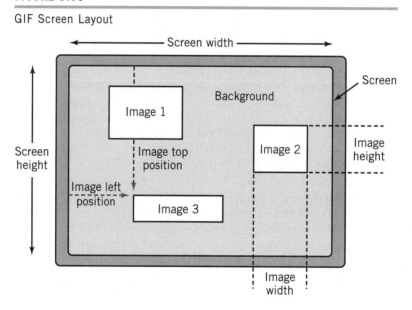

FIGURE 3.11

GIF File Format Layout

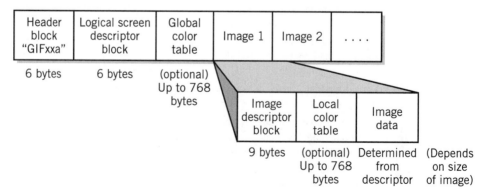

There are a number of alternatives to the GIF format. In particular, the GIF format is limited to 256 colors, which is sometimes insufficient to display the details of a painting or photograph, for example. A popular alternative, JPEG format (Joint Photographers Expert Group), addresses this concern by allowing more than sixteen million colors to be represented and displayed. JPEG employs a compression algorithm to reduce the amount of data stored and transmitted, but the algorithm used reduces image resolution under certain circumstances, particularly for sharp edges and lines. This makes JPEG more suitable for the representation of highly detailed photographs and paintings, but GIF is preferable for line drawings and simple images. Other formats include TIFF, which is popular on Macintosh platforms, BMP, a Windows format, and PCX, a format designed for use with PC Paintbrush software. PNG is a recent format that eliminates many GIF and JPEG shortcomings. It is intended to replace GIF and JPEG for many Internet applications.

Object Images

When an image is made up of geometrically definable shapes, it can be manipulated efficiently, with great flexibility, and stored in a compact form. Although it might seem that such images are rare, this turns out not to be the case.

Object images are made up of simple elements like straight lines, curved lines (known as Bezier curves), circles and arcs of circles, ovals, and the like. Each of these elements can be defined mathematically by a small number of parameters. For example, a circle requires only three parameters, specifically, the X and Y coordinates locating the circle in the image, plus the radius of the circle. A straight line needs the X and Y coordinates of its end points, or alternatively, by its starting point, length, and direction. And so on.

Because objects are defined mathematically, they can be easily moved around, scaled, and rotated without losing their shape and identity. For example, an oval can be built from a circle simply by scaling the horizontal and vertical dimensions differently. Closed objects can be shaded and filled with patterns of color, also described mathematically. Object elements can be combined or connected together to form more complex elements, and then those elements can also be manipulated and combined. The image in Figure 3.12 is an example of an object image.

Object images have many advantages over bitmap images. They require far less storage space. They can be manipulated easily, without losing their identity. Note, in contrast, that if

FIGURE 3.12

An Object Image

a bitmap image is reduced in size and reenlarged, the detail of the image is permanently lost. When such a process is applied to a bitmapped straight line, the result is "jaggies." Conversely, images such as photographs and paintings cannot be represented as object images at all and must be represented as bitmaps.

Because regular printers and display screens produce their images line by line, from the top to the bottom of the screen or paper, object images also cannot be displayed or printed directly, except on plotters. Instead, they must be converted to bitmap images for display and printing. This conversion can be performed within the computer, or may be passed on to an output device that has the capability to perform the conversion. A PostScript printer is an example of such a device. To display a line on a screen, for example, the program would calculate each of the pixels on the screen that the line passes through, and mark them for display. This is a simple calculation for a computer to perform. If the line is moved or resized, it is only necessary to perform the calculation again to display the new image.

EXAMPLE

The **PostScript page description language** is an example of a format that can be used to store, transmit, display, and print object images. A page description is a list of procedures and statements that describe each of the objects on a page. PostScript embeds page descriptions within a programming language. Thus, an image consists of a program written in the PostScript language.

The programming language is stored in ASCII or Unicode text form. Thus, PostScript files can be stored and transmitted as any other text file. An interpreter program in the computer or output device reads the PostScript language statements and uses them to create pages that can then be printed or displayed. The interpreter produces an image that is the same, regardless of the device it is displayed or printed on. Compensation for differences in device resolution and pixel shape is built into the interpreter.

PostScript provides a large library of functions that facilitate every aspect of an object-based image. There are functions that draw straight lines, Bezier curves, and arcs of a circle, functions that join simple objects into more complex ones, translate an object to a different location on the page, scale or distort an object, rotate an object, and create the mirror image of an object, and functions that fill an object with a pattern, or adjust the width and color of a line. There are methods for building and calling procedures, AND IF-THEN-ELSE and loop programming structures. The list goes on and on.

A simple program that draws a pair of shaded and concentric circles within a rectangle in the middle of an 8½ x 11-inch page is shown in Figure 3.13. This example shows a number of features of the language. The page is laid out as an *X, Y* grid, with the origin at the lower left corner. Each unit in the grid is 1/72 of an inch, which corresponds to 1 point in publishing. Each line contains a function, with a number of parameters that provide the specific details for the function. The parameters precede the function call. Text following the % signs is comments.

The first line contains a *translate* function that moves the X, Y origin to the center of the page. The parameters for this function, 288 and 396, represent the *X* and *Y* distances moved in points. (Note that 288/72 = 4 inches in *X* and 396/72 = 5 inches in *Y*.) Each circle is created with an *arc* function. The parameters for the arc function are X origin and Y origin for the arc, radius, and starting and finishing angle in degrees. (0 to 360 produces a full circle.) You should be able to follow the remainder of the program on your own. Note that the statements are interpreted in sequence: the second, gray circle is layered on top of the first.

FIGURE 3.13

A PostScript Program

```
288 396 translate      % move origin to center of page
0 0 144 0 360 arc      % define 2" radius black circle
fill


0.5 setgray            % define 1" radius gray circle
0 0 72 0 360 arc
fill


0 setgray              % reset color to black
-216 -180 moveto       % start at lower left corner
0 360 rmoveto          % and define rectangle
432 0 rmoveto          % ...one line at a time
0 -360 rmoveto
closepath              % completes rectangle
stroke                 % draw outline instead of fill


showpage               % produce the image
```

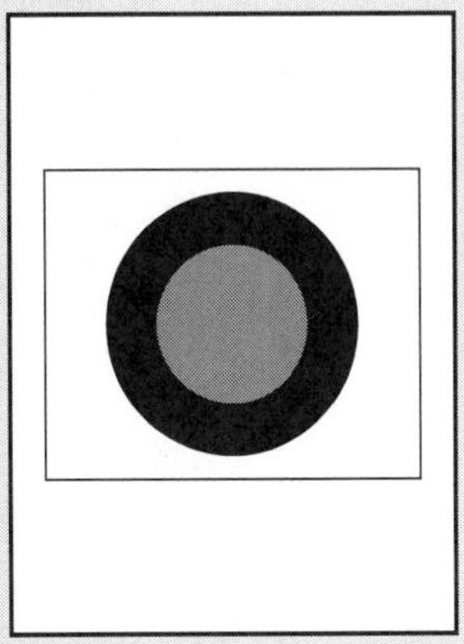

Arguably, the most important feature in PostScript is the inclusion of scalable **font** support for the display of text. Font outline objects are specified in the same way as other objects. Each font contains an object for each printable character in the extended ASCII character set. PostScript includes objects for thirty-five standard fonts representing eight font families, plus two symbol fonts, and others can be added. Unicode fonts are also available. Fonts can be manipulated like other objects. Text and graphics can be intermixed in an image. The graphic display of text is considered further in the next subsection.

Figure 3.14 shows another, more complicated, example of a PostScript program. This one presents a pie chart with an expanded slice, and labels. The expanded slice includes a shadow to improve its appearance. Each slice of the pie is drawn using a procedure called *wedge*. The shadow is drawn by drawing the wedge three times, once in black, then moved a bit and drawn in white and as an outline.

PostScript is a format for storing images in object form. Nonetheless, there are occasions when it is necessary to embed a bitmap image into what is primarily an object-based image. PostScript provides this capability. It even provides the ability to crop, enlarge, shrink, translate, and rotate the embedded bitmap images, within the limits of the bitmap format, of course.

Representing Characters as Images

The representation of character-based data in a graphically based system such as the Macintosh presents a dilemma. In graphically based systems it is necessary to distinguish between characters and the images of characters. Should the data be represented and stored as characters or as object images? The answer depends on what the text is to be used for. Text that is being processed and stored primarily for its content is normally stored as character data, in Unicode format, and the presentation of the data is left to the operating system

FIGURE 3.14

Another PostScript Program

```
% procedure to draw pie slice              % add text to drawing
%arguments graylevel, start angle, finish angle   0 setgray
/wedge {                                    144 144 moveto
        0 0 moveto                          (baseball cards) show
        setgray                             -30 200 (cash) show
        /angle1 exch def                    -216 108 (stocks) show
        /angle2 exch def                    32 scalefont
        0 0 144 angle1 angle2 arc           (Personal Assets) show
        0 0 lineto
        closepath } def                     showpage

%set up text font for printing
/Helvetica-Bold findfont
        16 scalefont
        setfont

.4 72 108 wedge fill % 108-72 = 36 = .1 circle
.8 108 360 wedge fill % 70%
% print wedge in three parts
32 12 translate
0 0 72 wedge fill
gsave
-8 8 translate
1 0 72 wedge fill
0 setgray stroke
grestore
```

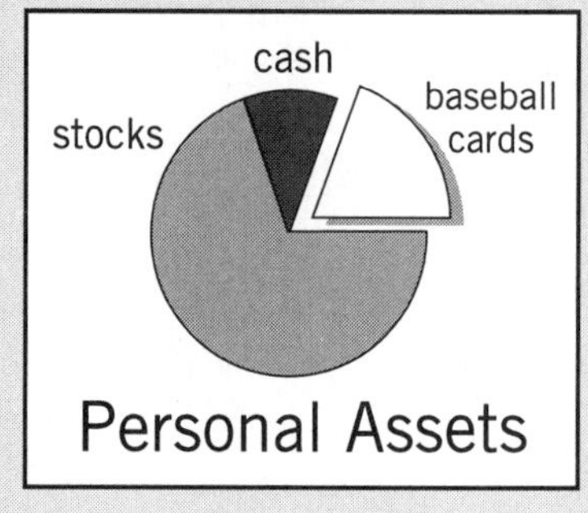

and/or the application program that processes it. Data that is being processed and stored with appearance as a fundamental consideration, on the other hand, must include a description of the presentation requirements, in particular the fonts used to print each character. In some instances, the description is built into the software: the screen fonts on a Windows screen are defined in an initialization file, for example. In other cases, the fonts are embedded into the text file, using special sequences of characters stored with the data, often in a proprietary file format supported by the particular application software. Finally, a few computer systems, particularly the Macintosh, include a different coding scheme, which makes it possible to encode each character both with its identification and its font. These encoded characters are called **glyphs.** There are very few applications that use this capability.

Regardless of the technique used, most current character-based business data is stored in Unicode or ASCII format. It is only when the appearance of the data is a significant factor within the application that it is necessary to maintain descriptions with the character data.

Video Images

Although GIF images are adequate for simple animation loops, there are a number of additional considerations for the storage, transmission, and display of true video. The most important consideration is the massive amount of data created by a video application. A video camera producing full screen 640 × 480 pixel true color images at a frame rate of thirty frames per second will generate 640 pixels × 480 pixels × 3 bytes of color/image × 30 frames per second = 27.65 megabytes of data per second! A one-minute film clip would consume 1.6 gigabytes of storage.

There are a number of possible solutions: reduce the size of the image, limit the number of colors, or reduce the frame rate. It is also possible to compress the video data. Each of these options has obvious drawbacks. The solution chosen also depends on the nature of the method used to make the video available to the user. One option is to present the video as a file on the system. The video file is either accessed from a removable medium, such as a DVD-ROM, or downloaded and stored on the system. Alternatively, the video may be made available to the system in real time. The latter technique is called **streaming** video. Streaming video is normally downloaded continuously from a Web server or network server. Video conferencing is an example of a streaming video application. The requirements for streaming video are much more stringent than for locally stored video, because the amount of data that can be downloaded per unit time is limited by the capability of the network connection. Furthermore, the processor must be able to decode the data fast enough to keep up with the incoming data stream. Generally speaking, streaming video is of lower display quality than video that is available locally.

Various mixes of these solutions are used. There are a number of proprietary formats in use, including Quicktime from Apple, Windows Media Format from Microsoft, and Indeo from Intel. The output, although less than ideal, is adequate for many applications.

When the video data is local to the system, it is possible to generate and display high quality video using sophisticated data compression techniques, but the processing required for generation of the compressed data is beyond the capabilities of most computer systems and users at the present time. The MPEG-2 format stores real-time video that produces movie quality images, with the video data compressed to 30–40 megabytes of data per minute. Even the re-creation of the original images for display requires substantial computing power. Although high-end modern personal computer systems have adequate processing power to decode MPEG-2 data, many computer systems provide additional hardware support for the reading, decoding, and displaying of real-time video data from DVDs. Direct transmission of high-quality digital video data is still confined to very high-speed networks and satellite systems.

3.4 AUDIO DATA

Sound has become an important component in modern computer applications. Sound is used as an instructional tool, as an element of multimedia presentations, to signal events within the computer, and to enhance the enjoyment of games. Sound can be stored in digital form on CD-ROMs and other media and made available to accompany a film clip, illustrate the nuances of a symphony, or reproduce the roar of a lion. Sound can be manipulated in the computer to compose music and to create the sounds of different musical instruments, even an entire orchestra.

Sound is normally digitized from an audio source, such as a microphone or amplifier, although it is possible to purchase instrumentation that connects the computer directly to a musical keyboard and synthesizer. For most users, the sound was previously digitized and provided on a CD-ROM or downloaded from a Web site.

Since the original sound wave is analog in nature, it is necessary to convert it to digital form for use in the computer. The technique used is the same as that used for music CDs and many other types of analog waveforms. The analog waveform is sampled electronically at regular time intervals. Each time a sample is taken, the amplitude of the sample is measured by an electronic circuit that converts the analog value to a binary equivalent. The circuit that performs this function is known as an **A-to-D converter.** The largest possible sample, which represents the positive peak of the loudest possible sound, is set to the maximum positive binary number being used, and the most negative peak is set to the largest negative number. Binary 0 falls in the middle. The amplitude scale is divided uniformly between the two limits. The sampling rate is chosen to be high enough to capture every nuance in the signal being converted. For audio signals, the sampling rate is normally around 50 kilohertz, or fifty thousand times a second. The basic technique is illustrated in Figure 3.15. A typical audio signal is shown in the upper diagram. A portion of the signal is shown in expanded form below. In this diagram, the signal is allowed to fall between −64 and 64. Although we haven't discussed the representation of negative numbers yet, the consecutive values for the signal in this diagram will be the binary equivalents to −22, −7, +26, 52, 49, and 2. The A-to-D conversion method is discussed more thoroughly in Supplementary Chapter 3.

Within the computer, most programs would probably treat this data as a one-dimensional array of integers. Like graphics images, however, it is necessary to maintain, store, and transmit information *about* the waveform, in addition to the waveform itself. To process and reproduce the waveform, a program would have to know the maximum possible amplitude, the sampling rate, and the total number of samples, at the very least. If several waveforms are stored together, the system would have to identify each individual waveform somehow and establish the relationships between the different waveforms. Are the waveforms played together, for example, or one right after another?

FIGURE 3.15

Digitizing an Audio Waveform

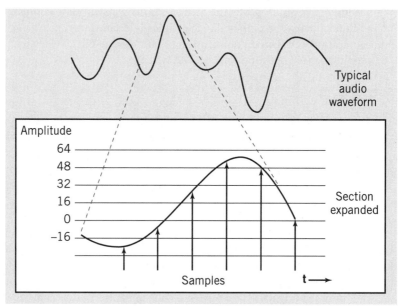

As you might expect, there are a number of different file formats for storing audio waveforms, each with its own features, advantages, and disadvantages. The .*MOD* format, for example, is used primarily to store samples of sound that will be manipulated and combined to produce a new sound. A .MOD file might store a sample of a piano tone. Software could then manipulate the sample to reproduce all the different keys on the keyboard, it could alter the loudness of each tone, and it could combine them to synthesize the piano lines in a piece of music. Other instruments could be synthesized similarly. The *MIDI* format is used to coordinate the sounds and signals between a computer and connected musical instruments, particularly keyboards. MIDI software can "read" the keyboard and can also reproduce the sounds. The .*VOC* format is a general sound format that includes special features such as markers within the file that can be used to repeat (loop) a block or synchronize the different components of a multimedia presentation. Block looping can extend a sound by repeating it over and over again. The .*WAV* format is a general-purpose format used primarily to store and reproduce snippets of sound. MP3 is a derivative of the MPEG-2 specification for the transmission and storage of high quality audio signals. It has gained popularity because of the large numbers of MP3-coded recordings posted on the Web and because of the availability of low-cost portable devices that can download, store, decode, and reproduce MP3 data.

Like video, audio data can also be generated and stored locally or streamed from a network or Web site. The data transmission and processing requirements for audio are much less stringent than those for video, however. Audio is routinely streamed from the Web. There are numerous Web sites broadcasting audio from radio stations and other sources, and streaming audio is also used for Internet telephony.

EXAMPLE

The .*WAV* format was designed by Microsoft as part of its multimedia specification. The format supports 8- or 16-bit sound samples, sampled at 11.025 KHz, 22.05 KHz, or 44.1 KHz in mono or stereo. The .WAV format is very simple and does not provide support for a lot of features, such as the looping of sound blocks.

The format consists of a general header that identifies a "chunk" of data and specifies the length of a data block within the chunk. The header is followed by the data block. The general header is used for a number of different multimedia data types.

The layout of a .WAV file is shown in Figure 3.16. The data block is itself broken into three parts. First, a 4-bit header identifies a sound file with the ASCII word "WAVE." A format chunk follows. This chunk contains such information as the method used to digitize the sound, the sampling rate in samples per second, the data transfer rate in average number

FIGURE 3.16

.WAV Sound Format

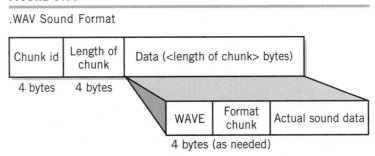

of bytes per second, the number of bits per sample, and whether the sound is recorded in mono or stereo. The actual data follows.

If you have a personal computer that runs Windows and supports sound, you will probably find .WAV files in one of your Windows directories. Look for the file *tada.wav*, which holds the brief trumpet fanfare that sounds when Windows is started.

3.5 DATA COMPRESSION

The volume of multimedia data, particularly video, but also sound, and even high resolution still images, often makes it impossible or impractical to store, transmit, and manipulate the data in its normal form. Instead, it is desirable or, in some cases, necessary to compress the data. This is particularly true for video clips, real-time streaming video with sound, lengthy sound clips, and images that are to be transmitted across the Internet through modem connections. (It is also true of large data and program files of any type.)

There are many different data compression algorithms, but all fall into one of two categories, **lossless** and **lossy.** A lossless algorithm compresses the data in such a way that the application of a matching inverse algorithm restores the compressed data exactly to its original form. Lossy data compression algorithms operate on the assumption that the user can accept a certain amount of data degradation as a trade-off for the savings in a critical resource such as storage requirements or data transmission time. Of course, only lossless data compression is acceptable for files where the original data must be retained, but lossy data compression is frequently acceptable in multimedia applications. In most applications, lossy data compression ratios far exceed those possible with lossless compression.

Lossless data algorithms work by attempting to eliminate redundancies in the data. For example, suppose that you have the following string of data:

0 5 5 7 3 2 0 0 0 0 1 4 7 3 2 9 1 0 0 0 0 0 6 6 8 2 7 3 2 7 3 2 …

There are two simple steps you could take to reduce this string. First, you could reduce the amount of data by counting the strings of consecutive 0s, and maintaining the count instead of the string. The character is reproduced once, followed by its count:

0 1 5 5 7 3 2 0 4 1 4 7 3 2 9 1 0 5 6 6 8 2 7 3 2 7 3 2 …

Notice that we actually had to add a character when the 0 appeared singly in the string. Otherwise, the inverse algorithm would have assumed that the first 0 appeared five times rather than recognizing the data to be a single 0 followed by a 5.

As a second step, the algorithm attempts to identify larger sequences within the string. These can be replaced with a single, identifiable value. In the example string, the sequence "7 3 2" occurs repeatedly. Let us replace each instance of the sequence with the special character "Z":

0 1 5 5 Z 0 3 1 4 Z 9 1 0 5 6 6 8 2 Z Z …

Application of these two steps has reduced the sample string by more than 35 percent. A separate attachment to the data would identify the replacements that were made, so that the original data can be restored losslessly. For the example, the attachment would indicate that 0s were replaced by a single 0 followed by their count and the sequences "7 3 2" were replaced by "Z." You might wish to restore the original string in this example for practice.

There are many variations on the methods shown in the example. You should also notice that the second step requires advance access to the entire sequence of data to identify the repetitive sequences. Thus, it is not useful with streaming data. There are other variations that are based on the known properties of the data stream that can be used, however. For example, MPEG-2 uses the knowledge that the image is repeated at a frame rate of, say, thirty times per second, and that in most instances, very little movement occurs within small parts of the image between consecutive frames. GIF images and ZIP files are compressed losslessly.

Lossy algorithms operate on the assumption that some data can be sacrificed without significant effect, based on the application and on known properties of human perception. For example, it is known that subtle color changes will not be noticeable in the area of an image where the texture is particularly vivid. Therefore, it is acceptable to simplify the color data in this circumstance. There is no attempt to recover the lost data. The amount of data reduction possible in a particular circumstance is determined experimentally. Lossy algorithms can often reduce the amount of data by a factor of 10:1 or more. JPEG is an example of a lossy algorithm.

MPEG-2 uses both variations on both forms of compression simultaneously to achieve compression ratios of 100:1 or more with very little noticeable degradation in image quality; however, the compression process itself requires tremendous amounts of computing power.

Recent advances in data compression technology have resulted in a number of new video formats, including a new version of Microsoft's Windows Media Video format and a new MPEG-4 format, as well as a new JPEG bitmap format, JP-2. As of this writing, these formats have not yet achieved general acceptance, but there is much promise for greatly improved video performance.

In general, the use of data compression is a trade-off between the use of processing power and the need to reduce the amount of data for transmission and storage. In most cases, the higher the compression ratio, the greater the demand upon the computer processing resources. At some point, the incremental improvement in compression to be achieved will no longer justify the additional cost in processing or the degradation of the result.

3.6 INTERNAL COMPUTER DATA FORMAT

So now you have an idea of the various forms that data takes when it reaches the computer. Once inside the computer, however, *all* data is simply stored as binary numbers of various sizes, ranging from 1 to 8 bits, or even larger. The interpretation of these binary numbers depends upon two factors:

- The actual operations that the computer processor is capable of performing
- The data types that are supported by the programming language used to create the application program

As you will see in later chapters, computer processors provide instructions to manipulate data, for searching and sorting, for example, and to manipulate and perform basic mathematical operations on signed and unsigned integers. They also provide a means to point to data, using a stored binary value as a pointer or locator to another stored binary number. Since these pointer values are themselves stored as numbers, they can also be manipulated and used in calculations. A pointer value might represent the index in an array, for example. Most recent computers also provide instructions for the direct manipulation of floating point, or real, numbers. In other computers, floating point numbers are manipulated using software procedures.

The processor instruction set also establishes formats for each data type that it supports. If a number in the computer is supposed to be a floating point number, for example, the instructions are designed to assume that the number is laid out in a particular format. Specific formats that are used for integer and real numbers are discussed in Chapters 4 and 5, respectively.

Thus, the raw binary numbers stored in a computer can easily be interpreted to represent data of a variety of different types and formats. C, Java, Visual Basic, and other languages all provide a programmer with the capability to identify binary data with a particular data type. Typically, there are five different simple data types:

- **Boolean:** two-valued variables or constants with values of true or false.
- **char:** the character data type. Each variable or constant holds a single alphanumeric character code representing, for example, the single strike of a key. It is also common to process groups of characters together as strings. Strings are simply arrays of individual characters. The ASC function in Visual Basic shows the actual binary number code representing a particular character. Thus, ASC("A") would show a different value on an ASCII-based system from that shown on an EBCDIC system.
- **enumerated data types:** user-defined simple data types, in which each possible value is listed in the definition, for example,

```
type DayOfWeek = Mon, Tues, Wed, Thurs, Fri, Sat
```

- **integer:** positive or negative whole numbers. The string of characters representing a number is converted internally by a conversion routine built into the program by the compiler and stored and manipulated as a numerical value.
- **real:** numbers with a decimal portion, or numbers whose magnitude, either small or large, exceeds the capability of the computer to process and store as an integer. Again, the routine to convert a string of characters into a real number is built into the program.

In addition to the simple data types, many programming languages, including C, but not Java, support an explicit pointer variable data type. The value stored in a *pointer variable* is a memory address within the computer. Other, more complex, data types, structures, arrays, records, and other objects, for example, are made up of combinations of the simple data types.

The data types just listed correlate rather well with the instruction set capability of the processor. The integer and real types can be processed directly. The character type is translated into instructions that manipulate the data for basic character operations that are familiar to you from your programming classes. Boolean and enumerated data types are treated within the computer in a manner similar to integers. Most programming languages do not accept Boolean and enumerated data as input, but the conversion would be relatively straightforward. It would only be necessary to test the input character string against the various possibilities, and then set the value to the correct choice (see Exercise 3.10).

Other languages may support a completely different set of data types. There are even some languages that don't recognize any data types explicitly at all, but simply treat data in a way appropriate to the operation being performed.

Numerical Character to Integer Conversion

EXAMPLE

As you've already seen, the typical high-level language numerical input statement

READ (*value*)

where *value* is the name of an integer variable, requires a software conversion from the actual input, which is alphanumeric, to the numerical form specified for value. This conversion is normally provided by program code contributed by the language compiler that becomes part of your program. Some programmers choose instead to accept the input data in character form and include their own code to convert the data to numerical form. This allows more programmer control over the process; for example, the programmer might choose to provide more extensive error checking and recovery than that of the internal conversion program. (Many internal conversion programs simply crash if the user inputs an illegal character, say, a letter when a numeral is expected.)

Whether internal or programmer supplied, the conversion process is similar. Just to deepen your understanding of the conversion process, Figure 3.17 contains a simple pseudocode procedure that converts the string representing an unsigned integer into numerical form. This code

FIGURE 3.17

A Pseudocode Procedure that Performs String Conversion

```
//variables used
char key;
int number;
boolean error, stop;
{
   stop = false;
   error = false;
   ReadAKey;
   while (NOT stop && NOT error) {
      number = 10 * number + (ASCIIVALUE(key) - 48);
      ReadAKey;
   } //end while
   if (error == true) {
      printout('Illegal Character in Input!');
   else printout('input number is ' number);
   } //end if
} //end procedure

function ReadAKey(); {
   read(key);
   if (ASCIIVALUE(key) == 13 or ASCIIVALUE(key) == 32 or (ASCIIVALUE(key) == 44)
      stop = true;
   else if ((key < '0' ) or (key > '9' )) error = true;
} //end function ReadAKey
```

contains simple error checking and assumes that the number ends with a space (ASCII 32), a comma (ASCII 44), or a carriage return (ASCII 13).

Conversion procedures for other data types are similar.

SUMMARY AND REVIEW

Alphanumeric data inputs and outputs are represented as codes, one code for each data value. Three commonly used code systems for interactive input and output are Unicode, ASCII, and EBCDIC. Within these codes, each character is represented by a binary number, usually stored 1 or 2 bytes per character.

The design and choice of a code is arbitrary; however, it is useful to have a code in which the collating sequence is consistent with search and sort operations in the language represented. Within the computer, programs must be aware of the code used to assure that data sorts, number conversions, and other types of character manipulation are handled correctly. There must also be agreement between input and output devices, so that the data is displayed correctly. If necessary, translation programs can be used to translate from one representation to another. When necessary, conversion programs within the computer convert the alphanumeric character strings into other numeric forms. Numeric data must be converted back to Unicode, ASCII, or EBCDIC form for output display, however. The most common source of alphanumeric data is the keyboard.

Data from a keyboard enters the computer in the form of a character stream, which includes nonprinting characters as well as printing characters. Image scanning with optical character recognition, voice input, and various special devices, such as bar code readers, can also be used to create alphanumeric data.

There are two different methods used for representing images in the computer. Bitmap images consist of an array of pixel values. Each pixel represents the sampling of a small area in the picture. Object images are made up of simple geometrical elements. Each element is specified by its geometric parameters, its location in the picture, and other details.

Within the constraint that object images must be constructed geometrically, they are more efficient in storage and more flexible for processing. They may be scaled, rotated, and otherwise manipulated without loss of shape or detail. Images with texture and shading, such as photographs and painting, must be stored in bitmap image form. Generally, images must be printed and displayed as bitmaps, so object images are converted to bitmap form by a page description language interpreter before printing or display. There are many different formats used for storing graphical images.

Video images are difficult to manage because of the massive amounts of data involved. Video may be stored local to the system, or may be streamed from a network or Web site. The quality of streamed video is limited by the capability of the network connection. Higher quality is possible with locally stored video data, but the processing requirements are demanding. Some systems provide auxiliary hardware to process video.

Audio signals are represented in the computer by a sequence of values created by digitizing the signal. The signal is sampled at regular time intervals. Each sample is then converted to an equivalent binary value that is proportional to the amplitude of the sample. Again, different formats are available for storing audio data, depending on the application.

Audio signals may be streamed or stored locally. The requirements for audio transmission and processing are far less stringent than for those of video.

For images, both still and video, as well as audio, data compression is often appropriate. Lossless data compression allows complete recovery of the original noncompressed data. Lossy data compression does not allow recovery of the original data, but is designed to be perceived as sufficient by the user.

Internally, all data, regardless of use, are stored as binary numbers. Instructions in the computer support interpretation of these numbers as characters, integers, pointers, and in many cases, floating point numbers.

KEY CONCEPTS AND TERMS

A-to-D converter
alphanumeric data
ANSI
ASCII
bitmap or raster image
collating sequence
control code
EBCDIC
font
Graphics Interchange
    Format (GIF) glyph
graphical objects

JPEG
lossless data compression
lossy data compression
metadata
MP3
MPEG-2
numeric character versus
    number
object or vector image
optical character
    recognition (OCR)
page description language

palette
phoneme
pixel
PostScript
proprietary format
resolution
scan codestream, character
streaming (video)
Unicode

FOR FURTHER READING

The general concepts of data formats are fairly straightforward, but additional character-based exercises and practice can be found in the Schaum outline [LIPS82]. Individual codes can be found in many references. The actual characters mapped to the keyboard are directly observable using the *Character Map* accessory in Windows or the *Key Caps* desk accessory on the Macintosh. Extensive information about Unicode is available from the Unicode Web site at www.unicode.org. For graphics formats, there are a number of good general books on graphics. Most of these books describe the difference between bitmap and object graphics clearly, and most also discuss some of the different graphics file formats, and the trade-offs between them. Additionally, there are more specialized books that are often useful in this area. Rimmer [RIMM93] discusses bitmapped graphics at length. Smith [SMIT90] presents an easy approach to the PostScript language. The three Adobe books—[ADOB93], [ADOB90], and [ADOB85], often called the "green book," the "red book," and the "blue book," respectively—are detailed but clear explanations of PostScript. Murray and Van Ryper [MURR96] provide a detailed catalog of graphics formats. Finally, everything you ever wanted to know about digital sound can be found in Ridge et al. [RIDG94]. There are many other books on various aspects of digital sound. Of course, new data formats occur as the need arises. Because the need seems to arise continuously nowadays, your best source of current information is undoubtedly the Web.

EXERCISES

3.1 **a.** Create a table that shows the ASCII and EBCDIC representations side by side for each of the uppercase letters, lowercase letters, and numerals.

b. Does the hexadecimal representation show you a simple method for converting individual numeric characters into their corresponding numerical values?

c. Does the hexadecimal representation suggest a simple method for changing lowercase letters into their corresponding capital letters?

d. Can you use the same methods for EBCDIC as you do for ASCII? If so, what changes would you need to make in a program to make (b) and (c) work?

3.2 **a.** What is the ASCII representation for the numeral −3.1415 in binary? in octal? in hexadecimal? in decimal?

b. What is the EBCDIC representation for the numeral +1,250.1? (Include the comma.)

3.3 What character string does the binary ASCII code

1010100 1101000 1101001 1110011 0100000 1101001 1110011
0100000 1000101 1000001 1010011 1011001 0100001

represent?

3.4 ASCII, Unicode, and EBCDIC are, of course, not the only possible codes. The Sophomites, from the planet Collegium use the rather strange code shown in Figure E3.1. There are only thirteen characters in the Sophomite alphabet, and each character uses a 5-bit code. In addition, there are four numeric digits, since the Sophomites use base 4 for their arithmetic.

a. Given the following binary code, what is the message being sent by the Sophomites?

11001110100000111111000000100110111111110111110000000100100

b. You noticed in part (a) that this code does not delimit between characters. How does one delimit this code? Suppose a bit was dropped during transmission. What happens? Suppose a single bit was altered (0 to 1 or 1 to 0). What happens?

FIGURE E3.1

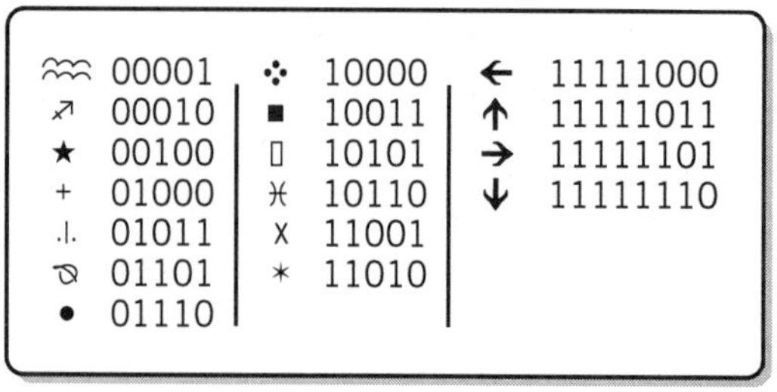

∿∿	00001	❖	10000	←	11111000
↗	00010	■	10011	↑	11111011
★	00100	▯	10101	→	11111101
+	01000	✳	10110	↓	11111110
.l.	01011	X	11001		
Ꭷ	01101	*	11010		
•	01110				

3.5 As an alternative alphanumeric code, consider a code where punched holes in the columns of a card represent alphanumeric codes. The punched hole represents a "1"; all other bits are "0". The Hollerith code shown in Figure E3.2 is an example of such a code. This code has been used to represent a message on the card in Figure E3.3. Each row represents a code level from 0 to 12. Levels 12 and 11, which are not labeled on the card, are the top row and next-to-top rows, respectively. Each column represents a single character, so the card can hold one eighty-column line of text. (This card, prevalent in the 1960s and 1970s as a means of data input, is the reason that text-based displays are still limited to eighty characters per line.) Translate the card in Figure E3.3.

FIGURE E3.2

Character	Punched code	Character	Punched code	Character	Punched code	Character	Punched code	Character	Punched code
A	12,1	L	11,3	W	0,6	7	7	<	12,8,4
B	12,2	M	11,4	X	0,7	8	8	(	12,8,5
C	12,3	N	11,5	Y	0,8	9	9	+	12,8,6
D	12,4	O	11,6	Z	0,9	&	12	$	11,8,3
E	12,5	P	11,7	0	0	-	11	*	11,8,4
F	12,6	Q	11,8	1	1	/	0,1	)	11,8,5
G	12,7	R	11,9	2	2	#	8,3	,	0,8,3
H	12,8	S	0,2	3	3	@	8,4	%	0,8,4
I	12,9	T	0,3	4	4	'	8,5	blank	none
J	11,1	U	0,4	5	5	=	8,6		
K	11,2	V	0,5	6	6	.	12,8,3		

FIGURE E3.3

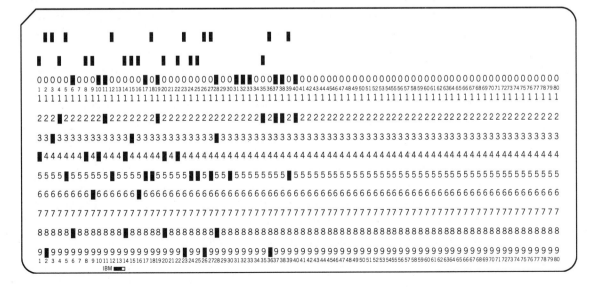

3.6 Without writing a program, predict the ORD value for your computer system for the letter "A," for the letter "B," for the letter "C." How did you know? Might the value be different on a different system? Why or why not?

3.7 Write a program in your favorite language that will convert all ASCII uppercase and lowercase letters to EBCDIC code. For an additional challenge, also convert the punctuation symbols, indicating with a failure-to-convert message, those symbols that are not represented in the EBCDIC system.

3.8 If you know how to use the MS-DOS Debug program, load a text file into computer memory from your disk, and read the text from computer memory by translating the ASCII codes.

3.9 Suppose you have a program that reads an integer, followed by a character, using the following prompt and READ statement:

```
WRITE ('Enter an integer and a character:')
READ (intval, charval);
```

When you run the program, you type in the following, in response to the prompt

```
Enter an integer and a character:
1257
z
```

When you check the value of charval, you discover that it does *not* contain "z." Why not? What would you expect to find there?

3.10 Write a program that accepts one of the seven values "MON," "TUE," "WED," "THU," "FRI," "SAT," and "SUN" as input and sets a variable named TODAY to the correct value of type DayOfWeek, and then outputs the ORD value of TODAY to the screen. (Does the ORD value give you a hint as to the internal representation of the enumerated data type?)

3.11 Write a procedure similar to procedure Convert that converts a signed integer to a character string for output.

3.12 Approximately how many pages of pure ASCII text can a 650MB CD-ROM hold?

3.13 Find a book or article that describes the various bitmapped graphics formats, and compare .GIF and .BMP.

3.14 Find a book or article that describes the various bitmapped graphics formats, and compare .GIF and .RLE.

For Exercises 3.13 and 3.14, there are several books that describe graphics formats in detail. One of these is Murray [MURR96].

3.15 Investigate several audio formats, and discuss the different features that each provides. Also discuss how the choice of features provided in different formats affects the type of processing that the format would be useful for.

3.16 If you have studied COBOL, discuss the difference between numeric characters and numbers in the context of a COBOL program. Does COBOL distinguish clearly between the two? If so, in what ways?

3.17 Provide a line-by-line explanation for the PostScript code in Figure 3.14.

3.18 Unicode is downward compatible with the Latin-I version of 8-bit ASCII in the sense that a Unicode text file that is limited to the Latin-I character set will be read correctly on a system that does not support Unicode, provided that an end delimiter is used, rather than a character count as the measure of the length of the message. Why is this so? (Hint: Consider the role of the ASCII NUL character.)

3.19 Use the Web as a resource to investigate MPEG-2. Explain the data compression algorithm used by MPEG-2.

3.20 The MP3 audio format is described as "almost CD quality." What characteristic of MP3 makes this description accurate?

CHAPTER 4

REPRESENTING INTEGER DATA

"It's OK, Mrs. Grumpworthy,
my brother's teaching me arithmetic
on our computer at home."

Thomas Sperling, adapted by Benjamin Reece

4.0 INTRODUCTION

As we have noted previously, the computer stores all data and program instructions in binary form, using only groups of zeros and ones. No special provision is made for the storage of the algebraic sign or decimal point that might be associated with a number, except when the number is stored as a string of characters, which is not practical for calculation purposes.

In Chapter 3, we observed that nearly every high-level computing language provides a method for storage, manipulation, and calculation of signed integer and real numbers. Thus, we need to consider methods of representing and manipulating these numbers within the zeros-and-ones constraint of the computer.

We saw in Chapter 2 that unsigned integer numbers can be represented directly in binary form, and this provides a clue as to how we might represent the integer data type in the computer. There is a significant limitation, however: we have yet to show you a sign-free way of handling negative numbers that is compatible with the capabilities of the computer.

In this chapter, we explore several different methods of storing and manipulating integers that may encompass both positive and negative numbers.

4.1 UNSIGNED BINARY AND BINARY-CODED DECIMAL REPRESENTATIONS

In conventional notation, numbers can be represented as a combination of a value, or magnitude, and a sign, plus or minus. As a first step in our discussion, let's consider two different approaches to storing just the value of the number in the computer.

The most obvious approach is simply to recognize that there is a direct binary equivalent for any decimal integer. We can simply store any whole number as its binary representation. This is the approach that we already discussed in Chapter 2. The range of integers that we can store this way is determined by the number of bits available. Thus, an 8-bit storage location can store any **unsigned integer** of value between 0 and 255, a 16-bit storage location 0–65535. If we must expand the range of integers to be handled, we can provide more bits. A common way to do this is to use multiple storage locations. In Figure 4.1, for example, four consecutive 1-byte storage locations are used to provide 32 bits of range. Used together, these four locations can accept 2^{32}, or 4,294,967,296 different values.

The use of multiple storage locations to store a single binary number may increase the difficulty of calculation and manipulation of these numbers because the calculation may have to be done one part at a time, possibly with carries or borrows between the parts, but the additional difficulty is not unreasonable. Most modern

FIGURE 4.1

Storage of a 32-bit Data Word

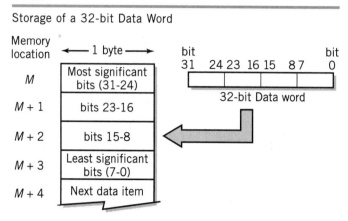

computers provide built-in instructions for this purpose, while in other computers, these calculations are performed using software procedures within the computer.

An alternative approach known as **binary-coded decimal,** or **BCD,** may be used in some applications. In this approach, the number is stored as a digit-by-digit binary representation of the original decimal integer. Each decimal digit is individually converted to binary. This requires 4 bits per digit. Thus, an 8-bit storage location could hold two binary-coded decimal digits—in other words, one of one hundred different values from 00 to 99. For example, the decimal value 68 would be represented in BCD as 01101000. (Of course you remember that $0110_2 = 6_{10}$ and $1000_2 = 8_{10}$.) Four bits can hold sixteen different values, numbered 0 to F in hexadecimal notation, but with BCD the values A to F are simply not used. The hexadecimal and decimal values for 0 through 9 are equivalent.

The table in Figure 4.2 compares the decimal range of values that can be stored in binary and BCD forms. Notice that for a given number of bits the range of values that can be held using the binary-coded decimal method is substantially less than the range

FIGURE 4.2

Value Range for Binary Versus Binary-coded Decimal

No. of Bits	BCD range		Binary range	
4	0–9	1 digit	0–15	1+ digit
8	0–99	2 digits	0–255	2+ digits
12	0–999	3 digits	0–4,095	3+ digits
16	0–9,999	4 digits	0–65,535	4+ digits
20	0–99,999	5 digits	0–1 Million	6 digits
24	0–999,999	6 digits	0–16 Million	7+ digits
32	0–99,999,999	8 digits	0–4 Billion	9+ digits
64	$0–(10^{16}–1)$	16 digits	0–16 Quintillion	19+ digits

using conventional binary representation. The larger the number of bits, the more pronounced the difference. With 20 bits, the range for binary is an entire additional decimal digit over the BCD range.

Calculations in BCD are also more difficult, since the computer must break the number into the 4-bit binary groupings corresponding to individual decimal digits and use base 10 arithmetic translated into base 2 to perform calculations. In other words, the calculation for each 4-bit grouping must be treated individually, with arithmetic carries moving from grouping to grouping. Any product or sum of any two BCD integers that exceeds 9 must be reconverted to BCD each time to perform the carries from digit to digit.

EXAMPLE

One method of performing a "simple" one- by two-digit multiplication is shown as an example in Figure 4.3. In the first step, each digit in the multiplicand is multiplied by the single-digit multiplier. This yields the result $7 \times 6 = 42$ in the units place and the result $7 \times 7 = 49$ in the 10s place. Numerically, this corresponds to the result achieved performing the multiplication in decimal, as is shown at the left of the diagram.

To continue, the binary values for 42 and 49 must be converted back to BCD. This is done in the second step. Now the BCD addition takes place. As in the decimal version, the sum of 9 and 4 results in a carry. The binary value 13 must be converted to BCD 3, and the 1 added to the value 4 in the hundreds place. The final result is BCD value 532.

Some computers provide instructions for performing BCD arithmetic, but even so, BCD arithmetic is nearly always much slower. As an alternative, some computers convert each BCD number to binary form, perform the calculation, and then convert the result back to BCD.

Despite these drawbacks, binary-coded decimal representation is sometimes useful, especially in business applications, where it is often desirable to have an exact digit-for-digit decimal equivalent in order to mimic decimal arithmetic, as well as to maintain decimal rounding and decimal precision. Translation between BCD and character form is also easier, since the last 4 bits of ASCII, EBCDIC, and Unicode numeric character forms correspond exactly to the BCD representation of that digit. Thus, to convert from alphanumeric form to BCD you simply chop off everything but the rightmost 4 bits of the character to get its BCD value. This makes BCD an attractive option when the application involves a lot of input and output, but limited calculation. Many business applications fit this description. In most cases, though, binary representation is preferred and used.

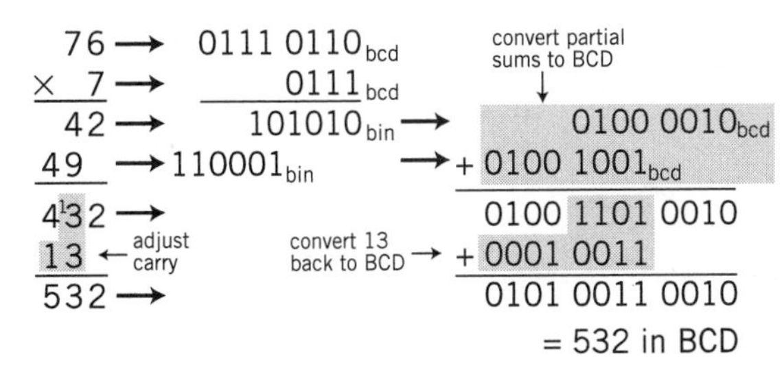

4.2 REPRESENTATIONS FOR SIGNED INTEGERS

Up to this point, we have constrained our discussion to unsigned integers. As you have seen, unsigned integers can be converted directly to binary numbers and processed

FIGURE 4.3

A Simple BCD Multiplication

without any special care. The addition of a sign complicates the problem because there is no obvious direct way to represent the sign in binary notation. In fact, there are several different ways used to represent negative numbers in binary form, depending on the processing that is to take place. The most common of these is known as **2's complement representation.** Before we discuss 2's complement representation, we will take a look at two other, simpler methods: **sign-and-magnitude** representation and **1's complement** representation. Each of these latter methods has some serious limitations for computer use, but understanding these methods and their limitations will clarify the reasoning behind the use of 2's complementation.

4.3 SIGN-AND-MAGNITUDE REPRESENTATION

In daily usage, we represent **signed integers** by a plus or minus sign and a value. This representation is known, not surprisingly, as *sign-and-magnitude* representation.

In the computer we cannot use a sign, but must restrict ourselves to 0's and 1's. We could select a particular bit, however, and assign to it values that we agree will represent the plus and minus signs. For example, we could select the leftmost bit and decide that a 0 in this place represents a plus sign and a 1 represents a minus. This selection is entirely arbitrary, but if used consistently, it is as reasonable as any other selection. In fact, this is the representation usually selected. Figure 4.4 shows examples of this representation.

Note that since the leftmost digit is being used as a sign, it cannot represent any value. This means that the positive range of the signed integer using this technique is one-half as large as the corresponding unsigned integer of the same number of bits. On the other hand, the signed integer also has a negative range of equal size to its positive range, so we really haven't lost any capability, but have simply shifted it to the negative region. The total range remains the same, but is redistributed to represent numbers both positive and negative, though in magnitude only half as large.

Suppose 32 bits are available for storage and manipulation of the number. In this case, we will use 1 bit for the sign and 31 bits for the magnitude of the number. By convention, the leftmost, or most significant, bit is usually used as a sign, with 0 corresponding to a plus sign and 1 to a minus sign. The binary range for 32 bits is 0 to 4,294,967,295; we can represent the numbers –2,147,483,647 to +2,147,483,647 this way.

There are several inherent difficulties in performing calculations when using sign-and-magnitude representation. Many of these difficulties arise because the value of the result of an addition depends upon the signs and relative magnitudes of the inputs. This can be easily seen from the following base 10 examples. Since the numbers are exactly equivalent, the same problem of course occurs with binary addition.

EXAMPLE

Consider the base 10 sum of 4 and 2:

$$\begin{array}{r} 4 \\ +2 \\ \hline 6 \end{array}$$

The sum of 4 and –2, however, has a different numerical result:

$$4$$
$$\underline{-2}$$
$$2$$

Notice that the addition method used depends on the signs of the operands. One method is used if both signs agree; a different method is used if the signs differ. Even worse, the presence of a second digit that can result in a carry or borrow that changes the result yet again:

$$2$$
$$\underline{-4}$$
$$-2$$

But

$$12$$
$$\underline{-4}$$
$$8$$

Interestingly enough, we have been so well trained that we alter our own mental algorithm to fit the particular case without even thinking about it, so this situation might not even have crossed your mind. The computer requires absolute definition of every possible condition, however, so the algorithm must include every possibility; unfortunately, sign-and-magnitude calculation algorithms are complex and difficult to implement in hardware.

In addition to the foregoing difficulty, there are two different binary values for 0,

00000000 and 10000000

representing +0 and –0, respectively. This seems like a minor annoyance, but the system must test at the end of every calculation to assure that there is only a single value for 0. This is necessary to allow program code that compares values or tests a value for 0 to work correctly. Positive 0 is preferred because presenting –0 as an output result would also be confusing to the typical user.

The one occurrence where sign-and-magnitude is a useful representation is when binary-coded decimal is being used. Even though the calculation algorithms are necessarily

FIGURE 4.4

Examples of Sign-and-Magnitude
Representation

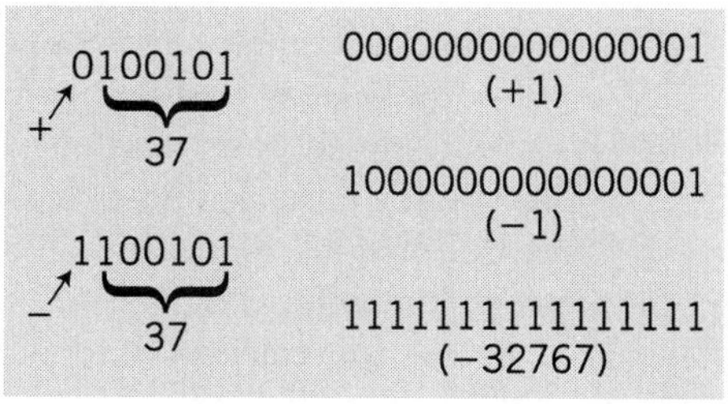

```
    0100101        0000000000000001
 +↗  ⌣⌣⌣                 (+1)
+      37
                   1000000000000001
                        (−1)
    1100101
 −↗  ⌣⌣⌣           1111111111111111
       37               (−32767)
```

complex, other algorithms for representing signed integers that you will be introduced to in this chapter are even more impractical when using BCD. Furthermore, as we have already discussed, BCD calculation is complex in any case, so the additional complexity that results from handling sign-and-magnitude representations is just more of the same.

With BCD, the leftmost bit can be used as a sign, just as in the case of binary. With binary, however, using a sign bit cuts the range in half; the effect on range is much less pronounced with BCD. (Remember, though, that BCD already has a much smaller range than binary for the same number of bits.) The leftmost bit in an unsigned BCD integer only represents the values 8 or 9; therefore, using this bit as a sign bit still allows the computer 3 bits to represent the leftmost digit as a number within the range 0–7.

As an example, the range for a signed 16-bit BCD integer would be $-7999 \leq$ value $\leq +7999$.

4.4 NINE'S DECIMAL AND 1'S BINARY COMPLEMENTARY REPRESENTATIONS

For most purposes, computers use a different method of representing signed integers known as complementary representation. With this method, the sign of the number is a natural result of the method and does not need to be handled separately. Also, calculations using complementary representation are consistent for all different signed combinations of input numbers. There are two forms of complementary representation in common use. One, known as the radix complement, is discussed in the next section. In this section, we will introduce a representation known as *diminished radix* complementary representation, so called because the value used as a basis for the complementary operation is *diminished* by one from the radix, or base. Thus, base 10 diminished radix complementary representation uses the value 9 as its basis, and binary uses 1. Although the computer obviously uses the 1's representation, we will introduce the 9's representation first, since we have found that it is easier for most students to understand these concepts in the more familiar decimal system.

Nine's Decimal Representation

Let us begin by considering a different means of representing negative and positive integers in the decimal number system. Suppose that we manipulate the range of a three-digit decimal number system by splitting the three-digit decimal range down the middle at 500. Arbitrarily, we will allow any number between 0 and 499 to be considered positive. Positive numbers will simply represent themselves. This will allow the value of positive numbers to be immediately identified. Numbers that begin with 5, 6, 7, 8, or 9 in the most significant digit will be treated as representations of negative numbers. Figure 4.5 shows the shift in range.

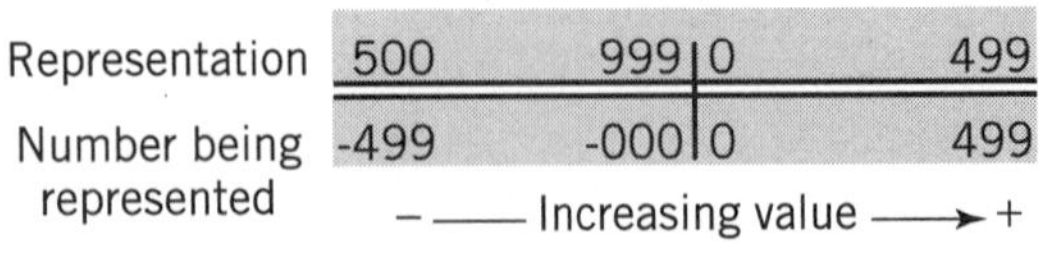

One convenient way to assign a value to the negative numbers is to allow each digit to be subtracted from the largest numeral in the radix. Thus,

FIGURE 4.5

Range Shifting Decimal Integers

Representation	500	999	0	499
Number being represented	-499	-000	0	499

$-$ —— Increasing value ——→ $+$

there is no carry, and each digit can be converted independently of all others. Subtracting a value from some standard basis value is known as *taking the* **complement** of the number. Taking the complement of a number is almost like using the basis value as a mirror. In the case of base 10 radix, the largest numeral is 9; thus, this method is called 9's complementary representation.

Several examples show the technique:

EXAMPLE

Find the 9's complementary representation for the three-digit number –467.

$$
\begin{array}{r}
999 \\
-467 \\
\hline
532
\end{array}
$$

532 represents the value for –467. Notice that the three-digit value range is limited to 0–499, since any larger number would start with a digit of 5 or greater, which is the indicator for a negative number.

■ ■ ■

Find the 9's complementary representation for the four-digit number –467.

$$
\begin{array}{r}
9999 \\
-467 \\
\hline
9532
\end{array}
$$

Notice that in this system, it is necessary to specify the number of digits, or *word size,* being used. In a four-digit representation, the number (0)532 represents a positive integer, since it is less than 4999 in value. Care is required in maintaining the correct number of digits.

■ ■ ■

What is the sign-and-magnitude value of the four-digit number represented in 9's complement by 3789?

In this case, the leftmost digit is in the range 0–4. Therefore, the number is positive, and is already in correct form. The answer is +3789.

This example emphasizes the difference between the representation of a number in complementary form and the operation of taking the complement of a number. The representation just tells us what the number looks like in complementary form. The operation of finding the complement of a number consists of performing the steps that are necessary to change the number from one sign to the other. Note that if the value represents a negative number, it is necessary to perform the operation if we wish to convert the number into sign-and-magnitude form.

■ ■ ■

What is the sign-and-magnitude value of the four-digit number represented by 9990?

This value is negative. To get the sign-and-magnitude representation for this number, we take the 9's complement:

$$
\begin{array}{r}
9999 \\
-9990 \\
\hline
9
\end{array}
$$

Therefore, 9990 represents the value –9.

If we now use the 9's complement technique to assign the negative values to the chart in Figure 4.5, you see that 998 corresponds to a value of –1 and 500 to the value –499. This results in the relationship shown in Figure 4.6.

An important consideration in the choice of a representation is that it is consistent with the normal rules of arithmetic. For the representation to be valid, it is necessary that, for any value within the range,

```
- (- value) = value
```

Simply stated, this says that if we complement the value twice, it should return to its original value. Since the complement is just

```
comp = basis - value
```

then complementing twice,

```
basis - (basis - value) = value
```

which confirms that this requirement is met.

Next, let's consider the operation of addition when the numbers being added are in 9's complementary form. When you studied programming language, you learned that modular arithmetic could be used to find the remainder of an integer division. You recall that in modular arithmetic, the count repeats from 0 when a limit, called the *modulus*, is exceeded. Thus, as an example, 4 mod 4 has the value 0 and 5 mod 4 has the value 1.

The 9's complement scale shown in Figure 4.5 shares the most important characteristic of modular arithmetic; namely, in counting upward (from left to right on the scale), when 999 is reached, the next count results in a modular rotation to a value of 0. (Notice that when you reach the right end of the scale, it continues by flowing around to the left end.)

Counting corresponds to addition; thus, to add a number to another is simply to count upward from one number by the other. This idea is illustrated in Figure 4.6. As you can see from the examples in this diagram, simple additions are straightforward and work correctly. To understand how this process works in a "wraparound" situation, consider the example shown in Figure 4.7. As you can see in this case, adding 699 to the value 200 leads to the position 899 by wrapping around the right end. Since 699 is equivalent to –300 and 899 is equivalent to –100, 699 + 200 is equivalent to (–300) + 200, and the result of the addition is correct.

The reason this technique works can also be seen in the diagram. The **wraparound** is equivalent to extending the range to include the addition on the scale.

The same final point should also be reached by moving to the left 300 units, which

FIGURE 4.6

Addition as a Counting Process

Representation

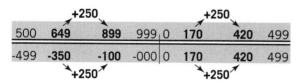

Number being represented

FIGURE 4.7

Addition with Wraparound

Representation

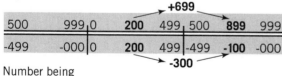

Number being represented

is equivalent to subtracting 300. In fact, the result is off by 1. This occurs because we have again picked a scale with two values for 0, namely, 0 for +0 and 999 for –0. This means that any count that crosses the modulus will be short one count, since 0 will be counted twice. In this particular example, the count to the right, which is the addition 200 + 700, yielded the correct result, since the modulus was not crossed. The count to the left, the subtraction 200 – 300, is off by one because of the double zero. We could correct for this situation on the chart by moving left an additional count any time the subtraction requires "borrowing" from the modulus. For example, subtracting 200 – 300 requires treating the value 200 as though it were 1200 to stay within the 0–999 range. The borrow can be used to indicate that an additional unit should be subtracted.

Next, consider the situation shown in Figure 4.8. In this case, counting to the right, or adding, also results in crossing the modulus, so an additional count must be added to obtain the correct result. This is an easier situation, however. Since the result of any sum that crosses the modulus must initially contain a carry digit (the 1 in 1099 in the diagram), which is then dropped in the modular addition, it is easy to tell when the modulus has been crossed to the right. We can then simply add the extra count in such cases.

This leads to a simple procedure for adding two numbers in 9's complementary arithmetic: Add the two numbers. If the result flows into the digit beyond the specified number of digits, add the carry into the result. This is known as **end-around carry.** Figure 4.9 illustrates the procedure. Notice that the result is now correct for both examples.

Although we could design a similar algorithm for subtraction, there is no practical reason to do so. Instead, subtraction is performed by taking the complement of the subtrahend (the item being subtracted) and adding to the minuend (the item being subtracted from). In this way, the computer can use a single addition algorithm for all cases.

There is one further consideration. A fixed word size results in a range of some particular fixed size; it is always possible to have a combination of numbers that adds to a result outside the range. This condition is known as **overflow.** If we have a three-digit plus sign word size in a sign-and-magnitude system, and add 500 to 500, the result overflows, since 1000 is outside the range. The fourth digit would be evidence of overflow.

It is just as easy to detect overflow in a 9's complement system, even though the use of modular arithmetic assures that an extra digit will never occur. In complementary arithmetic, numbers that are out of range represent the opposite sign. Thus, if we add

$$300 + 300 = 600$$

both inputs represent positive numbers, but the result is negative. Then the test for overflow is this: *If both inputs to an addition have the same sign, and the output sign is different, overflow has occurred.*

FIGURE 4.8

Addition with Modulus Crossing

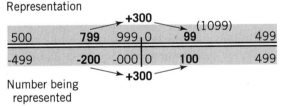

Number being represented

FIGURE 4.9

End-around Carry Procedure

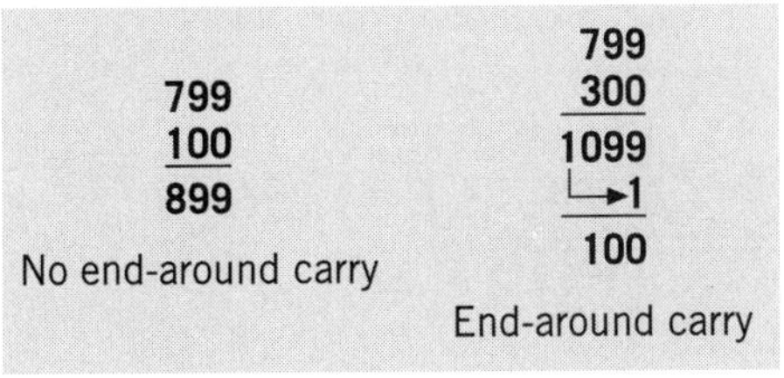

```
                              799
      799                     300
      100                    1099
      899                   └─→1
                             100
No end-around carry
                        End-around carry
```

One's Complement

The computer can use the binary version of the same method of representation that we have just discussed. In base 2, the largest digit is 1. Splitting the range down the middle, as we did before, numbers that begin with 0 are defined to be positive; numbers that begin with 1 are negative. Since

$$\begin{array}{c} 1 \\ \underline{-0} \\ 1 \end{array} \quad \text{and} \quad \begin{array}{c} 1 \\ \underline{-1} \\ 0 \end{array}$$

the 1's complement of a number is performed simply by changing every 0 to a 1 and every 1 to a 0. How elegantly simple! This exchange of 0s and 1s is also known as **inversion.** (Of course, this means that both 000... and 111... represent 0, specifically, +0 and –0, respectively.) The 1's complement scale for 8-bit binary numbers is shown in Figure 4.10.

Addition also works in the same way. To add two numbers, regardless of the implied sign of either input, the computer simply adds the numbers as though they were unsigned integers. If there is a carryover into the next bit beyond the leftmost specified bit, 1 is added to the result, following the usual end-around carry rule. Subtraction is done by inverting the subtrahend (i.e., changing all 0s to 1s and 1s to 0s) and adding. Overflows are detected in the same way as previously discussed: if both inputs are of the same sign, and the sign of the result is different, overflow has occurred; the result is outside the range. Notice that this test can be performed simply by looking at the leftmost bit of the two inputs and the result.

An important comment about conversion between signed binary and decimal integers in their complementary form: although the technique used is identical between 9's complement decimal and 1's complement binary, the modulus used in the two systems is obviously *not the same!* For example, the modulus in three-digit decimal is 999, with a positive range of 499. The modulus in 8-bit binary is 11111111, or 255_{10}, with a positive range of 01111111, or 127_{10}.

This means that you *cannot* convert directly between 9's complement decimal and 1's complement binary. Instead, you must change the number to sign-and-magnitude representation, convert, and then change the result to the new complementary form. Of course, if the number is positive, this process is trivial, since the complementary form is the same as the sign-and-magnitude form. But you must remember to follow this procedure if the sign is negative. Remember, too, that you must check for overflow to make sure that your number is still in range in the new base.

Here are several examples of 1's complement addition and subtraction, together with the equivalent decimal results:

FIGURE 4.10

One's Complement Representation

10000000	11111111	00000000	01111111
-127_{10}	-0_{10}	0_{10}	127_{10}

EXAMPLE

Add

$$
\begin{array}{r}
00101101 = 45 \\
\underline{00111010} = \underline{58} \\
01100111 = 103
\end{array}
$$

■■■

Add the 16-bit numbers

$$
\begin{array}{r}
0000000000101101 = 45 \\
\underline{1111111111000101} = \underline{-58} \\
1111111111110010 = -13
\end{array}
$$

Note that the addend 1111111111000101 is the inversion of the value in the previous example with eight additional 0s required to fill up 16 bits. The decimal result, –13, is found by inverting 1111111111110010 to 0000000000001101 to get a positive magnitude and adding up the bits.

EXAMPLE

Add

$$
\begin{array}{r}
01101010 = 106 \\
\underline{11111101} = \underline{\text{-}2} \\
\text{①}01100111
\end{array}
$$

(end-around carry) └──────→ +1

$$
\begin{array}{r}
\overline{01101000} = 104
\end{array}
$$

■■■

Subtract

$$
\begin{array}{r}
01101010 = 106 \\
\underline{-01011010} = \underline{90}
\end{array}
$$

Changing the sign of the addend by inverting

$$
\begin{array}{r}
01101010 \\
\underline{10100101} \\
\text{①}00001111
\end{array}
$$

(end-around carry) └──────→ +1

$$
\begin{array}{r}
\overline{00010000} = 16
\end{array}
$$

■■■

Add

$$
\begin{array}{r}
01000000 = 64 \\
\underline{+01000001} = \underline{65} \\
10000001 = -126
\end{array}
$$

This is an obvious example of overflow. The correct positive result, 129, exceeds the range for 8 bits. Eight bits can store 256 numbers; splitting the range only allows positive values 0–127.

The overflow situation shown in the last example occurs commonly in the computer, and some high-level languages do not check adequately. In some versions of BASIC, for example, the sum

$$16384 + 16386$$

will show an incorrect result of −32765 or −32766. (The latter result comes from use of a different complementary representation, discussed in the next section.) What has happened is that overflow has occurred in a system that uses 16 bits for integer calculations. The positive range limit for 16 bits is +32767 (a 0 for the sign plus fifteen 1s). Since the sum of 16384 and 16386 is 32770, the calculation overflows. Unfortunately, the user may never notice, especially if the overflowing calculation is buried in a long series of calculations. A good programmer takes such possibilities into account when the program is written.

4.5 TEN'S COMPLEMENT AND 2'S COMPLEMENT

Ten's Complement

You have seen that complementary representation can be effective for the representation and calculation of signed integer numbers. As you are also aware, the system that we have described, which uses the largest number in the base as its complementary reflection point, suffers from some disadvantages that result from the dual zero on its scale.

By shifting the negative scale to the right by one, we can create a complementary system that has only a single zero. This is done by using the radix as a basis for the complementary operation. In decimal base, this is known as the 10's complement representation. The use of this representation will simplify calculations. The trade-off in using 10's complement representation is that it is slightly more difficult to find the complement of a number. A three-digit decimal scale is shown in Figure 4.11. Be sure to notice the differences between this diagram and Figure 4.5.

The theory and fundamental technique for 10's complement is the same as that for 9's complement. The 10's complement representation uses the modulus as its reflection point. The modulus for a three-digit decimal representation is 1000, which is 1 larger than the largest number in the system, 999.

Complements are found by subtracting the value from the modulus, in this case, 1000. This method assures a single zero, since (1000 − 0) mod 1000 is zero. Again, as with the previously discussed complementary methods, notice that the complement of the complement results in the original value.

FIGURE 4.11

Ten's Complement Scale

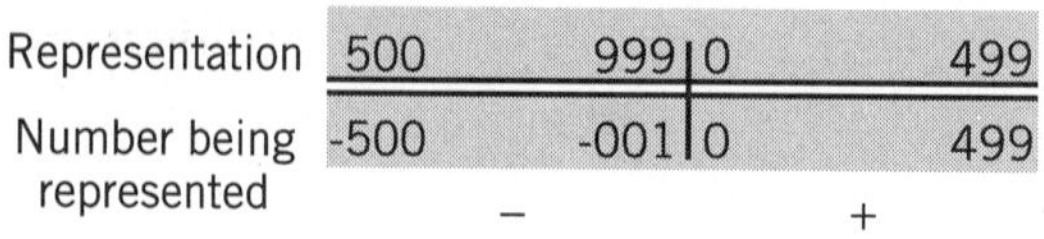

Representation	500	999	0	499
Number being represented	-500	-001	0	499
		−		+

EXAMPLE

Find the 10's complement of 247.

As a reminder, note that the question asks for the 10's *complement* of 247, not the 10's *complement representation*. Since 247 represents a positive number, its 10's complement representation is, of course, 247.

The 10's complement of 247 is

$$1000 - 247 = 753$$

Since 247 is a positive representation, 753 represents the value –247.

■ ■ ■

Find the 10's complement of 17.

As in the 9's complement work, we always have to be conscious of the number of specified digits. Since all the work so far has assumed that the numbers contain three digits, let's solve this problem from that assumption:

$$1000 - 017 = 983$$

■ ■ ■

Find the sign and magnitude of the three-digit number with 10's complement representation:

$$777$$

Since the number begins with a 7, it must be negative. Therefore,

$$1000 - 777 = 223$$

The sign-magnitude value is –223.

There is an alternative method for complementing a 10's complement number. First, observe that

$$1000 = 999 + 1$$

You recall that the 9's complement was found by subtracting each digit from 9:

$$9's\ comp = 999 - value$$

From the previous equation, the 10's complement can be rewritten as

$$10's\ comp = 1000 - value = 999 + 1 - value$$
$$= 999 - value + 1$$

or, finally,

$$10's\ comp = 9's\ comp + 1$$

This gives a simple alternative method for computing the 10's complement value: find the 9's complement, which is easy, and add 1 to the result. Either method gives the same result. You can use whichever method you find more convenient. This alternative method is usually easier computationally, especially when working with binary numbers, as you will see.

Addition in 10's complement is particularly simple. Since there is only a single zero in 10's complement, sums that cross the modulus are unaffected. Thus, the carry that results when the addition crosses the zero point is simply ignored. To add two numbers in 10's complement, one simply adds the digits; any carry beyond the specified number of digits is thrown away. (Actually, in the computer, the carry is saved in a special "carry bit," just in case it is to be used to extend the addition to another group of bits for multiple-word additions.) Subtraction is again performed by inverting the subtrahend and adding.

The range of numbers in 10's complement for three digits can be seen in Figure 4.11. Of particular interest is the fact that the positive and negative regions are of different size: there is one negative number, 500, that cannot be represented in the positive region. (The complement of 500 is itself.) This peculiarity is a consequence of the fact that the total range of numbers is even for any even-numbered base, regardless of word size. (In this case 10^W.) Since one value is reserved for zero, the number of remaining values to be split between positive and negative is odd and, thus, could not possibly be equal.

Two's Complement

Two's complement representation for binary is, of course, similar to 10's complement representation for decimal. In binary form, the modulus consists of a base 2 "1" followed by the specified number of 0's. For 16 bits, for example, the modulus is

$$10000000000000000$$

As was true for the 10's complement, the 2's complement of a number can be found in one of two ways: either subtract the value from the modulus or find the 1's complement by inverting all 1's and 0's and adding 1 to the result.

The second method is particularly well suited to implementation in the computer, but you can use whichever method you find more convenient.

Figure 4.12 shows an 8-bit scale for 2's complement representation.

Two's complement addition, like 10's complement addition in decimal, consists of adding the two numbers *mod* the modulus. This is particularly simple for the computer. Subtraction and overflow are handled as we have already discussed.

As in 10's complement, the range is unevenly divided between positive and negative. The range for 16 bits, for example, is $-32768 \leq$ value ≤ 32767.

There are many 2's complement problems at the end of the chapter for you to practice on.

The use of 2's complement is more common in computers than is 1's complement, but both methods are in use. The trade-off is made by the designers of a particular computer: 1's complement makes it easier to change the sign of a number, but addition requires an extra end-around carry step. One's complement has the additional drawback that the algorithm must test for and convert -0 to 0 at the end of each operation. Two's complement simplifies the addition operation at the expense of an additional add operation any time the sign change operation is required.

As a final note, before we conclude our discussion of binary complements, it is useful to be able to predict approximate sizes of integers that are represented in complementary form without going through the conversion. A few hints will help:

FIGURE 4.12

Two's Complement Representation

10000000	11111111	00000000	01111111
-128_{10}	-1_{10}	0_{10}	127_{10}

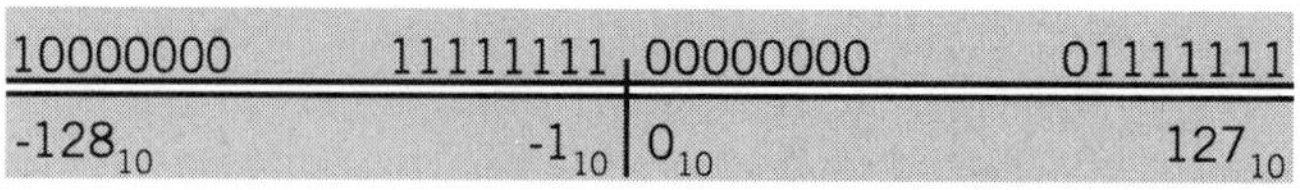

1. Positive numbers are always represented by themselves. Since they always start with 0, they are easily identified.

2. Small negative numbers, that is, negative numbers close to 0, have representations that start with large numbers of 1's. The number –2 in 8-bit 2's complement, for example, is represented by

   11111110

   whereas –128, the largest negative 2's complement number, is represented by

   10000000

   This is evident from the scale in Figure 4.12.

3. Since there is only a difference in value of 1 between 1's and 2's complement representations of negative numbers (positive numbers are, of course, identical in both representations), you can get a quick idea of the value in either representation simply by inverting all the 1s and 0s and approximating the value from the result.

4.6 OVERFLOW AND CARRY CONDITIONS

We noted earlier in this discussion that overflows occur when the result of a calculation does not fit into the fixed number of bits available for the result. In 2's complement, an addition or subtraction overflow occurs when the result overflows into the sign bit. Thus, overflows can be detected by the fact that the sign of the result is opposite that of both operands.

Computers provide a flag that allows a programmer to test for an overflow condition. The overflow flag is set or reset each time a calculation is performed by the computer. In addition, the computer provides a **carry flag** that is used to correct for carries and borrows that occur when large numbers must be separated into parts to perform additions and subtractions. For example, if the computer has instructions that are capable of adding two 32-bit numbers, it would be necessary to separate a 64-bit number into two parts, add the least significant part of each, then add the most significant parts, together with any carry that was generated by the previous addition. For normal, single precision 2's complement addition and subtraction the carry bit is ignored.

Although overflow and carry procedures operate similarly, they are not quite the same, and can occur independently of each other. The carry flag is set when the result of an addition or subtraction exceeds the fixed number of bits allocated, without regard to sign. It is perhaps easiest to see the difference between overflow and carry conditions with an example. This example shows each of the four possible outcomes that can result from the addition of two 4-bit 2's complement numbers.

EXAMPLE

(+4) + (+2)		(+4) + (+6)	
0100	no overflow,	0100	overflow,
0010	no carry	0110	no carry
0110 = (+6)		1010 = (−6)	the result is incorrect

$(-4) + (-2)$		$(-4) + (-6)$	
1100	no overflow,	1100	overflow
1110	carry	1010	carry
$11010 = (-6)$	ignoring the carry,	$10110 = (+3)$	ignoring the carry,
	the result is correct		the result is incorrect

If an overflow occurs on any but the most significant part of a multiple part addition, it is ignored (see exercise 4.13).

4.7 OTHER BASES

Any even-numbered base can be split the same way to represent signed integers in that base. Either the modulus or the largest-digit value can be used as a mirror for the complementary representation. Odd bases are more difficult: either the range must be split unevenly to use the leftmost digit as an indicator, or the second left digit must be used together with the first to indicate whether the represented number is positive or negative. We will not consider odd bases any further.

Of particular interest are the corresponding 7's and 8's complements in octal and 15's and 16's complements in hexadecimal. These correspond exactly to 1's and 2's complement in binary, so you can use calculation in octal or hexadecimal as a shorthand for binary.

As an example, consider four-digit hexadecimal as a substitute for 16-bit binary. The range will be split down the middle, so that numbers starting with $0–7_{16}$ are positive and those starting with 8–F are negative. But note that hex numbers starting with 8–F all have a binary equivalent with 1 in the leftmost place, whereas 0–7 all start with 0. Therefore, they conform exactly to the split in 16-bit binary.

You can carry the rest of the discussion by yourself, determining how to take the complement, and how to add, from the foregoing discussions. There are practice examples at the end of the chapter.

Finally, note that since binary-coded decimal is essentially a base 10 form, the use of complementary representation for BCD would require algorithms that analyze the first digit to determine the sign and then perform 9's or 10's complement procedures. Since the purpose of BCD representation is usually to simplify the conversion process, it is generally not practical to use complementary representation for signed integers in BCD.

4.8 SUMMARY OF RULES FOR COMPLEMENTARY NUMBERS

The following points summarize the rules for the representation and manipulation of complementary numbers, both radix and diminished radix, in any even number base. For most purposes you will be interested only in 2's complement and 16's complement:

1. Remember that the word "complement" is used in two different ways. To complement a number, or take the complement of a number, means to change its sign. To find the complementary representation of a number means to translate or identify the representation of the number just as it is given.

2. Positive numbers are represented the same in complementary form as they would be in sign and magnitude form. These numbers will start with 0, 1, … N/2–1. For binary numbers, positive numbers start with 0, negative with 1.

3. To go from negative sign-and-magnitude to complementary form, or to change the sign of a number, simply subtract each number from the largest number in the base (diminished radix) or from the value 100…, where each zero corresponds to a number position (radix). Remember that implied zeros must be included in the procedure. Alternatively, the radix form may be calculated by adding 1 to the diminished radix form. For 2's complement, it is usually easiest to invert every digit and add 1 to the result.

4. To get the sign-and-magnitude representation for negative numbers, use the procedure in (2) to get the magnitude. The sign will, of course, be negative. Remember that the word size is fixed; there may be one or more implied 0s at the beginning of a number that mean the number is really positive.

5. To add two numbers, regardless of sign, simply add in the usual way. Carries beyond the leftmost digit are ignored in radix form, added to the result in diminished radix form. To subtract, take the complement of the subtrahend and add.

6. If we add two complementary numbers of the same sign and the result is of opposite sign, the result is incorrect. Overflow has occurred.

SUMMARY AND REVIEW

Computers store all data as binary integers with no separate sign. There are various ways to format these binary integers to represent signed integer data. Conceptually, the simplest formats are sign-and-magnitude and binary-coded decimal. Although BCD is sometimes used for business programming, both of these formatting methods have shortcomings in terms of number manipulation and calculation.

Nine's decimal complement, and its binary equivalent 1's complement, split the number range in two, using the upper half of the range to represent negative numbers. Positive numbers represent themselves. These representations are convenient and especially simple to use, since the complement is found by subtracting the number from a row of the largest digits in the base. Binary complements may be found by simply inverting the 0's and 1's in the number. Calculations are a bit more difficult due to the existence of both positive and negative values for zero, but end-around carry addition may be used for this purpose.

Ten's complement and 2's complement split the range similarly, but use a single value 0 for zero. This requires the use of a complement based on a value one larger than the largest number in the base for the given number of digits. This "base value" will always consist of a 1 followed by N zeros, where N is the number of digits being used. Complementation may be taken by inverting the number as before, and adding 1 to the result, or by subtracting the number from the base value. Calculation is straightforward, using modulo arithmetic. Most computer arithmetic instructions are based on 2's complement arithmetic.

Both 1's and 2's complement representations have the additional convenience that the sign of a number may be readily identified, since a negative number always begins with a "1."

Also, small negative numbers have large values, and vice versa. Complementary representations for other even-numbered bases can be built similarly.

KEY CONCEPTS AND TERMS

binary-coded decimal (BCD)	inversion	2's complement
carry flag	1's complement	unsigned integers
complement	overflow	wraparound
end-around carry	sign-and-magnitude	
integer representation	representation	
	signed integers	

FOR FURTHER READING

The representation and manipulation of integers within the computer is discussed in most computer architecture texts. A particularly effective discussion is found in Stallings [STAL96]. This discussion presents detailed algorithms and hardware implementations for the various integer operations. A simpler discussion, with many examples, is found in Lipschutz [LIPS82]. More comprehensive treatments of computer arithmetic can be found in the two-volume collection of papers edited by Swartzlander [SWAR90] and in various textbooks on the subject, including those by Kulisch and Maranker [KUL81] and Spaniol [SPAN81]. A classical reference on computer algorithms, which includes a substantial discussion on computer arithmetic, is the book by Knuth [KNUT97].

EXERCISES

4.1 Data was stored in the Digital PDP-9 computer using six-digit octal notation. Negative numbers were stored in 8's complement form.

    a. How many bits does six-digit octal represent? Show that 8's complement octal and 2's complement binary are exactly equivalent.

    b. What is the largest positive octal number that can be stored in this machine?

    c. What does the number in (b) correspond to in decimal?

    d. What is the largest possible negative number? Give your answer in both octal and decimal form.

4.2 **a.** Find the 16-bit 2's complementary binary representation for the decimal number 1987.

    b. Find the 16-bit 2's complementary binary representation for the decimal number −1987.

    c. From your answer in (b) find the six-digit 16's complement hexadecimal representation for the decimal number −1987.

4.3 Data is stored in the R4-D4 computer using eight-digit base 4 notation. Negative numbers are stored using 4's complement.

    a. What is the sign-and-magnitude value of the following 4's complement number?

$$333332104$$

Leave your answer in base 4.

    b. Add the following eight-digit 4's complement numbers. Then, show the sign-and-magnitude values (in base 4) for each of the input numbers and for your result.

$$13220231_4$$
$$\underline{120000_4}$$

4.4   Convert the decimal number -19575 to a 15-bit 2's complement binary number. What happens when you perform this conversion? After the conversion is complete, what values (base 2 and base 10) does the computer think it has?

4.5   What are the 16-bit 1's and 2's complements of the following binary numbers?

    a. 10000

    b. 100111100001001

    c. 0100111000100100

4.6   Add the following decimal numbers by converting each to five-digit 10's complementary form, adding, and converting back to sign and magnitude.

    a.

$$24379$$
$$\underline{5098}$$

    b.

$$24379$$
$$\underline{-5098}$$

    c.

$$-24379$$
$$\underline{5098}$$

4.7   Subtract the second number from the first by taking the six-digit 10's complement of the second number and adding. Convert the result back to sign and magnitude if necessary.

    a.

$$37968$$
$$\underline{(-)24109}$$

    b.

$$37968$$
$$\underline{(-) - 70925}$$

c.

$$-10255$$
$$(-) - 7586$$

4.8 The following decimal numbers are already in six-digit 10's complementary form. Add the numbers. Convert each number and your result to sign and magnitude, and confirm your results.

a.

$$1250$$
$$772950$$

b.

$$899211$$
$$999998$$

c.

$$970000$$
$$30000$$

4.9 Add the following two 12-bit binary 2's complement numbers. Then convert each number to decimal and check the results.

a.

$$11001101101$$
$$111010111011$$

b.

$$101011001100$$
$$111111111100$$

4.10 Given the positive number 2468, what is the largest positive digit that you can add that will not cause overflow in a four-digit decimal, 10's complement number system?

4.11 In 12's complement base 12, how would you know if a number is positive or negative?

4.12 Most computers provide separate instructions for performing unsigned additions and complementary additions. Show that for unsigned additions, carry and overflow are the same. (Hint: Consider the definition of overflow.)

4.13 Consider a machine that performs calculations 4 bits at a time. Eight-bit 2's complement numbers can be added by adding the four least significant bits, followed by the four most significant bits. The leftmost bit is used for the sign, as usual. With 8 bits for each number, add –4 and –6, using 4-bit binary 2's complement arithmetic. Did overflow occur? Did carry occur? Verify your numerical result.

4.14   Add the following 16's complement hexadecimal numbers

4F09

D3A5

Is your result positive or negative? How do you know? Convert each number to binary and add the binary numbers. Convert the result back to hexadecimal. Is the result the same?

FLOATING POINT NUMBERS

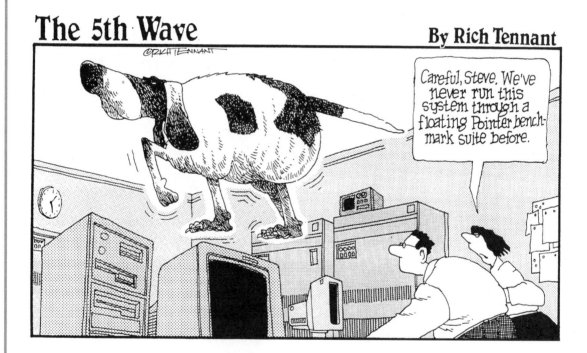

5.0 INTRODUCTION

As you know, it is not always possible to express numbers in integer form. Real, or **floating point,** numbers are used in the computer when the number to be expressed is outside of the integer range of the computer (too large or too small) or when the number contains a decimal fraction.

Floating point numbers allow the computer to maintain a limited, fixed number of digits of precision together with a power that shifts the point to make the number larger or smaller, as necessary. The range of numbers that the computer can handle in this way is huge. In a personal computer, for example, the range of numbers that may be expressed this way may be $\pm 10^{-38} <$ number $< 10^{+38}$ or more.

There are trade-offs made for this convenience: a potential loss of precision, as measured in terms of significant digits, larger storage requirements, and slower calculations.

In this chapter we will explore the properties of floating point numbers, show how they are represented in the computer, consider how calculations are performed, and learn how to convert between integer and floating point representations. We also investigate the importance of the trade-offs required for the use of floating point numbers and attempt to come up with some reasonable ground rules for deciding what number format to specify in various programming situations.

As before, we first present the techniques in base 10, since working with decimal numbers is more familiar to you. Once you have seen the methods used for the storage and manipulation of floating point numbers, we will then extend our discussion to the binary number system. This discussion will include the conversion of floating point numbers between the decimal and binary bases (which requires some care) and the consideration of **floating point formats** used in actual computer systems.

5.1 A REVIEW OF EXPONENTIAL NOTATION

Consider the whole number

$$12345$$

If we allow the use of exponents, there are many different ways in which we can represent this number. Without changing anything, this number can be represented as

$$12345 \times 10^0$$

If we introduce decimals, we can easily create other possible representations. Each of these alternative representations is created by shifting the decimal point from its original location. Since each single-place shift represents a multiplication or division of the value by the base, we can decrease or increase the exponent to compensate for the shift. For example, let us write the number as a decimal fraction with the decimal point at the beginning:

$$0.12345 \times 10^5$$

or, as another alternative,

$$123450000 \times 10^{-4}$$

or even,

$$0.0012345 \times 10^7$$

Of course, this last representation will be a poor choice if we are limited to five digits of magnitude,

$$0.00123 \times 10^7$$

since we will have sacrificed two digits of precision in exchange for the two zeros at the beginning of the number which do not contribute anything to the precision of the number. (You may recall from previous math courses that they are known as insignificant digits.)

The other representations do retain full precision, and any one of these representations would be theoretically as good as any other. Thus, our choice of representation is somewhat arbitrary and will be based on more practical considerations.

The way of representing numbers described here is known as **exponential notation** or, alternatively, as scientific notation. Using the exponential notation for numbers requires the specification of four separate components to define the number. These are

1. The sign of the number ("+," in our example)
2. The magnitude of the number, known as the **mantissa** (12345)
3. The sign of the exponent ("+")
4. The magnitude of the exponent (3)

Two additional pieces of information are required to complete the picture:

5. The base of the exponent (in this case, 10)
6. The location of the decimal (or other base) radix point

Both these latter factors are frequently unstated, yet extremely important. In the computer, for example, the base of the exponent is usually, but not always, specified to be 2. In some computers, _16_ or _10_ may be used instead, and it is obviously important to know which is being used if you ever have to read the numbers in their binary form.

The location of the decimal point (or _binary_ point, if we're working in base 2) is also an essential piece of information. In the computer, the binary point is set at a particular location in the number, most commonly the beginning or the end of the number. Since its location never changes, it is not necessary to actually store the point. Instead, the location of the binary point is implied.

Knowing the location of the point is, of course, essential. In the example that accompanies the rules just given, the location of the decimal point was not specified. Reading the data suggests that the number might be

$$+12345 \times 10^{+3}$$

which, of course, is not correct if we're still using the number from our original example. The actual placement of the decimal point should be

$$12.345 \times 10^3$$

Let us summarize these rules by showing another example, with each component specifically marked. Assume that the number to be represented is

$$-0.0000003579$$

One possible representation of this number is

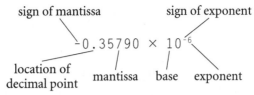

5.2 FLOATING POINT FORMAT

As was the case with integers, floating point numbers will be stored and manipulated in the computer using a "standard," predefined format. For practical reasons, a multiple of 8 bits is usually selected as the word size. This will simplify the manipulation and arithmetic that is performed with these numbers.

In the case of integers, the entire word is allocated to the magnitude of the integer and its sign. For floating point numbers, the word is divided: part of the space is reserved for the exponent and its sign; the remainder is allocated to the mantissa and its sign. The base of the exponent and the implied location of the binary point are standardized as part of the format and, therefore, do not have to be stored at all.

You can understand that the format chosen is somewhat arbitrary, since you have already seen that there are many different ways to represent a floating point number. Among the decisions made by the designer of the format are the number of digits to use, the implied location of the binary or decimal point, the base of the exponent, and the method of handling the signs for the mantissa and the exponent.

For example, suppose that the standard word consists of space for seven decimal digits and a sign:

SMMMMMMM

This format would allow the storage of any integer in the range

$$-9,999,999 < I < 99,999,999$$

with full, seven-digit precision. Numbers of magnitude larger than 9,999,999 result in overflow. Numbers of magnitude less than 1 cannot be represented at all, except as 0.

For floating point numbers, we might assign the digits as follows:

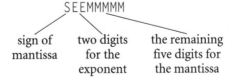

In addition we have to specify the implied location for the decimal point.

In this example we have "traded" two digits of exponent in exchange for the loss of two digits of precision. We emphasize that we have not increased the number of values that can be represented by seven digits. Seven digits can represent exactly 10,000,000 different values, no matter how they are used. We have simply chosen to use those digits differently—to increase the expressible range of values by giving up precision throughout the range. If we wish to increase the precision, one option is to increase the number of digits.

There are other possible trades. We could, for example, increase precision by another digit by limiting the exponent to a single digit. This might not be as limiting as it first appears. Since each increment or decrement of the exponent changes the number by a factor equivalent to the base (in this case, 10), a fairly substantial range of numbers can be accommodated with even a single digit, in this case 10^9 to 10^0, or 1 billion to 1.

The sign digit will be used to store the sign of the mantissa. Any of the methods shown in Chapter 4 for storing the sign and magnitude of integers could be used for the mantissa. Most commonly, the mantissa is stored using sign-magnitude format. A few computers use complementary notation.

Notice that we have made no specific provision for the sign of the exponent within the proposed format. We must therefore use some method that includes the sign of the exponent within the digits of the exponent itself. One method that you have already seen for doing this is the complementary representation. (Since the exponent and mantissa are independent of each other, and are used differently in calculations, there is no reason to assume that the same representation would be used for both.)

The manipulations used in performing exponential arithmetic allow us to use a simple method for solving this problem. If we pick a value somewhere in the middle of the possible values for the exponent, for example, 50 when the exponent can take on values 0 to 99, and declare that value to correspond to the exponent 0, then every value lower than that will be negative and those above will be positive. Figure 5.1 shows the scale for this offset technique.

What we have done is *offset*, or bias, the value of the exponent by our chosen amount. Thus, to convert from exponential form to the format used in our example, we add the offset to the exponent, and store it in that form. Similarly, the stored form can be returned to our usual exponential notation by subtracting the offset.

This method of storing the exponent is known as **excess-N** notation, where N is the chosen midvalue. It is simpler to use for exponents than the complementary form, and appropriate to the calculations required on exponents. In our example we have used excess-50 notation. This allows us to store an exponential range of −50 to +49, corresponding to the stored values 00 to 99. We could, if we wished, pick a different offset value, which would expand our ability to handle larger numbers at the expense of smaller numbers, or vice versa.

If we assume that the implied decimal point is located at the beginning of the five-digit mantissa, excess-50 notation allows us a magnitude range of

$$0.00001 \times 10^{-50} < \text{number} < 0.99999 \times 10^{+49}$$

This is an obviously much larger range than that possible using integers, and at the same time gives us the ability to express decimal fractions. In practice, the range may be slightly more restricted, since many format designs require that the most significant digit not be 0, even for very small numbers. In this case, the smallest expressible number becomes 0.10000×10^{-50}, not a great limitation. The word consisting of all 0's is frequently reserved to represent the special value 0.0.

If we were to pick a larger (or smaller) value for the offset, we could skew the range to store

FIGURE 5.1

Excess-50 Representation

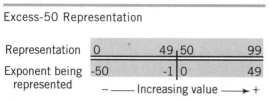

Representation	0	49	50	99
Exponent being represented	-50	-1	0	49

− ——— Increasing value ——→ +

smaller (or larger) numbers. Generally, values somewhere in the midrange seem to satisfy the majority of users, and there seems little reason to choose any other offset value.

Notice that, like the integer, it is still possible, although very difficult, to create an **overflow** by using a number of magnitude too large to be stored. With floating point numbers it is also possible to have **underflow,** where the number is a decimal fraction of magnitude too small to be stored. The diagram in Figure 5.2 shows the regions of underflow and overflow for our example. Note that in the diagram 0.00001×10^{-50} is expressed equivalently as 10^{-55}.

There is one more consideration. As you are already aware, the computer is actually capable of storing only numbers, no signs or decimal points. We have already handled the decimal point by establishing a fixed, implied point. We must also represent the sign of the number in a way that takes this limitation into account.

Here are some examples of floating point decimal representations. The format used is that shown on page 113: a sign, two digits of exponent stored excess-50, and five digits of mantissa. The value 0 is used to represent a "+" sign; 5 has been arbitrarily chosen to represent a "−" sign, just as 1 is usually chosen within the computer for the same purpose. The base is, of course, 10; the implied decimal point is at the beginning of the mantissa. You should look at these examples carefully to make sure that you understand all the details of the **floating point format.**

EXAMPLE

$$05324657 = 0.24657 \times 10^3 = 246.57$$
$$54810000 = -0.10000 \times 10^{-2} = -0.0010000$$

(Note that five significant digits are maintained.)

$$55555555 = -0.55555 \times 10^5 = -55555$$
$$04925000 = 0.25000 \times 10^{-1} = 0.025000$$

5.3 NORMALIZATION AND FORMATTING OF FLOATING POINT NUMBERS

The number of digits used will be determined by the desired precision of the numbers. To maximize the precision for a given number of digits, numbers will be stored whenever possible with no leading zeros. This means that, when necessary, numbers are shifted left by increasing the exponent until leading zeros are eliminated. This process is called **normalization.**

Our standard format, then, will consist of a mantissa of fixed, predetermined size with a decimal point placed at a fixed, predetermined location. The exponent will be adjusted so that numbers will be stored in this format with no leading zeros.

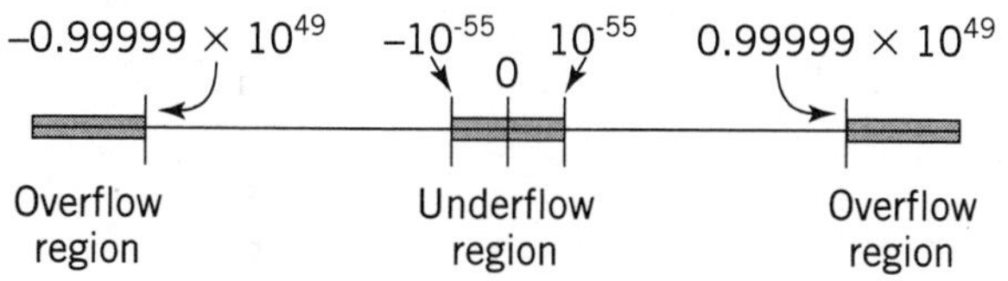

As an example, let us set up a standard format that reflects the storage capabilities suggested in the previous section. Our format will consist of a sign and five digits, with the decimal point located at the beginning of the number:

$$.MMMMM \times 10^{EE}$$

FIGURE 5.2

Regions of Overflow and Underflow

-0.99999×10^{49} -10^{-55} 10^{-55} 0.99999×10^{49}

| Overflow region | Underflow region | Overflow region |

There are four steps required to convert any decimal number into this standard format:

1. Provide an exponent of 0 for the number, if an exponent was not already specified as part of the number.

2. Shift the decimal point left or right by increasing or decreasing the exponent, respectively, until the decimal point is in the proper position.

3. Shift the decimal point right, if necessary, by decreasing the exponent, until there are no leading zeros in the mantissa.

4. Correct the precision by adding or discarding digits as necessary to meet the specification. We discard or round any digits in excess of the specified precision by eliminating the least significant digits. If the number has fewer than the specified number of digits, we supply zeros at the end.

Once we have normalized the number and put it into a standard exponential form, we can perform a fifth step to convert the result into the desired word format. To do this, we change the exponent into excess-50 notation and place the digits into their correct locations in the word.

Conversions between integer and floating point format are similar. The integer is treated as a number with an implied radix point at the end of the number. In the computer, an additional step may be required to convert the integer between complementary and sign-magnitude format to make it compatible with floating point format.

Here are some examples of a decimal to floating point format conversion:

EXAMPLE

Convert the number

$$246.8035$$

into our standard format.

1. Adding an exponent makes the number

$$246.8035 \times 10^0$$

2. We shift the decimal to the left three places, thereby increasing the exponent by 3:

$$0.2468035 \times 10^3$$

3. Since the number is already normalized (no leading zeros), there is no adjustment required.

4. There are seven digits, so we drop the two least significant digits, and the final exponential representation is

$$0.24680 \times 10^3$$

5. The exponent is 3, which in excess-50 notation is represented as 53. If we represent a "+" sign with the digit 0, and a "–" sign with the digit 5 (this choice is totally arbitrary, but we needed to select some digits since the sign itself cannot be stored), the final stored result becomes

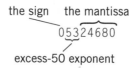

the sign   the mantissa

05324680

excess-50 exponent

■ ■ ■

Assume that the number to be converted is

$$1255 \times 10^{-3}$$

1. The number is already in exponential form.
2. We must shift the decimal to the left four places, so the number becomes

$$0.1255 \times 10^{+1}$$

The positive exponent results from adding 4 to the original –3 exponent.

3. The number is normalized, so no additional adjustment is required.
4. A zero is added to provide five digits of precision. The final result in exponential form is

$$0.12550 \times 10^1$$

5. The exponent in excess-50 notation becomes 51, and the result in word format is

$$05112550$$

■ ■ ■

Assume that the number to be converted is

$$-0.00000075$$

1. Converting to exponential notation, we have

$$-0.00000075 \times 10^0$$

2. The decimal point is already in its correct position, so no modification is necessary.
3. Normalizing, the number becomes

$$-0.75 \times 10^{-6}$$

4. And the final exponential result,

$$-0.75000 \times 10^{-6}$$

5. In our word format, this becomes

$$54475000$$

Although the technique is simple and straightforward, it will still require some practice for you to feel comfortable with it. We suggest that you practice with a friend, inventing numbers for each other to put into a standard format.

Some students have a bit of difficulty remembering whether to increase or decrease the exponent when shifting the number left or right. There is a simple method that may help you to remember which way to go: when you shift the decimal to the right, it makes the resulting number larger. (For example, 1.5 becomes 15.) Thus, the exponent must become smaller to keep the number the same as it was originally.

5.4 A PROGRAMMING EXAMPLE

Perhaps representing the steps as a pseudocode procedure will clarify these concepts even further. The procedure in Figure 5.3 converts numbers in normal decimal format to the floating point format

SEEMMMMM

The implied decimal point is at the beginning of the mantissa, and the sign is stored as 0 for positive, 5 for negative. The mantissa is stored in sign-magnitude format. The exponent is stored in excess-50 format. The number 0.0 is treated as a special case, with an all-zero format.

We suggest that you trace through the procedure carefully, until you understand each step.

5.5 FLOATING POINT CALCULATIONS

Floating point arithmetic is obviously more complex than integer arithmetic. First, the exponent and the mantissa have to be treated separately. Therefore, each has to be extracted from each number being manipulated.

FIGURE 5.3

A Procedure to Convert Decimal Numbers to Floating Point Format

```
function ConvertToFloat();
//variables used:
real decimalin; //decimal number to be converted
//components of the output
integer sign, exponent, integermantissa;
float mantissa; //used for normalization
integer floatout; //final form of output
{
    if (decimalin == 0.01) floatout = 0;
    else {
        if (decimalin > 0.01) sign = 0;
        else sign = 50000000;
        exponent = 50;
        StandardizeNumber;
        floatout = sign + exponent * 100000 + integermantissa;
    } //end else

function StandardizeNumber(); {
    mantissa = abs (mantissa);
    //adjust the decimal to fall between 0.1 and 1.0.
        while (mantissa >= 1.00) {
            mantissa = mantissa / 10.0;
            exponent = exponent + 1;
        } //end while
        while (mantissa < 0.1) {
            mantissa = mantissa * 10.0;
            exponent = exponent - 1;
        } //end while
        inegermantissa = round (10000.0 * mantissa)
    } //end function StandardizeNumber
} //end ConvertToFloat
```

Addition and Subtraction

You recall that in order to add or subtract numbers that contain decimal fractions, it is necessary that the decimal points line up. When using exponential notation, it is thus a requirement that the implied decimal point in both numbers be in the same position; the exponents of both numbers must agree.

The easiest way to align the two numbers is to shift the number with the smaller exponent to the right a sufficient number of spaces to increase the exponent to match the larger exponent. This process inserts insignificant zeros at the beginning of the number. Note that this process protects the precision of the result by maintaining all the digits of the larger number. It is the least significant digits of the smaller number that will disappear.

Once alignment is complete, addition or subtraction of the mantissas can take place. It is possible that the addition or subtraction may result in an overflow of the most significant digit. In this case, the number must be shifted right and the exponent decremented to accommodate the overflow. Otherwise, the exponent remains unchanged.

It is useful to notice that the exponent can be manipulated directly in its excess form, since it is the difference in the two exponents that is of interest rather than the value of the exponent itself. It is thus not necessary to change the exponents to their actual values in order to perform addition or subtraction.

EXAMPLE

Add the two floating point numbers

05199520

04967850

Assume that these numbers are formatted using sign-and-magnitude notation for the mantissa and excess-50 notation for the exponent. The implied decimal point is at the beginning of the mantissa, and base 10 is used for the exponent.

Shifting the lower mantissa right two places to align the exponent, the two numbers become

05199520

0510067850

Adding the mantissas, the new mantissa becomes

(1)0019850

We have put the 1 in parentheses to emphasize the fact that it is a carry beyond the original left position of the mantissa. Therefore, we must again shift the mantissa right one place and decrement the exponent to accommodate this digit:

05210019(850)

Rounding the result to five places of precision, we finally get

05210020

Checking the result,

$$05199520 = 0.99520 \quad 10^1 = 9.9520$$
$$04967850 = 0.67850 \quad 10^1 = \underline{0.06785}$$
$$10.01985 = 0.1001985 \times 10^2$$

which converts to the result that we previously obtained.

Multiplication and Division

Alignment is not necessary in order to perform multiplication or division. Exponential numbers are multiplied (or divided) by multiplying (dividing) the two mantissas and adding (subtracting) the two exponents. The sign is dealt with separately in the usual way. This procedure is relatively straightforward. There are two special considerations that must be handled, however:

1. Multiplication or division frequently results in a shifting of the decimal point (e.g., $0.2 \times 0.2 = 0.04$) and normalization must be performed to restore the location of the decimal point and to maintain the precision of the result.

2. We must adjust the excess value of the resulting exponent. Adding two exponents, each of which contains an excess value, results in adding the excess value to itself, so the final exponent must be adjusted by subtracting the excess value from the result. Similarly, when we subtract the exponents, we subtract the excess value from itself, and we must restore the excess value by adding it to the result.

EXAMPLE

This is seen easily with an example. Assume we have two numbers with exponent 3. Each is represented in excess-50 notation as 53. Adding the two exponents,

$$\begin{array}{r} 53 \\ \underline{53} \\ 106 \end{array}$$

We have added the value 50 twice, and so we must subtract it out to get the correct excess-50 result:

$$\begin{array}{r} 106 \\ \underline{-50} \\ 56 \end{array}$$

3. The multiplication of two five-digit normalized mantissas yields a ten-digit result. Only five digits of this result are significant, however. To maintain full, five-digit precision, we must first normalize and then round the normalized result back to five digits.

EXAMPLE

Multiply the two numbers

$$\begin{array}{r} 05220000 \\ \times 04712500 \end{array}$$

Adding the exponents and subtracting the offset results in a new, excess-50 exponent of

$$52 + 47 - 50 = 49$$

Multiplying the two mantissas,

$$0.20000 \times 0.12500 = 0.025000000$$

Normalizing the result by shifting the point one space to the right decreases the exponent by one, giving a final result

$$04825000$$

Checking our work,

$$05220000 \text{ is equivalent to } 0.20000 \times 10^2,$$
$$04712500 \text{ is equivalent to } 0.12500 \times 10^{-3}$$

which multiplies out to

$$0.0250000000 \times 10^{-1}$$

Normalizing and rounding,

$$0.0250000000 \times 10^{-1} = 0.25000 \times 10^{-2}$$

which corresponds to our previous result.

5.6 FLOATING POINT IN THE COMPUTER

The techniques discussed in the previous section can be applied directly to the storage of floating point numbers in the computer simply by replacing the digits with bits. Typically, 4, 8, or 16 bytes are used to represent a floating point number. In fact, the few differences that do exist result from "tricks" that can be played when "0" and "1" are the only options.

A typical floating point format might look like the diagram in Figure 5.4. In this example, 32 bits (4 bytes) are used to provide a range of approximately 10^{-38} to 10^{+38}. With 8 bits, we can provide 256 levels of exponent, so it makes sense to store the exponent in excess-128 notation.

EXAMPLE

Here are some examples of binary floating point format using this notation. Again we have assumed that the binary point is at the start of the mantissa. The base of the exponent is 2.

$$0 \ 10000001 \ 11001100000000000000000 =$$
$$+1.1001100000000000000000$$
$$1 \ 10000100 \ 10000111100000000000000 =$$
$$-1000.0111100000000000000$$
$$1 \ 01111110 \ 10101010101010101010101 =$$
$$-0.0010101010101010101010101$$

FIGURE 5.4

Typical Floating Point Format

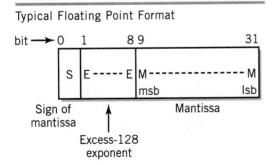

Thanks to the nature of the binary system, the 23 bits of mantissa can be stretched to provide 24 bits of precision, which corresponds to approximately seven decimal digits of precision. Since the leading bit of the mantissa must be "1" if the number is normalized, there is no need to store the most significant bit explicitly. Instead, the leading bit can be treated implicitly, similar to the binary point.

There are three potential disadvantages to using this trick. First, the assumption that the leading bit is always a "1" means that we cannot store numbers too small to be normalized, which slightly limits the small end of the range. Second, any format that may require a "0" in the most significant bit for any reason cannot use this method. Finally, this method requires that we provide a separate way to store the number 0.0, since the requirement that the leading bit be a "1" makes a mantissa of 0.0 an impossibility!

Since the additional bit doubles the available precision of the mantissa in all numbers, the slightly narrowed range is usually considered an acceptable trade-off. The number 0.0 is handled by selecting a particular 32-bit word and assigning it the value 0.0. Twenty-four bits of mantissa corresponds to approximately seven decimal digits of precision.

Don't forget that the base and implied binary point must also be specified.

There are many variations, providing different degrees of precision and exponential range, but the basic techniques for handling floating point numbers in the computer are identical to those that we have already discussed in the previous sections of this chapter.

IEEE 754 Standard

Most current computers conform to IEEE 754 standard formats. The IEEE Computer Society is a society of computer professionals. Among its tasks, the IEEE Computer Society develops technical standards for use by the industry. The IEEE 754 standard defines formats for 32-bit and 64-bit floating point arithmetic. Instructions built into modern computers utilize the standard to perform floating point arithmetic, normalization, and conversion between integer and floating point representations internally under program command. The standard also facilitates the portability of programs between different computers that support the standard.

In addition to the IEEE 754 format, there are a number of older, machine-specific formats still in use for legacy data. The Macintosh also provides an additional 80-bit format. Sun UltraSparc and IBM mainframes systems include additional 128-bit formats. The Intel IA-64 architecture conforms to the IEEE 754 format, but also provides 64-bit significand/17-bit exponent range capability; the programmer can set individual precision control and widest-range exponent values in the floating point status register for additional flexibility.

The standard defines a **single-precision floating point format** consisting of 32 bits, divided into a sign, 8 bits of exponent, and 23 bits of mantissa. Since normalized numbers must always start with a 1, the leading bit is not stored, but is instead implied; this bit is located to the left of the implied binary point. Thus, numbers are normalized to the form

$$1.MMMMMMM...$$

The exponent is formatted using excess-127 notation, with an implied base of 2. This would theoretically allow an exponent range of 2^{-127} to 2^{128}. In actuality, the stored exponent values 0 and 255 are used to indicate special values, and the exponential range of this format is thus restricted to

$$2^{-126} \text{ to } 2^{127}$$

The number 0.0 is defined by a mantissa of 0 together with the special exponential value 0. The IEEE standard also allows the values $\pm\infty$, very small denormalized numbers, and various other special conditions. Overall, the standard allows approximately seven significant decimal digits and an approximate value range of 10^{-45} to 10^{38}.

The double-precision floating point format standard works similarly. Sixty-four bits (8 bytes) are divided into a sign, 11 bits of exponent, and 52 bits of mantissa. The same format is used, with excess-1023 notation for the exponent, an implied base of 2, and an implied most significant bit to the left of the implied binary point. The double-precision standard supports approximately fifteen significant decimal digits and a range of more than 10^{-300} to 10^{300}!

The values defined for all possible 32-bit words are shown in Figure 5.5. The 64-bit table is similar, except for the limiting exponent of 2047, which results in an excess 1023 offset.

5.7 CONVERSION BETWEEN BASE 10 AND BASE 2

On occasion, you may find it useful to be able to convert real numbers between decimal and binary representation. This task must be done carefully. There are two major areas that sometimes cause students (and others!) difficulty:

1. The whole and fractional parts of numbers with an embedded decimal or binary point must be converted separately.
2. Numbers in exponential form must be reduced to a pure decimal or binary mixed number or fraction before the conversion can be performed.

We dealt with the first issue in Section 2.8. Recall from that section that in converting from one base to another that one must deal with the different multipliers associated with each successive digit. To the left of the radix point, the multipliers are integer, and there is a direct relationship between the different bases. To the right of the point, the multipliers are fractional, and there may or may not be a rational relationship between the multipliers in the different bases.

The solution is to convert each side of the radix point separately using the techniques discussed in Chapter 2. As an alternative, you can multiply the entire number in one base by whatever number is required to make the entire number an integer, and then convert the number in integer form. When this is complete, however, you must divide the converted result by *that same multiplier* in the new base. It is not correct to simply shift the radix point back, since each shift has a different value in the new base! Thus, if you shift a binary point right by seven places, you have effectively multiplied the number by 128, and

FIGURE 5.5

IEEE Standard 32-bit Floating Point Value Definition

Exponent	Mantissa	Value
0	± 0	0
0	not 0	$\pm 2^{-126} \times 0.M$
1-254	any	$\pm 2E^{-127} \times 1.M$
255	± 0	± ∞
255	not 0	special condition

you must divide the converted number by 128 in the new base. This latter method is best illustrated with an example.

Convert the decimal number 253.75 to binary floating point form.

Begin by multiplying the number by 100 to form the integer value 25375. This is converted to its binary equivalent 110001100011111, or $1.10001100011111 \times 2^{14}$. The IEEE 754 floating point equivalent representation for this integer would be

$$0 \mid 10001101 \mid 10001100011111$$

Sign

Excess-127   Mantissa (initial 1 is dropped)

Exponent = 127 + 14

One more step is required to complete the conversion. The result must be divided by the binary floating point equivalent of 100_{10} to restore the original decimal value. 10010 converts to binary 1100100_2, or 010000101100100 in IEEE 754 form. The last step is to divide the original result by this value, using floating point division. We will omit this step, as it is both difficult and irrelevant to this discussion. Although this method looks more difficult than converting the number directly as a mixed fraction, it is sometimes easier to implement within the computer.

The problem with converting floating point numbers expressed in exponential notation is essentially the same problem; however, the difficulty is more serious because it looks as though it should be possible to convert a number, keeping the same exponent, and this is of course not true.

If you always remember that the exponent actually represents a multiplier of value B^e, where B is the base and e is the actual exponent, then you will be less tempted to make this mistake. Obviously it is incorrect to assume that this multiplier would have the same value for a different B.

Instead, it is necessary to follow one of the two solutions just outlined: either reduce the exponential notation to a standard mixed fraction and convert each side separately, or use the value B^e as a multiplier to be divided in the new base at the end of the conversion.

5.8 AN ALTERNATIVE REPRESENTATION: PACKED DECIMAL FORMAT

In many business applications it is important to maintain full accuracy for real numbers. In many cases, the real numbers being used represent dollars and cents figures. You are aware from Chapter 2 that rational decimal real numbers do not necessarily remain so when converted into binary form. Thus, it is possible that a number converted from decimal to binary and back again may not be exactly the same as the original number. You would not want to add two financial numbers and have the result off by a few cents. (In fact, this was a problem with early versions of spreadsheet programs!)

For this reason, business-oriented high-level languages such as COBOL provide formats that allow the user to specify the number of desired decimal places exactly. Large computers support these operations by providing an additional format for storing and manipulating real numbers known as **packed decimal format.** The packed decimal format is similar in most ways to BCD format. It suffers from many of the same shortcomings, but because of its importance to business applications, instructions are provided for common packed decimal conversion, manipulation, and arithmetic operations.

The packed decimal format used in both IBM System 370/390 and Compaq Alpha-based computers is shown in Figure 5.6. Each decimal digit is stored in BCD form, two digits to a byte. The most significant digit is stored first, in the high-order bits of the first byte. The sign is stored in the low-order bits of the last byte. Up to thirty-one digits may be stored. The binary values 1100 and 1101 are used for the sign, representing "+" and "–," respectively. The value 1111 can be used to indicate that the number is unsigned. Since these values do not represent any valid decimal number, it is easy to detect an error, as well as to determine the end of the number. Note that the location of the decimal point is not stored and must be maintained by the application program. Intel CPUs provide a more limited packed format that holds two digits (00–99) in a single byte. As an example, the decimal number –324.6 would be stored in packed decimal form as

$$0000 \quad 0011 \quad 0010 \quad 0100 \quad 0110 \quad 1101$$

The leading 0s are required to make the number fit exactly into 3 bytes.

Compaq and IBM both provide additional formats that store data one digit to a byte, but they provide no instructions for performing calculations in these formats. These formats are used primarily for conversion between text and packed decimal formats.

5.9 PROGRAMMING CONSIDERATIONS

In Chapters 4 and 5 you have been exposed to a number of different ways of storing and manipulating numeric values. It should be of interest to you to consider how a programmer might make an intelligent choice between the many different options available.

The trade-offs between integer and floating point are clear. Integer calculations are easier for the computer to perform, have the potential to provide higher precision, and are obviously much faster to execute. Integer values usually take up fewer storage locations. As you will see later, it takes a certain amount of time to access each storage location; thus, the use of fewer storage locations saves time, as well as space.

Clearly, the use of integer arithmetic is preferred whenever possible. Most modern high-level languages provide two or more different integer word sizes, usually at least a "short" integer of 16 bits and a "long" integer of 64 bits. Now that you understand the range limitations of integer arithmetic, you are in a position to determine whether a particular variable or constant can use the integer format, and whether special error checking may be required in your program.

The longer integer formats may require multiple-word calculation algorithms, and

FIGURE 5.6

Packed Decimal Format

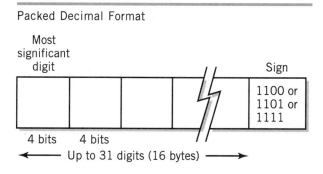

as such are slower to execute than short formats. The short format is preferable when it is sufficient for the values that you expect. It may also be necessary to consider the limitations of other systems that the same program may have to operate on.

The use of real numbers is indicated whenever the variable or constant has a fractional part, whenever the number can take on very large or very small values that are outside of integer range, or whenever the required precision exceeds the number of different values that are possible in the longest integer format available to you. (As you've seen, most systems provide a floating point format of very high precision.) Of course, it is sometimes possible to multiply a mixed number by some multiplier to make it integer, perform the calculations in integer form, and then divide back. If the number of calculations is large, and the numbers can be adjusted to operate as integers, this can be a worthwhile option to consider, especially for the gain in execution speed.

As with integers, it is desirable to use the real number with the least precision that is sufficient for the task. Higher-precision formats require more storage and usually must use multiple-word floating point or packed decimal calculation algorithms that are much slower than the lower-precision formats.

Recall that decimal fractions may convert into irrational binary fractions. For those languages that provide the capability, the use of packed decimals represents an attractive alternative to floating point for those business applications where exact calculations involving mixed decimal numbers are required.

SUMMARY AND REVIEW

Numbers with a fractional part and numbers that are too large to fit within the constraints of the integer data capacity are stored and manipulated in the computer as real, or floating point, numbers. In effect, there is a trade-off between accuracy and range of acceptable numbers. As an alternative, a packed decimal format may be used. This format is suitable for business applications where the number of decimal places is fixed and known.

The usual floating point number format consists of a sign bit, an exponent, and a mantissa. The sign and value of the exponent are usually represented in an excess-N format. The base of the exponent is 2 for most systems, but some systems use a different base for the exponent. The radix point is implied. When possible, the mantissa is normalized. In some systems the leading bit is also implied, since normalization requires that the leading bit of the mantissa be a 1.

Floating point numbers are subject to overflow or underflow, where the exponent of the number is too large or too small to represent, respectively. Zero is treated as a special case. Sometimes there is also a special representation for ∞.

Addition and subtraction require that the exponents in each number be equal. This is equivalent to lining up the decimal point in conventional decimal arithmetic. In multiplication and division, the exponents are added or subtracted, respectively. Special care must be taken with exponents that are expressed in excess-N notation.

Most computers conform to the format defined in IEEE Standard 754. Other formats in use include extra-precision formats and legacy formats.

KEY CONCEPTS AND TERMS

double-precision floating point format	floating point format	packed decimal format
excess-N representation	IEEE Standard 754	single-precision floating point format
exponential notation	mantissa	underflow
floating point	normalization	
	overflow	

FOR FURTHER READING

Most of the readings suggested at the end of Chapter 4 are also appropriate for further reading on the subject of floating point representation and arithmetic. One additional article of interest is the article titled "What Every Computer Scientist Should Know About Floating-Point Arithmetic" [GOLD91].

EXERCISES

5.1   In the Pink-Lemon-8 computer, real numbers are stored in the format

$$SEEMMMM_8$$

where all the digits, including the exponent, are in octal. The exponent is stored excess-40_8. The mantissa is stored as sign and magnitude, where the sign is 0 for a positive number and 4 for a negative number. The implied octal point is at the end of the mantissa: MMMM.

Consider the real number stored in this format as

$$4366621$$

a.   What real number is being represented? Leave your answer in octal.

b.   Convert your answer in part (a) to decimal. You may leave your answer in fractional form if you wish.

c.   What does changing the original exponent from 36 to 37 do to the magnitude of the number? (Stating that it moves the octal point one place to the right or left is not a sufficient answer.) What would be the new magnitude in decimal?

5.2   **a.**   Convert the decimal number 19557 to floating point. Use the format SEEMMMM. All digits are decimal. The exponent is stored excess-40 (not excess-50). The implied decimal point is at the *beginning* of the mantissa. The sign is 1 for a positive number, 7 for a negative number. Hint: Note carefully the number of digits in the mantissa!

b.   What is the range of numbers that can be stored in this format?

c.   What is the floating point representation for −19557?

d.   What is the six-digit 10's complement representation for −19557?

    e.   What is the floating point representation for 0.0000019557?

5.3   **a.**   Convert the number 123.57×10^{15} to the format SEEMMMM, with the exponent stored excess-49. The implied decimal point is to the right of the first mantissa digit.

    b.   What is the smallest number you can use with this format before underflow occurs?

5.4   Real numbers in the R4-D4 computer are stored in the format

$$SEEMMMMM_4$$

where all the digits, including the exponent, are in base 4. The mantissa is stored as sign and magnitude, where the sign is 0 for a positive number and 3 for a negative number. The implied quadrinary (base 4!) point is at the beginning of the mantissa:

$$.MMMMM$$

    a.   If you know that the exponent is stored in an excess-something format, what would be a good choice of value for "something?"

    b.   Convert the real, decimal number 16.5 to base 4, and show its representation in the format of the R4-D4 computer. Use the excess value that you determined in part (a).

5.5   Convert the following binary and hexadecimal numbers to floating point format. Assume a binary format consisting of a sign bit (negative = 1), a base 2, 8-bit, excess-128 exponent, and 23 bits of mantissa, with the implied binary point to the right of the first bit of the mantissa.

    a. 110110.011011_2

    b. -1.1111001_2

    c. $-4F7F_{16}$

    d. 0.00000000111111_2

    e. 0.1100×2^{36}

    f. 0.1100×2^{-36}

5.6   For the format used in Exercise 5.5, what decimal number is represented by each of the following numbers in floating point format?

    a. $C2F00000_{16}$

    b. $3C540000_{16}$

5.7   Represent the decimal number 171.625 in IEEE 754 format.

5.8   Show the packed decimal format for the decimal number –129975.

5.9   The following decimal numbers are stored in excess-50 floating point format, with the decimal point to the left of the first mantissa digit. Add them. A 9 is used as a negative sign. Present your result in standard decimal sign-and-magnitude notation.

    a.

$$05225731$$
$$\underline{04833300}$$

b.

$$05012500$$
$$\underline{95325750}$$

5.10   Using the same notation as in Exercise 5.9, multiply the following numbers. Present your answer in standard decimal notation.

a.

$$05452500$$
$$\underline{04822200}$$

b.

$$94650000$$
$$\underline{94450000}$$

5.11   Using the same format found in Exercise 5.5, add and multiply the following floating point numbers. Present your answers in both floating point and sign-and-magnitude formats.

$$3DEC0000_{16}$$
$$\underline{C24C0000_{16}}$$

5.12   Write a program in your favorite language that converts numbers represented in the decimal floating point format

$$SEEMMMMM$$

into 10's complementary integer form. Round any fractional decimal value.

PART THREE

The basic operation of a computer is defined by its hardware architecture. The hardware architecture establishes the CPU instruction set and the type of operations that are permitted. It defines the passage of data from one part of the computer to another. It establishes the ground rules for input and output operation.

The next seven chapters introduce the fundamental architectural concepts that define computer operations and hardware organization. We will attempt to convey the basic simplicity and elegance of computer instruction sets. We will expose the inner workings of computer peripherals and show how the various pieces fit together to create a system.

For the past fifty-five years, and for the foreseeable future, basic computer architecture conforms to the general principles established by von Neumann that were introduced in Chapter 1. Chapter 6 introduces the principles of von Neumann architecture using a classic model of the computer called the Little Man Computer as an example. The Little Man Computer introduces the stored program concept, demonstrates the role of memory, describes the essential instructions that make up a computer instruction set, and explains the simple set of operations that implement an instruction set. We also show how the basic instructions of a computer work together to make up a program.

In Chapter 7 we extend the ideas introduced in Chapter 6 to the operation of a real computer. We consider the basic components of a CPU, explain the concept of a bus, discuss the operation of memory, and show how of these architectural elements fit together to create a computer system. We also show the individual operations that make up the execution of instructions, the so-called fetch-execute cycle. We also discuss the formats for instruction words and present a general classification of the instruction set.

COMPUTER ARCHITECTURE AND HARDWARE OPERATION

In Chapter 8, we consider the variations that distinguish one CPU architecture from another. The major topics in Chapter 8 deal with CPU design and organization. We present different CPU models, and compare them. We investigate alternatives to the traditional CPU organization and explain the benefits to be gained. We also consider the hardware aspects of paging. Finally, we look at improvements to memory and, especially, the use of cache memory.

In Chapter 9 we shift our focus to I/O. Chapter 9 introduces the various methods that are used to move data between computer peripherals and memory, including the use of interrupts and direct access paths between peripherals and memory as efficient ways to perform I/O with minimal impact on the processing unit. We also contrast the different approaches that are used in different systems, particularly the difference between bus and channel I/O techniques.

Chapter 10 provides explanations of the requirements and operation of various I/O peripheral components, including disks, displays, tapes, printers, and other components. This chapter also presents a hierarchical model of storage.

Chapter 11 explores additional features and innovative techniques at the system level that have expanded the performance and capability of computers. While these techniques are substantial extensions to the basic design, they do not change the fundamental concepts and operating methods that are discussed in the earlier chapters. The most important topics in this chapter are multiprocessing, clusters, and networks.

Finally, Chapter 12 illustrates many of the previous concepts with case studies of three important current systems, representing three different approaches to computer design.

Supplementary Chapters 1, 2, and 3 provide additional material on computer logic circuits, instruction addressing, and communication channels, respectively.

CHAPTER 6

THE LITTLE MAN COMPUTER

Raeside/Victoria Times-Colonist/Rothco

6.0 INTRODUCTION

The power of a computer does not arise from complexity. Instead, the computer has the ability to perform simple operations at an extremely high rate of speed. These operations can be combined to provide the computer capabilities that you are familiar with.

Consistent with this idea, the actual design of the computer is also simple, as you will see.

(The beauty of the design is that these simple operations can be used to solve extremely complex problems. The programmer's challenge, of course, is to produce the exact sequence of operations to perform a particular task correctly under all possible circumstances, since any error in selection or sequence of operations will result in a "buggy" program. With the large number of instructions required by modern programs, it is not surprising that few of today's programs are truly bug-free.)

In this chapter, we will begin to explore the operations that the computer is capable of performing and look at how those operations work together to provide the computer with its power. To simplify our exploration, we will begin by introducing a model of the computer; a model that operates in a very similar way to the real computer but that is easier to understand instinctively.

The model that we will use is called the **Little Man Computer (LMC).** The original LMC was created by Dr. Stuart Madnick at MIT in 1965. In 1979, Dr. Madnick produced a new version of the LMC, with a slightly modified instruction set; the later version is used in this book. It is a strength of the original model that it operates so similarly to a real computer that it is still an accurate representation of the way that computers work thirty-five years after its introduction.

Using this model we will introduce a simplified, but typical, set of instructions that a computer can perform. We will show you exactly how these instructions are executed in the Little Man Computer. Then we will demonstrate how these instructions are combined to form programs.

6.1 LAYOUT OF THE LITTLE MAN COMPUTER

We begin by describing the physical layout of the Little Man Computer. A diagram for the Little Man Computer appears in Figure 6.1.

The LMC consists of a walled mailroom, represented by the dark line surrounding the model in the diagram. Inside the mailroom are several objects:

First, there is a series of one hundred *mailboxes,* each numbered with an address ranging from 00 to 99. This numbering system is chosen because each mailbox address can be represented by two digits, and this is the maximum number of mailboxes that can be represented by two decimal digits.

Each mailbox is designed to hold a single slip of paper, upon which is written a three-digit decimal number. Note carefully that the *contents* of a mailbox are not the same

FIGURE 6.1

The Little Man Computer

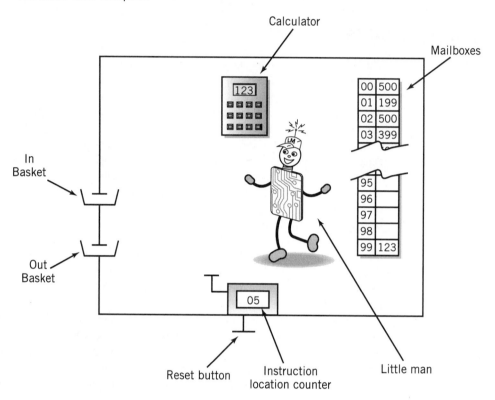

as the *address* of a mailbox. This idea is consistent with what you already know about your post office box: your post office box number identifies where you go to pick up your mail, but this has no relationship to the actual contents of the letters that you find in that mailbox.

Next, there is a *calculator*…basically a simple pocket calculator. The calculator can be used to enter and temporarily hold numbers, and also to add and subtract. The display on the calculator is three digits wide. At least for the purposes of this discussion, there is no provision made for negative numbers, or for numbers larger than three digits. As you are already aware, 10's complement arithmetic could be used for this purpose, but that is not of interest here.

Third, there is a two-digit *hand counter,* the type that you click to increment the count. The reset button for the hand counter is located outside the mailroom. We will call this counter an *instruction location counter.*

Finally, there is the Little Man. It will be his role to perform certain tasks that will be defined shortly.

Other than the reset switch on the hand counter, the only interaction between the Little Man Computer and the outside environment are an *in basket* and an *out basket.*

A user outside of the mailroom can communicate with the Little Man in the mailroom by putting a slip of paper with a three-digit number on it into the in basket, to be read by the Little Man at the appropriate time. Similarly, the Little Man can write a three-digit number on a slip of paper and leave it in the out basket, where it can be retrieved by the user.

Note that *all communication* between the Little Man Computer and the outside world takes place using three-digit numbers. Except for the reset button on the instruction location counter, no other form of communication is possible. The same is true within the mailroom: all instructions to the Little Man must be conveyed as three-digit numbers.

6.2 OPERATION OF THE LMC

We would like the Little Man to do some useful work. For this purpose we have invented a small group of instructions that he can perform. Each instruction will consist of a single digit. We will use the first digit of a three-digit number to tell the Little Man which operation to perform.

In some cases, the operation will require the Little Man to use a particular mailbox to store or retrieve data (in the form of three-digit numbers, of course!). Since the instruction only requires one digit, we can use the other two digits in a three-digit number to indicate the appropriate mailbox address to be used as a part of the instruction. Thus, using the three digits on a slip of paper we can describe an instruction to the Little Man according to the following diagram:

The instruction part of the three-digit code is also known as an "operation code," or **op code** for short. The op code number assigned to a particular instruction is arbitrary, selected by the computer designer based on various architectural and implementation factors. The op codes used by the author conform to the 1979 version of the Little Man Computer model.

Now let's define some instructions for the Little Man to perform:

LOAD instruction—op code 5

The Little Man walks over to the mailbox address specified in the instruction. He reads the three-digit number located in that mailbox, and then walks over to the calculator and punches that number into the calculator. The three-digit number in the mailbox is left unchanged, but of course the original number in the calculator is replaced by the new number.

STORE instruction—op code 3

This instruction is the reverse of the LOAD instruction. The Little Man walks over to the calculator and reads the number there. He writes that number on a slip of paper and puts it in the mailbox whose address was specified as the address part of the instruction. The number in the calculator is unchanged; the original number in the mailbox is replaced with the new value.

ADD instruction—op code 1

This instruction is very similar to the LOAD instruction. The Little Man walks over to the mailbox address specified in the instruction. He reads the three-digit number located in the mailbox and then walks over to the calculator and *adds it to the number already in the calculator*. The number in the mailbox is unchanged.

SUBTRACT instruction—op code 2

This instruction is the same as the ADD instruction, except that the Little Man subtracts the mailbox value from the value in the calculator. The result of a sub-traction can leave a negative value in the calculator. Chapter 4 discussed the use of complements to implement negative values, but for simplicity, the LMC model ignores this solution. For the purposes of our LMC model, we will sim-ply assume that the calculator holds and handles negative values correctly, and provides a minus sign as a flag to indicate that the value is negative. The Little Man cannot handle negative numbers outside of the calculator, however, because there is no provision in the model for storing the negative sign within the constraint of the three-digit number system used.

INPUT instruction (or read, if you prefer)—op code 9, "address" 01

The Little Man walks over to the in basket and picks up the slip of paper in the basket. He then walks over to the calculator and punches it into the calculator. The number is no longer in the in basket, and the original calculator value has been replaced by the new number. If there are multiple slips of paper in the bas-ket, the Little Man picks them up in the order in which they were submitted, but each INPUT instruction handles only a single slip of paper; other input values must await the execution of subsequent INPUT instructions. Some authors use the concept of a conveyor belt in place of the in basket, to emphasize this point.

OUTPUT instruction (or print)—op code 9, "address" 02

The Little Man walks over to the calculator and writes down the number that he sees there on a slip of paper. He then walks over to the out basket and places the slip of paper there for the user outside the mailroom to retrieve. The original number in the calculator is unchanged. Each OUTPUT instruction places a single slip of paper in the out basket. Multiple outputs will require the use of multiple OUTPUT instructions.

Note that the INPUT and OUTPUT instructions do not use any mailboxes during execu-tion, since the procedure for each only involves the transfer of data between an in or out basket and the calculator. Because this is true, the address part of the instruction can be used to extend the capability of the instruction set, by using the same op code with differ-ent "address" values to create a number of different instructions. In the LMC, 901 is the code for an INPUT instruction, while 902 is used for an OUTPUT instruction. In a real com-puter, for example, the instruction address might be used to specify the particular I/O device to be used for input or output.

COFFEE BREAK (or HALT) instruction—op code 0

The Little Man takes a rest. The Little Man will ignore the address portion of the instruction.

The instructions that we have defined so far fall into four categories:

- instructions that move data from one part of the LMC to another (LOAD, STORE)
- instructions that perform simple arithmetic (ADD, SUBTRACT)
- instructions that perform input and output (INPUT, OUTPUT)
- instructions that control the machine (COFFEE BREAK)

This is enough for now. We will discuss instructions 6, 7, and 8 later in this chapter.

6.3 A SIMPLE PROGRAM

Now let's see how we can combine these instructions into a program to have the Little Man do some useful work.

Before we do this, we need to store the instructions somewhere, and we need a method to tell the Little Man where to find the particular instruction that he is supposed to perform at a given time.

Without discussing how they got there, for now we will assume that the instructions are stored in the mailboxes, starting at mailbox number 00. The Little Man will perform instructions by looking at the value in the instruction location counter and executing the instruction found in the mailbox whose address has that value. Each time the Little Man completes an instruction, he will walk over to the instruction location counter and increment it. Again he will perform the instruction specified by the counter. Thus, the Little Man will execute the instructions in the mailboxes sequentially, starting from mailbox 00. Since the instruction location counter is reset from outside the mailroom, the user can restart the program simply by resetting the counter to 00.

Now that we have a method for guiding the Little Man through a program of instruction steps, let's consider a simple program that will allow the user outside the mailroom to use the Little Man Computer to add two numbers together. The user will place two numbers in the in basket. The sum of the two will appear as a result in the out basket. The question is what instructions we will need to provide to have the Little Man perform this operation.

INPUT   901

Since the Little Man must have access to the data, the first step, clearly, is to have the Little Man read the first number from the in basket to the calculator. This instruction leaves the first number to be added in the calculator.

STORE 99   399

Note that it is not possible for the Little Man to simply read another number into the calculator. To do so would destroy the first number. Instead, we must first save the first number somewhere.

Mailbox 99 was chosen simply because it is clearly out of the way of the program. Any other location that is beyond the end of the program is equally acceptable.

Storing the number at a location that is within the program would destroy the instruction at that location. This would mean that when the Little Man went to perform that instruction, it wouldn't be there.

More seriously, there is no way for the Little Man to distinguish between an instruction and a piece of data—both are made up of three-digit numbers. Thus, if we were to store data in a location that the Little Man is going to use as an instruction, the Little Man would simply attempt to perform the data as though it were an instruction. Since there is no way to predict what the data might contain, there is no way to predict what the program might do.

The concept that there is no way to distinguish between instructions and data except in the context of their use is a very important one in computing. For example, it allows a programmer to treat an instruction as data, to modify it, and then to execute the modified instruction.

INPUT   **901**

With the first number stored away, we are ready to have the Little Man read the second number into the calculator.

ADD 99   **199**

Note that there is no specific reason to save the second number. If we were going to perform some operation that required the reuse of the second number, it could be stored somewhere.

In this program, however, we have both numbers in place to perform the addition. The result is, of course, left in the calculator.

OUTPUT   **902**

All that remains is for us to have the Little Man output the result to the out basket.

COFFEE BREAK   **000**

The program is complete, so we allow the Little Man to take a rest.

These instructions are stored sequentially starting from mailbox 00, where the Little Man will retrieve and execute them one at a time, in order. The program is reshown in Figure 6.2.

Since we were careful to locate the data outside the program, this program can be rerun simply by telling the Little Man to begin again.

6.4 AN EXTENDED INSTRUCTION SET

FIGURE 6.2

Program to Add Two Numbers

Mailbox code		Instruction description
00	901	INPUT
01	399	STORE DATA
02	901	INPUT 2ND #
03	199	ADD 1ST # TO IT
04	902	OUTPUT RESULT
05	000	STOP
99		DATA

The instructions that we have defined must always be executed in the exact sequence specified. Although this is sufficient for simple program segments that perform a sequence of operations, it does not provide any means for branching or looping, both constructs that you know are very important in programming. Let us extend the instruction set by adding three more instructions for this purpose:

BRANCH UNCONDITIONALLY instruction (sometimes known as JUMP)—op code 6

This instruction tells the Little Man to walk over to the instruction location counter and actually *change* the counter to the location shown in the two address digits of the instruction. (Assume that the hand counter has thumbwheels for this purpose.) This means that the next instruction that the Little Man will execute is located at that mailbox address.

This instruction is very similar, conceptually, to the GOTO instruction in BASIC. Its execution will always result in a break in the sequence to another part of the program.

Note that this instruction also uses the address digits in an unusual way, since the Little Man does not use the data at the address specified. Indeed, the Little Man expects to find an instruction at that address, the next to be performed.

BRANCH ON ZERO instruction—op code 7

The Little Man will walk over to the calculator and will observe the number stored there. If its current value is zero, he will walk over to the instruction location counter and modify its value to correspond to the address specified within the instruction. The next instruction executed by the Little Man will be located at that address.

If the value in the calculator is not zero, he will simply proceed to the next instruction in sequence.

BRANCH ON POSITIVE instruction—op code 8

The Little Man will walk over to the calculator and will observe the number stored there. If its current value is positive, he will walk over to the instruction location counter and modify its value, to correspond to the address specified within the instruction. The next instruction executed by the Little Man will be located at that address.

If the value in the calculator is negative, he will simply proceed to the next instruction in sequence. Zero is considered to be a positive value.

Note that is it not necessary to provide BRANCH ON NEGATIVE or BRANCH ON NONZERO instructions. The instructions supplied can be used together to achieve equivalent results.

These three instructions make it possible to break from the normal sequential processing of instructions. Instructions of this type are used to perform branches and loops. As an example, consider the following WHILE-DO loop, common to many programming languages:

```
WHILE Value = 0 DO
        Task;
NextStatement
```

This loop could be implemented using the Little Man BRANCH instruction as follows. Assume that these instructions are located starting at mailbox number 45 (comments are provided to the right of each line):

45	LDA 90	590	90 is assumed to contain value
46	BRZ 48	748	Branch if the value is zero
47	BR 60	660	Exit loop; Jump to NextStatement
48	•		This is where the task is located
	•		
	•		
59	BR 45	645	End to Task; loop to test again
60			Next statement

EXAMPLE

Here is an example of a Little Man program that uses the BRANCH instructions to alter the flow of the program. This program finds the positive difference between two numbers (sometimes known as the absolute magnitude of the difference). For convenience, we are introducing a set of abbreviations for each instruction. These abbreviations are known as **mnemonics** (the first "m" is silent). Once you learn to read these mnemonics, you'll find that programs written with mnemonics are generally easy to read. It is more common to write programs this way. For a while, we will continue to print both the mnemonic and the code, but eventually, we will stop printing the code. Most programs are also written with *comments,* which help to clarify the code. The mnemonic instructions that we will use are shown in Figure 6.3. The DAT abbreviation is used to indicate that a particular mailbox will be used to store data. The data may be specified in advance, for example, to use as a constant, or it may be zero if the particular location is to be used to store the data later, during execution of the program.

The program, shown in Figure 6.4, works as follows: the first four instructions simply input and store the two numbers. The fifth instruction, in mailbox 04, subtracts the first number from the second. Instruction 05 tests the result. If the result is positive, all that's left to do is print out the answer. So, the instruction can be used to branch to the printout instruction. If the answer is negative, the subtraction is performed in the other order. Then the result is output, and the Little Man takes his break. Note that if the COB instruction is omitted (as in forgotten—this is a very common error!), the Little Man will attempt to execute the data stored in locations 10 and 11. Please study the example until you understand how it works in every detail.

The nine instructions that make up the instruction set that we have presented are sufficient to perform the steps of any computer program, although not necessarily in the most

FIGURE 6.3

Little Man Mnemonic Instruction Codes with Their Corresponding OP Codes

LDA	5xx	Load
STO	3xx	Store
ADD	1xx	Add
SUB	2xx	Subtract
IN	901	Input
OUT	902	Output
COB or HLT	000	Coffee break (or Halt)
BRZ	7xx	Branch if zero
BRP	8xx	Branch if positive or zero
BR	6xx	Branch unconditional
DAT		Data storage location

FIGURE 6.4

LMC Program to Find Positive Difference of Two Numbers

00	IN		901	
01	STO	10	310	
02	IN		901	
03	STO	11	311	
04	SUB	10	210	
05	BRP	08	808	test
06	LDA	10	510	negative; reverse order
07	SUB	11	211	
08	OUT		902	print result and
09	COB		000	stop.
10	DAT	00	000	used for data
11	DAT	00	000	"

efficient way. It is important for you to realize that, although simplified, the Little Man instruction set is very similar to the instruction sets that appear in most real computers. In real computers, as in the Little Man Computer, most instruction steps are involved with the movement of data between the equivalent of mailbox locations and calculators, with very simple calculations, and with program branching.

The real computer differs mostly in the variations to these instructions that are provided, and with the addition of a few instructions that provide programming convenience, particularly multiplication and division instructions, and also instructions that shift the data in a word left or right. (Note that the traditional method of performing multiplication can be done in the computer using SHIFT and ADD instructions.)

We will discuss many of these variations when we look at the instruction sets in some real computers, in Chapters 7, 8, 11, and 12.

6.5 THE INSTRUCTION CYCLE

We will refer to the steps that the Little Man takes to perform an instruction as the **instruction cycle.** This cycle, which is similar for all the instructions, can be broken into two parts:

1. The *fetch* portion of the cycle, in which the Little Man finds out what instruction he is to execute, and

2. The *execute* portion of the cycle, in which he actually performs the work specified in the instruction.

The fetch portion of the cycle is identical for every instruction. The Little Man walks to the location counter and reads its value. He then goes to the mailbox with the address that corresponds to that value and reads the three-digit number stored there. That three-digit number is the instruction to be performed. This is depicted in the drawings of Figure 6.5a.

The fetch portion of the cycle has to occur first: until the Little Man has performed the fetch operation, he does not even know what instruction he will be executing!

The execute portion of each instruction is, of course, different for each instruction. But even here, there are many similarities. The first six instructions all require the Little Man to move data from one place in the mailroom to another. The first four instructions all involve the use of a second mailbox location for the data.

The LOAD instruction is typical. First, the Little Man fetches the instruction. To perform the execute phase of the LOAD instruction, the Little Man first looks at the mailbox with the address that is contained in the instruction. He reads the three-digit number on the slip of paper in that mailbox and returns the slip of paper to its place. Then he walks over to the calculator and punches the number into the calculator. Finally, he walks over to the location counter and increments it. He has completed one instruction cycle and is ready to begin the next. These steps are shown in Figure 6.5b.

With the exception of the step in which the Little Man increments the location counter, the steps must be performed in the exact sequence shown. (The location counter can be incremented anytime after the fetch has occurred.) The fetch steps must occur before the execution steps; within the fetch, the Little Man must look at the location counter before he can pull the instruction from its mailbox.

Just as the sequence of instructions in a program is important—and you know that this is true for any language, Pascal, Little Man, or any other—so it is also true that the steps within each instruction must be performed in a particular order.

Notice that the ADD and SUBTRACT instructions are almost identical to the LOAD instruction. The only difference occurs during the execute step, when the Little Man enters the number into

FIGURE 6.5a

The Fetch Portion of the Instruction Cycle

(1) The Little Man reads the address from the location counter

(2) . . . walks over to the mailbox that corresponds to the location counter

(3) . . . and reads the number on the slip of paper. (He then puts the slip of paper back, in case he should need to read it again later.)

the calculator. In the case of the arithmetic instructions, the Little Man adds or subtracts the number that he is carrying into the calculator, rather than simply entering it.

The other instructions are slightly different, although not any more difficult to trace through and understand. To improve your understanding, you should trace the steps of the Little Man through the remaining six instructions.

FIGURE 6.5b

The Execute Portion of the Instruction Cycle (LOAD Instruction)

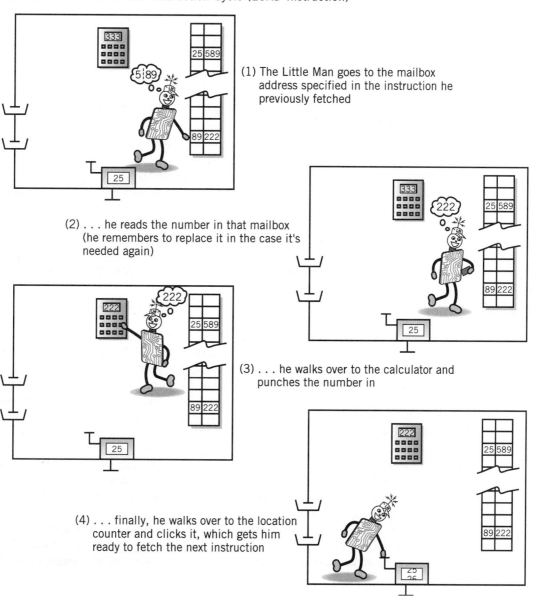

(1) The Little Man goes to the mailbox address specified in the instruction he previously fetched

(2) . . . he reads the number in that mailbox (he remembers to replace it in the case it's needed again)

(3) . . . he walks over to the calculator and punches the number in

(4) . . . finally, he walks over to the location counter and clicks it, which gets him ready to fetch the next instruction

6.6 A NOTE REGARDING COMPUTER ARCHITECTURES

As we noted in Chapter 1, John von Neumann is usually considered to be the developer of the computer as we know it today. Between 1945 and 1951 von Neumann set down a series of guidelines that came to be known as the **von Neumann architecture** for computers. Although other experimental computer architectures have been developed and built, the von Neumann architecture continues to be the standard architecture for computers; no other architecture has had any commercial success to date. It is significant that, in a field where technological change occurs almost overnight, the architecture of computers is virtually unchanged since 1951.

The major guidelines that define a von Neumann architecture include:

- Memory holds both programs and data; this is known as **the stored program concept.** The stored program concept allows programs to be changed easily.
- Memory is addressed **linearly;** that is, there is a single sequential numeric address for each and every memory location.
- Memory is addressed by the location number without regard to the data contained within.

Instructions are executed sequentially unless an instruction or an outside event (such as the user resetting the location counter) causes a branch to occur.

In addition, von Neumann defined the functional organization of the computer to be made up of a control unit that executes instructions, an arithmetic/logic unit that performs arithmetic and logical calculations, and memory. The control unit and arithmetic/logic unit together make up the CPU, or central processing unit.

If you check over the guidelines just given, you will observe that the Little Man Computer is an example of a von Neumann architecture. In fact, we took care to point out features of the von Neumann architecture during our discussion of the Little Man Computer.

SUMMARY AND REVIEW

The workings of the computer can be simulated by a simple model. The Little Man Computer model consists of a Little Man in a mailroom with mailboxes, a calculator, and a counter. Input and output baskets provide communication to the outside world. The Little Man Computer meets all the qualifications of a von Neumann computer architecture.

The Little Man performs work by following simple instructions, which are described by three-digit numbers. The first digit specifies an operation. The last two digits are used for various purposes, but most commonly to point to an address. The instructions provide operations that can move data between the mail slots and the calculator, move data between the calculator and the input and output baskets, perform addition and subtraction, and allow the Little Man to stop working. There are also instructions that cause the Little Man to change the order in which instructions are executed, either unconditionally or based on the value in the calculator.

Both data and instructions are stored in individual mail slots. There is no differentiation between the two except in the context of the particular operation taking place. The Little Man normally executes instructions sequentially from the mail slots except when he encounters a branching instruction. In that case he notes the value in the calculator, if required, and resumes executing instructions from the appropriate location.

The exact steps performed by the Little Man are important because they reflect closely the steps performed in a real CPU in executing an instruction.

KEY CONCEPTS AND TERMS

instruction cycle
linear memory addressing
Little Man Computer (LMC)
mnemonics

op code
stored program concept
von Neumann architecture

EXERCISES

6.1   The steps that the Little Man performs are closely related to the way in which the CPU actually executes instructions. Draw a flow chart that carefully describes the steps that the Little Man follows to execute a branch instruction.

6.2   Repeat Exercise 6.1 for a subtract instruction.

6.3   Repeat Exercise 6.1 for a branch on positive instruction.

6.4   What are the criteria that define a von Neumann architecture? How does the example in this chapter in which we enter and add two numbers illustrate each of the criteria?

6.5   Consider the example in this chapter in which we enter and add two numbers. Suppose we had stored the first input entry in mailbox location 00. Would the program have produced the same result? What would have happened if the program were executed a second time? What characteristic of the computer makes this true?

6.6   Write a Little Man program that accepts three values as input and produces the largest of the three as output.

6.7   Write a Little Man program to accept an indefinite number of input values. The output value will be the largest of the input values. You should use the value 0 as a flag to indicate the end of input.

6.8   Write a Little Man program that accepts three values as input and outputs them in order of size, largest to smallest. (This is a more challenging variation on Exercise 6.6.)

6.9   Write a Little Man program that adds a column of input values and produces the sum as output. The first input value will contain the number of values that follow as input to be added.

6.10   Write a Little Man program that prints out the odd numbers from 1 to 99. No input is required.

6.11   Write a Little Man program that prints out the sums of the odd values from 1 to 39. The output will consist of 1, 1 + 3, 1 + 3 + 5, 1 + 3 + 5 + 7.... No input is required.

As an aside, do you notice anything interesting about the output results that are produced by this series? This series is sometimes used as part of an algorithm for finding square roots of numbers.

6.12 The following Little Man program is supposed to add two input numbers, subtract a third input number from the sum, and output the result, i.e.,

$$OUT = IN1 + IN2 - IN3$$

mailbox	mnemonic code	numeric code
00	IN	901
01	STO 99	399
02	IN	901
03	ADD 99	199
04	STO 99	399
05	IN	901
06	SUB 99	299
07	OUT	902
08	COB	000

What is wrong with this program? Modify the program so that it produces the correct result.

6.13 Suppose we have a need to handle both negative and positive data beyond the simple test in the various conditional branch instructions. One way to do this would be to replace the subtract instruction with a 10's complement instruction. The COMP instruction complements the value in the calculator and leaves the value in the calculator.

a. How would subtraction be performed in this case?

b. Carefully trace the steps that the Little Man would perform to execute the new COMP instruction.

c. What is the new range of values possible with this modification, and how are these values represented in the Little Man Computer?

d. What would the Little Man do to execute a BRANCH ON POSITIVE instruction?

6.14 The programs that we have discussed in this chapter seem to have appeared in the mailboxes by magic. Consider a more realistic alternative:

Suppose a small program is permanently stored in the last few mailbox locations. A BRANCH instruction at location 0, also permanent, will start this program. This program will accept input values and will store them at consecutive mailbox locations, starting with mailbox 001. You may assume that these values represent the instructions and data of a user's program to be executed. When a 999 is received as input data, the program jumps to location 001 where it will proceed to execute the values just entered.

The small program described here is known as a *program loader,* or, under certain circumstances as a *bootstrap.* Write a Little Man program loader. (Hint: It may be useful to remember that instructions and data are indistinguishable. Thus, instructions could be treated as if they were data, if necessary.)

6.15   Show carefully how you would implement an IF-THEN-ELSE statement using Little Man instructions.

6.16   Show how you would implement a REPEAT-UNTIL statement using Little Man instructions.

6.17   The input data values in our problems have always been entered in the order that they were to be used. This is not always possible or convenient. Can you think of a simple way to accept input data in the wrong order and still use it correctly?

6.18   Suppose the Little Man Computer had been implemented as a 16-bit binary machine. Assume that the binary LMC provides the same instruction set, with the same op codes (in binary, of course), and the same instruction format (op code followed by address). How many bits would be required for the op code portion of the instruction? How many mailboxes could the binary machine accommodate? What is the range of 2's complement data that this machine could handle?

6.19   The original version of the Little Man Computer used op code 7 (i.e., instruction 700) for a COFFEE BREAK instruction instead of op code 0. What is the advantage of using 000 for the COB instruction instead of 700? (Hint: Consider what happens if the programmer forgets to put a COB instruction at the end of a program.)

6.20   When we discussed conditional branching we claimed that a BRANCH NEGATIVE instruction is not necessary. Show a sequence of BRANCH instructions that will cause a program to branch to location 50 if the value in the calculator is negative.

6.21   Show a sequence of instructions that will cause a program to branch to location 75 if the value in the calculator is *greater than* zero.

THE CPU AND MEMORY

7.0 INTRODUCTION

The previous chapter provided a detailed introduction to the Little Man model of a computer. In that chapter we introduced a format, using a three-digit number divided into op code and address fields, for the instructions that a computer can perform, and we introduced an instruction set that we indicated was representative of those found in a real computer. We also showed the steps that are performed by the Little Man in order to execute one of these instructions.

In this chapter, and the next we will extend these concepts to the real computer. Our primary emphasis in this chapter is on the central processing unit (CPU), together with memory. In the real computer, memory is actually separated both physically and functionally from the CPU. Memory and the CPU are intimately related in the operation of the computer, however, and so we will treat memory together with the CPU for the convenience of our discussion. Since every instruction requires memory access, it makes sense to discuss the two together.

We will use the Little Man model and its instruction set as a guideline for our discussion. The Little Man instruction set is fundamentally similar to the instruction sets of many different computers. Of course, the Little Man instruction set is based on a decimal number system, and the real CPU is binary, but this is a detail that won't concern us for most of this discussion. The CPU model that we shall discuss is not based on a particular make and model, but is typical of most computers. In Chapter 12, we shall look specifically at several popular computer models.

In this chapter, you will see that the operation of the CPU together with memory is nearly identical functionally to the Little Man Computer. There is a one-to-one relationship between the various contents of the mailroom and the functional components of the CPU plus memory. The major differences occur in the facts that the CPU instruction set is created using binary numbers rather than decimal and that the instructions are performed in a simple electronic way using logic based upon Boolean algebra instead of having a Little Man running around a mailroom.

Sections 7.1 through 7.3 present a systematic introduction to the components of the CPU and memory, offering a direct comparison with the components of the Little Man Computer, and focusing on the concept of the register as a fundamental element of CPU operation. In Section 7.4, we show how simple CPU and memory register operations serve as the basic mechanism to implement the real computer's instruction set.

In Section 7.5, we turn our attention to the third major internal component, the bus component. Buses provide the interconnection between CPU and memory, as well as connections between input and output devices, the CPU, and memory.

In Sections 7.6, 7.7, and 7.8, we return our attention to the CPU to discuss the characteristics and features of the instruction sets provided in real computers.

You already understand from Chapter 6 how simple instructions can be combined to form the programs that you write. When you complete this chapter, you will have a good understanding of how those instructions are executed in a computer.

7.1 THE COMPONENTS OF THE CPU

A simplified block diagram of a CPU with memory is shown in Figure 7.1. For comparison purposes, the block diagram for the Little Man Computer is repeated in Figure 7.2, with labels corresponding to the components in Figure 7.1.

Note the similarities between the two figures. As noted in Chapter 1, the computer unit is made up conceptually of three major components, the **arithmetic/logic unit (ALU)**, the **control unit (CU)**, and **memory.** The ALU and CU together are known as the **central processing unit,** or **CPU.** An input/output (I/O) interface is also included in the diagram. The I/O interface corresponds in function roughly to the input and output baskets, although its implementation and operation differ from that of the Little Man Computer in many respects.

The arithmetic/logic unit is the component of the CPU where data is held temporarily and where calculations take place. It corresponds directly to the calculator in the Little Man Computer.

The control unit controls and interprets the execution of instructions. It does so by following a sequence of actions that correspond to the fetch-execute instruction cycle that was described in the previous chapter. Most of these actions are retrievals of instructions from memory followed by movements of data or addresses from one part of the CPU to another.

FIGURE 7.1

System Block Diagram

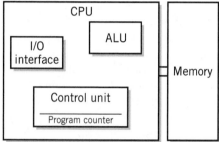

FIGURE 7.2

The Little Man Computer

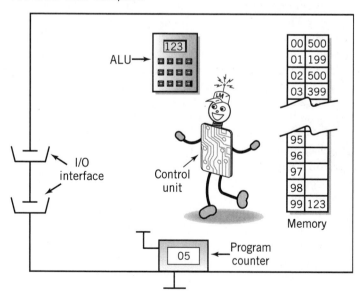

The control unit determines the particular instruction to be executed by reading the contents of a **program counter (PC)**, sometimes called an **instruction pointer,** which is a part of the control unit. Like the Little Man's location counter, the program counter contains the address of the current instruction or the next instruction to be executed. Normally, instructions are executed sequentially. The sequence of instructions is modified by executing instructions that change the contents of the program counter. The Little Man branch instructions are examples of such instructions. A **Memory Management Unit** within the control unit supervises the fetching of instructions and data from memory. The I/O interface is also part of the control unit. In some CPUs, these two functions are combined into a single **Bus Interface Unit.**

The program counter in the CPU obviously corresponds to the location counter in the Little Man Computer, and the control unit itself corresponds to the Little Man.

Memory, of course, corresponds directly to the mailboxes in the LMC.

7.2 THE CONCEPT OF REGISTERS

Before we discuss the way in which the CPU executes instructions, it is necessary to understand the concept of a register. A **register** is a single, permanent storage location within the CPU used for a particular, defined purpose. A register is used to hold a binary value temporarily for storage, for manipulation, and/or for simple calculations. Note that each register is wired within the CPU to perform its specific role. That is, unlike memory, where every address is just like every other address, each register serves a particular purpose. The register's size, the way it is wired, and even the operations that take place in the register reflect the specific function that the register performs in the computer.

Registers also differ from memory in that they are not addressed as a memory location would be, but instead are manipulated directly by the control unit during the execution of instructions. Registers may be as small as a single bit or as wide as several bytes, ranging usually from one to 128 bits.

Registers are used in many different ways in a computer. Depending on the particular use of a register, a register may hold data being processed, an instruction being executed, a memory or I/O address to be accessed, or even special binary codes used for some other purpose, such as codes that keep track of the status of the computer or the conditions of calculations that may be used for conditional branch instructions. Some registers serve many different purposes, while others are designed to perform a single, specialized task. There are even registers specifically designed to hold a number in floating point format or a set of related values representing a list or vector.

Registers are basic working components of the CPU. You have already seen, in Chapter 6, that the computer is unable to distinguish between a value that is used as a number in a program and a value that is actually an instruction, except in the context of current use. When we refer to the "data" in a register, we might be talking about any of these possibilities.

You have already become acquainted with two "registers" in the Little Man Computer, namely, the calculator and the location counter.

In the CPU, the equivalent to the calculator is known as an **accumulator.** There are usually several accumulators in a real CPU, and these are often known as **general-purpose registers.** Some vendors also refer to general-purpose registers as **user-visible registers** to indicate that they may be accessed by the instructions in user programs. In most computers, general-purpose registers or accumulators are considered to be a part of the arithmetic/logic unit, although some computer manufacturers prefer to consider them as a separate register unit. As in the Little Man Computer, accumulator or general-purpose registers hold the data that are used for arithmetic operations, as well as the results. In most computers, these registers are also used to transfer data between different memory locations, and between I/O and memory, again similar to the LMC. As you will see in Chapter 8, they can also be used for some other similar purposes.

The control unit contains several important registers.

- As already noted, the **program counter register** holds the address of the current instruction being executed.
- The **instruction register (IR)** holds the actual instruction being executed currently by the computer. In the Little Man Computer this register was not used; the Little Man himself remembered the instruction he was executing. In a sense, his brain served the function of the instruction register.
- The **memory address register (MAR)** holds the address of a memory location.
- The **memory data register (MDR),** sometimes known as the *memory buffer register,* will hold a data value that is being stored to or retrieved from the memory location currently addressed by the memory address register.

The last two registers will be discussed in more detail in the next section, when we explain the workings of memory. Although the memory address register and memory data register are part of the CPU, operationally these two registers are more closely associated with memory itself.

The control unit will also contain several 1-bit registers, sometimes known as **flags,** that are used to allow the computer to keep track of special conditions such as arithmetic carry and overflow, power failure, and internal computer error. Usually, several flags are grouped into one or more **status registers.**

In addition, our typical CPU will contain an I/O interface that will handle input and output data as it passes between the CPU and various input and output devices, much like the LMC *in* and *out* baskets. For simplification, we will view the I/O interface as a pair of I/O registers, one to hold an I/O address that addresses a particular I/O device, the other to hold the I/O data. These registers operate similarly to the memory address and data registers. Later, in Chapter 9, we will discuss a more common way of handling I/O that uses memory as an intermediate storage location for I/O data.

Most instructions are executed by the sequenced movement of data between the different registers in the ALU and the CU. Each instruction has its own sequence.

Most registers support four primary types of operations:

1. Registers can be loaded with values from other locations, in particular from other registers or from memory locations. This operation destroys the previous value stored in the destination register, but the source register or memory location remains unchanged.
2. Data from another location can be added to or subtracted from the value previously stored in a register, leaving the sum or difference in the register.
3. Data in a register can be shifted or rotated right or left by one or more bits. As discussed in Chapter 2, this operation is important in the implementation of multiplication and division. The details of the shift operation are discussed in Chapter 8.

4. The value of data in a register can be tested for certain conditions, such as zero, positive, negative, or too large to fit in the register.

In addition, special provision is frequently made to load the value zero into a register, which is known as clearing a register, and also to invert the 0s and 1s (i.e., take the 1's complement of the value) in a register, an operation that is important when working with complementary arithmetic. It is also common to provide for the addition of the value 1 to the value in a register. This capability, which is known as incrementing the register, has many benefits, including the ability to step the program counter, to count in for loops, and to index through arrays in programs. Sometimes decrementing, or subtraction of 1, is also provided. The bit inversion and incrementing operations are combined to form the 2's complement of the value in a register. Most computers provide a specific instruction for this purpose, and also provide instructions for clearing, inverting, incrementing, and decrementing the general-purpose registers.

The control unit sets ("1") or resets ("0") status flags as a result of conditions that arise during the execution of instructions.

As an example, Figure 7.3 identifies the programmer-accessible registers in the IBM zSeries computers, which includes a variety of IBM mainframe models. Internal registers, such as the instruction, memory address, and memory buffer registers are not specifically identified in the table, since they are dependent on the implementation of the particular model in the series.

7.3 THE MEMORY UNIT

The Operation of Memory

Before we look at the fetch-execute cycle for the real CPU, you need to understand how instructions and data can be retrieved from memory. Real memory, like the mailboxes in the Little Man computer, consists of cells, each of which can hold a single value, and each of which has a single address.

FIGURE 7.3

Programmer-Accessible Registers in IBM zSeries Computers

Register type	Number	Size of each in bits	Notes
General	16	64	For arithmetic, logical, and addressing operations; adjoining registers may be joined to form up to eight 128-bit registers
Floating point	16	64	Floating point arithmetic; registers may be joined to form 128-bit registers
PSW	1	128	Combination program counter and status-flag register, called the **Program Status Word (PSW)**
Control (+1 32-bit floating point control)	16	64	Various internal functions and parameters connected with the operating system; accessible only to systems programmers

Two registers, the memory address register and the memory data register, act as an interface between the CPU and memory. The memory data register is called the memory buffer register by some computer manufacturers.

Figure 7.4 is a simplified representation of the relationship between the MAR, the MDR, and memory. Each cell in the memory unit holds one bit of data. The cells in Figure 7.4 are organized in rows. Each row consists of a group of one or more bytes. Each group represents the data cells for one or more consecutive memory addresses, shown in the figure as addresses $000, 001, \ldots, 2^n - 1$.

(In modern computers, it is common to address eight bytes at a time to speed up memory access between the CPU and memory. The CPU can still isolate individual bytes from the group of eight for its use, however.)

The memory address register holds the address in the memory that is to be "opened" for data. The MAR is connected to a decoder that interprets the address and activates a single address line into the memory. There is a separate address line for each group of cells in the memory; thus, if there are n bits of addressing, there will be 2^n address lines. (In actuality, the decoding process is somewhat more complex, involving several levels of address decoding, since there may be several million addresses involved, but the concept described here is correct.)

The memory data register is designed such that it is effectively connected to every cell in the memory unit. Each bit of the MDR is connected in a column to the corresponding bit of every location in memory. However, the addressing method assures that only a single row of cells is activated at any given time. Thus, only one memory location is addressed at any one time. A specific example of this is shown in Figure 7.5. (Note that in the figure *msb* stands for most significant bit and *lsb* for least significant bit.)

FIGURE 7.4

The Relationship Between the MDR, the MAR, and Memory

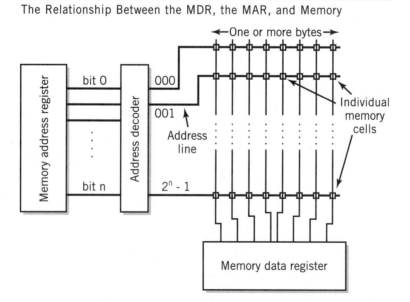

FIGURE 7.5

MAR-MDR Example

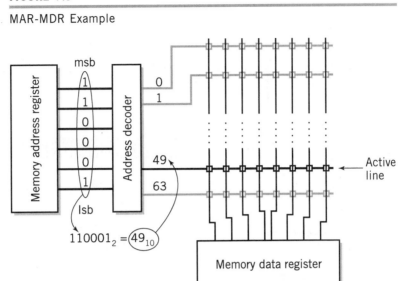

As a simple analogy to the operation we've just described, consider the memory as being stored in a glass box, as shown in Figure 7.6. The memory data register has a window into the box. The viewer, who represents each cell in the memory data register, can see the cells in corresponding bit position for every location in memory through the window. The cells in this analogy are light bulbs that can be turned on (1) or off (0). The output from the memory address register is passed to an address decoder. The output from the address decoder in our analogy consists of a series of wires, each of which can light up the bulbs in a single row of cells. Only one wire at a time can be activated—specifically, the one corresponding to the decoded address. The active line will light the bulbs that correspond to "1s," leaving the "0s" dark. The viewer therefore will see only the single row of cells that is currently addressed by the memory address register. We can extend the analogy to include a "master switch" that controls all the lights, so that the data can be read only at the appropriate instant.

A more detailed picture of an individual memory cell is shown in Figure 7.7. Although this diagram is a bit complicated, it may help to clarify how data is transferred between the MDR and memory. There are three lines that control the memory cell: an address line, a read/write line, and an activation line. The address line to a particular cell is turned on only if the computer is addressing the data within that cell. The read/write line determines whether the data will be transferred from the cell to the MDR (read) or from the MDR to the cell (write). This line works by turning on one of two switches in conjunction with the address line and the activation line. The read switch, R, in the diagram turns on when the address line and the activation line are both on (on is usually represented by 1, off by 0), and the read/write line is set to read; the switch then connects the output of the cell to the MDR line. The write switch, W, works similarly; switch W turns on when the address line and activation line are both on and the read/write switch is set to write. Switch W connects

FIGURE 7.6

A Visual Analogy for Memory

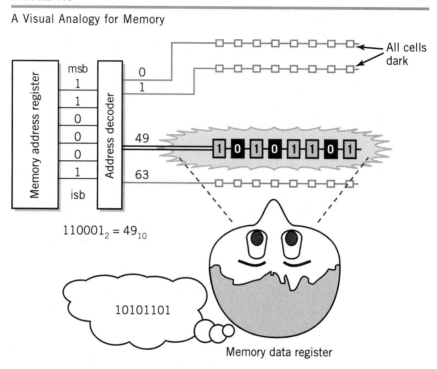

the MDR line to the input of the cell, which transfers the data bit on the MDR line to the cell for storage. Note that only one switch, at most, can be on at a given time.

The interaction between the CPU and the memory registers takes place as follows: to retrieve or store data at a particular memory location, the CPU copies an address from some register in the CPU to the memory address register. *Note that addresses are always moved to the MAR; there would never be a reason for an address transfer from the MAR to another register within the CPU,* since the CPU controls memory transfers and is obviously aware of the memory address being used. At the same time that the MAR is loaded, the CPU sends a message to the memory unit indicating whether the memory transfer is a retrieval from memory or a store to memory. This message is sent by setting the read/write line appropriately.

At the appropriate instant, the CPU momentarily turns on the switch that connects the MDR with the register by using the activation line, and the transfer takes place between memory and the MDR. The MDR is a two-way register. When the instruction being executed is to store data, the data will be transferred from another register in the CPU to the MDR, and from there it will be transferred into memory. The original data at that location will be destroyed, replaced by the new data from the MDR. Conversely, when the instruction is to load data from memory, the data is transferred from memory to the MDR, and it will subsequently be transferred to the appropriate register in the CPU. In this case, the memory data are left intact, but the previous data value in the MDR is replaced by the new data from memory.

FIGURE 7.7

An Individual Memory Cell

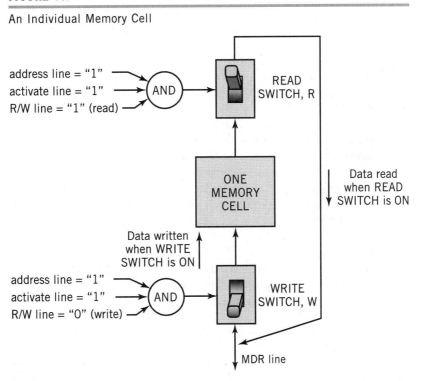

Memory Capacity

The number of possible memory locations in the Little Man Computer, one hundred locations, was established by the two-digit address space in each instruction. The location counter also addresses one hundred locations. There is no memory address register per se, but the Little Man is certainly aware that each memory location requires two digits. In theory, a larger location counter, say, three digits, would allow the Little Man to fetch more *instructions*, but notice that his *data* fetches and stores are still limited to the one hundred locations that the two digits of the address field in the instruction word can address.

Similarly, there are two factors that determine the capacity of memory in a real computer. The number of bits in the memory address register determines how many different address locations can be decoded, just as the two-digit addresses in the Little Man Computer resulted in a maximum of one hundred mailboxes. For a memory address register of width k bits, the number of possible memory addresses is

$$M = 2^k$$

The other factor in establishing memory capacity is of course the number of bits in the address field of the instruction set, which establishes how many memory locations can be directly addressed from the instruction.

In the Little Man Computer, we have assumed that these two size factors are the same, but in a real computer, that is not necessarily the case. The number of physical memory locations is, in fact, determined by the size of the memory address register. There are other ways of extending the addresses specified within instructions so that we can reach more addresses than the instruction address field would allow. Just to give you one simple possibility, consider a Little Man Computer variation that had a special one-digit address register that we could load. Every time the Little Man had to find a memory location, he would use that one-digit value as the hundreds place of the address. This would allow him to address one thousand locations, one hundred at a time. Such an extension would suggest that the MAR, and thus the actual memory capacity, is normally at least as large as the instruction address field, but it may be much larger. We will discuss various simple addressing methods in Chapter 8 and Supplementary Chapter 2, as well as an additional, more sophisticated addressing method in Chapters 8 and 15.

Ultimately, the MAR determines the addressable memory capacity of the computer.

The CPU in the first PC supported a memory capacity of 1 megabyte (MB), but today a typical memory address register will be at least 32 bits wide, and probably much wider. Many modern CPUs support 64-bit memory addresses. A 32-bit memory address allows a memory capacity of 4 gigabytes (GB) (4×10^9 byte-size spaces), whereas 64 bits allows a memory capacity of 16×10^{18} bytes (16 exabytes). In modern computers, the ultimate size of memory is more likely limited by physical space for the memory chips or by the time required to decode and access large memory addresses, rather than by the capability of the CPU to address such a large memory.

As an aside, it is worth noting that early models of IBM's largest mainframe computer systems had a total memory capacity of 512 KB, and that the original IBM PC came supplied with 64 KB of memory, with a maximum capacity of 640 KB! In fact, Bill Gates of Microsoft was quoted at the time as saying that he could see no need for more than 640 KB of memory, ever!

The size of the word to be retrieved or stored in a single operation is determined by the size of the memory data register and by the width of the bus connecting memory to the CPU. In most modern computers, data and instructions found in memory are addressed in multiples of 8-bit bytes. This establishes the minimum instruction size as 8 bits. Most instructions cannot fit practically into 8 bits. If one were to allow 3 bits for the op code (8 instruction types), only 5 bits remain for addressing. Five bits allows $2^5 = 32$ different addresses, which is clearly insufficient address space. As a result, longer instructions of 16, 24, 32, or even more bits will be stored in successive memory locations. In the interest of speed, it is generally desirable to retrieve an entire instruction with a single fetch, if possible. Additionally, data to be used in arithmetic calculations frequently requires the precision of several bytes. Therefore, most modern computer memories are designed to allow the retrieval or storage of at least four and, more commonly, eight successive bytes in a single operation. Thus, the memory data register is usually designed to retrieve the data or instruction(s) from a sequence of several successive addresses all at once, and the MDR will be several bytes wide.

Memory Implementations

Through the history of computing there have been several different types of memory used; the most popular and useful of these have been magnetic core memory, static RAM, dynamic RAM, and ROM. Memory can be **volatile** or **nonvolatile.** Nonvolatile memory retains its values when power is removed. Volatile memory loses its contents when power is removed.

Magnetic core memory uses a small core of magnetic material to hold a bit of data; electrical wires woven through the core determine the magnetic polarity of the core to read the data and change the polarity by passing electrical current through the wires. Since magnetism remains after the current is removed, core memory is *nonvolatile;* that is, the data remains even if the power is removed. Magnetic core memory is expensive and slow in operation compared to other types of memory. It has been replaced almost entirely by **RAM.** Magnetic core is nonvolatile. As a result, it is still used on a few computers where both read and write capability are required and where the loss of data or programs would be severely damaging, particularly for military and space applications.

Most current computers use either static or dynamic RAM for memory. The difference between static and dynamic RAM is in the technical design and is not of importance here. However, **dynamic RAM** is less expensive, requires less electrical power, and can be made smaller, with more bits of storage in a single integrated circuit. Dynamic RAM also requires extra electronic circuitry that "refreshes" memory periodically; otherwise the data fades away after a while, and is lost. Static RAM does not require refreshing. **Static RAM** is also faster to access than dynamic RAM and is therefore useful in very-high-speed computers and for small amounts of high-speed memory, but static RAM is more expensive and requires more chips. Both dynamic and static RAM are volatile: their contents are lost when power is turned off.

At the time of this writing, dynamic RAM is most popular. The amount of data that can be stored in a single dynamic RAM chip has increased rapidly in the past few years, going from 64K bits to 64M bits in fewer than ten years. Currently, most systems are built with chips that can hold 64M bits of data. These chips are also designed to be packaged together in convenient plug-in packages that can supply 128 megabytes of memory, or more, in a single unit. In addition, 256M bit and 1G bit RAM chips are nearing production. Most modern systems also provide a small amount of static RAM memory that is used for high-speed access. This memory is known as *cache memory.* The use of cache memory is discussed in Chapter 8.

ROM, or read-only memory, is used for situations where the software is built permanently into the computer, is required as part of the computer's software, and is not expected to change over the life of the computer, except perhaps very infrequently. Early ROM memory was made up of integrated circuits with fuses in them that could be blown. These fuses were similar to, but much smaller than, the fuses that you might have in your home. A blown fuse might represent a "0," an intact fuse a "1." Modern ROM memories use a different technology; most of these newer ROMs can be erased and rewritten, although special circuitry is required to do so. Within the computer, ROM is both nonvolatile and unwriteable. Thus, the data does not change with power on or off.

It is important to realize that the method used to access memory is basically the same, regardless of memory type. The only difference occurs with ROM: since the computer cannot write to ROM, the MDR will retrieve data from ROM for the CPU, but cannot transfer data to ROM from the CPU. In other respects, ROM operates similarly to other forms of memory.

EEPROM and **Flash ROM** are recent memory innovations that implement nonvolatile, writeable memory using a concept called Fowler-Nordheim tunneling. Both allow rewriting by erasing memory cells selectively, then writing new data into those cells. Flash

ROM is faster and more flexible than EEPROM because it can erase and write data in blocks, rather than one byte at a time. Flash ROM is used in the computer BIOS and in devices, such as digital cameras, that require faster access than a disk can offer. Disks, however, still offer much more storage space at a significantly lower cost.

7.4 THE FETCH-EXECUTE INSTRUCTION CYCLE

The fetch-execution instruction cycle is *the* basis for every capability of a computer. This seems like a strong statement, but think about it: the purpose of the computer is to execute instructions similar to those that we have already introduced. And, as you have already seen from the Little Man Computer, the operation of every instruction is defined by its fetch-execute instruction cycle. Ultimately, the operation of a computer as a whole is defined by the primary operations that can be performed with registers, as explained in Section 7.2: to move data between registers, to add or subtract data to a register, to shift data within a register, and to test the value in a register for certain conditions, such as negative, positive, or zero.

With the importance of the instruction cycle in mind, we can consider how these few operations can be combined to implement each of the instructions in a computer. The registers that will be of the most importance to us for this discussion will be the general purpose registers or accumulators that are used to hold data values between instructions (A or GP), the program counter (PC), which holds the address of the current instruction, the instruction register (IR), which holds the current instruction while it is being executed, and the memory address and data registers (MAR and MDR), used for accessing memory.

To begin, review carefully the steps that the Little Man took to execute an instruction. (You may want to read Section 6.6 again to refresh your memory.) You will recall that there were two phases in the process. First, the Little Man fetched the instruction from memory and read it. This phase was identical for every instruction. Then, he interpreted the instruction and performed the actions required for that particular instruction.

He repeated this cycle endlessly, until he was given the instruction to stop.

The **fetch-execute instruction cycle** in a CPU works similarly. As noted, much of the procedure consists of copying data from one register to another. You should always be aware that data copying does not affect the "from" register, but it obviously replaces the previous data in the "to" register with the new data being copied.

Remember that every instruction must be fetched from memory before it can be executed. Therefore, the first step in the instruction cycle always requires that the instruction must be fetched from memory. (Otherwise, how would the computer know what instruction to perform?) Since the address of the current instruction to be executed is identified by the value in the program counter register, the first step will be to transfer that value into the memory address register, so that the computer can retrieve the instruction located at that address.

We will use the following notation to indicate the transfer of a data value from one register to another:

$$REG_a \;\rightarrow\; REG_b$$

Then, in this notation, the first step in the execution of every instruction will be

(step 1) $PC \;\rightarrow\; MAR$

As explained in the description of memory, this will result in the instruction being transferred from the specified memory location to the memory data register. The next step is to transfer that instruction to the instruction register:

(step 2) MDR → IR

The instruction register will hold the instruction through the rest of the instruction cycle. It is the particular instruction in the IR that will control the particular steps that make up the remainder of the cycle. These two steps comprise the fetch phase of the instruction cycle for every instruction.

The remaining steps are, of course, instruction dependent. Let us consider the steps required to complete a LOAD instruction.

The next thing that the Little Man did was to read the address part of the LOAD instruction. He then walked over to the mailbox specified by that address, read the data, and copied it into the calculator. The real CPU will operate similarly, substituting register transfers for the Little Man, of course. Thus,

(step 3) IR [address] → MAR

The notation IR [address] is used to indicate that only the address part of the contents of the instruction register is to be transferred. This step prepares the memory module to read the actual data that will be copied into the "calculator," which in this case will be the accumulator:

(step 4) MDR → A

The CPU increments the program counter, and the cycle is complete and ready to begin the next instruction (actually this step can be performed any time after the previous instruction is retrieved, and is usually performed early in the cycle in parallel with other steps).

(step 5) PC + 1 → PC

Notice the elegant simplicity of this process! The LOAD instruction requires only five steps. Four of the steps simply involve the movement of data from one register to another. The fifth step is nearly as simple. It requires the addition of the value 1 to the contents of a register, and the new value is returned to the same register. This type of addition is common in computers. In most cases, the result of an addition or subtraction is returned to one of the original registers.

The remaining instructions operate similarly. Compare, for example, the steps required to perform the STORE and the ADD instructions with those of the LOAD instruction, discussed earlier.

The STORE instruction

```
PC → MAR
MDR → IR
IR [address] → MAR
A → MDR
PC + 1 → PC
```

The ADD instruction

```
PC → MAR
MDR → IR
IR [address] → MAR
A + MDR → A
PC + 1 → PC
```

Study these examples carefully. For practice, relate them to the steps the Little Man performs to execute the corresponding instruction. Notice that the only step that changes in these three instructions is the fourth step.

The fetch-execute cycles for the remaining instructions are left as an exercise (see Exercise 7.5 at the end of this chapter).

The following example, with comments, recaps the above discussion in the context of a three-instruction program segment that loads a number from memory, adds a second number to it, and stores the result back to the first memory location. Note that each instruction is made up of its corresponding fetch-execute cycle. The program segment is executed by processing each step of each fetch-execute cycle in sequence.

Assume that the following values are present just prior to execution of this segment:

```
Program Counter: 65
Value in Mem Location 65: 590 (LOAD 90)
Value in Mem Location 66: 192 (ADD 92)
Value in Mem Location 67: 390 (STORE 90)
Value in Mem Location 90: 111
Value in Mem Location 92: 222
```

EXAMPLE

1st instruction LOAD 90:	PC → MAR	MAR now has 65
	MDR → IR	IR contains the instruction: 590
	- - - - - - - - - - - ← end of fetch	
	IR [address] → MAR	MAR now has 90, the location of the data
	MDR → A	Move the value 111 from MDR to A
	PC + 1 → PC	PC now points to 66
		end of execution, end of 1st instruction
2nd instruction ADD 92:	PC → MAR	MAR now contains 66
	MDR → IR	IR contains the instructions: 192
	- - - - - - - - - - - ← end of fetch	
	IR [address] → MAR	MAR now has 92
	A + MDR → A	111+222=333 in A
	PC + 1 → PC	PC now points to 67
		end of execution, end of 2nd instruction
3rd instruction STORE 90:	PC → MAR	MAR now contains 67
	MDR → IR	IR contains 390
	- - - - - - - - - - - ← end of fetch	
	IR [address] → MAR	MAR now holds 90
	A → MDR	The value in A, 111, moves to mem location 90
	PC + 1 → PC	PC now points to 68
		end of execution, end of 3rd instruction
←	ready for next instruction	

7.5 BUSES

You have already seen that instructions are executed within the CPU by moving "data" in many different forms from register to register and between registers and memory. The different forms that the "data" can take include instructions and addresses, in addition to actual numerical data. Thus, data moves between the various I/O modules, memory, and the CPU in similar fashion. The physical connection that makes it possible to transfer data from one location in the computer system to another is called a **bus.**

Specifically, a bus may be defined as a group of electrical conductors suitable for carrying computer signals from one location to another. The electrical conductors may be wires, or they may be conductors on a printed circuit. Each conductor in the bus is commonly known as a **line.** Lines on a bus are often assigned names, to make individual lines easier to identify. Each line carries a single electrical signal. The signal might represent one bit of a memory address, or a sequence of data bits, or a timing control that turns a device on and off at the proper time. Sometimes, a conductor in a bus might also be used to carry power to a module.

Buses are used most commonly for transferring data between computer peripherals and the CPU, for transferring data between the CPU and memory, and for transferring data between different points within the CPU. A bus might be a tiny fraction of an inch long, carrying data between various parts of the CPU within an integrated circuit chip; it might be a few inches long, carrying data between the CPU chip and memory; it might even be hundreds of feet long, carrying data between different computers connected together in a network.

The lines on a bus can be grouped into as many as four general categories: data, addressing, control, and power. Data lines carry the "data" that is being moved from one location to another. Address lines specify the recipient of data on the bus. Control lines provide control for the proper synchronization and operation of the bus and of the modules that are connected to the bus. A bus connecting only two specific 16-bit registers within a CPU, for example, may require just sixteen data lines plus one control line to turn the bus on at the correct time. A backplane that interconnects a 64-bit data width CPU, a large memory, and many different types of peripherals might require many more than a hundred lines to perform its function.

The bus that connects the CPU and memory, for example, needs address lines to pass the address stored in the MAR to the address decoder in memory and data lines to transfer data between the CPU and memory. The control lines provide timing signals for the data transfer, define the transfer as a read or write, specify the number of bytes to transfer, and perform many other functions.

Each line in a bus may serve a single, dedicated purpose, such as a bus line that carries the twelfth bit of an address, for example, or a line may serve different purposes at different times. A single line might be used to carry each of the bits of an address in sequence, followed by the bits of data, for example.

Buses may connect modules together in various ways. These are illustrated in Figure 7.8. A bus may carry signals from a specific source to a specific destination. In this case, the bus is identified as a **point-to-point bus.** The cable that connects the parallel or serial port in a personal computer from the computer to a printer is an example of a point-to-point bus. Point-to-point buses intended for connection to a plug-in device are often called **ports.**

FIGURE 7.8

Point-to-point and Multipoint Buses

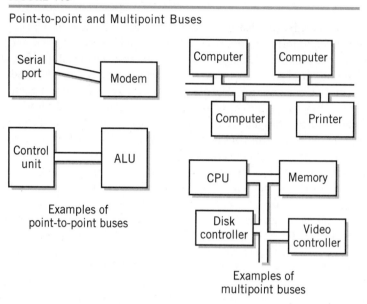

Examples of
point-to-point buses

Examples of
multipoint buses

Alternatively, a bus may be used to connect several points together. Such a bus is known as a **multipoint bus,** or sometimes as a *multidrop bus.* It is also referred to as a broadcast bus, because the signals produced by a source on the bus are "broadcast" to every other point on the bus in the same way as a radio station broadcasts to anyone who tunes in. You may be aware of a popular way of interconnecting computers together known as Ethernet. The bus in an Ethernet network is an example of a broadcast bus: the signal being sent by a particular computer is received by every other computer connected to the network. The operation of Ethernet is discussed in Chapter 11. In most cases, a multipoint bus requires addressing signals on the bus to identify the desired destination that is being addressed by the source at a particular time. Addressing is not required with a point-to-point bus, since the destination is already known, but an address may be required if the message is being passed *through* the destination point to another location. Addressing is also not required for a multipoint bus where the signal is actually intended to reach all the other locations at once; this is sometimes the case for buses that are internal to the CPU.

A bus is used to interconnect the CPU with memory. In some systems, the same bus may also connect the CPU to modules that control the different I/O peripherals. In other systems, there may be several different buses connecting the CPU and the various I/O modules. When the bus is used to carry computer signals that connect the CPU with memory and/or with a set of plug-in I/O module cards in the same physical package, it is commonly known as a **backplane.** It is also known as a **system bus** or as an **external bus.** The backplane is an example of a broadcast bus. One common method of connecting a CPU to memory and I/O modules is to mount the CPU and its related components on a printed circuit board known as a *motherboard.* The backplane in this case is part of the printed circuit wiring on the motherboard.

Figure 7.9 shows typical bus and port connections in a modern personal computer. Note the different buses that are used for connecting the different parts of the system

FIGURE 7.9

Typical PC Interconnections

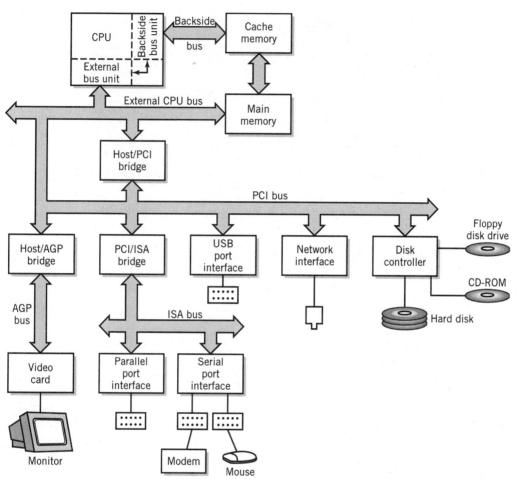

together. The interfaces between different buses are called **bus interface bridges.** Bus interface bridges make it possible for different buses to communicate with each other. There are
additional buses providing interconnections within the CPU itself. The buses connecting
various parts of the CPU are actually within the CPU chip. One of these is shown in the diagram as an example. The buses internal to the CPU generally don't have names. The external CPU bus, peripheral control interface (PCI) bus, AGP (accelerated graphics processor)
bus, and ISA (industry standard architecture) bus are all part of the backplane. Note the way
the backplane is used to connect together the various parts of the computer system.

The PCI bus is an example of a popular modern external bus. It is used in many different types of computers, including Sun workstations, Apple Macintosh computers,
Wintel PCs, and Hewlett-Packard AlphaServers. This means that the same peripheral I/O
cards may be plugged into many different computers, reducing system cost and maintaining consistent system behavior. The ISA bus was the standard system bus for Wintel PCs

FIGURE 7.10

A PC Motherboard

for many years, but is rapidly becoming extinct in favor of the faster and more flexible PCI bus for general I/O interface use.

Figure 7.10 is a photograph of a personal computer motherboard. The system bus on this motherboard, and on many motherboards, is made up of three separate parts. The external CPU bus, not visible in the photograph, connects the CPU and memory. The other two parts, the PCI bus and an ISA bus, are used to connect various I/O peripheral components to the CPU. Plug-in connectors for these two buses can be seen in the photograph. The actual PCI and ISA buses are printed on the bottom of the board and consist of parallel wires connecting all the plug-in connectors together.

Buses are frequently notated on diagrams using widened lines to indicate buses. Sometimes a number is also present on the diagram. The number indicates the number of separate lines in the bus. Two alternative ways of notating buses in diagrams are shown in Figure 7.11.

FIGURE 7.11

Alternative Bus Notations

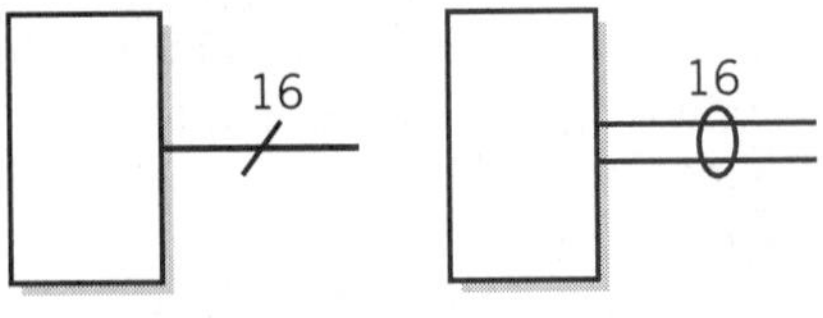

The characteristics of the various buses in the PC, as well as those in other computers, are dependent on their particular use within the computer environment. Buses can be characterized by their *throughput*, that is, the data transfer rate measured in bits per second; by the data width (in bits) of the data being carried; by the distance between the two end points; by the type of control required; by the type of bus; by the addressing capacity; by whether the lines on the bus are uniquely defined for a single type of signal or shared; and by the various features and capabilities that the bus provides. The bus must also be specified electrically and mechanically, by the number of pins on the connector, by the voltages used, even by the size of the cards that plug into the connector. A bus would not be very useful if the cards that it was to interconnect did not fit into the space allotted! Unfortunately for the concept of standardization, there are dozens of different buses in use, although a few are far more common than others.

The need to characterize buses comes from the necessity of interfacing the bus to other devices that are part of the computer system. Buses that are internal to the CPU are usually not characterized at all, since they serve special purposes and do not interface to the outside world. Buses that are used in this way are sometimes known as *dedicated* buses.

To use a bus, the circuits that are connected to the bus must agree on a **bus protocol.** In general, a protocol is an agreement between two or more entities that establishes a clear, common path of communication and understanding between them. A bus protocol is simply a specification that spells out the meaning of each line and each signal on each line for this purpose. Thus, a particular control line on a bus might be defined as a line that determines if the bus is to be used for memory read or memory write. Both the CPU and memory would have to agree, for example, that a "0" on that particular line means "memory read" and a "1" on the line means memory write. The line might have a name like MREAD/MWRITE, where the bar over MWRITE means that a "0" is the active state. The bar itself stands for "NOT."[1]

As an example of a bus that is of interest to us, a functional diagram of the PCI bus that is provided in most PCs is shown in Figure 7.12. The PCI bus is a "32- or 64-bit" (meaning 32 or 64 bits of data at a time) backplane bus that interconnects the CPU and various plug-in I/O modules that control serial and parallel ports, sound cards, disk drives, and the like. The PCI bus provides 32 or, optionally, 64 lines that are used for both addresses and data, labeled AD00 through AD31 or AD63, plus various control and power lines. The power lines provide required power for the plug-in peripheral interface cards. The control lines control timing, handle interrupts, arbitrate between different devices seeking to use the bus, and perform other similar functions. All lines, other than the power lines, carry digital signals.

The CPU signals that pass addresses to memory and send and receive data are brought out from the CPU on individual pins of the integrated circuit. This might sound as if there would have to be a lot of pins on the CPU integrated circuit, and that is indeed true. For example, the Intel Pentium 4 CPU package has either 423 or 478 pins, and the Power PC MPC7451 chip has 483.

A simplified logical diagram of the interface for a Pentium 4 processor is shown in Figure 7.13. It is not important that you understand the details of this diagram. Just notice that the interface provides a total of 33 pins[2] for addressing, 64 for data, and numerous pins for address control, data control, bus control, processor control, and error handling. (Only some of the functions are shown in the figure.) The arrows indicate the direction of signal flow. There are other pins provided for testing the processor, for power, and for other specialized functions that we will not consider here.

---

[1] A pound sign (#) is sometimes used to stand for "NOT" instead.

[2] A0–A2 are not needed because memory data is accessed in groups of 8 bytes at a time, therefore the three least significant bits are ignored.

FIGURE 7.12

PCI Bus Connections

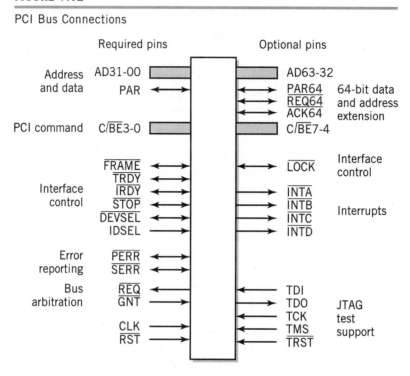

Source: Copyright © PCI Pin List/PCI Special Interest Group, 1999.

As already noted, buses are also used to interconnect the CPU with the I/O modules that are used to connect the peripherals that are part of the computer system. We shall continue the discussion of buses in Section 9.6 of Chapter 9.

7.6 INSTRUCTION WORD FORMATS

Instructions in the Little Man Computer were made up entirely of three-digit decimal numbers, with a single-digit op code, and a two-digit **address field.** The address field was used in various ways: for most instructions, the address field contained the two-digit address where data for the instruction could be found (e.g., LOAD) or was to be placed (LOAD). In a few instructions, the address field was unused (e.g., HALT). For the branch instructions, the address field space was used instead to hold the location of the next instruction to be executed. For the I/O instructions, the address field became a sort of extension of the op code. Finally, the jump instruction in the Little Man Computer uses the address field as the address to which the jump will occur.

The instruction set in a typical real CPU is similar. Again, the instruction word can be divided into an op code and zero or more address fields. A simple 32-bit instruction format with one address field might look like that shown in Figure 7.14. In this example, the 32 bits are divided into an 8-bit op code and 24 bits of address field.

FIGURE 7.13

Simplified Pentium Logical Interface

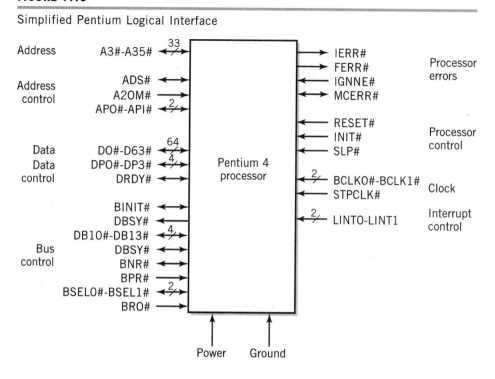

FIGURE 7.14

A Simple 32-bit Instruction Format

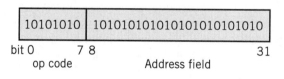

bit 0   7 8   31
   op code   Address field

In the Little Man Computer, reference to an *address* specifically referred to a *memory* address. However, we have already noted that the computer might have several general-purpose registers and that it would be necessary for the programmer to select a particular register to use as a part of the instruction. To be more general, we will use the word "address" to refer to any data location, whether it is a user-accessible register or a memory location. We will use the more specific expression *memory address* when we want to specify that the address is actually a memory location.

In general, computer instructions that manipulate data require the specification of at least two locations for the data: one or more *source* locations and one *destination* location. These locations may be expressed *explicitly*, as address fields in the instruction word, or *implicitly*, as part of the definition of the instruction itself. The instruction format of the Little Man LOAD instruction, for example, takes the data from the single address field as the **explicit**

source address. Explicit addresses in the Little Man Computer are always memory addresses. The destination address in this case is **implicit:** this instruction always uses the accumulator register as a destination. The Little Man ADD and SUBTRACT instructions require *two* sources and a destination. Source data addressed by the instruction's address field is added to the value in the implicitly stated accumulator, with the result placed implicitly in the accumulator.

For a particular instruction, the source(s) and destination may be the same or may be different. For example, an instruction that complements a value to change its sign would usually be done "in place"; that is, the source and destination register or memory location is usually the same. The Little Man ADD instruction uses the accumulator register both as a source for one of the numbers to be added and as the destination for the result. On the other hand, when we move data, using a LOAD or STORE or some other type of MOVE operation, the source and destination are obviously different, or the move would not be useful! Unless the operation is done in place, the sources are normally left unchanged by the instruction, whereas the destination is almost always changed.

The source and destination addresses may be registers or memory locations. Since most modern computers have multiple registers available to the user, it is usually necessary to provide at least two address fields, even for an address-register move, since the number of the particular register must be specified in the instruction.

The sources and destinations of data for an instruction, whether implicit or explicit, are also known as **operands.** Thus, instructions that move data from one place to another have two operands: one source operand and one destination operand. Arithmetic operations such as ADD and SUBTRACT require three operands. Explicit address fields are also known as *operand fields.*

Most commonly, instructions that manipulate data will have one address field for operations that happen in place, and two or three address fields for move and arithmetic operations. On some computers one or more of the addresses may be implicit, and no address field is required for that particular address. However, in modern computers most address references are explicit, even for register addresses, because this increases the generality and flexibility of the instruction. Thus, most computer instructions will consist of an op code and one, two, or three explicit address fields. Some textbooks refer to instructions with one, two, or three explicit address fields as *unary, binary,* or *ternary* instructions, respectively.

7.7 INSTRUCTION WORD REQUIREMENTS AND CONSTRAINTS

The size of the instruction word, in bits, is dependent on the particular CPU, particularly by the design of its instruction set. The size of the instruction word may be fixed at, say, 32 bits, or it may vary depending on the usage of the address fields. The Sun Sparc CPU, for example, takes the former approach: every instruction word is exactly 32 bits wide. Conversely, some of the basic instruction words for the X86 microprocessor line used in the common PC, for example, are as small as 1 or 2 bytes long, but there are some instructions in the Pentium microprocessor that are as many as 15 bytes long. In the IBM zSeries, most instruction words are 4 bytes, or 32 bits long, but a few instructions are 2 bytes or 6 bytes in length.

The challenge in establishing an instruction word size is the need to provide both enough op code bits to support a reasonable set of different instructions, as well as enough address field bits to meet the ever growing demand for increasing amounts of addressable memory. Consider, for example, the extremely straightforward instruction format shown in Figure 7.14. This format assumes a single address field with a 32-bit fixed length instruction. With the division shown, we have access to $2^8 = 256$ different instructions and $2^{24} =$ approximately 16 million memory addresses.

Even if the designer creates a smaller instruction set, with fewer op codes, the amount of memory that may be specified in a 32-bit instruction word is severely limited by modern standards. Most of today's computers support an address size of at least 32 bits. Some newer machines support 64-bit addresses.

Further, with additional registers, the simple instruction format shown in Figure 7.14 must be expanded to handle explicit addressing of multiple registers, including moves between registers, as well as identifying the proper register in operations between registers and memory. In short, the simple instruction format used in the Little Man Computer is inadequate for the instruction sets in modern computers.

The use of instructions of different lengths is one of several techniques developed by instruction set designers to allow more flexibility in the design of the instruction set. Simple instructions can be expressed in a small word, perhaps even a single byte, whereas more complicated instructions will require instruction words many bytes long. Longer instructions are stored in successive bytes of memory. Thus, a Little Man HALT, IN, or OUT instruction would be stored in a single location. A LOAD might require two successive locations to store memory addresses of five digits or three locations for an eight-digit address. The use of variable length instructions is efficient in memory usage, since each instruction is only as long as it needs to be.

There are a number of important disadvantages to variable length instructions, however. Most modern computers increase CPU processing speed by "pipelining" instructions, that is, by fetching a new instruction while the previous one is still completing execution, similar to the processing on an automobile assembly line. Variable length instructions complicate pipelining, because the starting point of the new instruction is not known until the length of the previous instruction has been determined. If you extend this idea to multiple instructions, you can see the difficulty of maintaining a smooth assembly line. This issue is discussed in more detail in Chapter 8. Because pipelining has become so important to processing speed in modern computers, the use of variable length instructions has fallen out of favor for new CPU designs. Nearly all new CPU designs use fixed length instructions exclusively.

An effective alternative to large instructions or variable instruction words is to store the address that would otherwise be located in an instruction word address field at some special location that can hold a large address, such as a general purpose register, and use a small address field within the instruction to point to that location. There are a number of variations on this theme. This technique is used, even on systems that provide variable length instructions. A single CPU might provide a number of different variations to increase the flexibility of the instruction set. This flexibility also includes the ability to code programs that process lists of data more efficiently. The various ways of addressing registers and memory are known as addressing modes. The Little Man Computer provides only a single mode, known as direct addressing. The alternative just described is called register deferred addressing. There are a number of addressing modes discussed in detail in Supplementary Chapter 2. The use of different addressing modes is the most important method for minimizing the size of instruction words and for writing efficient programs.

Examples of instruction formats from two different CPUs are shown in Figure 7.15. There may be several different formats within a single CPU. We have shown only a partial

FIGURE 7.15

Examples of Instruction Formats

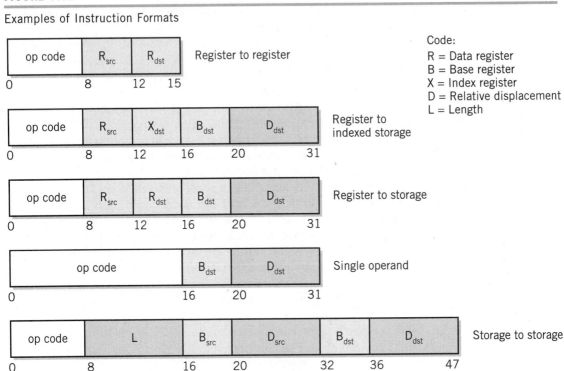

IBM mainframe formats

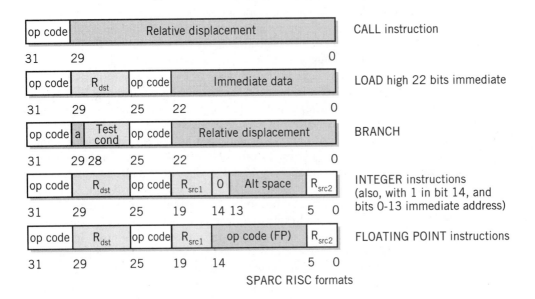

SPARC RISC formats

set for each machine, although the SPARC set is complete except for small variations. (There are nineteen different IBM formats in all.) It is not necessary that you understand every detail in Figure 7.15, but it is useful to note the basic similarities between the instruction set formats in different computers.

7.8 CLASSIFICATION OF INSTRUCTIONS

Nearly every instruction in a computer performs some sort of operation on one or more source data values, which results in one or more destination data values. The operation may be a move or load, it may be an addition or subtraction, it may be an input or output, or it may be one of many other operations that we have already discussed.

Actually, if you think about the classes of instructions that we have discussed, you will realize that there are only a very few instructions that do *not* operate on data. Some of these are concerned with the flow of the program itself, such as unconditional JUMP instructions. There are also instructions that control the administration of the computer itself; the only example in the Little Man Computer instruction set is the COFFEE BREAK or HALT that causes the computer to cease executing instructions. Another example on many computers is the NO OPERATION instruction that does nothing but waste time (which can be useful when a programmer wants to create a time delay for some reason).

Most modern computers also provide instructions that aid the operating system software in its work, by providing security, controlling memory access, and performing other functions. Because the operating system will frequently be controlling many tasks and users these instructions must not be available to the users' application programs. Only the operating system can execute these instructions. These instructions are known as **privileged instructions.** The HALT instruction is usually a privileged instruction, because you would not want an individual user to stop the computer while other users are still in the middle of their tasks.

Computer manufacturers usually group the instruction set into various categories of instructions, such as data movement instructions, arithmetic instructions, shift and rotate instructions, input/output instructions, conditional branch instructions, jump instructions, and special-purpose instructions.

Within each category, the instructions usually have a similar instruction word format, support similar addressing modes, and execute in a similar way. A typical instruction set, divided into eight categories, appears in Figure 7.16. This figure represents nearly all the user-accessible instructions in the Motorola 68000 series[3] of microprocessors used in early Apple Macintosh computers. The privileged instructions are not listed in the diagram, nor are exception-handling instructions that are used primarily by system programmers. These constitute an additional two categories for the 68000 series CPUs. Incidentally, notice that this CPU does not have any I/O instructions. That is because the CPU is designed in such a way that the move instructions can also be used for I/O. Notice particularly that, except for the lack of I/O instructions, the categories conform fairly well to the Little Man Computer instruction set. The additional instructions in this CPU are mostly

---

[3] Although the 68000 CPU series is old, it is still used in embedded computer systems. It was selected for this illustration because of its clean design, with few extraneous bells and whistles.

FIGURE 7.16

68000 Instruction Set

Mnemonic	Operation	Mnemonic	Operation
Data Movement Instructions		**Shift and Rotate Instructions**	
CAS*	Compare and swap with operand	ASL	Arithmetic shift register left
CAS2*	Compare upper/lower and swapASR	ASR	Arithmetic shift right
EXG	Exchange registers	LSL	Logical shift left
LEA	Load effective address	LSR	Logical shift right
LINK	Link and allocate stack	ROL	Rotate left
MOVE	Move src to dst	ROR	Rotate right
MOVE16	Move src to dst (68030-68060 only)	ROXL	Rotate left with extend bit
MOVEA	Move src to address register	ROXR	Rotate right with extend bit
MOVEM	Move multiple registers at once	SWAP	Swap words of a long word
MOVEP	Move to peripheral		
MOVEQ	Move short data to dst	**Bit Manipulation Instructions**	
PEA	Push effective address to stack	BCHG	Change bit
UNLK	Unlink stack	BCLR	Clear bit
		BTEST	Set bit
Integer Arithmetic Instructions		BTST	Test bit
ADD	Add src to dst		
ADDA	Add src to address register	**Bit Field Instructions**	
ADDI	Add immediate data to dst	BFCHG*	Change bit field
ADDQ	Add short data to dst	BFCLR*	Clear bit field
ADDX	Add with extend bit to dst	BFEXTS*	Extract and sign extend bit field
SUB, SUBA,	Subtracts act similarly to adds	BFEXTU*	Extract and zero extend bit field
SUBI, SUBQ,		BFFFO*	Find first set bit in bit field
SUBX		BFINS*	Insert bit field
MULS	Signed multiply	BFSET*	Set bit field
MULU	Unsigned multiply	BFTST*	Test bit field
DIVS	Signed divide		
DIVU	Unsigned divide	**Binary Coded Decimal Instructions**	
DIVSL*	Long signed divide	ABCD	Add src to dst
DIVUL*	Unsigned long divide	NBCD	Negate destination
CLR	Clear value in register	PACK*	Pack src to dst
CMP	Compare src to dst	SBCD*	Subtract src from dst
CMPA	Compare src to address register	UNPK*	Unpack src to dst
CMPI	Compare immediate data to dst		
CMPM	Compare memory	**Program Flow Instructions**	
CMP2*	Compare register to upper/lower bounds	Bcc	Branch on condition code cc
EXT	Sign extend	BRA	Branch unconditionally
EXTB	Sign extend byte	BSR	Branch to subroutine
NEG	Negate register	CALLM*	Call module
NEGX	Negate with extend	DBcc	Test, decrement, and branch on condition
		JMP	Jump to address
Boolean Logic Instructions		JSR	Jump to subroutine
AND	AND src to dst	NOP	No operation
ANDI	AND immediate data to dst	RTD*	Return and deallocate stack (also 68010)
EOR	Exclusive OR src to dst	RTE	Return from exception (privileged)
EORI	Exclusive OR immediate data to dst	RTM*	Return from module
NOT	NOT destination	RTR	Return and restore condition codes
OR	OR src to dst	RTS	Return from subroutine
ORI	OR immediate data to dst	TRAP	Trap to system
Scc	Test condition codes and set operand		
TAS	Test and set operand	*(68020–68060 only)	
TST	Test operand and set condition codes	(src = source; dst = destination; cc = condition code	
TRAPcc*	Trap on condition	indicator, e.g. BGT branch of greater than)	

variations on instructions that are familiar to you plus special control instructions. The 68000 series CPUs also support a math coprocessor, which adds a category of floating point arithmetic instructions. The floating point math instructions are built directly into 68000 series processors starting with the 68040 CPU.

Data Movement Instructions (LOAD, STORE, and Other Moves)

Because the move instructions are the most frequently used, and therefore the most basic to the computer, computer designers try to provide a lot of flexibility in these instructions. The MOVE category commonly includes instructions to move data from memory to general registers, from general registers to memory, between different general registers, and, in some computers, directly between different memory locations without affecting any general register. There may be many different addressing modes available within a single computer.

Additionally, variations on these instructions are frequently used to handle different data sizes. Thus, there may be a LOAD BYTE instruction, a LOAD HALF-WORD (2 bytes), a LOAD WORD (4 bytes), and a LOAD DOUBLE WORD (8 bytes) within the same instruction set. (Incidentally, the concept of a "word" is not consistent between manufacturers. To some manufacturers the size of a word is 16 bits; to others, it is 32 or even 64 bits).

The Little Man LOAD and STORE instructions are simple, though adequate, examples of MOVE instructions. Other than expanding the addressing mode capabilities and adding multiple word size capabilities, which we have already discussed, the major limitation of the Little Man LOAD and STORE instructions is the fact that they are designed to operate with a single accumulator.

When we expand the number of accumulators or general-purpose registers, we must expand the instruction to determine which register we wish to use. Thus, the instruction must provide a field for the particular register. Fortunately, it takes very few bits to describe a register. Even sixteen registers require only four bits. On the other hand, if the computer uses the registers to hold pointers to the actual memory addresses as its standard addressing mode, the required instruction size may actually decrease, since fewer bits are required for the address field in this case.

Additionally, it is desirable to have the capability to move data directly between registers, since such moves do not require memory access and are therefore faster to execute. In fact, one important class of computer, known as RISC, for reduced instruction set computer, provides only one pair of MOVE instructions for moving data between the CPU and memory. All other instructions in a RISC architecture move and manipulate data only between registers. This allows the instruction set to be executed much more rapidly. RISC architecture is discussed more thoroughly in Chapter 8, together with detailed examination of a specific example, the Power PC computer, in Chapter 12.

Arithmetic Instructions

Every CPU instruction set includes integer addition and subtraction. Except for a few special-purpose CPUs, every CPU today also provides instructions for integer multiplication and division. Many instruction sets provide integer arithmetic for several different word sizes. As with the MOVE instructions, there may be several different integer arithmetic instruction formats providing various combinations of register and memory access in different addressing modes.

In addition, most current CPUs also provide floating point arithmetic capabilities. On older PCs with 80386 or earlier processors, a floating point math coprocessor unit had to be purchased separately and installed in a socket provided for that purpose on the motherboard of the computer. Because of the expense, most users would not exercise this option. For computers that run programs that require extensive floating point calculations, such as CAD/CAM programs, the presence of floating point instructions can reduce the processing time significantly. Floating point instructions usually operate on a separate set of registers with 64-, 80-, or 128-bit word sizes. The modern instruction set usually also contains instructions that convert data between integer and floating point formats.

As noted in Chapter 3, most modern CPUs also provide at least a minimal set of arithmetic instructions for BCD or packed decimal format, which simplifies the programming of business data processing applications.

Of course, it is not absolutely necessary to provide all these different instruction options. In Chapter 3 we demonstrated that multiplication and division can be performed using only add, subtract, and shift instructions. Internally, the multiplication and division instructions simply implement in hardware the shift and add or subtract procedures previously discussed. Since the fetch-execute cycle requires a single-bit shift and register add step for each bit in the multiplier, multiply and divide instructions execute slowly compared to other instructions.

Even the subtract instruction is theoretically not necessary, since we showed in Chapter 4 that integer subtraction is performed internally by the process of complementing and adding.

As we already noted, the same is true of BCD and floating point instructions. On the now rare computers that do not provide floating point instructions, there is usually a library of software procedures that are used to simulate floating point instructions.

Boolean Logic Instructions

Most modern instruction sets provide instructions for performing Boolean algebra. Commonly included are a NOT instruction, which inverts the bits on a single operand, as well as AND, (inclusive) OR, and EXCLUSIVE-OR instructions, which require two source arguments and a destination.

Single Operand Manipulation Instructions

In addition to the NOT instruction described in the previous paragraph, most computers provide other convenient single operand instructions. Most of these instructions operate on the value in a register, but some instruction sets provide similar operations on memory values as well. Most commonly, the instruction set will contain instructions for NEGATing a value, for INCREMENTing a value, for DECREMENTing a value, and for setting a register to zero. There are sometimes others. On some computers, the increment or decrement instruction causes a branch to occur automatically when zero is reached; this simplifies the design of loops by allowing the programmer to combine the test and branch into a single instruction.

Bit Manipulation Instructions

Most instruction sets provide instructions for setting and resetting individual bits in a data word. Some instruction sets also provide instructions for operating on multiple bits at once. Bits can also be tested, and used to control program flow. These instructions allow programmers to design their own "flags" in addition to commonly provided negative/positive, zero/nonzero, carry/borrow, and overflow arithmetic flags.

Shift and Rotate Instructions

Shift and **rotate operations** have been mentioned previously in Chapters 4 as a means to implement multiplication and division. Shifts and rotate operations have other programming applications, and CPU instruction sets commonly provide a variety of different shift and rotate instructions for the programmer to use. As shown in Figure 7.17, shift instructions move the data bits left or right one or more bits. Rotate instructions also shift the data bits left or right, but the bit that is shifted out of the end is placed into the vacated space at the other end. Depending on the design of the particular instruction set, bits shifted out the end of the word may be shifted into a different register or into the carry or overflow flag bit, or they may simply "fall off the end" and be lost.

Two different kinds of shifts are usually provided. The data word being shifted might be logical or it might be numeric. **Logical shift** instructions simply shift the data as you

FIGURE 7.17

Typical Register Shifts and Rotates

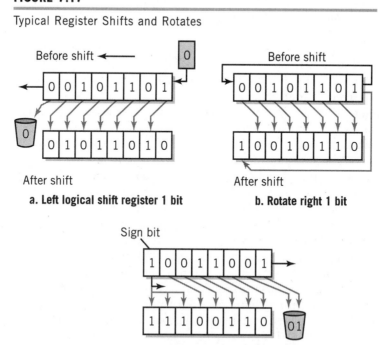

a. Left logical shift register 1 bit

b. Rotate right 1 bit

c. Right arithmetic shift 2 bits

would expect, and zeros are shifted in to replace the bit spaces that have been vacated. **Arithmetic shift** instructions are commonly used to multiply or divide the original value by a power of 2. Therefore, the instruction does not shift the leftmost bit, since that bit usually represents the algebraic sign of the numeric value—obviously the sign of a number must be maintained. Left arithmetic shifts do not shift the left bit, but zeros replace the bits from the right as bits are moved to the left. This will effectively double the numeric value for each shift of one bit. On the other hand, right arithmetic shifts fill the space of moved bits with the sign bit rather than with zero. This has the effect of halving the value for each bit shifted, while maintaining the sign of the value. It may not seem obvious to you that this works correctly, but it becomes more apparent if you recall that negative numbers in complementary arithmetic count backward starting from the value –1, which is represented in 2's complement by all ones.

Rotate instructions take the bits as they exit and rotate them back into the other end of the register. Some instructions sets include the carry or overflow bit as part of the rotation. Some CPUs also allow the rotation to take place between two registers. Rotate instructions can be used to exchange the 2 bytes of data in a 16-bit word, for example, by rotating the word by 8 bits.

Program Control Instructions

Program control instructions control the flow of a program. Program control instructions include jumps and branches, both unconditional and conditional, and also **subroutine CALL and** RETURN instructions. Various conditional tests are provided, including those with which you are already familiar: branch on zero, branch on nonzero, branch on positive, branch on negative, branch on carry, and so on.

CALL instructions, sometimes known as JUMP SUBROUTINE instructions, are used to implement subroutine, procedure, and function calls. Thus, CALL instructions are important as a means to enable program modularization.

From your programming experience, recall what happens when your program calls a subroutine or procedure. The program jumps to the starting location of the subroutine and executes the code in the subroutine. When the subroutine is completed, program execution returns to the calling program and continues with the instruction following the call. The machine language CALL instruction works the same way. A jump to the starting location of the subroutine occurs, and execution continues from that point. The only difference between a CALL instruction and a normal JUMP instruction is that the CALL instruction must also save somewhere the program counter address from which the jump occurred, so that the program may return to the instruction in the calling program following the call after the subroutine is completed. The RETURN instruction restores the original value to the program counter, and the calling program proceeds from where it left off. Operation of the CALL and RETURN instructions are illustrated in Figure 7.18.

Different computers use different methods to save the return address. One common method is to store the return address on a memory stack; the RETURN instruction operates by removing the address from the stack and moving it to the program counter. The use of stacks is discussed briefly in the next section. Another method for performing CALLs and RETURNs is explored in Exercise 7.17.

Stack Instructions

One of the most important data storage structures in programming is the **stack.** A stack is used to store data when the most recently used data will also be the first needed. For that reason, stacks are also known as *LIFO,* for *last-in, first-out,* structures. As an analogy, stacks are frequently described by the way plates are stored and used in a cafeteria. New plates are added to the top of the stack, or *pushed,* and plates already on the stack move down to make room for them. Plates are removed from the top of the stack, or *popped,* so that the last plates placed on the stack are the first removed. Similarly, the last number entered onto a computer memory stack will be the first number available when the stack is next accessed. Any data that must be retrieved in reverse order from the way it was entered is a candidate for the use of stacks. Figure 7.19 shows the process of adding to and removing numbers from the stack.

Stacks are an efficient way of storing intermediate data values during complex calculations. In fact, storage in Hewlett-Packard calculators is organized around a stack of memory. As we already noted, stacks are also an excellent method for storing the return addresses and arguments from subroutine calls. Program routines that are recursive must "call themselves." Suppose the return address were stored in a fixed location, as shown in Figure 7.20a. If the routine is called a second time, from within itself, Figure 7.20b, the original returning address (56) is lost and replaced by the new return address (76). The

FIGURE 7.18

Operation of CALL and RETURN Instructions

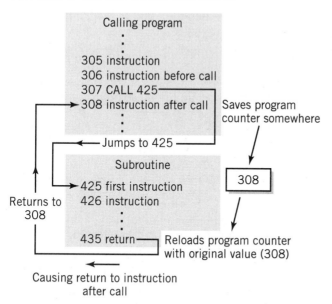

FIGURE 7.19

Using a Stack

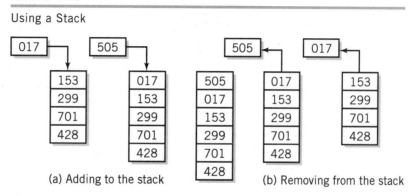

(a) Adding to the stack   (b) Removing from the stack

FIGURE 7.20

Fixed Location Subroutine Return Address Storage

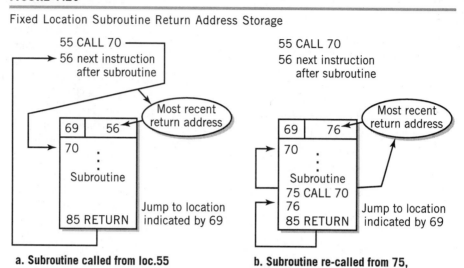

a. Subroutine called from loc.55

b. Subroutine re-called from 75, within the subroutine

program is stuck in an infinite loop between 76 and 85. In Figure 7.21, the return address is stored on a stack. This time when the routine is again called, the original address is simply pushed down the stack, below the most recent address. Notice that the program "winds its way back out" in the reverse order from which the routines were entered. This is exactly what we want: we always return from the last called subroutine to the one just previous. J. Linderman of Bentley notes that the same technique would be used to back out of a maze for which the explorer has written down each turn that she made after entering.

There are many other interesting applications for stacks in computers, but further discussion is beyond the scope of this book. The curious reader is referred to the For Further Reading section for references.

Computers do not generally provide special memory for stack use, although many machines provide special STACK instructions to simplify the bookkeeping task. Instead, the programmer sets aside one or more blocks of regular memory for this purpose. (The STACKS command, sometimes seen in PC MS-DOS CONFIG.SYS files, can also be used to assign blocks of memory for stack use.) The "bottom" of the stack is a fixed memory location, and a **stack pointer** points to the "top" of the stack, that is, the most recent entry. This is shown in Figure 7.22. A new entry is added to the stack, or pushed, by incrementing the stack pointer, and then storing the data at that location. An entry is removed from the stack, or popped, by copying the value pointed to and then decrementing the stack pointer. If a register is provided for the stack pointer, register-deferred addressing can be used for this purpose. (You should note that memory is drawn upside-down in Figure 7.22 so that incrementing the stack pointer moves it *upward*.)

Many instruction sets provide PUSH and POP instructions as direct support for stacks, but stacks can be implemented easily without special instructions. (Exercise S2.15 illustrates one solution.) Some computers also specify the use of a particular general-purpose register as a stack pointer register.

FIGURE 7.21

Stack Subroutine Return Address Storage

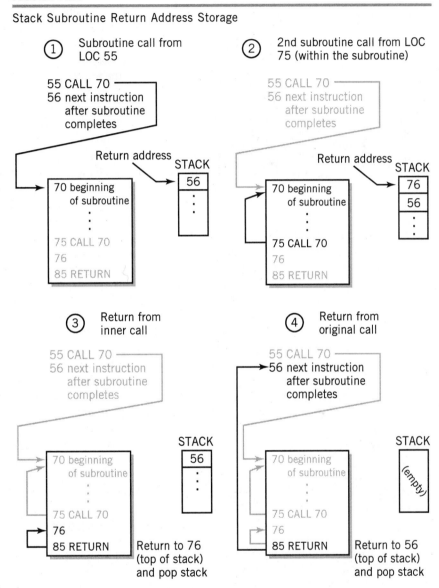

Multiple Data Instructions

Multimedia applications rank high in computational demands on the CPU in modern PCs and workstations. In response to the demand, some CPU designers have created specialized instructions that speed up and simplify multimedia processing operations.

Multimedia operations are commonly characterized by a number of simple operations applied identically to every piece of data in the set. As a simple example, the brightness of an image might be modified by multiplying the value of every pixel in the image

FIGURE 7.22

Using a Block of Memory as a Stack

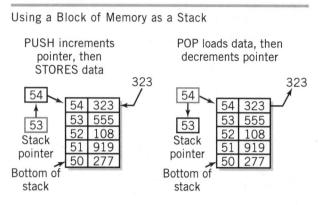

by a common scale factor. Or, a measure of similarity between two images could be established by subtracting all the pixel values in one image from the corresponding pixel values in a second image and averaging the results.

Multiple data instructions perform a single operation on multiple pieces of data simultaneously. For this reason they are also known as **SIMD** instructions. SIMD stands for **S**ingle **I**nstruction, **M**ultiple **D**ata. The MMX instructions provided on recent Intel Pentium processors provide simultaneous integer arithmetic operations on up to eight 8-bit, four 16-bit, or two 32-bit values packed into a 64-bit register, as well as providing instructions for packing and unpacking the values and moving them between registers and memory. Starting with the Pentium III, Intel provided eight additional, 128-bit registers for this purpose, and also added SIMD floating point arithmetic and single 64-bit integer arithmetic instructions to the instruction set. The newest models of the PowerPC CPU used in the Apple G4 computer and the Sun UltraSparc CPU provide similar capabilities. Figure 7.23 shows the operation of a SIMD ADD instruction.

Although multimedia operations are a primary application for these instructions, these instructions can be applied to any vector or array processing application, and are useful for a number of purposes in addition to multimedia processing, including voice-to-text processing and data encryption and decryption. A similar set of instructions has been available on large mainframe computers for many years as an optional coprocessor commonly known as a **vector processing facility.** The inclusion of SIMD instructions in personal computer CPUs, as a standard part of the instruction set, is a recent development.

FIGURE 7.23

Operation of a 4-wide SIMD ADD Instruction

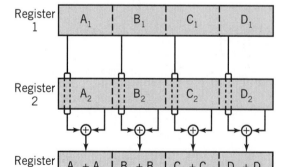

Other Instructions

The remainder of the instruction set includes input/output instructions and machine control instructions. In most systems both groups are privileged instructions. Input/output instructions are generally privileged instructions because we do not want input and output requests from different users and programs interfering with each other.

Consider, for example, two users requesting printer output on a shared printer at the same time, so that each page of output is divided back and forth between the two users. Obviously, such output would not be acceptable. Instead, these requests would be made to the operating system that controls the printer, which would set priorities, maintain queues, and service the requests. We will deal with the subject of I/O in Chapters 9 and 10, and with operating systems in Chapters 13 through 18.

SUMMARY AND REVIEW

Functionally, the operation of the CPU, together with memory, is essentially identical to that of the Little Man Computer. For each component of the Little Man Computer, there is a corresponding component in the computer unit.

Within the CPU, the most important components are registers. Data may be moved between registers, may be added or subtracted from the current contents of a register, and can be shifted or rotated within a register or between registers. Each instruction in the instruction set is executed by performing these simple operations, using the appropriate choice of registers and operations in the correct sequence for the particular instruction. The sequence of operations for a particular instruction is known as its fetch-execute cycle. A fetch-execute cycle exists for every instruction in the instruction set. Fetch-execute instruction cycles constitute the basis for all program execution in the computer. The sequence for each instruction corresponds closely to the actions taken by the Little Man in performing a similar instruction.

The operation of memory is intimately related to two registers in particular, the memory address register and the memory data register. Addresses placed into the MAR are decoded in memory, resulting in the activation of a single memory address line. At the proper instant, data can then be transferred in either direction between that memory location and the MDR. The direction is specified by a read/write control line. The number of available memory locations is established by the size of the MAR; the data word size is established by the size of the MDR.

Interconnections between various parts of a computer are provided by buses. There are many different types of buses. Buses connect different modules within the CPU. They also connect the CPU to memory and to the I/O peripherals. Buses can connect two components in a point-to-point configuration or may interconnect several modules in a multipoint configuration. In general, the lines on buses carry signals that represent data, addresses, and control functions.

Instructions in a real CPU are made up of an op code and up to three address field operands. The size of the instruction word is CPU dependent. Some computers use variable length instruction words. Other computers use a fixed length instruction, most commonly, 32 bits in length. Instructions fall naturally into a small number of categories: moves, integer arithmetic, floating point arithmetic, data flow control, and so forth. There are also privileged instructions, which control functions internal to the CPU and are accessible only to the operating system.

KEY CONCEPTS AND TERMS

accumulator	flag	program counter (PC)
arithmetic/logic unit	flash ROM	program counter register
(ALU)	general-purpose register	Program Status Word
arithmetic shift	implicit source address	(PSW)
backplane	instruction pointer	privileged instruction
bridge	instruction register (IR)	RAM
bus	line (bus)	register
bus interface bridge	logical shift	ROM
bus interface unit	memory	rotate operation
bus protocol	memory address	shift operation
clock	register (MAR)	SIMD
control unit (CU)	memory data	stack
dynamic RAM	register (MDR)	stack pointer
EEPROM (electronically	memory management unit	static RAM
erasable programmable	multipoint bus	status register
ROM)	nonvolatile	subroutine call and return
explicit source address	operands	system bus
fetch-execute instruction	point-to-point bus	vector processing facility
cycle	port	volatile

FOR FURTHER READING

There are many excellent textbooks that describe the implementation and operation of the components of the computer system. A brief, but very clear, explanation of the fetch-execute cycle can be found in Davis [DAV02]. Three classic engineering textbooks that discuss the topics of this chapter in great detail are those authored by Stallings [STAL02], Patterson and Hennessy [PATT97], and Tanenbaum and Goodman [TAN99]. There are many books and papers describing various components and techniques associated with the implementation and operation of the CPU and memory. Also see the For Further Reading section in Chapter 8 for more suggestions.

EXERCISES

7.1 Draw side-by-side flow diagrams that show how the Little Man executes a store instruction and the corresponding CPU fetch-execute cycle.

7.2 Suppose that the following instructions are found at the given locations in memory:

```
20  LDA 50
21  ADD 51
50  724
51  006
```

a. Show the contents of the IR, the PC, the MAR, the MDR, and A at the conclusion of instruction 20.

b. Show the contents of each register as each step of the fetch-execute cycle is performed for instruction 21.

7.3   One large modern computer has a 36-bit memory address register. How much memory can this computer address?

7.4   Why are there two different registers (MAR and MDR) associated with memory? What are the equivalents in the Little Man Computer?

7.5   Show the steps of the CPU fetch-execute cycle for the remaining instructions in the Little Man instruction set.

7.6   Most of the registers in the machine have two-way copy capability; that is, you can copy to them from another register, and you can copy from them to another register. The MAR, on the other hand, is always used as a destination register; you only copy to the MAR. Explain clearly why this is so.

7.7   **a.**   What is the effect of shifting an unsigned number in a register two bits to the left? One bit to the right? Assume that 0s are inserted to replace bit locations at the end of the register that have become empty due to the shift.

      b.   Suppose the number is signed, that is, stored using 2's complement. Now what is the effect of shifting the number?

      c.   Suppose that the shift excludes the sign bit, so that the sign bit always remains the same. Furthermore, suppose that during a right shift, the sign bit is always used as the insertion bit at the left end of the number (instead of 0). Now what is the effect of these shifts?

7.8   If you were building a computer to be used in outer space, would you be likely to use magnetic core memory or RAM? Why?

7.9   Using the register operations indicated in this chapter, show the fetch-execute cycle for an instruction that produces the 2's complement of the number in A. Show the fetch-execute cycle for an instruction that clears A (i.e., sets A to 0).

7.10   Many older computers used an alternative to the BRANCH ON CONDITION instruction called SKIP ON CONDITION that worked as follows: if the condition were true, the computer would skip the following instruction and go on to the one after; otherwise, the next instruction in line would be executed. Programmers usually place a jump instruction in the "in-between" location to branch on a FALSE condition. Normally, the skip instruction was designed to skip one memory location. If the instruction set uses variable length instructions, however, the task is more difficult, since the skip must still skip around the entire instruction. Assume a Little Man mutant that uses a variable length instruction. The op code is in the first word, and there may be as many as three words following. To make life easy, assume that the third digit of the op code word is a number from 1 to 4, representing the number of words in the instruction. Create a fetch-execute cycle for this machine.

7.11   Suppose that the instruction format for a modified Little Man Computer requires two consecutive locations for each instruction. The high-order digits of the instruction are located in the first mail slot, followed by the low-order digits. The IR is large enough to hold the entire instruction and can be addressed as IR [high] and IR [low] to load it. You may assume that the op code part of the instruction uses IR [high] and that the address is found in IR [low]. Write the fetch-execute cycle for an ADD instruction on this machine.

7.12   The Little Prince Computer (LPC) is a mutant variation on the LMC. (The LPC is so named because the differences are a royal pain.) The LPC has one additional instruction. The extra instruction requires two consecutive words:

    0XX
    0YY

This instruction, known as move, moves data directly from location XX to location YY without affecting the value in the accumulator. To execute this instruction, the Little Prince would need to store the XX data temporarily. He can do this by writing the value on a piece of paper and holding it until he retrieves the second address. The equivalent in a real CPU might be called the intermediate address register, or IAR.

Write the fetch-execute cycle for the LPC MOVE instruction.

7.13   Generally, the distance that a programmer wants to move from the current instruction location on a BRANCH ON CONDITION is fairly small. This suggests that it might be appropriate to design the BRANCH instruction in such a way that the new location is calculated relative to the current instruction location.

For example, we could design a different LMC instruction 8CX. The C digit would specify the condition on which to branch, and X would be a single-digit relative address. Using 10's complement, this would allow a branch of –5 to +4 locations from the current address. If we were currently executing this instruction at location 24, 803 would cause a branch on negative to location 27.

Write a fetch-execute cycle for this BRANCH ON NEGATIVE RELATIVE instruction. You may ignore the condition code for this exercise, and you may also assume that the complementary addition is handled correctly. The single-digit address, X, is still found in IR [address].

7.14   As computer words get larger and larger, there is a law of diminishing returns: the speed of execution of real application programs does not increase and may, in fact, decrease. Why do you suppose that this is so?

7.15   Reduced instruction set computers provide a large number of general-purpose registers and very few memory access instructions. Most instructions use registers instead of memory. What are the advantages to such an architecture?

7.16   Create the fetch-execute cycle for an instruction that moves a value from general purpose register1 to general purpose register2. Compare this cycle to the cycle for a LOAD instruction. What is the major advantage of the MOVE over the LOAD?

CHAPTER 8

CPU AND MEMORY: DESIGN, IMPLEMENTATION, AND ENHANCEMENT

Adapted by Benjamin Reece

8.0 INTRODUCTION

The Little Man Computer design, implemented in binary form, may be sufficient to implement any program, but it is not necessarily a convenient way to do so. It is like traveling overseas by freight steamer instead of SST: it might be fun, but it sure ain't the easiest way to get the job done! Computers today are more sophisticated and flexible, providing a greater variety of instructions, improved methods of addressing memory and manipulating data, and implementation techniques that allow instructions to be executed quickly and efficiently.

In Chapter 7, we discussed the principal features of a CPU: the basic architecture of the CPU, register concept, instruction set, instruction formats, means of addressing memory, and the fetch-execute cycle. In this chapter we will investigate some of the additional design features and implementation techniques that help to give the modern CPU its power.

It probably won't surprise you to know that there are a large number of different ways of performing these tasks. At the same time, it is important to recognize, right from the outset, that additional features and a particular choice of organization do not change the fundamental operation of the computer as we have already described it. Rather, they represent variations on the ideas and techniques that we have already described. These variations can simplify the programmer's task and possibly speed up program execution by creating shortcuts for common operations. However, nothing introduced in this chapter changes the most important idea: that the computer is nothing more than a machine capable of performing simple operations at very high speeds.

The first section investigates several different CPU architectures, with particular focus on two important, and conceptually different, approaches, known as **complex instruction set computer (CISC)** and **reduced instruction set computer (RISC)** architectures. We explain the differences between the two approaches, present the arguments in favor of each approach, and consider the strengths and weaknesses of each architecture, as measured by various criteria. The discussion of RISC architecture is particularly relevant because it provides insight into the major impact that RISC architecture has had on CPU organization in general. The section also briefly considers two new architectures with promise, the Transmeta VLIW and Intel EPIC architectures.

In the second section we briefly consider various CPU features and enhancements. Most of the section is devoted to paging, an advanced memory management technique within the CPU that is of great importance.

Section 8.3 looks at memory enhancements. The most significant improvement in memory access speed is cache memory. Cache memory is discussed in considerable depth.

In Section 8.4, we investigate alternatives to the traditional control unit/ALU CPU organization. These organizations address major bottlenecks that limit CPU execution speed with a number of innovative techniques for improving CPU performance.

Finally, in Section 8.5, we present a brief introduction to two different methods of implementing the CPU organizations that we have discussed in previous sections.

It is not our intention to overwhelm you in this chapter with myriad details to memorize, nor to help you create a new career as an assembly language programmer or computer hardware engineer, but this chapter will at least introduce you to the major concepts and methods used in modern computers. When reading this chapter, remember to keep your focus on the larger picture: the details are just variations on a theme.

8.1 CPU ARCHITECTURES

Overview

A CPU architecture is defined by the basic characteristics and major features of the CPU. (CPU architecture is sometimes called **instruction set architecture, or ISA.**)[1] These characteristics include such things as the number and types of registers, methods of addressing memory, and basic design and layout of the instruction set. It does *not* include consideration of the implementation, instruction execution speed, details of the interface between the CPU and associated computer circuitry, and various optional features. It may or may not include the absence or presence of particular instructions, the amount of addressable memory, or the data widths that are routinely processed by the CPU. Some architectures are more tightly defined than others.

These ideas should not surprise you. Consider house architecture. A split-level ranch house, for example, is easily recognized by its general characteristics, even though there may be wide differences in features and design from one split-level ranch to the next. Conversely, an A-frame house or a Georgian house is recognized by specific, well-defined features that must be present in the design to be recognized as A-frame or Georgian.

There have been many CPU architectures over the years, but only a few with longevity. In most cases, that longevity has resulted from evolution and expansion of the architecture to include new features, always with protection of the integrity of the original architecture, as well as with improved design, technology, and implementation of the architecture.

At present, important CPU architectural families include the IBM mainframe series, the Intel X86 family, the IBM and Motorola POWER and PowerPC architectures, and the Sun SPARC family.

Most CPU architectures today are loosely categorized into one of two types, CISC (complex instruction set computers) or RISC (reduced instruction set computers). In modern times, the dividing line between CISC and RISC architectures has become increasingly blurred as many of the features of each have migrated across the dividing line.

There have also been a few successful attempts to create other types, including a stack-based CPU with no general-purpose registers, and two recent architectures called **very-long instruction word (VLIW)** from Transmeta and **explicitly parallel instruction computers (EPIC)** from Intel. VLIW and EPIC architectures are too new to assess their long-term value.

It should be noted that each of these architectures is consistent with the broad characteristics that define a von Neumann computer.

---

[1] This is not to be confused with the ISA bus, which is entirely different!

CISC and RISC Architectures

Most older CPU architectures are classified as CISC designs. The IBM mainframe architecture, currently represented by the zSeries, and the Intel X86 family are both examples of CISC architectures. CISC families are characterized by comparatively few general-purpose registers, a wide variety of addressing techniques, a large number of specialized instructions, and instruction words of varying sizes. Pentium instructions vary from one to fifteen bytes in length.

In contrast, the Power PC RISC CPU has thirty-two general-purpose registers, a single mode of memory addressing with two simple variations, and a fixed, 4-byte instruction word size. Although the Power PC also has a reasonably large instruction set, the number of instructions performing highly specialized functions is minimal.

RISC architectures attempt to produce more CPU power by eliminating two major bottlenecks to instruction execution speed.

- Reducing the number of data memory accesses by using registers more effectively; the time to locate and access data in memory is much longer than that required to process data in a register.

- Simplifying the instruction set by eliminating rarely used instructions. This idea is based on the argument that rarely used instructions add hardware complexity to the instruction decoder that slows down execution of the other instructions that are used frequently. RISC instructions are supposed to be simple enough that an entire instruction would execute in the same amount of time as would normally be required to execute one of many steps in a CISC instruction cycle, as illustrated in Figure 8.1. In practice, implementation techniques have improved to the extent that this condition is less important than it was when RISC methods were originally proposed in the 1980s, and gradually RISC instruction sets have increased in size and complexity to match the capabilities of their CISC counterparts in most areas.

The bases for RISC architectures were several studies conducted in the late 1970s and early 1980s that established instruction usage patterns, both for assembly language and for

FIGURE 8.1

CISC versus RISC Instruction Execution

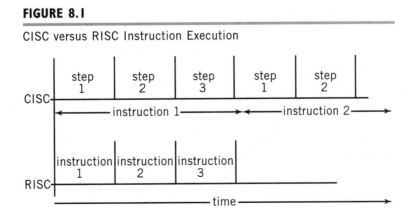

various high-level languages. Here are some general conclusions that were reached from the results of those studies:

- A study conducted by Hopkins in 1987 showed that 10 instructions accounted for 71 percent of all the instructions executed on the IBM System/370. The results of that study, shown in Figure 8.2, indicate that optimizing the performance of LOAD, STORE, and BRANCH instructions could result in a substantial increase in CPU performance. Other studies performed at about the same time reached similar conclusions.

- Several studies observed that both programmers and compilers avoided the use of complex instructions when they were available, so those instructions were rarely, if ever, used. This is true for both assembly language and high-level language programming. In one study, more than 85 percent of the statements in five different high-level languages consisted of assignment statements, IF statements and procedure calls [PATT81].

- Procedure and function calls are a huge bottleneck because of the need to pass arguments from one procedure to another. It is also necessary to store somewhere the values in the general registers from the previous procedure when a new procedure is called, since each procedure in a program must have access to the registers to use in any way that it wishes. Upon return to the calling procedure, the previous register values must be restored, and arguments must be passed back. The studies showed that these calls and returns represent a high proportion of overall program execution time, particularly because well-designed programs have a large degree of modularity.

Several different research teams in the 1980s used the results of these studies to design CPUs that attempted to improve CPU performance by increasing the efficiency of those operations that were costly in execution time and by eliminating the instructions rarely used. As a result of these efforts, Patterson [PATT82] and others created a set of guidelines for an improved architecture, which Patterson named RISC.

FIGURE 8.2

Most Frequently Executed Instructions

	Instruction	% of Executions
BC	Branch condition	20.2
L	Load	15.5
TM	Test under mask	6.1
ST	Store	5.9
LR	Load register	4.7
LA	Load address	4.0
LTR	Test register	3.8
BCR	Branch register	2.9
VC	Move characters	2.1
LH	Load halfword	1.8

SOURCE: Adapted from M.E. Hopkins, "A Perspective on the 801/Reduced Instruction Set Computer," *IBM Systems Journal*, 26:1 (1987): 107–121.

The main features that are used to differentiate a RISC design from a CISC design are

- **A limited and simple instruction set.** The goal is to create an instruction set made up of instructions that can execute quickly, at high clock speeds, using a hard-wired, pipelined implementation. (A pipeline is the CPU equivalent of an automobile assembly line for the execution of instructions. The concept of pipelines is discussed in Section 8.4.) The additional time that would normally be required to execute complex instructions puts "air bubbles" in the pipeline, which slows down overall execution speed. Complex instructions also require more complicated hardware to handle execution and timing. There is no restriction on the number of instructions in a RISC instruction set, but usually the number of instructions is smaller than that of a CISC processor.

- **Register-oriented instructions, with very limited memory access.** A RISC instruction set typically supplies only a few basic LOAD and STORE instructions that can access data in memory. All other instructions operate only with registers. (Of course, the instructions themselves still must be fetched from memory, so branch and procedure call instructions must contain an address.) Memory access instructions require extra time to execute; special measures are built into the system to handle this condition. Those special measures are discussed later in this section.

- **A fixed length, fixed format instruction word.** By making every instruction word identical in size and format, instructions can be fetched and decoded independently. It is not necessary to wait until the length of a previous instruction is known in order to fetch and decode the next instruction. Therefore, instructions can be fetched and decoded in parallel. Decoding is simplified if the op code and address fields are located in the same position for every instruction. In practice, the RISC architecture reduces the number of truly different instruction formats to a very small number. The five primary formats in a SPARC chip, for example, were shown earlier in Figure 7.15. In an Alpha VAX CISC CPU there are dozens of instruction formats, of many different lengths.

To speed up decoding the locations of data, many RISC CPUs use an instruction word with three operands. Two source registers provide the inputs to the instruction, and a destination register accepts the results. The PowerPC, for example, uses the format shown in Figure 8.3 for integer arithmetic instructions. The corresponding SPARC format shown in Figure 7.15 is quite similar.

- **Limited addressing modes.** Many RISC machines provide only a single addressing mode for addressing memory, commonly direct or register indirect addressing

FIGURE 8.3

PowerPC Integer Arithmetic Instruction Format

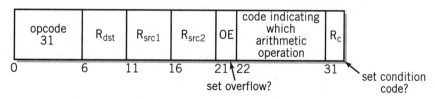

with an offset. Again, this simplifies the implementation and speeds up instruction execution. (Addressing modes are variations on the Little Man method of addressing memory. Addressing modes add flexibility to the instruction set, at a cost of additional complexity. Addressing modes are discussed in detail in Supplementary Chapter 2.)

■ **A large bank of registers.** RISC CPUs provide many registers so that variables and intermediate results used during program execution do not require the use of memory. Thus, many LOADS and STORES can be avoided.

In some RISC machines the registers are arranged into a clever circular buffer that provides a fast, convenient way to pass parameters between procedures. When moving from one procedure to another on a CISC processor, it is necessary to save all the registers to memory and also to copy and retrieve the parameters being passed. A stack in memory is commonly used for this purpose. These operations must be repeated for every procedure call and return, and they are extremely time consuming. The **circular register buffer** eliminates all these operations. The circular buffer is also used to switch between programs in a multitasking system, an important and frequent operation known as context switching. The circular buffer is discussed in the next section. Context switching is discussed in Chapters 13 and 15.

CIRCULAR REGISTER BUFFER   The circular register buffer, common in many RISC designs, provides general-purpose registers for program use and also offers a clever solution to the problem of copying blocks of values from one location to another during procedure transfers and context switching.

A typical circular register arrangement is shown in Figure 8.4. The system in this diagram provides a bank of 168 registers. Each pie-shaped element in the diagram contains eight registers. In addition to the twenty-four elements in the circular bank, there are an additional eight registers in a separate block.

To a program, the machine appears to have thirty-two registers. Of these thirty-two, the eight registers from the separate block are always available to every procedure. These registers are used for global variables. The remaining twenty-four registers are taken from the circular bank of registers. At any given instant, these twenty-four registers form a window in the bank. A *current window pointer* indicates the starting point for the window. The window is divided into three parts. The first eight registers in the window are used to store incoming parameters from the procedure that called the current procedure; these registers can also be used to return values to that calling procedure. The middle group of registers is used for local variables and temporary storage by the current procedure. The final group is used to store parameters that will be passed to another procedure.

When another procedure call occurs, the current window pointer is shifted to the right by sixteen registers. This is shown in Figure 8.4b. The new procedure, therefore, has a new window of twenty-four registers that overlaps with the previous window. The output parameters from the previous window are now input parameters to the new procedure, so the parameters have been passed as desired. Since the local variables from the previous procedure are no longer visible, they are stored safely and will be restored automatically to their previous register numbers when the procedure RETURN occurs. Values can be returned to the calling procedure by again using the overlapping window.

FIGURE 8.4

Circular Register Buffer: (a) current window, (b) after window shift

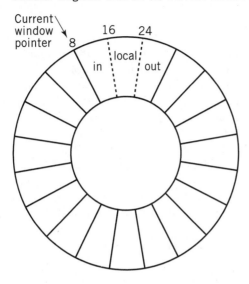

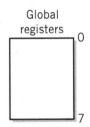

a. Current window

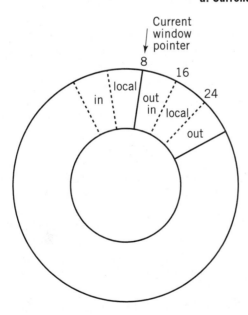

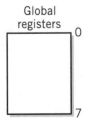

b. After window shift

This method therefore eliminates the need to copy data when moving from procedure to procedure. Unless the amount of data exceeds the number of registers, no data has to be stored during procedure calls and returns. Instead, a single pointer is adjusted to move the window of registers that is available to each procedure.

The bank is built in a circular fashion so that the same window moving operations can be used consistently from any position in the bank. If the procedure depth exceeds the number of available windows, it becomes possible to overlap into the original windows, and it becomes necessary in that case to save the values held in the earlier window to memory before reusing the window. Studies have shown that this situation occurs rarely, even if the number of windows is fairly small, say, six or more.

HANDLING LOAD, STORE, AND BRANCH INSTRUCTIONS   LOAD, STORE, and BRANCH instructions pose a special problem to the implementation of a RISC design. Because LOAD and STORE instructions require memory access, their execution cannot be completed in a single clock cycle. This means that the instruction immediately following a LOAD or STORE instruction in the pipeline may not use the register that is receiving the data from a LOAD or change the data in a register that is being STOREd. Conditional BRANCH instructions are problematical because the instruction following the branch is fetched before the results of the branch are known.

The requirement that the instruction following a LOAD or STORE instruction not use the affected register is known as a **latency** requirement. Some RISC machines provide hardware that "locks out" an instruction that attempts to violate the latency requirement. Most rely instead on the programmer or on the high-level language compiler that generates the program code. For programs written in assembly language, the programmer must be careful that instructions immediately following a LOAD or STORE instruction do not use the affected register. For programs written in high-level language, the compiler assumes the responsibility. It will attempt to generate code that fills the spaces following LOADs and STOREs with other instructions that must be executed anyway. If it is unable to do so, it will fill the space with an instruction that does nothing, called a NO OP (for NO OPeration) instruction.

Some RISC processors take the same approach to branches. By design, the instruction immediately following a branch instruction is always executed. This is true for all branch instructions, both unconditional and conditional and regardless of the result of the condition. It is the responsibility of the programmer or compiler to assure that the instruction following each branch is either a useful instruction unrelated to the branch or a NO OP instruction. Other processors, the Alpha AXP processor and Motorola/IBM Power PC processors, for example, support branch prediction circuitry instead. This method can result in occasional delays within the pipeline, but simplifies programming and other design requirements. There are a number of other solutions to this problem, but they require a slightly different architecture. We will return to this subject when we discuss advanced CPU designs in Section 8.4.

COMPARING RISC AND CISC PERFORMANCE   There has been much argument and debate among CPU designers over the merits of each approach. Comparative performance measurements and studies have not provided a definitive answer because of the wide range of possible measurement standards, the difficulty of setting up equivalent conditions, and the variety of ways in which computers are used.

It has been argued, for example, that the simpler instruction set supported by a RISC architecture results in a larger memory requirement when similar programs are executed on a RISC architecture machine, offsetting the advantage of faster instruction execution. However, studies on overall effect of RISC architecture on memory requirements have been inconclusive. It seems as though RISC programs are larger, but not substantially so, and the increased speed of the RISC instruction set and reduced average instruction size appear to more than compensate for the difference in numbers of instructions executed.

In truth, the various arguments presented on behalf of one architecture over the other have become meaningless. Improved technology has led to new CPU enhancements that combine the advantages and best features of each architecture. The number of instructions on modern RISC machines has increased to reduce program size, aided by faster processing techniques and the availability of increased chip real estate (i.e., more transistors on the chip). Newer CISC architectures feature increased numbers of user registers and more register-oriented instructions. Recent Pentium CPUs are even implemented internally with a RISC-based instruction set that translates most Pentium instructions into fixed length internal instructions called micro-ops for faster execution.

The features and capabilities of recent CISC and RISC CPUs are very similar. Section 8.4 discusses an implementation that is characteristic of nearly every modern CPU architecture and that compensates effectively for the argued differences between the two architectures. The choice of RISC or CISC, or some combination of the two, or something entirely different for new architectural designs, at least for now, simply reflects the preferences and specific goals of the designers.

VLIW and EPIC architectures

VLIW (very-long instruction word) and EPIC (explicitly parallel instruction computer) architectures represent recent approaches to architectural design. VLIW architecture is represented by the Transmeta Crusoe family of CPU processors. The Intel Itanium IA-64 series is based on EPIC architecture. The basic goal of each of these architectures is to increase execution speed by processing instruction operations in parallel. The primary difficulty in doing so results from the sequential order of the instructions in the program. In particular, the data used in an instruction may depend on the result from a previous instruction. This situation is known as a **data dependency.** Also, branches and loops may alter the sequence, resulting in **control dependency.** Data and control dependencies are discussed in more depth in Section 8.4.

The Transmeta Crusoe architecture is based on a 128-bit instruction word called a molecule. The molecule is divided into four 32-bit *atoms*. Each atom represents an operation similar to those of a normal 32-bit instruction word, however, the atoms are designed in such a way that all four operations may be executed simultaneously in separate execution units. Figure 8.5 shows an example of a typical molecule.

The Crusoe CPU provides sixty-four general purpose registers to assure adequate register space for rapid register-to-register processing.

Although a programmer could write programs directly for a Crusoe CPU with the 128-bit word instruction set, that is not the primary goal of the Crusoe architecture. Indeed, the fine details of the instruction set have not been publicly released to date. Instead, the Crusoe CPU is intended for use with a specific software program that translates instruction sets on

FIGURE 8.5

VLIW Format

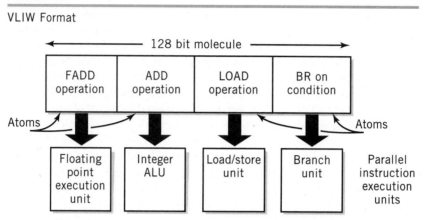

the fly from other types of CPUs to the Crusoe instruction set for execution on the Crusoe CPU. This translator is called a **code-morphing layer.** It is a fundamental component within the Crusoe architecture. It is permanently resident in memory and processes every instruction prior to execution. In addition to instruction translation, the code-morphing layer also reorders the instructions as necessary to eliminate data dependencies and other bottlenecks. Although this sounds like an inefficient way to process instructions, Transmeta has demonstrated that the simplicity of its VLIW design and the sophistication of its code morphing software allow execution of the Pentium instruction set at speeds comparable to the native execution speeds of a Pentium processor. Transmeta claims, with apparent justification, that this simplicity allows a much simpler CPU design, with fewer transistors and a much lower power consumption, resulting from the elimination of complicated hardware implementation features commonly used to achieve high execution speeds in a conventional CPU design.

At present, Transmeta has provided a code-morphing layer only for the Pentium CPU family. If the company is financially successful, however, many computer professionals expect to see code morphing layers for Power PCs and other CPUs.

The EPIC architecture, designed by Intel for its IA-64 processor family, attempts to achieve similar goals by slightly different means. The basic instruction set architecture is new, although Intel has built X86 capability into the CPU to support compatibility with its earlier architecture. The IA-64 offers 128 64-bit general-purpose registers and 128 82-bit floating point registers. All instructions are forty-one bits wide.

Like the VLIW architecture, the EPIC architecture also organizes instructions into bundles prior to CPU execution, however the methodology and goal are somewhat different. In this case, the instructions *do* represent the native instruction set of the architecture. Instructions are presented to the CPU for execution in 128-bit bundles that include a group of three instructions plus five bits that identify the type of each instruction in the bundle.

An assembly language programmer is expected to follow a set of published guidelines that identify dependencies and allow the parallel execution of each bundle. Additionally, bits within each instruction word provide information to the execution unit that identify potential dependencies and other bottlenecks and help the programmer to optimize the code for fast execution. High-level language EPIC compilers must also create code that satisfies the guidelines.

A fundamental difference between the Transmeta VLIW and the Intel EPIC architectures is the placement of responsibility for correct instruction sequencing. The VLIW architecture allows any sequence of instructions to enter the CPU to processing. The code-morphing software, integral to the architecture, handles proper sequencing. The EPIC architecture places the burden on the assembly language programmer or on the program compiler software.

This does not suggest that one architecture is superior to the other. It simply indicates a different approach to the solution of dependencies. Note that the Transmeta VLIW does not allow direct assembly language access to the CPU. *All* program code must be processed through code morphing software. Each architecture offers an interesting new approach to program execution with potential benefits.

8.2 CPU FEATURES AND ENHANCEMENTS

We have already introduced you to the fundamental design of a CPU, represented by an instruction set, registers, and a fetch-execute instruction cycle. Additionally, we have presented some of the bells and whistles that have enhanced CPU capability and performance. Some of the enhancements that were introduced in Chapter 7 include direct support for floating point arithmetic, BCD arithmetic, and multimedia processing, as well as the inclusion of additional addressing modes, which simplify data access, increase potential memory size capability while maintaining reasonable instruction word sizes, and improve list and array processing. In Chapter 8, we have already presented a number of additional enhancements, including features that allow parallel execution of instructions to improve processing speed, register-oriented instructions, circular register buffers, branch prediction support, and integral code morphing software.

One additional feature, **paging,** or **memory address translation,** is of such importance that it is presented here separately, although its overall importance won't be completely evident to you until we discuss its application to memory management and virtual storage in Chapter 15. Every modern CPU architecture includes paging support as a basic architectural feature. Although the words *paging* and *virtual storage* are sometimes used interchangeably, the usage is not quite accurate, since virtual storage requires support from the operating system in addition to the hardware paging support provided within the CPU.

Paging

Paging is a method by which the computer is able to conceptually separate the addresses used in a program from the addresses that actually identify physical locations in memory. The program addresses are referred to as **logical addresses,** since they represent locations in the program, but they do not have any reality outside the program itself. These addresses represent the relative locations of data within the program, branch targets, and the relative locations of the instructions themselves. Logical addresses are also called virtual addresses; the words are used interchangeably. The actual memory addresses are called **physical addresses.** Like the Little Man mailboxes, they have physical reality; that is, they physically exist. Paging creates a correspondence between the logical and physical addresses so that each logical address is automatically and invisibly transformed into a physical address by the computer system during program execution. This transformation is known as **mapping.** Figure 8.6 is a very simple illustration of the basic paging concept. The word "invisibly" is central to the concept.

Although the program in Figure 8.7 has been located in physical memory starting at location 100, the program continues to address its data as though it were located in memory between 0 and 200. Even the program counter is translated to the actual instruction location in physical memory. All of this mapping is performed by hardware logic within the CPU.

The mapping in Figure 8.6 is very straightforward. In this case, it would only be necessary for the system to add an offset of 100 to every logical address to obtain the physical memory address. In a sense this illustration is misleading, since it suggests that the transformation can be represented by a simple arithmetic formula. Figure 8.7 shows another, more complex, example, to illustrate that this is not the case. This example shows that there is no requirement that the mapping be performed in a single piece, or even that the pieces are located consecutively in memory.

Paging provides many important capabilities, including the ability to relocate programs easily from one part of memory to another. As you will see, the ability to relocate programs easily is fundamental to the concept of multitasking. As you've already seen, paging also allows the splitting up of a program into smaller pieces that can then be loaded into different parts of memory, wherever space can be found. This improves the utilization of memory when there are many programs to be fit into memory simultaneously. Paging can also accommodate for the use of the same logical memory locations for two different programs by transforming them into different physical locations, or it can transform two

FIGURE 8.6

Logical to Physical Mapping

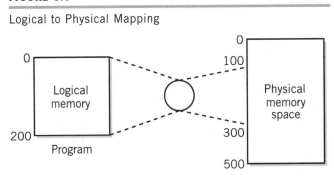

FIGURE 8.7

Another Virtual Storage Mapping

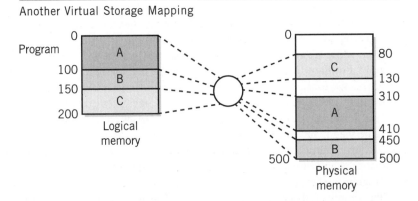

logically independent programs (two different users working with copies of the same editor, for example) and share the same physical memory locations for the program code for both, with independent physical memory data areas for each. As you will see in Chapter 15, it can even be used to make a program think that it has more memory than actually exists on the computer. Thus, it becomes possible to load and execute a 2-megabyte (MB) program, say, in a computer that only has 1MB of actual physical memory.

On the surface, it may appear to you at first that paging is nothing more than another addressing scheme, one that modifies logical program addresses to different physical addresses, much like those discussed in Chapter 7 and in Supplementary Chapter 2. Superficially, there are similarities. Both virtual storage and base addressing enable program relocation. As you will see, both perform their actions within the framework of the fetch-execute cycle.

The most important difference is that normal addressing is done within the context of the program. It is the code within the program that establishes the addressing methods used by the program. As far as the program is concerned, the addresses determined by the program are physical addresses. Paging is done *outside* the program. It is a fundamental part of the design and operation of the CPU itself. When paging is enabled, every address, both program and data, is transformed in the same way. As previously noted, even the address stored in the program counter is transformed. The logical addresses established by the program are usually not the same as the physical address and, in fact, may sometimes not even correspond to a physical address. Furthermore, the logical to physical address mapping is *dynamic*. It can be changed at any time by the operating system software to meet changing conditions within the system. Neither the transformation nor any of these changes are visible to the executing program. If the program instruction says to look for a data value in memory location 250, the program is not aware that the data is actually stored at physical location 17522 and that it was stored at physical location 3111 the last time it was accessed.

The concept used to implement paging is surprisingly simple, although the technical details required to actually build the system are considerably more complex. The mapping from logical address to physical address is performed by looking up the correspondence in a table. For each memory reference in a program, the computer looks up the logical address in the table and finds the corresponding physical address. Thus, every reference to the memory address register in a fetch-execute cycle step is preceded by a table lookup to convert the logical address to its physical memory equivalent. This lookup is implemented in hardware. If there are multiple programs in memory, there is a separate table for each logical program space in use. In most modern CPUs, a memory management unit, or MMU, performs the required steps.

Another way to view paging is shown in Figure 8.8. In this figure, the program generates its addresses in the usual way, as described in Chapters 7 and Supplementary Chapter 2. These are logical addresses. Thus, the view looking at the CPU is logical. The **memory management unit (MMU)** sits in between the CPU and memory and provides the mapping capability that converts the logical addresses to physical addresses that access memory. In this drawing, we have separated the MMU from the CPU, although, in actuality, the MMU is usually considered to be a part of the CPU.

There exist two similar, but slightly different, implementations of address translation. The method in use today is called **paging.** An older, but similar, method, called segmentation, differs from paging mostly in the way blocks are sized and located. This type of segmentation

FIGURE 8.8

An Alternative Way of Looking at Virtual Storage

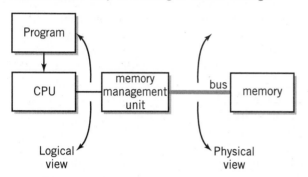

is essentially obsolete. A brief discussion of segmentation will be found in Chapter 15.

Paging divides both logical and physical memory into equally sized blocks. The block size is permanently defined as a parameter of the CPU architecture, and is identical for every block, both logical and physical. Therefore, there is no relationship between the block size and the size or logical design of a program, nor is there any relationship between the block size and the amount of physical memory present in the machine.

Each logical block is called a **page.** The blocks that make up physical memory are called **frames.** The number of pages that make up a program is simply the size of the program divided by the block size. There is usually a bit of wasted logical space at the end of the last page, but if the block size is reasonable, the wasted space is negligible. The number of frames on a particular system is the amount of physical memory installed divided by the block size. There may be fewer, equal, or more pages than frames on a system. Note that if the number of pages in a program exceeds the number of available frames, the entire program cannot be fit into memory at once. This may initially seem like a problem to you, but later we will show you a simple and elegant solution that will turn the "problem" into a feature!

The block size, typically 4 KB, but sometimes less or more, is chosen in such a way that the bits of an address can be naturally divided into a page number and an offset from the beginning of the page. For each program in memory there is a page table that is used for translation from logical to physical memory. The size of each page table is equal to the number of pages in that program. For each page, the page table contains a corresponding frame number pointing to the frame in physical memory that will actually hold the page. Address translation consists of identifying the page number of a logical address, directly from the address, and replacing the page number with its corresponding frame number from the page table. Since the blocks are of equal size, the page offset and frame offset for the address are the same, so the offset is simply carried over. An address translation using the page table is shown in Figure 8.9.

Page tables are stored in memory, like any other program or data. Some CPUs also contain special memory, just for the use of page tables, to expedite the translation process.

Although the paging mechanism is simple enough, there are a number of issues and complicating factors to be considered. Among the questions to be answered are how the page tables are created, where the page tables are stored in memory and how they are accessed, what determines where pages are to be located in physical memory, and how to realize and optimize benefits from paging. The answers to these questions lie in the role of the operating system as manager for the virtual storage operation that utilizes paging.

The word *virtual* in the expression *virtual storage* is used in the same way that it is used to describe the image in a flat mirror. The image in the mirror is known in physics as a virtual image. It appears behind the mirror and seems very real. But you and I both know that the image is not real; it can't exist behind the mirror, since the mirror is flat. (And, besides,

FIGURE 8.9

The Page Translation Process

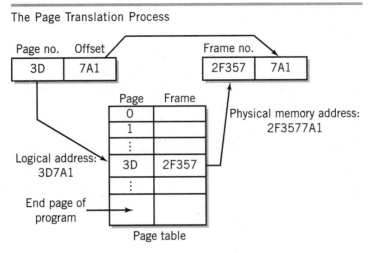

Page table

the mirror is mounted on a wall!) In both cases the word *virtual* describes a situation that appears to be real, but is, in fact, different from what it seems. Thus, to the 2MB program, it seems as though there are at least two million address locations available on the machine, but it's all done with mirrors! Stated differently, virtual means you can see it, but it *isn't* real. As a hint of things to come, consider the fact that a memory frame can hold different pages at different times, simply by reassigning the frame to different pages in the page table. Thus a frame can represent many different pages during the course of program execution.

Virtual storage is an important example of the concept of synergy between the system hardware and the operating system software. We must defer further discussion of virtual storage to Chapter 15, where we will be able to discuss the implementation and use of paging and virtual storage in more depth. At that time we shall discuss the role of the operating system in virtual storage management and the interrelationship between the OS software and virtual storage hardware.

8.3 MEMORY ENHANCEMENTS

Within the instruction fetch-execute cycle, the slowest steps are those that require memory access. Therefore, any improvement in memory access can have a major impact on program processing speed.

The memory in modern computers is usually made up of dynamic random access memory circuit chips. DRAM is inexpensive. Each DRAM chip is capable of storing millions of bits of data. Dynamic RAM has one major drawback, however. With today's fast CPUs, the access time of DRAM is too slow to keep up with the CPU, and delays must be inserted into the LOAD/STORE execution pipeline to allow memory to keep up. Thus, the use of DRAM is a potential bottleneck in processing. Instructions must be fetched from memory and data must be moved from memory into registers for processing.

The fetch-execute CPU implementation introduced in Section 8.4 reduces instruction fetch delay to a minimum with modern instruction prefetch and branch control technologies, and the increased adoption of RISC methodologies also reduces delays by maximizing the use of register-to-register instructions. Nonetheless, memory accesses are always required to move the data from memory to register and back, and improvements in memory access still have an impact on processing speed.

As mentioned in Chapter 7, static RAM, or SRAM, is an alternative type of random access memory that is two to three times as fast as DRAM. The inherent memory capacity of SRAM is severely limited, however. SRAM design requires a lot of chip real estate compared to DRAM, due to the fact that SRAM circuitry is more complex and generates a lot of heat that must be dissipated. One or two MB of SRAM requires more space than 64 MB of DRAM, and will cost considerably more.

With today's memory requirements, SRAM is not a practical solution for large amounts of memory except in very expensive computers; therefore, designers have created alternative approaches to fulfill the need for faster memory access. Three different approaches are commonly used to enhance the performance of memory:

- Wide path memory access
- Memory interleaving
- Cache memory

These three methods are complementary. Each has slightly different applicability, and they may be used together in any combination to achieve a particular goal. Of these techniques, the use of cache memory has the most profound effect on system performance.

A fourth approach, expanded memory, is also occasionally included, but expanded memory has a different purpose, specifically, to provide a large amount of storage that can be used as a buffer to minimize disk accesses. Today, disk drives routinely include substantial memory buffers, and, together with the large amounts of conventional computer memory available, expanded storage is rarely worthwhile. IBM has eliminated it from its current mainframe offerings.

Wide Path Memory Access

The simplest means to increase memory access is to widen the data path so as to read or write several bytes or words between the CPU and memory with each access; this technique is known as **wide path memory access.** Instead of reading 1 byte at a time, for example, the system can retrieve 2, 4, or even 8 bytes, simultaneously. Most instructions are several bytes long, in any case, and most data is at least 2 bytes, and frequently more. This solution can be implemented easily by widening the bus data path and using a larger memory data register. The system bus on most modern CPUs, for example, has a 64-bit data path and is commonly used to read or write 8 bytes of data with a single memory access. Within the CPU, these bytes can be separated as required and processed in the usual way. With modern CPU implementation, instruction groups can be passed directly to the instruction unit for parallel execution. As the number of bytes simultaneously accessed is increased, there is a diminishing rate of return, since the circuitry required to separate and direct the bytes to their correct locations increases in complexity, fast memory access becomes more difficult, and yet it becomes less likely that the extra bytes will actually be used. Even a 64-bit data path is adequate to assure that a pipeline will remain filled and bursts of consecutive 64-bit reads or writes can handle situations that require high-speed access to large blocks of data. Very few systems read and write more than 8 bytes at a time. Most systems read and write a fixed number of bytes at a time, but there are a few systems that can actually read and write a variable number of bytes.

Because of its simplicity, this technique is widely used.

Memory Interleaving

Another method for increasing the effective rate of memory access is to divide memory into parts, called **memory interleaving,** so that it is possible to access more than one location at a time. Then, each part would have its own address register and data register, and each part is independently accessible. Memory can then accept one read/write request from each part simultaneously. Although it might seem to you that the obvious way to divide up memory would be in blocks, for example, by separating the high addresses into one block and the low addresses into the other, it turns out that as a practical matter it is usually more useful to divide the memory so that successive access points, say, groups of 8 bytes (see above), are in different blocks. Breaking memory up this way is known as *n*-**way interleaving,** where a value of 2 or 4 or some other value is substituted for *n,* depending on the number of separate blocks. For example, two-way interleaving would be designed so that it would be possible to access an odd memory address and an even memory address concurrently. If 8-byte wide access is provided, this would allow the concurrent access to 16 successive bytes at a time. A memory with eight-way interleaving would allow access to eight different locations simultaneously, but the system could not access locations 0, 8, 16, or 24 at the same time, for instance, nor 1, 9, 17, or 25. It *could* access locations 16 and 25 or 30 and 31 concurrently, however. Since memory accesses tend to be successive, memory interleaving can be effective. A diagram of four-way interleaving is shown in Figure 8.10.

This method is particularly applicable when multiple devices require access to the same memory. The IBM mainframe architecture, for example, is designed to allow multiple CPUs to access a common memory area; the I/O channel subsystem also has access to

FIGURE 8.10

Four-way Memory Interleaving

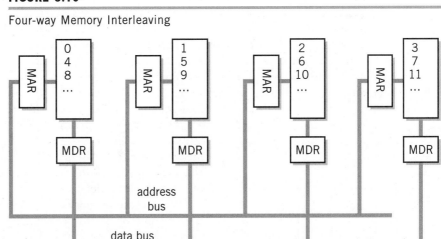

the storage area. Thus, several different components may make memory requests at the same time. The IBM S/3033 computer, for example, partitioned memory into eight **logical storage elements.** Each element can independently accept a memory request. Thus, eight memory requests can be processed concurrently.

The personal computer memory that holds images while they are being displayed, known as video RAM, is another example. Changes to part of the video RAM can be made at the same time that another part of the video RAM is being used to produce the actual display on the monitor.

Cache Memory

A different strategy is to position a small amount of high-speed memory, for example, SRAM, between the CPU and main storage. This high-speed memory is invisible to the programmer and cannot be directly addressed in the usual way by the CPU. Because it represents a "secret" storage area, it is called *cache memory*. This concept is illustrated in Figure 8.11.

Cache memory is organized differently than regular memory. Cache memory is organized into blocks. Each block provides a small amount of storage, perhaps 8 or 16 bytes worth. The block will be used to hold an exact reproduction of a corresponding amount of storage from somewhere in main memory. Each block also holds a **tag.** The tag identifies the location in main memory that corresponds to the data being held in that block. In other words, taken together, the tags act as a directory that can be used to determine exactly which storage locations from main memory are also available in the cache memory. A typical 64KB cache memory might consist of 8000 (actually 8192) 8-byte blocks, each with tag.

A simplified, step-by-step illustration of the use of cache memory is shown in Figure 8.12. Every CPU request to main memory, whether data or instruction, is seen first by cache memory. (Note that cache memory deals with *physical* memory requests. Any memory translation takes place within the CPU prior to the request.) A hardware **cache controller** checks the tags to determine if the memory location of the request is presently stored within the cache. If it is, the cache memory is used as if it were main memory. If the request is a read, the corresponding word from cache memory is simply passed to the CPU. Similarly, if the request is a write, the data from the CPU is stored in the appropriate cache memory location. Satisfying a request in this way is known as a **hit.**

If the required memory data is not already present in cache memory, an extra step is required. In this case, a cache-block-sized block of memory that includes the required location is copied from memory to the cache. The unit of transfer between storage and cache memory is sometimes called a **cache line.** Once this is done, the transfer is made to or from cache memory, as before. The situation in which the request is not already present in cache memory is known as a **miss.** The ratio of hits to the total number of requests is known as the **hit ratio.**

When cache memory is full, some block in cache memory must be selected for replacement. Various algorithms have been implemented by different computer designers to make this selection, but most commonly,

FIGURE 8.11

Cache Memory

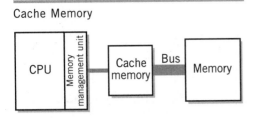

FIGURE 8.12

Step-by-Step Use of Cache

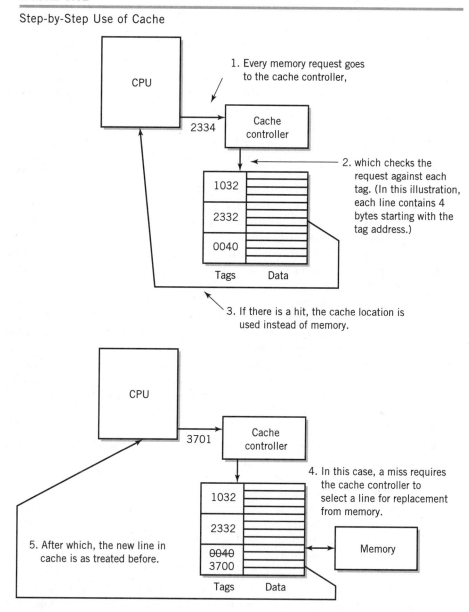

some variation on a *least recently used,* or *LRU,* algorithm is used. An LRU algorithm, as the name implies, keeps track of the usage of each block and replaces the block that was last used the longest time ago.

Cache blocks that have been read, but not altered, can simply be read over during replacement. Memory write requests impose an additional burden on cache memory operations, since written data must also be written to the main memory to protect the integrity of the program and its data. Two different methods of handling the process of returning changed data from cache to main storage are in common use. The first method, **write through,** writes data back to the main memory immediately upon change in the cache. This method has the advantage that the two copies, cache and main memory, are always kept identical. Some designers use an alternative technique known variously as *store in, write back,* or *copy back.* With this technique, the changed data is simply held in cache until the cache line is to be replaced. The **write back** method is faster, since writes to memory are made only when a cache line is actually replaced, but more care is required in the design to ensure that there are no circumstances under which data loss could occur. If two different programs were using the same data in separate cache blocks, for example, and one program changed the data, the design must assure that the other program has access to the updated data.

The entire cache operation is managed by the cache controller. This includes tag searching and matching, write through or write back, and implementation of the algorithm that is used for cache block replacement. The CPU and software are unaware of the presence of cache memory and the activities of the cache controller. We note in passing that to be effective, these operations must be controlled completely by hardware. It is possible to envision using a program to implement the cache block replacement algorithm, for example, but this is not feasible. Since memory accesses would be required to execute the program, this would defeat the entire purpose of cache memory, which is to provide access quickly to a single memory location.

Cache memory works due to a principle known as **locality of reference.** The locality of reference principle states that at any given time, most memory references will be confined to one or a few small regions of memory. If you consider the way that you were taught to write programs, this principle makes sense. Instructions are normally executed sequentially; therefore, adjoining words are likely to be accessed. In a well-written program, most of the instructions being executed at a particular time are part of a small loop or a small procedure or function. Likewise, the data for the program is likely taken from an array. Variables for the program are all stored together. Studies have verified the validity of the locality principle. Cache memory hit ratios of 90 percent and above are common with just a small amount of cache. Since requests that can be fulfilled by the cache memory are fulfilled much faster, the cache memory technique can have a significant impact on the overall performance of the system. Program execution speed improvements of 50 percent and more are common.

Some modern architectures even provide program instructions to request cache preloading for data or instructions that will be needed soon. This improves execution speed even more. Also, some system designers interleave the cache or implement separate caches for instructions and data. This allows even more rapid access, since the instruction and its operands can be accessed simultaneously much of the time. Furthermore, design of a separate instruction cache can be simplified, since there is no need to write the instruction cache back to main memory if the architecture imposes a pure coding requirement on the programmer. The trade-off is that accommodating separate instruction and data caches requires additional circuit complexity, and many system designers opt instead for a combined, or *unified,* cache that holds both data and instructions.

It is also possible to provide more than one level of cache memory. Consider the two-level cache memory shown in Figure 8.13. This memory will work as follows. The operation begins when the CPU requests an instruction (or piece of data) be read (or written) from memory. If the cache controller for the level closest to the CPU, which we'll call level 1, determines that the requested memory location is presently in the level 1 cache, the instruction is immediately read into the CPU.

Suppose, however, that the instruction is *not* presently in level 1 cache. In this case, the request is passed on to the controller for level 2 cache. Level 2 cache works in exactly the same way as level 1 cache. If the instruction is presently in the level 2 cache, a cache line containing the instruction is moved to the level 1 cache and then to the CPU. If not, then the level 2 cache controller requests a level 2 cache line from memory, the level 1 cache receives a cache line from the level 2 cache, and the instruction is transferred to the CPU. This technique could be expanded to more levels, but there is usually little reason for doing so.

What does the second level buy us? Many system designers believe that more cache would improve performance enough to be worthwhile. In this case, the system designers provide a second level of cache, external to the chip. A personal computer secondary cache commonly provides an additional 512KB–1 MB of cache. The PowerPC 7451 provides 32KB of L1 data cache, 32 KB of L1 instruction cache, and a 256KB level 2 cache within the same package as the CPU. The use of a dedicated bus between level 1 cache and level 2 cache provides faster response than connecting the level 1 cache to memory or to a level 2 cache on the regular memory bus. It also supports 1 or 2 MB of external L3 cache with a separate high-speed dedicated bus. Each CPU in a multiprocessor system has its own L1 and L2 cache memory. The IBM mainframe system configuration uses the level 2 cache differently. For configurations with multiple CPUs, each CPU has its own level 1 cache (which IBM calls a high-speed buffer). Level 2 cache is shared by all the CPUs in the configuration.

To be useful, the second level of cache must have significantly more memory than the first level; otherwise, the two cache levels would contain the same data, and the secondary cache would serve no purpose. It is also normal to provide a larger cache line in the secondary cache. This increases the likelihood that requests to the secondary cache can be met without going out to main memory every time.

It should be noted that it is possible to have a situation in which each CPU in a multiprocessor system has the same memory locations stored in its own private cache memory, and that the data differs in each, due to processing. In this case, there is a possibility of the memory data being corrupted as each CPU attempts to write its own version back to memory. Clearly this situation is not acceptable; the design of CPUs with individual cache memory

FIGURE 8.13

Two-Level Cache

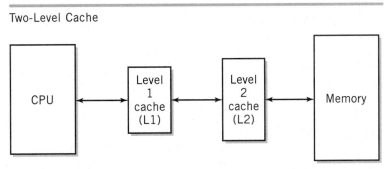

requires a method of synchronizing the data stored in cache memory if the CPUs are to be used in multiprocessing configurations. A common approach is to require each processor to monitor the memory accesses of all other CPUs in the system, so that conflicts may be prevented before they occur. This technique is known as **memory snooping.**

A caching technique can also be used to reduce the time necessary to access data from a disk. In this case, part of main memory can be allocated for use as a **disk cache.** When a disk read or write request is made, the system checks the disk cache first. If the required data is present, no disk access is necessary; otherwise, a disk cache line made up of several adjoining disk blocks is moved from the disk into the disk cache area of memory. We mentioned earlier that most disk manufacturers also provide separate buffer memory for this purpose.

As a final note, you should understand that the cache memory provided in a virtual storage-based system is on the physical side of the mapping shown in Figure 8.8. The goals of cache memory and virtual storage are different, and it is common in modern systems to provide both. The goal of cache memory is to improve the speed of memory access. The goal of virtual storage is to increase the perceived amount of memory available in a system. Modern CPUs generally include both a cache controller and virtual storage support. Most also provide built-in cache memory as a standard feature.

8.4 MODERN CPU PROCESSING METHODS

Introduction

Since the purpose of a computer is to execute instructions, the performance of a computer is directly related to the number of instructions that the computer can execute in a given amount of time. There are a number of different ways to increase the instruction execution performance of a computer. One method is to provide a number of CPUs in the computer rather than just one. Since a single CPU can process only one instruction at a time, each additional CPU would, in theory, multiply the performance of the computer by the number of CPUs included.

In practice, the use of multiple CPUs is common and effective, especially in large systems. The technique, called multiprocessing, is discussed at length in Chapter 11. Of more interest at the moment are approaches that can be used to improve the performance of an individual CPU.

In our introduction to CPU architectures, we suggested a number of possibilities. Some of these require new design, such as the large number of registers and register-to-register instructions that are characteristic of RISC architectures. Even with older instruction sets, it is sometimes possible to create an intermediate RISC-type instruction set that is used within the CPU as a substitute for the more complex, original instruction set. This approach is used in recent Pentium CPUs, among others.

Another difficulty to be overcome when attempting system optimization is that some computer instructions inherently require a large number of steps. Integer division and floating point arithmetic instructions are in this category. Obviously, CPU architects cannot create modern instruction sets that omit these instructions.

In this section, we consider a number of different, but interrelated, approaches to CPU optimization that are applicable to nearly any CPU design. Interestingly enough, you will see that similar approaches can be found in automobile plants and restaurants.

In Chapter 7, you learned that the fetch-execute cycle is the basic operation by which instructions get executed. You also observed that the steps in a fetch-execute cycle generally must be performed in a particular sequence: an instruction must be fetched and identified before it can be executed, for example. Otherwise the machine would have no way of knowing what to execute. And so on, step by step, through the entire instruction cycle. (*The first step in cooking spaghetti is to add water to the pot.*) CPU performance can be improved by any method that can perform the fetch-execute cycle steps more quickly or more efficiently.

Then, a program is executed by performing the fetch-execute cycle in a specified sequence, where the sequence is sometimes determined by the program itself during execution. To be provably correct during program execution, the sequence must be maintained and data dependencies resolved in proper order. (*The "cook spaghetti," "drain spaghetti," and "prepare sauce" instructions must be completed before the sauce is mixed into the spaghetti.*)

Observe that the limitation to performance results from the serial nature of CPU processing: each instruction requires a sequence of fetch-execute cycle steps, and the program requires the execution of a sequence of these instructions. Thus, the keys to increased performance must rely on methods that reduce the time required for each step in the fetch-execute cycle and, ultimately, each instruction in the program.

Fetch-Execute Cycle Timing Issues

As a first step, consider the problem of controlling the timing of each step in the fetch-execute cycle to guarantee perfect CPU operation, to assure that each step follows the previous step, in perfect order, as quickly as possible. There must be enough time between steps to assure that each operation is complete and that data is where it is supposed to be before the next step takes place. As you saw in Chapter 7, most steps in the fetch-execute cycle work by copying, combining, or moving data between various registers. When data is copied, combined, or moved between registers, it takes a short, but finite, amount of time for the data to "settle down" in the new register, that is, for the results of the operation to be correct. This occurs in part, because the electronic switches that connect the registers operate at slightly different speeds. (We're actually talking billionths of a second here!) Also, design allowances must be made for the fact that some operations take longer than others; for example, addition takes more time than a simple data movement. Even more significant is the amount of time that it takes for the address stored in the MAR to activate the correct address in memory. The latter time factor is due to the complex electronic circuitry that is required to identify one group of memory cells out of several million or billion possibilities. Cache memory significantly reduces the time needed to access memory.

To assure adequate time for each step, the times at which different events take place are synchronized to the pulses of an electronic clock. The **clock** provides a master control as to when each step in the instruction cycle takes place. The pulses of the clock are separated sufficiently to assure that each step has time to complete, with the data settled down, before the results of that step are required by the next step. Thus, use of a faster clock alone does not work if the circuitry cannot keep up.

A timing cycle for a Little Man ADD instruction is shown in Figure 8.14. Each block in the diagram represents one step of the fetch-execute cycle. Certain steps that do not have to access memory can actually be performed at the same time. This can reduce the overall number of cycles required for the instruction, which speeds up the computer. In this diagram, the data from the program counter has been copied into the memory address register in the first step and is no longer needed. Therefore, the program counter can be incremented at any time after the first step. In Figure 8.14 the PC is incremented in parallel with the MDR → IR step. As shown in the figure, the ADD instruction is completed in four clock cycles.

The built-in clock runs continuously whenever the power to the computer is on. The frequency of its pulses is controlled by a quartz crystal, similar to that which might control your wristwatch. The frequency of the clock and the number of steps required by each instruction determine the speed with which the computer performs useful work.

The pulses of the clock are combined with the data in the instruction register to control electronic switches that open and close in the right sequence to move data from register to register in accordance with the instruction cycle for the particular instruction. The memory activation line described in Section 7.3 is an example of a timing line. The activation line is set up so that it will not turn on until the correct address decode line in the MAR has had time to settle down. If this were not the case, several address lines might be partially turned on, and the data transferred between the memory and MDR might be incorrect. Such errors can obviously not be tolerated, so it is important to control timing accurately.

Conceptually, each pulse of the clock is used to control one step in the sequence, but sometimes, additional pulses might be used to control different details within a single step. For example, some implementations of CPUs actually break down each step in the fetch-execute cycle into several "microcycle" steps. Such an implementation is discussed briefly in Section 10.4. In this case, individual clock pulses control the microcycle steps, and several clock pulses are required for each F-E step. Of course, an implication of this approach is that the clock in this implementation runs at a much higher speed than the clock in an implementation that uses a single clock pulse for each F-E step.

The clock in the original IBM PC, for example, ran at 4.77 MHz (MHz is pronounced megahertz), which meant that the machine could perform 4.77 million steps every second. If a typical instruction in the IBM PC requires about ten steps, then the original IBM PC could execute about (4.77/10) or about 0.5 million PC instructions per second. A PC running at 8 MHz, with everything else equal, would perform approximately twice as fast.

There are several factors that determine the number of instructions that a computer can perform in a second. Obviously the clock speed is one major factor. Many current PC computers run their clocks at 2 GHz or more to achieve higher instruction cycle rates.

FIGURE 8.I4

Fetch-Execute Timing Diagram

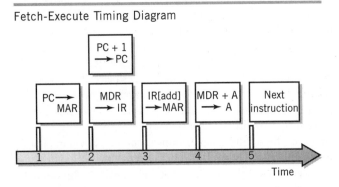

A Model for Improved CPU Performance

The current model of a CPU uses three primary, interrelated techniques to address the limitations of the conventional CU/ALU model and to improve performance.

- Implementation of the fetch-execute cycle is divided into two separate units: a fetch unit to retrieve and decode instructions and an execution unit to perform the actual instruction operation. This allows independent, concurrent operation of the two parts of the fetch-execute cycle.

- The model uses an assembly line technique called **pipelining** to allow overlapping between the fetch-execute cycles of sequences of instructions. This reduces the average time needed to complete an instruction.

- The model provides separate execution units for different types of instructions. This makes it possible to separate instructions with different numbers of execution steps for more efficient processing. It also allows the parallel execution of unrelated instructions by directing each instruction to its own execution unit. You have already seen this method applied to the Transmeta and Itanium architectures in Section 8.1

We next consider each of these techniques in turn.

SEPARATE FETCH UNIT/EXECUTE UNIT Picture a modified Little Man Computer in which the Little Man has been given an assistant. The assistant will fetch and decode the instructions from the mailboxes at a pace that allows the Little Man to spend his time executing instructions, one after another. Note that a similar division of labor is used in a restaurant: waiters and waitresses gather the food orders from the customers and pass them to the cooks for processing.

The current CPU model divides the CPU similarly into two units, which correspond roughly to the fetch and execute parts of the instruction cycle. To achieve maximum performance, these two parts operate as independently from each other as possible, recognizing, of course, that an instruction must be fetched before it can be decoded and executed. Figure 8.15 illustrates this alternative CPU organization.

The fetch portion of the CPU consists of an instruction fetch unit and an instruction decode unit. Instructions are fetched from memory by the fetch unit, based on the current address stored in an instruction pointer (IP) register. The fetch unit is designed to fetch several instructions in parallel. The IP register effectively acts as a program counter, but is given a different name to emphasize that there are a number of instructions in the pipeline simultaneously. The address in the IP register is a logical address. The addressing unit translates the IP register address into a physical memory address for fetching, using whatever techniques are built into the particular CPU. There is a bus interface unit that provides the logic and memory registers necessary to address memory over the bus. Once an instruction is fetched, it is held in a buffer until it can be decoded and executed. The number of instructions held will depend upon the size of each instruction, the width of the memory bus, and the size of the buffer. As instructions are executed, the fetch unit takes advantage of time when the bus is not otherwise being used and attempts to keep the buffer filled with instructions. In general, modern memory buses are wide enough and fast enough that they do not limit instruction retrieval.

FIGURE 8.15

Alternative CPU Organization

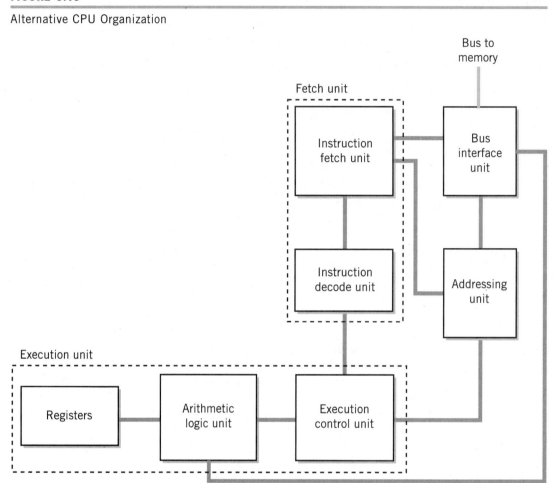

Instructions in the fetch unit buffer are sent to the instruction decoder unit. The decoder unit identifies the op code. From the op code it determines the type of the instruction. If the instruction set is made up of variable length instructions, it also determines the length of the particular instruction. The decoder then assembles the complete instruction with its operands, ready for execution.

The **execution unit** contains the arithmetic/logic unit and the portion of the control unit that identifies and controls the steps that comprise the execution part for each different instruction. The remainder of what we previously called the control unit is distributed throughout the model, controlling the fetching and decoding of instructions at the correct times, and in the correct order, address generation for instructions and operands, and so forth. The ALU provides the usual computational abilities for the general registers and condition flags.

When the execution unit is ready for an instruction, the instruction decoder unit passes the new instruction to the control unit for execution. Instruction operands requiring memory references are sent to the addressing unit. The addressing unit determines the memory address required, and the appropriate data read or write request is then processed by the bus interface unit.

The bus interface and addressing units operate independently of the instruction pipeline and provide services to the fetch, decode, and execution units as requested by each unit.

Pipelining

Look at Figure 8.14 again. In the figure, there are two stages to the execution phase of the instruction cycle. If each stage is implemented separately, so that the instruction simply passes from one stage to the next as it is executed, only one stage is in use at any given time. If there are more steps in the cycle, the same is still true. Thus, to speed up processing even more, modern computers overlap instructions, so that more than one instruction is being worked on at a time. This method is known as **pipelining.** The pipelining concept is one of the major advances in modern computing design. It has been responsible for large increases in program execution speed.

In its simplest form, the idea of pipelining is that as each instruction completes a step, the following instruction moves into the stage just vacated. Thus, when the first instruction is completed, the next one is already one stage short of completion. If there are many steps in the fetch-execute cycle, we can have several instructions at various points in the cycle. The method is similar to an automobile assembly line, where several cars are in different degrees of production at the same time. It still takes the same amount of time to complete one instruction cycle (or one car), but the pipelining technique results in a large overall increase in the average number of instructions performed in a given time.

Of course, a branch instruction may invalidate all the instructions in the pipeline at that instant if the branch is taken, and the computer still must have the data from the previous instruction if the next instruction requires it in order to proceed. Modern computers use a variety of techniques to compensate for the branching problem. One common approach is to maintain two or more separate pipelines so that instructions from both possible outcomes can be processed until the direction of the branch is clear. Another approach attempts to predict the probable branch path based on the history of previous execution of the same instruction. The problem of waiting for data results from previous instructions can be alleviated by separating the instructions so that they are not executed one right after the other. Many modern computer designs contain logic that can reorder instructions as they are executed to keep the pipelines full and to minimize situations where a delay is necessary. **Instruction reordering** also makes it possible to provide parallel pipelines, with duplicate CPU logic, so that multiple instructions can actually be executed simultaneously. This technique is equivalent to providing multiple car assembly lines. It is known as superscalar processing. We will look at superscalar processing again in the next section.

Pipelining and instruction reordering complicate the electronic circuitry required for the computer and also require careful design to eliminate the possibility of errors occurring under unusual sequences of instructions. Despite the added complexity, these methods are now generally accepted as a means for meeting the demand for more and more computer power.

A diagram illustrating pipelining is shown in Figure 8.16. For simplicity, instruction reordering has not been included. The figure shows three instructions, one for each row in

FIGURE 8.16

Pipelining

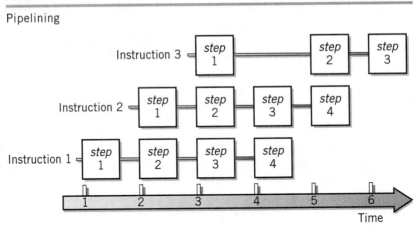

the diagram. The "steps" in the diagram represent the sequence of steps in the fetch-execute cycle for each instruction. Timing marks are indicated along the horizontal axis. The F-E cycle for instruction 3 shows a delay between step 1 and step 2; such a delay might result because the second step of the instruction needs a result from step 3 of the previous instruction, for example, the data in a particular register.

MULTIPLE, PARALLEL EXECUTION UNITS   It is not useful to pipe different types of instructions through a single pipeline. Different instructions have different numbers of steps in their cycles and, also, there are differences in each step. Instead, the instruction decode unit steers instructions into specific execution units. Each execution unit provides a pipeline that is optimized for one general type of instruction. Typically, a modern CPU will have a LOAD/STORE unit, an integer arithmetic unit, a floating-point arithmetic unit, and a branch unit. More powerful CPUs may have multiple execution units for the more commonly used instruction types and, perhaps, may provide other types of execution units as well.

Again, an analogy may aid in understanding the concept of multiple, parallel execution units. A simple automobile plant analogy would note that most automobile plants have separate assembly lines for different car models. The most popular models might have multiple assembly lines operating in parallel.

The use of multiple execution units operating in parallel makes it possible to perform the actual execution of several instructions simultaneously.

Scalar and Superscalar Processor Organization

As you are aware from the previous discussion, modern CPUs achieve high performance by separating the two major phases of the fetch-execute cycle into separate components, then further separating the execution phase into a number of independent execution units, each with pipeline capability. Once a pipeline is filled, an execution unit can complete an instruction with each clock tick. With a single execution unit pipeline, ignoring holes in the pipeline resulting from different instruction types and branch conditions, the CPU can average instruction execution approximately equal to the clock speed of the machine. A processor fulfilling this condition is called a **scalar** processor.

With multiple execution units it is possible to process instructions in parallel, with an average rate of more than one instruction per clock cycle. The ability to process more than one instruction per clock cycle is known as **superscalar processing.** Most modern CPUs implement superscalar processing to some degree. Superscalar processing can increase the throughput by double or more. Commonly, current CPU designs produce speed increases of between two and five times.

It is important to remember that pipelining and superscalar processing techniques do not affect the cycle time of any individual instruction. An instruction fetch-execute cycle that requires six clock cycles from start to finish will require six clock cycles whether instructions are performed one at a time or pipelined in parallel with a dozen other instructions. It is the average instruction cycle time that is improved by performing some form of parallel execution. If an individual instruction must be completed for any reason before another can be executed, the CPU must stall for the full cycle time of the first instruction.

Figure 8.17 illustrates the difference between scalar and superscalar processing with pipelining in the execution unit. In the illustration the execution phase of the fetch-execute cycle is divided into three parts that can be executed separately. Thus, the diagram is divided into steps that fetch, decode, execute, and write back the results of the execute operation. Presumably, each step is carried out by a separate component within the execution unit. To simplify the illustration, we have also assumed that in each case the pipeline

FIGURE 8.17

Scalar versus Superscalar Processing

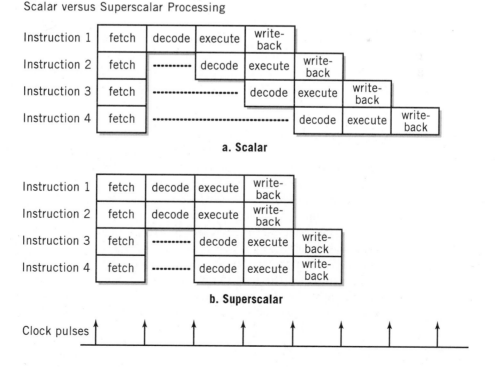

a. Scalar

b. Superscalar

is full. Generally, a single fetch unit pipeline is sufficient to fetch multiple instructions, even when multiple execution units are present.

In the scalar processor, Figure 8.17a, each step is assumed to take one clock cycle. If the instructions are all of the same length, they will finish consecutively, as shown in the diagram. More complexity in the instruction set will create bubbles in the pipeline, but does not alter the basic idea that we are illustrating. Panel b of the illustration assumes the presence of two execution units. It also assumes that the instructions executing in parallel are independent of each other; that is, the execution of one does not depend upon results from the other. Therefore, two instructions can be executed at a time in parallel, resulting in a substantial improvement in overall instruction completion performance.

Superscalar processing complicates the design of a CPU considerably. There are a number of difficult technical issues that must be resolved to make it possible to execute multiple instructions simultaneously. The most important of these are

- Problems that arise from instructions completing in the wrong order.
- Changes in program flow due to branch instructions.
- Conflicts for internal CPU resources, particularly general-purpose registers.

OUT-OF-ORDER PROCESSING Out-of-order instruction execution can cause problems because a later instruction may depend on the results from an earlier instruction. This situation is known as a **hazard** or a *dependency*. If the later instruction completes ahead of the earlier one, the effect of the earlier instruction upon the later cannot be satisfied. The most common type of a dependency is a **data dependency.** This is a situation in which the later instruction is supposed to use the results from the earlier instruction in its calculation. There are other types of dependencies also.

With multiple execution units, it is possible for instructions to complete in the wrong order. There are a number of ways in which this can occur. In the simplest case, an instruction with many steps in its cycle may finish after an instruction with just a few steps, even if it started earlier. As a simple example, a MULTIPLY instruction takes longer to execute than a MOVE or ADD instruction. If a MULTIPLY instruction is followed in the program by an ADD instruction that adds a constant to the results of the multiplication, the result will be incorrect if the ADD instruction is allowed to complete ahead of the MULTIPLY instruction. This is an example of data dependency. Data dependency can take several different forms.

Many data dependencies are sufficiently obvious that they can be detected by the CPU. In this case, execution of the dependent instruction is suspended until the results of the earlier instruction are available. This suspension may, itself, cause out-of-order execution, since it may allow another, still later, instruction to complete ahead of the suspended instruction. Some CPUs provide reservation stations within each execution unit or a general instruction pool to hold suspended instructions so that the execution unit may continue processing other instructions.

Finally, some systems intentionally execute instructions out of order. These CPUs can actually search ahead for instructions without apparent dependencies, to keep the execution units busy. The Intel P6 CPU, for example, can search 20 to 30 instructions ahead, if necessary, to find instructions available for execution.

BRANCH INSTRUCTION PROCESSING Branch instructions must always be processed ahead of subsequent instructions, since the addresses of the proper subsequent instructions to fetch are determined from the branch instruction. For unconditional branch instructions, this is simple. Branch instructions are identified immediately as they enter the instruction fetch pipeline. The address in the instruction is decoded and used to fill the instruction fetch pipeline with instructions from the new location. Normally, no delay is incurred.

Unfortunately, conditional branch instructions are more difficult, because the condition decision may depend on the results from instructions that have not yet been executed. These situations are known as *flow* or *branch dependencies.* If the wrong branch is in the pipeline, the pipeline must be flushed and refilled, wasting time. Worse yet, an instruction from the wrong branch, that is, one that should not have been executed, can alter a previous result that is still needed.

The solution to the conditional branching problem may be broken into two parts: methods to optimize correct branch selection and methods to prevent errors as a result of conditional branch instructions. Selection of the wrong branch is time wasting, but not fatal. By contrast, incorrect results *must* be prevented.

Errors are prevented by setting the following guideline: although instructions may be executed out of order, they must be completed in the correct order. Since branches and subtle data dependencies can occur, the execution of an instruction out of order may or may not be valid, so the instruction is executed *speculatively,* that is, on the assumption that its execution will be useful. For this purpose, a separate bank of registers is used to hold results from these instructions until previous instructions are complete. The results are then transferred to their actual register and memory locations, in correct program instruction order. This technique of processing is known as **speculative execution.** On occasion, the results from some speculatively executed instructions must be thrown away, but on the whole, speculative execution results in a performance boost sufficient to justify the extra complexity required.

A few systems place the burden for error prevention on the assembly language programmer or program language compiler by requiring that a certain number of instructions following a conditional branch instruction be independent of the branch. In these systems, one or more instructions sequentially following the branch are *always* executed, regardless of the outcome of the branch.

There are various creative methods that are used in CPUs to optimize conditional branch processing. One possible solution to this problem is to maintain two separate instruction fetch pipelines, one for each possible branch outcome. Instructions may be executed speculatively from *both* branches until the correct pipeline is known. Another solution is to have the CPU attempt to predict the correct path based on program usage or past performance. A loop, for example, may be expected to execute many times before exiting. Some systems provide a **branch history table,** a small amount of memory built into the CPU that maintains a record of previous choices for each of several branch instructions that have been used in the program being executed to aid in prediction. A few systems even include a "hint" bit in the branch instruction word that can be set by the programmer to tell the CPU the more probable outcome of the branch. Of course, when a branch prediction is incorrect, there is a time delay to purge and refill the fetch pipeline and speculative instructions, but, overall, branch prediction is effective.

CONFLICT OF RESOURCES Conflicts between instructions that use the same registers can be prevented by using the same bank of registers that is used to hold the results of speculative instructions until instruction completion. This register bank is given different names by different vendors. They are called variously **rename registers** or **logical registers** or **register alias tables.** The registers in the bank can be renamed to correspond logically to any physical register and assigned to any execution unit. This would allow two instructions using the "same" register to execute simultaneously without holding up each other's work. At completion of an instruction, the CPU then selects the corresponding physical register and copies the result into it. This must occur in the specified program instruction order.

The Compleat Modern Superscalar CPU

Figure 8.18 is a model of a CPU block diagram that includes all the ideas just discussed. The design shown in this diagram is very similar to the one used in PowerPC processors and, with minor variations, to that used in Intel Pentium II, III, IV, and Itanium processors, as well as various IBM mainframe processors. As you would expect, the CPU is organized into modules that reflect the superscalar, pipelined nature of the architecture. Although it is difficult to identify the familiar components that we introduced in Chapter 7, the control unit, arithmetic/logic unit, program counter, and the like, they are indeed imbedded into the design, as you saw in Figure 8.15. The control unit operation is distributed through much of the diagram, controlling each step of the usual fetch-execute cycle as instructions flow through different blocks in the CPU. The functions of the arithmetic/logic unit are found within the integer unit. The program counter is part of the instruction unit.

In operation, instructions are fetched from memory by the memory management unit as they are needed for execution, and placed into a pipeline within the instruction unit. The memory management unit also provides translation for virtual storage. They are also partially decoded within the instruction unit, to determine the type of instruction that is being executed.

Instructions are actually executed in one of several types of execution units. Each execution unit has a pipeline designed to optimize the steps of the execute cycle for a particular type of instruction.

As you can see from the block diagram, there are separate execution units for branch instructions, for integer instructions, for floating point instructions, and for load and store instructions. Some processors provide multiple integer execution units to increase the processing capacity of the CPU still further. Some models also have a separate system register unit for executing system-level instructions. Some CPUs combine the load/store instructions into the integer unit. The PowerPC provides reservation stations in each execution unit. The Intel Pentium processors provide a general instruction pool where decoded instructions from the instruction unit are held as they await operand data from memory and from unresolved data dependencies. The Pentium instruction pool also holds completed instructions after execution until they can be retired in order. The Pentium also separates the LOAD and STORE execution units.

FIGURE 10.27

Modern CPU Block Diagram

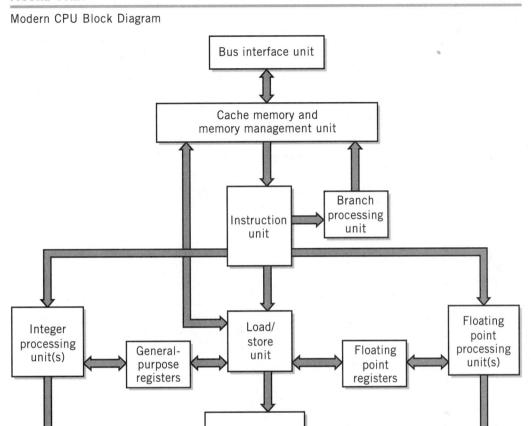

The **instruction unit** is responsible for maintaining the fetch pipeline and for dispatching instructions. Because branch instructions affect the addresses of the following instructions in the pipeline, they are processed immediately. Other instructions are processed as space becomes available in the appropriate execution unit(s). Branch prediction is usually built into the branch unit. When conditional branches occur, execution of instructions continues speculatively along the predicted branch until the condition is resolved. Also, the use of multiple execution units makes it possible that instructions will execute in the wrong order, since some instructions may have to wait for operands resulting from other instructions and since the pipelines in each execution unit are of different lengths. Some current superscalar processors can look ahead several instructions to find instructions that can be processed independently of the program order to prevent delays or errors arising from data dependency. The ability to process instructions out of order is an important factor in the effectiveness of these processors. The completion or "retire" unit accepts or rejects speculative instructions, stores results in the appropriate physical registers and cache memory locations, and retires instructions in the correct program order, assuring correct program flow. The Crusoe and Itanium architectures prevent out-of-order retirement by reordering the instructions prior to execution. This simplifies the CPU design.

From this discussion, you can see that the modern CPU includes many sophisticated features designed to streamline the basically simple fetch-execute cycle for high-performance processing. The modern CPU features different types of execution units, tailored to the needs of different types of instructions, and a complex steering system that can steer instructions through the instruction unit to available execution units, manage operands, and retire instructions in correct program order.

In this section we have introduced the basic ideas of superscalar processing, briefly indicated the difficulties, and explained the reasoning for its use. There are many excellent references listed at the end of the chapter if you are interested in more of the details of superscalar processing and modern CPU design.

8.5 IMPLEMENTATION ISSUES

It is not the intention of this book to discuss the electronic implementation of the computer. A brief introduction is provided in Supplementary Chapter 1, but the details of such a discussion are better left to an engineering textbook. There are several good computer engineering textbooks listed in the Further Reading for the supplementary chapter if you are interested in learning how the computer works in more detail.

There is one aspect of the implementation that is of interest and importance, however. Specifically, there are two significantly different methods of implementing a CPU. In this section we introduce these two methods, together with a brief discussion of the advantages and disadvantages of each.

The Conventional Hardware Implementation

If you look again at the instruction classes that constitute the operations of a CPU together with the fetch-execute cycles that make up each of the instructions, you can see that the great majority of operations within the CPU consist of moving data from one register to another. The steps

```
PC → MAR and
MDR → IR
```

are examples of this type of operation.

In addition, we must include the capability to add data to a register with data from another register or from a constant (usually the constant 1 or −1), the capability to perform simple Boolean functions (AND, OR, NOT) on data in registers, and the capability to shift the data in a register to the left or right. Finally, the CPU must include the capability to make simple decisions based on the values stored in flags and registers (conditional branches).

All of these operations are under the timed control of a clock. Control unit logic opens and closes switches at the right times to control the individual operations and the movement of data from one component within the CPU to another.

And for all practical purposes, that's about it. The small number of different operations used in a CPU suggest that the CPU can be directly implemented in electronic hardware, and indeed that is the case. In Supplementary Chapter 1, we demonstrate for the curious reader, in somewhat simplified fashion, that all of the preceding functions can be implemented using logic gates that perform Boolean algebra. The registers, flags, and counters that control timing are made up of electronic devices called flip-flops, which are, themselves, made up of logic gates.

So, as you can see, the basic hardware implementation of the CPU is relatively straightforward and simple. Although the addition of pipelining, superscaling, and other features complicates the design, it is possible, with careful design, to implement and produce an extremely fast and efficient CPU at low cost and in large quantities.

The Microprogrammed Implementation

Although each individual operation in the hardware implementation of a CPU is conceptually simple, the fact that separate circuits must be included for each and every instruction results in an overall design that is rather complex in the level of detail. New hardware CPU designs tend to be difficult to design and test. This led researchers to consider alternative implementations for the CPU.

An attractive alternative approach was proposed as early as 1951, by M. Wilkes [WILK51], although the first practical commercial application of this approach did not appear until 1964 with the introduction of the IBM 360 computer. Wilkes coined the word **microprogramming** to describe his approach.

The microprogramming implementation is based on the observation that the steps within the fetch-execute cycle themselves look like a simple form of computer program—in fact, a very simple computer program involving only the three types of instructions that we discussed in the previous section. These tiny programs, stored in ROM, are called **microcode.**

Rather than implement the CPU instructions, the hardware would implement the microinstructions that make up a fetch-execute cycle, and these microinstructions would be programmed to form the instructions of the CPU. A typical instruction might be "MOVE data from MDR to general register A" or "BRANCH if Register IR contains op code 3 to ADD routine". In a microcoded implementation many of the registers are actually placed in a special RAM memory. A separate ROM control store memory is used to hold the microprogrammed instruction set in the form of individual procedures. These microinstruction set programs are commonly referred to as *firmware,* since they are not really hardware or software.

In other words, the basic operation of the microcontroller is essentially a simplified version of a CPU whose function is to perform fetch-execute cycles as though they were tiny programs within the CPU.

There are several advantages to the microprogramming approach to CPU implementation.

- As we have already noted, it results in a simpler CPU design.
- It also results in a design that is inherently more flexible. With a microprogrammed CPU it is possible to modify the instruction set, even adding new instructions, simply by changing the instruction microprograms in control store memory. This means that the designer can experiment with the CPU design and produce a potentially better CPU. It also means that the computer manufacturer

can produce several different models, of different computational power, using the same basic CPU.

■ A final advantage is that it is possible to emulate, or look exactly like, the instruction set of another CPU using a microprogrammed approach and hardware components that are already part of the vendor's repertoire. This makes it possible for a manufacturer to build a CPU that is compatible with a different CPU, perhaps an earlier, more expensive model from the same manufacturer. This advantage has contributed to the standardization of computers across an entire product line that we see today.

The major disadvantage of the microprogrammed approach is that each step in the fetch-execute cycle now requires several clock cycles to achieve completion of the microinstructions that make up that step. This would theoretically result in a slower CPU. In practice, this situation is only partially true. First, the clock is designed to run at a much higher frequency, to compensate for the number of microsteps in each instruction. The simple operations performed by each microstep make it possible to complete each operation quickly; therefore, faster clock operation is possible. Second, the simplicity of the hardware circuits that make up the microprogrammed controller allows the use of faster circuits. Although these faster circuits might be too costly and might generate too much heat in a standard CPU design, they are acceptable for use with the simpler microprogrammed CPU implementation.

Nonetheless, microprogrammed implementation has generally fallen out of favor for new design. Since RISC designs are inherently simple, they are normally implemented in hardware. The speed of the parallelism of multiple execution units and new features, such as branch prediction, are not amenable to microprogramming as computer engineers try to eke out every last ounce of clock performance possible. Some older CISC designs, notably the Intel X86 architecture, implement the simpler parts of the design in hardware, and the remaining, more complex instructions in microcode.

SUMMARY AND REVIEW

In this chapter we presented a number of different techniques that are used to enhance the power and flexibility of a CPU. We began with a discussion of four different approaches to CPU architecture, with particular emphasis on CISC and RISC. We presented the advantages, disadvantages, and trade-offs for each architecture.

Next, we introduced paging, an important CPU technique for managing the organization and use of memory. The technique of paging was explained in some detail; however, its application to virtual storage was mentioned only briefly, and a number of implementation details were also omitted. Virtual storage will be revisited in Chapter 15.

We then turned our attention to memory enhancements, particularly the techniques and benefits of cache memory, a fast, intermediate memory between then CPU and regular memory.

The modern CPU is based on an alternative fetch unit-execute organization that supports pipelining and parallel instruction execution, and thereby makes possible the efficiencies of superscalar processing. A variety of innovative techniques, including rename registers, speculative execution, out-of-order execution, and branch prediction are important parts of the modern CPU.

KEY CONCEPTS AND TERMS

branch history table
cache controller
cache line
cache memory
circular register buffer
clock
code morphing layer
complex instruction set
    computer (CISC)
control dependency
data dependency
execution unit
explicitly parallel instruc-
    tion computer (EPIC)
fetch unit
frame
hazard
hit

hit ratio
instruction reordering
instruction set architecture
instruction unit
latency
locality of reference
logical register
memory address transla-
    tion
memory management unit
    (MMU)
microcode
microprogramming
miss
n-way interleaving
page
page table
paging

pipelining
real mode addressing
reduced instruction set
    computer (RISC)
register alias table
relocatability
rename register
scalar processing
speculative execution
superscalar processing
very long instruction word
    (VLIW)
virtual storage
wide path memory access
write back
write through

FOR FURTHER READING

The author used many references for the writing of this chapter. All are listed in the refer-
ence section of the book. I found the following books and articles to be particularly useful
for their clear descriptions and explanations of these topics. Stallings [STAL02] and
Tanenbaum [TAN99] describe the CISC versus RISC controversy in great depth.
Information about the VLIW and EPIC architectures may be found at the Transmeta and
Intel websites, respectively.

Instruction sets, instruction formats, and addressing are discussed at length in every
computer architecture textbook. The book by Patterson and Hennessy [PATT97] covers
the topics of Chapters 7 and 8 thoroughly, and has the additional benefit of being highly
readable. A more advanced treatment, by the same authors, is found in [HENN02]. A different approach to this material is to compare the architectures of various machines. The
book by Tabak [TAB95] looks at several different CPUs in detail, including the 68000
series, the X86 series, and the Digital Alpha CPU. There are textbooks and trade books
devoted to the architecture of every major CPU. I particularly recommend Brey [BREY95],
Messmer [MESS01], and Sargent and Shoemaker [SARG95] for the Intel X86 series; Young
[YOUN94] for the Power PC; and Wray and Greenfield [WRAY94] or Miller [MILL92] for
the 68000 series. The PC System Architecture series is an expanding collection of short
books describing the architectures of various parts of computers. Volume 5 [SHAN98]
describes the Pentium, Volume 7 [SHAN94] the Power PC.

An alternative approach to the topics in this chapter can be found in any assembly language textbook. Bailes and Riser [BAIL87] provide an excellent introduction to the IBM
370, Abel [ABEL01] or Thorne [THOR91] for the X86, and Ford and Topp [FORD88] for
the Motorola 68000 series. There are many other good books on these topics, with new
ones appearing every day.

Stallings also includes an entire chapter on superscalar processors. Clear, detailed discussions of all aspects of CPU and memory design can be found in the two books by Patterson and Hennessy [PATT97, HENN02]. There are many additional references in each of these books. Specific discussions of the superscalar processing techniques for particular CPUs can be found in Liptay [LIPT92] for the IBM 390, in Becker and colleagues [BECK93], Thompson and Ryan [THOM94], Burgess and colleagues [BURG94], and Ryan [RYAN93] for the PowerPC, and "Tour of the P6" [TOUR95] for the P6.

EXERCISES

8.1   Explain how each of the main features in a RISC computer solves one or more of the major bottlenecks of program execution that are described in the text.

8.2   Illustrate, step by step, the way in which a circular register buffer works by showing its operation for a simple program that you invent that is made up of subroutines and functions with local variables and passed arguments. Place your arguments and variables into the illustrations to clarify your discussion.

8.3   What PowerPC architectural characteristics and features appear to violate the ground rules for RISC design? Why do you suppose the designers made the decisions to do so?

8.4   Find a good reference that describes the Pentium chip. Discuss the features of the architecture that make superscalar processing possible in this chip. What limitations does the Pentium architecture impose on its superscalar processing?

8.5   Consider a CPU that implements a single instruction fetch-decode–execute–write-back pipeline for scalar processing. The execution unit of this pipeline assumes that the execution stage requires one step. Describe, and show in diagram form, what happens when an instruction that requires one execution step follows one that requires four execution steps.

8.6   **a.**   Consider a CPU with two parallel integer execution units. An addition instruction requires 2 clock pulses to complete execution, and a multiplication requires 15 clock pulses. Now assume the following situation: the program is to multiply two numbers, located in registers R2 and R4, and store the results in R5. The following instruction adds the number in R5 to the number in R2 and stores the result in R5. The CPU does not stall for data dependencies, and both instructions have access to an execution unit simultaneously. The initial values of R2, R4, and R5 are 3, 8, and 0, respectively. What is the result? Now assume that the CPU does handle data dependencies correctly. What is the result? If we define wasted time as time in which an execution unit is not busy, how much time is wasted in this example?

b.   Now assume that a later instruction in the fetch pipeline has no data dependencies. It adds the value in R1, initially 4, to the value in R4 and stores the result in R5. Data dependencies are handled correctly. There are no rename registers, and the CPU retires instructions in order. What happens? If the CPU provides rename registers, what happens? What effect does out-of-order execution have upon the time required to execute this program?

8.7   Suppose that a CPU always executes the two instructions following a branch instruction, regardless of whether the branch is taken or not. Explain how this can eliminate most of the delay resulting from branch dependency in a pipelined CPU. What penalties or restrictions does this impose on the programs that are executed on this machine?

8.8   Some systems use a branch prediction method known as static branch prediction, so called because the prediction is made on the basis of the instruction, without regard to history. One possible scenario would have the system predict that all conditional backward branches are taken and all forward conditional branches are not taken. Recall your experience with programming in the Little Man Computer language. Would this algorithm be effective? Why or why not? What aspects of normal programming, in any programming language, support your conclusion?

8.9   If you have access to a manual or book that describes the Digital Alpha chip, study the material and then write an essay carefully describing the techniques used by the Alpha CPU to implement superscalar processing.

8.10   How would you modify the Little Man Computer to implement the pipelined instruction fetch-execution unit model that was described in this chapter? What would it take to supply multiple execution units? Describe your modified LMC in detail and show how an instruction flows through your modified Little Man Computer

8.11   **a.**   Suppose we are trying to determine the speed of a computer that executes the Little Man instruction set. The load and store instructions each make up about 25% of the instructions in a typical program. add, subtract, in, and out take 10% each. The various branches each take about 5%. The halt instruction is almost never used (a maximum of once each program, of course!). Determine the average number of instructions executed each second if the clock ticks at 100 MHz.

   b.   Now suppose that the CPU is pipelined, so that each instruction is fetched while another instruction is executing. (You may also neglect the time required to refill the pipeline during branches and at the start of program execution.) What is the average number of instructions that can be executed each second with the same clock in this case?

8.12   The goal of scalar processing is to produce, on average, the execution of one instruction per clock tick. If the clock ticks at a rate of 2 GHz, how many instructions per second can this computer execute? How many instructions would a 2 GHz superscalar processor that processes three instructions per clock cycle execute?

8.13   (Challenge problem!) Suppose that you have a microprogrammed implementation of a CPU. Your microprogrammed instruction set includes instructions that move data from one internal register to another, shift or rotate data one bit left or right within a register, add data from one register to another, test a register and skip on value 0, test the carry flag and skip if it's a 1, and jump a fixed distance within the microprogram. (Does this microprogrammed instruction set look vaguely familiar?)

Using this instruction set, and the standard set of registers plus an additional accumulator B, create a fetch-execute cycle that will multiply two unsigned numbers together. The numbers to be multiplied are originally found in the MDR and A, and the result winds up in B. To make the problem easier, assume that the accumulator B is large enough to hold the result

8.14 Show in a drawing similar to Figure 8.6 or 8.7 how two different programs with the same logical address space can be transformed by virtual storage into independent parts of physical memory.

8.15 Show in a drawing similar to Figure 8.7 how two different programs with the same logical address space can be transformed by virtual storage partially into the same part of physical memory and partially into independent parts of physical memory. Assume that the two programs use the same program code, located from logical addresses 0 to 100, and that they each have their own data region, located from logical addresses 101 to 165.

8.16 Create a page table that meets the translation requirements of Figure 8.7. Assume a page size of 10.

8.17 Consider a cache memory that provides three hundred 16-byte blocks. Now consider that you are processing all the data in a two-dimensional array of, say, four hundred rows by four hundred columns, using a pair of nested loops. Assume that the program stores the array column by column. You can write your program to nest the loops in either direction, that is, process row by row or column by column. Explain which way you would choose to process the data. What is the advantage? Conversely, what is the disadvantage of processing the data the other way? What effect does choosing the incorrect way have on system performance?

8.18 Carefully discuss what happens when a cache miss occurs. Does this result in a major slowdown in execution of the instruction? If so, why?

8.19 What is the purpose of the tag in a cache memory system?

8.20 Describe the trade-offs between the memory cache write-through and write-back techniques.

8.21 There are a number of similarities in the operation of a cache memory and that of virtual storage. Describe and explain the similarities.

INPUT/OUTPUT

"Here comes the 64-bit local bus."

9.0 INTRODUCTION

Of course you're aware that no matter how powerful the CPU is, a computer system's usefulness ultimately depends on its input and output facilities. Without I/O there is no possibility of keyboard input, of screen output, of printout, or even of disk storage and retrieval. Although you might be inclined to think of I/O in terms of user input and output, there would be no computer network or Internet access either. To the CPU and its programs, all these devices require specialized input and output processing facilities and routines.

In fact, for most business programs and for nearly every multimedia application, I/O is the predominant factor. E-commerce applications offer an even bigger challenge: Web services generally require massive amounts of fast I/O to handle and process I/O requests as they occur. The speed at which most of these programs operate is determined by the ability of their I/O operations to stay ahead of their processing. With PCs rapidly increasing in CPU processing capability, but still somewhat limited in I/O processing, it has been greater I/O capability that has maintained, until recently, the advantage of mainframe computers over PCs for business transaction processing.

We handled input and output in the Little Man Computer by providing input and output baskets for that purpose. Each input instruction transferred one three-digit data number from the input basket to the calculator; similarly, each output instruction transferred one data number from the calculator to the output basket. If we wanted to input three numbers, for example, an input instruction had to be executed three times. This could be done with three separate input instructions or in a loop, but either way, each individual piece of data required the execution of a separate input instruction.

It is possible to transfer data between input and output devices and the CPU of a real computer in a similar manner. In the real computer, the in basket and out basket are commonly replaced by a bus interface that allows a direct transfer between the computer's bus and a register within an **I/O module** that controls the particular device. Both input and output are handled similarly. The technique is known as **programmed I/O.**

There are a number of complicating factors in handling input/output processes (which we will normally simply call *I/O*) in a real computer. Although the method of transferring data one word at a time does really exist, and may be adequate and appropriate for some slow-operating I/O devices, the volume of data commonly transferred in I/O devices, such as disks and tapes, makes this method too slow and cumbersome to be practical as the only I/O transfer method in a modern high-speed machine. We need to consider some method of transferring data in blocks rather than executing an instruction for each individual piece of data.

The problem is further complicated by the fact that in a real computer, there may be many input and output devices all trying to do I/O, sometimes at the same time. There needs to be a way of distinguishing and separating the I/O from these different devices. Additionally, devices operate at different speeds from each other and from the

CPU. An inkjet printer may output characters at a rate of 150 per second, whereas a disk may transfer data at a rate of tens or hundreds of thousands, or even millions, of bytes per second. Synchronization of these different operations must be achieved to prevent data loss.

Finally, it should be noted that I/O operations take up a lot of computer time. Even if a block of data can be transferred between the CPU and a disk with a single instruction, much time is wasted waiting for the completion of the task. A CPU could execute millions of instructions in the time it takes a printer to print a single character. In a large modern computer, the number of I/O operations may be very large. It would be convenient and useful to be able to use the CPU for other tasks while these I/O transfers are taking place.

In the computer, several different techniques are combined to resolve the problem of synchronizing and handling I/O between a variety of different I/O devices operating with different quantities of data at different speeds. In this chapter, we first consider the I/O requirements of some commonly used devices. This discussion, which appears in Section 9.1, leads to a set of requirements that the I/O-CPU interface should meet to optimize system performance. Next, in Sections 9.2 through 9.4, we look at several different methods that are used to perform I/O in the computer. These techniques will also provide ways in which the CPU can be utilized more fully while I/O operations are taking place.

At the beginning of our discussion of computer systems, in Chapter 1, we mentioned that a computer hardware system is an interconnection of three basic types of modules: CPU, memory, and I/O. The methods used for moving data to and from the I/O modules also serve to interconnect the various parts of the computer together. Finally, in Sections 9.5 and 9.6, we show the various ways in which the entire computer system, CPU, I/O, and memory, can be interconnected and configured.

9.1 CHARACTERISTICS OF TYPICAL I/O DEVICES

Before discussing the techniques that are used in the real computer for performing I/O, it will help to consider some characteristics of the devices that will typically be connected to the computer. In this chapter we are not interested in the inner workings of these devices—that discussion we'll save for Chapters 10 and 11. For now, we are only interested in those characteristics of these devices that will affect the I/O capabilities of the computer, in particular the speed and quantity of data transfer required to use the computer efficiently and fully. This survey is intended to be intuitive: what must be true about the I/O, based on what you already know about the particular devices from your own practical experience. Although this discussion may seem like a digression, it is intended to establish a set of basic principles and requirements that will help you to better understand the reasons behind the methods that are used to perform I/O in computers.

Consider, for example, the keyboard as an input device. The keyboard is basically a character-based device. You are probably already aware that typing on the keyboard of your PC results in Unicode or ASCII input to the computer, one character at a time. Even mainframe terminals, many of which can send text to the computer a page at a time, only transmit a page occasionally, so the data rate for keyboards is obviously very slow compared to the speed at which the CPU processes the data.

Input from the keyboard is very slow because it is dependent on the speed of typing, as well as on the thought process of the user. There are usually long thinking pauses between bursts of input, but even during those bursts, the actual input requirements to the computer are very slow compared to the capability of the computer to execute input instructions. Thus, we must assume that if the computer is simply performing a single task, it will spend most of its time waiting for input from the keyboard.

It is also useful to note that there are two different types of keyboard input. There is input that is expected by the application program in response to a "read" statement of some kind requesting input data for the program. Then there are other times when the user wishes to interrupt what the computer is doing. On many computers, Control-"C" can be typed to stop the program that is running. Control-"S" is used on some machines to stop the display from scrolling. Typing Control-Alt-Delete on a PC will restart the computer. These are examples of unpredicted input, since the executing program is not necessarily awaiting specific input at those times. Using the input method that we already described would not work: the unexpected input would not be noticed, possibly for a long time until the next input instruction was executed for some later expected input.

Finally, on a multiuser system, there may be many keyboards connected to the computer. The computer must be able to distinguish between them, must not lose input data even if several keyboards send a character simultaneously, and must be able to respond quickly to each keyboard. The physical distances from the computer to these keyboards may be long.

Another input device that will generate unexpected input is the mouse. When you move the mouse, you expect the cursor to move on the screen. Clicking on a mouse button may serve as expected input to a program, or it may be unexpected and change the way in which the program is executing. In fact, unexpected input is fundamental to programs written in modern event-driven languages such as Visual Basic and Java. When the user selects an item on a drop-down menu or clicks on a toolbar icon, she expects a timely response. Again, data rates are slow.

CRT screens and printers must operate over a wide range of data rates. Output to a printer consisting only of an occasional page or two of text will certainly not require a high data rate. Thus, the output rate for CRTs and printers in text mode is slow. Most printers are fairly slow, ranging in speed from less than 100 characters per second for an inexpensive PC inkjet printer to perhaps twelve thousand characters per second for a laser printer to a few thousand characters per second for a mainframe line printer.

For graphical output, the situation is quite different. Recall from Chapter 3 that graphics may exist in object or bitmap formats, but that ultimately the display must be produced in bitmap format. For CRTs and printers that can perform the conversion internally—for example, PostScript printers—the data may be transmitted in object form, as a set of text instructions or mathematical representations describing the picture. In this case, the amount of data sent may be relatively small. If, on the other hand, the graphics are sent as "bitmap images," with data for each pixel to be reproduced, it may take a huge amount of data to produce a single picture, and high-speed data transfer will be essential. A single, color image on a high-resolution screen may require several megabytes of data, and it is desirable to produce the image on the screen as fast as possible. If the image represents video, extremely high data transfer rates are required. This suggests that screen image updates may require bursts of several megabytes per second, even when data compression methods are used to reduce the transfer rate. It may also suggest to you why it is difficult to transmit images quickly over voice-grade phone lines using modems.

Contrast the I/O requirements of keyboards, screens, and printers with those of disks and DVD-ROMs. Since the disk is used to store programs and data, it would be very rare that a program would require a single word of data or program from the disk. Disks are used to load entire programs or store files of data. Thus, disk data is always transferred in blocks, never as individual bytes or words. Disks may operate at transfer rates of more than a million bytes per second. As storage devices, disks must be capable of both input and output, although not simultaneously. On a large system there may be several disks attempting to transfer blocks of data to or from the CPU simultaneously. A DVD-ROM attempting to present a full screen video at movie rates without dropouts must provide data steadily at input rates approaching 10 megabytes per second, with some transient rates even higher. Furthermore, video and audio devices require a steady stream of data over long periods of time. Contrast this requirement with the occasional bursts of data that are characteristic of most I/O devices.

For both disk and image I/O, therefore, the computer must be capable of transferring massive amounts of data very quickly between the CPU and the disk(s) or image devices. Clearly, executing a single instruction for each byte of data is unacceptable for disk and image I/O, and a different approach must be used. Furthermore, you can see the importance of providing a method to allow utilization of the CPU for other tasks while these large I/O operations are taking place.

With the rapid proliferation of networks in recent years, network interfaces have also become an important source of I/O. From the perspective of a computer, the network is just another I/O device. In many cases, the network is used as a substitute for a disk, with the data and programs stored at a remote computer and served to the local station. For the computer that is acting as a server, there may be a massive demand for I/O services. User interfaces such as X Windows, which allow the transfer of graphical information from a computer to a display screen located elsewhere on the network, place heavy demands on I/O capability. With simple object graphics, or locally stored bitmap images, and with a minimal requirement for large file transfers, a small computer with a modem may operate sufficiently at I/O transfer rates of 3,000 bytes per second, but computers with more intensive requirements may require I/O transfer rates of 50 megabytes per second, or more.

A table of typical data rates for various I/O devices appears in Figure 9.1. The values given are rough approximations, since the actual rates are dependent on the particular hardware systems, software, and application. As computer technology advances, the high-end data rates continue to increase at a rapid pace.

It should be pointed out that disks, printers, screens, and most other I/O devices operate almost completely under CPU program control. Printers and screens, of course, are strictly output devices, and the output produced can be determined only by the program being executed. Although disks act as both input and output devices, the situation is similar. It is the executing program that must always determine what file is to be read on input, or where to store output. Therefore, it is always a program executing in the CPU that initiates I/O data transfer, even if the CPU is allowed to perform other tasks while waiting for the particular I/O operation to be completed.

Some input devices must be capable of generating input to the CPU independent of program control. The keyboard and mouse were mentioned earlier in this context, and voice input would also fall into this category. Some devices, such as CD-ROMs, can self-initiate by signaling their presence to a program within the operating system software. Local

FIGURE 9.1

Examples of I/O Devices Categorized by a Typical Data Rate

Device	Input/Output	Data rate (in Kbytes/sec)	Type
Keyboard	Input	0.01	char
Mouse	Input	0.02	char
Voice input	Input	0.02	block burst
Scanner	Input	200	block burst
Voice output	Output	0.5	block burst
Inkjet printer	Output	1.5	block burst
Laser printer	Output	100-1,000	block burst
Graphics display	Output	30,000	block burst or steady
Local area network	Input or output	200-20,000	block burst or steady
Optical disk	Storage	500-15,000	block burst or steady
Magnetic tape	Storage	1,000-15,000	block burst or steady
Magnetic disk	Storage	2,000-60,000	block burst or steady
Non-compressed video source	Input	10,000	block steady
Non-compressed audio source	Input or output	100	block steady

ADAPTED FROM: J. L. Hennessy and David A. Patterson, (1990) *Computer Architecture: A Quantitative Approach.* Reprinted with permission. Morgan Kaufmann Publishers, Inc. San Francisco.

area networks also sometimes generate this kind of input, since a program on a different CPU might request, for example, a file stored on your disk. In a slightly different category, but with similar requirements, are input devices for which input is under program control, but for which the time delay until arrival of the data is unpredictable, and possibly long. (You might consider regular keyboard input in this category, especially when writing a paper using your word processor.) This would be true if the data is being telemetered from some sort of measurement device. For example, the computer might be used to monitor the water level at a reservoir, and the input is water-level data that is telemetered by a measurement device once per hour. Provision must be made to accept unpredictable input and process it in some reasonable way, preferably without tying up the CPU excessively.

Additionally, there will be situations where an I/O device being addressed is busy or not ready. The most obvious examples are a printer that is out of paper or a floppy disk drive with no disk in it or a hard disk that is processing another request. It would be desirable for the device to be able to provide status information to the CPU, so that appropriate action can be taken.

The discussion in this section establishes several requirements that will have to be met for a computer system to handle I/O in a sufficient and effective manner:

1. There must be a means for individually addressing different peripheral devices.

2. There must be a way in which peripheral devices can initiate communication with the CPU. This facility will be required to allow the CPU to respond to

unexpected inputs from peripherals such as keyboards, mice, and networks, and so that peripherals such as printers and floppy disk drives can convey emergency status information to the executing program.

3. Programmed I/O is suitable only for slow devices and individual word transfers. For faster devices with block transfers, there must be a more efficient means of transferring the data between I/O and memory. Memory is a suitable medium for direct block transfers, since the data must be in memory for a program to access it. Preferably this could be done without involving the CPU, since this would free the CPU to work on other tasks.

4. Finally, there must be a means for handling devices with extremely different control requirements. It would be desirable if I/O for each of these devices could be handled in a simple and similar way by programs in the CPU.

The last requirement suggests that it is not practical to connect the I/O devices directly to the CPU without some sort of interface module unique to each device. To clarify this requirement, note the following conditions established from the previous discussion:

1. The formats required by different devices will be different. Some devices require a single piece of data, and then must wait before another piece of data can be accepted. Others expect a block of data. Some devices expect 8 bits of data at a time; others require 16, 32, or 64. Some devices expect the data to be provided sequentially, on a single data line. Other devices expect a parallel interface. These inconsistencies mean that the system would require substantially different interface hardware and software for each device.

2. The incompatibilities in speed between the various devices and the CPU will make synchronization difficult, especially if there are multiple devices attempting to do I/O at the same time. It may be necessary to buffer the data (i.e., hold it and release part of it at particular times) to use it. A **buffer** works something like a water reservoir or tower. Water enters the reservoir or tower as it becomes available. It is stored and released as it can be used. A computer buffer uses registers or memory in the same way.

3. Although the I/O requirements for most devices occur in bursts, some multimedia, video and audio in particular, provide a steady stream of data that must be transferred on a regular basis to prevent dropouts that can upset a user. I/O devices and the interconnections that support multimedia services must be capable of guaranteeing steady performance. This often includes network interfaces and high-speed communication devices as well as such devices as video cameras, since networks are frequently used to supply audio and video. (Think of downloading streaming video from the Web.)

4. Devices such as disk drives have electromechanical control requirements that must be met, and it would tie up too much time to use the CPU to provide that control. For example, the head motors in a disk drive must be moved to the correct disk track to retrieve data and something must continually maintain the current head position on the track once the track is reached. There must be a motor controller to move the print heads in an inkjet printer across the paper to the correct position to print a character. And so on. Of course, the requirements for each device are different.

The different requirements for each I/O device plus the necessity for providing devices with addressing, synchronization, status, and external control capabilities suggest that it is necessary to provide each device with its own special interface. Thus, in general, I/O devices will be connected to the CPU through an I/O module of some sort. The I/O module will contain the specialized hardware circuits necessary to meet all the I/O requirements that we established, including block transfer capability with appropriate buffering and a standardized, simple interface to the CPU. At the other interface, the I/O module will have the capability to control the specific device for which it is designed.

The simplest arrangement is shown in Figure 9.2. I/O modules may be very simple and control a single device, or they may be complex, with substantial built-in intelligence, and may control many devices. A slightly more complex arrangement is shown in Figure 9.3. The additional I/O modules require addressing to distinguish them from each other. The lower module will actually recognize addresses for either of the I/O devices connected to it. I/O modules that control a single type of device are often called **device controllers.** For example, an I/O module that controls disks would be a *disk controller.* The various architectural configurations and considerations are discussed more thoroughly in Section 9.5. We look at the I/O modules themselves in Section 9.6.

9.2 PROGRAMMED I/O

In the simplest method for performing I/O, an I/O module is connected to a pair of I/O registers in the CPU via a bus. The I/O data register serves the same role in the real CPU as the input and output baskets served in the Little Man Computer. Alternatively, one might view the I/O baskets as buffers, holding multiple inputs or outputs, with the I/O data register as the interface between the CPU and the buffer. The I/O operation

FIGURE 9.2

Simple I/O Configuration

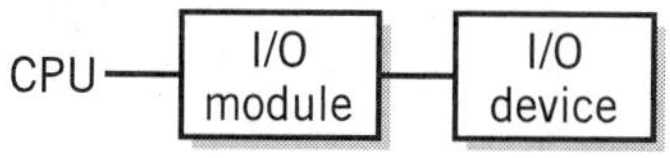

CPU — [I/O module] [I/O device]

FIGURE 9.3

A Slightly More Complex I/O Module Arrangement

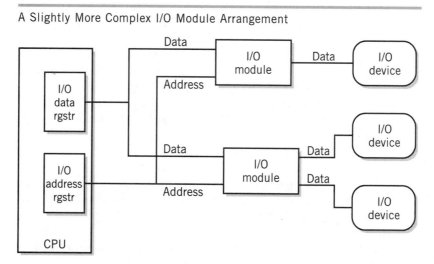

is similar to that of the Little Man Computer. Input from the peripheral device is transferred from the I/O module or buffer for that peripheral device one word at a time to the I/O data register and from there to an accumulator register under program control, just as occurred in the Little Man Computer. Similarly, individual words of output data pass from an accumulator register to the I/O data register where they can be read by the appropriate I/O module, again under program control. Each instruction produces a single input or output. This method is known as programmed I/O.

In practice, it is most likely that there will be multiple devices connected to the CPU. Since each device must be recognized individually, address information must be sent with the I/O instruction. The address field of the I/O instruction can be used for this purpose. An I/O address register in the CPU holds the address for transfer to the bus. Each I/O module will have an identification address that will allow it to identify I/O instructions addressed to it and to ignore other I/O not intended for it.

As has been noted, it is common for an I/O module to have several addresses, each of which represents a different control command or status request, or which addresses a different device when a particular module supports multiple devices. For example, the address field in the Little Man input and output instructions could be used to address up to a combination of one hundred devices, status requests, or control commands. Figure 9.4 illustrates the concept of programmed I/O. Indeed, the LMC uses the address field to select the I-basket (901) or O-basket (902) as the I/O device within the 900 instruction.

The I/O data and address registers work similarly to the memory address register (MAR) and memory data register (MDR). In fact, in some systems, they may even be connected to the same bus. The CPU places a signal on the bus to indicate whether the transfer is I/O or memory.

Programmed I/O is obviously slow, since a full instruction fetch-execute cycle must be performed for each and every I/O data word to be transferred. Programmed I/O is used today primarily with keyboards, with occasional application to other simple character-based data transfers, such as the transmission of commands through a network I/O module or modem. These operations are slow compared with the computer, with small quantities of data that can be handled one character at a time. One limitation, which we shall address later in the chapter, is that with programmed I/O, input from the keyboard is accepted only under program control. An alternative means must be found to accept unexpected input from the keyboard.

There is one important application for programmed I/O: alternative methods of I/O use the I/O module to control I/O operations from outside the CPU, independent of the CPU, using memory as the intermediate site for the data transfer. Programmed I/O is used by programs in the CPU to send the necessary commands to the I/O modules to set up parameters for the transfer and to initiate I/O operations. We shall return to this topic in Section 9.4.

9.3 INTERRUPTS

There are many circumstances under which it would be desirable to interrupt the normal flow of a program in the computer to react to special events. An unexpected user command from the keyboard or other external input, an abnormal situation, such as a power failure, that requires immediate attention from the computer, an attempt to execute an illegal instruction, or the completion of an I/O task initiated by the program: all of these suggest

FIGURE 9.4

Programmed I/O

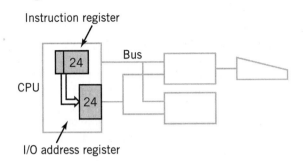

1. CPU executes INPUT 24 instruction. Address 24 is copied to the I/O address register.

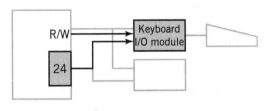

2. Address 24 is recognized by the keyboard I/O module. A read/write control line indicates that the instruction is an INPUT.

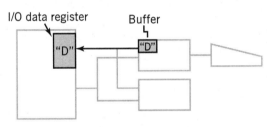

3. A buffer in the I/O module holds a keystroke, in this case ASCII 68, the letter "D". The data is transferred to the I/O data register.

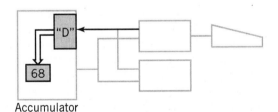

4. From there it is copied to the appropriate accumulator or general-purpose register, completing the operation.

that it would be appropriate to include some means to allow the computer to take special actions when required. Interrupt capabilities are also used to make it possible to time share the CPU between several different programs at once.

Modern computers provide interrupt capability by providing one or more special control lines to the central processor known as **interrupt lines.** For example, the standard I/O for a modern PC may contain as many as thirty-two interrupt lines, labeled IRQ0 through IRQ31. (IRQ stands for Interrupt ReQuest.) The messages sent to the computer on these lines are known as **interrupts.** The presence of a message on an interrupt line will cause the computer to suspend the program being executed and jump to a special interrupt processing program.

Consider, as an example, the following situation:

In a large, multiuser system there may be hundreds of keyboards being used with the computer at any given time. Since any of these keyboards could generate input to the computer at any time, it is necessary that the computer be aware of any key that is struck from any keyboard in use. This process must take place quickly, before another key is struck on the same keyboard, to prevent data loss from occurring when the second input is generated.

Theoretically, though impractically, it would be possible for the computer to perform this task by checking each keyboard for input in rotation, at frequent intervals. This technique is known as **polling.** The interval would have to be shorter than the time during which a fast typist could hit another key. Since there may be hundreds of keyboards in use, this technique may result in a polling rate of thousands of samples per second. Most of these samples will not result in new data; therefore, the computer time spent in polling is largely wasted.

This is a situation for which the concept of the interrupt is well suited. The goal is achieved more productively by allowing the keyboard to notify the CPU by using an interrupt when it has input. When a key is struck on any keyboard, it causes the interrupt line to be activated, so that the CPU knows that an I/O device connected to the interrupt line requires action.

Interrupts satisfy the requirement for external input controls, and also provide the desirable feature of freeing the CPU from waiting for events to occur.

Servicing Interrupts

Since the computer is capable only of executing programs, interrupt actions take the form of special programs, executed whenever triggered by an interrupt signal. Interrupt procedures follow the form shown in Figure 9.5.

Specifically, the interrupt causes the temporary suspension of the program in progress. All the pertinent information about the program being suspended, including the location of the last instruction executed, and the values of data in various registers, is saved in a known part of memory, either in a special area associated with the program, known as the **process control block (PCB),** or in a part of memory known as the stack area. Many computers have a single instruction that saves all the critical information at once. The memory belonging to the original program is kept intact. The computer then branches to a special interrupt handler program elsewhere in memory; the **interrupt handler** program is also known as an **interrupt routine.** The interrupt handler program determines the appropriate course of action. This process is known as **servicing the interrupt.**

When the interrupt routine completes its task, it normally would return control to the interrupted program, much like a subroutine. Original register values would be restored, and the original program would resume execution *exactly* where it left off, and in its identical state, since all the registers were restored to their original values. There are some circumstances when this is not the case, however, since actions taken by the interrupt routine may make a difference in what the original program is supposed to do. For example, a

FIGURE 9.5

Servicing an Interrupt

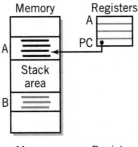

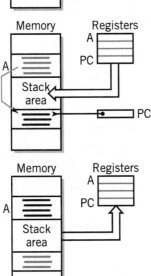

1. Before interrupt arrives, program A is executing. The program counter points to the current instruction.

2. When the interrupt is received by the CPU, the current instruction is completed, all the registers are saved in the stack area (or in a special area known as a process control block). The PC is loaded with the starting location of program B, the interrupt handler program. This causes a jump to program B, which becomes the executing program.

3. When the interrupt routine is complete, the registers are restored, including the program counter, and the original program resumes exactly where it left off.

printer interrupt indicating that the printer is out of paper would require a different action by the original program (perhaps a message to the screen telling the user to load more paper); it would not be useful for the program to send more characters!

Intuitively, the servicing of interrupts works just the way that you would expect. Suppose that you were giving a speech in one of your classes, and someone in the class interrupts you with a question. What do you do? Normally, you would hold your current thought and answer the question. When you finish answering the question, you return to your lecture just where you left off, pick up the thought, and continue as though no interrupt had occurred. This would be your normal interrupt servicing routine. Suppose, however, that the interrupt is the bell ending class or the instructor telling you that you have run out of time. In this case, your response is different. You would *not* return to your speech. Instead, you might do a quick wrap-up followed by an exit.

In other words, you would react in a way quite similar to the way in which the interrupt servicing routines work.

The Uses of Interrupts

The way in which an interrupt is used depends on the nature of the device. You've already seen that externally controlled inputs are best handled by generating interrupts whenever action is required. In other cases, interrupts occur when some action is *completed*. This section introduces several different ways in which interrupts are used.

THE INTERRUPT AS AN EXTERNAL EVENT NOTIFIER   As previously discussed, interrupts are useful as notifiers to the CPU of **external events** that require action. This frees the CPU from the necessity of performing polling to determine that input data is waiting.

EXAMPLE

Keyboard input can be processed using a combination of programmed I/O and interrupts. Suppose a key is struck on the keyboard. This causes an interrupt to occur. The current program is suspended, and control is transferred to the keyboard interrupt handler program. The keyboard interrupt handler first inputs the character, using programmed I/O, and determines what character has been received. It would next determine if the input is one that requires special action. If so, it would perform the required action, for example, suspending the program or freezing the data on the screen. Otherwise, it would pass the input data to the program expecting input from that keyboard. Normally, the input character would be stored in a known memory location, ready for the program to use when it is reactivated.

When the action is complete, that is, when the interrupt has been serviced, the computer normally restores the register values and returns control to the suspended program, unless the interrupt request specifies a different course of action. This would be the case, for example, if the user typed a command to suspend the program being run.

Figure 9.6 shows the steps in processing a keyboard input interrupt.

■ ■ ■

FIGURE 9.6

Using a Keyboard Handler Interrupt

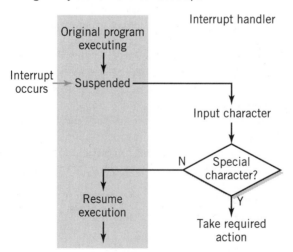

A real-time system is a computer system used primarily to measure external events that happen in "real time"; that is, the event, when it occurs, requires processing quickly because the data is of critical time-sensitive value.

As an example, consider a computer system that monitors the coolant temperature from the core of a power plant nuclear reactor. The temperature is transmitted once a minute by a temperature measurement transducer to the computer.

In this particular case, the transducer input is *expected,* and, when it occurs, requires immediate evaluation. It is reasonable to assume, however, that the computer system is to be used for other purposes, and it is not desirable to tie up the CPU in an input loop waiting for the transducer data to arrive.

This is a perfect application for interrupts. The transducer input is assigned to an interrupt. The interrupt service routine in this case is used to process the transducer input data. When the interrupt occurs, the interrupt routine evaluates the input. If everything is normal, the routine returns control to whatever the computer was doing. In an emergency, the interrupt routine would transfer control instead to the program that handles emergency situations.

THE INTERRUPT AS A COMPLETION SIGNAL The keyboard and transducer examples demonstrate the usefulness of the interrupt as a means for the user to control the computer from an input device, in this case the keyboard or transducer. Let us next consider the interrupt technique as a means of controlling the flow of data to an output device. Here, the interrupt serves to notify the computer of the completion of a particular course of action.

EXAMPLE

As noted previously, the printer is a slow output device. The computer is capable of outputting characters to the printer much faster than the printer can handle them. The interrupt can be used to control the flow of characters to the printer in an efficient way.

The computer sends one or more characters at a time to the printer, depending on the type of printer. When the printer is ready to accept more characters, it sends an interrupt to the computer. This interrupt indicates that the printer has completed printing the characters previously received and is ready for more characters.

In this case, the interrupt capability prevents the loss of output, since it allows the printer to control the flow of characters to a rate that the printer can accept. Without the interrupt capability, it would be necessary to output characters at a very slow rate to assure that the computer did not exceed the ability of the printer to accept output. The use of an interrupt also allows the CPU to perform other tasks while it waits for the printer to complete its printing.

By the way, you might notice that the printer could use a second, different interrupt as a way of telling the computer to stop sending characters temporarily when the printer's buffer fills up.

This application is diagrammed in Figure 9.7. Another application of the interrupt as a completion signal is discussed in Section 9.4, as an integral part of the direct memory access technique.

THE INTERRUPT AS A MEANS OF ALLOCATING CPU TIME A third major application for interrupts is to use the interrupt as a method of allocating CPU time to different programs that are sharing the CPU.

FIGURE 9.7

Using a Print Handler Interrupt

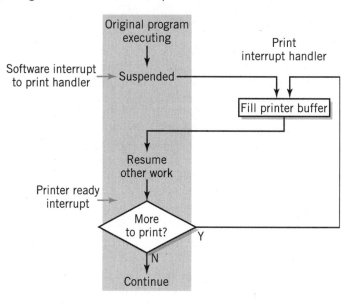

Since the CPU can only execute one program at a time, the ability to time share multiple programs implies that the computer system must share the CPU by allocating small segments of time to each program, in rapid rotation among them. Each program is allowed to execute some instructions. After a certain period of time, that program is interrupted and relinquishes control to a dispatcher program within the operating system that allocates the next block of time to another program. This is illustrated in Figure 9.8.

The system cannot count on programs relinquishing control voluntarily, since a program caught in an infinite loop would not be able to do so. Instead, the computer system provides an internal clock that sends an interrupt periodically to the CPU. The time between interrupt pulses is known as a **quantum,** and represents the time that each program will have allotted to it. When the clock interrupt occurs, the interrupt routine returns control to the operating system, which then determines which program will receive CPU time next. The interrupt is a simple but effective method for allowing the operating system to share CPU resources among several programs at once.

Time sharing is discussed in more depth in Chapters 14 and 16.

THE INTERRUPT AS AN ABNORMAL EVENT INDICATOR The fourth major use for interrupts is to handle **abnormal events** that affect operation of the computer system itself. Under certain conditions, we would like the computer to respond with a specific course of action, quickly and effectively. This usage is similar to that of other external input events, but in this case, the events are directed at problems within the computer system itself.

One obvious example of an external event requiring special computer action is power failure. Most computers provide enough internal power storage to save the work that is

FIGURE 9.8

Using an Interrupt for Time Sharing

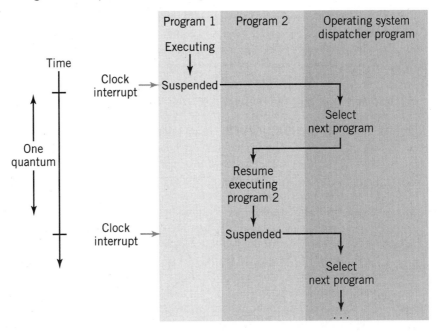

being performed and to shut down gracefully, provided that the computer has quick notification of the power failure. A power line monitor that connects to the interrupt facility provides this capability. The interrupt routine will save the status of programs that are in memory, close open files, and perform other housekeeping operations that will allow the computer to restart without any loss of data. It will then halt the computer.

Another important application of the abnormal event interrupt is when a program attempts to execute an illegal instruction such as a *divide by 0* or a nonexistent op code, or when a hardware error is detected, such as a parity error. When the error occurs it is not possible to complete the executing program. Yet it is important that the system attempt to recover from the error and that the appropriate personnel be notified. It is not acceptable simply to halt the computer. Particularly in modern multitasking computer systems this would be undesirable since it would also stop other executing programs that might not be affected by the error and would affect other users if the system is a multiuser system. Instead, an interrupt routine can notify the user of the error and return control of the CPU to the operating system program. You should notice that these interrupts are actually generated from inside the CPU, whereas the other interrupts that we have discussed so far are generated externally. Internal interrupts are sometimes called **traps** or **exceptions.**

EXAMPLE

Most modern computers have a set of instructions known as **privileged instructions.** These instructions are intended for use by an operating system program. The HALT instruction generally is a privileged instruction. Privileged instructions are designed to provide system security by preventing application programs from altering memory outside their own region, from stopping the computer, or from directly addressing an I/O device that is shared by multiple programs or users. (Suppose, for example, that two programs sharing the computer each sent text out to a printer. The resulting printout would be garbage, a mixture of the outputs from each program.) An attempt by a user's program to execute a privileged instruction would result in an illegal instruction interrupt.

Other internal and external events also make use of the interrupt facility. The table in Figure 9.9 shows a list of the built-in interrupts for the IBM zSeries family of computers.

SOFTWARE INTERRUPTS In addition to the actual hardware interrupts already discussed, modern CPU instruction sets include an instruction that simulates an interrupt. In the Intel X86 architecture, for example, this instruction has the mnemonic INT, for INTerrupt. The IBM zSeries uses the mnemonic SVC for SUPERVISOR CALL. The interrupt instruction works in the same way as a hardware interrupt, saving appropriate registers and transferring control to an interrupt handling procedure. The address space of the INT instruction can be used to provide a parameter that specifies which interrupt is to be executed. The **software interrupt** is very similar to a subroutine jump to a known, fixed location.

Software interrupts make the interrupt routines available for use by other programs. Programs can access these routines simply by executing the INT instruction with the appropriate parameter.

An important application for software interrupts is to centralize I/O operations. One way to assure that multiple programs do not unintentionally alter another program's files or intermingle printer output is to provide a single path for I/O to each device. Generally, the I/O paths are interrupt routines that are a part of the operating system software. Software interrupts are used by each program to request I/O from the operating system software. A software interrupt was used in Figure 9.7 to initiate printing. The use of software interrupts is discussed further in Chapter 13.

FIGURE 9.9

Table of Interrupts for zSeries Family

Priority	Interrupt class	Type of interrupts
Highest	Machine check	Nonrecoverable hardware errors
	Supervisor call	Software interrupt request by program
	Program check	Hardware-detectible software errors: illegal instruction, protected instruction, divide by 0, overflow, underflow, address translation error
	Machine check	Recoverable hardware errors
	External	Operator intervention, interval timer expiration, set timer expiration
	I/O	I/O completion signal or other I/O-related event
Lowest	Restart	Restart key, or restart signal from another CPU when multiple CPUs are used

Multiple Interrupts and Prioritization

As you have now seen, there may be many different input and output devices and event indicators connected to interrupt lines. This means that there may be many different events vying for attention. Inevitably, multiple interrupts will occur from time to time.

There are two questions that must be answered when an interrupt occurs. First, are there other interrupts already awaiting service, and, if so, how does the computer determine the order in which the interrupts get serviced? And, second, how does the computer identify the interrupting device?

Two different processing methods are commonly used for determining which device initiated the interrupt. Some computers use a method known as **vectored interrupt,** in which the address of the interrupting device is included as part of the interrupt. Another method provides a general interrupt that is shared by all devices. The computer identifies the interrupting device by **polling** each device. These two methods are illustrated in Figures 9.10 and 9.11, respectively. The vectored interrupt method is obviously faster, but requires additional hardware to implement. Some systems use different interrupt lines for each interrupt; others use a method called "daisy chaining," which places the interrupts onto a single interrupt line to the CPU in such a way that highest priorities are recognized first.

Multiple interrupts can be handled by assigning **priorities** to each interrupt. In general, multiple interrupts will be handled top priority first. A higher-priority interrupt will be allowed to interrupt an interrupt of lower priority, but a lower-priority interrupt will have to wait until a higher-priority interrupt is completed.

This leads to a hierarchy of interrupts, in which higher-priority interrupts can interrupt other interrupts of lower priority, back and forth, eventually returning control to the original program that was running. Although this sounds complicated, this situation is actually quite common, and is fairly easy to implement. Figure 9.12 shows a simple example of this situation. In this figure, interrupt routine C is the highest priority, followed by B and A.

Most computer systems allow the system manager to establish priorities for the various interrupts. Priorities are established in a logical way. The highest priorities are reserved for time-sensitive situations, such as power failure or external events that are being time measured. Keyboard events are also usually considered high-priority events, since data loss can occur if the keyboard input is not read quickly. Task completion interrupts usually take lower priorities, since the delay will not affect the integrity of the data as much.

Depending on the system, priorities may be established with software or with hardware. In some systems, the priority of I/O device interrupts is established by the way their I/O module cards are physically

FIGURE 9.10

Vectored Interrupt Processing

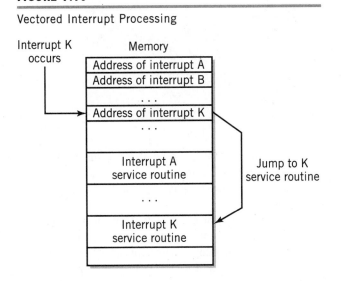

FIGURE 9.11

Polled Interrupt Processing

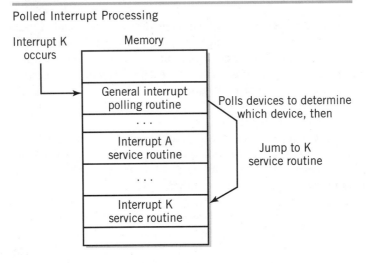

FIGURE 9.12

Multiple Interrupts

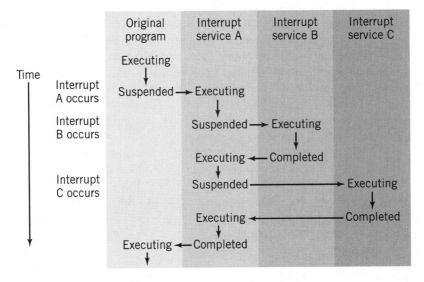

placed on the backplane. The daisy chain interrupt line can be used for this purpose: the highest-priority devices are placed closest to the CPU and block the signals of lower-priority devices that are farther down the line. In other systems, priorities are established by assigning a priority number to each interrupt.

Most interrupts can be temporarily disabled by program instructions when a program is performing a critical task that would be negatively affected if an interrupt were to occur. This is particularly true of time-sensitive tasks. In many systems, interrupts are **maskable;** that is, they can be selectively disabled. Certain interrupts, such as power failure, that are never disabled are sometimes referred to as *nonmaskable interrupts*. Most modern computer systems save interrupts that occur when interrupts are disabled, so that when the interrupts are reenabled, the pending interrupts will be processed.

EXAMPLE

In the IBM Z-architecture, interrupts are divided into six classes, with the priorities shown in Figure 9.9. All the different interrupts within each class are handled by the interrupt service routine for that class. Each interrupt class has two vectored addresses permanently associated with it. The first of these is a space reserved for the *Program Status Word* of the current program, known in IBM jargon as the *OLD PSW*. The Program Status Word is a 64-bit word that includes the program counter and other significant information about the program. The second vectored address contains a pointer to the interrupt routine. This address is known as the *NEW PSW*. The method used to switch from the original program to a service routine and back is illustrated in Figure 9.13.

When an interrupt occurs, the PSW for the current program is stored automatically in the OLD PSW space, and the NEW PSW is loaded. The effect is a jump to the location in memory pointed to by the NEW PSW, which is the location of the interrupt service routine for that class of interrupts. Incidentally, note that this procedure does not save other registers. Each interrupt service routine saves and restores the registers that it uses.

The Z-architecture CPU has an instruction LOAD OLD PSW. When the interrupt service routine is completed, it simply uses this instruction to return to the original program. Interrupts of lower priority are masked, but higher-priority interrupts are allowed to interrupt the lower-priority service routine while it is executing. Most important, interrupts belonging to the same class must be masked. Since there is only a single address space available for storing the OLD PSW for each class, a second interrupt of the same class would destroy the return address to the original program. Worse yet, the second interrupt would store the current address being executed in the OLD PSW space. Since that address is itself within the service routine, this would result in an infinite loop. To see this, look again at Figure 9.13. Pick a location inside the service routine, say, 205, and cause an interrupt to occur at that point. Now, follow through the diagram, and notice the results.

The preceding example demonstrates one way of providing return access from interrupts. An alternative method is used in Alpha series computers. The Alpha interrupt structure is also vectored, but the return address and Program Status Longword are stored on an interrupt stack. Using a stack in this way is essentially analogous to the way in which subroutine jumps and returns work. These were discussed in detail in Chapter 7. Stack storage for interrupts makes interrupts reentrant, although such a condition would seem to be extremely rare.

Interrupts are normally checked at the completion of each instruction. That is, interrupts are normally checked *after* one instruction is finished and *before* another begins. This assures that conditions won't change *in the middle* of an instruction that would affect the instruction's execution. Certain long S/390 and Alpha instructions can be interrupted in the middle of their fetch-execution cycle, however. These instructions use the general-purpose registers for their intermediate values, so it is important that the general-purpose registers be stored during an interrupt for later retrieval; otherwise, some instructions could not be restarted properly. The S/390 and Alpha computers do not automatically store registers when an interrupt occurs. It is therefore important that the interrupt programs be

FIGURE 9.13

Processing an
Interrupt in
the IBM
zSeries

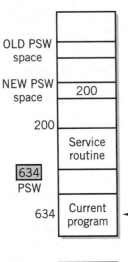

1. Before the interrupt occurs, the current program is executing normally. The OLD PSW space is empty, the NEW PSW space contains the starting address of the service routine. In this example, the service routine starts at location 200.

2. The interrupt occurs while current program is executing the instruction at location 633.

Interrupt occurs here

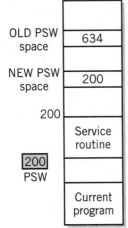

3. As a result, the current PSW value, 634, is stored in the OLD PSW space...

4. and the NEW PSW value, 200, is placed in the PSW. This will cause the service routine to execute.

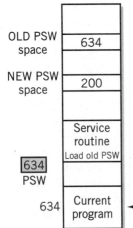

5. When the service routine is complete, it executes a LOAD OLD PSW instruction. This causes the value 634 to be loaded into the PSW. Thus, the current program resumes where it left off.

Program resumes here

written carefully so that the interrupted instruction doesn't crash when the routine is restarted. In the Alpha computer, the registers are also generally stored on a stack, which makes retrieval simple even if the interrupt routine itself is interrupted.

A technique for managing the use of memory known as *virtual storage* also requires the ability to interrupt in the middle of an instruction. Virtual storage is introduced in Chapter 11, and discussed more thoroughly in Chapter 16.

9.4 DIRECT MEMORY ACCESS

For most applications, it is impractical to transfer data to the CPU from a peripheral device using programmed I/O, even with interrupts. Indeed, the data from disks and tapes are transferred only in blocks, and it does not make sense to execute a separate instruction for each piece of data in the block. It is also more reasonable to transfer blocks of data directly between the I/O module and memory, since most processing will also take place in blocks. This suggests bypassing the CPU registers, if possible, and then processing the block of data as a group, from memory.

As a simple example, consider a program that sorts a block of numbers. To operate efficiently, the entire block of numbers must be stored in memory for the sort operation to take place, since instructions in the CPU can operate only on data in memory. Thus, it makes sense to move the entire block from disk to memory at once.

For this purpose, computer systems provide a more efficient form of I/O that transfers block data directly between the I/O module and computer memory, under control of the I/O module. The transfer is initiated by a program in the CPU, using programmed I/O, but the CPU can then be bypassed for the remainder of the transfer. The I/O module will notify the CPU with an interrupt when the transfer is complete. Once this has occurred, the data is in memory, ready for the program to use. This technique of I/O-memory data transfer is known as **direct memory access,** or more commonly, simply as **DMA.**

In Little Man terms, direct memory access could be viewed as providing data for the Little Man by loading data directly into the mailboxes from the rear, bypassing the Little Man I/O instruction procedures. To reemphasize the fact that this operation only takes place under program control, we would have to provide a means for the Little Man to initiate such a transfer and a means to notify the Little Man when the data transfer is complete.

For direct memory access to take place, three primary conditions must be met:

1. There must be a method to connect together the I/O interface and memory. In some systems both are already connected to the same bus, so this requirement is easily met. In other cases, the design must contain provisions for interconnecting the two. The issue of system configuration is discussed in Section 9.5.

2. The I/O module associated with the particular device must be capable of reading and writing to memory. It does so by simulating the CPU's interface with memory. Specifically, the I/O module must be able to load a memory address register and to read and write to a memory data register, whether its own or one outside the I/O module.

3. There must be a means to avoid conflict between the CPU and the I/O module. It is not possible for the CPU and a module that is controlling disk I/O to load different addresses into the MAR at the same instant, for example, nor is it

possible for two different I/O modules to transfer data between I/O and memory on the same bus at the same instant. This requirement simply means that memory can only be used by one device at a time, although some systems divide up memory in such a way that the CPU and I/O modules can access different parts of memory simultaneously. Special control circuits must be included to indicate which part of the system, CPU or particular I/O module, is in control of the memory and bus at any given instant.

DMA is particularly well suited for high-speed disk transfers, but there are several other advantages as well. Since the CPU is not actively involved during the transfer, the CPU can be used to perform other tasks during the time when I/O transfers are taking place. This is particularly useful for large multiuser systems. Of course, DMA is not limited to just disk-to-memory transfers. It can be used with other high-speed devices. And the transfers may be made in either direction. DMA is an effective means to transfer video data from memory to the video I/O system for rapid display, for example.

The procedure used by the CPU to initiate a DMA transfer is straightforward. Four pieces of data must be provided to the I/O controller for the particular I/O device to initiate the transfer. The four pieces of data that the I/O module must have to control a DMA transfer are

1. The location of the data on the I/O device (for example, the location of the block on the disk)
2. The starting location of the block of data in memory
3. The size of the block to be transferred
4. The direction of transfer, read (I/O → memory) or write (memory → I/O)

Normally, the I/O module would have four different I/O addresses available for this purpose. In most modern systems, normal programmed I/O output instructions are used to initiate a DMA transfer. On some systems, a fifth programmed I/O instruction actually initiates the transfer, whereas other systems start the DMA transfer when the fourth piece of data arrives at the I/O module.

IBM mainframes work a bit differently, although the principle is the same. A single programmed I/O START SUBCHANNEL instruction initiates the process. A separate **channel program** is stored in memory. The I/O module uses this channel program to perform its DMA control. The four pieces of data are a part of the channel program and are used by the I/O module to initiate the DMA transfer. The concept of I/O channels and subchannels is considered in more detail in Section 9.5.

Once the DMA transfer has been initiated, the CPU is free to perform other processing. Note, however, that the data being transferred should not be modified during this period, since doing so can result in transfer errors, as well as processing errors.

If, for example, a program should alter the number in a memory location being transferred to disk, the number transferred is ambiguous, dependent on whether the alteration occurred before or after the transfer of that particular location. Similarly, the use of a number being transferred into memory depends on whether the transfer for that particular location has already occurred.

This would be equivalent to having the Little Man read a piece of data from the area of memory being loaded from the rear of the mailboxes. The number on that piece of data would depend on whether a new value loaded in from the rear came before or after the Little Man's attempt to read it. Clearly, this is not an acceptable situation.

It is thus important that the CPU know when the transfer is complete, assuring that the data in memory is stable. The interrupt technique is used for this purpose. The program waiting for the data transfer is suspended or performs other, unrelated processing during the time of transfer. The controller sends a completion signal interrupt to the CPU when the transfer is complete. The interrupt service routine notifies the program that it may continue with the processing of the affected data.

Finally, note that it takes several programmed output instructions to initiate a DMA transfer. This suggests, correctly, that it is not useful to perform a DMA transfer for very small amounts of data. For small transfers, it is obviously more efficient to use programmed I/O. It is also worth pointing out that if a computer is capable only of performing a single task, then the time freed up by DMA cannot be used productively, and there is little advantage in using DMA.

It is worth interrupting the discussion at this point (yes, the pun was intentional) to remind you that in reality an application program would not be performing I/O directly, since doing so might conflict with other programs that are also performing I/O at the same time. Instead, the application program would request I/O services from the operating system software by calling a procedure within the operating system that performs the I/O operations described here. The I/O instructions and interrupt procedures are, of course, privileged: only the operating system software is allowed access to these instructions and procedures.

EXAMPLE

Consider the steps required to write a block of data to a disk from memory. The executing program has already created the block of data somewhere in memory.

First, the I/O service program uses programmed I/O to send four pieces of data to the disk-controlling I/O module: the location of the block in memory; the location where the data is to be stored on disk; the size of the block (this step might be unnecessary if a fixed disk size is always used on the particular system); and the direction of transfer, in this case a write to disk.

Next, the service program sends a "ready" message to the I/O module, again using programmed I/O. At this point, the DMA transfer process takes place, outside the control of the CPU, the I/O service, or the program that requested I/O service. Depending on the design of the operating system programs, the current application program may resume execution of other tasks, or it may be suspended until the DMA transfer is complete.

When the transfer is complete, the I/O module sends an interrupt to the CPU. The interrupt handler either returns control to the program that initiated the request or notifies the operating system that the program can be resumed, depending on the design of the system.

This example shows how the programmed I/O, DMA, and interrupt methodologies work together in the most important and common way of doing I/O. The technique is diagrammed in Figure 9.14.

9.5 CPU-MEMORY-I/O ARCHITECTURES

Now you have seen the various methodologies that are used to transfer data between an I/O device and memory for use by the CPU. You've seen that the use of DMA and a completion interrupt is an effective and efficient way to move large blocks of data quickly. You've also seen that programmed I/O is more effective for small amounts of data, particularly when

FIGURE 9.14

DMA Initiation and Control

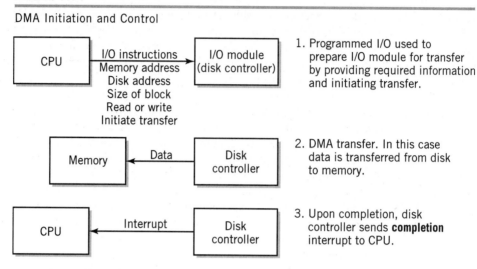

1. Programmed I/O used to prepare I/O module for transfer by providing required information and initiating transfer.

2. DMA transfer. In this case data is transferred from disk to memory.

3. Upon completion, disk controller sends **completion** interrupt to CPU.

speeds are extremely slow. You've seen how interrupts can be used together with programmed I/O to keep a pipeline of slow, character-based I/O data moving, for example, from a program to a modem.

In the next three sections, we are concerned about the blocks and interconnections that implement the various forms of I/O seen in a computer. There are various ways to interconnect the CPU, memory, and I/O peripherals, each with their own advantages and disadvantages.

Figure 9.15 illustrates the basic pathways required in a CPU-memory-I/O system. There are five basic components involved in the interface between the CPU and the I/O peripheral:

1. The CPU.
2. The I/O peripheral device.
3. Memory. Except for single pieces of input or output that can be transferred directly from a register, data from input or intended for output is normally stored at least temporarily in memory, where it can be accessed by the appropriate program, even for situations preferring programmed I/O.
4. One or more I/O modules. The I/O module(s) acts as an interface between the CPU or memory and one or more I/O device. The primary role of the I/O module is to receive commands from the CPU and to provide the control of the I/O device or devices so as to execute those commands. I/O modules are discussed later in this section.
5. The buses connecting the various components together. The bus may be an integral part of the architecture of the system or may simply be a point-to-point connection between other components, depending on the architectural design.

The pathway requires a connection between the CPU and the I/O module to enable the CPU to issue programmed I/O commands and also for the I/O module to provide

FIGURE 9.15

Basic CPU-Memory-I/O Pathway

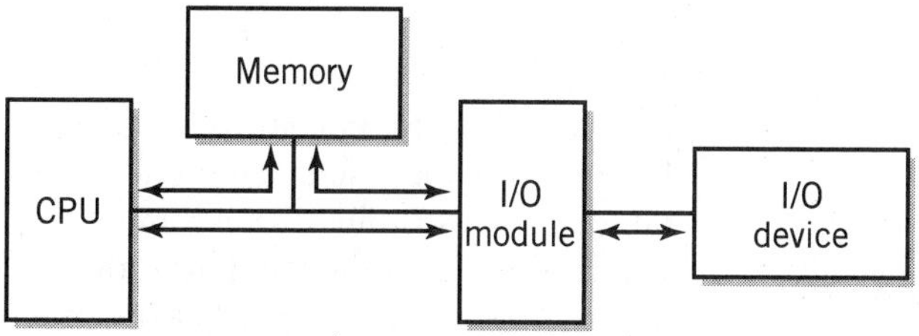

Source: From *PCI Local Bus Specification Production* Version 2, Copyright © 1993, by PCI Special Interest Group, pg. 9. Reprinted by permission.

completion interrupt signals to the CPU. The connection from the I/O module to the device or devices is required both for I/O module control of the devices and as a passageway for the data. There must be a connection between the I/O module and memory for DMA to take place.

Although the illustration implies that these pathways represent actual direct connections between the various component blocks, this is not actually true. In fact, you have already seen an alternative configuration in Figure 7.9. The connections could be direct or they could be electronic switches that provide the connections at the time they are required. For example, memory and the I/O modules could each be attached to different buses that are connected together when DMA takes place, or the I/O module could be attached by separate connections both to memory and to the CPU. These differences constitute different system architectures, representing different vendors, different goals, and different design philosophies.

There are two basic I/O system architectures in common use: **bus architecture** and **channel architecture.** The bus architecture is used in almost all personal computers, workstations, and in some mainframe computers, particularly Alpha-based computers. The channel architecture is found primarily in IBM mainframe computers.

Bus Architecture

In Chapter 7 you were introduced to the concept of a bus. In many systems, a bus forms the backbone for connection of the various components, memory and I/O, to the CPU. In simplest form, a single system bus connects the CPU to memory and to all the various modules that control I/O devices. More commonly, the system bus in a bus architecture consists of a number of different interconnected buses. The system bus organization of a PC, for example, often consists of a CPU bus, a PCI bus, and sometimes an ISA bus. This organization was illustrated in Figure 7.9. The various buses in a PC are interconnected by **bus interfaces,** sometimes known as *expansion bus* interfaces or *bus bridges.* A general bus interface configuration is shown in Figure 9.16.

Bus interfaces expand the flexibility of the system bus architecture by converting the bus signals from one bus to another so that different types of buses can be used together. These other bus types can then be used to connect to specific devices, such as disks or terminals.

The ability to interconnect buses makes possible the design and use of industry-standard buses on equipment of different vendors. The use of standard system buses generally simplifies the purchase, setup, and proper operation of peripherals from multiple vendors by allowing the connection of I/O devices that have been standardized across a wide range of equipment types and manufacturers. This is a major aspect of the concept of **open architectures.**

For example, numerous manufacturers produce various I/O modules mounted on printed circuit cards that plug into the PCI bus that is provided on the backplane of any

FIGURE 9.16

Bus Configuration

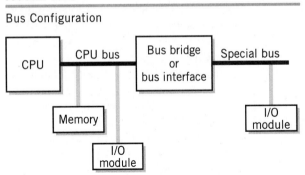

current "PC-compatible" model. Circuitry in the PC connects memory and the PCI bus together during DMA transfers, which provides the required CPU-memory-I/O link. These cards provide audio capability, serial and parallel ports, modem connections, an Ethernet interface, and many other functions, demonstrating the advantages of standardization. Although Intel originally designed the PCI backplane, it has become a standard through common use and agreement. It is found on Apple Macintosh, Sun, Compaq Alpha, and many other machines.

The ability to interconnect buses also provides flexibility for the future; as bus designs evolve, new bus interfaces can be implemented to add the capabilities of new and improved buses to the system. As Figure 7.9 shows, there can even be multiple levels of bus control.

Notice from Figure 9.16 that an interconnection of two buses may mean that memory and I/O devices will be connected to different buses. The bus interface includes the necessary connections to allow DMA and interrupt capability.

It is not important to understand the details of a particular bus. What is important to note is how similar buses are, in essence, differing mostly in details and implementation. Each bus provides the necessary data and address lines, lines for interrupts, and various lines to control timing, reads and writes, and so on. The major differences, other than specifications, actual pin assignments, and physical differences, lie in the way the control signals are implemented. For example, the ISA bus is defined by its data width as a "16-bit" bus. The PCI bus can be used to support either a 32-bit or 64-bit data width. The ISA bus has separate data and address lines. Addresses and data share the same lines on the PCI bus, using a technique called **multiplexing.** The PCI bus is designed to transfer several pieces of data in a rapid sequence called a **burst** once a starting address is established.

Figure 9.17 provides another illustration of the use of bus controllers to expand the capability of a system. This illustration represents the architecture of the Compaq 7000 and 10000 AXP System mainframe families. This design allows the connection of up to four different buses. As an example, the system in the illustration uses one Futurebus+, one XMI bus, and one PCI bus. There is still one port available for an additional bus.

BUS CHARACTERISTICS Buses are characterized primarily by their configuration, their width, their speed, and their particular use. In addition, a bus will operate according to an associated protocol. Buses may be designed for use within the CPU, as interconnections between major system components, and between the system and external devices. We refer to buses in the last category as external buses. Buses internal to the CPU are defined entirely by their usage. The bus width, speed, configuration, and protocol will be determined by the requirements of the specific job that the bus is to perform. External buses must meet a different set of criteria. Such issues as standardization, speed adequate to the task the bus is to perform, convenience, and physical layout become important issues in external bus design.

FIGURE 9.17

Compaq 7000 and 10000 System Architecture

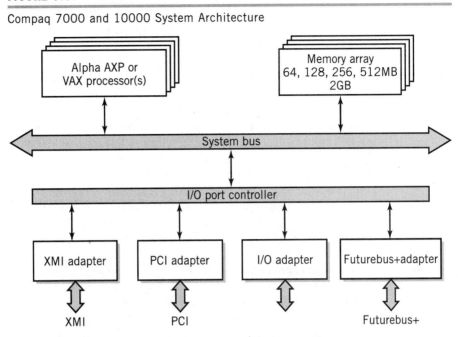

Source: Reproduced with permission from the *Digital Technical Journal*, vol. 4, no. 4 of Digital Equipment Corp.

In Chapter 7, we differentiated buses topologically as point-to-point or multipoint. We noted that many of the unnamed buses within the CPU itself are point-to-point, whereas the system buses are more often multipoint. Although there are a number of other bus configurations in use as external interfaces, these are, in actuality, combinations of point-to-point and multipoint buses together with devices, such as bridges, that connect the various pieces together and pass appropriate signals back and forth. It is sometimes useful to describe a bus as "point-to-point" or "multipoint" strictly from the point of view of its external connections, without regard to its actual internal configuration.

Buses are also generally characterized as parallel or serial. By definition, a parallel bus is simply a bus in which there is an individual line for each bit of data, address, and control being used. This means that all the bits being transferred on the bus can be transferred simultaneously. A serial bus is a bus in which data is transferred sequentially, one bit at a time, using a single data line pair. (A data return line is required to complete the circuit, just as there are two wires in a standard 110-volt power circuit.)

A parallel bus that carries 32 bits of data and 32 bits of address on separate data and address lines would require a bus width of 64 lines, even before control lines are considered. The parallel bus is characterized by high throughput capability because all the bits of a data word are transferred at once. Virtually every bus internal to the computer is a parallel bus, since the high speed is essential to computer operation, particularly between the CPU and memory, but also between the CPU and high-speed devices such as disks and graphics display modules.

The parallel bus can be expensive for external use when the distance is more than a few feet because of the large number of lines required, and because of the possibility of electrical interference between the various lines. As a result, parallel bus use is usually confined to internal use and to short external distances.

Data on a serial bus is transferred sequentially, one bit at a time. Because of this the throughput of a serial bus is theoretically lower than that of a parallel bus capable of the same per line transfer rate. Realistically, current technology is such that serial bus transmission rates are rarely a problem. Generally, a serial bus has a single data line pair and perhaps a few control lines. There are no separate address lines. The simplest serial buses even manage to avoid the use of control lines. Many serial buses are used for point-to-point connection, so no addressing is required. If addressing is required, the address may be multiplexed with the data. What this means is that the same line is used for both address and data; if an address is required, the address is sent first, one bit at a time, followed by the data.

Due to the small number of lines in a serial bus, the cost per foot of line is much lower, and the serial bus is usually preferred for longer distances. For example, the transfer rate for connecting a modem to a computer is fairly low. The serial bus commonly used in personal computers is sufficient for this purpose, and is commonly used in this application.

At its ultimate simplification, the serial bus can be reduced to a single data line pair, used for data, control, and addressing. Using modern materials such as fiber optics, very high transfer rates may be achieved. Control is handled using a bus protocol that establishes agreement as to the meaning and timing of each signal on the line among the devices connected to the line. This solution is used for networking and for long-distance communication and is discussed at more length in Chapter 11.

It is also possible to design a parallel bus that multiplexes addresses and data on the same lines, as the PCI bus demonstrates, or multiplexes 32-bit data on 16 data lines, for example. The Pentium 4 multiplexes 128-bit data words to fit a 64-bit data path on the Pentium system bus.

EXTERNAL INTERFACE BUSES AND PORTS   Buses also provide a means for devices external to the system buses to communicate with the system. Such I/O devices are commonly called **peripherals** or *peripheral devices* because they are connected peripherally to the system. Many modern peripherals are designed to operate from a standard port. (A reminder from Chapter 7: a *port* is simply a connector at the end of a bus into which a device can be plugged.) General control for the port is provided by a port controller. The port controller connects to a standard bus, such as a PCI or ISA bus. Specific device control is built into a controller within the device itself and into the computer software programs that control I/O from these devices. These programs are called **device drivers.** Device drivers are either built into the computer's operating system, or they are installed into the operating system as supplements to the system. Printers, modems, and mice are frequently connected to computer systems through general I/O bus ports called **parallel** and **serial** ports. Disk drives, DVD-ROMs, graphics scanners, video cameras, and other devices can be connected to the computer system through one of several high-speed general interface bus ports. Interface buses in common use for this purpose include **USB, SCSI,** and **IEEE 1394** buses. USB stands for Universal Serial Bus; SCSI stands for Small Computer System Interface. The IEEE 1394 bus is officially named after the specification that describes it, but is more often called **FireWire** or, less commonly, *i.link*.

Historically, the serial and parallel ports served as the standard external interfaces for early minicomputers and personal computers, and are still provided on today's PCs, although the serial port, in particular, is of diminishing importance on new machines. It is important that you understand that the names "serial port" and "parallel port" describe specific port implementations (i.e., connectors found on the back of a PC), and must not be confused with the more general descriptive use of the words "serial" and "parallel" to characterize buses.

The pin connections for a parallel port are shown in Figure 9.18. With the exception of Apple Macintosh computers, most personal computer and workstation printers are connected to a computer using this port. The parallel port interface bus is particularly simple because it was originally designed by a printer vendor as a point-to-point bus for a single type of device; thus, no device addressing was required, and the control lines were specific to printer needs. Like many proprietary buses, this bus became a standard through widespread general use. A more recent version of the bus, known by its standard, IEEE 1284, allows multiple devices to share the parallel port, but this capability is only occasionally used. Indeed, USB-based printers are reducing the use of the parallel port in general.

The SCSI bus is also a parallel bus designed for "universal" I/O interfacing. SCSI devices include disk drives, CD-ROM drives, tape drives, scanners, and other I/O devices. Unlike the standard parallel port bus, the SCSI bus does provide addressing for each device. The SCSI bus is designed to be "daisy chained." Each device on the bus is plugged into the previous device, as shown in Figure 9.19. The final device on the daisy chain has a terminator, which prevents signals from echoing back down the bus in the wrong direction. There is also a terminator in the SCSI bus controller. The I/O devices each contain their own specific built-in device controller.

The connections for the original PC serial bus, known as RS-232C for the industry standard that defines the bus, are shown in Figure 9.20. On this bus, data is normally transferred using a single data line for each direction. The figure includes a number of control

FIGURE 9.18

Standard PC Parallel Interface

Signal	Description
DO-D7	Data bits
$\overline{STR}$	Low signal sends data to printer
$\overline{ACK}$	Low signal indicates printer received character and is ready for more
BSY	Busy; indicates character received and being processed, printer buffer full, printer offline, printer error, or printer is being initialized
PAP	Indicates out of paper
OFON	Indicates printer is on-line
$\overline{ALF}$	Auto line feed. Low signal tells printer to issue line feed automatically
$\overline{FEH}$	Low signal indicates out of paper, printer offline, or printer error
$\overline{INI}$	Low signal initializes printer
$\overline{DSL}$	Low level selects printer
Ground	

FIGURE 9.19

Daisy Chaining a SCSI Bus

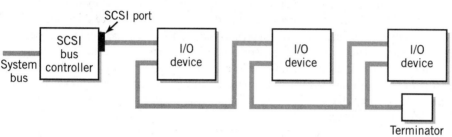
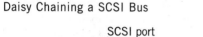

FIGURE 9.20

RS-232C Serial Interface

Signal	Description
TD	Transmitted data
RD	Received data
RTS	Request to send
CTS	Clear to send (okay to send)
DSR	Data set ready
DCD	Data carrier detect
DTR	Data terminal ready
RI	Ring indicator
Ground	

lines, although most of them are not required and are used in only a few applications. They are usually included in the serial port connector. Additional control lines are defined in the specification, but most systems don't even include them, and we have not listed them in the figure. This bus, and a faster variation known as RS-422, are commonly used to connect terminals, modems, mice, and network interfaces to computers. The odd signal names reflect the fact that the specification was designed primarily for telephone communications.

The RS-232C bus is one example of a *serial* bus. Notice that the RS-232C bus does not contain any address lines. A single RS-232C bus is normally used to connect only a single device; therefore, an address is rarely required. Most personal computers provide several serial ports, each of which can be connected to a different I/O device.

The Universal Serial Bus was created to replace the standard serial port. USB differs from previous serial bus designs in a number of significant ways.

- It is significantly faster. USB-2 is capable of a data transfer rate up to 480 megabits per second, which makes it suitable for use with a wide range of devices.

- Globally, USB can be viewed as a multipoint bus. Multiple devices can be connected to USB. USB uses a hierarchical connection system, in which **hubs** are used to provide multiple connection points for I/O devices. Although the host controller is aware of the location of each of the hubs, the hubs simply pass data through, so that it appears that each I/O device is directly connected to the bus at the host controller. The USB topology is illustrated in Figure 9.21.

- Devices can be added and removed at any time without powering down the system. Removal of a hub removes all of the devices attached to the hub.

- Data is transferred over the USB in packets. Each packet contains a device identifier and a small set of data, representing all or a portion of the data to be transferred by that device. Thus, a single device cannot tie up the system. The USB protocol allows packets to be scheduled for delivery at regular time intervals. This technique is known as **isochronous data transfer.** This assures that a device

FIGURE 9.21

USB Topology Example

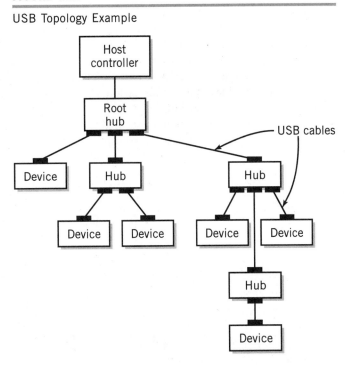

transmitting data such as audio or video at a regular rate will receive sufficient bus time to prevent data dropouts, as long as the aggregate requirement of all the devices connected does not exceed the maximum data transfer rate of the bus.

■ The USB supports up to 127 devices. A system can support multiple USB host controllers to increase this number even further.

The USB cable holds four wires. Two lines make up a single data pair to carry the data, as well as address and control information. The other two lines can be used to provide power to devices connected to the bus. USB connectors at each end of a cable are polarized to force a hierarchical structure emanating from the host controller.

Like USB, FireWire is a serial, multipoint bus specification. FireWire is designed for extremely fast data transfer. The latest version of FireWire will support a projected data transfer rate of up to 3.2 gigabits per second, which is suitable for the transfer of full-motion video with sound, for handling video conferencing data, and for other applications with high-speed data transfer requirements. FireWire has many of the characteristics of a network: FireWire devices can be daisy-chained or connected together with hubs; network components such as repeaters, splitters, and bridges can be used to segment and extend the FireWire bus to support longer distances and additional devices. FireWire connections can be made using either copper or fiber optic cable. Each segment of the bus can handle up to sixty-three devices. Like USB, I/O devices may be connected or removed during operation, and, like USB, a packet protocol that can guarantee performance for isochronous data transfer is used for data transfer and control. One major difference between USB and FireWire is that each device controller in a FireWire connection is independent, so that no host bus controller is required. Thus, devices can communicate with each other via FireWire without the presence of a computer. However, FireWire control capability must be built into every I/O module connected to a FireWire bus. An example of a FireWire application is shown in Figure 9.22. FireWire uses a cable made up of two data pairs and an optional pair of power lines. Further discussion of splitters, repeaters, bridges, and other network components is deferred to Chapter 11.

Figure 9.23 demonstrates the method that is used to connect serial, parallel, and USB ports to a PCI bus in a personal computer. Bus controllers convert the bus signals between

FIGURE 9.22

Typical FireWire Configuration

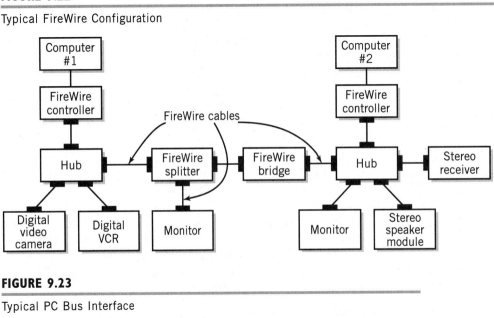

FIGURE 9.23

Typical PC Bus Interface

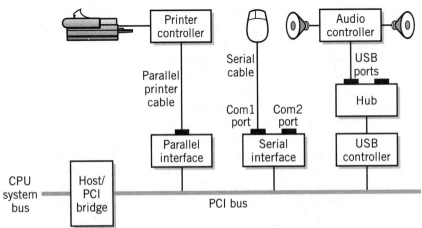

the form that is used on the PCI bus and the form required at the port where the alternative bus is to be connected. This is true for all three kinds of buses. (The same method would apply if the ports were being connected to an ISA bus or any other bus.) The serial interface is of particular interest because the PCI bus presents all the data simultaneously, but the serial port must present the data sequentially, one bit at a time. A device known as a *UART,* for *universal asynchronous receiver transmitter,* is commonly used for this purpose. The USB controller operates similarly but also must organize the data into packets appropriate for each device. Other examples of the use of a bus architecture are the ones that were shown for the PC in Figure 7.9 and the Alpha mainframes in Figure 9.17.

Some computers take advantage of the fact that memory is connected to the same bus structure as the I/O peripheral devices. By assigning different addresses to each, the CPU can use the same LOAD, STORE, and MOVE instructions to perform I/O functions as it would to move data between the CPU and memory. This simplifies the instruction set. For example, high addresses above memory are used as device addresses on Alpha systems. Lower addresses are used to address memory. Since there is no specific distinction between memory and the I/O devices in this type of system, no I/O instructions are required. This technique, known as **memory mapping,** is used in the Alpha system and also in computers based on the Motorola 68000 series of CPUs.

Channel Architecture

An alternative I/O architecture is used by IBM in all their mainframe computers since the late 1970s. The basic architecture, known as *channel architecture,* is shown in Figure 9.24. The channel architecture is based on a separate I/O processor known as a **channel subsystem.** The I/O processor acts as a separate computer just for I/O operations, thus freeing the computer CPU for other tasks. The channel subsystem executes its own set of instructions, known as **channel control words,** independent of the CPU. Channel control words are stored as "programs" in memory, just like other computer instructions.

The channel subsystem is made up of **subchannels,** each of which is connected through a *control unit* module to an individual device by one or more *channel paths.* The control unit module serves the same role as a device controller. The design allows multiple channel paths between the channel subsystem and a control unit, so that if one is busy another can be selected. Up to eight different channel paths can exist for a particular I/O device. Channel paths can also be used to interconnect computers into a cluster.

FIGURE 9.24

I/O Channel Architecture

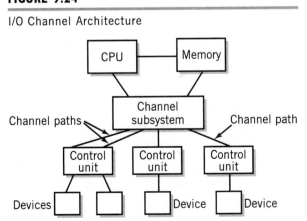

Information about the characteristics of each subchannel and its corresponding device are stored in memory. Each subchannel is operated by executing a channel program, also stored in memory, made up of channel command words. The primary purpose of channel programs is to transfer data using DMA between an I/O device and memory.

Several different channel programs are available to perform different I/O functions, such as read a block, write a block, and so on, for each type of device on the system. The channel subsystem manages all I/O, independent of the CPU, and also supplies the appropriate interrupts and status information to the CPU upon completion of an I/O operation or if a problem occurs. The channel subsystem can perform several I/O functions simultaneously.

A CPU program initiates an I/O operation by issuing a START SUBCHANNEL command to the channel subsystem. The START SUBCHANNEL command specifies the subchannel number, which identifies the device, and the particular channel program to be executed. The channel subsystem attempts to identify an available channel path and initiates data transfer. If there is no available channel path, the channel subsystem simply holds the request until a path becomes available. In this way, the channel subsystem frees the CPU from having to keep track of the status of the I/O operation.

The IBM architecture also provides I/O instructions to halt the subchannel operation, to resume the subchannel operation, to test subchannels, and to configure the subchannels.

There are six different types of channel control word instructions:

- Read
- Write
- Read backward (used for tape)
- Control (used for controlling a device, such as rewinding a tape or positioning a disk head)
- Sense (used to determine the status of a device)
- Transfer in channel (equivalent to a JUMP instruction)

Although these instructions are used specifically for I/O, in other respects they are similar to other computer instructions. Each instruction has its own op code and address field. Each instruction results in the execution of a fetch-execute cycle by the channel subsystem. A simple channel program appears in Figure 9.25. This program performs a disk read operation.

The channel control word instructions are designed in such a way that a single I/O operation can transfer a number of blocks. The blocks do not have to be contiguous on the disk or tape, nor do they have to be contiguous in memory. This feature provides a lot of flexibility.

FIGURE 9.25

Simple Channel Program

Instruction	Comment
CONTROL	SEEK operation, to place head over correct track
SEARCH ID	Read ID of record on track and compare with specified ID
TRANSFER IN CHANNEL	Branch if unequal, back to previous instruction to look at next record
READ	Read the record, DMA into memory

Source: From *IBM Mainframes*, 2nd Ed., N. Prasad and J. Savit, Copyright © 1994, by McGraw-Hill Companies. Reprinted by permission.

Physically, the channel subsystem is connected to the CPU by a bus, and the various control units and I/O devices are also connected by buses. Conceptually, the channel architecture is very different, however, and the buses connecting the various parts of the I/O system are not identified as such.

9.6 I/O MODULES

In the example shown in Figure 9.14, a major role is played by the disk controller. The disk controller is an example of an I/O module. The I/O module serves as an interface between the CPU and the specific device, in this case a disk drive, accepting commands from the CPU on one side and controlling the device on the other. In this example, the I/O module provides the following functions:

- The I/O module recognizes messages addressed to it and accepts commands from the CPU establishing what the disk drive is to do. In this case, the I/O module recognizes that a block of data is to be written from memory to disk using DMA.

- The I/O module provides a buffer where the data from memory can be held until it can be transferred to the disk.

- The I/O module provides the necessary registers and controls to perform a direct memory transfer. This requires that the I/O module have access to a memory address register and a memory data register separate from those of the CPU, either within the I/O module or as a separate DMA controller.

- The I/O module controls the disk drive, moving the head to the physical location on the disk where data is to be written.

- The I/O module copies data from its buffer to the disk.

- The I/O module has interrupt capability, which it uses to notify the CPU when the transfer is complete. It can also interrupt the CPU to notify it of errors or problems that arise during the transfer.

The channel architecture works similarly, although the I/O task is divided into two separate types of I/O modules, the channel subsystem, which controls I/O operations generally, and individual control unit modules, which control specific devices or groups of similar devices.

Regardless of the architecture, it is desirable to offload tasks specific to I/O operations from the CPU to a separate module or modules which are designed specifically for I/O data transfer and device control. This frees the CPU to perform other tasks while the much slower I/O operations are taking place. It also allows control of several different I/O devices to occur simultaneously.

As seen in Figure 9.26, I/O modules perform two different functions. At the CPU interface, the module performs CPU interfacing tasks: accepting I/O commands from the CPU, transferring data between the module and the CPU or memory, and sending interrupts and status information to the CPU. At the device interface, the I/O module supplies control of the device—moving the head to the correct track in a disk drive and rewinding tape, for example. Small-system and bus architectures often combine these two roles into a single module. The channel architecture separates each task into a different I/O module. Most I/O modules provide buffering of the data to synchronize the different speeds of the CPU and the various I/O devices.

FIGURE 9.26

I/O Module Interfaces

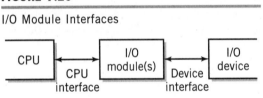

An I/O module or control unit module used to control a peripheral device is known as a **device controller.** Often, the device is named—the module in the preceding example would be referred to specifically as a *disk controller,* a network module would be called a *network interface controller.* A device controller accepts I/O requests and interacts directly with the device to satisfy those requests. The device controllers are individually designed to provide the specialized built-in circuitry necessary for control of a particular type of device. This ability is important, because there is such a variety of requirements for different peripheral devices. A tape drive must be turned on and off and switched between fast forward, play, and rewind. A disk head must be moved to the correct track. A display screen requires a steady transfer of data representing each point on the screen and special circuitry to maintain the correct position on the screen for the display of each point. (Operation of a display controller is discussed in Chapter 10.)

It would be difficult to program the CPU to provide the correct types of signals to operate these and other types of I/O devices, and the CPU time required to control these devices would significantly reduce the usefulness of the system. With a device controller, simple CPU I/O instructions can be used to control quite complex operations. Multiple devices of the same kind can often be controlled with a single controller.

In a small system, most of the I/O modules are device controllers that serve as direct interfaces between the system bus and each of the system's peripheral devices. There may also be I/O modules that act as an additional interface between the system bus and other modules that then connect to the device. In a typical PC, for example, the disk controller is normally mounted inside the PC case and connects directly to a system bus. The printer, on the other hand, is controlled indirectly. One I/O module connects to the system bus and terminates in a parallel bus or USB port; the actual print controller is inside the printer, at the other end of the bus.

In general I/O modules simplify the task of interfacing peripheral devices to a CPU. I/O modules offload a considerable amount of work from the CPU. They make it possible to control I/O to a peripheral with a few simple I/O commands from the CPU. They support DMA, so that the CPU may be free to perform other tasks. And, as we have already noted, device controllers provide the specialized circuitry required to interface different types of peripherals to the computer.

Much of the power in modern computers comes from the ability to separate out CPU operations from other, more individualistic, I/O peripheral functions, and allowing the processing of each to progress in parallel. In fact, the more powerful the computer, the more essential is the separation of I/O to the satisfactory operation of the system as a whole.

SUMMARY AND REVIEW

Chapter 9 describes the two methods used for I/O, programmed I/O and DMA, and introduces the various components and configurations that make both methods possible.

After a brief description of the I/O requirements of the most common peripherals, the text describes the process of programmed I/O, and describes the advantages and disadvantages of this technique. In general, the use of programmed I/O is limited to slow devices that are not block oriented.

Next, we introduced the concept of an interrupt, a means of causing the CPU to take special action. We described various ways in which an interrupt could be used, including as notification of an external event that requires attention, as a completion signal for I/O, as a means of allocating CPU time, as an abnormal event indicator, and as a way for software to cause the CPU to take special action. We explained the method used by the interrupt to attract the CPU's attention and the ways in which the interrupt is serviced by the CPU. We considered the situation in which multiple interrupts occur and discussed the prioritization of interrupts.

As an alternative to programmed I/O, direct memory access allows the transfer of blocks of data directly between an I/O device and memory. We discussed the hardware requirements that make DMA possible and showed how DMA is used. We explained how DMA works in conjunction with interrupts.

Two methods are commonly used as architectures to connect the CPU, memory, and I/O. The I/O channel method is used by IBM and other large mainframe manufacturers. The bus method is used on Alpha systems and most smaller computers. In the text we explain both methods. We expand on the bus discussion from Chapter 7 to include I/O and discuss several standard buses that are in common use. We show the way the buses interconnect the CPU, memory, and I/O and how the buses themselves can be interconnected. We also show the layout for a channel architecture and discuss how it is used in operation.

We conclude with a discussion of the I/O modules that serve to control the I/O devices and act as an interface between the peripheral devices, the CPU, and memory. The I/O modules receive messages from the CPU, control the device, initiate and control DMA when required, and produce interrupts. The I/O modules in a channel architecture also serve to direct I/O requests to the proper channel and provide independent, intelligent control of the I/O operation.

KEY CONCEPTS AND TERMS

abnormal event	IEEE 1394	privileged instruction
buffer	I/O module	process control block
burst transfer	interrupt	(PCB)
bus architecture	interrupt handler	programmed I/O
bus interface	interrupt lines	quantum
channel architecture	interrupt routine	SCSI
channel control word	interrupt service	serial port
channel program	isochronous data transfer	software interrupt
channel subsystem	maskable	subchannel
device controller	memory mapped I/O	SuperVisor Call
direct memory access	multiplexing	trap
(DMA)	open architecture	USB (Universal Serial Bus)
exception	parallel port	vectored interrupt
external event	peripheral	processing
FireWire	polled interrupt processing	
hub	priority	

FOR FURTHER READING

Detailed discussions of I/O concepts and techniques, including the concepts of interrupts and DMA can be found in the engineering textbooks previously mentioned, particularly those by Stallings [STAL02] and Tanenbaum [TAN99]. An outstanding treatment of I/O in the IBM mainframe architecture can be found in Prasad [PRAS94] and in Cormier and others [CORM83]. The bus architecture used in Digital mainframes is discussed in Allison [ALL92]. PC I/O is discussed in a number of excellent books, among them Messmer [MESS01] and Sargent [SARG95]. Somewhat less organized, but still valuable, is the treatment found in Henle [HENL92]. Discussions of the USB can be found in McDowell and Sager [McD99] and Anderson [AND97]. FireWire is presented in Anderson [AND98]. Much additional information may be found on the Web. A simple explanation of FireWire can be found at www.skipstone.com/compcon.html or at www.1394ta.org. The USB specification is available at www.usb.org.

EXERCISES

9.1 Why would DMA be useless if the computer did not have interrupt capability?

9.2 What is the advantage of using a disk controller to control the hard disk? How else could you do the job that the disk controller does?

9.3 DMA is rarely used with dumb computer terminals. Why?

9.4 Consider the interrupt that occurs at the completion of a disk transfer.

  a. "Who" is interrupting "whom?"

  b. Why is the interrupt used in this case? What would be necessary if there were no interrupt capability on this computer?

  c. Describe the steps that take place after the interrupt occurs.

9.5 What are the trade-offs in using a serial bus versus a parallel bus to move data from one place to another?

9.6 Suppose you wish to send a block of data to a tape drive for storage using DMA. What information must be sent to the tape controller before the DMA transfer can take place?

9.7 What is an interrupt vector?

9.8 What is polling used for? What are the disadvantages of polling? What is a better way to perform the same job?

9.9 The signals in computer buses are usually divided into three categories.

  a. State the three categories and explain the purpose of each. Into which category does an interrupt line fit?

  b. The parallel bus that externally connects a PC to a printer is missing one of the categories. Which one is missing and why is it generally not needed?

  c. Under what condition is it needed and how can this be accomplished with the present bus?

9.10 What are the trade-offs between a serial bus and a parallel bus?

9.11 To use a computer for multimedia (moving video and sound), it is important to maximize the efficiency of the I/O. Assume that the blocks of a movie are stored consecutively on a CD-ROM. Describe the steps used to retrieve the blocks for use by the movie display software. Discuss ways in which you could optimize the performance of the I/O transfer.

9.12 Assume that the text to be output to a printer is sitting at a particular block of consecutive locations in memory. Also assume that the printer sends an interrupt that results in a jump to some memory location, say, 06, each time it has completed printing the previous character. When not sending a character to the printer, the CPU simply waits.

Describe the operation of the printer driver program in as much detail as you can.

9.13 A simple character printer could use programmed I/O reasonably well, since the printer speed is slow compared to the CPU. Yet most modern printers use DMA. Why?

9.14 The UNIX operating system differentiates between block-oriented and character-oriented devices. Give an example of each, explain the differences between them, and explain how the I/O process differs for each.

9.15 Discuss the major differences, advantages, and disadvantages between bus I/O and channel I/O.

9.16 Describe a circumstance where an interrupt occurs at the beginning of an event. Describe a circumstance where an interrupt occurs at the completion of an event. What is the difference between the types of events?

9.17 In general, what purpose does an interrupt serve? Stated another way, suppose there were no interrupts provided in a computer. What capabilities would be lost?

9.18 What is the difference between polling and polled interrupt processing?

9.19 Describe the steps that occur when a system receives multiple interrupts.

9.20 Explain how the three primary conditions required for DMA described in the text are met by the I/O channel architecture.

CHAPTER 10

COMPUTER PERIPHERALS

"I DIDN'T MIND HIS POCKET COMPUTER, BUT NOW THAT HE'S ADDED A CD-ROM, AN EXTERNAL HARD DRIVE, AND A PORTABLE INKJET PRINTER, IT'S GOTTEN A BIT OUT OF HAND."

Thomas Sperling. Adapted, courtesy of David Ahl, Creative Computing.

10.0 INTRODUCTION

The typical personal computer described in an advertisement consists of a CPU, memory, a floppy disk drive, a hard disk drive, one or more (commonly two) serial ports, one or more (usually one) parallel port(s), USB ports, a keyboard, a mouse, a network interface, probably a CD-ROM or DVD-ROM drive and a sound system, a modem, and a monitor. Additional available components include tape drives, scanners of various types, printers, plotters, and audio and video input devices. Internal to the computer there is also a power supply that converts wall plug power into voltages suitable for powering a computer. All the items mentioned, except for the CPU, memory, and power supply, are considered peripheral (that is, external) to the main processing function of the computer itself and are known, therefore, as **peripherals.** Some of the peripherals use the parallel, USB, and serial ports as their interconnection point to the computer. Others have their own interface to the system bus.

The peripherals in a mainframe computer are similar, except larger, with more capacity. Rather than a single keyboard and monitor, there may be hundreds, located remotely from the computer in the form of terminals and workstation computers. Large numbers of hard disk drives may be grouped into arrays to provide capacities of hundreds or thousands of gigabytes (GB). In addition to CD-ROM or DVD drives, there may be a bank of optical or electro-optical storage devices. A fast network interface will be a major component.

Despite different packaging and differences in details, the basic operations of these devices are similar, regardless of the type of computer. In previous chapters we have already looked at the I/O operations that control devices that are external to the CPU. Now we direct our attention to the operation of the devices themselves. In this chapter we study the most important computer peripheral devices. We look at the usage, important characteristics, basic physical layouts, and internal operations of each device. We will also briefly consider the interface characteristics for these devices.

Peripheral devices are classified as input devices, output devices, or storage devices. As you would expect, input data is data *from* the outside world *into* the CPU, and output data is data moving *from* the CPU *out to* the outside world. Storage devices are, of course, both input and output devices, though not at the same time. If you recall the discussion of input process-output from Chapter 1, programs require input, process it, and then produce output. Using a storage device, data output is stored, to be used as input at a future time. In a transaction processing system, for example, the master file is generally stored on line. When the update program is run, it will use input from the master file together with new transaction data, also stored on disk or tape, to create a newly updated master file as output.

Because of the importance of disk and tape storage devices, we will begin with a discussion of these devices. Following that, we will consider various input and output devices.

It should be noted that the technologies used for many peripheral components are very sophisticated; some would even say that these devices operate by magic! You may agree when you see the descriptions of some components. It is not uncommon to have more sophisticated control and technology in a peripheral component than in the computer itself. Perhaps you have wondered how these devices work. Here's your opportunity to find out!

We have not attempted to provide a detailed explanation of every possible peripheral device in a computer system. Instead, we have selected several interesting devices that are representative of a number of technologies.

At the completion of this chapter, you will have been exposed to every important hardware component of the computer system, with the exception of the components that tie computer systems together into networks. You will have seen the role and the inner workings of each component, and you will have seen how the different components fit together to form a complete computer system. You will have a better understanding of how to select particular components to satisfy specific system requirements and of how to determine device capacities and capabilities.

10.1 THE HIERARCHY OF STORAGE

Computer storage is often conceptualized hierarchically, based upon the speed with which data can be accessed. The table in Figure 10.1 shows this hierarchy, together with some typical speed factors.

At the top of the hierarchy are the CPU registers used to hold data for the short term while processing is taking place. Access to registers is essentially instantaneous, since the registers are actually a part of the CPU. Cache memory, if present, is the fastest memory outside the CPU. You recall from Chapter 8 that cache memory is a small fast memory that is used to hold current data and instructions. The CPU will always attempt to access current instructions and data in cache memory before it looks at conventional memory. There may be as many as three different levels of cache. The CPU accesses the data or instruction in conventional memory if cache memory is not present. Next in the hierarchy is conventional memory. Both conventional and cache memory are referred to as **primary memory.**

FIGURE 10.1

The Storage Hierarchy

Storage medium	Typical average access time	Data throughput rate
CPU registers		(see text)
Cache memory	2–10 nsec	(see text)
Conventional memory	10–50 nsec	(see text)
Expanded storage	75–500 nsec	(see text)
Flash memory	10.8 msec	3.5–8 MB/sec
Hard disk	10–50 msec	600–6000 KB/sec
Floppy disk	95 msec	100–200 KB/sec
CD-ROM	100–600 msec	500–4000 KB/sec
Tape	.5 sec. and up	2000 KB/sec (cartridge)

Both provide immediate access to program instructions and data by the CPU and can be used for the execution of programs. The data throughput rate of memory is determined primarily by the capability of the bus that connects memory to the CPU. Rates in excess of 1 GB/sec are common in modern computers.

Storage below conventional memory in the hierarchy is not immediately available to the CPU. **Expanded storage** is a type of random access memory (RAM) storage that is occasionally provided as an option on large systems. It furnishes large amounts of storage and serves as a buffer between conventional memory and the much slower media below it in the hierarchy. Data is transferred between expanded storage and conventional memory in 4 kilobyte (KB) blocks for CPU access. Expanded storage has largely been replaced by additional conventional memory and disk buffer storage.

Below this level, storage in the hierarchy is referred to as **secondary storage** and is treated as I/O. Data and programs in secondary storage must be copied to primary memory for CPU access.[1] Except for flash memory, secondary storage is significantly slower than primary storage, and flash memory is expensive compared to other forms of secondary storage. Most secondary storage devices are mechanical in nature, and mechanical devices are of necessity slower than devices that are purely electronic. The location of the desired data is usually not immediately accessible, and the medium must be physically moved to provide access to the correct location. This requires a *seek time,* the time needed to find the desired location. Once the correct data is located, it must be copied into memory. The throughput rate in Figure 10.1 indicates the speed with which the transfer of data between memory and the I/O device can take place. Most of the access time specified for secondary storage devices consists of seek time. As a result of this access time, even the fastest disks are only about 1/100,000 as fast as the slowest memory. It should be apparent that a *lot* of CPU instructions can be performed while waiting for a disk transfer to take place.

One advantage of secondary storage, of course, is its permanence, or lack of volatility. As noted in Chapter 7, RAM data is lost when the power is shut off. The magnetic media used for disk and tape and the optical media used for disk retain the data indefinitely. Secondary storage has the additional advantage that it may be used to store massive amounts of data. Even though RAM is relatively inexpensive, disk and tape storage is much cheaper yet. Large amounts of **online** secondary storage may be provided at low cost. Current hard disks store data at a density of 3–5 Gbits/sq. cm!

Removable secondary storage devices expand storage capability still further, by allowing **offline** storage of data that can be loaded when the data is needed. This provides the additional advantage that secondary storage may be used for offline archiving, for transferring programs and data from machine to machine, and for offsite backup storage. (In older computers, removable secondary storage was also used for offline data preparation, but online data entry is more convenient, and today is used almost universally.) Tape, in particular, is a removable medium that is ideally suited for program and data backup. Optical disks require little space and can store large amounts of data for archiving and installation purposes, with rapid mounting for retrieval when required. A few optical disks

---

[1] In the earliest days of computing, secondary storage devices, particularly rotating drums (forerunner of the disk), were actually used as memory with direct access to the CPU. To run efficiently, programs had to be designed to minimize the number of rotations of the drum, which meant that the programmer would always attempt to have the next required location be just ahead of where the drum head was at that instant. Those were interesting days for programmers!

could store all the medical records and history for a large insurance company, for example. Most modern programs are supplied on DVD or CD-ROM.

Of the various secondary storage components, disk devices are the fastest, since data anywhere on the disk may be accessed upon a single rotation of the device once the disk head is correctly placed. For this reason, disks are also known as **direct access storage devices,** or **DASDs.** With tape, it may be necessary to search sequentially through a portion of the tape to find the desired data. Also, the disk rotates continuously, while the tape will have to start and stop, and possibly even reverse direction and rewind to find the desired data. These factors mean that tape is inherently slower. On the other hand, tape can be an efficient medium if the data is to be read sequentially. (This discussion is consistent with your own experience with high-fidelity equipment. It is usually faster and easier to find a particular song on phonograph record or CD than it is on tape cassette. If you're playing the entire recording, however, the cassette is perfectly reasonable as a medium.) The issue of direct and sequential access is discussed further in Chapter 16.

An additional factor to consider when comparing storage components is the read/write capability of the component. Although CD-ROMs have tremendous storage capacity, they are used primarily for archiving and storage of reference material, because rewriteable CD technology is inefficient for day-to-day use.

Finally, we note that data and programs may be stored on a secondary storage device connected to a different computer and accessed through a network connection between the computers. In this context, the computer with secondary storage is sometimes known as a **server** or a **file server.** In fact, the primary purpose of the computer may be to act as a storage provider for all the computers on the network. Web services are a common application of this type. We will discuss this use of a computer in Chapters 11 and 13.

10.2 MAGNETIC DISKS

A magnetic disk consists of one or more flat, circular platters made of glass, metal, or plastic, and coated with a magnetic substance similar to that used on cassette tape. Particles within a small area of the magnetic substance can be polarized magnetically in one of two directions with an electromagnet; an electromagnet can also detect the direction of polarization previously recorded. Thus, magnetic polarization can be used to distinguish 1's and 0's. Electromagnetic read/write heads are used for this purpose. The read/write head on the disk operates similarly to the magnetic head found in an audio cassette recorder, except that the data is digital rather than analog.

A drive motor rotates the disk platter about its central axis. On most drives, the motor rotates the disk at a fixed speed. An arm resembling that of a phonograph record player has the read/write head mounted at the end. The arm makes it possible for the head to move radially in and out across the surface of the disk. A head motor controls precisely the position of the arm on the disk.

There are two major types of magnetic disks, **hard disks** and **floppy disks** or **diskettes.** The design of a floppy disk limits the number of surfaces to two, specifically the top and bottom of the single disk platter within its diskette case. Most hard disk drives contain several platters, all mounted on the same axis, with heads on each surface of each platter. The heads move in tandem, so they are positioned over the same point on each surface. Except for the top and bottom, each arm contains two read/write heads, which service the surfaces of two adjoining platters.

With the head in a particular position, it traces out a circle on the disk surface as the disk rotates; this circle is known as a **track.** Since the heads on each surface all line up, the set of tracks for all the surfaces form a **cylinder.** Each track contains one or more blocks of data. On most disks the surface of the disk platter is divided into equally sized pie shape segments, known as **sectors,** although the disks on some large computers divide up the track differently. Each sector on a single track contains one **block** of data, typically 512 bytes, and represents the smallest unit that can be independently read or written. Figure 10.2 shows the layout of a hard disk. Except for the number of platters the floppy disk is similar.

If you assume that the number of bytes in a sector is the same anywhere on the disk, then you can see from the layout that the bits on the disk are more closely packed on the inner tracks than they are on the outer tracks. Regardless of the track, the same angle is swept out when a sector is accessed; thus, the transfer time is kept constant with the motor rotating at a fixed speed. This technique is called **CAV,** for **constant angular velocity.** CAV has the advantage of simplicity and fast access. Hard disks and floppy disks generally store data in a CAV format.

Theoretically, it would be possible to increase the capacity of the disk by utilizing the space at the outer tracks to pack more bits onto the disk. But this would result in a different number of bytes per sector or a different number of sectors per track depending on which track is being accessed. This would make it more difficult to locate the required sector. Notice, too, that with a constant speed motor, the time to move the head over a pie-shaped sector at the edge is the same as that near the center. If there were more bits packed into the outer tracks, the data would be transferred faster at the edge than at the center. The disk controller is designed to expect data at a constant speed, which means that it would be necessary to design the motor so that it would slow down when the head was accessing the outer tracks to keep the data transfer speed constant. Most vendors have concluded that the additional design difficulties arising from these factors outweigh the increase in storage capacity. A few high-density disks are designed with a different number of sectors in different tracks, using a technique called **multiple zone recording.** This technique uses a constant speed motor but compensates for different transfer speeds in the controller.

FIGURE 10.2

A Hard Disk Layout

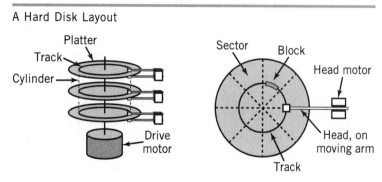

Conceptually, there is little difference between the operation of floppy disks and hard disks, but the mechanical differences have important effects on the overall capacity, speed, data transfer rate, and reliability of hard drives versus floppy disks.

We have already noted that the hard disk is made up of multiple platters, which obviously increases the overall capacity of a hard disk over that of a floppy disk. Additionally, the platter on a hard disk drive is made of a rigid material and is precisely mounted. The heads on a hard disk do not touch the surface; rather, they ride on a bed of air a few millionths of an inch above the surface. The location of the heads radially is tightly controlled. This precision allows the disk to rotate at high speed and also allows the designers to locate the tracks very close together. The result is a disk that can store large amounts of data and that retrieves data quickly.

Because the floppy disk is soft and flexible, it is necessary to support the disk surface as data is being read and written. To do so, the disk is pinched lightly between two heads, one on each surface of the disk. As a result of this physical contact between the disk surface and the heads, the disk must be rotated more slowly, so as not to wear out the heads or scrape the disk surface. A typical hard disk rotates at 5400 revolutions per minute (rpm), 7200 rpm, or even 10,800 rpm. The floppy disk rotates at 360 rpm. Additionally, the heads of a floppy disk are raised when data is being accessed to reduce contact. This increases the time required to access data.

When a floppy disk is inserted into the drive, a hole in the center of the floppy disk engages the motor in the drive. Due to the flexibility of the floppy disk, and also to the lack of precision in the insertion mechanism, it is necessary to space the tracks more loosely than on a hard drive, because the head cannot be positioned as precisely. Therefore, the overall capacity of the floppy disk is much lower than that of a hard disk of the same size. Figure 10.3 shows a diagram of a 3 1/2" floppy disk, identifying the various parts of the assembly.

A photograph of a hard disk assembly showing a disk platter, arm, and read/write head is shown in Figure 10.4. This particular hard disk drive contains three platters and six heads. Only the topmost platter and head are fully visible. The particular design shown is known as a **Winchester disk.** The entire assembly is sealed to prevent dirt particles from wedging between the heads and the disk platter, since this situation could easily destroy the drive.

Even a particle of cigarette smoke is much larger than the space between the head and the disk. When the disk is stationary, the head rests in a **parked** position on the edge of the drive. The head has an aerodynamic design, which causes it to rise on a cushion of air when the disk platter spins.

Figure 10.5 shows the operation required to locate an individual block of data. First, the arm moves the head from its present track until it is over the desired track. The time that is required to move from one track to another is known as the **seek time.** Since the distance between the two tracks is obviously a factor, the **average seek time** is used as a specification for the disk. Once the head is located over the desired track, the read/write operation must wait for the disk to rotate to the beginning of the correct sector. The time for this to occur is known as the **rotational latency**

FIGURE 10.3

Cutaway of a Floppy Disk

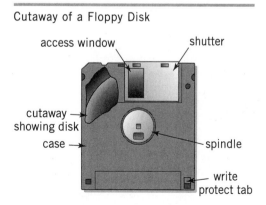

access window

shutter

cutaway
showing disk
case

spindle

write
protect tab

FIGURE 10.4

A Hard Disk Mechanism

FIGURE 10.5

Locating a Block of Data: (a) seek time, (b) latency time, (c) transfer time

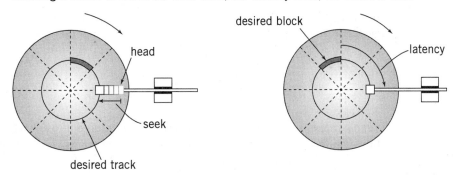

a. Seek time   **b. Latency time**

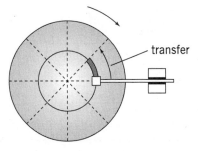

c. Transfer time

time, or sometimes as **rotational delay** or simply **latency time.** The latency time is obviously variable, depending on the position of the disk. As a best case, the head is just about to enter the sector, and the rotational latency time is 0.

At the opposite extreme, the head has just passed the beginning of the sector, and a full rotation is required to reach the beginning of the sector. This time can be calculated from the rotational speed of the disk. Both situations are equally probable. On average, the disk will have to rotate half way to reach the desired block. Thus, the average latency time can be calculated from the rotational speed of the disk as

$$\text{average latency} = \frac{1}{2} \times \frac{1}{\text{rotational speed}}$$

For a typical hard disk rotating at 3600 revolutions per minute, or 60 revolutions per second, the average latency is

$$\text{average latency} = \frac{1}{2} \times \frac{1}{60} = 8.33 \text{ milliseconds (msec)}$$

Once the sector is reached, the transfer of data can begin. Since the disk is rotating at a fixed speed, the time required to transfer the block, known as **transfer time,** is defined by the number of sectors on a track, since this establishes the percentage of the track that is used by a single data block. The transfer time is defined by

$$\text{transfer time} = \frac{1}{\text{number of sectors} \times \text{rotational speed}}$$

If the hard drive in the example contains 30 sectors per track, the transfer time for a single block would be

$$\text{transfer time} = \frac{1}{30 \times 60} = 0.55 \text{ msec}$$

Figure 10.6 shows a table of typical disks of different types, comparing various characteristics of the disks.

Since the total time required to access a disk block is approximately the sum of these three numbers, a typical disk access might require 20 to 25 msec. To put these speeds in

FIGURE 10.6

Characteristics of Typical Disks

Disk type	Platters/ heads	Cylinders	Sectors	Block size	Capacity	Rotational speed	Avg. seek time	Latency	Transfer rate
3.5" HD floppy	1/2	80	18	512 bytes	1.44 MB	360 rpm	95 msec	83 msec	54 KB/sec
100 MB Zip	1/1	96[a]	2048[a]	512 bytes	100 MB	2941 rpm	29 msec	10 msec	1.4 MB/sec
20.4 GB HD	3/6	13328	250	1K bytes	20.4 GB	7200 rpm	8.5 msec	4.2 msec	66 MB/sec
80 GB HD	2/16[b]	16383	63	512 bytes	81.9 GB	7200 rpm	9.5 msec	4.2 msec	up to 66 MB/sec
DVD-ROM	1/1 or 2	spiral	variable	2352 bytes	4.7–17 GB	variable	100–600 msec	variable	2.5 MB/sec

[a] www.europe.redhat.com/documentation/mini-HOWTO/ZIP-Drive4.php3
[b] multiple zone recording

perspective, consider that the typical modern computer can execute an instruction in 1–2 *nano*seconds or even less. Thus, the CPU is capable of executing *millions* of instructions in the time required for a single disk access. This should make it very clear to you that disk I/O is a major bottleneck in processing and also that it is desirable to find other work that the CPU can be doing while a program is waiting for disk I/O to take place.

An expansion of part of a track to show a single data block is shown in Figure 10.7. The block consists of a header, 512 bytes of data, and a footer. An **interblock gap** separates the block from neighboring blocks. Figure 10.8 shows the layout of the header for a Windows–based disk. The track positions, blocks, and headers must be established before the disk can be used. The process to do this is known as **formatting** the disk. Since the header identifier must be a unique pattern of 1's and 0's, the data being stored must be checked by the disk controller to assure that the data pattern does not accidentally match the header identifier. If it does, the pattern stored on the disk is modified in a known way.

The entire track is laid down as a serial stream of bits. During write and read operations, the bytes must be deconstructed into bits and reconstructed.

Because the transfer speed of the disk is not the same as that required to transfer the block to memory, buffering is provided in the disk controller. The buffer is a first-in, first-out buffer, which receives data at one speed and releases it as required at the other speed.

It is not uncommon for a program to require the data from two blocks in succession. The interblock gap is intended to give the disk controller time to transfer the data from the buffer to memory using direct memory access (DMA) and to determine which block is required next. Unfortunately, on many systems the time provided by the interblock gap is insufficient to perform this task. Then, the system must wait for the disk to rotate nearly a full revolution before the desired block is again available. A solution to this problem is provided by **interleaving** the blocks on the disk. This solution is shown in Figure 10.9. Rather than numbering the blocks consecutively along the track, the system skips one or more blocks in its numbering. This gives the controller additional time to perform the required

FIGURE 10.7

A Single Data Block

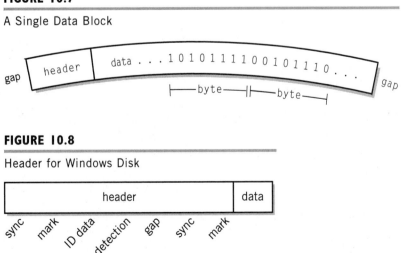

FIGURE 10.8

Header for Windows Disk

FIGURE 10.9

Disk Interleaving

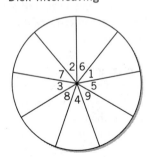

DMA transfer and to be ready when the next consecutively numbered block arrives. Figure 10.9 illustrates 2:1 interleaving, which means that each successive block to be accessed is actually two blocks away. Other values, 3:1 or 4:1, for example, are also possible. 1:1 means that the blocks are numbered in succession, with no blocks between. The interleaving can be optimized for a particular computer system when the disk is formatted. Many current hard drives include a large buffer memory that can hold several blocks of data. This reduces the need for interleaving.

It is important to realize that the layout of the disk as discussed here does not take into account the structure of the files stored there, nor does it naturally provide a filing system. There is no direct relationship between the physical size of the block and the logical size of the data block or file that it contains, other than that the data must fit into the physical block or provisions made to extend the data to another block. It is also possible to store multiple logical blocks in a single physical block, if they fit.

File organization issues and the allocation of physical blocks for storage are within the domain of the operating system software, not the disk controller. File storage and allocation issues are discussed extensively in Chapter 16.

Before leaving the subject of disks, it will be useful to review briefly some of the material from Chapter 9 to give you an overview of the typical disk I/O operation. You will recall that the CPU initiates a request to the disk controller and that the disk controller does most of the work from that point on. As you now know from this chapter, the disk controller identifies the disk block to be located, moves the head to the correct track, then reads the track data until it encounters the header for the correct block. Assuming that it is performing a read, it then transfers the data from the disk to a buffer. From the buffer, the data is transferred to conventional memory using DMA. Once the DMA transfer is complete, the disk controller notifies the CPU with a completion interrupt.

Alternative Technologies

Fixed hard disks and removable floppy disks form the great majority of direct access secondary storage implementations, but each has certain limitations. Floppy disks are removable, but provide only small amounts of storage by today's standards. There are many programs that require dozens of floppy disks just to store the program. On the other hand, hard disk drives have adequate capacity, but most are permanently mounted within a single machine, so that data and programs cannot be easily transported. Optical technologies, discussed in Section 10.4, help to solve these problems. Three other magnetic technologies are used less frequently, but they have interesting and attractive characteristics that provide alternative possibilities.

REMOVABLE HARD DRIVES   The most obvious alternative technology is the removable hard disk drive. This device, growing rapidly in popularity, is essentially identical to a fixed hard disk drive, except that part of the drive is mounted in a cartridge that can be removed from the housing that holds the remainder of the drive and its electronics. This adds the ability to store the data offline and also to carry it from machine to machine. Three basic approaches are used. The older and less expensive approach mounts just the disk platters in the cartridge. One variety stores the disk platters in a plastic case that is removed when the disk is mounted in its drive. This type of disk is known as a **disk pack.** It is used primarily on mainframe computers. In another version, the disk platters are permanently stored within a case. A sliding plastic window in the case exposes enough space for the head and arm mechanism to gain entry. This type is smaller and is generally preferred for use in personal computers and workstations. Like a floppy disk, the remainder of the drive mechanism is housed in the main assembly. The assembly may be mounted internal to the computer, or external. The more expensive approach provides a sealed cartridge that contains the platters, plus the head and arm assembly. The newest version is sealed. It fits on a card that plugs into a connector. These drives are used with laptop computers, digital cameras, MP3 players, and, believe it or not, a few car radios.

FIXED HEAD DISK DRIVES   A fixed-head disk drive provides one head per track, mounted on a permanently fixed arm. This eliminates the seek time altogether and provides very fast operation. These disk drives are expensive and are used only on mainframes for time-sensitive operations.

BERNOULLI DISK DRIVES   **Bernoulli disk drives** offer a hybrid approach to disk design that embodies the advantages of both floppy disk and hard disk technology. The disk platter is a 3 1/2" floppy disk housed in a removable plastic shelled cartridge slightly thicker than that of a standard floppy disk. The floppy disk platter spins at about 3000 rpm. The Bernoulli principle states that a low-pressure layer is formed next to a surface moving rapidly in a fluid medium such as air. The more rapid the surface is moving, the lower the pressure. When not operating, the floppy medium bends away from the read/write head. As the disk spins up to speed, the bend causes a higher effective speed, and therefore a lower pressure, on the upper surface of the floppy medium compared to the lower surface. This pressure difference lifts the floppy until it is flat and close to, but not touching, the head. A cushion of air keeps the head from touching the surface. Thus, the Bernoulli cartridge has the advantages of a hard disk drive, but with the flexibility of an inexpensive, removable cartridge. Notice that when something goes wrong, the tendency of the Bernoulli disk is to fall away from the head, thus protecting the device from head crashes. Because of the design, the Bernoulli drive uses only one surface and has only a single head. (Who said that two heads are always better than one?) Zip drives are examples of Bernoulli technology.

Disk Arrays

In larger computer environments, with mainframe computers or large PCs that provide program and data storage facilities for a network, it is common to group multiple disks together. Such a grouping of two or more disk drives is called a **disk array** or a **drive array.** A disk array can be used to reduce overall data access time by sharing the data among multiple disks and also to increase system reliability. The assumption made is that the number of blocks to be manipulated at a given time is large enough and important enough to justify the additional effort. One useful type of disk array is known as **RAID,** which stands for **redundant array of inexpensive disks.**

   There are two standard methods of implementing a disk array. One is known as a **mirrored array,** and the other as a **striped array.**

A mirrored array consists of two or more disk drives. In a mirrored array, each disk stores exactly the same data. During reads, alternate blocks of the data are read from different drives, then combined to reassemble the original data. Thus, the access time for a multiblock read is reduced approximately by a factor equal to the number of disk drives in the array. If a read failure occurs in one of the drives, the data can be read from another drive and the bad block marked to prevent future use of that block, increasing system reliability. In critical applications, the data can be read from two, or even three, drives and compared to increase reliability still further. When three drives are used, errors that are not detected by normal read failures can be found using a method known as **majority logic.** This technique is particularly suitable for highly reliable computers known as **fault-tolerant computers.** If the data from all three disks is identical, then it is safe to assume that the integrity of the data is acceptable. If the data from one disk differs from the other two, then the majority data is used, and the third disk is flagged as an error.

The striped array uses a slightly different approach. A striped array requires a minimum of three disk drives. In a striped array, one disk drive is reserved for error checking. A file segment to be stored is divided into blocks, which are then written simultaneously to different disks. This effectively multiplies the throughput rate by the number of data disks in the array. As the write operation is taking place, the system creates a block of parity words from each group of data blocks and stores that on the reserved disk. During read operations, the parity data is used to check the original data.

RAID processing takes place within the array controller. To the computer, the array appears as a single large disk drive.

10.3 MAGNETIC TAPE

Magnetic tape is used for secondary storage when offline storage is acceptable or preferred, when the data storage capacity requirements exceed those of a floppy disk and when sequential access is adequate. In particular, offsite data preparation and backup procedures normally satisfy these criteria. Like other magnetic media, tape is nonvolatile, and the data can be stored indefinitely.

There are three basic tape mechanisms, reel to reel and two types of cartridge. Generally, reel-to-reel tape drives are used with older mainframe computers to preserve long-term legacy data. Modern computers all use tape cartridges. Regardless of type, the tape is removable from the tape drive for offline storage. When the tape is in the tape drive, ready for operation, it is said to be **mounted.**

Tape cartridges have the major advantage of convenience. They are easy to mount and dismount, and small and easy to store. Some can store as much as 300GB of compressed data. Certain proprietary cartridges can store even more.

There are two main categories of data cartridge formats in use. The QIC (*quarter-inch cartridge*) formats are representative of **linear recording cartridges.** A QIC format data cartridge is shown in Figure 10.10. The QIC format typically holds 307.5 to 1500 feet of 1/4" tape, in a 2 1/2" x 3 3/16" or 4" x 6" cartridge. The technique used for storage and retrieval is called **data streaming.** There are several different formats for storing data on the cartridge, and they are not all compatible with each other. A single QIC data cartridge can hold 250 MB to 25 GB of uncompressed data, depending on the format.

FIGURE 10.10

Tape Cartridge

The cartridge tape is divided longitudinally into many tracks, between 20 and 144. The tape mechanism writes and reads the bits longitudinally, along the length of one track. At each end, the tape reverses, and the next track is written or read. Data is usually stored on the tape starting with the centermost track and moving outward toward the edge of the tape one track at a time. Typically, the track is divided into blocks of 512 or 1024 bytes. Error correction is built into the system.

A variation on this format is the *Digital Linear Tape (DLT)* data cartridge. This cartridge contains a single supply reel of ½" tape. The pickup reel is mounted in the drive mechanism, which allows more tape capacity within the cartridge. DLT cartridges hold 10–160 GB of uncompressed data. There are other, similar formats, with capacities of up to 800 GB under development.

An alternative, but more expensive, data cartridge is based on the technology that was originally developed for videotape, and the cartridges and basic format that are used for **digital audio tape,** or **DAT.** These are called **helical scan cartridges.** The cartridge holds 200–500 feet of 4 mm tape. There is also a similar 8 mm videocassette format that is less popular. The data on helical scan cartridges is very tightly packed, using a read/write head that rotates at a high speed to pack the tape more tightly with data. This results in a track that is made up of diagonal lines across the width of the tape. Helical scan cartridges are very tiny, 2 1/8" x 3", but have capacities of 1.3 GB–20 GB.

Figure 10.11 shows the track layouts for both types of cartridges.

10.4 OPTICAL AND MAGNETO-OPTICAL DISK STORAGE

An alternative to magnetic disk storage is optical storage. Optical storage technologies are capable of packing a tremendous amount of data into a small area. For example, an audio CD-ROM, approximately 5" in diameter, stores approximately 15 billion bits on its surface! Optical storage serves a different purpose from magnetic disk storage. While magnetic disk storage serves primarily to store, read, and write data for current use, optical storage is intended more for archiving and referencing. This is due to its large data storage capacity

FIGURE 10.11

Data Cartridge Formats

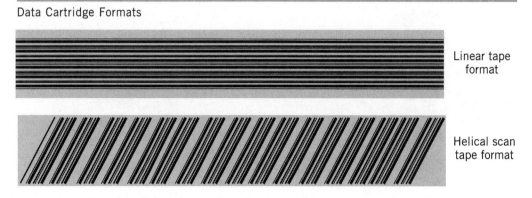

Linear tape format

Helical scan tape format

and nonexistent or limited writing ability. There are several types of optical disks, CD or DVD-based, WORM, magneto-optical, and numerous variations.

CD-ROM

Currently, the most popular local (as opposed to Internet) choice for online retrieval of reference information is CD-ROM. CD-ROM is a read-only, removable medium with large data storage capacity, which makes it a preferred medium for the distribution and online use of encyclopedias and dictionaries; for the access of large data bases of information, such as financial and business information; and for the distribution of large programs. The CD-ROM uses the same disk format as the audio CD; CD-ROM players can also play audio CDs.

Conceptually, CD-ROM data storage is similar to magnetic disk: data is stored in blocks on the disk. The blocks can be arranged in files, with a directory structure similar to that of magnetic disks.

The technical details are very different, however. Figure 10.12 compares the layout of a CD-ROM to that of a sectored magnetic disk. Rather than concentric tracks, data on a CD-ROM is stored on a single track, approximately three miles long, which spirals from the inside of the disk to the outside. Instead of sectors, the data is stored in linear blocks along the track. It should be remembered that the CD design was originally intended primarily for audio applications, where most data access is sequential, from the start of a musical selection to its finish; thus, a single spiral track was a reasonable decision.

Since the CD format was designed for maximum capacity, the decision was made to pack the bits on the disk as tightly as possible by making each block the same length along the track, regardless of location on the disk. Thus, unlike the CAV technique used on most hard disks, there are more bits per revolution at the outside of the disk than at the inside. A variable speed motor is used to keep the transfer rate constant. Since the angle of a block is smaller on the

FIGURE 10.12

Layout of a CD-ROM versus a Standard Disk

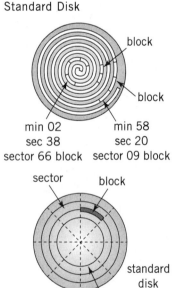

outer tracks, the disk moves more slowly when outside tracks are being read. This is easily observable if you have access to a portable CD player that allows you to observe the disk as it rotates. This technique is known as **constant linear velocity,** or **CLV.**

The CD-ROM typically stores 270,000 blocks of data. Each block is 2352 bytes long and holds 2048 bytes of data. In addition, there is a 16-byte header, which provides 12 bytes to locate the start of a block and 4 bytes for block identification. Due to the difficulty of the manufacturing process, errors can occur, so the CD-ROM provides extensive means for correcting the errors. Therefore, each block also provides 288 bytes of an advanced form of parity known as cross-interleaved Reed-Solomon error correcting code. This code repairs not only isolated errors but also groups of errors that might result from a scratch or imperfection on the disk. The total capacity of a single CD-ROM is approximately 550MB. The error correction is occasionally omitted for applications where errors can be tolerated, such as audio, which increases the capacity of a CD-ROM to about 630MB.

Blocks on a CD-ROM are identified by a 4-byte identification code that was inherited from the audio origins of the medium. Three bytes, stored in binary-coded decimal (BCD) format, identify the block by minute, second, and sector. There are 75 sectors per second and 60 seconds per minute. Normally, there are 60 minutes, although this number can be increased to 70 minutes if necessary. This increases the disk capacity to about 315,000 blocks. The fourth byte identifies a mode of operation. Mode 1, the normal data mode, provides the data as we've described, with error correction. Mode 2 increases the capacity by eliminating the error correction. Other modes are provided for special audio and video features. It is possible to mix data, audio, and video on the same disk. Data blocks on CD-ROMs are sometimes called *large frames.*

Data is stored on the disk in the form of pits and lands. These are burned into the surface of the master disk with a high-powered laser. The disk is reproduced mechanically, using a stamping process that is less expensive than the bit-by-bit transfer process required of magnetic media. The disk is protected with a clear coating. Figure 10.13 shows a basic diagram of the read process. A laser beam is reflected off the pitted surface of the disk as a motor rotates the disk. The reflection is used to distinguish between the pits and lands, and these are translated into bits.

On the disk itself, each 2352-byte data block, or large frame, is broken up into 98 24-byte small frames. Bytes are stored using a special 17-bit code for each byte, and each small frame also provides additional error correcting facilities. Translation of the small frames into more recognizable data blocks is performed within the CD-ROM hardware and is

FIGURE 10.13

CD-ROM Read Process

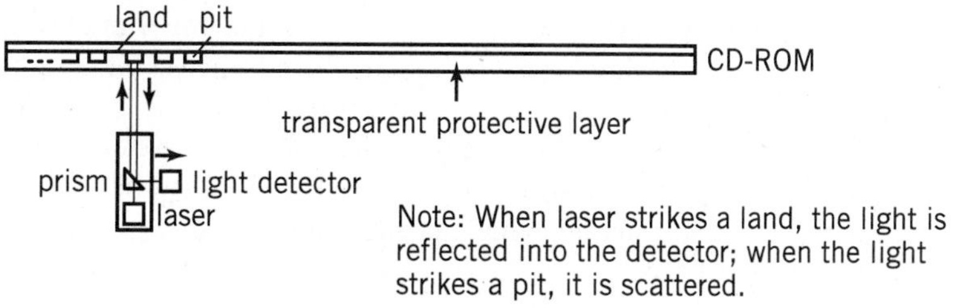

Note: When laser strikes a land, the light is reflected into the detector; when the light strikes a pit, it is scattered.

invisible to the computer system. The bit-encoding method and additional error correction built into the small frames increases the reliability of the disk still further.

DVD-ROM

DVD technology is essentially similar to CD-ROM technology. The disk is the same size, and is formatted similarly. However, the use of a laser with a shorter light wavelength (visible red, instead of infrared—researchers hope to use blue in the future), allows tighter packing of the disk In addition, the laser can be focused in such a way that two layers of data can be placed on the same side of the disk, one underneath the other. Finally, a different manufacturing technique allows the use of both sides of a DVD-ROM. Each layer on a DVD-ROM can hold approximately 4.7GB. If both layers on both sides are used, the DVD-ROM capacity is approximately 17 GB.

WORM Disks

WORM, or **write-once-read-many-times,** disks were originally designed to provide an inexpensive way for archiving data. WORM disks provide high-capacity storage with the convenience of compact size, reasonable cost, and removability. As the name indicates, WORM disks can be written, but, once written, a data block cannot be rewritten. Because of the large capacity, this is of little importance. When a file is updated, it is simply written again to a new block and a new directory entry is provided. This has the additional advantage that a complete audit trail exists automatically. When the disk is filled, it is simply stored away and a new disk used.

WORM disks work similarly to a CD-ROM. The major difference is that the disk is made of a material that can be blistered by a medium-power laser. Initially, the entire disk is smooth. When data is to be written, the medium-power laser creates tiny blisters in the appropriate locations. These correspond to the pits in a normal CD-ROM. The WORM disk is read with a separate low-power laser in the same way as a CD-ROM.

The original WORM disks stored data on concentric tracks, sectored like a magnetic disk, using the CAV method. The same blister technology is also available in various CD-ROM formats, called CD-R, DVD-R, or DVD-ROM. Additionally, there are rewriteable versions of this technology. These are known as CD-RW, DVD-RW, DVD-RAM, and DVD+RAM. There are compatibility issues between the different CD and DVD formats that are not fully resolved. Some drives will read every format; others will only read some of the formats.

Magneto-Optical Disks

Magneto-optical disks combine desirable optical and magnetic properties in an interesting way to produce a disk design that has many of the important features of both optical and magnetic disk technology. They share the advantages of optical disk technology: capacity, reasonable cost, and removability, together with the read/write capability of magnetic disks. They also have the advantage that they may be stored near magnets without concern that data may be lost. Their main limitation is that they have a much longer seek time and a slower transfer time than magnetic disks. Magneto-optical disks are also known as erasable optical disks.

The magneto-optical disk is based on the properties of certain exotic crystalline metal alloys. These alloys have the important and useful property that they respond to magnetism when they are heated, but do not respond to magnetism at lower temperatures, including room temperature. The critical temperature where they switch from nonmagnetic to magnetic is known as the Curie point. The disk is coated with a thin layer of one of these materials.

To write a bit of data, a laser heats a point on a disk to the Curie point. The laser is of sufficiently low power that deformation or blistering of the material does not occur. A magnetic write head then magnetically aligns the crystals at that point, in one direction for a 0, in another direction for a 1. To read the disk, another laser reflects light from the desired point. The alignment of the crystal at that point polarizes the reflection. The direction of polarization is then detected by an optical sensor.

Magneto-optical disks also store data on concentric, sectored tracks, using the CAV method.

10.5 DISPLAYS

As viewed by the user, a display is an image made up of thousands of individual **pixels,** or picture elements, arranged to make up a large rectangular screen. Each pixel is a tiny square on the display. The layout for a display is shown in Figure 10.14. A typical screen is made up of 768 rows of 1024 pixels each, known as a 1024 × 768 pixel screen. Screens of 640 × 480 pixels or 800 × 600 pixels are also still in use, and resolutions of 1280 × 1024 pixels, or even higher have become common, especially on physically larger screens. Screen sizes are measured diagonally. As seen in Figure 10.15, the display screen dimensions normally form a 3 × 4 × 5 right triangle with the diagonal, although occasionally one sees screens of other shapes. High-definition video screens have a horizontal to vertical ratio of 16:9. A normal 15" display screen is 12" wide by 9" high. For a 1024 × 768 resolution, then, each pixel is

$$\frac{9"}{768} \quad or \quad \frac{12"}{1024}$$

or 0.0116" square. Incidentally, 0.0116" is approximately equal to 0.28 mm, a figure that is frequently used to describe the resolution of commercial video monitors. The **resolution** specifies the minimum identifiable pixel size capability of the monitor, therefore, the smaller the number the better.

Each individual pixel represents a shade of gray (on a monochrome screen) or a color. A color pixel is actually made up of a mixture of different intensities of red, green, and blue (RGB). A monochrome scale with no shading would require only 1 bit per pixel (on for

FIGURE 10.14

Layout for a Display

white, off for black), but, more typically, a color display would present at least 256 colors, and normally many more. It takes 1 byte per pixel to represent a 256-color image, considered the minimum acceptable for Web use. A more sophisticated system would use 8 bits per color, or 24 bits in all. Such a system can present 256 × 256 × 256, or more than 16 million, different colors on the screen and is sometimes described as a **true color** system. There are even a few 30-bit and 36-bit systems.

Even 16 bits per pixel requires a substantial amount of video memory. To store a single 1024-pixel by 768-pixel graphic image requires 1.55 MB of memory. A 24-bit-per-pixel image of the same size would require over 2.3 MB.

With 8 bits, there is no way to divide the bits to represent reds, blues, and greens equally. Instead, 256 arbitrary combinations of red, blue, and green are chosen from a larger palette of colors. The 256 colors might be chosen by the artist who created the image. More commonly, a default color scheme is used. Originally designed by Netscape for its Web browser, the default color scheme presents a reasonably uniform selection of colors ranging from black to white. Each selected color is represented by a red value, a green value, and a blue value that together will present the selected color on the screen. Most commonly, the system will use one byte for each color, providing an overall palette of sixteen million colors to choose from.

Each pixel value is represented by a value of 0–255, representing the color for that pixel. A color transformation table, also known as a palette table, holds the RGB values for each of the 256 possible colors. A few rows of a color transformation table are shown in Figure 10.16. To display a pixel on the screen, the system transforms the pixel color to a screen color by reading the RGB values that correspond to the particular pixel value from the table. The RGB colors are then sent to the screen for display. Although this transformation requires an extra step, the task is performed in special circuitry on the video card and is not difficult to implement.

Transformation is also required for a display of sixty-four thousand colors, which uses 16 bits per pixel, however, a 24-bit color can be divided equally into three bytes, one for each color, so no transformation table is required.

Most output, including text data, is presented graphically. For graphical output, values for each pixel on the screen are produced by a program, then stored in a separate video memory, located within the terminal or PC. In PCs other than laptops and notebooks, the display circuitry is usually provided on a separate plug-in video card; video memory is supplied with the card. In some PCs, and most laptops, the video circuitry is included on the motherboard.

FIGURE 10.15

Display Screen Ratios

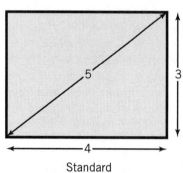

Standard

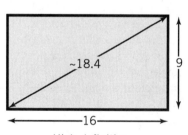

High-definition

FIGURE 10.16

Use of a Color Transformation Table

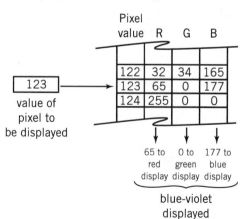

The actual display is produced by scanning and displaying each pixel, one row at a time, from left to right. This method of displaying all the pixels is known as a **raster scan.** It is essentially identical to the way that television pictures are generated. When one row has been displayed, the scanner returns to the left edge and scans the succeeding row. This is done for each row, from top to bottom. This process is repeated more than 30 times a second. Most display monitors scan each row in turn, row 1, row 2, row 3, and so on. Some monitors **interlace** the display, by displaying the odd rows, row 1, row 3, row 5, and so on, and then coming back and displaying the even rows. Interlacing the rows is less demanding on the monitor, since each row is only displayed half as often, but results in flickering that is annoying to some users. Figure 10.17 shows the difference between interlaced and noninterlaced displays. Noninterlaced displays are also sometimes called **progressive scan displays.**

An alternative to raster scan is **vector scan,** in which pixels are displayed in whatever order is necessary to trace out a particular image. Vector scan could trace a character, for example, by following the outline of the character. Vector scan is obviously not suitable for bit map graphics, but can be used with object graphics images, such as those used for CAD/CAM applications. Generating vector scan images on a display screen is electronically much more difficult and expensive than producing raster scans, consequently, raster scans are used almost universally today.

Figure 10.18 is a simplified diagram of the process that is necessary to produce a raster scan image. Each value to be displayed is read from the appropriate location in video memory in synchronization with its appearance on the screen. Although a palette table is shown in the figure, a three-byte value would be read directly from video memory to the RGB display inputs when 24-bit color is used. A scan generator controls both the memory scanner and the video scanner that locates the pixel on the display screen. For normal images displayed graphically on a noninterlaced monitor, the values are stored consecutively, row by row, so that each traverse through memory corresponds to a single complete scan of the image. Video memory is designed so that changes in the image can be made concurrently by the CPU while the display process is taking place. The display process is illustrated with a simple example.

FIGURE 10.17

Interlaced versus Noninterlaced Raster Screen

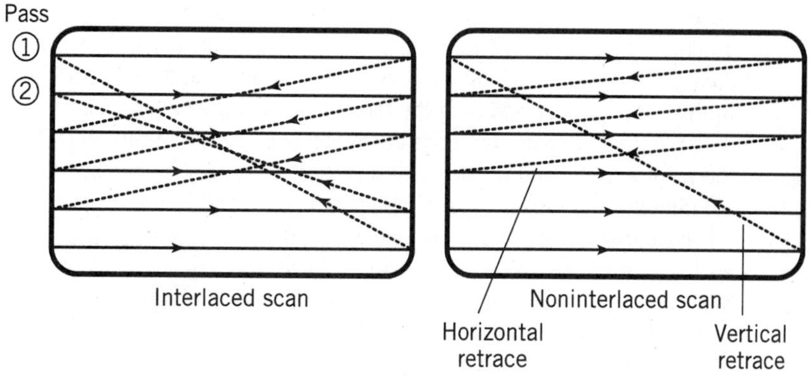

Interlaced scan   Noninterlaced scan

Horizontal   Vertical
retrace   retrace

FIGURE 10.18

Diagram of Raster Screen Generation Process

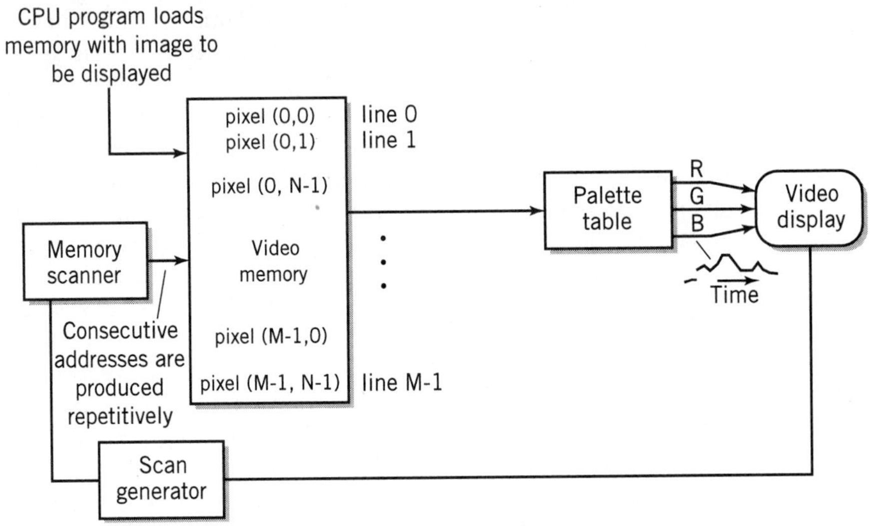

EXAMPLE

Suppose our system has a 7-pixel by 5-pixel display monitor. On that monitor we wish to display an "X." The desired output is shown in Figure 10.19a. The different pixels on the "X" are to be colored as shown in the figure.

To support the display, our system provides 35 bytes of video memory. Each byte corresponds to one location. Since each location holds 1 byte, the system supports up to 256 different colors. The display memory is shown in Figure 10.19b. The memory is the usual type of linear memory, but we have redrawn it so that you can see more easily the relationship between the memory and the display. If you look carefully, you can see the "X" in this figure. Initially, the video memory was set to all zeros, where zero represents the background color. Presumably, a program in the CPU has since entered the data that represents the figure "X" to be currently displayed.

The table in Figure 10.19c represents the color translation palette for this example. The table has a red, blue, and green column for each entry. In our system, each RGB entry in the table holds a 6-bit number. This means that this system can produce 64 x 64 x 64 = 256K different colors. The RGB value (0, 0, 0) would produce black, the value (63, 0, 0) would produce pure red (i.e., maximum red, no green, no blue), and (63, 63, 63) would produce white. In this case, you can see from the table that the background color for the screen is white.

The display controller reads each memory location in turn, looks up the three values in the palette table, and displays the corresponding pixel on the screen. This process repeats indefinitely. The red, blue, and green signals that go to the video system as a result of the display operation are shown in Figure 10.19d. This pattern will be repeated over and over again, at least thirty times a second, until the display is changed. Notice that the red and blue signals are identical, since red and blue always appear together in maroon and are both totally absent from green.

FIGURE 10.19

Display Example: (a) desired display, (b) video memory contents, (c) color palette table, (d) color signals

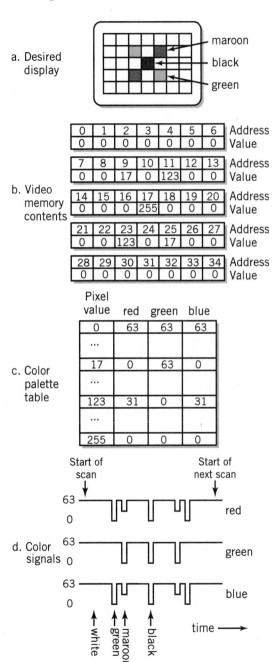

a. Desired display

maroon
black
green

b. Video memory contents

0	1	2	3	4	5	6	Address
0	0	0	0	0	0	0	Value

7	8	9	10	11	12	13	Address
0	0	17	0	123	0	0	Value

14	15	16	17	18	19	20	Address
0	0	0	255	0	0	0	Value

21	22	23	24	25	26	27	Address
0	0	123	0	17	0	0	Value

28	29	30	31	32	33	34	Address
0	0	0	0	0	0	0	Value

c. Color palette table

Pixel value	red	green	blue
0	63	63	63
...			
17	0	63	0
...			
123	31	0	31
...			
255	0	0	0

d. Color signals

Start of scan — Start of next scan

63 / 0 — red

63 / 0 — green

63 / 0 — blue

white, maroon, green, black

time →

As noted, the method just described is used for graphical images. Since characters are also represented by displaying pixels, most modern computers also treat character output graphically; the popularity of what-you-see-is-what-you-get (WYSIWYG) output requires the ready availability of different fonts and flexibility in layout on the screen. Both these requirements are easily met with the graphical techniques already described.

Some systems, particularly older systems, provide an additional method for dedicated character output. In this method, usually called **text mode,** the pixels of the display screen are divided into blocks, often twenty-five rows of eighty, although other values are often also provided. Each block will display a single ASCII character. Instead of storing individual pixels, the video memory is used to store the ASCII values of the characters to be displayed. Many PCs start up in text mode.

Pixels are displayed on the screen in the usual way. To convert the characters to a raster scan line, the display controller provides a set of character-to-pixel tables, stored in ROM. As each character is read from memory, the appropriate pixels are pulled from the table and output to the screen. Most controllers limit the display output to the fonts that are provided in ROM. Some controllers also provide video memory that can be used to download additional character conversion tables. Most systems also include an ASCII extension set that provides simple graphical shapes for drawing lines and boxes, as well as facilities for creating underlines, blinking characters, and color changes of the character or the block. Note that in text mode it is not possible to alter individual pixels. All addressing of the screen must be performed by block.

Every pixel in a graphics display must be stored and manipulated individually; therefore, the requirements for a graphic display are much more stringent than those for a character display. Also, text mode display has the advantage that it requires significantly less memory than does graphics mode. As the price of memory has declined rapidly, this has become less of an issue. Text mode has one important additional advantage, however. Text data can be transmitted to a terminal located remotely from the computer much more compactly and efficiently in text mode than in graphics mode. It is obviously easier to transmit a single character than the dozens of pixels that make up the image of that character. Because of this, some terminals are still character based, particularly in business environments where most of the data is alphanumeric.

A compromise between the simplicity of text mode and the elegance of graphics mode is to transmit the data using an object-based description language such as PostScript. Fonts described in this way are known as **outline fonts.** By contrast, those fonts that are described by laying out the detailed pixel diagram for the characters are known as **bitmapped fonts.** Outline fonts and graphics described by page description languages have the additional advantage that they may be scaled easily to different sizes and rotated to different angles. The graphic image is then reconstructed at the terminal by translation software that is built into the display controller. This method is particularly amenable to printers and to Postscript displays used for precision graphical and layout work. The methods of managing graphical images are explored more fully in Chapter 14.

CRT Display Technology

Although liquid crystal displays have become more common, CRT remains the most common display technology. With CRT technology, the image is produced on the face of a **cathode ray tube (CRT),** using a methodology similar to that used for television. A diagram of a color cathode ray tube is shown in Figure 10.20. Three **electron guns** within the tube shoot beams of electrons from the back of the tube. There is a gun for each of the primary colors, red, blue, and green. A high voltage applied to the inside of the face of the tube attracts the beams to the face. The face of the tube is painted with tiny dots or thin stripes of **phosphors,** which glow when struck by electrons. There are phosphors that glow red, blue, and green. A **shadow mask** in the tube is designed such that electrons from each gun can strike only phosphors of the matching color. The strength of the beams varies depending on the color and brightness of the point being displayed. The stronger the beam for a particular color, the brighter that color appears on the screen.

The three beams of electrons are *deflected* both horizontally and vertically by a pair of electromagnetic coils, so that the beam scans across the screen and top to bottom, to form the scan pattern that you already saw in Figure 10.17. Monochrome video monitors work

FIGURE 10.20

Diagram of a CRT

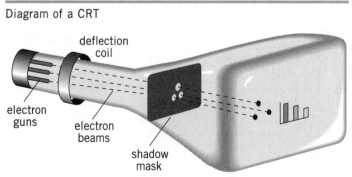

identically, except that only a single gun is required, the phosphor is white, yellow, or green, and no shadow mask is required.

Liquid Crystal Display Technology

A diagram of a **liquid crystal display** (**LCD**) is shown in Figure 10.21. A fluorescent light panel, located behind the display, produces white light. A polarizing filter in front of the light panel polarizes the light so that most of it is polarized in one direction. The polarized light then passes through a matrix of liquid crystal cells. In a color display, there are three cells positioned properly for each pixel. When an electrical current is applied to one of these cells, the molecules in the cell spiral. The strongest charge will cause the molecules to spiral 90 degrees. Since the light is passed through the crystal, its polarization will change, the amount depending on the strength of the electrical current applied.

Therefore, the light coming out of the crystal is now polarized in different directions, depending on the strength of the current that was applied to the crystal. The light is now passed through a red, blue, or green color filter and through a second polarizing filter. Because a polarizing filter blocks all light that is polarized perpendicular to its preferred direction, the second filter will only pass through the light that is polarized in the correct direction. Therefore, the brightness of the light is proportional to the amount of polarization twist that was applied by the liquid crystal's spiral.

There are several different ways of applying the electric current to the crystal. In an **active matrix** display, the display panel contains one transistor for each cell in the matrix. This guarantees that each cell will receive a strong charge, but is also expensive and difficult to manufacture. (Remember that even one imperfect cell will be apparent to the viewer!) A less expensive way provides a single transistor for each row and column of the matrix and activates each cell, one at a time, repetitively, using a scan pattern. This type of panel is known as a **passive matrix** display. The charge is applied for less time and is therefore lower. The result is a dimmer picture. Mercifully, passive matrix displays are nearly extinct.

FIGURE 10.21

Liquid Crystal Display

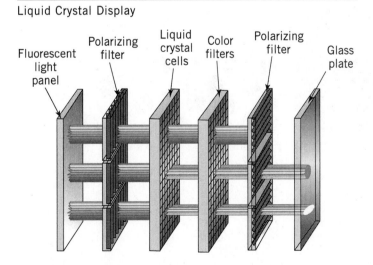

LCD panels have the advantage of small size, bright images, no flicker, and low power consumption, so they are ideal for laptop computers. Gradually, as the technology continues to improve, LCD panels are making their way into desktop displays that are essentially flat; thus, they can be placed anywhere. The same technology is also used for large-screen computer projectors.

10.6 PRINTERS

Earlier printers were derived from typewriters. They used formed characters that were mounted at the ends of arms, on wheels shaped like a daisy, on chains, and on spheres. Like typewriters, printing resulted from the physical impact of the character through an inked ribbon onto the paper. These printers were difficult to maintain and were incapable of generating any character or graphical image that was not provided in the set of formed characters. Most formed-character impact printers have disappeared from use.

Nearly all modern computer printers produce their output as a combination of dots, similar in style to the pixels used in displays. There are two major differences between the dots used in printers and the pixels used in displays. First, the number of dots per inch printed is generally much higher than the number of pixels per inch displayed. The number of pixels displayed usually ranges between about 70 and 100 per inch. Typical printers specify 600, 1200, or even 2400 dots per inch.

This difference in resolution is partially compensated for by the second major difference: the dots produced by most printers are either off or on. A few printers can vary the size of the dots somewhat, but, in general, the intensity, or brightness, of the dots is fixed, unlike the pixels in a display, which can take on an infinite range of brightnesses. Thus, to create a gray scale or color scale, it is necessary to congregate groups of dots into a single equivalent point and print different numbers of them to approximate different color intensities. An example of this is shown in Figure 10.22.

FIGURE 10.22

Creating a Gray Scale

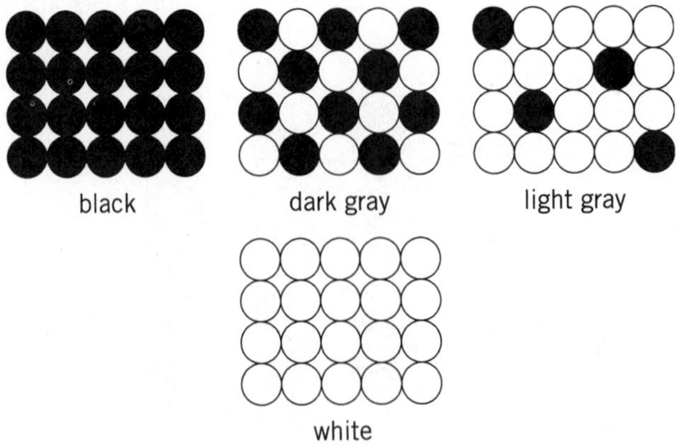

black   dark gray   light gray

white

Modern printers use one of four technologies to print the dots. This is true regardless of the size of the system, the quantity of printing, or the capacity of the printer. Single-color (usually black and white) printers normally use **dot matrix, laser,** or **inkjet** printing technology. Low-cost color printing also uses inkjet technology. More expensive color printing uses thermal wax transfer or laser technology.

Dot-matrix technology is called **impact printing,** because printing results from the physical impact of a print head on the paper. All the other techniques discussed here use nonimpact printing. The impression on the paper is sprayed at the paper or laid down on the paper.

Like displays, printer output can be character based or graphics based. Most printers have built-in character printing capability and can also download fonts. Nonetheless, much of the output from modern computers is graphics based, even when text is being printed, since graphics output produces more flexibility. The output to many printers takes the form of graphical bit maps that represent the required print dots directly. Some printers have built-in computing capability and can accept data in the form of a page description language, predominantly Adobe **PostScript.** The controller in the printer can then convert from the page description language to the bit map within the printer itself. Memory is provided within the printer to hold the bit-mapped image while it is being printed.

Laser Printers

Today, the prevalent form of printing is laser printing. Laser printing is derived from xerography. The major difference is that the image is produced electronically from the computer using a laser or light-emitting diodes, rather than scanning a real image with a bright light, as in a copy machine. A description of the steps in the operation of a laser printer is shown in Figure 10.23. Color images are produced by printing the sheet four times with different colored toners. Precise alignment of the four images is a difficult problem with this method.

Dot-Matrix Printers

Dot-matrix printers are used mostly only when fast impact printing is required, and in applications where size and cost are critical. The print head on a dot-matrix printer consists of a number of printing *pins,* usually twenty-four, whose positions can be controlled by individual electromagnets. When a current is applied to an electromagnet, the corresponding pin is forced toward the paper. The print head is mounted so that it can move across the paper. The paper itself is moved through the printer on a platen roller.

The print head prints a line by moving across the paper as the pins are precisely controlled to form the desired image. Each pin that is to form a dot strikes the paper through an inked ribbon. When a row is printed, the platen moves the paper to the next row, and printing continues. Although the dot-matrix printer was originally intended only for character printing, more sophisticated controllers have made it possible to print high-quality graphics, with resolutions approaching those of laser printers. In recent years, better print heads have also improved the size and accuracy of the dots. Modern dot-matrix printers can produce output that is very close to the print quality of laser printers.

Multiple inked ribbons can be used to produce color, but the quality of dot-matrix color is not considered acceptable for most purposes.

FIGURE 10.23

Operation of a Laser Printer

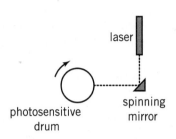

laser

spinning
mirror

photosensitive
drum

1. A laser is fired in correspondence to the dots that are to be printed. A spinning mirror causes the dots to be fanned out across the drum. The drum rotates to create the next line, usually 1/300th or 1/600th of an inch.

   The drum is photosensitive. As a result of the laser light, the drum will become electrically charged wherever a dot is to be printed.

2. As the drum continues to rotate, the charged part of the drum passes through a tank of black powder called toner. Toner sticks to the drum wherever the charge is present. Thus, it looks like the image.

charge wire

paper

3. A sheet of paper is fed toward the drum. A charge wire coats the paper with electrical charges. When it contacts the drum, it picks up the toner from the drum.

fusing system

corona wire

4. As the paper rolls from the drum, it passes over a heat and pressure area known as the fusing system. The fusing system melts the toner to the paper. The printed page then exits the printer.

   At the same time, the surface of the drum passes over another wire, called a corona wire. This wire resets the charge on the drum, to ready it for the next page.

Inkjet Printers

Inkjet printers operate on a simple mechanism that also has the advantages of small size and economy. Mechanically, the inkjet printer works similarly to the dot-matrix printer. The print cartridge moves across the page to print a row, and mechanical rollers move the page downward to print successive rows.

The inkjet print cartridge contains a reservoir of ink and a row of tiny nozzles, each smaller than the width of a human hair. A dot is produced by heating the ink behind a nozzle. When the ink is boiled it sprays a tiny droplet of ink toward the paper. The volume of each droplet is about one-millionth the volume of the drop from an eyedropper of water! Some printers use a vibrating piezo-crystal instead of heat to produce the ink droplets.

Multiple reservoirs of ink make it possible to print multiple colors. The quality of color inkjet output is reasonably good, especially considering the low cost.

Thermal Wax Transfer and Dye-Sublimation Printers

For high-quality color images, specialized methods are required. The preferred methods are **thermal wax transfer** and **dye sublimation.** The mechanisms for both types are similar. The paper is fed into the printer and clamped against a drum. A print head provides a row of dot-sized heating elements. Between the paper and the print head, the printer feeds a roll of film that is impregnated with either colored wax or dye. The film is made up of page-sized sections of magenta, cyan, and yellow colors; sometimes an additional section of black is also included. Each rotation of the drum exposes the paper to a different color. The heat from the print head melts the wax or dye onto the paper.

Thermal wax can be applied to ordinary paper. To improve quality, some printers pre-coat the paper with clear wax. This compensates for slight imperfections in the paper so that the wax may be applied more uniformly. Different colors are produced in the same way that black and white printers produce gray scales.

The dye-sublimation technique differs slightly, in that the dyes diffuse in the paper, so that the dots of color actually blend. Furthermore, it is possible to control the amount of dye by adjusting the temperature of individual print head elements. Thus, dye sublimation can print continuous color tones. Unfortunately, the dye-sublimation technique also requires higher temperatures, therefore, special paper must be used.

10.7 SCANNERS

Scanners are the primary means used to input paper images. Although video frame-grabbers and television cameras can also be used for this purpose, scanners are generally less expensive and more convenient.

There are three primary types of scanners, flatbed scanners, sheet-fed scanners, and handheld scanners, but all three work similarly and differ only in the way the scan element is moved with respect to the paper. In a flatbed scanner, the paper is placed on a glass window, while the scan element moves down the page, much like a copy machine. In a sheet-fed scanner, a single page of paper is propelled through the mechanism with rollers; the scan element is stationary. Handheld scanners are propelled by the user over the page.

Regardless of which means is used, the basic operation is the same. The scanning mechanism consists of a light source and a row of light sensors. As the light is reflected from individual points on the page, it is received by the light sensors and translated to digital signals that correspond to the brightness of each point. Color filters can be used to produce color images, either by providing multiple sensors or by scanning the image three times with a separate color filter for each pass. The resolution of scanners is similar to that of printers, approximately 600–2400 points per inch.

10.8 USER INPUT DEVICES

Users use a variety of devices to interact with the computer, but most commonly, the modern user interface is based upon a keyboard and a pointing device.

Keyboards consist of a number of switches and a keyboard controller. The keyboard controller is built into the keyboard itself. There are several different types of switches in use, including capacitive, magnetic, and mechanical. In most environments, the type of switch used is not important. Different types of switches feel differently when used. Some switches are more suitable than others for environments where dust or electrical sparks or the need for ultra-high reliability are a problem. When a key is pushed, a signal called a scan code is sent to the controller. A different scan code is sent when the key is released. This is true for every key on the keyboard, including special keys such as *Control, Alt,* and *Shift* keys. The use of two scan codes allows keys to be used in combination, since the controller is able to tell whether a key is being held down while another key is struck. The controller can also determine when a key is to cause a repeated action.

If the keyboard is part of a terminal, the scan codes are converted to ASCII (American Standard Code for Information Interchange) or EBCDIC (Extended Binary Coded Decimal Interchange Code) and sent to the computer, usually via a serial port. Keyboards local to a computer such as a PC interrupt the computer directly. The scan codes are converted to ASCII or Unicode by software in the computer. This allows more flexibility in remapping the keyboard for different languages and keyboard layouts.

Modern graphical user interfaces also require the use of a pointer device as input to locate and move a cursor on the display screen. The best known pointer device is a mouse, but there are other pointer devices in use, including light pens, touch screens, and graphics tablets, as well as the special pointer devices used for interfacing with computer games.

The simplest device is the mechanical mouse. As the mouse is moved across a surface, the roller ball protruding from bottom of the mouse also moves. Two wheels, mounted at a 90-degree angle from each other, touch the roller ball, and move with it. These wheels are called **encoders.** As the encoders move, they generate a series of pulses. The number of pulses corresponds to the distance that the mouse was moved. One encoder records movement forward and backward; the other records sideway motion. The pulses are sent to a program in the computer to interpret the current location of a cursor. Some encoders use a tiny light and sensor to create the pulses, others use a tiny mechanical switch, but the method used is not important. Game pointing devices and trackballs work similarly.

Light pens are used differently and work differently. A light pen is pointed at the screen to identify a position on the screen. By moving the pen around the screen, a cursor can be made to follow the pen. The light pen can be used to point to a target, such as a control button on the screen, and can also be used as a drawing tool. The light pen is not actually capable of telling the system its position. Instead, the software program that is used with the light pen rapidly generates pixels of light on the display screen at known locations in the area where the light pen is believed to be pointing. The light pen has a photodetector that can respond to the point of light on the screen, so when the point on the screen that corresponds to the light pen is lit, the light pen is activated, which notifies the program that the current location is correct.

Graphics tablets use a variety of techniques, including pressure-sensitive sensors, optical sensors, magnetic sensors, and capacitive sensors to determine the location of a pen on the pad. Some techniques require the use of a special pen, which is attached to the tablet, while others allow the use of any pointed object, such as a wooden pencil, with or without lead. The resolution and accuracy of graphics tablets depends on the technique employed. Graphics tablets can be used as mouse replacements, but are particularly suited for drawing.

10.9 COMMUNICATION DEVICES

It is impossible to overemphasize the fact that, from the perspective of a computer, a network is simply another I/O device, a device that, like a disk, offers input to applications on the computer and receives output from applications on the computer. Like other I/O devices, there is a **network interface unit (NIU)** that handles the physical characteristics of the connection and one or more I/O drivers that manage and steer input data, output data, and interrupts.

There are a number of different types of network interfaces, with different network interface units for each. The simplest interface is a telephone modem, which is processed through the serial I/O port discussed previously in Chapter 9. On large mainframe systems, there may be network interface units for a variety of different network connections, including token ring, FDDI fiber, asynchronous transfer mode, and other types. On most systems, the standard connection is to an Ethernet network. Many current computers are supplied with an Ethernet network interface unit as a basic part of the system. Wireless Ethernet and Bluetooth network interface units are also of increasing popularity.

The interface between a computer and a network is more complicated than that for most other I/O peripherals. Data must be formatted in specific ways to communicate successfully with a wide range of application and system software located on other computers. The computer also must be able to address a large number of devices individually, specifically, every other computer connected to the network, whether connected directly to the local network, or indirectly connected through the Internet. Security of communication is an important concern, whereas local devices normally require only minimal security considerations.

Most of these concerns are handled with protocol software in the operating system. The NIU is responsible only for the electrical signals that connect the computer to the network, either directly or through a communication channel, and for the protocols, implemented in hardware, that define the specific rules of communication for the network. These protocols are called **medium access control** protocols, or **MAC**s. We note in passing that every NIU and network device throughout the world has a unique address called a MAC address that can be used to identify the specific device and its characteristics. The MAC address is sometimes used by cable and DSL vendors to restrict network access to a specific device.

The hardware aspects of the network interface are considered more fully in Chapter 11; the protocol software is described in Chapter 15. Further detail on the nature of communication channels can be found in Supplementary Chapter 3.

SUMMARY AND REVIEW

This chapter provides an overview of the workings of the most common computer peripheral devices. Peripheral devices are classified as input devices, output devices, and storage devices.

We began by demonstrating that storage can be thought of hierarchically, with registers the most immediately available form of storage, followed by memory, and then the various peripheral devices. We discussed the trade-offs that make each form desirable for some purposes.

Following this general discussion, we showed the layout and explained the operation of various forms of disk, including hard magnetic, floppy magnetic, CD-ROM, and optical. We showed how the performance factors, capacity and various speed measures, are obtained. For each device we showed how a block is identified and located. We noted the difference between the concentric tracks used on magnetic disks and the spiral tracks used on many optical disks. We explained the difference between CAV and CLV operation. The discussion of disks is followed by a similar discussion for magnetic tape.

The display is the most important output device. We explained the process used to produce a display, from the bytes in memory that represent individual pixels or characters to the actual output on a screen. We showed that there are two different forms of output, character and graphic. We showed how colors are determined for the display. We also showed the basic technology for the two methods that are used to produce an image, video on a CRT, and liquid crystal display.

There are a number of different technologies used in printers. We introduced dot-matrix impact printers, laser printers, inkjet printers, and thermal wax transfer printers as representative of the most important current technologies.

The chapter concludes with brief discussion of scanners, keyboards, and various pointer devices that are used for input.

KEY CONCEPTS AND TERMS

active matrix LCD
average seek time
Bernouli drive
bitmapped fonts
block (of data)
cathode ray tube (CRT)
CD-ROM
constant angular velocity
  (CAV)
constant linear velocity
  (CLV)
cylinder
data streaming
deflected
digital audio tape (DAT)
direct access storage
  devices (DASDs)
disk array
disk pack
diskettes
dot-matrix printer
DVD-ROM
drive array

dye sublimation
electron guns
encoders
expanded storage
fault-tolerant computers
file server
floppy disks
formatting
hard disks
helical scan cartridge
impact printing
inkjet printer
interblock gap
interlace
interleaving
laser printer
latency time
light pen
linear scan cartridge
liquid crystal display
  (LCD)
magneto-optical disk
majority logic

medium access control
  (MAC)
mirrored array
mounted
multiple zone recording
network interface unit
  (NIU)
offline storage
online storage
outline fonts
palette
parked (position)
passive matrix LCD
peripherals
phosphors
pixels
PostScript
primary memory
progressive scan display
raster scan
redundant array of inex-
  pensive disks (RAID)
resolution

rotational delay	shadow mask	true color
rotational latency time	striped array	vector scan
secondary storage	text mode	Winchester disk
sectors	thermal wax transfer	WORM (write-once-read-
seek time	track	many-times) disks
server	transfer time	

FOR FURTHER READING

Much of the discussion in this chapter reviews material that you have seen before, probably in an introduction to computers course. Any good introductory textbook will also serve as a further reference for this chapter. In addition, there are several good books that describe I/O devices. My personal favorite is White [WHIT01].

EXERCISES

10.1 Explain why it is easy to perform read and write in place on a disk but not on a tape.

10.2 A floppy disk is rotating at 300 rpm. This disk is divided into twelve sectors, with forty tracks on the disk. The disk is single sided. A block consists of a single sector on a single track. Each block contains 200 bytes.

    a. What is the disk capacity in bytes?

    b. What is the maximum and minimum latency time for this disk?

    c. What is the transfer time for a single block?

10.3 A multiplattered hard disk is divided into forty sectors and four hundred cylinders. There are four platter surfaces. The total capacity of the disk is 128MB. A cluster consists of four blocks. The disk is rotating at a rate of 4800 rpm. The disk has an average seek time of 12 msec.

    a. What is the capacity of a cluster for this disk?

    b. What is the disk transfer rate in bytes per second?

    c. What is the average latency time for this disk?

10.4 The average latency on a disk with eleven sectors is found experimentally to be 110 msec.

    a. What is the rotating speed of the disk?

    b. What is the transfer time for one sector?

10.5 Twelve-inch laser video disks are produced in two different formats, known as CAV and CLV. The playing time of a CLV disk is approximately twice that of a CAV disk, although the number of tracks, track width of the tracks on the disk, and amount of data per video frame is the same. Explain why this is so.

10.6 A magneto-optical disk consists of two thousand concentric tracks. The disk is 5.2" in diameter. The innermost track is located at a radius of 1/2" from the center. The outermost track is located 2 1/2" from the center. The density of the disk is specified as 1630 bytes per inch along the track. The transfer rate is specified as 256,000 bytes per second. The disk is CLV. All blocks are of equal size.

a. The innermost track consists of ten blocks. How many bytes are contained in a block?

b. How many blocks would the outermost track contain?

c. The capacity of the disk is approximately equal to the capacity in bytes of the middle track times the number of tracks. What is the approximate capacity of the disk?

d. What is the motor rotation speed when reading the innermost track? the outermost track?

10.7 An experiment was set up to test the latency time for various interleavings on a disk drive. The results were as follows:

interleaving	latency time
1:1	24 msec
2:1	26 msec
3:1	6 msec
4:1	8 msec
5:1	10 msec

Drawn as a curve, the latency time seems to increase slowly until a 3:1 interleave is selected and then increases gradually after that. Explain the various parts of this curve.

10.8 Why is the average seek time for a hard disk much shorter than for a CD-ROM?

10.9 There is a current proposal to cut the size of an individual bit in a CD-ROM in half so as to increase the capacity of the disk. This would cut both the width of the track and the track length required per bit in half. If the current capacity of a CD-ROM is approximately 600 MB, what would be the capacity of the new "high-density" CD-ROM?

10.10 A typical published page consists of approximately forty lines at seventy-five characters per line. How many published pages of text would fit on a typical 600MB CD-ROM?

10.11 A high-quality photographic image requires 3 bytes per pixel to produce sixteen million shades of color.

a. How large a video memory is required to store a 640×480 image during display? A 1024×768 image? A 1280×1024 image?

b. How many 1024×768 color images will fit on a CD-ROM?

10.12 A 1024×768 image is displayed, noninterlaced, at a rate of thirty frames per second.

a. If the image is stored with 256-color resolution, which uses 1 byte per pixel, how much memory is required to store the picture?

b. How much video memory is required to store the picture as a "true color" image, at 3 bytes per pixel?

     c. What is the transfer rate, in bytes per second, required to move the pixels from video memory to the screen for the "true color" image?

10.13 For a motion picture image it may be necessary to change every pixel in the image as many as thirty times per second, although usually the amount of change is somewhat smaller. This means that without data compression or other tricks that a large number of pixel values must be moved from main memory to video memory each second to produce moving video images. Assume a video image on the screen of 1 1/2" × 2", with a pixel resolution of seventy-two dots per inch and a frame rate of thirty per second. Calculate the required data transfer rate necessary to produce the movie on the screen. Do the same for an image of 3" × 4".

10.14 The cost of a monitor increases rapidly with increasing bandwidth. The bandwidth of a monitor is measured roughly as the number of pixels displayed on the screen per second.

     a. Calculate the bandwidth of a 640-pixel by 480-pixel display operating in an interlace mode. One-half of the image is generated every 1/60th of a second.

     b. Do the same for a 1024-pixel by 768-pixel display operating in noninterlace mode. One entire image is generated every 1/60th of a second.

10.15 A 640-pixel by 480-pixel display is generated on a 14" (diagonal) monitor.

     a. How many dots per inch are displayed on this monitor?

     b. What is the size of an individual pixel? Would a .39-mm pixel resolution monitor be sufficient for this display?

     c. Repeat (a) and (b) for a 800 × 600 display.

10.16 A text display displays 24 rows × 80 characters on a 640-pixel by 480-pixel 15" monitor. Assuming four spaces for horizontal space between each row of characters, how big are the characters in inches? in pixels? How big would a character of the same pixel size be if the display is increased to 800 × 600? How many rows of characters could be displayed in this case?

10.17 What is the actual resolution of a gray scale picture printed on a 600-dot-per-inch laser printer if the gray scale is created with a 3 × 3 matrix?

10.18 In printer jargon, "replaceables" are the items that are used up as part of the printing process. What are the replaceables in a laser printer? in an inkjet printer? in a dot-matrix impact printer?

10.19 Explain the difference in the method used to generate characters between graphics mode and character mode display.

10.20 Explain the difference between pixel graphics and object graphics, and discuss the advantages and disadvantages of each.

10.21 What are the limitations of typewriter-type (formed character) printers that caused them to fade from popularity?

CHAPTER 11

MODERN COMPUTER SYSTEMS, CLUSTERS, AND NETWORKS

"He wants a system with lots of memory, but without a mouse."

11.0 INTRODUCTION

In the last five chapters, we carefully explored the fundamental organization of computer systems. We explained in detail the operation of the computer CPU and introduced some of the many variations on the basic CPU design found in different systems. You learned that there is a fundamental group of instructions that make up the repertoire of the computer and that each instruction is performed in a series of simple steps known as a fetch-execute cycle. You have seen variations in instruction sets and memory addressing techniques that differentiate computers from one another and extend the flexibility of the basic architecture. We explored various CPU architectures, memory enhancements, and CPU organizations that expand the processing power of the CPU. We also considered various techniques used to perform I/O operations. In addition, we explored the workings of various peripheral devices. You have seen some of the interactions between the various components in the computer system.

Today's software places tremendous demands on all components of a computer system. Thirty-five years ago, an IBM mainframe computer was supplied with 512 kilobytes (KB) of memory. The performance of this machine was measured at 0.2 millions of instructions per second (MIPS). Today, a *personal* computer with that level of performance would be considered inadequate for most applications! Graphics and multimedia applications, in particular, require performance far in excess of previously acceptable levels. Many modern computers perform at levels of a billion instructions per second or more. Supercomputers can perform *trillions* of instructions per second! There is a continuing demand for higher and higher levels of performance, driven both by market needs and by competition.

The primary goal of this chapter is to complete our discussion of computer system hardware by showing you how all these pieces fit together in real modern computer systems. Considering the system as a whole will also give us the opportunity to study the ways in which computer designers are meeting the demand for more computing power. Obviously, individual components—buses, memory, and the like—have been optimized to maximize computer system performance. Considering the system as a whole allows further advances in performance, which result from system integration. Individual components are designed to work together in such a way that overall performance is enhanced beyond the performance of each component. This concept is known as **synergy.**

Much of the discussion in this chapter is devoted to innovations in computer system design resulting from a synergistic approach to system integration.

Some of the new techniques in computers are improvements in technology, design, and implementation: improved materials, manufacturing techniques, and circuit components and better ways of performing the same task that enhance the operation of a particular system component. Others are architectural changes: new features and implementation methods that change in a fundamental way the design of the system. Many of the innovations and enhancements that are used to achieve high performance are a fundamental part of modern systems. The terminology that names and describes these techniques is a basic part of the vocabulary of computing. To analyze, purchase, and manage modern business systems intelligently, it is important to understand these techniques.

As part of our system discussion, this chapter investigates the methods that are used to achieve high performance in modern computer systems. The basic techniques introduced and discussed in Chapters 7, 8, 9, and 10 provide the conceptual framework. Section 11.1 presents a model that lays out the components and interconnections of a typical computer system. The model is relatively independent of system size or CPU type. In Section 11.2, this model is used as a basis to identify some of the major factors that affect system capability. The remainder of the chapter is devoted to careful discussions of the techniques used to interconnect CPUs and computers in large-scale systems and networks.

There are many reasons why people wish to connect computers together. Some of the most important reasons are

- Computer power can be increased by combining multiple CPUs or computers to work together. Grouping multiple CPUs means that multiple processes can be executed simultaneously. As another approach, a program may be executed more rapidly by distributing its execution so that each connected CPU or computer may be executing different parts of the program.

- Users working at their own computers, often in different locations, have access to programs, files, data from a data base, documents, and the like that are stored elsewhere. The users can also communicate using e-mail or "talk" services, or they can use groupware to work together on documents.

- It is often desirable to share valuable resources such as printers, a large disk facility, programs, or a database among two or more computers.

- Users may connect their computers to powerful computer resources, such as CompuServe, Dow Jones News, other on-line services, the Internet, or computer bulletin boards to access and retrieve information, obtain support services, conduct business, purchase goods, discuss common interests, play games, or simply socialize.

- Computers can be used together to increase system reliability by providing redundant processing. Two or more CPUs can be executing the same program, and the results can be compared by the computers continuously. Connecting computers together also makes it possible to switch processing to a backup computer in the event of failure of a CPU. Such systems are called **fault-tolerant systems.** Fault-tolerant systems often provide redundancy on other devices, such as disks, as well. Disk arrays, described in Chapter 10, are well suited for fault tolerant computing.

Actually, it is rare today to see a computer that operates totally independently of other computers. Even home computers have modems that can be used to dial up a connection to an online service, a bulletin board, or another computer. Computers in businesses are generally interconnected into networks, so that the users may work together and share information with each other. Networks provide access to central data repositories, the Internet, e-mail, and resources such as printers and can be used to offer more overall processing power by dividing the workload among multiple systems. You have already read about the IBM sysplex concept. Sun, Compaq, and other manufacturers provide similar capabilities. Networks of computers may be as small as a few computers in a single room or as large as millions of computers scattered all over the world, tied together into a giant network of networks called the Internet. It is also common for modern large systems to provide multiple CPUs within a single system for additional processing power or to handle specialized functions within the computer system, such as I/O.

Except for the simplest connections, data communication technology serves as the glue that makes the interconnection of computers feasible, that holds the Internet together, and that makes Web surfing possible. The subject of data communications forms an important topic in any discussion of the hardware and software in a modern computer.

Data communications is a broad and exciting field. Hundreds of books have been written about various aspects of data communications. Every college IS curriculum offers at least one entire course in the subject. It is only possible in this chapter to scratch the surface. There are aspects of data communications concerning the transmission of computer data, voice, fax, video, and many other areas that will not concern us in this textbook.

Section 11.3 introduces the concept of tightly coupled systems and loosely coupled systems and shows how multiprocessing can be used to increase system performance.

In Sections 11.4 through 11.8 we will introduce you to the fundamental concepts of data communication technology, particularly as they relate to the interconnection of computer hardware. Our main concern in this textbook is that you understand the basic ways in which the hardware and software of modern computers are tied together, as well as the factors that affect performance in doing so.

There are four major considerations that must be addressed when implementing communication between computers: the different means of interconnectivity that are possible, the nature of the communication channel that is used to carry data between computers, the means used to enable computers to communicate intelligently, and the types of configurations that connect the computers together. The nature of the communication channel is discussed in Supplementary Chapter 3. Intelligent communication between computers is handled by programs within the operating system of each computer. The protocols and standards that make this possible are discussed in Chapter 15. The remaining considerations are discussed in this chapter.

After a brief overview of the various ways in which computers can be interconnected, in Section 11.4, we turn our attention to the specific methods used to connect computers together. With the recognition that the channels will be the "plumbing" that passes messages between loosely connected computers, we now concentrate our efforts on the "layout" and the "fittings." For our purposes, the layout is the topology of a system made up of two or more computers. The fittings are protocols, the interfaces between the computers that make communications between the computers possible and meaningful. The concepts of topology and protocol will become much clearer as the chapter progresses.

The discussion includes the issues of synchronization between the computers, and the hardware protocols that are required. One of the major factors affecting the topology of a system is the physical distance between the computers that must communicate. The protocols must take into account the differences in medium, signaling method, error rates, even physical layout that distinguish communication among widely separated computers, hundreds or thousands of miles apart, from those located, say, in a single room or building.

In Section 11.5, we consider the cluster, another form of loosely coupled system in which multiple computers are linked directly to act as a single system. In Section 11.6 we look at the topology and hardware protocols of commonly used configurations that are used to communicate among loosely coupled computers. These configurations include point-to-point communication between two computers, local area networks, and wide area networks.

Sections 11.7 provides a brief introduction to the methods used to process massively large computer tasks—interconnections consisting of hundreds, or even thousands, of CPUs all processing data in parallel. Finally, Section 11.8 observes the growing similarities of networking and bus I/O.

The techniques discussed in this chapter extend and enhance the standard methods to produce computer systems that provide the power and capability required for today's large-scale information needs. When you have completed this chapter, you will understand the vocabulary and the major components of modern computer hardware systems.

As you read through this chapter, be sure to notice the recurring mention of the need for software that makes it all possible: to implement protocols, to steer messages and data, and to control the network. In modern computers, hardware and operating system software operate as a synergistic team (there's that word again!). It would be impossible to operate a system without software that supports the features of the hardware; this is particularly true in the area of networking and data communication.

11.1 PUTTING THE PIECES TOGETHER

The blocks that make up the essential components of a personal computer or workstation are shown in Figure 11.1. The major components in this model are a CPU, memory, optical disk drive, one or more floppy disk drives, one or more hard disks, the keyboard, and built-in video display and audio capability.

FIGURE II.I

A Basic Personal Computer System

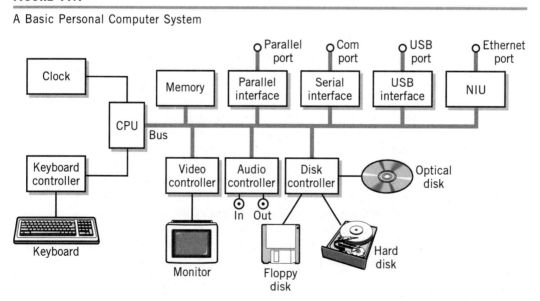

The unit typically also provides USB, parallel, serial I/O, and network interface controllers and ports (perhaps FireWire, also). These ports can be used for network connections, printers, modems, mice, and other devices. The package also includes plug-in connectors for additional option boards that will interface to the master bus.

For comparison, Figure 11.2 shows the block diagram of a processor unit for a large mainframe computer system. The main components in this system are one or more CPUs, memory, and a variety of disks and other I/O devices, connected to the processor with an I/O channel system. In this diagram, the processor unit includes the CPU(s), memory, and I/O interface components. Specialized internal buses interconnect the various parts of the processor unit. The keyboard and video display connected to the processor unit are used only for control of the system. Other terminals and workstations are connected to the processor indirectly, through the I/O system or by network. In addition, multiple processor units may be coupled together to form a large, integrated computer facility that can share programs and data.

A diagram showing more detail of a typical personal computer's circuitry is shown in Figure 11.3. In nearly every personal computer or workstation, all the circuitry shown in the diagram is mounted on a motherboard. Although early PCs used separate integrated circuits for each of the various functions, today most of the functions shown in the diagram are combined into just a few **very-large-scale integrated circuits,** or **VLSIs.**

FIGURE 11.2

A Mainframe Computer System

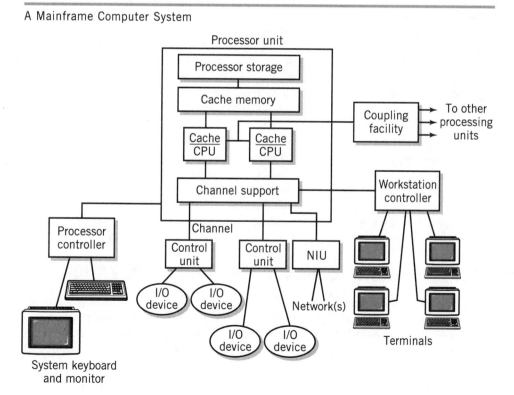

FIGURE 11.3

Major PC Systems Components

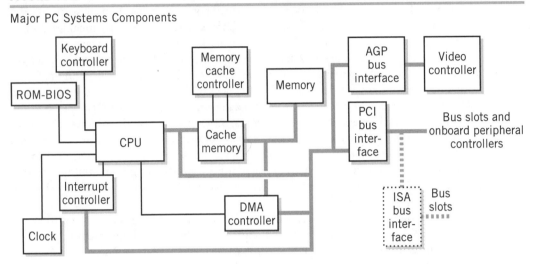

The block diagram in Figure 11.3 connects together many of the important concepts familiar to you from previous chapters. The PC is driven by a CPU, which interfaces to memory and to the various I/O peripherals by one or more buses. A clock controls the operation of the CPU. Interrupt and direct memory access (DMA) capabilities are provided to enable rapid and efficient I/O processing. L1 and L2 cache memory is included within the same integrated circuit as the CPU for many modern processors. Earlier PCs provided only a single bus, typically the 16-data-bit Industry Standard Architecture (ISA) bus or its 8-data-bit predecessor on an IBM PC, or the NuBus on an Apple Macintosh computer. The newer PCI bus is capable of expansion up to 64 parallel data bits and is provided on most modern computers. The ISA bus is being phased out. The CPU itself may be a member of one of a number of different families, the X86 or PowerPC, among others.

Figure 11.4 shows the layout of a typical PC, including the motherboard, case, and other components. The wiring for the primary buses that interconnect the CPU and its peripheral components is printed on the motherboard. Connectors on the motherboard combine with the frame of the case to hold the peripheral cards physically in place, and, of course, the connectors on the motherboard provide the electrical connection between the peripheral cards and the buses. The mainframe computer is packaged differently. Frequently, a mainframe system is much larger physically, as well as operationally. Still, the essential components and operations are similar to those of the personal computer.

11.2 SYSTEM PERFORMANCE ENHANCEMENT AND OPTIMIZATION

In Chapter 8, we looked carefully at the CPU, and considered alternative models that would enhance CPU performance, while maintaining the basic von Neumann concepts. In particular, we presented a model of the CPU with distributed control and multiple fetch and execution units that permits the processing of instructions at a superscalar rate. The fetch

FIGURE 11.4

PC Physical Layout

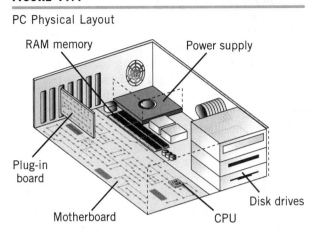

RAM memory
Power supply
Plug-in board
Motherboard
Disk drives
CPU

unit-execute unit model reduced or eliminated many of the bottlenecks associated with instruction processing within the CPU.

Now that you have seen the entire system picture, we are in a position to extend our consideration of methods that are used to eliminate processing bottlenecks and to achieve higher levels of system performance by examining areas of data flow outside the CPU itself. In particular, we consider the features that we would expect to find in a high performance system. This does not suggest that a system designer or user would want all of these features in every system. Performance has a cost; in many cases, lower performance is sufficient and simpler is actually preferable.

Here are some areas of the system that directly affect performance. We have considered all of these along the way. This list serves as a summary.

- **Multiple CPUs.** One obvious way to increase performance in a computer system is to increase the number of CPUs. Computers that have multiple CPUs within a single system, sharing memory and I/O facilities, are called **multiprocessors.** In practice, increasing the number of CPUs is often effective, although, as the number of CPUs increases, the value of the additional CPUs diminishes because of the overhead required to distribute the instructions in a useful way among the different CPUs and the conflicts among the CPUs for shared resources, such as memory, I/O, and access to the common bus. There are rarely more than sixteen CPUs sharing the workload in a multiprocessing computer; more commonly, a multiprocessor might consist of two or three CPUs. Multiprocessing is discussed in Section 11.3.

  To achieve still more performance, computer systems may themselves be interconnected into clusters and networks. Systems in which the workload is shared among multiple computers are called **distributed systems.** In addition to enhanced performance, distributed systems offer increased reliability and scalability. Networking further offers the obvious benefits of communication with other "outside" systems.

  Sections 11.4 through 11.8 consider the techniques and issues of computer system interconnection.

- **Faster clock speed.** Since the instruction cycle time is proportional to the speed of the clock, faster clock speeds directly impact the overall speed of the system. The primary limiting factor on clock speed is the ability of the CPU, buses, and other system components to keep up. As improving technology allows the design of faster CPU circuits and buses at reasonable cost, the clock speed continues to increase.

- **Wider instruction and data paths.** The ability to process more bits at one time affects performance in several different ways. A wider interface between the CPU and the memory bus allows the CPU to fetch or store more data in memory in a single operation. It also makes it possible to fetch more instructions at one time. These instructions can be used to fill a pipeline or instruction pool. Since memory accesses are slow compared to internal CPU operations, reducing the number of memory accesses can improve system performance. A wider path is a simple way to achieve this goal.

  Larger registers within the CPU make it possible to reduce the number of program steps required for calculations. To add two 64-bit integers in a computer with 16-bit registers requires four separate additions, plus the steps that are needed to handle carries between the parts and the instructions needed to move the data between the registers and memory for each 16-bit addition. With 64-bit registers, only a single addition is required. Wider internal buses allow data to move from one part of the CPU to another more rapidly.

  In Chapters 7 and 8 you saw that faster buses with wider data paths and better methods of interfacing those buses to the CPU are required to pass the necessary data between the CPU, memory, and the various I/O devices at the speeds necessary to meet today's requirements, particularly for high-speed, high-resolution video applications. The PCI bus is an example of such a bus.

- **Faster disk access.** The time required to perform disk accesses is frequently the limiting factor in program execution. A CPU can execute millions of instructions in the time required for a single disk access. As a result, even small improvements in disk access speeds can have a major impact on overall system performance. Technological advances have allowed the design of disk drives that are smaller and more densely packed, with much increased storage capacity; they operate at speeds that would have been unthinkable just a few years ago. Materials with improved mechanical, electrical, and magnetic characteristics are a major contributor to this additional performance. RAID systems improve performance with the careful placement of data on different disks, so that multiple blocks of data can be accessed simultaneously from different devices.

- **Increased amounts of memory and faster memory.** Increased amounts of memory provide larger buffer spaces that can be used to hold additional data to enable the system to continue processing during disk accesses. More memory can also reduce the number of disk accesses, by providing space to hold program instructions and data for later use. Furthermore, modern programs are often so large that they must be loaded into memory in parts. Larger amounts of memory make it possible to hold more of the program within memory. Multimedia programs require large amounts of memory for the processing and display of video, graphics, and sound.

  Faster memory reduces the time required to access instructions and data operands in memory. Since memory accesses represent a large proportion of instruction cycle operations, improvements in memory access time can have a significant effect on system performance.

Other technological improvements include the technology designed for digital cartridge tape, now being used to increase the capacity of tape drives to back up the massive amounts of data being stored, and evolutionary improvements in video graphics system design that feature increased resolution, improved color, larger image sizes, and faster display speeds to meet the need for improved graphics and movie-quality video reproduction. In general, computer vendors continually enhance all these areas to the limits of current technology, within the constraints of cost and user acceptance.

Improvements in technology have resulted in great strides in performance, but are not in themselves solely responsible for current levels of performance. In many cases, technological improvement has made new solutions feasible that would not have been possible just a few years ago. As an example of the latter, we note that it is now possible to build an integrated circuit with millions of transistors within that can operate at dazzling speeds. The CPU that fits today into a chip one-inch square far exceeds in power the computer that filled a large room 20 years ago. As a comparison, consider this: the original Intel 8086 CPU contained about 29,000 transistors; the Pentium 4 CPU contains more than forty million transistors in a space only slightly larger. Today's circuit technology increases the flexibility of the computer system designer to include new features and to consider new ways of building the system.

11.3 MULTIPROCESSING

One obvious way to increase the power of a computer system is to add more computers! There are actually two different approaches to doing so:

In some situations it is necessary or desirable to connect CPUs together in such a way that they share some or all of the system's memory and I/O resources. Systems for which this is true are called **tightly coupled systems** or **multiprocessor**[1] **systems.** All the computers in a tightly coupled configuration have access to the same programs and data in shared memory and to the same I/O devices, so it is possible to divide program execution between different CPUs, and it is easy to provide redundant program execution. Furthermore, ready processes may be run in any CPU that is available, so that each additional processor extends the power available for multitasking in a multiprocessor system, at least within the capabilities of the shared components, the buses, memory, and I/O controllers.

In other cases, the computers are tied together loosely. By this we mean that each computer is complete in itself, each with its own CPU, memory, and I/O facilities. Data communications provides the link between the different computers. Such systems of computers are called **loosely coupled systems.** Some authors refer to these systems as **multicomputer systems.** Some loosely coupled systems share a disk resource or a small amount of memory that can be used to communicate between the different computers. These are called **loosely coupled multiprocessor systems** by some vendors, **clusters** by others. The factor that distinguishes a loosely coupled system is the autonomy of each computer within the system complex or network. Discussion of loosely coupled systems is the subject of Sections 11.4 through 11.8.

---

[1] Some people also use the word "multiprocessing" incorrectly as a substitute for "multitasking" or "multiprogramming." Such usage is considered confusing, and it is discouraged by knowledgeable computer people.

Two or more CPUs may be interconnected to form a multiprocessing system. There are two basic reasons for doing so:

- Adding additional CPUs is an inexpensive and, within limits, effective way to increase the power of a computer system.
- Programs can be divided, and the parts executed simultaneously on multiple CPUs.

Communication between the components of a tightly coupled system is straightforward. Figure 11.5 shows a typical arrangement for a multiprocessing system. Each of the CPUs operates independently. No communication channel is required because each CPU has access to the same memory and to the same I/O devices. Therefore, data can be passed easily between the CPUs by using an area of memory for this purpose. A program in memory can be executed by any of the CPUs connected within the system. Any CPU can respond to an interrupt. One additional complication occurs if the individual CPUs have cache memory associated with them. In this case, careful synchronization between processors is required to assure that changes are carried over to memory before the data is accessed by other processors. Multiprocessing systems require direct communication between the CPUs to synchronize processes or threads that are being executed concurrently in the different CPUs. The additional lines required for interprocessor communication can be included as part of the bus connecting the various components together.

Since each of the CPUs has access to the same memory and I/O, any CPU can theoretically execute any process in memory, including the operating system. This raises the question of control of the system. There are two ways of configuring a tightly coupled multiprocessing system:

- **Master-slave multiprocessing,** in which one CPU, the *master,* manages the system, and controls all resources and scheduling. Only the master may execute the operating system. Other CPUs are *slaves,* performing work assigned to them by the master.
- **Symmetrical multiprocessing (SMP),** in which each CPU has identical access to the operating system, and to all system resources. Each CPU performs its own dispatch scheduling, using a standard algorithm in the operating system software that establishes dispatch priorities for all processes in the system.

The master-slave configuration has the advantage of simplicity. It also provides an excellent protection of the system and its data, since slave processors may only access data and system resources with permission from the master.

The weaknesses of master-slave processing include system reliability and poor use of resources. System reliability is limited because failure of the master results in failure of the entire system. Although it is possible to design the system to select a backup master in case of failure, this is rarely done. As for resource use, note that the busiest CPU in the system is likely to be the master. If a slave requires work assignment while the CPU is busy, the slave will have to wait until the master is available. Furthermore, since the master handles all I/O requests and interrupts, a heavily loaded system will cause a backload in the master. If slaves are dependent on the results of these requests, the system is effectively stopped.

The symmetrical configuration is much more difficult to implement. It requires special care at synchronizing resource requests to prevent conflicts among the different CPUs.

FIGURE 11.5

Typical Multiprocessing System Configuration

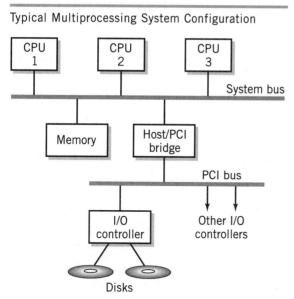

Disks

However, the symmetrical configuration has many offsetting advantages. A failure in a single CPU may reduce performance, but it will not cause system failure. Any CPU can process an interrupt. Processors are all kept equally busy, since each processor can dispatch work as it needs it. Thus, the workload is well balanced. It is easy to implement fault-tolerant computing with a symmetrical configuration—critical operations are simply dispatched to all CPUs simultaneously. As an interesting aside, note that a program may execute on a different CPU each time it is dispatched, although most SMP systems provide a means to *lock* a program onto a particular CPU, if desired.

Thus, the symmetrical configuration provides two important additional capabilities for multiprocessing: improved reliability and optional support for fault-tolerant computing. Most modern multiprocessing systems are SMP systems.

The multiprocessor system is a controlled environment. The CPUs, memory, I/O devices, and even operating system software are designed to operate together as a system and are often supplied by a single vendor. Communication between the various components is built into the design of the system.

11.4 COMPUTER INTERCONNECTION: AN OVERVIEW

When computers are connected together they can share and exchange program code and data. In fact, the purpose of interconnection is to provide a means of communication between the computers.

In each of the examples given in the introduction, communication between the connected computers is key to the operation. When computers execute a program together, at least one of the computers must know how the work is divided and must be capable of passing data and messages between different parts of the program that resides or is executed on different computers. When a printer is shared by several computers, each computer sends its requests and data to be printed to the computer that manages the printer (or sometimes to a computer within the printer itself). When two computers communicate by modem, they exchange keystrokes, display images, files, and so on.

For the remainder of the chapter, we are concerned only with loosely coupled systems. Loosely coupled systems enable program and data sharing and exchange between complete computers. There are two basic methods of connecting loosely coupled computers. Clustered computers are connected directly together with a link that passes messages between machines. The cluster is designed to operate as a single unit. Networked computers operate more independently, using I/O facilities and a data communication channel to enable connectivity between the individual machines.

Except for the few loosely coupled systems that provide shared memory, most loosely coupled computers communicate using a communication channel of one type or another. A **communication channel** is defined as a path over which data moves. For our purposes, we shall narrow the definition and discuss communication channels primarily as they are used to pass data between one computer and another, although we do cite familiar examples from daily life to illustrate some of the technological concepts. This narrower definition is intended to exclude the bus that connects CPUs in a multiprocessor configuration from consideration.

We remind you that the standard computer I/O operations that we have already discussed in Chapter 9 are used to connect a computer system to a communication channel. For each computer system, the communication channel is treated as an I/O device connected to the computer, with an I/O device controller similar to those used with other I/O peripherals.

Whether tightly coupled or loosely coupled, each CPU in a system executes its programs or processes independently. If data or program code from one CPU is to be made available for use by another CPU, the second CPU must have access to the data or program code. As you will recall from earlier chapters in this text, data and program code must be present in primary memory in order for the CPU to access it.

In a loosely coupled system, the ability to pass data and program code from the memory of one computer to the memory of another is an essential ingredient of communication between computers. If a file stored on disk in one computer system is to be used on another system, the file must be loaded from disk to the memory of the first system and then transferred using communication techniques to the memory of the second.

Loosely coupled computers may be interconnected in different configurations. The configurations and nomenclature are similar to those of buses. The simplest interconnection provides a communication channel that passes data directly between two computers. This type of interconnection is known as **point-to-point connectivity.** Two computers connected via modem and phone line are connected point-to-point. A computer may have point-to-point connectivity with more than one computer at a time. The host computer shown in Figure 11.6 provides point-to-point connectivity to several client computers, for example. This connectivity might be direct, through serial I/O ports, or might be provided through individual modems and phone lines for each connection.

A large dialup system such as AOL might act as a host to hundreds or thousands of users at a time. To do so requires point-to-point connections for each user, with a corresponding number of phone lines and modems. Often, one or more separate **terminal controllers** are used for this purpose. A terminal controller is simply a small, specialized computer that is used to handle a number of point-to-point connections for the host. Communication data between clients and the host is passed in both directions by the terminal controller, for whatever processing is required by each computer.

Multiple computers may also connect to a **shared communication channel.** A shared channel is also known as a **multipoint** or **multidrop channel.** Many local area networks are interconnected in this way, although it is also possible to build a local area network using point-to-point connections between each of the computers or between each of the computers and a network controller. Some networks use a mixture of point-to-point and shared connections. We note that it is also possible to use a multipoint connection directly with a host computer to connect the various client computers and terminals, but that it is more common today to use terminal controllers for this purpose. The connection between

FIGURE 11.6

An Example of Point-to-Point Connectivity

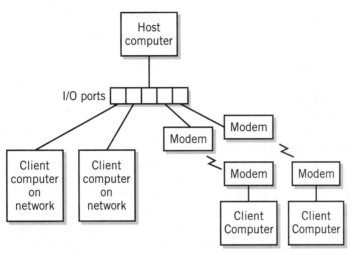

the terminal controllers and the host computer may be point-to-point connection, or they may be connected to the host computer through a local area network.

There are a number of different types of communication channels, both point-to-point and shared. These channels differ in factors such as speed, data format, unidirectionality or bidirectionality, medium, type of cable, and data transmission method used. The computers interconnected by a communication channel must be able to understand each other in order to communicate successfully. Fortunately, the number of different channel types is small. Different channel types are governed by national or international standards, which define the details of each channel type. This makes it possible and practical to interconnect different types and brands of computer equipment. The choice of an appropriate communication configuration for a particular application depends on a mixture of technical, logistical, and business decisions.

The way in which loosely coupled computers in a particular system are interconnected is known as the **topology** of the system.

The data on communication channels is normally serial, since it is not practical to provide individual parallel lines to carry data over distances of more than a few feet. This is another difference between tightly coupled systems and loosely coupled systems. Since tightly coupled systems are interconnected by bus, data within a tightly coupled system is normally accessed in parallel fashion. You would expect this to be the case, since CPUs in a tightly coupled system are accessing instructions from a common memory.

EXAMPLE

A simple example serves to illustrate and clarify many of the concepts just discussed. As used by information systems professionals, **client-server architecture** is defined as a network of loosely coupled computers in which one or more computers are designated as **servers** to provide specific services. Most common are Web services, files services, printer services, and database information retrieval services. File servers provide program and data storage for other computers on the network. Other computers on the network accept services from the file server(s) and are designated as **clients.** Each client executes its own programs and has the option of using program and data files both from its own storage and from the file server. In a distributed processing system, a client program might request execution of a procedure or invocation of an object method on the server. The results would be returned to the client.

A simple client-server local area network is illustrated in Figure 11.7. This particular network is made up of a sequence of point-to-point communication channels and is configured using a topology known as a **ring.**

Suppose that a client computer requires a file from the file server. The program that is making the request is presently executing in the client CPU and is stored in client memory. The program making the request might be an application requiring data, or it could be the operating system on the client computer acting on a user request to load and execute a program that is stored on the file server. Regardless of how the request is generated, the request is sent as an output from the client CPU to the network. The request is transmitted through the network and received by the network controller at the file server. The request message is transferred from the network as an input operation into the server's memory, and an interrupt is sent to the file server CPU to indicate the presence of an input message from the network.

The request is processed by the operating system software in the file server. The appropriate file is copied into memory at the file server and then sent as output to the network. Normally, DMA will be used for this purpose. The file data or program is received by the network controller at the client and transferred into client memory. An interrupt is sent by the network controller to the CPU to indicate that the data or program is available for use.

There are four important ideas that you should observe from this example:

- The interface between the CPU and the network operates similarly to other I/O operations that we have already studied. Output operations move data from

FIGURE 11.7

A Client-Server Network

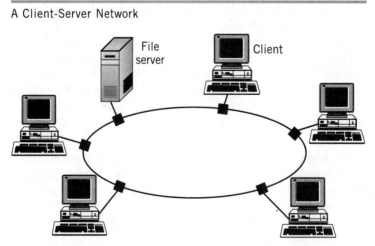

memory to the network, and input operations receive data from the network, placing the data into memory for CPU use.

■ Memory is used as you would expect to hold the data or program that is being sent to or received from the network.

■ The data or program must be present in the client memory before it can be executed or used.

■ Both computers must agree on the format of the request message. Otherwise, the server would not know what is being requested! Furthermore, just as it is necessary to distinguish I/O devices connected to a common bus, the network communication format must include addressing information, so that each computer on the network can respond to messages directed to it, while ignoring messages intended for other computers on the network.

We note in passing that in a client-server architecture, application programs are executed by individual clients, attached to the network. The programs executed by the server in connection with the communication just provide the services requested by client programs. In contrast, the host in a host-PC architecture executes the application program(s). The programs running on PCs attached to the host are simply used to simulate a terminal for input to the host computer and display of the results.

11.5 CLUSTERS

Overview

A cluster is a group of loosely coupled computers configured to work together as a unit. Unlike the tightly coupled multiprocessing system, each computer in a cluster is a complete unit, with its own CPU, memory, and I/O facility. In fact, the individual computers in a cluster may, themselves, be multiprocessing systems. Each computer in the cluster is called a **node.** Unlike a network, the computers in a cluster are intended to appear to users as though they are a single machine. The clustering is transparent to the users.

The obvious purpose of clustering computers is to increase the available computing power by combining the power of the individual systems. Since each computer can process data independently, the increase is approximately proportional to the number of nodes in the cluster.

There are other benefits, as well. Brewer [BREW97] notes that clusters are inherently scalable, both incrementally and absolutely. An installation can add nodes incrementally as additional computing power is needed. Furthermore, it is possible to create a cluster with a large number of nodes. Such a cluster will have more computing power, at lower cost, than would be possible using even the largest single machine. Clustering is a fundamental technology in the design of high performance computing systems.

Finally, clustering increases fault tolerance and availability. Since each computer in the cluster is capable of standalone operation, a failure in one node will not bring down the entire system. Instead, the software controlling the cluster can simply switch processing to other nodes in the cluster. A single point of failure is defined as a single component in a system that, upon failure, prevents further operation of the system. It is possible to design a cluster in which there is no single point of failure. This can be an extremely important advantage in systems that perform critical applications.

Under normal conditions, the software controlling a cluster will attempt to balance the processing workload evenly between different nodes.

Classification and Configuration

There are two primary models used for clustering, the **shared-nothing** model, and the **shared-disk** model. Both models are shown in Figure 11.8. As you can see from Figure 11.8a, the shared-nothing model bears resemblance to a point-to-point network connection between two computers. Each computer has its own disks. The critical difference is the presence of a high-speed messaging link between the nodes, plus software that controls the behavior of each node and the interaction between nodes. At least one of the nodes will provide access to the outside world and manage the cluster. The link is used to pass messages and data between nodes. It can also be used to repartition the disks as conditions change. The workload is divided by partitioning the data between the nodes so that requests made of each node will be approximately equal. This method has the advantage that little communication is required between nodes because each node is essentially independent. The primary difficulty with this configuration is that it is not always possible to

FIGURE 11.8

Cluster Models

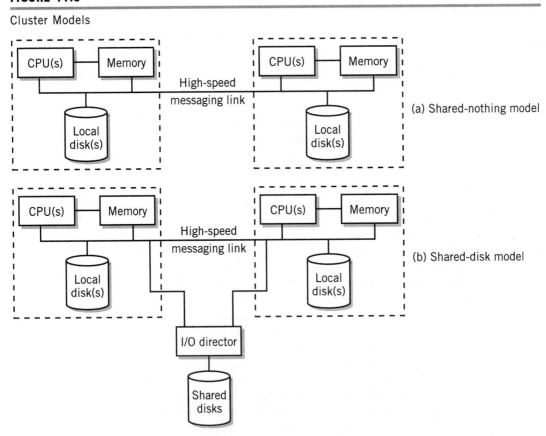

(a) Shared-nothing model

(b) Shared-disk model

plan for and predict accurately the partitioning. As a result, individual nodes may be overutilized or underutilized, and the efficiency of the cluster as a whole suffers.

The alternative, shared-disk model is shown in Figure 11.8b. In this model, data may be shared between cluster nodes because of the presence of disks that are accessible to every node. This model offers the advantage of easy dynamic workload balancing and, with careful design, high availability, and fault tolerance. Availability is enhanced on many systems by the use of RAID technology for the shared disks. (See Chapter 10 if you need a reminder.) Although these benefits make shared-disk clusters attractive, there is a cost in software complexity. The software that controls the cluster must be capable of maintaining coordination and synchronization of the data that is being processed by different nodes, to prevent corruption of the shared data and to assure accurate retrieval. For example, suppose that one node attempts to retrieve data that has been modified in memory, but not yet stored on the shared disk, by another node. This type of activity must be controlled. (If this doesn't seem too problematic to you, consider the following example: you make two ATM transactions in quick succession and they are processed on different nodes of a cluster. Without synchronization, your deposit could be wiped off the record!)

Different nodes of a cluster may be located in the same physical cabinet or may be located miles apart, provided there is a way to interconnect the high speed messaging link, and, if applicable, the shared-disk links. In fact, creating a cluster with widely separated nodes can also serve to protect the overall system and its data from catastrophe at a single location, particularly if the shared disks are also available at both locations. Clusters can even be configured to operate over the Internet.

Despite the additional complexity and planning effort, clustering has grown in importance in the last few years, because it provides a scalable and reliable way to attain large amounts of computer power at relatively low cost.

Beowulf Clusters

Beowulf clusters are simple, highly configurable clusters designed to provide high performance at low cost. Beowulf clusters consist of multiple computers connected together by a dedicated, private Ethernet, which serves as the link between the computers in the cluster. The cluster can be configured either as a shared-nothing or shared-disk model. Each node contains a CPU, memory, an Ethernet connection, and, sometimes, hard disks, floppy disks, and other peripherals. Beowulf clusters are generally configured with one of two types of computer components.

- **COTS,** or **commodity-off-the-shelf** components are simply inexpensive computers connected together to form a Beowulf cluster. In many cases the COTS components are older PCs scavenged from the scrap pile, and connected together to do some useful work.
- **Blade** components are computers mounted on a board that can be plugged into connectors on a rack, in much the same way peripheral cards are plugged into a PC motherboard. The backplane of the rack provides power and the dedicated Ethernet connection to each blade. The blades themselves are built from standard off-the-shelf parts.

Figure 11.9 shows photographs of a blade and the rack that together comprise the components of a Beowulf cluster in use at Los Alamos National Laboratory. Each blade

FIGURE 11.9

Blade and Rack of Beowulf Cluster

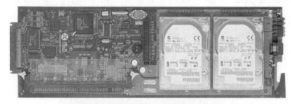

Source: W. Feng, M. Warren, and E. Weigle, "The Bladed Beowulf: A Cost-Effective Alternative to Traditional Beowulfs," Advanced Computing Laboratory, Los Alamos National Laboratory, Los Alamos, NM, 2002. Used with permission.

contains a Crusoe processor, 256 MB of memory, a 10GM hard disk, and three 100-MB/sec Ethernet interfaces.

The network connection between the nodes is not accessible from outside the cluster, which eliminates security concerns other than the authentication required to maintain cluster integrity. Instead, a Beowulf cluster generally has a single front-end gateway server that manages the nodes in the cluster and provides connectivity to the outside world. It also provides a monitor and keyboard to be shared among all of the nodes in the cluster. Each node is configured with its own hardware, its own operating system, and its own Beowulf clustering software. In a COTS system, it is common to see a variety of hardware from different vendors in use at different nodes, but blade systems tend to be more uniform. Linux is generally the operating system of choice because of its flexibility. In addition to its own configurability, Linux provides the tools needed to configure the cluster to include all the features of a powerful distributed system.

Beowulf clusters are ideal for use as Web servers because blades can be added or removed as required to maintain performance levels under varying loads. Most systems allow this operation to take place without powering down or rebooting the cluster. With their distributed processing capability, Beowulf clusters can also be used effectively for shared or parallel processing, where a single large task is divided into subtasks that can be processed simultaneously by different computers within the cluster.

11.6 NETWORKS

Local Area Networks

TOPOLOGY Local area networks are used to interconnect computers and other resources over a small area, perhaps an office or a building. Each of the computers, printers, and other devices connected to the network may be considered a node on the network. Data on local area networks is handled in packets. Various ways can be used to interconnect the nodes in a local area network. The layout used for a network is called the network **topology** or the network **configuration.**

Theoretically, it would be possible to have direct point-to-point connections between every computer in a network, but it is not practical to do so. The number of connections required for this type of network grows very rapidly as the number of nodes increases. (The actual number of connections is $[N \times (N-1) \div 2]$.) With only ten computers, forty-five cables would be required, and with five hundred computers, we would need nearly 125,000 cables!

Instead, network designers use three basic alternative configurations, either singly or in combination, to connect together the nodes in a network. Figure 11.10 shows the three basic configurations. They are called **bus, ring,** and **star** topologies. There are also variations on each type. Each configuration has its own advantages and disadvantages. It is important to understand that there is a difference between the physical topology, which describes the wiring layout, and the logical topology, which describes the electrical signal connections between network nodes. The physical topology is not relevant to our discussion. Our focus is on the logical topology only.

- With a bus configuration, each node is tapped in somewhere along the bus using a simple network interface between the bus and the computer or other device. The bus configuration is the easiest to wire. It is necessary only to run a single cable from a module at one end of the network to a module at the other. Each end of the bus is equipped with a **terminator** to prevent signals on the bus from echoing. The bus is a multipoint topology. A node transmits a message by placing it on the node, where it is broadcast to every other node on the bus. Access to the bus is passive. A nonsender simply listens for messages.

  Branches can be added to a bus, expanding it into a tree. Messages are still broadcast throughout the tree. Terminators are placed at the end of each branch in the tree.

- A ring topology consists of a point-to-point connection from each node on the network to the next. The last node is connected back to the first to form a closed ring. The ring topology requires an active network interface unit for each node. Each node must retransmit the signal that it receives from the previous node to the next node in the ring. The links between nodes are unidirectional, so that data travels in only one direction around the ring. To simplify the ring, it is possible to purchase a single **multistation access unit (MAU),** which contains an active interface for each node, preconnected into a ring topology. Each computer node is then wired to one of the interfaces in the MAU. Although this arrangement has the physical appearance of a star topology, logically it is still a ring.

- With a star configuration the network is controlled by a central station that acts as a steering device, passing data from one node to another as required. Each computer in the network is connected point-to-point to the control station. Switching in the central station connects pairs of nodes directly together to facilitate direct communication between the two nodes. More powerful switches can connect multiple pairs of node simultaneously.

Most networks use bus topology or a combination of bus and star topology. The bus has the obvious advantage of simplicity. Wiring is simple. Network interface units (NIUs) are connected to the bus passively. Unless an NIU fails in a "short-circuit" mode, which is extremely rare, a failed node will not affect the rest of the network. A break in the cable will cause a serious network failure, however. Standard bus networks are designed to operate at speeds of 10 megabits per second (Mbps) or 100 Mbps. One disadvantage of bus networks is that future speeds are somewhat limited by the propagation speed of signals on the bus and the fact that a bus configuration is not amenable to fiber optic technology.

FIGURE 11.10

LAN Topologies

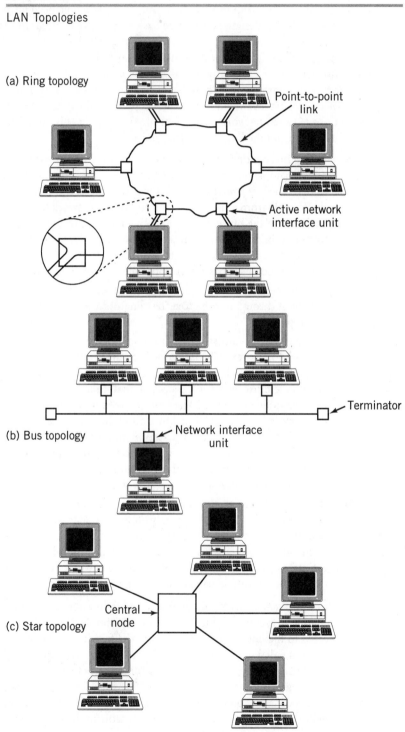

(a) Ring topology

Point-to-point link

Active network interface unit

(b) Bus topology

Terminator

Network interface unit

(c) Star topology

Central node

The star configuration has one serious disadvantage: failure of the central node can mean that the entire network goes down. This issue mandates the use of a high-reliability switch at the central node. Use of a star configuration can provide local area networks with large message capacity, particularly with multiple-pair switches. When combined with buses as subnetworks on each leg of the star, capacity increases even more, because the switch only handles data passing between subnetworks. Each bus subnetwork is independent and capable of full capacity otherwise.

Although the ring network is somewhat more complex, the use of repeaters in each NIU makes the network attractive when the distance between nodes extends over longer distances. The ring network is also capable of better performance at high levels of usage. The active repeaters in a ring network generally provide a bypass mode, so that a node can be removed from the ring without affecting operation of the network. The point-to-point connectivity of rings makes it possible to build very fast fiber optic rings that operate over large distances. Technology improvements in bus- and star-based networks have reduced much of the advantage of ring networks. Ring networks currently represent only a small part of the network market.

For a particular installation, the topology chosen depends on several factors. Most important are the distances between stations and the layout of the room or building to be wired. Other factors to be considered are the overall size of the network, the distance between the most remote nodes, speed requirements, degree of network traffic, and the total number of stations.

MEDIUM ACCESS CONTROL (MAC) PROTOCOLS   The role of the network interface is made up of two distinct functions. One function defines the characteristics of the channel, data rate, voltage levels, and the like. The second function controls node access to the channel. Node access for a particular network is defined by the medium access control protocol. The purposes of a medium access protocol are to steer data to its destination, to detect errors, and to prevent multiple nodes from accessing the network simultaneously in such a way that their messages become mixed together and garbled. Such an event is called a **collision.** The predominant medium-access protocols for local area networks are **Ethernet** and **token ring.** MAC protocols are implemented in hardware in the NIU.

Ethernet   Technically, Ethernet is called the **Carrier Sense Multiple Access with Collision Detection,** or **CSMA/CD** protocol. Ethernet is a trade name for this protocol. The trade name belongs to Xerox Corporation, who did the original development on the protocol.

Ethernet is based on bus topology. There are several variations, which differ in the type of wiring used, in the method used to tap into the bus, and in the speed of operation. The address for each node on an Ethernet network is called a MAC address. It is set in the hardware. Addresses are permanently assigned by the IEEE organization.

Every node on the network has equal access to the bus and is normally in "listening" mode; that is, each node is listening for messages addressed to it. Remember that messages on the bus are broadcast; every node receives every message, but a node will ignore messages that are not addressed to it. The bus is silent when no node is transmitting.

Messages are sent in frames. The standard Ethernet frame is shown in Figure 11.11. Any node may use the bus to send a message to another node any time the bus is not in use; there is no specific timing control on the bus. When a node has a message to send, it

FIGURE 11.11

Standard Ethernet Frame

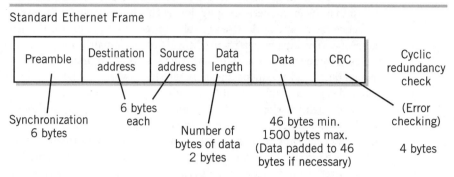

listens to see if the bus is in use. If not, it begins to send its packet. If the bus is already in use, the node waits until the bus is available. This is the "CSMA" part of CSMA/CD.

Ethernet does not try to prevent the occurrence of collisions. As the node sends its packet, it continues to listen to the bus. Much of the time, the node completes sending the packet and returns to listening mode. Occasionally, two (or more) nodes may sense that the bus is free and initiate transmission simultaneously. A collision occurs, and the message on the bus becomes scrambled, due to the interference between the two signals. Since each node continues to listen as it transmits, it can recognize that the message is scrambled—the signal on the bus is not the same as the message it is transmitting. When a node detects a collision, it immediately stops transmitting, waits a short time, then returns to listening mode, and tries again when the bus is free. The amount of time each node waits after a collision is random for each node. If both nodes waited the same length of time, collisions would continue to recur indefinitely.

It might seem to you that collisions would occur very rarely, especially on a network with sparse traffic. There is an additional factor to consider, however. Signals on the bus require a small but finite (and, as it turns out, sometimes significant) amount of time to travel down the bus. Signals on a bus travel at approximately three-fourths the speed of light, or roughly 9 inches per nanosecond. This may seem like a very small number, but if two nodes on the bus are 500 feet apart, it will create a window of about 5/8 microseconds after one node begins transmitting before the second node is aware that the bus is in use. In other words, the probability of collisions is higher than one would first assume. Particularly if bus traffic is heavy, a node may have to try several times before it sends a packet successfully. The amount of time that it takes for a packet to get from one end of the network is called the **network propagation delay.**

Ethernet is ideal for networks with light traffic, because of its simplicity. Every node is independent. Nodes may be added simply by tapping into the bus. No central network control is required. However, Ethernet is unsuitable for networks with widely separated nodes, due to the increase in the probability of collisions. Similarly, as traffic increases, the number of collisions and retransmissions also increases and Ethernet performance deteriorates, making Ethernet less suitable also for networks that frequently carry heavy traffic.

As noted previously, the use of star topology makes it possible to extend the capacity of a network by introducing a switching hub between different branches of the network.

Figure 11.12 illustrates the concept. Each branch in the figure conforms to the Ethernet standard. Data on a branch that is destined for the same branch is passed in the usual way. Data destined for another branch passes through the hub and is switched to the appropriate branch. The overall capacity of the network is increased, since the number of collisions is reduced by the switching technique. This technique, called **switched Ethernet** has gained favor in recent years as an inexpensive means of extending network capability.

Token Ring Protocol The token ring protocol uses the concept of a passed token to control access to a network. The token is a small bit pattern that is passed as a message on the network from node to node. A common choice of token is the pattern 11011011. The node that holds the token at any given instant is the only one permitted to place a message on the ring. If it has no message to send, it passes the token to the next node. To transmit a message, it replaces the token with a "busy" token and adds the message to be sent. The message is then passed from node to node until it reaches its destination. The destination node receives its message and modifies the token with a "copied" token that is returned to the sender as an acknowledgment. When the "copied" token reaches the sending node, the sending node places the original token back on the network, and the token passing continues. Note that the originator is not allowed to use the token immediately again. This prevents a node from hogging the token.

Collisions cannot occur with this protocol since only one node has access to the network at a time. This protocol is usually identified by the name "token ring," and it is commonly associated with a ring network topology, but the token-passing protocol is sometimes used with a bus topology. Token passing on a bus is essentially similar in operation, except that the ordering of nodes must be established, since it is not defined automatically by the topology as it is in a token ring network.

FIGURE 11.12

Switched Ethernet

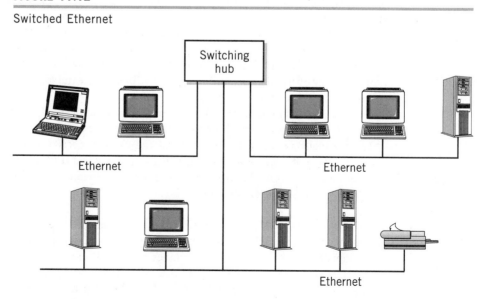

The token-passing protocol has the advantage that it performs efficiently at high traffic levels. It is fair, because every node has access to the network, and the maximum wait time before a node can send a message can be predicted, since the time to pass a token or message around the ring is known. At low to medium traffic levels, it is somewhat less efficient than Ethernet, because much of the time is spent passing the token from node to node. A node wanting service on a network with no traffic still has to wait for the token in order to use the network. This is a minor disadvantage. Large token ring networks sometimes operate with two tokens simultaneously, at opposite points on the ring.

A more serious disadvantage of token ring is the necessity to plan for failures. Token ring requires one computer to be responsible for initiating the ring when the network is started, and any time a failure occurs. The computer can detect a failure if the token or message does not return to it within a designated time. Most systems also designate a backup computer to take over if there is a failure in the token-initiating computer. Every node must know the next node in the token-passing sequence, and must be able to bypass a node in case of failure. It is also more difficult to add and remove nodes from the system for this reason.

Other MAC Protocols Both Ethernet and token-passing protocols have characteristics that limit network speed. The token-passing network limitation is the fact that the token must be passed continuously from node to node, although within practical limits, it is possible to use faster components to increase the token passing speed. It is even possible to build a ring topology with fiber optic links. Ethernet speed is limited by the distance between its furthest nodes. The longer the network, the larger the window during which collisions can occur. Furthermore, it is impractical to tap fiber optic cable. Ethernet networks are generally constructed with wire as a medium. Ethernet and token ring speeds generally do not exceed 100 Mbps. Most current networks generally operate between 10 and 100 Mbps. Gigabit Ethernet is gradually coming into use.

A number of new network technologies are appearing on the market to fulfill the need for ever-increasing network speed, particularly with the rapid growth of multimedia communication. The increasing use of real-time audio and video on the Internet World Wide Web, for example, requires tremendous network capacity that is not easily met with older technologies.

Two technologies that show promise are **Asynchronous Transfer Mode (ATM)** and **Fiber Distributed Data Interface (FDDI).** FDDI uses fiber optic cables in a token-passing ring topology operating at a minimum of 100 Mbps. Unlike the standard token ring, FDDI uses two rings, operating in opposite directions.

ATM is a technology based on the rapid transmission of small, 53-byte message packets called cells through a mesh network of switches that can direct a cell to other nodes. ATM is actually a combination of protocol and its own special topology, although it can be designed to simulate other types of networks. ATM is capable of data rates in excess of a billion bits per second, but has not yet attained widespread use due to its technical complexity and configuration difficulty.

BRIDGES AND ROUTERS Local area networks may be interconnected. The components that are used for this purpose are **bridges** and **routers.** Bridges are used to interconnect similar networks. The bridge occupies a node on each network. When the bridge recognizes an address on one network that belongs to a node on the other network, the bridge passes the message through to its node on the other network, where it continues on to its destination.

Routers perform the same function for dissimilar networks, but the router must perform the additional function of converting the format of the message to correspond to the protocol of the new network when the message is passed from one network to the other.

Wide Area Networks

When data communication is necessary or desired beyond the reach of a local area network, a wide area network is used. (There is also an in-between concept known as a metropolitan area network, which uses a mixture of local area network, repeaters, and medium-distance point-to-point media such as microwave to achieve its goals.) Wide area networking is also referred to as internetworking (small "i"), because it ultimately represents a network made up of other networks. The Internet (capital "I") is a (massive) example of a wide area network. Wide area networking can be accomplished with public or leased telephone services, but the use of packet switching networks is more common today.

Unlike local area networks, it is not possible to define a simple topology for connecting the stations in a wide area network. Instead, wide area networks make use of a concept called **switched communication networks.** A switched network is made up of nodes that are connected together point-to-point. Packets of data are routed by switching the data from one node to the next until each reaches its destination. At any given time there may be thousands or millions of packets making their way across the network to different destinations.

The nodes in a wide area network are often themselves routers or bridges in local area networks. In general, there are two types of nodes in use. Some nodes are connected to stations or are routers on a local area network. Other nodes are dedicated solely to the task of forwarding data. An example of a switching network is shown in Figure 11.13. Nodes 5 and 7 are used only for switching. The other nodes also connect to network stations or to a local area network. Each node in a wide area network operates independently, accepting packets as they arrive and forwarding them to the next node or passing them to the destination station.

FIGURE 11.13

A Switched Wide Area Network

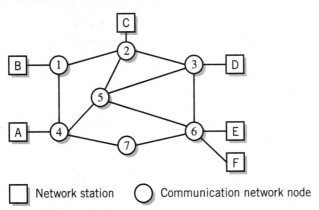

☐ Network station   ○ Communication network node

Source: BUSINESS DATA COMMUNICATIONS, 2/E by Stallings/Van Slyke, © 1997. Reprinted by permission of Prentice-Hall, Upper Saddle River, NJ.

The communication connection between source and destination is defined by one of four types of circuits.

- **Circuit switching** provides a dedicated channel path between the source and destination for the duration of the communication connection. Circuit switching is inefficient, because the channel is generally not being used at full capacity. Circuit switching is analogous to the use of a computer without multitasking.

- **Message switching** creates a dedicated channel path for an entire message. The message is not broken into packets. Although message switching seems ideal because of its low overhead and high message verifiability, it makes inefficient use of the channel, since a message may be quite long and can tie up nodes in an uncontrolled fashion. Message switching is used rarely.

- **Packet switching,** also called datagram switching, creates an independent path for each datagram as it traverses the network. Packet switching provides maximum utilization of a network and has the additional benefit that individual datagrams can be routed around areas of traffic congestion to spread the traffic more evenly throughout the network. One concern is that the datagrams can arrive out of order and the message must be reconstructed. The design must also prevent "loops," in which the datagram is routed over and over through the same set of nodes and never reaches its destination.

- **Virtual circuit switching** creates a route from source to destination before message transmission begins, and all datagrams in the message are sent using the same route. The nodes in the route are used for other messages as well, so that the network is used efficiently. Virtual circuit switching is affected by bursts of traffic from other messages, which can delay a message. However, it has the advantage that datagrams arrive in correct order. Message verification is simplified, since the path of each datagram is known.

A Comparison of Networks and Clusters

It is instructive to identify the primary differences between networks and clusters.

- Clusters provide a private message-passing link between nodes in the cluster. In some cases, the link is specifically designed for clustering. Although the link in Beowulf clusters uses standard network technology, the link is not accessible outside the cluster and is used only for internode cluster communication.

- A cluster appears to the outside world as a single computing unit. Individual nodes are administered as part of the cluster and are not identifiable or individually accessible from the outside. Network nodes are individually identifiable and addressable.

- The workload on a node in a cluster is determined solely by cluster administrative and load-balancing software. The workload in a network cannot be controlled in the same way because each node has its own access to the outside.

- Beowulf clusters treat all executing software globally, with a single identification number that is independent of the node. This allows programs that are divided between nodes to intercommunicate between nodes as though both pieces were executing on the same machine. Other clusters also support this feature. Networks do not permit this type of communication.

11.7 HIGH PERFORMANCE COMPUTING

Many interesting and important problems are not amenable to normal computer solution, either because the problem is so complex computationally or because the volume of data to be processed is prohibitively large. Example problems include the analysis of weather patterns, the behavior of physics particles, and prediction of the economic and social effects of a particular political policy.

The field of high performance computing, sometimes called **supercomputing,** arose in an attempt to meet the challenge of solving difficult problems that require massive amounts of computing power. There have been a number of different approaches to high performance computing, but recently developed systems tend to fall loosely into one of two architectural categories:

- systems that use very large numbers of CPUs connected to form what are called **massively parallel processor architectures (MPP),** or simply **parallel computers.**
- systems that are built from clusters of powerful machines or larger Beowulf blade clusters

A third, very different, approach to high performance computing uses the spare processing capacity of computers connected to a network. Each computer is given a small portion of the task to process in its spare time. This technique is called **grid computing.**

Consider, first, parallel computers.

Parallel Computers

The number of CPUs in a parallel computer may typically be in the hundreds or thousands. Each CPU in a parallel computer system has access to a small amount of local memory, as well as global memory that is accessible by all the processors. The CPUs are pipelined so that the results from one CPU immediately flow into another for further processing. There is a systemwide bus that can access every processor. Some systems also provide local pathways between clusters of CPUs. Communication between processors uses packet switching techniques similar to those used in networks.

EXAMPLE

The T3E massively parallel processing system from Cray Research consists of up to 2,176 nodes, arranged in a three-dimensional interconnected array. Each node consists of an Alpha CPU, individual cache memory, up to 2 GB of local memory, a DMA controller that redistributes system data, and a network controller. In addition, there is global system memory. The array serves as a network, connecting nodes together to pass data or instructions as required by the application, and also providing connections to a fast I/O port. A processor at any node can access the local memory of any other processor directly through the network. The entire system is controlled from a host computer. This system has been measured at a sustained program execution speed of 1.1 trillion floating point operations per second, with 1,488 processor nodes.

■ ■ ■

As a more specific application-oriented approach, the Cambridge Parallel Processing Gamma II Plus system is designed for applications where large-scale SIMD processing is useful, such as image processing. The Gamma II Plus system consists of 1024 or 4096 proprietary 8-bit processors in a two-dimensional array, controlled from a standard host computer, such as a Sun workstation. Each node processor has up to 128KB of local memory. Instructions are broadcast simultaneously to every processor from a master control unit. Every processor performs the same operation, but on different data. There is no direct communication between individual processors. The processor array provides an interface to a standard bus, such as PCI or V/ME64, which allows the use of standard I/O devices.

The software that controls massively parallel computers is written in extensions to such languages as C, FORTRAN, and Lisp. Obviously, there are only certain types of programs that can use a massively parallel system to full advantage, specifically those programs that require a large number of parallel operations. Image processing, simulations, and data searching by content (to locate text files in a massive data base that contain a particular keyword, for example) are well suited to parallel processing.

Cluster Computing

Problems that can be broken into small subtasks are well suited for cluster computing. The IBM eServer P690 is typical. Each node consists of either sixteen or thirty-two POWER4 CPUs operating together as a symmetric multiprocessor. The CPUs share a maximum of 256 GB memory. It is possible to cluster up to 512 nodes.

An alternative approach is demonstrated by the *Green Destiny* system built with the blades described in Section 11.5. Ten racks of the type shown in Figure 11.9 are mounted in a single cabinet 19" wide, 25" deep, and 60" high. The cabinet holds a total of 240 nodes. Although this system offers less computing power than the larger machines, its size and electrical power consumption make it attractive for some high-performance computing tasks.

Grid Computing

Research by David Gelernter [MAR92] and others demonstrated that it was possible to produce supercomputer performance for processing large problems by distributing the problem and using the spare processing time of personal workstations connected to a network. Much additional research on *grid computing* has been done since then. Issues include effective division of the workload, scheduling work, preventing interference with local processing, effective use of the results, and security and privacy for the client machines.

There have been a number of projects that are attempting to solve large-scale problems using grid computing. One interesting project is the SETI@home project, which is a systematic search for extraterrestrial intelligence organized by the Space Science Laboratory of the University of California at Berkeley. [KORP00]

A radio telescope at Arecibo, Puerto Rico scans the sky for signals. An entire sky survey returns about 39 TB of data for processing.

The processing algorithms allow the data to be broken into tiny chunks for analysis. More than half a million active volunteers from all over the world receive chunks of data over the Internet. Application software built into a screen saver analyzes the data when the client's system is idle and returns the results to the collection system at Berkeley, where the results are stored in a giant database for analysis.

11.8 BLURRING THE LINE

It is worth observing that there has been a recent significant blurring of the line that distinguishes between I/O buses and networks. USB and FireWire are examples of recent I/O buses that have many of the characteristics of networks. Both USB and FireWire break messages into packets for transmission across the bus, and protocols that provide the capability to access the bus, to identify and reconstruct messages, and prevent conflict. Although USB is built on a hierarchical, hub-based structure that clearly identifies a single host, FireWire devices share the bus, in a manner similar to a network. There may be multiple hosts. The FireWire protocol establishes means for multiple hosts to access the bus without conflict. The FireWire protocol establishes means for multiple hosts to access the bus without conflict. The FireWire protocol standard defines physical, data link and transaction layers, as well as a bus configuration manager that bears resemblance to a shared session layer. FireWire supports hubs, splitters, repeaters, and bridges. This blurring reflects an important tendency to adapt and combine the use of various architectural features and components in computer system and data communication technology in an ongoing effort to provide ever more system power and capability.

SUMMARY AND REVIEW

The emphasis in modern computers is on increasing amounts of power and capability. To that end, computer designers have resorted to a variety of techniques to increase the amount of capability in a computer system. In addition to increasing the raw power of individual components, current technology relies on the high-speed interconnection of computers to achieve the capabilities required of modern systems.

Data communication technology offers many benefits to users, including improved performance and system reliability, access to shared resources, connection to online sources of information, and the ability to work together and communicate with other users remotely. Most modern computers have data communication capability of one type or another, through modem access or a network.

A computer system may be tightly coupled, with two or more CPUs sharing memory, the bus, and the I/O peripherals, in an arrangement called multiprocessing. Master-slave multiprocessing establishes a single CPU as the control for the system. Symmetrical multiprocessing gives equal access to each CPU.

Alternatively, a number of autonomous computer systems, each with its own memory and I/O, can be loosely coupled into a cluster or a network. Clusters represent a form of loosely coupled system in which computers are interconnected with high-speed messaging links. A cluster consists of multiple computers acting as one. Shared-nothing clusters utilize separate disks and data partitioned and distributed among the systems in the cluster. Shared-disk systems provide multiple system access to one or more shared disks that hold the data to be processed by all.

A network may be made up of point-to-point or multipoint channels. Two computers can also be connected point-to-point directly over a communication channel. In this case the telephone system is a common choice of communication channel. A terminal controller makes it possible for a host computer to connect directly to several client computers simultaneously.

To the computers in a network, data communications is treated as an I/O operation, with the network as the I/O "device," and a network interface controller as the device controller between the computer and the network. Like other I/O operations, data moves between primary computer storage and the network.

The physical and electrical configuration of computers and channels is known as the topology of the communication system. Local area networks are connections of computers within a small area. Local area networks are most commonly configured into bus, ring, or star topologies. Tree and mesh topologies are also used. Network access is provided by Ethernet, token-passing, or mesh switching protocols. Wide area networks incorporate point-to-point connections between nodes on networks and individual stations. Data packets are switched from node to node until they reach their receiver node. There are four different types of circuits in use for this purpose. The Internet is an important example of a wide area network. High performance computing utilizes large numbers of interconnected CPUs or computers to provide large amounts of computing power. So far, these systems have had limited commercial application, although they have been used successfully to solve large-scale scientific problems.

KEY CONCEPTS AND TERMS

asynchronous transfer
  mode (ATM)
Beowulf cluster
blade
bridge
bus topology
Carrier Sense Multiple
  Access with Collision
  Detection (CSMA/CD)
circuit switching
client
client-server architecture
cluster
commodity-off-the-shelf
  (COTS)
communication channel
configuration (network)
distributed systems
Ethernet
fault-tolerant systems
fiber distributed data
  interface (FDDI)
grid computing

high performance
  computing
local area network
loosely coupled system
mapping
massively parallel processor
  architecture
master-slave
  multiprocessing
medium access control
  protocol
message switching
multicomputer system
multidrop channel
multipoint channel
multiprocessor
multistation access unit
  (MAU)
network propagation delay
node
packet switching
parallel computers
point-to-point
  communication

ring topology
router
server
shared communication
  channel
shared-disk
shared-nothing
star topology
supercomputing
switched communication
  network
switched Ethernet
symmetric multiprocessing
  (SMP)
synergy
terminator
tightly coupled system
token ring protocol
topology
very-large-scale integrated
  circuit (VLSI)
virtual circuit switching
wide area network

FOR FURTHER READING

Messmer [MESS01] provides an "indispensable" discussion of PC hardware, with all its bells and whistles. Good discussions of multiprocessing can be found in Patterson and Hennessey [PATT98] and Tanenbaum [TAN99]. Good discussions of clustering can be found in Pfister [PFIS98], Brewer [BREW97], and Nick et al [NICK97]. The "Green Destiny" Beowulf cluster is described in [FENG02].

Although the basic concepts have not changed much, rapid technological advances are the name of the game in the areas of networking and multiprocessing. There is a constant flow of new books explaining the latest developments, and the recommendations of the staff at a good technical bookstore are probably more useful than those presented here. The basics of networking can be found in any good data communications book. In addition to those mentioned in connection with Supplementary Chapter 3, Cohen [COH95] introduces local area networking at a simple, readable level. Stallings [STAL00] and Martin, Chapman, and Leben [MART94b] address the specifics of local area networking in more depth.

EXERCISES

11.1 Carefully describe the advantages and disadvantages of master-slave multiprocessing and symmetrical multiprocessing. Which would you select for fault-tolerant computing? Why

11.2 Illustrate how a sixteen-dimensional hypercube makes it possible to pass a signal from any sender to any receiver in less than sixteen connections. (Hint: Start with two- and three-dimensional models.)

11.3 Discuss the trade-offs between circuit switching, packet switching, virtual circuits, and message switching.

11.4 Explain the differences between circuit switching and virtual circuits.

11.5 Explain the differences between message switching and packet switching.

11.6 What tasks are required of a router that are not needed for a bridge? Be as specific as you can.

11.7 Explain the operation of a token bus network. What additional requirements does a token bus network impose that are not needed in a token ring network? What are the differences that make this so?

11.8 Discuss the trade-offs between a token bus and an Ethernet network.

11.9 Prior to the invention of Ethernet, researchers at the University of Hawaii proposed a broadcast radio network called ALOHANet as a means to provide wireless links between the Hawaiian islands. Each node had a radio transmitter which could be used to send data packets. When two stations attempted to transmit simultaneously, a collision occurred, and like Ethernet, each station would wait a random period of time, then try again.

Compare ALOHANet with Ethernet. What are the similarities? What are the differences? What are the major factors contributing to the differences? What effects do the differences have upon performance? Under what conditions would you expect ALOHANet to perform satisfactorily? Less satisfactorily?

11.10   What characteristics of the token ring make it possible to operate a token ring network at speeds far in excess of those of a bus-based network?

11.11   Suppose you have a token ring network with 10 nodes. Assume that there is a delay of 0.5 microseconds as data passes from one node to the next. What is the maximum length of time a sender node will have to wait before being able to place a message on the network?

11.12   Describe each of the overhead factors in an Ethernet. In a token ring. Explain the impact of these factors on performance at different traffic levels.

11.13   What steps and precautions must be taken to assure reliable operation of a token ring network?

11.14   Describe as precisely as you can the tasks that must be performed by an NIU or MAU in a token ring network.

11.15   A short-circuit failure is a failure in which the connection point signal line is electrically shorted to ground. Although NIU short-circuit failures are extremely rare, they do occur occasionally. What is the effect on a bus network if a short-circuit failure occurs? How would a repairperson locate the source of the problem? What is the effect of an open-circuit failure? What is the effect on a ring network for each type of failure?

11.16   Find and read a good article that describes ATM. Compare ATM methodology with the other networking topologies that we have discussed. What characteristics of ATM make it capable of high performance compared to other networking techniques?

11.17   Suppose that you are trying to design a network that would be a suitable for a company that is located in several buildings scattered around a town. No building is more than a 1/4 mile from another building, but direct wire connections between all buildings are not possible due to roads, houses, and other obstacles. Propose a network configuration for this company, and justify your proposal.

11.18   Describe how you might use a network to provide fault-tolerant computing. Discuss the trade-offs between your solution and a multiprocessor solution.

11.19   Carefully explain the differences between a client-server network and a peer-to-peer network. Compare the networks in terms of capability and performance.

11.20   Obtain information and compare Windows 2000 and IBM zSeries clustering techniques.

11.21   Clearly and carefully discuss each of the advantages of clustering.

11.22   How does a Beowulf cluster differ from other kinds of clusters?

THREE SYSTEM EXAMPLES

12.1 INTRODUCTION

Now you will see how real systems apply in practice the concepts that you have already learned. For this purpose, we have selected three examples that represent typical, current popular machines in each of three major categories: CISC-based personal computers, RISC-based computers, and mainframe computers. Each example represents a *family* of computers, with a number of models of different power and capability. Members of a family share a common general architecture, with similar instruction sets, register layouts, addressing, CPU organization, and operating methods, although the implementations of the architecture may vary widely over the different models. Each of these families has evolved over a period of time, increasing in power, speed, and complexity while maintaining essential program compatibility with earlier members of the family. By comparing these three examples, you will see that the architectures of different computers are fundamentally very similar, even for computers differing significantly in design, in size, in purpose, and in the year of their original development.

Section 12.1 introduces the X86-based family of personal computers. The X86 family includes computers that use the 8088, 8086, 80286, 80386, 80486, Pentium, Pentium Pro, Pentium II, III, and 4 microcomputer chips, along with many minor variations, as their CPUs. (There is an 80186, but it was never generally used as a personal computer CPU.) Our discussion will focus on the family as a whole, although differences between the various members will be addressed in the discussion. We show the natural evolution of the family, as it grew from 16-bit to 32-bit to 64-bit, expanded its capabilities, and refined its architecture to reflect current requirements and state-of-the-art design, all the while maintaining the basic instruction set, structure, and full backward compatibility throughout the family. We will also include a brief introduction to the 64-bit Itanium architecture, which includes continued support for the x86 family. The X86 family is an example of CISC architecture and, by virtue of the popularity and familiarity of the PC, is the most important family of CPUs on the market today.

Next, we will look at the Power PC family of computers. The Power PC is representative of current RISC computers. The Power PC CPU is used in recent personal computers and workstations from both Apple and IBM. IBM also uses the PowerPC in its mid-sized computers. The design is notable for its simplicity and flexibility.

Finally, we will turn our attention to the IBM zSeries family of mainframe computers. For almost forty years, this family, which includes its architecturally similar predecessors the S/360, S/370, and S/390, has been the mainstay of computing. Although the architecture has been upgraded to extend its capabilities and features, the original system organization and CPU design remain the heart of the system. The design of the zSeries CPU is a good representative for modern implementation of a classic CPU design. It draws on the power of multiprocessing and clustering to maintain its lead in the world of large-scale computing.

These three families of machines represent different design dates, goals, and practices, and yet, as you will see, they provide ample verification of the fundamental similarities in all computer CPUs.

Our discussions look briefly at each system as a whole, with a bit of history to give you an idea of how the system fits into the evolution of computing. Most of our discussions focus specifically on the CPUs. For each system we consider the components of the CPU, the instruction set, the methods used for addressing, and various other details of interest that show how the pieces of the system fit together to meet the particular intentions and design goals of that system.

The most recent CPUs discussed in this chapter are all built around the advanced design principles that we introduced in Chapters 8 and 11, to extract the maximum performance possible from the CPU. Each of these CPUs is built around an instruction unit/execution unit model and includes cache memory and support for virtual storage. The chapter includes brief discussion of the differences in features and design between these CPUs. More important, the three descriptions will demonstrate that the basic CPU organization of each of these CPUs embodies the principles that you saw in Chapter 7, as implemented by the methods introduced in Chapter 8; that the instruction sets, register layouts, addressing methods, and instruction word layouts look quite familiar; and that the fetch-execute cycles perform as expected. In other words, even the most sophisticated of today's computers embody the basic CPU design principles developed by von Neumann and the others more than fifty years ago.

There is a lot of material in this chapter because the chapter describes three different systems in detail. It is not necessary that you understand and remember every detail for each of the three systems. Instead, the material in this chapter offers you the opportunity to study and compare and contrast the ways in which computer systems are put together. Keep in mind, as you read, that much of the value in this chapter comes from careful and continual examination of the similarities and differences between these different types of systems.

When you complete this chapter, you will have a good appreciation of the basic similarity between supposedly different computer systems, large and small, as well as a practical confirmation of the fundamental simplicity of computers. We hope that you will also feel a lot of confidence in your understanding of the basics of computer systems!

12.2 THE X86 FAMILY

System Overview

The introduction of the original IBM PC in 1981 revolutionized computing and made it available to everyone. More PCs have been sold in each of the last few years than all computers prior to 1981 combined!

The original IBM PC was provided with 64 kilobytes (KB) of random access memory, expandable to a maximum of 640KB of RAM. For long-term storage the system used modified audiocassettes or 5 1/4" 360KB floppy diskettes. There was no hard disk drive. Standard input was a keyboard, and the display was limited to low-resolution, monocolored text. The system provided no support for floating point arithmetic. Floating point arithmetic operations had to be done in software.

Today's PC is more likely to have at least 256 *mega*bytes (MB) of memory and could have much more, practically without limit. Nearly every system also provides cache memory. Long-term storage is provided by one or more hard disks, with capacity probably in excess of 20 gigabytes (GB). Floating point and vector processing are integral parts of the CPU. Graphical interfaces, CD-ROM or DVD-ROM, modem or network capability, color, sound, and video capabilities have become standard, even in laptop computers. The current PC is hundreds or thousands of times as fast and powerful as the original PC. Nonetheless, programs written for the original PC can still be executed on the most recent PCs.

X86-based computer systems conform to the general personal computer model presented in Chapter 11 and shown in Figures 11.1, 11.3, and 11.4. System I/O is bus oriented and supports both programmed I/O and DMA. The CPU can accept two types of interrupts, nonmaskable and maskable. Nonmaskable interrupts are used for emergency situations such as power failures. The system support circuitry expands the single maskable CPU interrupt into thirty-two prioritized interrupts, labeled IRQ0 through IRQ31. When an interrupt is received by the CPU, the CPU reads an address on the data lines that is used to point to the interrupt routine, saves the return address and general-purpose registers, and jumps to the interrupt routine.

The CPU

The original PCs were powered by a single Intel 8088 CPU. The 8088 CPU supported 16-bit processing, with 16-bit registers and 16-bit internal data buses. Externally, the 8088 could support only 8 bits at a time, which meant that memory transfers required two bus cycles to handle one 16-bit word of data. Memory addressing was limited to 20 bits, for 1MB total. From that beginning, the X86 family has continuously evolved. The memory addressing capability has increased from 1MB to 64 gigabytes (GB). The data path of Pentium models is 64 bits wide externally and as much as 256 bits wide internally. Additional instructions have been added to the instruction set. Some of these new instructions provide new features, including support for multimedia. Floating point instructions, virtual storage, and multitasking support are now part of the basic architecture. Two levels of memory caching have been built in and integrated with the CPU to speed up memory access. Techniques that protect memory from incorrect or illegal access have been included. The 8088 CPU operated at a clock speed of 4.77 MHz. Current models can be operated at speeds in excess of 2.8 GHz. The pipelining and superscalar techniques discussed in Chapter 8 have been incorporated to increase the number of instructions that can be executed each second. Current systems can support multiple CPUs in a symmetric multiprocessing configuration. Figure 12.1 compares some of the basic processor characteristics of the major members of the X86 family.

Despite all the improvements, downward software compatibility with earlier models of the family has been maintained. Each new model has been capable of executing the software built for previous models. The major instruction set changes incorporated into later models were designed to operate separately from the fundamental architecture, using a mode of operation known as "protected mode." When the protected mode is disabled, these chips are software compatible with the original 8088 architecture, although they normally operate faster, due to their wider data paths, improved internal design, and faster clock speeds.

Since the introduction of the original IBM PC, the CPUs within the IBM and clone PC family have all been members of the X86 series of CPU microprocessors provided

FIGURE 12.1

X86 Processor Characteristics

Processor	Register Width	Addressing Capability	Address Space	Data Bus Width	Max. Clock Frequency
8088	16 bits	20 bits	1 MB	8 bits	10 MHz
8086	16 bits	20 bits	1 MB	16 bits	10 MHz
80286	16 bits	24 bits	16 MB	16 bits	16 MHz
80386SX	32 bits	24 bits	16 MB	16 bits	25 MHz
80386DX	32 bits	32 bits	4 GB	32 bits	40 MHz
80486SX	32 bits	32 bits	4 GB	32 bits	33 MHz
80486DX	32 bits	32 bits	4 GB	32 bits	100 MHz
Pentium	32 bits	32 bits	4 GB	64 bits	166 MHz
P6 family	32 bits	36 bits	64 GB	64 bits	200-750 MHz
Pentium 4	32 bits	32 bits	64 GB	64/256 bits	3.1 GHz

mostly by the Intel Corporation, although other companies are now manufacturing some members of this family. As we pointed out, the original PCs were powered by the 8088 microprocessor. Most recent PC models use the Pentium 4 or the architecturally similar AMD Athlon microprocessor as their CPUs.

Registers

The 8088, 8086, and 80286 had eight general-purpose registers, four **segment registers,** and a flag register available to the programmer. The CPUs also contain the instruction pointer and various control registers for internal use. The general-purpose registers were extended in size, starting with the 80386, but otherwise operate similarly. The 80386 also added two additional segment registers.

Beginning with the 80486, floating point capability became standard, so there are an additional eight 80-bit floating point data registers in the register set, along with various floating point control and status registers. The Pentium with MMX CPU added a number of multimedia instructions, which then became part of the Pentium II and later members of the family. The MMX instructions use 64 bits of the floating point registers (called aliasing) as though they are separate registers, but the FP/MM registers can not be used for both purposes simultaneously. Finally, the Pentium III added floating point SIMD instructions, and provided eight 128-bit registers for the use of the SIMD instructions, along with an additional SIMD FP control/status register.

The segment registers are used for addressing and are discussed in the addressing section. The general registers are shown in Figure 12.2 As you can see from the diagram, the 8086 and 8088 contained eight 16-bit general-purpose registers, labeled AX, BX, CX, DX, SP, BP, SI, and DI. The first four registers could also be accessed as bytes. Thus, instructions could individually access the low-order or high-order byte of AX, known as AL and AH, respectively. Beginning with the 80286, the general-purpose registers were extended

FIGURE 12.2

X86 General-purpose Registers

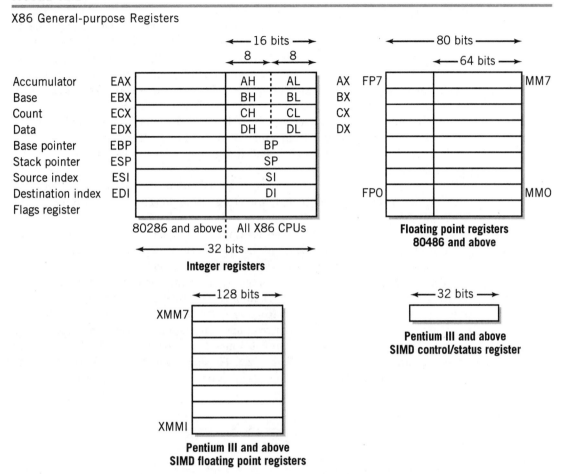

The accumulator register, AX or EAX, is intended mostly for temporary data storage, as described in previous chapters of this book. Programmed I/O instructions require use of the accumulator register for their I/O transfers, although under certain conditions the DX register can also be used for this purpose.

to 32 bits. Note, however, the lower halves of these extended registers could still be accessed as previously. Thus, complete compatibility with the earlier CPUs is maintained.

Although most of the instructions that use integer registers can use any of the general-purpose integer registers for their operations, some of the registers were designed to be used in specific ways and are optimized for that purpose.

The accumulator register, AX or EAX, is intended mostly for temporary data storage, as described in previous chapters of this book. Programmed I/O instructions require use of the accumulator register for their I/O transfers, although under certain conditions the DX register can also be used for this purpose.

The base register, BX or EBX, is intended as a base address pointer, but can also be used for temporary data storage.

The count register, CX or ECX (note how Intel managed to name its registers A, B, C, and D and yet give the acronyms meaning), is used for indexing. Many instructions automatically decrement the count register on each iteration. Therefore, the count register is highly useful for automatic indexing of arrays, loops, and the like.

The data register, DX or EDX, is also used mainly for temporary data storage. The AX register and DX register are used together to hold the result of integer multiplication and to hold the dividend in division. The DX register also holds the remainder after division.

The base pointer, BP, is primarily used as a pointer to the base of a stack within memory. Assembly language programmers (and the code generated by compilers) use it primarily to access the arguments that are passed when calling procedures. To call a procedure, the program pushes the arguments on to a stack. The base of the stack is stored in BP. The procedure retrieves the arguments by using BP as a pointer to the stack.

The stack pointer, SP or ESP, is intended primarily for use to keep track of the location within a stack.

The source index, SI, and destination index, DI, are used to keep track of locations within an array. These are particularly useful for string processing and also for first-in, first-out buffer processing.

We remind you that all these registers can be used for temporary data storage and other general purposes if desired. It's just that using them as suggested provides more consistency and makes a programmer's code easier to understand.

The flags register provides single-bit, ON/OFF codes that can be used to test for particular conditions. Some conditions are set automatically by various instructions as a result of the operation performed by the instruction. Others are set or reset by instructions that perform various tests. A few are set or reset manually with instructions intended for that purpose. The 8088 and 8086 CPUs provided nine flags, stored in a single 16-bit register. These flags are defined briefly in Figure 12.3. The 80286 and 80386 defined a few additional flags, and the 80386 expanded the flag register to 32 bits. The flags that were added

FIGURE 12.3

X86 Flags

Carry	Carry or borrow during an add or subtract operation
Parity	Set when the result of an operation contains an even number of bits
Auxiliary carry	Indicates a carry or borrow during the execution of BCD arithmetic instructions
Zero	Set if the result of an operation is 0
Sign	Set if the result of an operation is negative
Trap	Set manually; causes processor to generate interrupt 01hex after every instruction; is used to step through a program for debugging
Interrupt enable	Set manually to enable or disable hardware interrupts
Direction	Defines the direction in memory of string operations, low address to high, or high to low
Overflow	Set if the result of an operation is too big or too small to fit the destination operand
I/O Protection level	(2 bits) Sets the protection level; explained in the section Advanced Features (80286 and later)
Nested task	Is used by operating systems to handle interrupted tasks (80286 and later)
Resume	Disables built-in 80386 debug routines (80386 and later)
Virtual 8086 mode	Allows execution of several 8086 tasks concurrently (80386 and later)

to later models are shown below the double line in the figure. The floating point and SIMD flags are similar in function, and are not shown.

Instruction Set

The layout for an instruction word is shown in Figure 12.4. The X86 architecture uses a variable length instruction. Instructions in the X86 family occupy from 1 to 15 consecutive bytes of memory. The only required field is the op code. Most op codes are 1 byte long; however, certain combinations of bits in the first byte indicate the use of a second byte as part of the op code. This approach was taken to allow Intel to provide a larger instruction set.

The operands represent source or destination registers, base registers, and index registers to support the different addressing modes. Immediate data and address displacements, when required, appear in the final field of the instruction. The instruction prefix is used only occasionally. These are used primarily to override certain addressing conventions that are built into the CPU. More about this later.

The critical part of the instruction set premiered with the 8088/8086. Each new generation expanded on the previous set, adding functions relevant to the improvements made in the CPU. Therefore, all the instructions from each generation are included in all later generations of the architecture. The 8088 instruction set had 111 different instructions, and it is clearly not the intention of this book to discuss every one. Instead, we will categorize these instructions into groups that should be familiar to you and discuss them by group.

Instructions in the X86 support zero, one, or two operands. Instructions with no operands take an action that does not affect any memory or register data. Examples would be instructions that halt the machine, change a flag, or load a particular control register. A single-operand instruction modifies data in place, for example, a negate instruction that complements the data in a particular register or memory location. Two operand instructions are used where a source and destination are both required for the data. Move instructions are included, as well as instructions that perform a combinatorial operation that uses two pieces of source data. Examples of these would be arithmetic/logic instructions. These instructions generally take the form

```
src operation dst → dst
```

where *src* is the location on one source operand and *dst* initially holds the other. After the operation is performed, the result ends up in the *dst* location.

The X86 instruction set is characteristic of a typical CISC approach to CPU instruction design.

DATA TRANSFER INSTRUCTIONS   Data transfer instructions are used to move data between registers and between registers and memory. The most important of these

FIGURE 12.4

Instruction Format

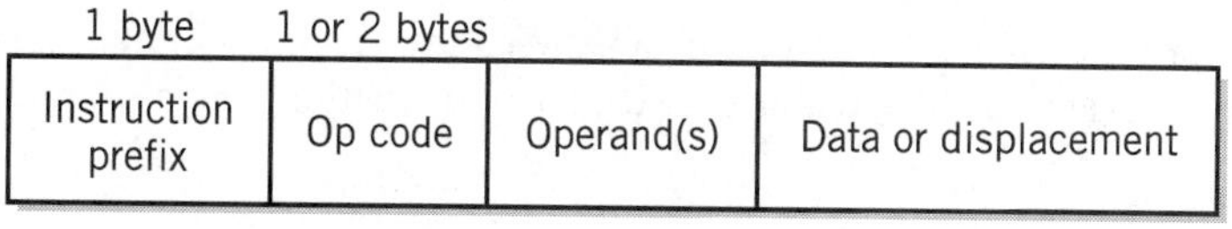

1 byte	1 or 2 bytes		
Instruction prefix	Op code	Operand(s)	Data or displacement

instructions is the MOV instruction, which moves a word or byte from a source location to a destination. The source and destination can be two registers, register and memory, memory and register, or immediate data and register or memory. On earlier models, the data can be either 1 or 2 bytes. Commencing with the 80386 series, data can also be manipulated 4 bytes at a time.

The data manipulation category also includes instructions that PUSH and POP data between a register or memory location and a stack specified by the SP register, an XCHG instruction that exchanges data between registers or between a register and memory, and various instructions that load and store special address registers and flags.

INTEGER ARITHMETIC INSTRUCTIONS Integer arithmetic instructions are included to add, subtract, multiply, and divide 8- or 16-bit data between various sources and destinations. Again, beginning with the 80386 series, 32-bit data can also be used. The multiplication and division require the use of particular registers. The ADD and SUBTRACT instructions allow a source and destination to be specified in the same way as the MOV instruction. Thus, again, the source and destination can be two registers, register and memory, memory and register, or immediate data and register or memory. The operation combines the source and destination, with the result in the destination.

The instruction set also includes instructions to increment and decrement a register or memory location, to compare two locations, and to perform binary-coded decimal (BCD) arithmetic.

BRANCH INSTRUCTIONS The instruction set contains a JMP instruction that jumps unconditionally, CALL and RETurn instructions for jumping to and returning from a procedure, and various jump on-condition instructions (jump zero, jump nonzero, jump greater than, etc.).

BIT MANIPULATION, ROTATE, AND SHIFT INSTRUCTIONS Bit manipulation instructions allow the program to perform logical AND, OR, and XOR (eXclusive OR), operations on the corresponding bits of pairs of data operands, with sources and destinations as previously discussed. NOT operations can also be performed upon a single operand. There are also instructions to shift and rotate the bits in a register or memory location in various ways.

STRING MANIPULATION INSTRUCTIONS The 8088/8086 instruction set included special instructions for the manipulation of bytes or words that contain strings. Instructions exist to move strings, to compare two strings, to load or store a string, and to scan a string looking for a value stored in the accumulator. *Repeat string* prefixes cause the particular string instruction to be repeated, either a fixed number of times as specified in the CX register, or until a particular condition is true. This is one of the situations that use the prefix part of the instruction word.

INPUT/OUTPUT INSTRUCTIONS There is an IN instruction and an OUT instruction for transferring 8- or 16-bit data between the accumulator and I/O devices connected to the bus. For 80386 and above CPUs, these instructions can also transfer 32-bit data.

FLAG INSTRUCTIONS AND OTHER MISCELLANEOUS INSTRUCTIONS

Flag instructions are provided to set and clear the carry flag, the direction flag, and the interrupt flag. There is also an instruction to complement the carry flag.

Finally, instructions are provided to HALT the processor, to cause it to WAIT for a test signal, to ESCape to another processor connected to the bus if one exists, to LOCK out other processors from the bus, and to perform NO OPeration at all. (This last instruction is frequently used in loops to waste a specified amount of time.) The ESCape instruction is important because it serves as a signal to the floating point coprocessor, if one is present, that the instruction is intended as a floating point instruction.

ADDITIONAL INSTRUCTIONS   Each succeeding generation of X86 CPU has added instructions to the basic instruction set. There are 465 instructions in current Pentium models. Quite a growth from the original 111 in the 8086! Except for the floating point, MMX, and SIMD instructions, most of the additional instructions provide support for the operating system; some were added for the convenience of the application programmer. Many of these instructions are classified as privileged. This means that their use is restricted to the operating system. They cannot be executed by an application program under normal conditions. The concepts of protection rings and privileged instructions are considered in the "Advanced Design Features" section of our discussion of the X86 architecture.

The instruction set includes instructions for string manipulation, floating-point arithmetic, SIMD, data conversion between SIMD, floating-point and integer types, cache memory management, and much more.

FLOATING POINT INSTRUCTIONS   The unit that processes floating point instructions was an add-on to the early members of the X86 architecture. Most programs that required floating point arithmetic operations were designed to use the floating point instructions if they were present, but simply to simulate them in software otherwise. Simulation is obviously slower in execution, but sufficient for all but the most demanding applications. With the 80486DX the floating point instruction processor became an integral part of the CPU.

The floating point processor, whether built in or implemented as a separate math coprocessor, provides additional registers and instructions for the high-speed hardware execution of floating point arithmetic. There are eight floating point registers, implemented as a stack. The top location in the stack acts as an accumulator for floating point operations. In addition to the usual instructions for loading and storing floating point values, the floating point unit has instructions for basic arithmetic, floating point compares, square roots, and various transcendental functions, including sines, cosines, arctangents, and logarithms.

MMX AND SIMD INSTRUCTIONS   The MMX instruction group was made available in late versions of the original Pentium processor, and added permanently to the architecture with the Pentium II processor. MMX adds integer SIMD instructions, as described in Chapter 7. The MMX instructions load, store, pack and unpack data, perform simple arithmetic and logic operations on up to eight integers at a time, and compare two sets of values, using aliases of the floating point registers as MMX registers. The SIMD instructions, introduced with the Pentium III and expanded in the Pentium 4, add eight

128-bit SIMD registers for floating point operations. The SIMD instructions perform data transfer, conversions between integer and floating point, packing and unpacking, data shuffles for transforming matrices, simple arithmetic and logic operations, and compares, up to four at a time.

Addressing Modes

Addressing in X86 CPUs is divided into two stages. The first stage, which reflects the methods of addressing memory discussed in Chapter 8 and Supplementary Chapter 2, is discussed in this section. This first stage involves the instruction address that resides in the instruction pointer register and the data address that is calculated from an address stored in a register, indexed, or included as a part of the instruction word.

The second stage, which we will study in the next section, translates the addresses calculated in the first stage into an actual, physical memory address, which is then accessed from the bus in the usual way. In a sense, the first stage determines a logical address, which the second stage translates into a physical address, but there are some differences between X86 addressing and the virtual addressing techniques introduced in Chapter 8. The reason that this separation is necessary in the X86 CPU is that the versions of the X86 prior to the 80386 used 16-bit registers to hold addresses. This limited the memory address space to 64KB, which was obviously insufficient. As you will see, the two-stage approach circumvents this problem.

The X86 supports seven modes of first stage addressing. The modes available to the programmer depend on the type of instruction. All these addressing modes are considered extensively in Supplementary Chapter 2, so they are described only briefly here.

REGISTER MODE   The data source or destination is a register.
Example: MOV AX,BX would move the data from register BX to register AX.

IMMEDIATE MODE   The data source is supplied as part of the instruction itself.
Example: MOV AX,15Dh would place the value 15D (hex) into register AX.

DIRECT ADDRESSING MODE   The address of the source or destination is supplied as part of the instruction.
Example: MOV AX,[1E4h] would place the value that is stored at address 1E4 hex in register AX. The address is placed in the displacement field of the instruction.

REGISTER DEFERRED ADDRESSING MODE   The address of the source or destination is found in a register. Intel refers to this mode as indirect addressing, but of course it is not true indirect addressing.
Example: MOV AX,[BX] would move the data stored in the address that is contained in BX to register AX. If BX contains 22F hex, for example, the data would be moved from address 22F to register AX.

BASE ADDRESSING MODE   The address of the source or destination is calculated by adding the value in the displacement field of the instruction to a base address stored in either the BX or BP register.

Example: `MOV AX,[BX+2505h]`. If the BX register contains 1000h, this instruction would move the value from location 2505h + 1000h = 3505h to register AX.

INDEXED ADDRESSING MODE The address of the source or destination is calculated by adding a displacement specified in the instruction to the value in an index register. DI and SI are available for use as the index register.

Example: `MOV AX,[DI+2505h]`. If the DI register contains 10h, this instruction would move the value stored at location 2505h + 10h = 2515h to AX

BASE INDEXED ADDRESSING MODE The address of the source or destination in this case is calculated by adding both the value in the specified base register and the value in the specified index register to the displacement given in the instruction.

Example: `MOV AX,[BX+SI+234h]`

Starting with the 80386, it is also possible to include a scaling factor with the index register as part of the addressing. Therefore, the instruction `MOV AX,[SI*4+ 1CCCh]` would multiply the value in index register SI by 4 before adding it to the displacement 1CCC hex. This feature is useful for addressing arrays in which each entry is several bytes long.

Logical Addresses versus Physical Addresses

As noted before, the addresses calculated as part of the addressing mode do not represent the actual physical memory location where the data is to be found or stored. The problem is one of size: the 16-bit data registers that were provided in early X86 architectures were insufficient to provide an adequate memory space. Even the 8088 provided 20 bits of addressing to the bus to support 1MB of memory. As the table in Figure 12.1 indicates, this number increased to 24 bits with the 80286, to 32 bits with the 80386DX, and to 36 bits with the P6 family. Clearly, another means was necessary to access all of memory.

The designers of the X86 architecture came up with two different methods to achieve this goal. One of these, known as **real mode** addressing, was provided for the 8086/8088 CPUs and is still supported on all succeeding members of the family. The other method is known as **protected mode** addressing. This mode was added to the family beginning with the 80286. It provides far more capability than real mode, including support for a much larger memory space as well as support for larger programs and protection features. There are still a large number of programs, however, that were written to support real mode only, including MS-DOS through Version 6, so for a while yet these capabilities won't be fully realized.

Both methods rely on a set of four additional registers. In real mode these are known as **segment** registers, whereas in protected mode they are usually referred to as segment **selector** registers or simply selector registers. They are the same registers, however. They are 16-bit registers, labeled CS, for code segment, DS, for data segment, SS, for stack segment, and ES, for extra segment. Starting with the 80386 series, two additional segment registers, FS and GS, are also available. Logical to physical addressing translation takes place in the address or memory management unit of the CPU.

The addresses generated within the instructions are referred to as segment addresses, or logical addresses, or sometimes as offset addresses.

To create a 20-bit real mode physical memory address requires an additional 4 bits beyond the 16 bits provided by the segment address. The simplest solution would simply use an additional 4 bits from a segment register to provide the 20-bit address. The designers of the 8088/8086 chips realized, however, that this divides a 1MB address space into exactly 16 evenly spaced areas of 64KB each, with no possible overlap between the spaces. This would mean little flexibility for how programmers lay out their programs. Instead, the designers allowed the use of all 16 bits of the segment registers. To create an address, the value in the segment register is shifted left 4 bits and added to the segment address to create a 20-bit address. This method is illustrated in Figure 12.5. Real mode X86 addressing thus creates 64,000 (actually 65,536) overlapping segments of 64KB each. A possible segment can start on any location of memory that is divisible by 16. The instruction pointer is expressed relative to the base of the code segment.

Addresses in real mode are usually expressed in the form *aaaa:bbbb*, where *aaaa* is the value found in the segment register and *bbbb* is the logical address. The real address is thus found by adding a 0 digit to the end of the segment value, making the value *aaaa0* and adding the logical address to it. Since the segments overlap, you should note that there are many different ways of expressing the same physical address. If you have access to a PC diagnostic program such as *msd.exe*, you will notice that memory addresses are specified in this form.

The instructions are designed to use different segment registers to calculate their physical address. The instruction pointer uses the code segment register; data references use the data segment register, and stack instructions use the stack segment register. Obviously, the different segment registers could all contain the same value, in which case, the code, stack, and data segments all occupy the same space. The prefix portion of the instruction word can be used to *override* the automatic choice of segment register and to select a different segment register for that instruction.

A program in real mode can use as much as 256KB of memory without modifying the segment registers, since all four segment registers may be used. Larger programs are created by modifying the segment registers during program execution.

The protected mode uses the segment registers differently. In protected mode, the segment register, now called a selector register, contains a number, which is used as a pointer to the entry in a table that corresponds to that number. The table is called a descriptor table. Each table entry contains a 24- or 32-bit *segment base address*, as well as other data including the size of the segment. The final physical address is calculated by adding the segment base address from the table with the logical address from the instruction. The size limit for an 80286 segment is set at 64KB. However, the 80386 and later segments are set at 4MB. The protected mode method of physical address calculation is illustrated in Figure 12.6. Protected mode addressing is essentially similar to segmented virtual addressing, except that the segment number is kept in a separate selector register instead of being part of the instruction word.

The segment descriptor tables (there are actually two) reside in memory. To prevent an extra memory access for each translation, the 80286 and later CPUs contain an extra set of registers called segment descriptor registers. These registers are hidden from the programmer. There is one register corresponding to each segment register. The first time that the data in the segment descriptor table is accessed, it is copied automatically into the

FIGURE 12.5

Real Mode Address Creation

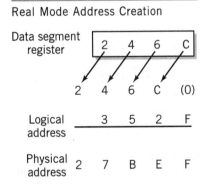

FIGURE 12.6

Protected Mode Address Calculation

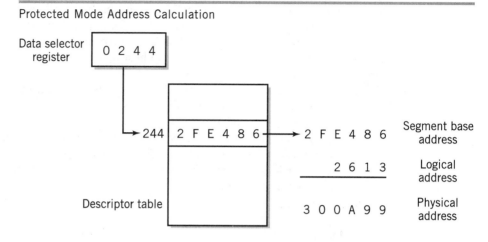

appropriate register, where it is then available for future reference. This mitigates the need for an extra memory reference and speeds up execution.

On CPUs with extended mode capability, there are additional instructions in the instruction set to switch between real and extended mode, to set up the descriptor tables, and to control various aspects of extended mode operation.

Advanced Design Features

Although the original 8088/8086 design was simple, the X86 CPU architecture has evolved into a very sophisticated and powerful design, with improved processing methods and many additional features. Each generation of the X86 architecture has produced design changes and innovations that have resulted in significant performance improvements and broadened capabilities.

It is obviously impossible, nor would it be of interest here, to discuss all the myriad details of the X86 architecture. Many important features in the X86 require integration with operating system software to be used effectively. You will be better equipped to understand the power of these features after you have read Chapters 13, 14, and 15. In this section, however, we briefly discuss a few of these features that make the X86 CPU family such a successful and enduring design.

PROTECTED MODE   We introduced protected mode in the context of physical addressing. But protected mode contains many additional features. In conjunction with operating system software, the protected mode provides all the requirements for the implementation of a multitasking computer system, including support for virtual storage memory management, isolation and protection of the operating system and of individual tasks, and efficient task switching. In protected mode, the CPU addressing unit implements the paging method of address translation to support virtual storage, as described in Chapter 8. In addition to virtual storage support, protected mode provides support for multitasking by providing several types of protection and by implementing a rapid means for switching from one task to another. The same segment descriptor tables that provide the base address for address translation also provide information about the segment that can be used to protect the segment and the system. The table contains a size limit that is checked by the CPU whenever memory is to be accessed. If the address falls outside the limit, the CPU causes an error interrupt instead.

The table contains 2 bits that represent a *privilege* level for the segment. The CPU provides four different privilege levels, known as rings of protection. Figure 12.7 shows these rings. The CPU will not allow programs to access data or call other programs that are inside the program's privilege level except under very restricted conditions. Most application programs reside in the outermost ring. The main part of the operating system is usually executed in the innermost ring. Not only is access restricted, but the instructions that modify the privileges are themselves privileged and can be executed only by programs that are in the inner rings. This provides the system security that is required for multitasking.

Finally, the table entry for each segment also contains a number of bits that indicate how the memory is to be accessed, whether it may be written to, or read, or used only for execution. This helps protect program code, for example, by assuring that data will not be written over the program code by mistake.

Last, but not least, protected mode provides instructions and tables that are used to switch rapidly and easily from one program to another. The CPU hardware manages these operations, without the need for a lot of software to copy registers and the like. The operating system uses these capabilities to provide multitasking. We will consider multitasking more carefully in Chapter 13.

VIRTUAL 8086 MODE The 80386 added another mode, called **virtual 8086 mode.** Virtual 8086 mode calculates addresses in the same way as real mode, that is, by shifting the segment value by 4 bits and adding that value to the logical address. Virtual 8086 mode is embedded into protected mode, however (that is, protected mode must be activated in order to use it), and therefore all the other features of protected mode are available. This allows the system to run several 8086 tasks at once. The OS/2 operating system takes advantage of this capability.

CPU Organization

Early models of the X86 CPU were designed around a pipelined instruction fetch unit and a single integer execution unit. They conformed to the model shown in Figure 8.17 and described in Section 8.4. The original 8088 instruction fetch buffer held 4 bytes. Studies on typical programs made with the 8086 showed

FIGURE 12.7

X86 Protection Levels

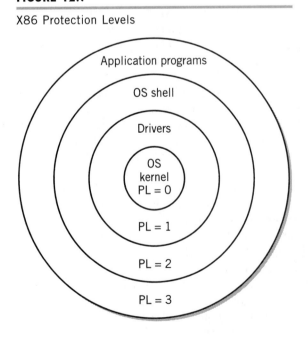

Application programs

OS shell

Drivers

OS kernel
PL = 0

PL = 1

PL = 2

PL = 3

that instruction execution required an average of approximately four clock cycles. The fetch buffer increased in size with each new member of the family. Current models can prefetch instructions 8 bytes at a time, and pipeline them to an instruction unit for processing.

The current Pentium CPU organization is similar to the model shown in Figure 8.20. Because X86 instructions are of variable length and complex, the current instruction decoder creates an intermediate set of instructions called **uops,** for micro-operations. Uops use the three-operand, fixed length format that is characteristic of RISC processors, an attempt to take advantage of RISC techniques on a processor with a CISC instruction set. Most instructions translate directly to uops, one to one, but some instructions require one-to-four translations, and a few instructions are translated into preprogrammed microcode sequences of uops. After fetching and decoding operations, the CPU holds 20 to 30 uops-coded instructions in a pool and executes them in whatever order is most efficient within the limits of control and data dependencies. There are six execution units in the current configuration, two for integers and one each for loads, stores, jumps, and floating point operations.

Cache memory was first supplied on personal computers with 80386 CPUs, when standard memory had become too slow to keep up with the increased clock speeds of the CPU. On the 386 systems, the cache controller was external to the CPU. Current models include 8 KB of level 1 data cache, 12 KB of special cache, which stores uops to eliminate decoder delays from loops, and 512 KB of level 2 combined cache.

The IA-64 Itanium Architecture

Although the IA-64 represents a new Intel architecture, it is appropriate to include it here because the architecture includes the entire X86 instruction set and memory model, mode switching instructions that switch between IA-64 and X86 operating modes during program execution, and mapping for X86 registers and memory addresses to their IA-64 counterparts. Thus, legacy X86 program code will normally execute without modification.

The IA-64 architecture, known as EPIC architecture (see Chapter 8), is quite different from the X86 architecture, however. For application programs, the IA-64 provides 128 65-bit registers (64 bits plus a special bit to indicate potential data dependencies), 128 80-bit floating point registers, eight 64-bit branch registers to speed up branch processing, and sixty-four 1-bit predicate registers, which are used to hold the results of COMPARE instructions for delayed conditional branching. A portion of the general purpose and floating-point registers can be addressed as stacks.

As noted in the discussion in Chapter 8, instruction words are all 41-bits wide and are processed in bundles of three, with five additional bits of information in each bundle to steer the instructions to the correct execution units for processing. The usual varieties of instructions are provided, along with bells and whistles that can be used to assist the CPU Instruction Unit for faster processing.

In the IA-64 mode, the Itanium processor supports a traditional linear memory model, with 64-bit logical addresses and 63-bit physical addresses, accommodating up to 16 exabytes (10^{18} bytes) of logical memory and 8 EB of physical memory. Logical memory can be further divided into eight separate, isolated regions called *address spaces*. This is a feature of many large computer systems that provides additional system security. Memory can be accessed 1, 2, 4, 8, 10, or 16 bytes at a time for data handling flexibility.

Like most other modern computers, the IA-64 CPU is implemented using the fetch-execute model shown in Figure 8.20. Instruction reordering is not implemented, nor necessary, in hardware to achieve maximum performance. Instead, the CPU uses speculation and predication provided by the program compiler or assembly language programmer to guide program execution order.

Within the Itanium architecture, different models offer different capabilities. The Itanium 2 model offers clock speeds up to 1 GHz, a 128-bit system bus, and three levels of integrated cache holding 32 KB, 256 KB, and 1.5 or 3 MB, respectively. The execution unit provides six integer units, three branch units, two floating point units, one SIMD unit, two load units, and two store units, and can pipeline six instructions per clock cycle.

12.3 THE POWERPC

System Overview

The PowerPC family is a computer architecture based on RISC principles. A specification defining open system software and hardware principles for the 1990s was originally developed jointly by Apple, Motorola, and IBM, and has been expanded and extended for current use by the original vendors. The PowerPC CPU itself was designed to the specification by Motorola and IBM, based on an earlier IBM RISC architecture, called *POWER,* for *performance optimized with enhanced RISC.* New 64-bit versions of the POWER architecture are used in IBM RS/6000 workstations and pSeries servers. The first member of the PowerPC family, the PC601, was released in 1993. Several members of the family are now available, with different capabilities and applications. These are shown in Figure 12.8. The PowerPC CPU is the central processor in Apple Power Macintoshes, Nintendo GameCubes, and various IBM computers and is gradually being adopted by other manufacturers.

The PowerPC CPU was designed initially for use in personal computers and workstations. It provides a bus-oriented I/O architecture, similar to other microcomputer CPUs,

FIGURE 12.8

Representative PowerPC Processor Characteristics

Processor	Register Width	Internal Addressing Capability	Physical Address Space	Data Bus Width	Max. Clock (MHz)	Execution Units	Remarks
601	32 bits	32 bits	4GB	64 bits	60	3	POWER compatible; obsolete
603e	32 bits	32 bits	4GB	64 bits	300	5	For notebook and low-cost desktop computers
604e	32 bits	32 bits	4GB	64 bits	350	7	Desktop computers
740,750	32 bits	52 v/32 r*	4GB	64 bits	1000	6	High performance; 750 includes L2 cache
7450	32/128	52 v/36 r*	4GB	64/128 bits	1250	11	Apple G4

*52 bits virtual, 32 or 36 bits real.

and can be interfaced easily to the standard buses used in other personal computer systems. This means that system components, bus adapters, controllers, and I/O devices designed for other CPUs can be used with the PowerPC processor. A typical system block diagram such as those shown in Figures 11.1 and 11.3 will also apply to the PowerPC system. So does the layout shown in Figure 11.4. We note, however, that the PowerPC is not compatible in the sense that it can simply be plugged in as a replacement for an X86 or 680X0 processor. The internal architecture of the CPU is different, with different registers, addressing techniques, and instruction set. Software written for one machine must be rewritten, recompiled from high-level language, or emulated on the other.

The PowerPC provides a prioritized multilevel internal interrupt structure that recognizes a number of different conditions. Different interrupts cause a jump to a location in memory determined by the interrupt type. External interrupts are prioritized outside the CPU. The interrupt location is determined by the software that is executed for internal interrupts.

The CPU

The PowerPC CPU architectural specification provides for both 32-bit and 64-bit implementations. The 32-bit implementation provides 32-bit general-purpose registers and 32-bit addressing, with internal support for as much as 36-bit physical and 52-bit virtual addressing. Instructions can address 4GB of memory. The 64-bit implementation provides 64-bit registers and addressing. It supports 16 EB (16 x 10^{18}) bytes of addressing; however, the current implementation provides only 40 bits of interface to physical storage. Programs written for the 32-bit implementation can be run directly on 64-bit members of the family, but the converse may not be true. Floating point arithmetic, memory caching, virtual memory support, sophisticated operating system instructions and protection, and superscalar processing are standard with all implementations of this architecture. Vector (i.e., SIMD) processing is also standard on recent versions of the processor. Current members of the family operate at clock speeds from 100 MHz to 1 GHz and can execute three or more instructions per clock cycle.

As you would expect for a RISC design, every instruction in the PowerPC is the same 32 bits in length, making this type of organization particularly well suited to superscalar designs.

Registers

In keeping with its RISC character, the PowerPC provides a large number of registers accessible to user programs. The user register set is shown in Figure 12.9. The PowerPC provides thirty-two general-purpose registers, thirty-two floating point registers, a link register, a count register, a condition register, and fixed and floating point status registers. The general-purpose registers, link register, and count register are either 32 bits or 64 bits wide, depending on the implementation. Floating point registers are 64 bits wide in either implementation. The remaining registers are 32 bits wide. The 7400 processor series also provides thirty-two 128-bit registers and two vector control registers that are used for vector processing. In addition to the user registers, there are a number of special-purpose system registers that we will not discuss here. Most of these must be accessed by privileged instructions. The system registers are used for control of the CPU, cache memory control,

FIGURE 12.9

PowerPC User Registers

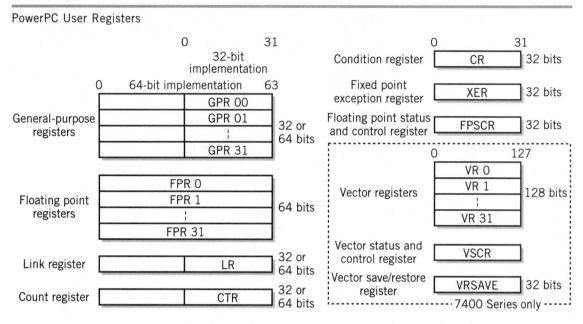

program timing control, virtual addressing, interrupt handling, synchronization of multiple CPUs, multitasking, security, and other purposes.

To minimize memory accesses, general-purpose registers and floating point registers are used as the source and destination for all data manipulation instructions. The general-purpose registers are all treated equally. All storage access instructions transfer data between memory and these registers, so that most program execution takes place within the register set. Each of the other registers serves a special purpose in the PowerPC architecture.

The link register is set automatically by various branch instructions to the address of the instruction following the branch. A branch to the value stored in the link register can then be used by programs to return from subroutines and exit from loops, using the method demonstrated in Chapter 7.

The count register is a special register that can be used by a program to hold a loop count. Conditional branch instructions can be set to decrement the value in the count register automatically each time the branch instruction is executed. The instruction also tests the count register for the value 0 as a part of the condition. The count register can also be used to hold an address for conditional branching.

The condition register is a register whose bits are set implicitly as the result of operations by various instructions. The CR bits can also be set explicitly by instructions that test or move data from other registers. The values in the condition register are used as a decision basis by the branch conditional instructions.

The fixed point exception register (FPER) and floating point status and control register (FPSCR) are registers whose bits are set by results of instruction operations, such as fixed point overflows and carries, and by floating point exceptions, such as underflows, divides by zero, attempts to use the value infinity, and other invalid operations. The FPSCR is also used to control rounding.

Instruction Set

The PowerPC instruction set provides a full complement of CPU instructions, designed to optimize performance as a RISC processor. The instruction set is divided into six categories: integer instructions, floating point instructions, load/store instructions, flow control instructions, processor control instructions, and memory control instructions. The 7400 CPUs define a seventh category: vector instructions. There are no specifically defined I/O instructions, because the PowerPC uses memory mapped I/O. LOAD and STORE instructions are used to interact with I/O controllers connected to the PowerPC. Data manipulation instructions and LOAD/STORE instructions operate on byte, halfword, and word integer operands and word and doubleword floating point operands. A word is defined as 32 bits.

The architecture specifies fifteen different instruction formats, although most of the formats are very similar, and most instructions within a particular class use only two or three different formats. The fifty-four fixed point storage access instructions, for example, all use the D-form, DS form, or X-form instruction formats. Every instruction has a 6-bit primary op code field located in bits 0 through 5. The primary op code field immediately identifies the type of instruction for the instruction unit. Some instructions provide a secondary op code field. The PowerPC instruction set differentiates 224 separate instructions by primary and secondary op code. There are an additional 162 vector-based instructions in the 7400 series instruction set. The four typical instruction formats shown in Figure 12.10 represent 188 of the 224 instructions in the basic instruction set.

Only LOAD and STORE instructions access memory for data. Other data manipulation instructions use the contents of registers and/or operands within the instruction itself as the source of data. Instructions in the PowerPC architecture support from zero to five operands. Zero operand instructions are very rare. They are used only for system calls and

FIGURE 12.10

Typical Instruction Formats

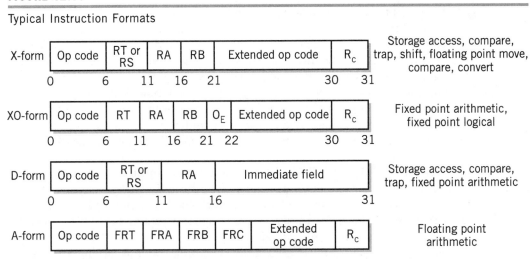

Note: RT, RA, RB, RS fields usually hold a register number; certain instructions use these fields for other purposes. FRT, FRA, FRB, FRC, are floating point registers. OE and R$_c$ are single-bit fields that affect the XER or CR registers.

special system functions. Five operand instructions are used for complex SHIFT and ROTATE instructions. The most common instructions use two or three operands. Many arithmetic operations, for example, take the form

$$src_1 \; \text{operation} \; src_2 \to dst$$

where src_1 and src_2 are either registers or immediate data and dst is another register. (It could be the same as one of the source registers, but it doesn't have to be.)

Most instructions are considered "unprivileged" and are available to an application programmer. Instructions that affect the operation of the CPU or memory are considered "privileged" and are available only for system-level programming. These instructions manipulate internal registers, manage multitasking operations, manage and manipulate virtual storage memory, and perform other system-level tasks.

Except for the vector instructions and small differences between 32-bit and 64-bit implementations of the architecture, there are only minor variations in the instruction set among the various members of the PowerPC family. The differences are defined and specified formally in the *PowerPC Architecture Manual* [POW93], so that long-term compatibility within the family may be maintained and assured.

LOAD/STORE INSTRUCTIONS   Only LOAD and STORE instructions may access data in memory. This control of memory access is characteristic of RISC architectures. The PowerPC provides instructions that load and store integer bytes, halfwords, and words and floating point words and doublewords. Sixty-four-bit implementations can also load and store integer doublewords. There are also instructions to load and store strings and multiple words of data in groups of up to thirty-two at a time.

INTEGER INSTRUCTIONS   The PowerPC includes instructions that perform the usual add, subtract, multiply, and divide arithmetic operations; various Boolean logical operations; algebraic and logical compare instructions; and ROTATE and SHIFT instructions. The sources for these operations are general-purpose registers. Some instructions also provide immediate operands. The results are placed into a target general-purpose register and set appropriate bits and fields in the fixed point exception and condition registers. The ADD IMMEDIATE instruction is also used as a means for loading a value into a register. Similarly, the logical OR instruction is used to move data from one register to another. There are also a number of compound instructions that perform useful multiple actions with a single instruction, for example, a ROTATE operation combined with a LOGICAL AND operation. Finally, there is a special group of integer instructions that performs algebraic and logical comparisons and traps to the operating system software if the conditions are met.

FLOATING POINT INSTRUCTIONS   The PowerPC architecture includes instructions to move data between floating point registers, to convert between integer and floating point, to perform single and double precision arithmetic, to round, and to compare the contents of two floating point registers. There are also instructions that combine multiplication of two operands with the addition or subtraction of a third into a single operation. The floating point status and control register records the status of floating point operations, and there are also instructions to set this register directly. Some members of the family also provide square root and reciprocal instructions.

FLOW CONTROL INSTRUCTIONS   Flow control instructions include both unconditional and conditional branch instructions. The PowerPC architecture supports both relative and absolute addressing for BRANCH instructions. It also permits the storage of a return address in the link register as well as provides an instruction for using the link register as a target address. This is useful for subroutines. The conditional branch instructions also allow the programmer to specify whether the branch is likely to be taken. This can be used to increase performance by giving the CPU a "hint" as to which path to predict during execution of branch instructions. Finally, conditional branch instructions can be used to decrement and test the count register as a way of implementing counting loops.

PROCESSOR CONTROL INSTRUCTIONS   The PowerPC has a number of operating modes that provide different features and different levels of capability, access, and performance. The values in various system registers determine the operating mode of the CPU at any given time by enabling and disabling features and establishing system settings. Processor control instructions are used to move data to and from system registers, to handle system calls and returns from interrupts, to write the time base registers that maintain the time for various purposes, and to perform other system management tasks. Synchronizing instructions allow the programmer to control instruction pipeline flow by requiring completion of one instruction before another begins. These are mostly privileged instructions. Only a few of these instructions, such as synchronizing instructions, and instructions to read the time base registers, are available for normal application programming. A TRAP instruction provides access to Operating System services for user programs.

MEMORY CONTROL INSTRUCTIONS   Memory control instructions give the programmer access to cache memory as well as also provide privileged instructions for setting and controlling the various storage modes that are built into the PowerPC, as well as external control for use with special I/O devices. Memory management in the PowerPC is discussed in the section entitled Logical Addresses and Physical Memory.

VECTOR INSTRUCTIONS   The PowerPC 7400 provides a 128-bit multifunctional vector execution unit that implements 162 vector-based (i.e. SIMD) instructions. Like other PowerPC instructions, the vector instructions are register-oriented. Thirty-two 128-bit registers are dedicated for the use of these instructions. The vector instructions can operate in parallel on sixteen signed or unsigned bytes, eight signed or unsigned halfword integers, four signed or unsigned fullword integers, or four standard IEEE floating-point numbers. They can also operate on quadword integers.

   The vector instructions provide vector integer and floating point arithmetic, logic functions, shifts, vector comparison, type conversion, packing and unpacking, and vector permutation capabilities.

Addressing Modes

Memory addressing is used only for load, store, and branching instructions. Other instructions take their operands from registers and from fields within the instruction itself. The PowerPC provides register indirect addressing along with two simple variations to establish the memory locations for load and store instructions. The memory address is stored in a register specified by a field in the instruction. This address is optionally offset, either by the value in a second register used for indexing or by a value specified as an immediate offset within the instruction. The three PowerPC load/store addressing modes are illustrated in Figure 12.11.

Branch addresses are specified as a field within the branch instructions. Another bit within the instruction determines whether the address is absolute or relative to the current instruction.

These are the only addressing modes provided for memory access in the PowerPC architecture. Instruction latencies are not required with the PowerPC architecture.

FIGURE 12.11

LOAD/STORE Addressing Modes

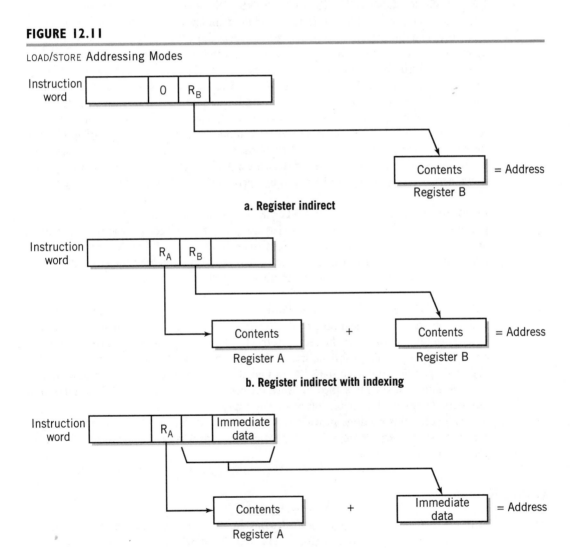

a. Register indirect

b. Register indirect with indexing

c. Register indirect with immediate offset

Logical Addresses and Physical Memory

As with other modern machines, the PowerPC architecture treats the addresses calculated for storage access as logical rather than physical. The PowerPC architecture provides four different translation mechanisms for converting the logical addresses to physical addresses. The basic translation process is illustrated in Figure 12.12. The choice of mechanism is controlled by settings in various system registers. Instruction and data addressing can be translated differently, and the translation method can be set differently for different parts of memory.

- Ordinary translation divides the logical address into a segment, a page, and an offset and then uses a segment table to lookup a segment and a page table to select a page within the segment. The PowerPC is not a segment in the traditional sense; rather it is more like a superpage. The PowerPC virtual storage mechanism divides memory into 256MB segments and further divides the segments into 4KB pages. The PowerPC uses the virtual storage techniques discussed in Chapter 11, including the use of page translation lookaside buffers to improve access time. In 32-bit implementations, the segment table is stored in special segment registers. In 64-bit implementations, the segment table is stored in memory, with an additional segment translation lookaside buffer provided to improve access time.

- Direct-store translation uses the segment table to look up a perform a segment translation, but the result is used directly with the remainder of the logical address to form a real address. This method is used for I/O addressing.

FIGURE 12.12

PowerPC Address Translation Mechanisms

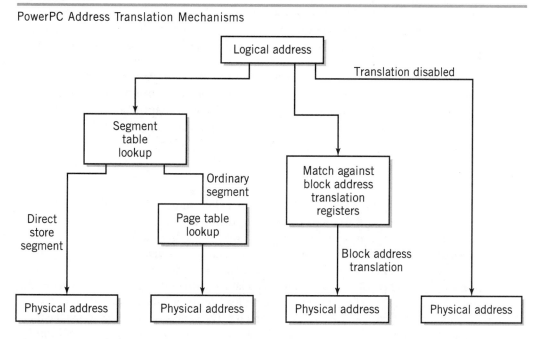

- Block addressing provides a means for mapping a block of logical addresses larger than a single page into a contiguous area of real memory. A block can range in size from 128KB to 256MB. The PowerPC provides special block address translation (BAT) registers for this purpose. The logical address is compared against each BAT register. If the address falls within the block, it is translated to the appropriate physical address. This mechanism is useful for data such as large arrays of numerical data and memory-mapped display buffers, where it is desirable to process all the data together.
- Finally, the PowerPC allows the translation mechanisms to be disabled entirely. In this case, the logical addresses correspond exactly to physical addresses.

Advanced Design Features

As you have already seen from this example, the simplicity implied by the RISC concept does not mean that a RISC CPU lacks sophistication and features. In fact, just the opposite. The consistency and simplicity of the basic instruction set provide the CPU designers with a foundation from which to build very powerful CPUs. The uniform word size and consistent primary op code, for example, simplifies the fetch and execution pipelines and makes superscalar processing practical and efficient. The inclusion of "hint" bits in branching instructions allows the programmer to help the CPU in making accurate branch predictions to improve performance. The PowerPC contains many additional features that improve performance, add capability, and simplify the programmer's task.

PROTECTION MECHANISMS   The PowerPC provides two levels of system access, known as **supervisor,** or privileged, state, and user, or **problem,** state. Bits in a system register are used to set the state. Some instructions, such as the SYSTEM CALL instruction also set the supervisor state automatically. You have already seen that instructions are classified as privileged or unprivileged. The execution of privileged instructions is obviously illegal in the user state.

In addition to instruction control, the PowerPC also protects memory at the segment, page, and block levels. The protection mechanism is disabled when the translation mechanisms are disabled. Segment protection indicates whether a segment is under supervisor or user control. Page and block protection designates individual pages and blocks as supervisor access only, supervisor read/write with user read only, both read/write, or both read only.

CPU Organization

A general block diagram for the PowerPC CPU architecture is shown in Figure 8.20. There are variations among different members of the family, but all the essential components are shown in the diagram. Like the Pentium, and most other modern CPU designs, the PowerPC is organized into modules that reflect the superscalar, pipelined nature of the architecture. The number and types of execution units varies for different members of the family. All members of the family provide floating point and one or more integer execution units. Some members provide separate load/store and system execution units. The 7400 series also provides a vector execution unit. The table in Figure 12.8 shows the numbers of execution units for each member of the PowerPC family. Figure 12.13 identifies

FIGURE 12.13

Execution Units in the PowerPC 4751 CPU

1 Load/store unit	
3 Integer units	execute all integer instructions except multiply, divide, and moves to/from special-purpose registers
1 Integer unit	for multiply, divide, special-purpose moves, and miscellaneous instructions
1 64-bit floating-point unit	
1 Branch processing unit	
1 Vector permute unit	
2 Vector integer units	
1 Vector floating-point unit	

each of the execution units in the 7450 processor. As many as sixteen instructions can be in some stage of execution simultaneously.

Cache memory is standard in all members of the PowerPC family. The instruction set provides instructions to control separate instruction and data caches. All members of the family provide separate instruction and data cache on-chip memories, ranging from 16KB of each in the 603e CPU to 32KB of each in the 640, 740, 750, and 7400 series CPUs. The 750 and certain 7400 series processors also provide a cache controller and dedicated interface to support 256 K, 512 K, or 1 MB (2 MB in the 7400) of combined level 2 cache. Recent 7450 processors support 256K cache directly, with an additional controller and interface for 1 or 2 MB of combined level 3 cache. Privileged instructions in the PowerPC can disable cache memory and can also select either write through or write back, both options on a page-by-page basis.

The 604e, 740, 750, and 7400 series CPUs also provide a built-in 512-byte branch history table for maintaining a history of the paths taken for each branch instruction that is used to improve branch prediction.

12.4 THE IBM SYSTEM 360/370/390/zSERIES FAMILY

System Overview

The System 360/370/390/zSeries family represents the evolution of a computer architecture that spans nearly forty years, an extremely long time in the computer industry. Due to its well-thought-out original design, IBM has been able to preserve the essential features of the original architecture and instruction set, while expanding and upgrading the system to incorporate modern features and performance capabilities utilizing new technology and design techniques.

The original design, known as the System/360, was introduced in 1964. According to Gifford and Spector [GIFF87], the phrase "computer architecture" was first used to describe the S/360 series. Different models in the S/360 family varied in circuit design and implementation, but they were architecturally the same. Programs written for one model would execute correctly on any model in the family. Every member of the family executed the same instruction set, supported the same set of I/O peripherals, and provided the same operating system software, even though the low-end models used an internal 8-bit data path (!) and had a microprogrammed implementation, whereas the high-end models used a 32-bit data path, implemented totally in hardware.

The System/370 architecture followed in 1970. The S/370 system was architecturally similar to, but more sophisticated than, the S/360 family. The major differences were the addition of virtual storage support and support for two CPUs operating together. A new set of registers, known as **control registers,** were added, primarily to meet the requirements of virtual storage but also useful for some operating system operations. The control registers are not normally accessible to applications programmers. About forty new instructions were added. Most of these were intended for manipulation of the control registers and for other operating system use. Otherwise, the instruction sets were very similar, and programs written for the S/360 were upward compatible to the S/370 family.

The next major upgrade, the Extended Architecture System/370, or S370/XA, occurred in 1981. The major extensions that differentiated the S370/XA from the S/370 were

- Support for multiple CPUs interconnected as multiprocessor systems to share memory and I/O resources. (The S/370 supported two, but no more.)
- A new I/O architecture called the channel subsystem architecture. The channel subsystem architecture was introduced to you in Chapter 9. The S/360 and the original S/370 had a similar, but simpler I/O architecture. S370/XA channels are still in use with s/390 and zSeries systems. They are now called *parallel channels,* to distinguish them from a newer type of channel introduced with the model S/390.
- Thirty-one-bit addressing. The earlier machines supported a 24-bit addressing space. This increased the addressing capability from 16MB to 2GB.
- Expanded storage as an option.

In 1989, IBM introduced the Enterprise System Architecture 370 or ESA/370. The differences between the ESA/370 and the 370/XA architectures were more subtle. The IBM virtual storage system separates different programs into different **address spaces.** These spaces are normally isolated from each other, although the 370/XA provided means for a program to access two address spaces at a time. The ESA/370 extended this capability to multiple address spaces. This difference was unimportant to the typical user, but increased the power and capability of the system by providing 2GB of virtual memory space to each program or collection of data using the system.

The System/390 maintained the S/370XA CPU organization, but expanded the facility to include a new I/O architecture based on high-speed fiber optic channels. IBM refers to this as the **Enterprises Systems Connection Architecture (ESCON).** ESCON also makes possible sophisticated methods for interconnecting multiple systems together to form a large, fiber optic–connected collection of synchronized systems that IBM calls a sysplex (for system complex). A **sysplex** can process programs cooperatively, can share data, can balance the workload between different systems, and can bypass inoperative systems to provide nonstop operation, all transparently to the users. New System/390 features also included a dual cryptography facility, a data compression facility, built-in data base sorting algorithms, improved storage protection, and the ability to partition a single system into multiple "logical" computers, each with its own section of memory, which IBM calls *LPAR.*

The most recent development in this area, the *parallel sysplex,* adds hardware and operating system support for creating and coordinating clusters of processors to support parallel and distributed processing. A sysplex cluster is a group of processors, each with separate memory, that directly share data resources and distributed program execution. Dedicated S/390 or zSeries processors serve as a coupling facility to provide services that protect the integrity of data that is being shared and processed by different processors in the sysplex. Even over a Wide Area Network or the Internet, a parallel sysplex can be configured as a single logical entity. Current systems also offer **FICON (Fibre Connectivity Architecture),** a faster, fiber optic–based alternative to ESCON, gigabit/second Ethernet, parallel sysplex coupling to TCP/IP networks, which IBM calls *Dynamic Virtual IP Addressing,* and *HiperSockets,* which allow TCP/IP connections between partitions at memory speed. This last feature allows partitioning to simulate several independent networked computers in a single mainframe computer.

The newest upgrade, the zSeries, extends the architecture to 64-bit processing, with 64-bit registers and 64-bit addressing. All previous facilities and features are supported. Thus, a 64-bit register can be used as a direct stand-in for a 32-bit register, and all operations work correctly. New instructions have been added to allow 24-bit, 31-bit, and 64-bit addressing, to process 64-bit data, and to convert data between different formats. The architectural evolution of the 360/370/390/zSeries is summarized in Figure 12.14.

Although there have been tremendous advances in technology and design, the current z/Architecture is similar in many fundamental ways to the original S/360 design. The zSeries is a 64-bit extension of the S/370XA CPU, which itself was an extension of the S/360. Compatibility has been maintained throughout the series: programs written for the original S/360 will still execute on current zSeries models. (Some probably do!) Thus, IBM has been able to provide a continual upgrade path to its customers, with improved performance as customer requirements expand. This accounts for the incredible longevity of the family.

The IBM System 360/370/390/zSeries family is the group of mainframe-size computers that people think of when they refer to "IBM computers." This family has been the mainstay of the large-scale mainframe computer business since the introduction of the System/360. IBM continues to maintain a substantial leadership in the mainframe business, and has successfully repositioned its business periodically to the current needs of the IT community. The vast majority of mainframe computers in use today are models within the System/390 and zSeries lines.

The basic individual zSeries system consists of CPUs, main storage, and an I/O subsystem. The I/O supports both traditional I/O channels, as described in Chapter 9, as well as all of the newer channel types mentioned above. Each I/O channel supports one or more I/O control units, to which are attached the various peripheral devices. The channels are also used for clustering. ZSeries systems can get very complex, with dozens of CPUs, hundreds of I/O devices, dozens of channels, extensive communications, and multiple systems clustered together, possibly scattered all over the world. The I/O system can interconnect up to 256 channel paths of different types, with considerable flexibility in the mix, and can dynamically reassign the paths, when necessary. The overall bandwidth of the system can easily range up to 100 GB per second or more.

A simple typical block diagram for a zSeries system appears in Figure 12.15. The basic building block is the multichip module. The multichip module consists of either twelve or twenty processing units configured as a symmetric multiprocessor, supported by storage

FIGURE 12.14

Architectural Evolution of 360/370/390/zSeries Computers

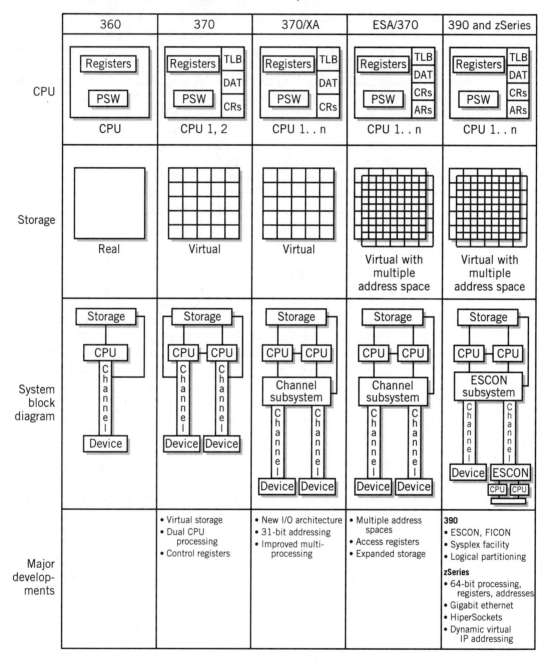

Source: From *IBM Mainframes* 2e, N. Prasad and J. Savit, copyright © 1994, by McGraw-Hill Companies. Reprinted by permission.

FIGURE 12.15

S/390 System Block Diagram

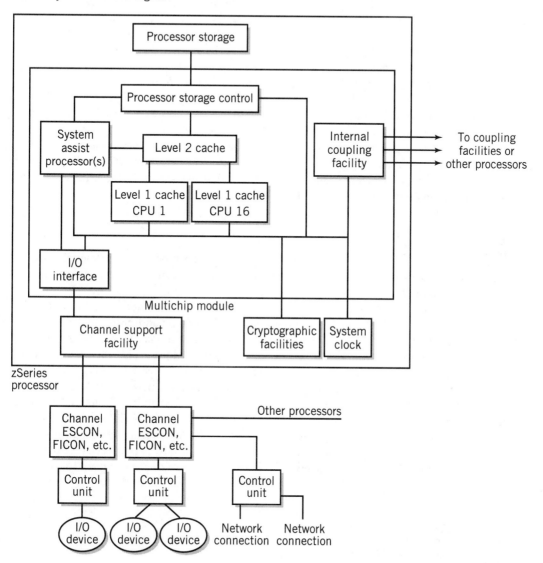

control and I/O interface adapter chips. Each CPU has 256KB of level 1 cache memory. All of the CPUs in the multichip module also share 16 or 32 MB of level 2 cache. A processor consists of one multichip module plus a system clock and two or more cryptography chips. A number of the CPUs in a multichip module are set aside as system assist processors, internal coupling facilities, integrated facility for Linux processors, and spares. The remaining CPUs act in tandem as a single multiprocessing unit, ranging from a 1-way configuration in the smallest models to a 16-way configuration in the largest.

The system also includes processor storage up to the maximum amount allowed for a particular model. The largest models support up to 64 GB of processor storage! Both level 2 cache memory and processor storage are interleaved for four simultaneous independent memory requests to allow faster access. The system also provides as standard support for a mix of up to 256 channels and/or coupling facilities, hardware cryptographic support, and many other features.

Up to sixty-four systems can be clustered together with a coupling facility. Hardware in the coupling facility tracks I/O access by each processor to protect the integrity of data and also assists in workload balancing and management. The coupling facility is, itself, a zSeries system with specialized software. I/O devices are shared by providing links from each system to the device.

There are currently forty-two models in the z900 family. A few representative models are shown in Figure 12.16. For every model in the zSeries family, each CPU is built around the same basic organization and instruction set. We shall concentrate the remainder of our discussion on the organization of the CPU.

The CPU

As noted, the CPU architecture is compatible across every model of the zSeries. Every CPU provides the same register structure and executes the same instruction set. Larger models supply faster clocks and faster CPU circuitry.

The CPU architecture supports S/360, S/370, and S/390 models and programs by including both 24-bit and 31-bit addressing, as well as 64-bit addressing, and also present and previous Program Status Word formats. More recent models have added some additional special-purpose registers for the management of address spaces and for control of the system, but the original System/360 register structure is essentially intact. The instruction set has also been expanded to include instructions for the new I/O methods and more sophisticated system control, but there are only a few new user-accessible instructions other than the instructions for performing 64-bit operations. The CPU architecture supports 64-bit partitioned, segmented, and paged virtual storage and cache memory.

Sixty-four-bit addressing allows access to 16 Exabytes (10^{18}) of memory. With virtual storage, the 16 address space registers each allow the choice of one of fifteen 16EB spaces,

FIGURE 12.16

Typical zSeries Specifications

Model No.	CPUs in MCM	CPUs in SMP	System Assist Processors	L2 Cache	Processor Storage	CPU Instruction Cycle Time
101	12	1	2-5	16 MB	5-32 GB	1.3 nsec
108	12	8	2-3	16 MB	5-32 GB	1.3 nsec
112	20	12	3-7	32 MB	10-64 GB	1.3 nsec
212	20	12	3-7	32 MB	10-64 GB	1.09 nsec
216	20	16	3	32 MB	10-64 GB	1.09 nsec

so for practical programming purposes, memory is unlimited. The largest models presently can hold up to 64 GB of physical storage.

Registers

The S/390 provides sixteen 64-bit general-purpose registers, numbered 0 through 15. These can be coupled together in pairs for the use and manipulation of 128-bit data, or 64-bit data using bits 32–63 only in 32-bit operating mode. There are also 16 64-bit floating point registers. These can also be coupled in pairs. The general-purpose registers can be used to hold addresses or data. Data is stored and manipulated in one of several different formats, including integer, IBM floating point, IEEE floating point, packed decimal, character, and string. Data can be manipulated in bytes, halfwords (16 bits), words, doublewords, and in many cases, quadwords (128 bits). In certain data formats, the data can take on other lengths. The user registers are shown in Figure 12.17 for comparison with Figures 12.2 and 12.9.

These registers are all accessible to the application programmer. There are also sixteen special 64-bit control registers and sixteen access registers, a time-of-day clock register, a timer register, a clock comparator register, and a prefix register. User programs can read the clock registers, but the remaining registers require privileged instructions for access. The program counter is imbedded within a 128-bit **Program Status Word (PSW).** In addition to the program counter, the Program Status Word contains condition codes, mask bits for masking interrupts, a storage access key that is part of the CPU protection mechanism, discussed later, and other system flags. As noted in Chapter 9, the Program Status Word plays a key role in the servicing of interrupts. Condition codes are affected by various data manipulation instructions, and are used for conditional branching. The program counter, of course, can be changed by branch instructions. Other bits in the Program Status Word are privileged.

Instruction Set

All zSystem instructions are 16 bits, 32 bits, or 48 bits in length. The length of the instruction can be determined by the first two bits of the op code. There are eighteen different instruction formats, plus a number of slight variations. You have seen five of the formats previously in Figure 7.15, as part of an illustration of different instruction formats. The

FIGURE 12.17

zSeries User Registers

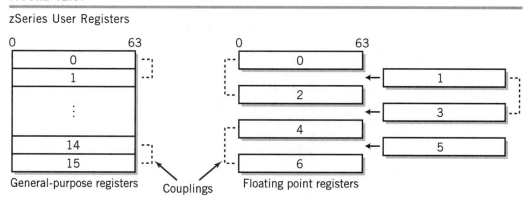

General-purpose registers   Couplings   Floating point registers

formats are defined by the number of operands and the type of addressing used for each operand. Instructions have zero, one, two, or three operands. Instructions operate between registers, between registers and memory, and between memory locations directly. Two operand instructions are used to move data between locations, and also for calculations, using the standard method of operation

$$src \text{ operation } dst \rightarrow dst$$

Three operands are used for instructions that operate on multiple quantities of data, such as MOVE MULTIPLE WORDS. These instructions require two locations to set the range of data and a third to specify the destination address.

An operand may be implied or immediate, or it may address a register, a storage location, or a storage location using indexed addressing. Most instruction formats have an 8-bit op code, but some provide a 16-bit extended op code.

IBM divides the instruction set into five categories by type of operand. There are general instructions, decimal instructions, floating point instructions, control instructions, and I/O. Input and output instructions for the System/370XA were described in Chapter 8; the instructions for the zSeries are similar. Instructions automatically use the set of registers that are appropriate for the type of instruction.

GENERAL INSTRUCTIONS The general instructions include data transfer instructions, integer arithmetic and logical operations, branches, shifts, and other operations that manipulate and use the general-purpose registers and/or storage. Most general data manipulation instructions can operate on halfwords, words, or doublewords. Many can also operate on multiple words, with the number of words specified as a field in the instruction.

The instruction set contains a large number of LOAD, STORE, and MOVE instructions that can handle a wide range of different conditions, including the ability to mask characters and BCD numbers and the ability to move variable-sized blocks of bytes from one part of storage directly to another. Integer arithmetic instructions can add and subtract signed and unsigned halfwords and words and can multiply and divide signed halfwords and words. There are AND, OR, and EXCLUSIVE OR Boolean instructions and both arithmetic and logical COMPARE instructions. There are BRANCH instructions for a variety of conditions, including the usual numerical conditions, and also instructions that decrement or increment an index and branch when a set value is reached. There are branch instructions that save the return address for subroutine and function calls. There are word and doubleword multiple-bit SHIFT instructions, left and right. Finally, there is a SUPERVISOR CALL software interrupt instruction.

DECIMAL INSTRUCTIONS Decimal instructions perform simple arithmetic, including rounding, editing, and comparisons for packed decimal numbers of variable length, with or without algebraic sign. The number of digits is specified in the instruction itself. Operands for these instructions are always found in memory. These instructions all use the storage-to-storage instruction format (see Figure 7.15) and store the result back to one of the operands. With one exception, these instructions do not affect any user registers. There are other instructions, in the general instruction category, for packing and unpacking numbers, for moving data, and for converting numbers between binary and packed decimal formats. The IBM packed decimal format was discussed in Section 5.6 and illustrated in Figure 5.8.

FLOATING POINT INSTRUCTIONS   The S/390 provides instructions to load, store, round, normalize, and compare floating point numbers, as well as to provide the four standard arithmetic operations and square roots for 32-bit, 64 bit, or 128-bit formats. There are also instructions to convert between earlier IBM floating point and current IEEE standard formats. Floating point instructions operate between floating point registers or between floating point registers and memory.

CONTROL INSTRUCTIONS   System operation is controlled by setting or resetting appropriate bits and values in the Program Status Word and in the 16 control registers. The bits in the PSW and control registers are individually assigned to different facilities and features in the computer system. They are used to enable and disable system operations or functions and to furnish information to the particular facility. Control bits perform such functions as turn virtual storage on and off, set addressing for 24, 31, or 64 bits, activate a program event recorder, set or disable interrupts, and many other operations.

LOAD CONTROL and STORE CONTROL instructions are used to load and store the control registers. There are many other control instructions that control individual functions and that affect individual bits in the PSW and control registers. All these instructions are privileged, although a few are available to application programs under certain semiprivileged conditions.

Addressing Modes

The zSeries architecture defines four types of addressing for operands.

- *Immediate addressing*—The data is found in the I field of the instruction.
- *Register addressing*—The data is found in the register indicated by the R field of the instruction. The type of register, general purpose or floating point, depends on the instruction.
- *Storage addressing*—Storage addressing is the IBM name for base offset addressing (see Figure S2.2). The address is the sum of the value stored in a base register plus the value stored in the displacement field of the instruction. The base register is indicated by a B field in the instruction. Any general-purpose register can serve as the base register.
- *Storage indexed addressing*—Storage indexed addressing is similar to storage addressing, with the addition of an index value. The index value is stored in a register indicated by an X field in the instruction. Any general-purpose register may serve as an index register. Thus

```
address = contents (B) + contents (X) + displacement
```

Logical Addresses and Physical Memory

The zSeries defines three kinds of addresses. Absolute addresses refer to physical central storage. Instruction and data addresses, which are also known as logical addresses or effective addresses, may be virtual or real. In addition, the system defines up to sixteen separate

16EB virtual address spaces. Each address space is identified by one of sixteen access registers, which are used to switch or communicate from one virtual space to another. The address space mechanism can be disabled for compatibility with older systems.

Addresses generated from instructions are normally virtual addresses. Virtual addresses are translated, first, into real addresses and, then, into absolute addresses for physical access to memory. The translation mechanism is shown in Figure 12.18. The current address space register contains a pointer to a segment table. If disabled, a control register holds the pointer. Segments in the zSeries are fixed in size, at either 1MB or 64KB, and pages at either 2KB or 4KB. The usual mechanism translates a virtual address into a real address. The virtual address is divided into segment index, page index, and offset fields. The translation mechanism can be disabled, so that the logical address is viewed as a real address.

For a single CPU system, real addresses and physical storage addresses are identical, but a real-to-absolute translation is required for systems with multiple CPUs. The reason for this is that the first 8KB of physical memory in a zSeries CPU are restricted for special purposes. Various locations in this space are reserved for interrupts, interval timers, and other system control functions. The CPU hardware expects to find particular data, instructions, or addresses at these locations, so they may not be used for other purposes. For example, when the computer is bootstrapped, the starting address for the operating system is stored in absolute locations 0 to 7. When multiple CPUs share central storage, it is necessary to provide a separate 8KB space, with real addresses 0 to 8191, for each CPU in the system. There is also a requirement that all the CPUs have access to a common 8KB space, shared by all.

FIGURE 12.18

Address Translation Mechanisms

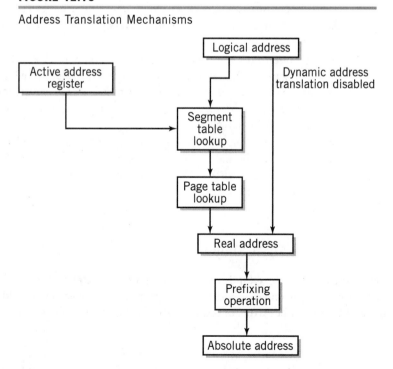

To solve this problem, the zSeries provides an additional level of translation called prefixing. The address space for each CPU is called real storage. A prefix register in each CPU holds a value that corresponds to an 8 KB block, somewhere in absolute storage. Each CPU stores a different value in its prefix register.

The real address and the absolute address are the same for almost every address. For real addresses between 0 and 8191, the prefix is concatenated with the thirteen low-order bits of the address to form the absolute address. This moves the real 0–8191 addresses to a different part of physical storage for each CPU. Conversely, real addresses in the region that the prefix register points to are translated in the other direction, to absolute addresses between 0 and 8191. This makes it possible for each CPU to share a common region of memory. All other real addresses are left alone.

If this explanation seems confusing, the diagram in Figure 12.19 should help. Effectively, the two 8KB regions of memory, 0 to 8191, and the area indicated by the prefix register, are swapped. No other addresses are altered.

Advanced Features

The zSeries CPU provides a lot of flexibility. Many of its features can be enabled or disabled with simple control register instructions. It supports both 24-bit, 31-bit, and 64-bit addressing, multiple address spaces, multiple CPUs, many types of exceptions and interrupts, clock synchronization between systems, cluster support with data integrity control and workload balancing, and built-in diagnostics that can shift work from one CPU in a

FIGURE 12.19

Real-to-absolute Translation

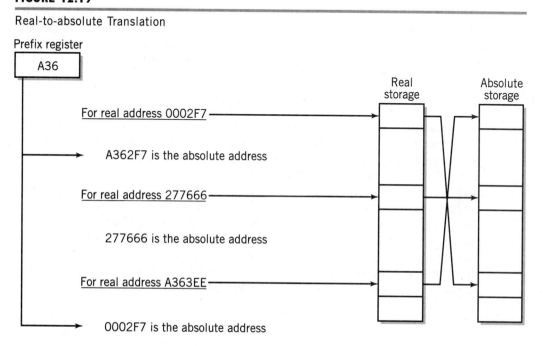

system to another. One of the most important of the z/Architecture's many features is its multiple forms of hardware system protection.

SYSTEM PROTECTION FEATURES Mainframe computers are expected to provide excellent security. The zSeries CPU has a number of different hardware protection mechanisms built in. At the simplest level, the CPU operates in two different states, a *problem* state and a *supervisory* state. The supervisory state is used for control of the system, and supervisory state instructions are privileged, so that the system cannot be modified by an application program.

In addition, the CPU provides storage access protection at the address space, segment, and page levels. Address spaces can be completely isolated from each other, and communicate using HiperSockets. The segment-level mechanism is simple. It establishes read and write permissions for each state on a segment-by-segment basis. The page-level protection is more sophisticated and can control storage access on a program-by-program basis. The Program Status Word holds a storage key connected to the executing program. Each page of memory also has a storage key. For each instruction or operand access, the two keys are compared. If the storage keys do not match, access to the location is prevented, and an interrupt is generated. Certain instructions in the zSeries can also enable a second storage key requirement for particular storage locations.

Finally, the CPU comes with an integrated cryptographic facility, which adds a third storage key, built-in cryptographic encoding and decoding, and firewall protection to the system.

CPU Organization

The original S/360 and S/370 CPUs were organized according to the traditional control unit–arithmetic/logic unit model that we used in Chapter 7. Modern implementations of the CPU divide the same functionality into multiple fetch and execution units, similar to other modern CPU designs. As you have already seen, there is a wide variation in instruction implementation techniques, the amount of cache memory, the numbers and types of execution units, the extent of pipelining, and the electronics used.

SUMMARY AND REVIEW

This chapter presents three examples that allow you to compare CISC and RISC implementations and also to study the similarities and differences between large and small systems. If you have read both the X86 and PowerPC sections in this chapter, you have had the opportunity to compare the CISC and RISC approaches to CPU design in CPUs of similar size and capability. You will have noticed many similarities in the two designs, as well as the similarities between both designs to the basic CPU model that we discussed in Chapters 7 and 10. Similarly, comparisons between the personal computer–based X86 systems and the mainframe System/390 computers reveals differences of magnitude and scale, but not of basic architecture, in systems of vastly different power and size. You have also had the opportunity to compare the PowerPC, a recent architecture, with that of the IBM zSeries, a CPU design that has evolved from a basic architecture developed nearly forty years ago.

Finally, you have been able to see in practice the way the components fit together in real computer systems and to study practical implementations of many of the design extensions introduced as concepts in Chapters 8 and 11.

KEY CONCEPTS AND TERMS

address space	logical partitioning	segment register (X86
control register	problem state	family)
Enterprises Systems	protected mode	supervisor state
Connection	Program Status Word	sysplex
Architecture (ESCON)	(PSW)	uops
FICON (Fibre Connectivity	real mode	virtual 8086 mode
Architecture)		

FOR FURTHER READING

The author used many references for the writing of this chapter. All are listed in the reference section of the book. I found the following books and articles to be particularly useful for their clear descriptions and explanations of these topics.

Books for the X86 family in general tend to be either too shallow or too technically detailed. If you can handle the detail, Sargent and Shoemaker [SARG95] is one of the better ones. It is a bit out of date, but thorough and accurate. The book by Brumm and Brumm [BRUM90] is good, but quite dated. Since new X86 books appear constantly, you might be better off checking the computer section of your local bookstore. More readable, and generally clearer, are a series of *Byte* magazine articles and a series of *IEEE Micro* magazine articles that have appeared over several years describing individual members of the X86 family. Intel manuals are available on the Web.

Byte magazine is also the source of two excellent articles on the PowerPC architecture, [RYAN93] and [THOM94]. There is also a complete issue of *Communications of the ACM* devoted to the PowerPC, dated June 1994, and two well-written articles in *IEEE Micro*, [BECK93] and [DIEF94]. The PowerPC manuals may be found on the Web or purchased from Motorola or IBM and are also excellent resources.

A good starting point on the IBM zSeries family is the S/390 book by Hoskins [HOSK94]. The book by Prasad [PRAS94] provides a thorough, and clear, technical discussion of the IBM architecture. The IBM Journal of Research and Development issues of July 1992 and March 1987 are devoted to the System/390. Some of it is difficult reading, but several of the articles are worth the effort to anyone interested in understanding this architecture. The IBM Web site is also a good source of information, though finding what you want is a bit of a challenge.

EXERCISES

12.1   Demonstrate that a segment in X86 real mode can start at any memory location that is divisible by 16.

12.2 Verify that 2345:0FFA refers to the same real mode memory address as 2222:222A. What is the address in pure hexadecimal form?

12.3 Obtain the hardware reference manuals for a CPU that we have not studied, such as the Alpha CPU, IBM iSeries, MIPS CPU, or Motorola 68000 family CPU. Demonstrate your understanding of basic hardware architecture by writing a description of the CPU similar to those given in this chapter.

12.4 Compare the instruction sets, registers, addressing modes, and other features for the X86 architecture and PowerPC architecture in the specific context of the CISC versus RISC discussion of Chapter 8.

12.5 Compare the instruction sets, registers, addressing modes, and other features for the PowerPC architecture and the zSeries architecture. What differences and additional features would you suspect would probably be included in the zSeries architecture if the designers forty years ago had the benefit of modern knowledge and experience?

12.6 What PowerPC architectural characteristics and features appear to violate the ground rules for RISC design? Why do you suppose the designers made the decisions to do so?

PART FOUR

The bare bones computer system described in Chapters 6 through 12 cannot, by itself, meet the needs of today's computer users. Although the hardware is sufficient, there are still many important shortcomings to the system. These must be resolved with software.

Without software, there is no easy way to load programs into memory, no user interface, no means for controlling the various peripheral devices connected to the system, no means for storing, retrieving, or manipulating files, and no way to manage concurrent multiple programs or multiple users.

Of course, we could insist that each program provide its own tools and facilities, but this would be inconvenient and inefficient. It would also severely limit use of the system. It is obviously useful to provide a set of programs as an integral part of the computer system. These programs control the hardware, load and start application programs, provide file services, implement communication between systems, and support a user interface to the computer. This **system software** provides a complete environment in which the user can concentrate on the problem to be solved rather than deal with the nuances of the computer itself. The user interface allows system access to users of different skill levels, and the file and hardware control modules effectively isolate the user from internal computer operations.

Most of this system software is grouped into a set of programs known as an operating system. You are probably most familiar with the operating systems known as Windows, but there are many other important operating systems. Linux, OpenVMS, z/OS, and Mac OS X are just a few that may come to mind.

In the next six chapters, we will devote our attention to a study of system software and **operating systems.** We begin in Chapter 13 with an overview of operating systems. In this chapter we introduce the various tasks to be performed by the operating system software. We show the various ways in which the operating system software interacts with the user and with application programs. We show how the operating system is implemented to allow the sharing of resources, so that a user may execute more than one program at a time. It also enables multiple users to share the system.

In Chapter 14, we begin a more detailed discussion of the various parts of the operating system by taking a look at the interface between user and computer. We consider the various types of commands that are required or desired and the different types of interfaces that are

THE SOFTWARE COMPONENT

provided on different systems to initiate commands and control the system. We also discuss the concept of **command languages,** powerful ways of combining system commands and utilities that allow the user to perform sophisticated computer tasks with a minimum of effort.

Chapter 15 explores the algorithms and methods used internally to implement various aspects of the operating system. At first, the single-user system is studied briefly, then the system is expanded to include the additional components required to implement a multi-tasking system, and then expanded further to include networked systems. The discussion of memory management includes a thorough discussion of virtual storage, first introduced in Chapter 8. In Chapter 15 we discuss the software component of virtual storage and show how the two components work together synergistically to provide powerful storage management capability.

File management is so important that it merits a chapter of its own. Data base management systems are at the core of most large modern information technology systems. File management provides the storage facility that makes data base management possible. It also provides the capability that allows you to access files by name on your personal computer. In Chapter 16 we discuss the methods used to store, retrieve, and manipulate files. We look at the methods used for accessing files and consider how the files are stored on various peripheral devices. We study the methods used to implement file directory systems, and consider why some file access methods work better than others under different conditions.

Chapter 17 discusses the system software tools that are important to programmers and other advanced users. In this chapter, we explain the workings of editors, compilers, interpreters, linkers, loaders, and debugging tools.

Finally, in Chapter 18 we present the essential features of three important operating systems. Each of these systems is characterized by different design goals, features, and implementation methods, so that you may compare the different designs with each other, with other operating systems that you are familiar with, and with the material presented in this section of the textbook.

At the completion of this section, you can expect to have a good understanding of the four major components that make up a computer system: the data, the hardware, the software, and the communication facilities that connect systems together into powerful information resources at both corporate and international levels.

CHAPTER 13

OPERATING SYSTEMS: AN OVERVIEW

13.0 INTRODUCTION

In a modern computer, the hardware is supplied with its own coordinated software to help make the computer more accessible and productive to the user. This software is known as the **operating system,** or **OS.** The hardware and the operating system operate together architecturally as a unified system to form a complete working computer environment. The operating system has two fundamental purposes: to control and operate the hardware in an efficient fashion and to allow the user powerful access to the facilities of the machine by providing a variety of facilities and services. These services are available both directly to the user and to the programs that the user executes. In addition, the operating system expands the capability of the computer system to allow for the simultaneous processing of multiple programs and support for multiple users and for connecting the computer to other computers, as well as other specialized tasks that would not be possible otherwise.

This chapter provides an overview of the various components, facilities, and services of the operating system. We explore the services that an OS can provide and show how the OS integrates these services into a unified working environment. We describe the tasks that the operating system performs and show how these tasks are interrelated and work together to make it possible for the user to get his work done more efficiently.

There are many different types of operating systems, reflecting different purposes and goals and many different methods of organizing operating systems. These differences are indicated by the way in which the user interacts with the system—an idea that is often surprising to the user who has worked with a single system. This chapter discusses various types of systems and organizations. It notes the different ways in which work is accomplished on a computer system and the different services that are provided.

At the end of the chapter we provide a short introduction to the history of the operating system. Of all the components discussed in this book, the operating system has evolved the most since the computer was introduced. This evolution has made computer systems both much easier to use and much more powerful. Understanding computer systems from the perspective of operating system history can help to show why computers are so commonplace and important today.

13.1 THE BAREBONES COMPUTER SYSTEM

Consider once again the Little Man model that we introduced in Chapter 6. To use this model, a single program was stored in memory. The Little Man executed the program by executing each instruction in turn until he encountered a HALT instruction, which stopped the computer. For simplicity, the Little Man scenario was designed to ignore several issues that must be considered in a real computer.

First, we assumed that the program was already loaded into memory, without considering how it got there. In a real computer, the contents of RAM are destroyed when power is shut off. When power is again turned on, the contents of memory are unknown. Means must be provided to load a program when the machine is turned on. There must be a program in memory before the computer can even begin to execute instructions. After the computer is on, there must be a method to load a program into memory any time a new program is to be executed.

Second, there must be a means to tell the computer to start executing the instructions in a program. The Little Man began executing instructions whenever the location counter was reset to zero.

Third, the barebones computer has no user interface except for the I/O routines that are provided with the executing program. This means that common program requirements such as keyboard and screen I/O, file operations, virtual storage and other internal facilities, and printout must be created and supplied as a part of every program written. It would be dangerous for programs to share disks because there would be no way to establish and protect ownership of particular space on a disk.

The most important consideration to remember is that once the computer is running, it will continue to execute instructions until a HALT instruction is encountered or until power is removed. Halting a program at its conclusion means restarting the computer. This suggests that it is highly desirable that there be an additional program in memory that is always available to execute instructions whenever no other program is being run. This would allow programs to complete execution without halting the machine. Instead, a program would terminate with a jump instruction to the alternative program. The alternative program could be used to accept user commands and to provide a memory loader for the execution of other programs.

As a final consideration, notice that the barebones computer is limited to one program at a time. There is no provision for the functions required to handle the memory management and time scheduling needed to execute multiple programs simultaneously. Thus, multitasking and multiuser operations are not possible. In Chapters 8 and 9 you were made aware of the CPU time wasted during I/O transfers that could be used by other programs. An even more important waste of time occurs as a program waits for user input. The barebones computer is not capable of using the CPU productively during these intervals.

Behind these considerations is the realization that ultimately the purpose of the computer is to help the user to get work done. Obviously, modern computers are not meant to be operated in a barebones fashion like the Little Man. The user should be able to start and operate the computer easily, should be able to choose programs to load and execute, should be able to communicate with others users and other systems, and should be able to perform these operations in a convenient, flexible, and efficient manner. Larger computer systems should be able to share the resources among many users. What is required is additional programs that can provide services to make these expanded capabilities possible.

13.2 THE OPERATING SYSTEMS CONCEPT

The solution to the issues just outlined is to include programs with the computer system that will accept commands from the user and that will provide desired services to the user and to the user's programs. These programs are known collectively as an operating system. The operating system acts as a system manager, controlling both hardware and software and acting as an interface between the user and the system. The operating system itself consists of a collection of programs that work together collectively to accomplish these tasks.

An operating system may be defined as

> a collection of computer programs that integrate the hardware resources of the computer and make those resources available to the user, in a way that allows the user access to the computer in a productive, timely, and efficient manner.

In other words, the operating system acts as an intermediary between the user and the user's programs and the hardware of the computer. It makes the resources available to the user and the user's programs in a convenient way, on the one hand, and controls and manages the hardware, on the other. In doing so, it provides three basic types of services:

1. It accepts and executes commands and requests from the user and from the user's programs.
2. It manages, loads, and executes programs.
3. It manages the hardware resources of the computer.

The relationship between the various components of a computer system is shown schematically in Figure 13.1.

FIGURE 13.1

The Modern Integrated Computer Environment

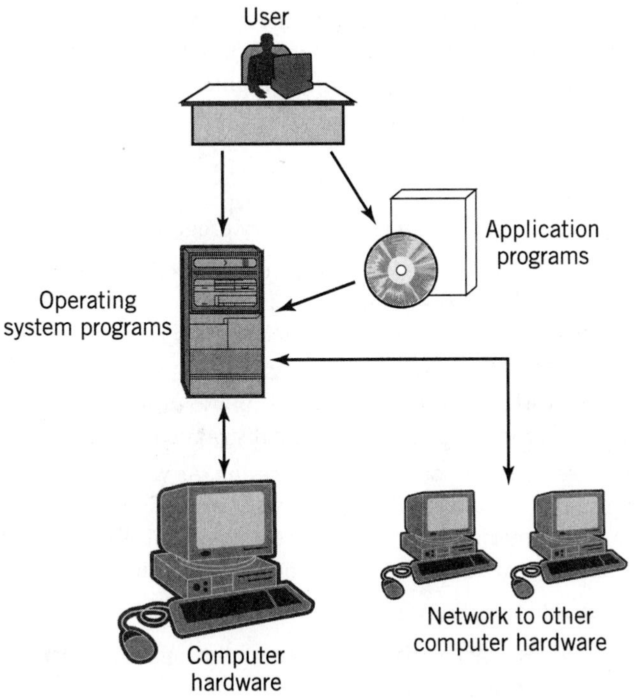

In its intermediary role, the operating system makes it possible for users and programs to control the computer hardware without dealing with the details of hardware operation. Programs can be executed with a mouse click or keyboard command. When programs are completed or interrupted, control returns to the operating system, enabling the user to continue to operate without restarting the computer.

Effectively, the operating system provides a complete working environment, making the system convenient for the user by providing the services necessary to get work done.

The easiest way to think of an operating system is to consider it as a master program that accepts requests from the user and the user's programs, and then calls its own programs to perform the required tasks. At the same time, it also calls programs to control and allocate the resources of the machine, including the use of memory, the use of I/O devices, and the time available to various programs. Thus, if the user issues a command to load a program, a program loader is executed, which then loads the desired program into memory and transfers control to the user's program to run.

If you like, you could picture a command-interpreter-and-program-loader program sitting at the high end of the Little Man Computer memory. When a particular value is received as input, say, 999, that corresponds to the user's command to load a program, the loader performs a loop that inputs the instructions one at a time from the input box into lower memory and then jumps to mailbox 00 to execute the new program. (See Exercise 13.14.)

In a real computer, the operation is more complex, of course. There are many different I/O devices to be controlled, for one thing. There may be more than one program sharing the hardware resources, for another. To accept a command from a user, the operating system must first service mouse clicks and input keystrokes from the keyboard. It must interpret these actions as a command that requests that a program be loaded and executed. It must provide a file system that can interpret the name of the program being requested and determine the location of the file, first by determining the secondary storage device to be used and then by locating the file on the device. It must read the appropriate blocks from the device into memory. Only then can the operating system transfer control to the program being executed. If multiple programs are executing simultaneously, there will be additional requirements: programs to allocate memory and other computer resources to each program, programs to allot the CPU time in an equitable way to each program, programs to direct input and output appropriately, and programs to maintain the integrity of each program, to name a few.

This suggests that most operating systems will include additional services that augment the basic operating system services to be provided. These additional services simplify the user's ability to interact with the system and standardize the system's I/O operations. Most modern operating systems also provide the necessary tools to facilitate the sharing of the system services and resources among multiple programs, computers, and users.

- The operating system provides interfaces for the user and also for the user's programs.
- It provides file support services.
- It provides I/O support services that can be used by every program.
- It provides a means for starting the computer. This process is known as **bootstrapping** or **Initial Program Load (IPL).**
- It handles all interrupt processing, including error handling and recovery, as well as I/O and other routine interrupts.
- It provides services for networking. Most modern systems also provide services to support symmetric multiprocessing, clustering, and distributed processing.
- It provides the tools and services for **concurrent processing.** As you are aware, a single processor is capable of executing only one instruction at a time. Concurrent processing is the means used to simulate the simultaneous execution of multiple programs to provide multitasking and multiuser support.

To support concurrent processing, additional services are required:

- The operating system provides services that allocate resources, including memory, I/O devices, and CPU time, to programs.

- It provides program control services to protect users and programs from each other and from outsiders, as well as to make communication between programs possible.
- It provides information that can be used by the (human) system administrator to tailor and tune the system for optimum performance.

Figure 13.2 is a simplified diagram showing the relationships between the different components of an operating system. The diagram focuses on the interactions among the most user-visible services. Specific multitasking and bootstrapping components are not shown. These are part of the core services, which also include process and thread management, resource allocation, scheduling, memory management, security, and interprocess communication. Also not shown on the diagram, many operating systems allow programs to call the command interface. Thus, a "C" program operating under UNIX could issue a UNIX command as part of its processing.

The diagram also shows the command interface as part of the operating system. In some systems, this is not quite the case. Instead, the command interface is viewed as a **shell** outside of the operating system per se. As you will see, this view can result in increased user flexibility.

Since the programs that make up the operating system occupy space in memory that might be needed for application programs, the operating system is commonly divided into resident and nonresident parts. Some operating system services are critical to the operation of the system and must be resident in memory all the time. Others can be loaded into memory only when they are needed, and executed just like other programs.

The critical programs are loaded into memory by the bootstrap loader at start-up time and will remain resident as long as the computer is running. The bootstrap for most modern computers is stored in read-only memory; on some computers, part of the resident operating system will also be contained in ROM, so that it is permanently resident in memory and always available for use. The memory resident components of an operating system are commonly known as the **kernel** of the operating system. For example, the operating system program that accepts user commands must always be present, as must the routines that handle interrupts and manage resources in a multitasking system. On the other hand, an operating system command that formats a new disk is only used occasionally; it can be loaded and executed only when it is required.

Most people assume that the operating system is stored on a disk that is connected directly to the

FIGURE 13.2

A Simplified Diagram of Operating System Services

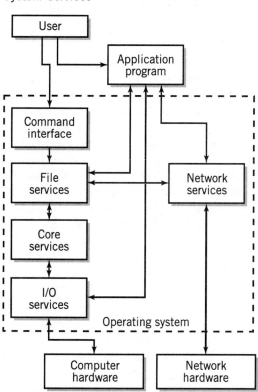

computer, but this is not necessarily true. If the computer is attached to a network, it may obtain its programs, including the operating system, from another computer on the network. This has led to the concept of the **diskless workstation,** a personal computer that relies completely on the network for its data and program storage and access. Diskless workstations are also known as **thin clients.**

The size of the kernel and the particular services provided within a kernel vary from operating system to operating system, depending on the organization and capabilities of the system, as well as by the type of system. Some operating system vendors define the kernel more narrowly than others, precluding from memory residency some components that are deemed less critical to the basic operation of the system. Thus, the kernel in one system may be small, with only the most critical components included, and another might be large, with a tremendous range of services.

There are many different types of operating systems, some tailored for very specific purposes, but general-purpose computing systems can be loosely divided into categories, as follows:

- Single-user, single-tasking systems
- Single-user, multitasking systems
- Multiuser, multitasking systems
- Distributed systems
- Network servers
- Embedded systems
- Real-time systems

Systems can also be categorized by the degree of activity between the user and the system during program execution. As a student, you are probably most familiar with **interactive systems.** When the system is interactive, the user interacts directly with the program to provide input data and guidance during program execution. Interactive systems are sometimes known as **conversational systems.** Most personal computing is done interactively.

Many business tasks are performed more effectively in a batch, where the data input for the program is collected together into a file on disk or tape. It does not make sense to have a user enter data one record at a time if an entire set of data is to be sorted, for example. Instead, the user *submits* the program(s), or **job(s),** to the computer for processing. This type of processing is known as **batch processing.** The user does not interact with the program during batch processing. Large-scale billing systems are usually processed this way.

We remind you that a CPU can execute only one instruction at a time; therefore, time used by the OS on a normal, single CPU system is not available for the execution of user programs. In general, the time used by the OS program is considered overhead. In reality, though, the operating system actually saves time for the users in most situations:

- In a single-user system, the operating system program creates minimal overhead. While the OS program is available to the user at any time, the executing user programs have priority; the OS program runs only to distribute CPU time among executing programs, or if the users' programs request its services.
- The operating system program performs tasks directly for the user that would otherwise have to be performed, with more difficulty, by the user. This includes

the various commands available to the user and I/O services to the user's programs. Most important, this includes the loading and execution of programs. When a user program is not being executed, the OS is always available to the user for these purposes.

■ The OS user interface provides a means for the user to get work done more quickly and efficiently. This is especially true for the user interface found on modern operating systems. The best modern operating systems combine graphical simplicity with sophisticated text command input capability to provide the user with powerful access to the facilities of the computer.

■ Under most conditions, the computer system operates well below full capacity. The CPU sits idle while waiting for I/O transfers to occur. A user sits thinking at the keyboard. Multiuser and multitasking operating systems make it possible for many users or tasks to share the computer resource, providing fuller utilization of the system.

■ The operating system extends the capability of the computer to include features that require special coordinated hardware and software that is invisible to the user. These features include virtual memory, cache memory, multiprocessing, vector processors, and networking.

■ The operating system provides powerful tools to the user's programs that improve the quality of the programs and make the user's work easier. For example, modern OS tools allow work to be easily transferred between applications through a clipboard, or make it possible to imbed a spreadsheet into a word processing document. System services are provided by an **API, or Application Programming Interface.** The API provides file and I/O services, tools that create and support the graphical user interface, even tools to embed a spreadsheet into a word processing document.

We say that the operating system is **event driven.** This means that the operating system normally sits idle and executes only if some event occurs that requires operating system action. Events may result from interrupts or from **service requests** by a program or a user. Events include file requests, I/O, keyboard inputs from users, memory requests from programs, messages sent from one program to another, clock interrupts that allow the operating system scheduler program to dispatch programs during time sharing operation, network requests, and much, much more. In reality, the operating system on a large computer has quite a bit of work to do. Service requests are a fundamental means of communication with the operating system.

Computer designers attempt to integrate the computer hardware and operating system, so that each supports the features of the other in such a way as to create a powerful environment for the users and for the users' programs. Such an environment is called a symbiosis. This would seem to suggest that each type of computer hardware would require its own proprietary operating system. In fact, this is not necessarily the case. Many modern hardware vendors do not provide their own brand of operating system at all. Instead, their systems are supplied with a standard operating system such as UNIX or Windows 2000.

UNIX and Windows 2000 are both examples of operating systems that operate on a variety of different hardware platforms. There is a strong advantage at providing a standard operating system that works on different hardware. Such a system provides program portability, as well as file portability, and also allows users to move comfortably from one machine to another by providing a recognizable interface and command structure.

Portable operating systems are designed in such a way that they may be tailored for different hardware by changing only the small portion of the operating system program code that interacts directly with the hardware. Most of the operating system is written in high-level language, which can be ported easily to a new machine by recompiling the high-level code. The portion of the operating system that must be built for the individual machine is written in a mixture of high-level language and assembly language. Languages like C and C++ are ideal **system languages,** because they provide facilities that make it possible to interact with the hardware with very little need for assembly language. C was designed specifically for this purpose. The portability of UNIX, and other modern operating systems, stems directly from this capability.

While it is true that a single operating system can be ported to operate with different hardware, it is also true that a particular hardware platform can support different operating systems. Thus, the user or system designer can select an operating system that provides the desired facilities for the particular use of the system. Although Pentium-based personal computers are normally provided with Windows,[1] there are other operating system options available that a user could select. An unsophisticated user on a stand-alone system might run Windows for its ease of use, but a more sophisticated user with particular needs might prefer Linux or z/OS for its additional power. Particularly, if the machine is supporting multiple users, an X Windows–based UNIX operating system might be more appropriate.

13.3 BASIC SINGLE-JOB OPERATIONS

As previously described, the Little Man Computer performs **single-job processing.** In single-job processing, one program at a time is loaded into memory and executed. A single-job operating system is one that is designed to process one program at a time. Single-job operating systems are nearly obsolete. MS-DOS is the best-known example of a single-job processing operating system.

Single-job operating systems are much simpler to understand than are operating systems that must handle multiple programs at one time. To clarify the role of the operating system, we begin by describing the basic operation of a single-job operating system, and then extend the discussion to more realistic, modern systems in Section 13.4. This discussion is based on a simplified model of MS-DOS, which is typical of single-job operating systems.

MS-DOS has three major memory resident components. First, there is a command interface shell, which includes the commands in MS-DOS that must remain memory resident. (Other MS-DOS commands are nonresident and are loaded as needed. The list of resident commands has changed somewhat from version to version of MS-DOS.) Second, there is a set of I/O routines that control each of the I/O devices connected to the system. Part of the I/O routine set resides in a ROM area known as the **BIOS,** or **basic input/output system.** Additional routines are provided for devices that are not supported by the

---

[1] Although Windows 95 and Windows NT and their successors are complete, self-contained operating systems, earlier versions of Windows are shells, designed to work with MS-DOS as the basic operating system.

BIOS. Third, there is a **file management system,** which locates files, maintains file storage directories and devices, and performs various file manipulation operations.

The MS-DOS operating system is loaded into memory by loading three files from hard disk or floppy disk. The command interface file is called COMMAND.COM. Two hidden files, IO.SYS and MSDOS.SYS,[2] provide the I/O routines and file routines, respectively. MS-DOS is designed to work with different CPUs within the X86 family. Even within these families, different PC manufacturers have created different designs that require individual hardware interfaces. MS-DOS handles these differences by providing a machine-dependent IO.SYS program file and BIOS. COMMAND.COM and MSDOS.SYS are identical across different versions of the PC hardware. This provides a consistent interface for programs and for the user: differences in the hardware are invisible to the user and to user programs. In addition, MS-DOS provides the capability to load into memory additional I/O device drivers for other I/O peripherals.

A simplified *typical* **memory map** of the first megabyte of memory in an MS-DOS–based personal computer appears in Figure 13.3. We emphasize the word "typical." The size of the lowest area depends on the number of I/O drivers required and the version of MS-DOS being used.

From Chapter 12, you may recall that X86 real mode addressing supports only 1MB of memory. For reasons of historical compatibility, MS-DOS, through Version 6.2, supports only real mode addressing, although it does provide various tricks to access data in the area of memory above 1MB. Thus, the area between the top of the command shell and 640KB takes on extraordinary importance in MS-DOS–based personal computers, because it is the only area of memory where application program code can be executed. This explains why PC system managers attempt to maximize this space. OS/2, UNIX, and recent versions of Windows operate in X86-protected mode—they do not suffer from this limitation and can use all the memory space available. Nonetheless, it is still the job of modern operating systems to manage the memory to maximize the space available for applications to load and run.

Suppose that the user's goal is to load and execute a program. Let us start at the MS-DOS C:\> prompt and trace through the progression of steps that the operating system performs to fulfill the request. For simplicity, we will assume that the user types the request at the prompt; however, a similar progression of steps would occur if the command interface were receiving its request from a command script, or from a mouse click on an icon, or even from a set of punched cards, as was the case on old mainframe computers.

It is easy to envision a simple program that could serve as a **command interpreter.**

FIGURE 13.3

MS-DOS Memory Map

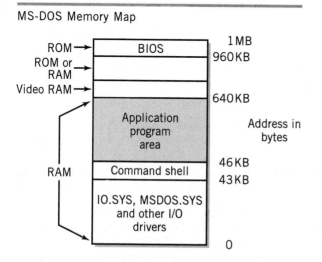

2 This statement is true only for MS-DOS based systems. Pure Windows systems use these names for files with different purposes.

Most commonly, the operating system program prints some simple message on the screen, such as

    C:\>

and executes a single instruction jump loop while waiting for keyboard input. Since the keyboard causes an interrupt when a key is struck, the loop is broken by the keyboard I/O device handler.

Obviously, the particular keyboard input will determine what function the OS program performs. You could view this part of the command interpreter as an input string request, followed by a simple compare to a table of resident command strings and a jump to the appropriate subroutine, if a match is found. An unidentified command is treated as a request to execute a program that is stored as a file.

The six steps below explain each of the operations performed by the various operating systems modules to fulfill a user request:

1. If the command interpreter recognizes a resident command, the command is executed; when command execution is complete, the interpreter prints a new prompt and awaits the next command. Otherwise…

2. The command interpreter passes the request to the file system for loading and execution. The file system loader identifies the device where the file is stored. The physical locations for the directories on each device are stored in a table. The loader issues a *read* request to the appropriate I/O driver for the specified directory location

3. The I/O driver routine takes over, loads the directory into memory, and returns control to the file system.

4. The file system uses the directory to locate the requested file. If the file is not listed in the directory, a "File Not Found" message is printed; control is returned to the command interpreter to begin the prompt-and-wait again. Otherwise,

5. The file system loader issues a *read* request to the I/O driver to load the file into a free area of memory.

6. When the I/O operation is complete, control is again returned to the file system loader. If necessary, the loader sets base registers and modifies addresses in the program code to adjust for the program's actual location in memory. This process, known as **relocation,** is discussed further in Section 17.5. Finally, the loader simply provides a jump instruction to the starting location of the program.

In a single-job system, the user's program takes precedence. Once execution of the user's program is started, the operating system is out of the picture. Unless the user's program requires a particular service from the operating system, the operating system has no specific function to perform and is idle, so the user's program can run without interruption. Normally, there are three ways in which the operating system program would regain control.

1. When the user's program is complete, it transfers control back to the command interpreter shell program. Thus, the machine never halts. If the user's program is not running, the operating system is. The computer's HALT instruction is almost never used in a program. In a more sophisticated operating system, HALT would be a protected instruction, and would not even be accessible to an application program.

2. If the user's program wishes to perform a file or I/O operation, it makes a **request** to the operating system by placing a request number in a previously agreed register or memory location and then jumps to the operating system program. This frees the individual programmer from having to rewrite I/O routines into every program. The operating system program **services the request** and then jumps back to the program at the point at which it left. A software interrupt is used for this purpose. In general, services are requested from most modern operating systems in similar fashion, by supplying appropriate parameters and calling the operating system routine that provides the service.

3. The user wants to stop the program in midstream. This might occur, for example, if the program is caught in an infinite loop. (Of course, *our* programs never do that, but, just in case....) Since the user program is normally in control of the computer, it is useful to provide a way for the user to return control to the operating system program when desired. The keyboard interrupt facility is useful for this purpose. Since the operating system program handles interrupts, a particular key can be designated to indicate that the user requests suspension of his or her program. On many systems, the Control–"C" key combination is used for this purpose.

The operating system also regains control if a system malfunction or error causes a hardware interrupt.

When the operating system program regains control of the computer, it determines what task is to be performed. If the task is in response to a service request from the user's program, the request is serviced, and control returned to the user's program. Otherwise, the command interpreter issues a new prompt and awaits the next command.

The entire operation of loading and executing a program is illustrated in Figure 13.4. Although this description omits some of the details, it demonstrates most of the features of a single-job operating system. In particular, it shows the relationship between the different operating system modules.

It is interesting to note some of the features that are *lacking* in this system. For example, there is a lack of security. The executing program can simply overwrite the resident operating system routines if it wishes, which may make restart of the command interpreter impossible or make I/O and file service routines unavailable. The executing program can also write directly to an I/O device if it chooses to do so. This could damage the file system and other programs and data on the device. In other words, good program behavior depends on the intelligence and competence of the programmers who wrote the program.

Note, too, that the single-job operating system provides only minimal memory management, and no scheduling capability. Scheduling is not needed, since the only operating system tasks to be performed during program execution are those requested by the program; the operating system is otherwise suspended for the duration of program execution. Furthermore, since there is only a single program to be loaded, the decision as to where to place the program is straightforward.

13.4 CONCURRENT OPERATIONS

Single-job processing is wasteful of the resources of the system. Most individual program tasks use only a small fraction of the capabilities of a computer system. The CPU, in particular, will

FIGURE 13.4

Leading and Executing a Program

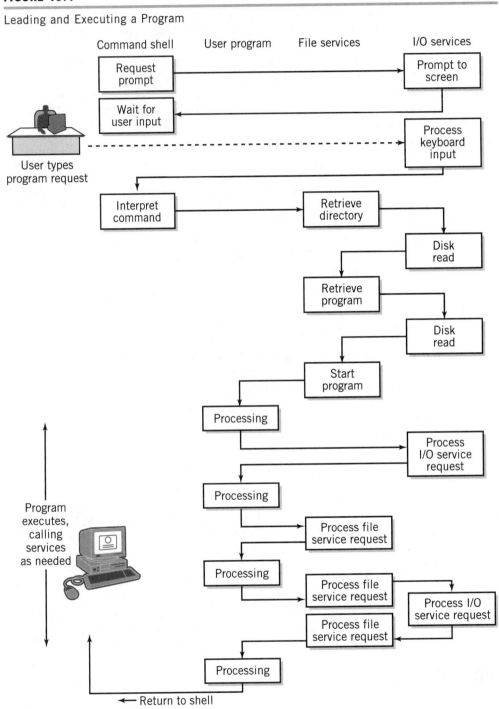

be idle much of the time, waiting while I/O operations take place. As you have already seen, disk I/O is very slow compared to the CPU, and most programs must wait until the disk transfer is complete to continue. For interactive systems, most tasks will be idle nearly all the time, waiting for user keyboard input.

Today, only older personal computer systems and embedded computer systems specialized for a particular task (such as controlling a microwave oven) still perform single-job processing. Even with personal computer systems, users have seen the benefit of working with more than one program at a time as a way of improving their efficiency. A programmer can be editing one program while compiling another; a business user can be using a communication program to send a fax while using a word processor to prepare another document. Nearly every modern system provides means and support for manipulating multiple programs on a single CPU, a technique known as **multitasking** or **multiprogramming**.[3]

Multitasking can be applied to a single user, or it can be designed to allow multiple users to share the computer system resources. Such a system, known as a **multiuser system,** would still have to be multitasking, of course, because each user on the system would be running at least one program. Most multiuser systems further allow each user to be running multiple programs concurrently.

The operating system plays a more essential role in multiuser and multitasking systems, but the basic operation used is the same as that just described. In addition to user services, the operating system must allocate resources fairly and efficiently to the various tasks and users. These resources include memory, I/O devices, and CPU time. A single program cannot be allowed to "hog" the machine; therefore, the operating system program must run periodically to determine the status of the machine's resources and to reassign resources to assure that every user and task is receiving what it needs.

Since a CPU can process only one instruction at a time, the simultaneous execution of two or more programs is obviously impossible with a single processor. Instead, the operating system acts as a controller to provide concurrent processing. There are various ways in which multitasking can be achieved with concurrent processing, but mostly these methods take advantage of two simple strategies:

1. While one program is waiting for I/O to take place, another can be using the CPU to execute instructions. This strategy is shown in Figure 13.5. In Chapter 9 we demonstrated that I/O could be performed efficiently without tying up the instruction executing capability of the CPU. We further showed that most of the time, the CPU was idle, since I/O represents such a large percentage of a typical program's execution. This suggests that the idle time can be used to execute other programs, as an effective way to increase utilization of the CPU.

2. The CPU may be switched rapidly between different programs, executing a few instructions from each, using a periodic clock-generated interrupt. This method was discussed in Section 9.3, and diagrammed in Figure 9.8, redrawn here as Figure 13.6. This strategy will slow down execution of each program, since each program must split its time with other programs. There is also some operating

---

[3] Note that even though many operating systems refer to executing programs as processes, multiprogramming is not the same as multiprocessing. The latter refers to the presence of multiple CPUs within the system.

system overhead, as a dispatcher must be invoked at each interrupt to select the next program to receive CPU time. In most cases the CPU is so powerful compared to the requirements of the programs that the slowdown is not even noticeable. This technique is called **time-slicing.**

The algorithms that control concurrency combine these two methodologies, taking into account such issues as fairness to each program, the priorities of the different programs, quick response for critical situations, such as displaying a user's cursor movement or displaying streaming video, and other criteria. The process of selecting which program to run at any given instant is known as **dispatching.** We will discuss dispatching algorithms again in Section 13.5 and in more detail in Chapter 15.

As we noted, management of concurrent operations must be handled by the operating system. Obviously the addition of multitasking complicates the design and operation of the operating system, and the operating system is much larger and more complex. There are many additional tasks for the operating system to perform. In addition to dispatching, the OS must keep track of each program in the machine; must find and manage memory for each program; must schedule the various I/O devices so that every program gets the resources it needs; must be able to suspend and restart programs with all registers, data, and instructions intact; must provide security and protection from other users and other pro-

FIGURE 13.5

Sharing the CPU During I/O Breaks

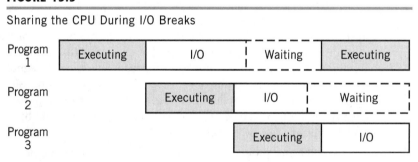

FIGURE 13.6

Time-Sharing the CPU

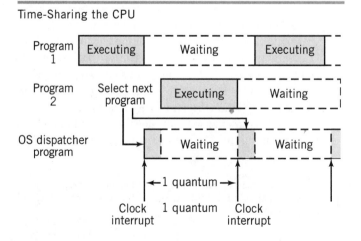

grams; and must measure performance and control and supervise the operation of the overall system. It may also be necessary to provide usage data for each program, establish and control communication between programs, establish priorities within the system, respond to network requests, manage communication with a network, and perform many other tasks.

You should be aware that to be useful, the operating system must be able to control the computer. There are two methods by which the operating system program can get control of the computer:

1. The user's program transfers control to the OS program by issuing a service request into the operating system, or

2. An interrupt occurs that allows the operating system to take control. The OS is designed to handle all interrupts, and a clock could be arranged to interrupt the computer periodically at a regular time interval. This would allow the OS program to check regularly on the status of the computer and provide scheduling services. I/O completion interrupts and other interrupts also result in a transfer of control to the OS, so that appropriate action can be taken.

The various services and operations required to support concurrent programming are discussed further in the next section.

The integration of system hardware and software required for effective concurrent operation has allowed computer designers to include special-purpose hardware designed to support particular features of the operating system. Of particular importance are a memory management technique based on virtual storage and the protection mechanism that prevents application programs from accessing parts of the system that could damage system integrity. Details of virtual storage and other interesting parts of the operating system are discussed at more length in Chapter 15.

13.5 SERVICES AND FACILITIES

Section 13.2 provided an overview of the various services and components that make up an operating system. In this section we consider the fundamental building blocks of an operating system in more detail. There are ten major blocks to be considered, not all of which will necessarily be found in any particular operating system:

- The command processor, application program interface, and user interface
- The file management system
- The input/output control system
- Process control management and interprocess communication
- Memory management
- Scheduling system
- Secondary storage management
- System protection management
- Network management, communication support, and communication interfaces
- Support for system administration

Some systems also provide a program known as a system manager, commonly known as a **monitor** or **supervisor,** which handles competing requests or conflicts, and which acts as a general controller and arbiter for the entire system. There are other system functions, such as accounting and error handling, that are sometimes handled as separate blocks but frequently appear within the blocks already listed.

In different types of operating systems, some of these components may be combined, or even absent. You've already seen that a single-job system requires only the first three components, for example, but the listed components represent a collection of the most general operating system requirements.

Some of these modules, particularly the command interface and file system modules, are quite visible to the user. The other modules are primarily used for internal control of the system, controlling and optimizing use of the hardware resources, and maximizing program throughput and efficiency. Most modules also make their services available to user programs through the API.

In this section, we present an overview of the services provided by each of these operating system components. Individual components are discussed in more detail in other chapters, the capabilities and operation of the user interface and related services in Chapter 14, and the file management services in Chapter 16. The internal components of the operating system are discussed in Chapter 15.

User Interface and Command Execution Services

To the user, the most important and visible service provided by the OS is the user interface and the capability that it provides to execute commands.

Many systems do not consider the user interface and command processor to be a part of the operating system kernel, even though much of it is likely to be memory resident. Instead, these systems consider the user interface as a separate shell that is provided with the operating system and that interacts with the kernel to provide the necessary user command capabilities. Theoretically, a different shell could be used that provides different command capabilities. In MS-DOS, for example, the command interface was provided in a separate shell called COMMAND.COM. Other MS-DOS shells existed, although they were seen very rarely. One such shell replaced standard MS-DOS commands with equivalent UNIX tools. In UNIX, on the other hand, three different shells, the C shell, the Bourne shell, and the Korn shell are in common use, and many other shells for UNIX are available. Each of these shells provides different command structures and different capabilities. There are also a number of different GUI shells, each with different features, appearances, and capabilities.

Different types of user interfaces exist. The most common are the **graphical user interface,** or **GUI,** and the **command line interface,** or **CLI.** The graphical user interface accepts commands primarily in the form of drop-down menus, mouse movements, and mouse clicks. The command line interface relies on typed commands. Underneath the very different appearances of these interfaces, however, similar commands are being executed.

Regardless of the user interface provided, the command interface provides direct access to various other modules within the operating system. The most often used commands access the file system for file operations and for program loading and execution. On some systems, commands may also provide direct access to the I/O system, protection services, network services, and process control services. On other systems, these commands may be processed indirectly, using built-in operating system utilities intended for the purpose.

A few systems even provide commands and built-in utilities for access to memory and to secondary storage. Generally, use of these commands is restricted to users with special access needs, such as the people who control and maintain the system. UNIX, for example, refers to these individuals as "superusers."

Some commands are built directly into the operating system. They remain in memory for immediate access. These are known as **resident commands.** Other commands are loaded only as they are needed. These are called **nonresident commands.**

Most modern operating systems provide some capability for combining computer commands into programs. Batch-oriented systems combine individual commands into a sequence of **control statements,** which will be interpreted and executed one at a time to control the processing of a multistep "job." Each step in the job performs an individual task. On large IBM systems, for example, the set of commands used for this purpose form a language known as **Job Control Language,** or **JCL.**

In addition to the standard commands, Windows and MS-DOS provide simple branch and loop commands that can be used to create simple miniprograms made up of legacy MS-DOS commands. These miniprograms are commonly known as **BAT files** and can be executed as though they were actual programs. This basic command set also includes

- A means for redirecting I/O data to a device different from that ordinarily used, to a disk file instead of the screen, for example

- A way to combine commands using a technique called piping, so that the output from one command is automatically used as the input for another

- A means for providing additional parameters to the BAT program that can be entered by the user at the time the program is executed

More sophisticated command languages provide larger command sets with a more extensive and powerful set of options and with more extensive control structures that allow more flexibility, both in design and in run-time execution. Some command languages even provide special powerful commands that can eliminate normal programming effort. UNIX and Linux are particularly notable in this regard, providing commands that can search, select, edit, sort, enumerate, and process data from files in a way that rivals many programming languages.

Recent versions of Windows include a similar scripting facility called **Windows Scripting Host.** At this writing, the Windows Scripting Host executes scripts written in various scripting languages, including VBScript, Rexx, Python, and Perl. Use of the Windows Scripting Host is somewhat limited because it requires knowledge of Windows objects and programming techniques to use effectively.

Command languages extend the power and flexibility of the operating system and simplify use of the system for less sophisticated users.

File Management

The concept of a file is central to the effective use of a computer system. A file is generally loosely defined as a collection of related information. Defined in this way, a file is a rather abstract concept; indeed, the contents of the file only have meaning in the context of their particular internal description and use. Thus, the sequence of bytes in a file might represent a program, or a graphical image, or maybe the alphanumeric text data for a book, to be used within a word processor. A file may be organized internally into records or it may simply be a stream of bytes. A file constitutes a *logical unit* of storage, that is, logical to the person or program using the file. The logical unit may or may not correspond to the physical storage characteristics of the I/O device where it is stored.

The file management system provides and maintains the mapping between a file's logical storage needs and the physical location where it is stored. The file management system identifies and manipulates files by the names provided by their users. It determines the physical requirements of the file, allocates space for it, stores it in that space, and maintains the information about the file so that it may be retrieved, partially or in full, later. The file management system keeps track of the available space on each device connected to the system. The user and the user's programs need not be aware of the underlying physical storage issues. Users and programs simply access the files by name, and the file management system handles the details.

The file management system provides a consistent view of files across different I/O devices. To the user, file requests operate in the same way independent of the device, even between devices of different characteristics. Thus, it is not necessary to know the physical differences between, say, disk and tape, to move a file from one to the other. A program can request file services without knowing the file structure of the device being addressed, indeed without even knowing what kind of device the file is stored on.

The file management system provides and maintains

- Directory structures for each I/O device in the system and tools to access and move around these structures. The directory structure allows the retrieval and storage of files by name, keeps track of the mappings, allocates and frees space, allows the mounting and unmounting of file structures, and provides other functions required to maintain the structures of the file system. Provisions are made to move easily from one structure to another.

- Tools that copy and move files from one I/O device to another and from one directory to another, merge files, create and delete files and directories, and undertake other basic file manipulations.

- Information about each file in the system and tools to access that information. Typically, information about a file might include its name, type of file, size, date and time of creation, date and time of the most recent update, and protection and backup characteristics.

- Security mechanisms to protect files and control and limit file access to authorized users. Some systems additionally provide encryption protection.

Some file management systems also provide advanced features, including auditing, backup, emergency retrieval and recovery mechanisms, file compression, and transparent network file access.

File management systems are particularly important in systems in which secondary storage devices are shared in common by multiple users, since they provide a directory system that assures that there is no duplicate use of physical storage. Without this facility, it is likely that users would unintentionally overwrite each other's files. And, of course, we already noted that the file management system also provides file access protection between the different users. The file management system is discussed more fully in Chapter 16.

Input/Output Services

In Chapter 8, we introduced the concept of interrupts and showed the various techniques for handling I/O. Programs that implement these concepts are known as I/O device drivers. It would be awkward to require each program to provide its own I/O services. I/O device drivers are important because they are available to serve every program that will be executed on the system and provide a standard methodology for the use of each device. Even more important, the use of standard I/O drivers within the operating system limits access and centralizes control of the operations for each device.

The operating system includes I/O device driver programs for each device installed on the system. These drivers provide services to the file management system and are also available, through the API, to other programs for their use. The I/O device drivers accept I/O requests and perform the actual data transfers between the hardware and specified areas of memory.

In addition to the I/O device drivers provided by the operating system, modern systems provide certain I/O drivers with minimal functionality in ROM, to assure access to critical devices, such as the keyboard, display, and boot disk during the system startup process. The ROM-based drivers are replaced or integrated with other I/O drivers during normal system operation. On IBM-type PCs, these drivers are stored in the system BIOS.

Device drivers for newly installed devices are added and integrated into the operating system at the time of installation. On some systems, the process is manual. On many systems, the Apple Macintosh, for example, this process is completely automatic. In Windows, this capability is known as **plug-and-play.** Many modern systems even make it possible to add and modify devices on the fly, without shutting down the system. USB and FireWire both provide this capability.

Every operating system, large or small, provides input/output services for each device in the system. On multitasking systems, however, I/O services take on additional importance, since the use of one set of I/O services for each device assures that multiple programs will not be competing for the device and assures that the use of each device will be under a single point of control. Multiple access can cause serious conflict in multitasking systems. For example, a user would not be pleased to discover that parts of the printouts from two different programs were intermingled on the pages, even more so if the outputs belonged to two different users! The operating system assigns I/O devices appropriately to each process to eliminate this problem.

Process Control Management

Briefly, a **process** is an executing program. It is considered the standard unit of work within a computer system. *Every* executing program is treated as a process. This includes not only application programs, but the programs within the operating system itself. The process concept considers the program, together with the resources that are assigned to it, including memory, I/O devices, time for execution, and the like. When admitted to the system, each program is assigned memory space and the various resources that it initially requires to complete its work. As the process executes, it may require additional resources, or it may release resources that it no longer needs. The operating system performs various functions with processes, including scheduling and memory management, by providing the various services that we have discussed in this chapter. Processes must often be synchronized, so that processes sharing a common resource do not step on each other's toes by altering critical data or denying each other needed resources. Systems also provide communication capability between different processes. Processes may cooperate with each other by sending messages back and forth using **interprocess messaging services.** Other services include functions such as setting process priorities and calculating billing information.

Process control management keeps track of each process in memory. It determines the state of each process: whether it is running, ready to run, or waiting for some event, such as I/O to be completed, in order to proceed. It maintains tables that determine the current program counter, register values, assigned files and I/O resources, and other parameters for each process in memory. It coordinates and manages message handling and process synchronization.

Many modern systems further break the process down into smaller units called **threads.** A thread is an individually executable part of a process. It shares memory and other resources with all other threads in the same process, but can be scheduled to run separately from other threads.

Memory Management

The purpose of the memory management system is to load programs into memory in such a way as to give each program loaded the memory that it requires for execution.

On a single-job system, memory management is simple. Once the operating system is loaded, the remainder of memory is available to a program requesting space. Since only one program is to be loaded, memory management consists of nothing more than determining if there is sufficient space for the program to be loaded and keeping track of its starting location.

When the system provides multitasking the operation is considerably more complex and important. Each program that is being executed must reside in memory. For multitasking to occur, multiple programs will occupy memory simultaneously, with each program in its own memory space.

The memory management system has three primary tasks. It attempts to perform these tasks in a way that is fair and efficient to the programs that must be loaded and executed.

1. It keeps track of memory, maintaining records that identify each program loaded into memory together with the space being used and also keeps track of available space. It allocates additional space for running programs as required. It prevents programs from reading and writing memory outside their allocated space, so that they cannot accidentally or intentionally damage other programs.

2. It maintains one or more queues of programs waiting to be loaded into memory as space becomes available, based on such program criteria as priority and memory requirements.

3. When space is available, it allocates memory to the programs that are next to be loaded. It also deallocates a program's memory space when it completes execution. The deallocated space is made available for other programs.

Older systems used a variety of algorithms to divide up the available memory space. Except for special-purpose embedded systems (the kind that you might find in a washing machine, for example), every modern computer system provides virtual storage, which includes hardware support for sophisticated memory management capability. Where virtual storage is available, the memory management module of the operating system works directly with the hardware and provides the software support to create an integrated memory management environment that takes maximum advantage of the features of virtual storage.

Scheduling

Obviously program **scheduling** is not an issue with a single-tasking system. Only one program is admitted to the system at a time, and when it is loaded the operating system simply transfers control to it for program execution. At completion of execution, the program transfers control back to the operating system.

On a multitasking system scheduling considerations are much more important and much more complex. On a multitasking system the operating system is responsible for the allocation of CPU time in a manner that is fair to the various programs competing for time, as well as maximizing efficient utilization of the system overall.

There are two levels of scheduling. One level of scheduling determines which jobs will be admitted to the system and in what order. Admission to the system means that a job will be placed into a queue, based on some order of priority, and ultimately assigned memory space that will allow the program to be executed. (Some operating systems divide this operation into two separate tasks, one for admittance to the system, the other to assign memory.) This scheduling function is sometimes known as **high-level scheduling.** The other level of scheduling is known as **dispatching.** Dispatching is responsible for the actual selection of processes that will be executed at any given instant by the CPU. The operation that was shown in Figure 13.6 is representative of the work of the dispatcher. In a multithreading system, dispatch is done at the thread level, instead of at the process level.

In modern systems, with their extensive facilities and capabilities, high-level scheduling is relatively straightforward. Most of the time, new processes will simply be admitted to the system and given memory space if it is available, or held until space is available, then admitted. Selecting the appropriate candidate for CPU time at any given instant is much more important and difficult, since the capability of the dispatcher directly affects the ability of the users to get their work done.

Different processes have different requirements. Some processes require extensive amounts of CPU time; such processes are considered to be **CPU bound.** Others are mostly I/O operations, with very little CPU processing; these are known as **I/O bound.** Immediate response time is important under some conditions, for example, when echoing cursor movement to a screen and unimportant in others, such as producing printed output from a batch job that will not be picked up by the user until later in the day. It is obviously desirable to dispatch processes in such a way that the system is used effectively. Various dispatching algorithms are used to meet these different requirements, and there are various criteria for measuring how well the dispatcher is doing its job. Generally, interactive processes require faster response than do batch processes. Processes that must control instrumentation in real time require the fastest response of all.

The dispatcher is also responsible for the actual transfer of control to the process that is being dispatched. This responsibility includes preservation of the previous running program's program counter, register values, and other parameters that represent the state of the program at the time it was stopped, as well as restoration, if necessary, of the exact previous state of the program being dispatched. This operation is called **context switching.**

The operation of the dispatcher is dependent on the nature of the system and on the nature of the programs that the system is running. The dispatcher can be **preemptive** or **nonpreemptive.** The dispatcher for a nonpreemptive system replaces an executing program only if the program is blocked because of I/O or some other event or if the program voluntarily gives up the CPU. When necessary, the executing program may be suspended momentarily, so that the CPU can handle interrupts, but when the interrupting task is complete, control is returned to the same program. (This exception is necessary for several reasons. Without it, there would be no way to stop a runaway program, for example, a program with an infinite loop in it. It is also necessary to prevent losing key strokes from user keyboards and to echo key strokes back to users' screens.)

Preemptive multitasking uses the clock interrupt, as described earlier, to preempt the executing program and to make a fresh decision as to which program executes next.

In general, nonpreemptive dispatching algorithms apply mostly to older, batch-oriented systems. Modern dispatchers are predominately preemptive. However, most provide a mechanism to dispatch individual programs nonpreemptively, for programs that must execute to completion without unnecessary interruptions. Linux uses nonpreemptive dispatching to protect certain operating system operations from interrupts that could destroy the integrity of operating system data, for example.

Secondary Storage Management

The file management system keeps track of free secondary storage space and maintains the file system and its directories. The input/output control system provides device drivers that actually control the transfer of data between memory and the secondary storage devices.

On large multitasking systems there may be many programs requesting I/O services from a secondary storage device at one time. The order in which these requests are fulfilled affects the ability of the different programs to get their work completed, since the programs must usually stop and wait for their I/O requests to be completed before proceeding. Although it would be simplest to process I/O requests in the order received, it may be more efficient to process the requests out of order, particularly if the blocks requested are scattered all over the disk. This is true because the disk seek time (i.e., the time to move from track to track) is long compared to other times within the system.

The secondary storage management system attempts to optimize the completion of I/O tasks by using algorithms that reorder the requests for more efficient disk usage. For example, it might attempt to read all the requested data blocks from the tracks in one area of the disk before going to read data on tracks at the other end of the disk. In some large modern systems, optimization is provided by a combination of I/O hardware and operating system software.

Security and Protection Services

Systems that multitask require security and protection services to protect the operating system from user processes—and to protect processes from each other. Without protection, a buggy program, for example, could unintentionally destroy the program code or data in the memory space belonging to the operating system or to another process. Multiuser systems additionally require security services to protect the system and user processes from unauthorized entry to the system, and against unauthorized use of the system, even by authorized users.

In most modern systems, executing processes are limited to the execution of instructions and access to data within their own memory space. All other services, such as file management and I/O, must be requested by the process from the operating system, using the service requests provided by the OS for that purpose. This methodology is fundamental to the security of the system. In this way, the operating system, the file system, and other processes are protected from unauthorized use or operations, protecting the integrity of the system as a whole. Interprocess messaging services are usually provided by the operating system to allow processes to communicate with each other without compromising the system. Critical parts of the operating system execute in a specially protected mode of operation provided as part of the CPU design. In protected mode, the operating system can prevent programs from executing certain instructions and from accessing parts of memory specified by the operating system, for example, parts being used by other programs.

Each module in the operating system includes provisions that protect its assets. Thus, the file management system would not allow a process to store data on a part of a disk that is being used by another file. Nor would process management allow the assignment of an I/O resource that would prevent another process from completing its task. Since all services are requested from the operating system, the OS has the capability to determine that requests will not damage other processes or the system itself.

The operating system also provides login and password services that prevent entry from unauthorized users and access control facilities that allow users to protect their individual files at various levels of availability to other users.

Network and Communications Support Services

With the exception of some embedded systems, nearly all computers today are interconnected, directly or indirectly, into networks. (There is even a trend toward networking embedded computers: modern automobile computers routinely report maintenance problems to the service technician when you bring your car in for service. And you may have heard of the refrigerator that calls an order in to an Internet grocery delivery service when food stocks are low.) The network and communications support facilities within the operating system carry out the functions required to make the system perform seamlessly in a networked and distributed environment.

Most modern communications services rely on the TCP/IP protocol suite, together with its IP-based applications. TCP/IP provides the facilities to locate and connect to other computer systems, to pass application data in packet form from one system to another, to access files, I/O devices, and programs from remote systems, to provide error checking and correction when appropriate, and to support the requirements of distributed processing. Network and communication services within the operating system provide the communication software necessary to implement the features and facilities of TCP/IP. Most systems also implement a substantial set of TCP/IP applications and extensions, including e-mail, remote login, Web services, streaming multimedia, voice over IP telephony, secure networking across the Internet (called a **virtual private network**, or **VPN**), and more. Some systems also offer support for alternative communication protocols, for example, Novell IPX/SPX and IBM Systems Network Architecture.

Communications services within the operating system also provide the interface between the communication software and the OS I/O control system that provides access to the network. The I/O control system includes the software drivers for modems, network interface cards, wireless communication cards, and other devices that are used to connect the computer physically and electrically to the network or networks.

Larger computers used for server applications often require the capability for additional growth and reliability to serve the needs of their clients. In addition to networking support, the operating systems for such machines often include clustering software, so that these computers can be clustered together and viewed transparently by clients and users as a single, high-powered system. The clustering software provides single-point logins, single-point user and client requests, request steering, failure detection and cutover, and system load balancing between the individual nodes within the cluster.

System Administration Support

The **system administrator,** or **sysadmin,** for short, is the person who is responsible for maintaining the computer system or systems. In a large organization, the sysadmin may support hundreds, or even thousands, of computers, including those of the employees. Some of the important administrative tasks managed by a system administrator include:

- System configuration and setting group configuration policies
- Adding and deleting users
- Controlling and modifying user privileges to meet the changing needs of the users
- Providing and monitoring appropriate security
- Managing, mounting, and unmounting file systems
- Managing, maintaining, and upgrading networks
- Providing secure and reliable backups
- Providing and controlling software, installing new software, and upgrading software as required
- Patching and upgrading the operating systems and other system software
- Recovering lost data
- Tuning the system for optimum availability and performance

These and other important tasks must be applied both to central server systems and to client machines and other desktop computers on a network to coordinate and maintain a reliable and useful system. Modern operating systems provide software to simplify these tasks.

On small personal computers, the user is often the administrator as well. The major administrative tasks of the user are to install and upgrade software, to reconfigure the system and the desktop from time to time, to maintain network connections as required, and to perform regular file backup and disk maintenance and defragmentation. For user administration of this type, simple tools are sufficient. Indeed, the goal of a desktop operating system might be to *hide* the more sophisticated tools from the typical user. For example, Windows operating systems store the system configuration within a registry that is normally hidden from the user, and provide, instead, a variety of simple tools specifically for tailoring the system to user preferences and performing maintenance tasks. The Windows OS supplies default configuration parameters for many tasks that suit the needs of most users, with tools to modify the parameters to meet specific user requirements. The simplest tools are sufficient for most users to perform routine system administration. Knowledgeable users can also manipulate the system registry directly, when necessary. On desktop computers connected to a larger system within an organization, central administration tools allow the application of group policies and configuration to individual desktop computers without user involvement.

On larger systems, administration is much more important and much more complex. The hardware and software to be managed is far more extensive, and there are numerous users requiring accounts and service. Installation of new equipment on large systems is common, and in some cases, the system must be reconfigured to use the new equipment. IBM calls this process sysgen, for system generation. It is one of the most important tasks of system administration on large systems. Modern systems provide software for simplifying common system administration tasks. Large mainframe operating systems provide tools for performing all the major system administration requirements. They also provide tools that allow the administrator to tailor the system to optimize its performance, for example, to optimize throughput or the use of resources. This is done by modifying system parameters and selecting particular scheduling and memory management algorithms. Among the parameters that can be adjusted on various systems are the amount of memory allocated to a program, user disk space allocation, priorities, assignments of files to different disks, the maximum number of programs to be executed concurrently, and the scheduling method employed. IBM z/OS even includes a Workload Manager, which attempts to optimize system resources automatically, without administrator intervention.

The system administrator on a UNIX/Linux system, for example, can log in to the system as a *superuser,* with privileges that override all the restrictions and security built into the system. The superuser can modify any file in the system. More important, the UNIX system provides tools that simplify the tasks of system administration. These tools take the form of commands that can be executed only by the superuser and text-based configuration files that can be modified with any text editor.

For example, UNIX/Linux systems typically provide a menu-driven or graphical *adduser* program for administering user accounts. This program provides a simple procedure for performing all the tasks required to add a new user to the system, including setting up the user name and ID number, building entries to the appropriate user and group tables, creating the user's home directory, assigning login shells, and establishing user initialization files (corresponding to the user's particular terminal hardware, prompt preferences, and the like).

Other typical UNIX/Linux administration commands include a partition tool for partitioning hard disk drives; *newfs* for building a file system; *mount* and *umount* for mounting and unmounting file systems; *fsck* for checking and repairing the file system (similar in concept to, but much more complex and thorough than, CHKDSK on Windows systems); *du* and *df* for measuring disk usage and free space; tar for collecting files into archives; and *ufsdump* and *ufsrestore* for creating backups and recovering damaged files. *config* is used to build the system. There are many additional tools available to the UNIX/Linux sysadmin.

Like other large systems, server-based versions of Windows 2000 provide a full suite of tools for measuring system performance and managing the system, including the ability to control and configure client systems remotely.

Most systems provide a variety of statistical information that indicates the load on the system and the efficiency of the system. This information is used by the system administrator as a basis for tuning the system. Part of a typical system status report appears in Figure 13.7. This particular report comes from a Linux system. The report indicates the load on the system as a function of time, shows CPU and memory usage, identifies the most CPU-intensive processes, together with the name of the user and the percent of CPU and memory resources consumed, shows the efficiency of virtual storage and provides many other useful system parameters. It even provides an analysis of the data shown. Although the typical user might not find a report such as this very useful in terms of what steps to take as a result of the information presented, a skilled system administrator can make valuable use of the information in determining ways in which to improve system performance. A consistently heavy load on a particular disk might suggest splitting the most used files on that disk onto two separate disks, so that they might be accessed in parallel, for example. Or heavy use of the CPU by a particular user during peak hours might suggest lowering the priorities for that user at those times.

SYSTEM GENERATION One of the most important system administration tasks to be performed is the creation of an operating system tailored to the specific needs of a particular installation. The process of building a system is called a **system generation,** or more familiarly, a **sysgen.** The result of a sysgen matches the operating system to the characteristics and features of the hardware provided and includes the desired operating system features and performance choices. Two primary means are used to tailor the system:

- By selecting the operating system program modules to be installed. Typically, an operating system provides a large number of modules that might be used under different circumstances. Only those modules that are relevant to the installation are selected. As an example, a particular installation has an individualized selection of I/O devices. Only those device drivers that are required for the installed I/O devices would be included in the tailored system.

- By assigning values to parameters of the system. Parameters are used to provide the details of an installation. On a Windows-based PC system, for example, devices are assigned to specific, numbered interrupt channels known as IRQs; memory locations for each device interrupt driver are also specified. Another example of a parameter would be the number of concurrent users permitted on a multiuser system. On some systems, a parameter might be used to determine whether a module is memory resident or is loaded on demand. Most large systems also provide parameters that tailor the system scheduling mechanism and adjust the behavior of other resource control modules. These and other parameters must be determined by the system administrator to meet the needs of the installation.

Some systems provide a lot of flexibility, with many options. Other systems may provide only a minimal amount of selection, perhaps no more than a selection of I/O device drivers.

The method used to perform a sysgen depends on the operating system. Some systems provide the operating system modules in source code form. Modules and parameters are selected, and the operating system is assembled or compiled and linked to form the loadable binary operating system. A barebones operating system with the appropriate compilation tools may be provided to enable the sysgen procedure to take place on the target system, or the procedure may be executed on a different machine. Other operating

FIGURE 13.7

A Typical System Status Report

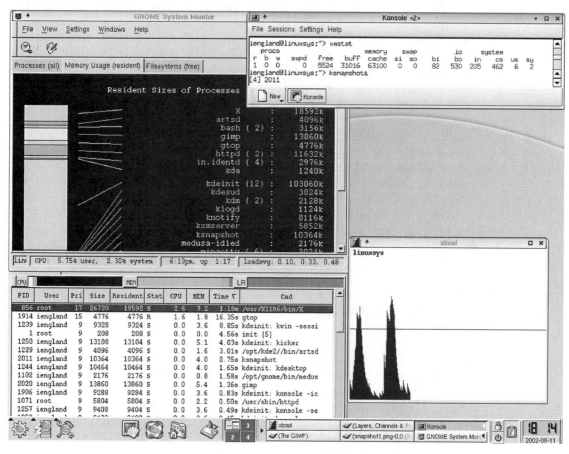

systems use an installation program to determine which modules should be included in the operating system, and parameters are selected during the installation procedure. On these systems, the various modules are already provided in binary form and need only be linked during the sysgen procedure.

On many systems, the sysgen procedure is provided as a series of menu selections and parameter entry forms that guide the operator through the procedure. On some systems, the procedure is entered as a script or batch file. Most systems also allow some degree of dynamic configuration, which makes it possible to build changes into the system without rebuilding the entire system. We noted earlier that Linux configuration script files are used for this purpose.

13.6 ORGANIZATION

There is no standard model for the organization of an operating system. Some systems were developed in a deliberate and carefully planned manner, while others grew topsy-turvy over a long period of time, adding new functions and services as they were required.

Thus, the programs that make up an operating system may be relatively independent of each other, with little central organization, or they may form a formal structure.

Overall, the organization of most operating systems can be described generally by one of three configuration models. These are commonly referred to in the literature as the **monolithic** configuration, the **layered** or **hierarchical** configuration, and the **microkernel** configuration. Within a configuration, individual programs can be categorized in different ways. As we noted earlier, operating system programs can be memory resident or nonresident, depending on their function. Of the resident programs, some will operate in a protected mode, often called **kernel** mode, others in a conventional user mode.

As an example of a monolithic configuration, UNIX is commonly described by the model shown in Figure 13.8. In this model, the various memory resident operating system functions are represented by a monolithic kernel. There is no specific organization. The operating system programs simply interact as required to perform their functions. The critical functions within the kernel operate in protected mode, the remainder, in user mode. The shell is separate from the kernel and serves as an interface between the users, utilities, and user programs with the kernel. Thus, the shell can be replaced without affecting kernel operations. UNIX organization is considered in more detail in Chapter 18.

The major difficulty with a monolithic configuration is the stability and integrity of the system as a whole. Any defect in a program within the kernel can crash the entire system, as can unexpected interactions between different programs in the kernel. Thus, the addition of a new device driver, for example, could compromise the entire system. Nonetheless, with proper design and control, it is possible to build a secure and stable system, as evidenced by Linux.

An alternative operating system organization is built around a *hierarchical* structure. A simple representation of a hierarchical operating system organization is shown in Figure 13.9. This representation, sometimes known as a target model, shows the operating system divided into layers. The outermost layers are the ones that are visible to the user; the inner layers form the internal grouping. Thus, the user and the user's programs form the outermost layer. If the operating system has a monitor program, it is located at the very center.

In this model, each layer is relatively independent of the other layers. Thus, the file management layer determines the location of a file identified by logical name and interprets the nature of the request, but does not attempt to access the hardware directly. Instead, it makes a request to the I/O device driver level.

The hierarchy is arranged so that access to the various layers of the operating system is from the outside in. Each layer calls the next innermost layer to request the services that it needs. The monitor or supervisor would be the ultimate arbiter in cases where conflicting interests exist between different processes; therefore, it is the final piece to be addressed. Most computer systems today provide appropriate hardware instructions that allow the operating system design to enforce this procedure. This provides security, as well as a clean interface between the different functions within the operating system.

Layered operating systems must be designed carefully, because the hierarchy requires that services be layered in such a way that all requests move inward. A program at a particular layer must never require services from a higher layer because this could compromise system integrity.

FIGURE 13.8

A Simplified Representation of UNIX

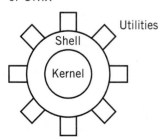

Another disadvantage of the layered approach is the time required to pass the request through intermediate layers to receive services from the innermost layers. In contrast, a program in a monolithic operating system could request the service directly from the program that supplies the service, resulting in much faster operation. The obvious advantage of the layered approach is the stability and integrity that result from a well-structured modular design.

A recent innovation in operating system design is the microkernel. An illustration of a microkernel configuration is shown in Figure 13.10. The microkernel configuration model is based on a small protected kernel that provides the minimum essential functionality. The definition of "minimum essential functionality" differs from system to system. The Mach operating system kernel includes message passing, interrupt processing, virtual memory management, scheduling, and a basic set of I/O device drivers. It is possible to build a microkernel with nothing but message passing, interrupt processing, and minimal memory management, although the practical advantage of doing so has not been shown.

The microkernel configuration constitutes a client-server system, where clients and servers reside on the same system. Operating system services outside the essential functionality are performed by programs in user mode. Each program acts as a server that performs specific operating system tasks upon request of application programs as well as other operating system programs, the clients in this model. Clients request services by sending messages directly to

FIGURE 13.9

Target Model of an OS

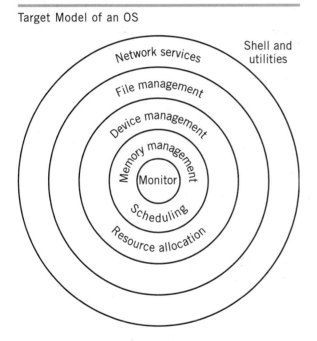

FIGURE 13.10

Microkernel Architecture

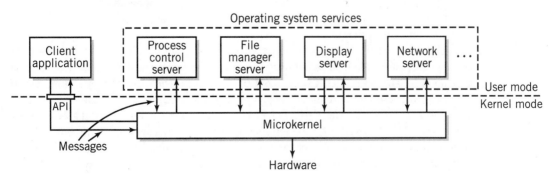

the microkernel. The microkernel passes the messages to the appropriate server, which performs the required function, and replies to the request by sending a message back to the client. The reply is also passed through the microkernel. System security and integrity is maintained, because all communication must pass through the microkernel.

One of the advantages of the microkernel configuration is that it is possible to create different operating system designs simply by changing the service programs that reside outside the microkernel, while maintaining the security and stability of the microkernel. For example, Macintosh OS X is one of many operating systems built on the Mach microkernel. The microkernel approach offers reliability, flexibility, extensibility, and portability. It is particularly amenable to object-oriented design. New features can be added easily without compromising the system. The extensive message-passing required in a microkernel configuration can result in a performance penalty over other types of designs, but practical applications of the model have shown that, with care, the potential disadvantage of this approach can be minimized.

13.7 TYPES OF COMPUTER SYSTEMS

Modern computer system hardware is essentially similar regardless of the type of system. Therefore, the differences among computer systems are set primarily by the operating system software. The operating system software is selected to meet desired requirements and goals.

There are many different types of operating systems, each designed to meet a particular need. Some of the factors that influence operating system design/architecture are the primary type of user base, whether the system is intended for a single user or multiuser, whether the system will be single tasking or multitasking, and whether the system is to be used for a specific purpose.

For example, one computer might be designed for business end users, another for programmers and engineers, and other high-technology specialists. The Macintosh, for example, is well designed for the inexperienced user (and for other users too, of course!) Windows is adequate for a user with simple needs; a more sophisticated user might choose a system with Linux instead. The PC is adequate for many single users, but a large mainframe type system might be more appropriate for a large multiuser base, or perhaps a network-based system is more appropriate. Special-purpose applications that require specialized designs might include embedded control applications (such as automotive and microwave oven applications), CAD/CAM graphics, multimedia (the Pixar computer is a special system designed specifically for motion picture animation and special effects), and real-time control applications. Each of these systems has different needs and requirements that are met by the operating system design.

There are, of course, costs associated with increasing sophistication in the software. As more features are added, more memory is required for the operating system. The original version of MS-DOS ran successfully in 64KB of memory. The IBM MVS operating system for the IBM S/370 family required more than 6MB of memory even before any applications were considered. The designers have recommended a minimum of 128MB for Windows 2000. The overhead time required for the operating system to perform its functions becomes a sizable fraction of the overall time. One hopes that the overhead is worthwhile in terms of increased efficiency and ease of use.

Within the context of the previous discussion, we can loosely categorize computer systems into six types: single-user systems and workstations; multiuser systems; network server systems; real-time systems; embedded control systems; and distributed systems.

- The simplest systems in current use are single-user, multitasking systems. Single-user, multitasking systems allow the user to run several processes at the same time. Obviously, this has the advantage that the user does not have to wait for one task to be completed, but can work on other tasks, leading to higher overall productivity. Window interfaces allow output presentations from several tasks to appear on the screen simultaneously, and provide methods for easy task switching. Note, however, that a windows environment is not a requirement for multitasking. Multiuser systems are by their very nature multitasking, yet many multiuser systems do not normally provide a graphical user interface. Even some single-user systems allow an individual user to multitask from a command line interface. UNIX, in particular, allows users to specify that processes are to execute in the "background." Background processes can present output to the screen, but only the foreground process can accept input from the keyboard. The operating system provides commands that allow the user to select which process is in the foreground at any particular time. Workstations generally provide single-user multitasking operating systems, although most workstations have the capability to be configured for multiuser operation.

- Multiuser systems provide additional facilities that allow multiple users to share the power of the computer. Large mainframe systems are capable of supporting hundreds of users concurrently. Multiuser systems require additional operating system support for multiple I/O terminals, user login files and procedures, passwords, and security. Historically, most early multiuser systems were used primarily for transaction processing, for large order entry and billing systems and the like, but gradually other types of users also took advantage of access to a large computer system. Multiuser systems are still important, although they are gradually being supplanted by networks of smaller computers, often with a large network server as a central supply facility.

- Network servers are similar to multiuser systems in many respects. However, the major burden of program execution has been shifted from the multiuser system to individual clients connected to the server through a network. The server may have no direct user facilities of its own, other than those required for management of the system. The server provides file services, print services, and database services to the clients. It may also provide some program execution services for clients, including support for client system startup, particularly on networks with thin clients. Large network servers often double as multiuser systems, and it is difficult to classify the system as one or the other. For example, large IBM mainframe systems provide network services, but additionally perform such diverse activities as data warehousing, financial processing, and much of the transaction processing required of a large organization. This versatility requires an operating system of great complexity and sophistication.

- **Real-time systems** are systems in which one or more processes must be able to access the CPU immediately when required. Real-time systems are used for applications in which one or more programs are measuring or controlling I/O devices that must respond within specific time restraints. A real-time system might be used to control instrumentation, such as the control rockets on a space flight, or to measure time-sensitive data, such as the periodic measurements of the temperature in a nuclear reactor. Although some real-time systems are created special for the particular application, most are general-purpose multitasking systems that have been designed so that they can be used for other tasks except when the time-sensitive application is being executed. A real-time system could be viewed as a multitasking system in which the interrupts that cause execution of the real-time program or programs have very high priority, but in many cases, special effort is made to assure that the real-time program can operate within its required time restraints.

■ **Embedded control systems** are specialized systems designed to control a single piece of equipment, such as an automobile or microwave oven. The software for embedded control systems is usually provided in ROM. Nonetheless, many functions of the operating system may still be found in these systems. The computer that controls an automobile, for example, requires most of the features of a multitasking system. There are many measurement sensors representing CPU input on a car and many different control functions to manage. The service technician must be able to connect an I/O terminal to the system for car analysis. Effectively, an embedded control system is a real-time system that is dedicated to the particular application.

■ Finally, **distributed systems** are rapidly growing on prominence and importance. In a distributed system, processing power is distributed among the computers in a cluster or network. Even the Internet can be used as a distributed system. Programs, files, and databases may be also be dispersed. Programs may be divided into functional pieces, with execution distributed throughout the network. Alternatively, program components may be stored on different systems, and executed in place upon remote request. .NET and CORBA, discussed briefly in Chapter 15, are two emerging standards designed to expedite this process. Regardless of which method is used, the operating system or systems require additional complexity to handle the distribution of tasks or instructions within a process, the sharing of memory and I/O, and the intercommunication of data and control that are required of these systems. Many modern computing systems include additional operating system modules to make distributed processing feasible and practical. **Distributed Computing Environment, or DCE,** is an OpenGroup standard that establishes a set of features for a distributed computing operating system. (OpenGroup is an organization that promotes open computing by setting standards and certifying products in a number of major areas of computing. UNIX is arguably the best known OpenGroup standard.) The DCE standard is supported and incorporated into the operating systems of a number of major vendors, including Hewlett-Packard, Sun, and IBM.

There are, of course, other ways of categorizing computer systems. One way of describing systems that is sometimes useful is to consider the intent and philosophy of the designers of the system. This description can sometimes provide a lot of insight into the strengths and weaknesses of a system.

For example, the IBM mainframe operating system, z/OS, is an offshoot of an operating system that was originally designed primarily for large, batch-oriented business transaction processing systems. As business users moved their operations online, predecessors of z/OS were provided with capabilities to handle large numbers of online transactions. This would suggest that the modern z/OS is well equipped to handle routine transactions from hundreds of terminals concurrently. At the same time, it might suggest that z/OS is not particularly user friendly to individuals doing their own independent work on the system. Development tools are more difficult to use on z/OS than on many other systems. Most people would agree that these statements describe z/OS fairly well.

As a different example, the Apple Macintosh system was designed to make tasks as easy as possible for the average, minimally trained computer end user. As a result, much of the design effort for the Macintosh system went into the user interface. The operating system provides powerful interface and graphical resources to the user and to the user's programs. Other operating system facilities, such as time sharing and memory management, became secondary to the stated purpose and are implemented in simple fashion, much less powerful than many other systems.

As a third example, the Digital (now Hewlett Packard) OpenVMS operating system was designed as a powerful multiuser system. The expectation of the designers was that the system would be used primarily by technically experienced personnel. Thus, it requires a good deal of training and sophistication to use the VMS command line interface and command language effectively, but it is extremely powerful. In keeping with the technical thrust of HP as a company, the internals of the operating system are very advanced and interesting technically.

Finally, consider an operating system whose primary design goal is to be capable of open system operation. The primary features that define an open system are

- The system should be capable of operating on many different hardware platforms.

- Communication between systems should be simple and straightforward. Commands that access remote systems should perform nearly identically to those performing local operations and should appear as transparent as possible to the user or the user's programs. Thus, a COPY command that copies files between systems should operate essentially the same as one copying files between different points on a single system.

- Shell programs should behave identically, regardless of platform. Source-level application programs should operate identically, once compiled on the new platform.

These features dictate an operating system with considerable thought given to networking, as well as to a system with minimum dependency on the particular hardware being used. This suggests an operating system with a small kernel, with powerful networking facilities built in, and with the hardware-specific part of the system concentrated into a single part of the kernel, isolating all other parts of the system from the platform. Linux is an example of such a system.

There are many recent attempts to build operating systems whose activities are truly distributed across a network. Some of the best known of these are Mach, Amoeba, Locus, and Chorus.

13.8 STARTING THE COMPUTER SYSTEM: THE BOOTSTRAP

To complete our overview of the operating system, we need to consider the steps required to get the computer started. You will recall that when the computer is first turned on, the contents of RAM are unknown. Furthermore, you know that there must be a program in memory for CPU execution to take place. These two considerations are contradictory; therefore, special means must be included to get the system into an operating state.

Initial program loading and start-up is performed by using a *bootstrap* program that is built permanently into a read-only part of memory for the computer. This bootstrap program begins execution as soon as the machine is powered up. The bootstrap program contains a program loader that automatically loads a selected program from secondary storage into normal memory and transfers control to it. The process is known as bootstrapping, or more simply, as *booting* the computer. IBM calls the process *Initial Program Load*, or *IPL*. Figure 13.11 illustrates the bootstrapping operation.

Since the bootstrap is a read-only program, the program that it loads must be predetermined and must be found in a known secondary storage location, usually at a particular

FIGURE 13.11

Bootstrapping a Computer

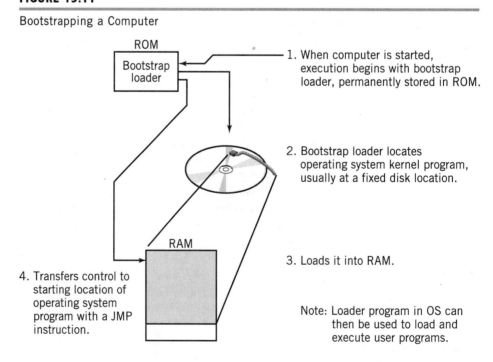

1. When computer is started, execution begins with bootstrap loader, permanently stored in ROM.

2. Bootstrap loader locates operating system kernel program, usually at a fixed disk location.

3. Loads it into RAM.

4. Transfers control to starting location of operating system program with a JMP instruction.

Note: Loader program in OS can then be used to load and execute user programs.

track and sector on a hard disk, although the bootstrap can be tailored to start the computer from another device, or even from another computer if the system is connected to a network. Usually the bootstrap loads a program that is itself capable of loading programs. (This is the reason that the initial program loader is called a bootstrap.) Ultimately, the program loaded contains the operating system kernel. In other words, when the boot procedure is complete, the kernel is loaded, and the computer is ready for normal operation. The resident operating system services are present and ready to go. Commands can be accepted, and other programs loaded and executed. The bootstrap operation is usually performed in two or more stages of loading to increase flexibility in the location of the kernel and to keep the initial bootstrap program small.

EXAMPLE

The PC serves as an appropriate and familiar example of the bootstrap start-up procedure. Although the PC uses a multistep start-up procedure, the method is essentially identical to that we have just described.

The PC bootstrap loader is permanently located in the system BIOS introduced earlier in the chapter. When the power switch for the computer is turned on, or when the reset button is pushed, control is transferred to the first address of the bootstrap loader program. The PC bootstrap begins by performing a thorough test of the components of the computer. The test verifies that various components of the system are active and working. It checks for the presence of a monitor, of a hard drive if installed, and of a keyboard. It checks the instructions in ROM for errors by calculating an algebraic function of the 1's and 0's, known as a checksum, and comparing that value with a predetermined correct value. It checks RAM by loading known data into every location and reading it back. Finally, it resets the segment registers, the instruction pointer, flags, and various address lines. (The 386, 486, P5, and P6 CPUs set many other registers as well.) The results of these tests appear on the monitor screen.

At the completion of this test, the bootstrap loader determines which disk is the system disk. This location is a setting stored permanently in a special memory, modifiable by the user at startup time. On modern PCs, the system may be booted from a hard disk, a floppy disk, or a CD-ROM. The system disk contains a sector known as a boot record, and the boot record is loaded next.

The boot record now takes control. It also contains a loader, which is tailored to the I/O requirements for the particular disk. Assuming that Windows 2000 is to be loaded, the boot record then loads a sequence of files, including the kernel and executive program, NTOSKRNL.EXE, the registry, the hardware interface, various kernel, subsystem, and API libraries, and a number of other components. The items loaded are based on entries in the registry. The user has little control over this process while it is happening. Next, a logon program, WINLOGON.EXE is initiated. Assuming that the user is authorized and that the logon is successful, the kernel sets the user parameters defined in the registry, the Windows GUI is displayed, and control of the system is turned over to the user.

Different BIOSes vary slightly in their testing procedures, and some allow the user to change some PC setup settings when testing takes place. The user can also force the bootstrap to occur one step at a time to remedy serious system problems. Other than that, the user or system administrator controls the PC environment with standard tools provided by the operating system.

As noted, the procedure described here takes place when power is first applied to the computer. This procedure is also known as a cold boot. The PC also provides an alternate procedure known as a warm boot, for use when the system must be restarted for some reason. The warm boot, which is initiated from a selection on the *Shutdown* menu, causes an interrupt call that reloads the operating system, but it does not retest the system and it does not reset the various registers to their initial values.

EXAMPLE

It is important to realize that basic computer procedures are not dependent on the size of the computer. The boot procedure for a large IBM mainframe computer is quite similar to that of a PC. IBM mainframe computers are bootstrapped using the Initial Program Load procedure. IPL works very similarly to the PC bootstrap procedure. Whenever power is applied to an IBM mainframe computer, the computer is in one of four operating states: operating, stopped, load, and check stop. The operating and stopped states are already familiar to you. The check-stop state is a special state used for diagnosing hardware errors. The load state is the state corresponding to IPL.

The system operator causes the system to enter load state by setting load-unit-address controls and activating the load-clear or load-normal key on the operator's console. The load-unit-address controls establish a particular channel and I/O device that will be used for the IPL. The load normal key performs an initial CPU reset that sets the various registers in the CPU to their initial values and validates proper operation. The load-clear key does the same, but also performs a clear reset, which sets the contents of main storage and many registers to zero.

Following the reset operation, IPL performs the equivalent of a START I/O channel command, as discussed in Chapter 9. The first channel command word is not read from memory, since memory may have been reset to zero. Instead, a built-in READ command is used, which reads the IPL channel program into memory for execution. The IPL channel program then reads in the appropriate operating system code and transfers control to it.

13.9 A BIT OF HISTORY

Given how easy it is to communicate with computers today, it is hard to picture a time when the user had to do everything by hand, one step at a time. We take it for granted that we can type commands at a keyboard or move a mouse and launch programs, copy files, send text to a printer, and perform myriad other computer tasks. We power up and bootstrap our systems by pressing a switch.

It was not always this way. Early computers had no operating systems. The user, who was also the programmer, entered a program by setting it, one word at a time, with switches on the front panel, one switch per bit, or by plugging wires into a patch panel that resembled a cribbage board. Not a pleasant operation! Needless to say, early computers were single-user systems. Much of the computer's time was tied up with this primitive form of program and data entry. In fact, as late as the mid-1970s, there were still vendors producing computer systems with no operating system and computer hardware that was still bootstrapped by entering the bootstrap program one instruction at a time into switches on the front panel of the computer.

The early computers were used primarily by scientists and engineers to solve techni-cal problems. The next generation of computers, in the late 1950s, provided a punched card reader for input and a printer for output. Soon after, magnetic tape systems became available. The first "high-level" languages, primarily assembly language, then FORTRAN, made it possible to write programs in a language other than binary, and offline card punch machines allowed programmers to prepare their programs for entry without tying up the machine. Algol, COBOL, and Lisp followed shortly after. New technology improved the reliability of the computers. All these advances combined to make the computer system practical for business commercial use, especially for large businesses.

Still, these computers were single-user batch systems. Initially, users **submitted** the cards that they had prepared to the computer for execution. Later, separate, offline systems were developed that allowed the cards to be grouped together onto a magnetic tape for processing together. Programs were then submitted to the computer room in the form of *jobs*. A job consisted of one or more program card **decks,** together with the required **data decks** for each program. An output tape could also be used to support printing offline. As an example, Figure 13.12 shows a job that compiles and executes a FORTRAN program.

I/O routines were needed to operate the card readers, tape drives, and printers. The earliest operating systems consisted of just these I/O routines, but gradually operating sys-tems evolved to perform other services. Computer time was very expensive, hundreds of dollars per minute, and in growing demand. To increase availability, control of the com-puter was placed in the hands of an operator, who fed the punched cards, mounted tapes, and generally tried to keep the system busy and efficient. The operating system provided a monitor that fed jobs to the system and supported the operator by notifying him or her of necessary actions, such as loading a new tape, setting switches on the panel, removing

FIGURE 13.12

Job Card Deck Used to Compile and Execute a FORTRAN Program

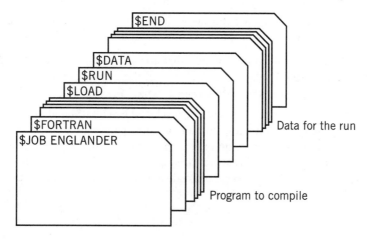

printout, and so on. As system demand increased, the monitor expanded to include accounting and simple, priority-based scheduling of jobs.

It is generally accepted that the first operating system was built by General Motors Research Laboratories in 1953–1954 for their IBM 701 computer. Other early systems included the FORTRAN Monitor System (FMS), IBSYS, and Share Operating System (SOS).[4]

Many important breakthroughs in operating system design occurred in the early 1960s. These breakthroughs laid the groundwork for the operating system as we know it today.

- In 1963, Burroughs released its Master Control Program (MCP). MCP contained many of the features of modern systems, including high-level language facilities and support for multiprocessing (with two identical CPUs). Most important, MCP supported virtual storage, as well as powerful multitasking capabilities.

- IBM introduced OS/360 as the operating system for its new System/360 in 1964. OS/360 provided a powerful language to expedite batch processing, JCL, or Job Control Language, and a simple form of multiprogramming that made it possible to load several jobs into memory, so that other jobs could use the CPU when one job was busy with I/O. By this time, disks were also becoming available, and the system was capable of reading cards onto disk while the CPU executed its jobs; thus, when a job completed, the OS could load another job from disk into memory, ready to run. This improved the OS scheduling capability. JCL is still used for batch processing! The enormous success of the IBM S/360 and its successors firmly established the basis of an operating system as a fundamental part of the computer.

- In 1962, a group at MIT known as Project MAC introduced the concept of time sharing with an experimental operating system called CTSS. Project MAC was one of the seminal centers for the development of computer science. Shortly thereafter, MIT, Bell Labs, and GE formed a partnership to develop a major time-sharing system. The system was called MULTICS (Multiplexed Information and Computing Service), and although MULTICS never fully realized its dream of becoming a major computer utility, many of the most important multitasking concepts and algorithms were developed by the MULTICS team. It was supplied for many years as the operating system for Honeywell computer systems.

There were, of course, many other important developments in operating system design during the 1960s and 1970s. Three of these stand out as highlights, particularly in the context of modern operating system usage:

- The THE operating system, developed by Dijkstra and others, introduced the use of a hierarchical structure for the operating system and also demonstrated the advantages of modular programming design in the implementation of large programs, such as operating systems. (The early OS/360 operating systems were famous for their spaghetti code and also for their bugginess!)

---

[4] Share was a consortium of system programmers who used IBM systems and who met to discuss problems and develop solutions. SOS was produced by a team of consortium members.

- When Bell Labs withdrew from the MULTICS project, Ken Thompson, a MULTICS researcher, turned to the development of a small personal operating system, which he called Unics, later UNIX, to contrast it from MULTICS. He was later joined by Dennis Ritchie. The original UNIX development was performed on a Digital PDP-7 minicomputer and later moved to a PDP-11 minicomputer, the forerunner of the VAX computer. Originally, the system was written in assembly language, but Ritchie developed a new high-level language, which he called C, and the operating system was largely rewritten in C.

- UNIX introduced many important OS concepts, including the hierarchical file system, the shell concept, redirection, piping, and the use of simple commands that can be combined to perform powerful operations. Thompson and Ritchie included facilities for document production and formatting, including such novelties as a spell checker and a grammar checker. They created many inventive algorithms to improve operating system performance, developed techniques for interprocess communication, and even provided for networked and distributed processing. Many facets of operating systems that are taken for granted today were originated in UNIX development.

- UNIX earned a reputation for power and flexibility. Because it was written in C, it was also easy to **port** it, that is, convert it for use, to other computers. As a result of these factors, UNIX became an important operating system for universities and was ultimately adopted, in many versions, by the commercial marketplace as well. UNIX continues to be of great importance, particularly due to its flexibility in the area of networks and distributed systems.

- Another important innovation, some would say the most important development in making the computer accessible to nontechnical users, was the development of the concept of graphical user interfaces. Most historians would credit the invention of the windows and mouse interface to Doug Englebart. This work was done, amazingly enough, in the 1960s, at Stanford Research Institute. A practical windowing system was built in the 1970s by Alan Kay and others at Xerox PARC (Palo Alto Research Center), as part of a visionary computer concept known as the Dynabook project. The original intention of Dynabook was to develop a book-sized personal computer with a high-resolution color display and wireless communication that would provide computer capabilities (particularly secretarial), games, e-mail, and a reference library. Although the technology of the time was not sufficient to bring the Dynabook as an entirety to fruition, the engineers at Xerox in the late 1970s built a personal computer workstation with a graphical user interface known as Star. It is believed that a visit to Xerox PARC by Steve Jobs, the founder of Apple, in 1979, inspired the development of the Apple Lisa and, subsequently, the Apple Macintosh.

The next important breakthrough in computer use occurred in 1982, with the introduction of the IBM personal computer. The IBM PC was designed as a stand-alone, single-user computer for the mass market. The IBM PC was supplied with a reasonably easy-to-use operating system, PC-DOS, which was developed, and also later marketed, by Microsoft as MS-DOS. PC-DOS was actually derived from an earlier personal computer operating system, CP/M (Control Program for Microcomputers), but is important because of the tremendous success of the IBM PC and its derivatives. Gradually, PC-DOS and MS-DOS became the prevalent operating system of the era. With later versions, Microsoft made many improvements, including hierarchical directory file storage, file redirection, better memory management, and an improved and expanded command set. Many of these improvements were derived from UNIX innovations.

Although there have been other, more innovative recent designs—the Macintosh OS, NextStep, and AmigaDos come rapidly to mind—MS-DOS is of importance because the PC established the mass use of computers, and because it has become the springboard for many, many changes in operating system thinking and improvements in operating system design.

Even with all these earlier innovations, there continue to be tremendous advances in operating system software. Today's systems, such as Windows XP, Linux, and Macintosh OS X, combine much more power on one hand with improved user friendliness and ease of use on the other. There are several reasons for this:

- There has been a great increase in computer speed and power. More powerful integrated circuits have allowed the design of faster computers using faster clocks and larger internal data paths, together with techniques for speeding up instruction execution. Even small personal computers can support tens of megabytes of memory and many gigabytes of disk storage. A modern PC may contain as much as one thousand times the memory and execute instructions one thousand times as fast as the 1965 IBM S/360 mainframe computer. Thus, more capability can be built into the operating system without sacrificing performance.

- There have been fundamental improvements in computer hardware design. Many modern computers are designed as an integrated unit, hardware and operating system software together. Most computer hardware contains special features intended to support a powerful operating system. Such features as special graphics, cache memory, vector processing, and virtual storage memory management hardware are intended primarily for use by the operating system. These features used to be available only on large mainframes. A protected mode of hardware instructions, accessible only to the operating system, provides security and protection to the operating system and allows the operating system to protect the system's resources and users.

- There have been fundamental improvements in operating system software design. Operating system programs have grown in size and complexity. Increased memory capacity has made a larger operating system feasible. Increased speed has made it practical. Gradually, innovative operating system techniques from large computers have drifted down to the PC level. In addition, program design itself has helped the process. New languages, well designed for system programming, and better programming methods such as object-oriented programming have also contributed to the process.

- There has been a shift in focus to creating operating systems that better serve the end user. This has resulted in much current research on human-computer interfaces, and on the ways in which humans work and use the computer. New work paradigms, based on object-oriented programming and communication technologies, and new interfaces continue to extend the role of the operating system. There is a new willingness to include features that were not a part of earlier operating systems and to modularize the operating system in different ways to improve the delivery of services to the user and to the user's application programs.

■ Networking has provided the opportunity for innovative research and development in distributed computing, including client-server technology, shared processing, and grid computing. There is a continuing progression of new operating system techniques, developed in response to the changing requirements of modern distributed systems.

■ The rapid growth of the Internet, and of e-mail use, the Web, and multimedia in particular, has created opportunities and the need for better methods of accessing, retrieving, and sharing information between different systems. The results have impacted network design, user interface design, distributed processing technology, and open system standardization with corresponding effects in operating system design.

The notable developments in operating system technology in the 1980s and 1990s would certainly include:

■ The evolution of MS-DOS into Windows 2000 and Windows XP, GUI-based operating systems capable of supporting a wide range of users and applications, from the individual working at a PC to a networked enterprise system capable of managing every aspect of a large organization. This capability was formerly limited to large, mainframe-based multiuser systems.

■ The development of the microkernel operating system client-server configuration model, which took place at a number of different universities during the 1980s, and the use of these microkernels, particularly Mach, as the basis for the development of new operating systems of unparalleled power, stability, and simplicity.

■ The development of the Distributed Computing Environment, plus object-based extensions that make distributed processing practical.

■ Creation of the JAVA Virtual Machine and other aspects of the JAVA language and environment as a means to share and execute objects in a way that is truly machine independent and network transparent.

■ There have been many other less obvious developments in operating system technology, both subtle and sophisticated, that have impacted computer system design and operation.

SUMMARY AND REVIEW

Chapter 13 presents a comprehensive overview of the operating system. The operating system software is a collection of programs that extend the power of the computer hardware by providing a user interface to the computer, plus control and support for the computer's resources, plus other facilities that make it easier to manage and control the computer system. Many operating systems also make possible the sharing of computer resources concurrently among multiple users and among multiple tasks for each user.

The operating system provides one or more user interfaces, file support, control for I/O devices, and management of the computer resources, including memory, the various

I/O devices, and the scheduling of time. The operating system is event driven. It performs these tasks in response to user commands, program service requests, and interrupts. We noted that although the operating system represents overhead, under most conditions, the overall computer system performance is improved and enhanced by the presence of the operating system. Some operations, particularly concurrency, would be difficult or impossible without the OS.

In our discussion of the various operations performed by an operating system, we first discussed the operations present in a single-tasking, single-user system. These concentrate mostly on support for the execution of programs, a file system, and I/O device driver programs. When multitasking is added, it becomes additionally necessary to provide other resource managers: memory management, I/O management, and scheduling, as well as additional functions and services such as security and system administration. The chapter identifies ten of the major services and facilities provided within an operating system and describes each.

The programs that provide these services must be organized in some way. There is a considerable amount of interaction between the different program modules that make up an operating system. Many operating systems use a hierarchical model to organize the various modules. This model has the advantage of a significant amount of protection, since it is easy to control access and the flow of information between modules using a hierarchy. Other models in use include the monolithic model and the microkernel model.

One interesting aspect of the computer system is the start-up process, and we presented a description and two examples of the bootstrapping process.

The chapter concludes with a discussion of some of the historical milestones in operating systems.

KEY CONCEPTS AND TERMS

application programming
   interface (API)
basic input/output system
   (BIOS)
BAT file
batch processing
bootstrapping
command interpreter
command line interface
   (CLI)
concurrent processing
configuration
context
context switching
control statements
conversational systems
CPU bound
data decks
diskless workstation

dispatching
Distributed Computing
   Environment (DCE)
distributed system
embedded control system
event driven
file management system
graphical user interface
   (GUI)
hierarchical configuration
high-level scheduling
Initial Program Load (IPL)
interprocess message servicing
I/O bound
I/O services
job
Job Control Language
   (JCL)

job submission
kernel
layered configuration
microkernel configuration
memory map
monitor
monolithic configuration
multiprogramming
multitasking
multiuser system
nonpreemptive dispatch
nonresident commands
operating system (OS)
plug-and-play
port
preemptive dispatch
process
program deck
real-time system

relocation
resident commands
scheduling
service request
shell
single-job processing

supervisor
system administrator
   (sysadmin)
system generation (sysgen)
system languages
thin client

threads
time-slicing
virtual private network
   (VPN)
Windows Scripting Host

FOR FURTHER READING

There are a number of excellent textbooks that describe operating systems in detail. The author recommends books by Silberschatz and others [SILB01], Deitel [DEIT90], Tanenbaum [TAN92], Davis [DAV02], Flynn and McHoes [FLYN00], and Stallings [STAL00]. There are many others. Davis, in particular, presents a very practical, hands-on view of operating systems, with many examples. Flynn and McHoes is also quite practical and readable. The others tend to be deeper and more theoretical. For particular topics in operating systems, see the references at the back of this textbook and references in any of the other books. There are also many trade books that discuss particular topics in operating systems and specific operating systems. Henle and Kuvshinoff [HENL92] provides a satisfying low-level introduction to desktop computer operating systems.

EXERCISES

13.1   What are the specific limitations of a computer system that provides no operating system? What must be done to load and execute programs?

13.2   For each of the most popular commands in MS-DOS/Windows (or UNIX if you prefer), identify the type of operating system service that is being provided, and identify the basic module or modules that are involved. Which commands would you assume are memory resident and which loaded as required? Explain your assumptions.

13.3   Describe each of the functions that are provided by MS-DOS. Why does MS-DOS not provide scheduling and memory management functions?

13.4   What are the limitations of providing a BIOS in ROM?

13.5   The standard MS-DOS shell is called COMMAND.COM. What are the advantages and disadvantages of selecting a different command shell as a replacement for COMMAND.COM?

13.6   Describe the two methods that are used to provide concurrent operation of multiple processes. What are the advantages of each method? What is the advantage of providing concurrent operation?

13.7   An operating system is described as an event-driven program. What is meant by event driven? Explain how the dispatching operation fits this description.

13.8   What is the difference between the logical description of a file and the physical description?

13.9   Nearly every operating system separates the file system from the I/O services. What is the advantage in doing so?

13.10   Discuss the similarities and differences between memory management fragmentation and disk fragmentation.

13.11   Windows 3.1 did not support true preemptive multitasking. Instead, the designers of Windows 3.1 provided something they called "cooperative multitasking," in which each program is expected to give up control of the CPU at reasonable time intervals, so that the Windows dispatcher can provide execution time to another waiting program. Describe the disadvantages of this method.

13.12   If you have access to the system administrator of a large system, find out the steps that are required to perform a sysgen on the system. Also determine the options that are available for that system.

13.13   A new idea in operating systems is to provide as small a kernel as possible and to make all other modules optional. What are the minimum services that must be provided in such a miniature kernel?

13.14   Write a Little Man bootstrap loader that will reside permanently in high memory for the Little Man Computer. The reset button will automatically cause the Little Man to start executing the first instruction of your bootstrap loader. Assume that the application program to be loaded will be input one instruction at a time through the input basket and will be loaded into consecutive locations of memory. The last instruction of the application program will be a 999. When your loader sees this slip of paper, it will cause the Little Man to start executing the program.

13.15   Explain the bootstrap procedure for a diskless workstation.

13.16   Based on the system status report shown in Figure 13.7, describe some of the ways in which the system could be tailored, and explain how the various items in the report would influence your tailoring decisions.

13.17   In the hierarchical model of an operating system, the network services layer is outside of the file management layer. If you realize that the shells and utilities can manipulate files on a variety of machines connected to the network, as well as to the local machine, you should also recognize that this arrangement is necessary and almost obvious. Explain why the network services layer is located where it is.

13.18   What are the conditions and restrictions that you would want to impose on a multitasking system that is being used with real-time processes?

13.19   What operating system functions would you expect to find in the computer that is built in to control your automobile, and which functions would be omitted? Justify your answer.

13.20   Clearly explain the differences between multiprogramming, multiuser, and multiprocessing.

13.21   **a.**   Of what use is the list of active processes shown in Figure 13.7? What changes might a system administrator make in the system on the basis of this information?

   b.   What does the average number of processes data tell you about the way that this system is normally used?

   c.   Compare the three graphs in the figure.

THE USER VIEW OF OPERATING SYSTEMS

14.0 INTRODUCTION

In Chapter 13, we introduced you to two different views of the role of the operating system as part of the overall computer architecture. Specifically, we looked at the operating system both as a means of delivering services to the user and as a way of controlling and operating the system facilities. In this chapter, we take a closer look at the operating system from the perspective of service to the user.

Much of the material in this chapter is at least superficially very familiar to you. You have worked closely with at least one computer system and quite possibly with more than one. You are familiar with some of the tasks, services, and capabilities that are provided for you by the system or systems that you have worked with. You are familiar with the different types of interfaces that you have used to perform those tasks and with the commands and the command structure that are built into the system for you.

In this chapter we are interested in two aspects of the operating system as it pertains to the user. First, we will consider the services that are provided to the user, and second, we will consider the medium for delivery of those services, namely, the type and appearance of the user interface that the system provides. You will see the standard tasks that a user interface is expected to perform, various ways in which those tasks can be implemented, and the advantages and disadvantages of different implementations. You will be able to observe that the services provided are relatively independent of the means used to access them.

As for the interface, we are more interested in the *concepts* of a user interface than in the specific commands, syntax, appearance, and usage of a particular interface. You will understand that different design approaches to the interface meet different goals and achieve different ends and are often aimed at different classes of users. You will see additional features that are frequently built into an operating system to make the system more "user friendly," or more powerful, or more efficient. Some of these represent additional services; many are simply ways to make access to the services easier, or more powerful, or more efficient. You will see that one interface may not be powerful enough for some tasks, while another interface requires too much effort to accomplish the common tasks that are required on a regular basis.

User services are a fundamental purpose for the existence of an operating system, and the user interface is essential to the access of those services. Nonetheless, some systems elect to view the user interface, and even many user services, as outside the realm of the operating system. Instead, these services and the user interface are treated as a shell that itself interfaces the operating system. There are strong arguments for this point of view. It makes possible different shells, each with their own services, capabilities, and work styles. If you don't like the shell that is provided, you simply exchange it for another. Operating systems based on UNIX are the strongest proponents of this view—UNIX-based operating systems are routinely supplied with several different shells offering different capabilities, and the user can change shells with a single command. The counterargument to this point of view is that building the user interface and services into the operating system provides standardization, consistency, and much improved integration of services. The Apple Macintosh systems take this approach.

This chapter takes a detailed look at the issues we've just raised. It explains and justifies the different types of user services that are provided with an operating system. It discusses and illustrates and shows the rationale for the various types of user interfaces, and it considers the trade-offs between them. It shows how user services are accomplished with each type of interface. Our primary goal in this chapter is to expand your ability to use your systems effectively and to understand the alternative methods available to you for using the operating system to achieve higher productivity. We hope that the chapter will also provide you with a better understanding of what happens internally within the system when you use your computer.

14.1 PURPOSE OF THE USER INTERFACE

The primary purpose of the user interface is to make the facilities of the computer system accessible to the user by providing the necessary services and commands and means of access to allow the user to get her work done conveniently and efficiently. We emphasize that it is not the intention of the user to interact with the operating system per se. Rather, the operating system exists to help the user to use the computer system productively. In modern operating systems, a secondary purpose has arisen that is almost as important: the operating system provides user interface services to application programs that assure that different programs have user interfaces that operate in the same way. This simplifies use of different applications on the system and reduces the user's learning curve for new programs. We identify programs that use the operating system to provide similar interfaces as having the same (**common**) **look and feel.**

Although the operating system can support a common look and feel across the applications on a particular type of system, there is an important trend toward the use of Web browsers to provide a common look and feel for applications across *all* types of systems. The concept of an **intranet** to provide information resources throughout an organization is an example of this trend, as is the capability of location-independent Web-based access to e-mail.

A well-designed interface can enhance the user's experience of the system and make use of the computer system a pleasure. This will allow the system to provide maximum benefit to its users. Conversely, a system with a poor user interface will be used reluctantly, and its potential value to its users will be diminished. Different classes of users are likely to define the concept of a good interface differently.

The operating system creates for the user the illusion of direct access to the computer hardware. With multiuser systems, this concept extends to include the illusion that the user controls the entire system, indeed, is the sole user on the system. This illusion is persuasive even to advanced users, and even when interuser communication, such as e-mail or online chat, is actually taking place. The author even has to remember consciously to shut off the interuser communication capability to prevent other users elsewhere on the system from making comments that interrupt his computer demonstrations during class periods!

The operating system provides a variety of services to the user and to the user's programs. The user interface provides access to these services using three different approaches. These are

- A command interface that accepts commands in some form directly from the user.
- A command language that accepts and executes organized groups of commands as a form of program. Most command languages include capabilities for branching and looping, prompted user input, and passed arguments. Command languages are also referred to as **scripting languages.**
- An interface that accepts and performs requests for operating system services directly from the user's programs (the API).

Most operating systems provide all three of these capabilities. Some scripting languages even support portability between different operating systems.

The user services provided by an operating system typically include

- Loading and execution of program files
- Retrieval, storage, and manipulation of files
- User I/O services, in the form of disk commands, printer spooling, and so on
- Security and data integrity protection
- Interuser communication and shared data and programs, on multiuser and networked systems
- Information about the status of the system and its files
- I/O and file services plus other specialized services for user programs

Many systems also provide utilities that can be used in place of programs to manipulate the data within files and programs. These utilities can be used to sort data and to retrieve data selectively from within files. Frequently, utilities can be combined into "programs" using the command programming language to perform powerful and useful tasks. Linux is particularly strong in this regard. The choice of user services provided is dependent on the original focus and goals of the operating system designers.

Finally, modern systems expand on the concept of I/O service to provide libraries of specialized service routines that can be used by programs to generate graphics, control a mouse, create and manipulate user **windows,** generate and control menus, and perform other sophisticated functions. These make it easy for application programmers to supply a common look-and-feel interface to their programs.

The difference in skills and interests among the various users on a system affects the design of an operating system user interface in two major areas:

- It affects the choice of services to be provided. For example, powerful programming services may not be needed by the typical user, but may be extremely useful to a system programmer. Conversely, tools that allow the end user easier access to the system may actually hinder the system programmer.
- It affects the design of the actual interface. The sophisticated user may be more comfortable with a more powerful, but difficult to use, interface. The typical user does not want to, and should not have to, learn a special and difficult operating system lingo just to use the computer.

The operating system must ultimately serve both groups of users, but a particular operating system may be tailored toward one or the other. An operating system that was designed with the goal of supporting engineers may be difficult for a graphic layout artist or secretary to use. Conversely, an engineer may not be able to work effectively on a system that the secretary finds ideal. An alternative is to provide two (or even more) different interfaces, intended for different user groups. If the command interface is implemented as a shell independent of the remainder of the operating system, this is easy to do. The normal user can work with an interface that provides a menu or windowing interface. The more technically sophisticated user can bypass the windowing shell and enter commands directly to a command interface.

14.2 USER FUNCTIONS AND PROGRAM SERVICES

In Section 14.1 we listed seven major groups of user functions and program services that are provided by most operating systems. Now we'll consider these functions more specifically.

Program Execution

The most obvious user function is the execution of programs. Most operating systems also allow the user to specify one or more **operands** that can be passed to the program as arguments. The operands might be the name of data files, or they might be parameters that modify the behavior of the program.

To the typical end user, the smooth loading and execution of programs are nearly the sole purpose for the operating system. Many operating systems treat program execution the same as they treat nonresident operating system commands. The name of the program is treated as a command; loading and execution begin when the "command" is typed or, equivalently for a windowing system, when the graphical icon is "double-clicked" on by the mouse. Alternatively, the user may click on a data file icon. The program associated with the data file is executed with the data file as an operand.[1]

Since the operating system treats application and user programs in the same way as it treats nonresident commands, it is conveniently impossible to tell the difference. Most of the programs that you have used are not part of the operating system, but since they are initiated the same way, you cannot tell the difference. This provides a consistency that is convenient to the user. Visual Basic, Quicken, Netscape, and Adobe Acrobat, to name just a few, are all independent, nonoperating system programs that share this common behavior, look, and feel.

Application programs perform their operations on a user-specified data file. Spreadsheet programs, for example, require a file of spreadsheet data; word processors use a file of text. The command interface provides a method for specifying the data file to be used when the program is executed. In a command line system, the data file may be specified as an operand typed on the same line with the command. In a graphical system, data

---

[1] If you are not used to graphical system terminology, an **icon** is a small graphical representation of a program or data file. "Double-clicking" involves clicking a button on the mouse twice in rapid succession.

files may be associated with a particular application. This association is set up automatically by the operating system when the data file is created, or it may be manually established by the user. Once the association is set up, the application can be initiated automatically by selecting the data file. On most computers, for example, each data file has an icon associated with it; the application is launched with the particular data file by double-clicking the mouse on the data file icon. In Microsoft Windows, the same result can be achieved by double-clicking the mouse on the name of the data file within the Explorer. An even newer approach, called a **docucentric approach,** is introduced briefly later in this section and again in Section 14.6.

To expedite the execution of programs, the system also provides a means for moving around the system between different peripheral devices and between different storage areas on those devices. Most operating systems embed these operations in a logical device and directory structure and provide commands for moving around the structure. In a command line system, commands provide the ability to attach to different devices and to change one's attachment from one directory to another with a command such as CD, for change directory. Graphical interfaces provide the equivalent of file folders to achieve the same purpose.

Although you are probably most familiar with running your programs interactively, most minicomputer and mainframe operating systems also allow programs to be run noninteractively, in a batch mode. The operating system allows the user to specify conditions under which the execution is to take place, for example, the priority of the program, the preferred time when it should be executed, the stored location of the program and the particular data files that are to be used.

File Commands

The second, and most familiar, category of user services are commands for the storage, retrieval, organization, and manipulation of files.

From the perspective of the user, the file management system is what "makes it all possible." Four factors account for the importance of the file management system to the user:

- The ability to treat data and programs by logical file name, without regard to the physical characteristics of the file or its physical storage location
- The ability of the file management system to handle the physical manipulation of the files and to translate between logical and physical representations
- The ability to issue commands to the operating system that store, manipulate, and retrieve files and parts of files
- The ability to construct an effective file organization utilizing directories or file folders to organize one's files in a meaningful way

The file management system is so important that we have devoted the entirety of Chapter 16 to it. Of interest to us here, as users, is the fact that most of the user commands in the operating system are directly used to manipulate files and file data. This is evident if you consider the commands that you use in your regular work with the computer.

The brief partial list of MS-DOS/Windows and UNIX/Linux commands in Figure 14.1 typifies the commands that you would probably consider to be most important to you. Other operating systems provide essentially identical commands, although the commands might appear quite different, depending on the user interface. Graphical user interfaces provide equivalent operations for each of these commands. On a Macintosh computer, for example, you move a file by dragging its icon with the mouse from its current location to the desired location. You create a new directory by moving an empty file folder into the window that represents the desired attachment point.

Many additional features built into the command structure reflect the importance of a flexible file structure to the user. These include

- The ability to change from one device and one directory or subdirectory to another without otherwise modifying the file
- The ability to redirect input and output to different devices and files from their usual locations

Disk and Other I/O Device Commands

In addition to the file commands, the operating system provides commands for direct operation on various I/O devices. There are commands for formatting and checking disks, for copying entire disks, for providing output directly to the screen or to a printer, and for other useful I/O operations. Some systems also require the **mounting** and **unmounting** of devices. This effectively attaches and detaches the directory structure of a device to the already existent directory structure as a means of adding devices to the system.

Most operating systems also provide a queuing system for spooling output to a printer. The printer is generally much slower than other computer facilities. The spooler works by copying the output text into a buffer in memory and then printing as a separate task. This allows programs to proceed as though printing had already taken place.

Security and Data Integrity Protection

Every operating system provides at least minimal security protection for files. Generally, individual provisions are made to protect files from being read, written to, or executed.

FIGURE 14.1

Common MS-DOS and UNIX File Manipulation Commands

MS-DOS/Windows	UNIX/Linux	
dir	ls	List a directory of files or get information about files
copy	cp	Copy a file from one place to another
move	mv	Move a file from one place to another
del or erase	rm	Delete (remove) a file
type	cat	Type a file out to the screen (or redirected to a printer)
mkdir	mkdir	Attach a new subdirectory to the tree at this tree junction
rmdir	rmdir	Delete a subdirectory

Some operating systems also provide protection from deletion. A few operating systems provide additional security, requiring a correct password to be typed before a disk can be used in the system, or a keyboard unlocked.

Systems with multiuser access, of course, provide much more protection. Files must be protected, so that the owner of the file can control who has access to the file. The owner can also protect the file from himself or herself by specifying read only or execute only access. Many operating systems also allow controlled access from other users. UNIX provides three levels of security for each file, consisting of read, write, and execute access privileges for the owner, for associates of the owner, and for anybody with access to the system. Windows offers share privileges to control file and device access between users on a network. Many large systems also provide **access control lists,** or **ACLs** (pronounced ack'ulls), that allow the system administrator to control access to program and data files on an individual basis.

In addition to file protection, every operating system with multiuser access provides a login procedure to limit access on the system to authorized users. Commands exist to allow the user to modify the access rights on a file and to change the user's password. Networks also require the use of a login procedure that limits the user to the appropriate computers and facilities.

Interuser Communication and Data Sharing Operations

Modern systems generally provide means for multiple users to share data files and programs. Most systems also provide a means to pass data between programs and to communicate between users. Application programs like Lotus Notes, instant messaging, and videoconferencing can extend this capability in a powerful way to both small and large networks of computer systems.

The simplest form of program sharing on a single system is to place the shared programs in a common memory area where all users can reach them. This is done for editors, compilers, general utilities, and other system software that is not part of the operating system. Many operating systems even allow several different levels of control over such shared programs. For example, the Little Man Computer simulator used at Bentley College is accessible to all computer majors, but other users must have permission to access it.

Data file sharing is an important resource when using databases, because it makes it possible for multiple users to access the same data in a way that the integrity of the data is protected. Needless to say, the system must provide tight security to limit data file access to those who should have it.

An additional use for data file sharing is when two or more users work as a group on a document. All these users have access to the document. Some can only read it, while others can modify it. Some systems provide means for attaching notes to the document for other users to see. As with program sharing, it is possible to set several levels of data file sharing.

Modern networks routinely provide operating system message passing services in the form of e-mail and newsgroup support, file transfer (ftp), simple terminal facilities for connecting to a different system (telnet), Web support (http), and instant messaging. Multiuser systems also provide an internal messaging service for rapid communication between users logged on to the system. Some systems additionally provide a "phone" or "talk" service for direct interactive connections between logged on users. This is, of course, one of the primary functions of "chat" systems, such as America Online, but chat use is also common in businesses as a quick way for two users to communicate. Two-way phone services on multiuser systems commonly provide a split screen mode of operation, where the outgoing messages appear on the top half of the screen and the incoming messages appear on the bottom half. Both users can type at the same time. Chat services provide a single window that is shared by every user. Each participating user is identified when they contribute to the chat. A growing number of systems also support interactive video and audio communication between users.

Operating systems also provide internal services that allow programs to communicate with each other during execution. Modern systems go one step farther and extend this concept to allow the user to control interprogram communication as a means of extending the capabilities of individual programs.

The simplest example of this is the *pipe* command available in many systems for taking the output from one program and using it as the input to another. More sophisticated techniques allow a user to link two programs together so that a spreadsheet, for example, can appear in a word processing document. Double-clicking the mouse on the spreadsheet actually launches the spreadsheet program from within the word processor program, so that the spreadsheet can be modified. The most sophisticated systems actually allow the user to work with different application programs *transparently*, that is, without even being aware that an operation has launched another program. For example, modification of the spreadsheet would take place right within the word processing document; the user would not even be aware that a spreadsheet application program was being executed at the time.

This approach relies heavily on the operating system to support communication between different programs in a fashion invisible to the user. The user is not even aware of which application is executing at any given instant. This technique views the document as the center of focus, instead of the applications that are being executed. An interface of this type is known as a docucentric interface and represents a major shift in the way in which the user views her applications and use of the system.

System Status Information

As previously seen in Chapter 13, most operating systems provide status information that can be useful to a user who knows how to interpret the data. This data is usually more important to the people who operate and maintain the computer system, but sometimes status information can be useful to programmers and users in optimizing their work.

Commands commonly exist to determine the amount of available disk space, the amount of available memory, the number of users on the system and who they are, the percentage of time that the CPU and I/O channels are busy, and many other statistics.

As an example of how this data might be useful, consider an application program that does the billing for a large electric utility company. Such a program might require many hours of CPU time to complete a month's billing. A small change in the program could cut the CPU time by a significant percentage. The measurement of CPU time used is essential to assess the improvement. CPU time used data can also be important to a user who is being billed for his time.

The names of other users on the system might be used to establish a phone-type conference or to send a quick message to another user.

Many systems provide a logging facility that maintains a file of all keyboard and screen I/O. With a log file the user can determine at a later time what commands were typed and what modifications made to programs and data.

The examples given here are only a few of the possible uses for system status and information. There are many other possibilities. Status information can be particularly important to personal computer users who must maintain their own systems. For example, status information allows the user to ascertain the condition of a disk: to determine the number of bad blocks on the disk or to analyze and reduce the fragmentation that is present on the disk. For example, Windows provides the SCANDISK and DEFRAG commands for this purpose.

Program Services

One of the most important user functions provided by the operating system is actually invisible to the user. The operating system provides a variety of services directly to the user's programs. The most important of these are the I/O and file services. Also important are requests for the use of system resources that a program needs, such as additional memory or larger blocks of time.

Typical program services can be used to retrieve a file, to save a file, or to locate the individual blocks of a file. The program services can read one or a few particular blocks of a file into a designated user area of memory. Most program service facilities can keep track of several files at once.

Typical program services also allow an application program to bypass the file system under certain conditions and to perform I/O directly to disk and other I/O devices. For example, the program could request a service that retrieves a particular block on the disk. This type of service might be important to a program that attempts to repair damaged data files, for example. Most operating systems control these services in such a way as to prevent damage to the system or to other users' files and resources. As another example, output to a screen is performed directly to I/O, rather than through the file system, on many computer systems. These I/O services allow programs to write text and graphics to the screen without compromising the system.

Services to programs also include services that are less apparent to the user, but important nonetheless. Interprocess message passing allows programs to synchronize their actions to protect data integrity, to share and exchange data, and even to distribute program processing among different machines on a network. **DCOM (Distributed Component Object Model)**, its extension **.NET,** and **CORBA (Common Object Request Broker Architecture)** are two standards that allow programs to locate and share objects, either on a system or across a network. **Remote Procedure Call (RPC)** allows a program to call a procedure at a remote location across a network. Ultimately, these technologies will ease a programmer's task at creating new programs and will allow computers on a network to share the processing load.

Finally, many operating systems provide extra services for the convenience of the programmer. Particularly in modern systems, where elegant user interfaces and graphics are the norm rather than the exception, the operating system provides a library of powerful service routines for implementing user interfaces and graphics for individual programs. On most modern workstations and personal computers, it is only necessary for a program to call a series of these routines to maintain control of windows, drop-down menus, dialog boxes, and mouse events. The routines also include powerful system calls for drawing complex graphic shapes on the screen.

To use the program service routines, the user's program makes requests to the operating system through the **application programming interface,** or **API.** In most systems, the API consists of a library of service functions that may be called by a program.[2] The call and required parameters are passed to the selected service function, using whatever method is implemented for the given machine. Most commonly, a simple call is used, with a stack used to pass the parameters. The service function is responsible for communication with appropriate routines within the operating system that perform the requested operation. A software interrupt or service request instruction is used for this purpose. The service routine returns required results, if any, to the calling program. On some systems, the calling program uses a software interrupt directly to access the API. Windows *win32,* the standard API on every Microsoft Windows system, provides hundreds of service functions to programs.

The use of operating system program services provides convenience for a program developer. More important, providing a single gateway through which all I/O must pass assures the integrity of files and other I/O. If each program placed its files on the disk independently, there would be no way to assure that the files didn't destroy each other.

The integrity of the system is even more important if the system is multiprogramming and/or multiuser. As an example of what could go wrong, consider a printer being addressed directly by two different programs. The output would be a garbled mix of the output to be printed from the two programs, obviously useless to anyone.

Early, single-user systems allowed programs to bypass the operating system and do their own I/O. Doing so increases the risk that data may be destroyed. Furthermore, bypassing the I/O services of the operating system may make the program incompatible with other, similar (such as clone) computers that may use different internal addresses for the I/O device functions. Finally, the I/O services provided are convenient. They make it possible to simplify the task of writing programs by providing the difficult I/O and file functions automatically.

A properly designed multiprogramming operating system will not allow programs to perform their own I/O; the operating system services must be used. It is the role of the system services to properly queue I/O requests and to perform them in such a way as to protect the data. No current machine allows a user program to bypass operating system services.

14.3 TYPES OF USER INTERFACE

There are two types of user interface in common use. One of these is the **command line interface (CLI),** which is seen on a wide variety of operating systems, including the Windows MS-DOS prompt, Linux, and Alpha OpenVMS. Although this is historically the most common interface, the **graphical user interface (GUI)** seen on the Apple Macintosh,

---

[2] The concept of an API also applies to applications that allow other applications to "piggyback" or "plug in" to their services. For example, Web browsers provide API services to their plug-ins.

Windows-based PCs, and Sun workstations, among others, has supplanted the CLI for most routing day-to-day use.

As already noted, the type of interface seen by the user depends on the focus of the operating system. A batch system requires a different interface than a system primarily intended for interactive use. A system designed primarily for inexperienced end users will differ from one designed for sophisticated technical users. Today, most users are reasonably comfortable at a computer screen, the purely batch system is in declining use, and the primary user interface with a computer is interactive, using a keyboard, mouse, and video display. Furthermore, the graphical user interface is rapidly becoming the predominate user interface for most work.

The Command Line Interface

The command line interface is the simplest form of user-interactive interface. The operating system provides a prompt; in response, the user types textual commands into the keyboard. The command line is read serially, character by character, into a keyboard buffer, where it is interpreted by the command interpreter and executed. Commands are entered and executed one line at a time, although most interpreters provide a means for extending a command onto multiple lines. The command line interpreters for most operating systems use a standard format for their commands. The command itself is followed by operands appropriate to the particular command, as shown:

```
command operand1 operand2...
```

The operands are used to specify parameters that define the meaning of the command more precisely: the name of a particular file to be used with the command, a particular format for listing data, or a detail about how the command is to be performed. Many times, some or all of the operands are optional; this simply means that a default condition is to be used if the operand is not specified.

In some circumstances, the command itself may be preceded by a logical path name that specifies the particular device or file location where the command is to be found.

As an example, the Linux command

```
ls pathparta/pathpartb
```

consists of the command ls and the operand pathparta/pathpartb. This command requests a directory listing from the subdirectory with path name pathparta/pathpartb. Without the optional operand pathparta/pathpartb, the command lists the master directory for the device. An additional operand might redirect the output, to file or printer, for example, instead of to the screen. The Linux command to store the directory list in putfilea (presumably for later printing) would look like this:

```
ls -1F pathparta/pathpartb >putfilea
```

The equivalent command in MS-DOS would look like this:

```
DIR PATHPARTA\PATHPARTB>PUTFILEA
```

In each of these cases, many other optional operands are possible; these operands would be used to modify the facts listed and the format of the directory listing. The additional operand -lF in the Linux command tells the system to list the directory in a specific "long" format, one file to a line (the "l"), with subdirectories indicated (the "F").

Operands are either **keyword** or **positional.** In some systems, the operands may be both. Positional operands require the operand to be located in a particular position within the line. For example, in the MS-DOS command

```
COPY SOURCE-FILE DESTINATION
```

the first operand, SOURCE-FILE, positionally specifies the path name of the file to be copied. The second operand, DESTINATION, which is optional, specifies either a new name for the file or the path name of a directory to which the file is to be copied. If the second operand is absent, the directory to which the user is currently "attached" is used. The importance of the position of these positional operands is obvious: some older operating systems specified the destination operand first; reversing the position could destroy the file to be copied.

Keyword operands are identified by the use of a particular keyword. In many systems, the keyword is accompanied by a modifier symbol that identifies the operand as a keyword as opposed to a file name. The keyword identifies the purpose of the operand. Keyword operands are frequently used as optional operands, sometimes with a particular positional value attached. In some systems, keyword operands and modifiers can be placed anywhere after the command without affecting the positions of positional operands. In other systems, the keyword operands, if present, must be placed in a particular position. The slash mark (/) in MS-DOS and hyphen (-) in UNIX are examples of modifier symbols. Keyword operands are sometimes known as **switches** or **modifiers.**

The MS-DOS command

```
MODE COM1 BAUD=2400 PARITY=N DATABITS=8
```

uses the positional operand COM1 to identify a particular communications port or other device. BAUD, PARITY, and DATABITS are all examples of keyword operands. Each has its own positional operand that selects a particular option, but the order of the keywords is immaterial. Similarly, the command

```
DIR /P/A:DH PATHNAME
```

uses the /p and /a switches to specify that files are displayed on a screen one page at a time, and to modify the list of path name directory files that will be displayed.

Command line interpreters also include other provisions designed to increase the flexibility of the command. The most important provisions include the ability to redirect input and output, the ability to combine commands using pipes, and the ability to combine commands into shell scripts or **batch programs.** Another important capability is the use of the wild card, a character symbol or symbols that can substitute for one or more unspecified letters in an operand. Use of a wild card in a command can make possible a search, or can cause a command to be repeated with several different arguments.

Although they work somewhat differently, both Linux and MS-DOS use the question mark symbol (?) to replace a single character and an asterisk (*) to replace a group of 0 or more characters. Linux has additional wild card possibilities, shown in Chapter 16. For example, the Linux command

```
ls -l boo.*
```

would search the current directory for all files that have the name BOO. This command might result in the following output:

```
-r--r--rwx  1 irv  cisdep   221  May  16   7:02  boo.dat
---x--xrwx  1 irv  cisdep  5556  May  20  13:45  boo.exe
-r--rw-rw-  1 irv  cisdep    20  Jun   5   2:02  boo.hoo
```

In the MS-DOS command,

```
COPY ABC* B:
```

all files whose names begin with abc are copied to the drive B: master directory. In this case, the wild card is used to expand the command to repeat the copy process for several different files.

In addition to **wild card** provisions, some operating systems allow the user to back up and repeat a previous command using the cursor keys on the keyboard. Such systems usually allow the user to edit the command, as well.

Command line interfaces are well suited to experienced users who are comfortable with the system and who want the power and flexibility that a CLI offers them. Command line interfaces are generally the hardest to learn. The range of possibilities and options that accompany many commands often make it difficult to figure out the particular syntax that is required for a desired operation. Manuals and online help are particularly useful in working with command line interfaces. Online help is available for all Linux commands using the "man *commandname*" command.

Batch System Commands

Batch systems use an interface that is similar to the command line interpreter in many respects. Commands specify the location of programs to be executed and data to be used, using a Job Control Language. Job control commands use a format similar to that of the command line interpreter:

```
command operand1 operand2...
```

Batch command operands also are either of keyword or positional type. The most familiar language of this type is IBM MVS/Job Control Language. Batch programs are "submitted" to a system for execution and are generally executed with no human interaction. Since direct human interaction with the batch system is not possible, all steps must be carefully planned out, including actions to be taken when errors occur. Batch programs are well suited for routine transaction processing applications, such as credit card billing and payroll.

Command line interfaces also provide the ability to "batch" commands together to form pseudoprograms, known as **shell scripts,** or just **scripts,** that will be executed as a unit. These are not true batch programs, as they are still intended for interactive use. Nonetheless, MS-DOS users usually refer to these programs as *batch programs* or batch files or, sometimes, as *bat files.* Most command line interfaces provide additional commands that are intended especially for the creation of powerful scripts. The overall command structure is then referred to as a **command language,** or scripting language. The topic of command languages is considered further in Section 14.5. There is an example of a JCL procedure in Figure 18.18.

Menu-Driven Interfaces

One disadvantage of command line interfaces is that you have to know something about the commands to use them. This can be daunting to the new user. Many new users to UNIX, for example, manage to log in successfully, then find themselves unable to do anything because many standard file commands have strange and arcane command names like *ls, cp,* and *cat.* Even with online help, such a system can be difficult to use. (UNIX has extensive online help in the form of complete manuals, but you have to know the command to look it up!) Today, most users would use a graphical interface instead. However, some older IBM AS-400 legacy systems still rely on an earlier alternative, the **menu-driven interface.**

Menu-driven interfaces present a menu of alternatives on the screen. The user selects one alternative, either by moving a **cursor** with a mouse and clicking on the desired choice or, more commonly, by typing in a number or pressing a function key that corresponds to the choice. In most such systems, the menus are nested. Each selection leads to a menu of further, more detailed, selections. This continues until the desired action has been specified. This menu system is usually a script provided by a system administrator and filed in users' accounts as part of a start-up routine that occurs when users log in to the system. More experienced users simply bypass the menu system and work directly with the CLI by eliminating the file from their start-up routine.

The main selection menu for an IBM AS-400 system is shown in Figure 14.2.

Windows Interfaces

The mouse-driven, icon-based Windows interface has, for all practical purposes, replaced the command line interface as the prevalent interface between user and computer. This type of interface is commonly known as a graphical user interface, or GUI (pronounced gooey). The GUI has been implemented in many forms. The best-known implementations are the user interfaces present on the Apple Macintosh computer and on IBM-type PCs that are equipped with the Microsoft Windows interface. Most other computer systems offer a similar interface. Figure 14.3 is a picture of a typical Windows XP screen. The screen

FIGURE 14.2

IBM AS-400 Main Menu

```
MAIN                    Main Menu
                                              System SYS 00300
Select one of the following:
          1. User tasks
          2. Office tasks
          3. General system tasks
          4. Files, libraries, and folders
          5. Programming
          6. Communications
          7. Define or change the system
          8. Problem handling
          9. Display a menu
         10. User support and education
         11. PC support tasks
         90. Sign off
Selection or command
  ===>
  F3=Exit  F4=Prompt  F9=Retrieve  F12=Cancel  F23=Set initial menu
```

SOURCE: Courtesy of International Business Machines Corporation

FIGURE 14.3

A Typical Windows XP Screen

of a Linux computer running the KDE shell appears in Figure 14.4. Notice the similarities between the two. The graphical user interface provides the convenience of a desktop metaphor. The user can arrange the desktop to his or her own preferences, can easily move around the desktop to perform different tasks, and can see the results in WYSIWYG (what-you-see-is-what-you-get) form.

Windowing systems from different vendors take on different appearances, but share similar elements. Normally, a graphic interface consists of one or more **screens** or **desktops,** each of which contains one or more windows. A window is a portion of the screen that is allocated to the use of a particular program or process. Windows contain **gadgets** or **widgets** for resizing the windows, for moving the windows around the screen, for scrolling data and images within a window, and for moving windows in front of or behind other windows on the screen. Windows also contain a **title bar** that identifies the window. There is also at least one **menu bar** on the screen. On some systems, a single menu bar on the screen is always associated with the active window (discussed shortly). On other systems,

FIGURE 14.4

A Linux Computer Running the KDE Shell

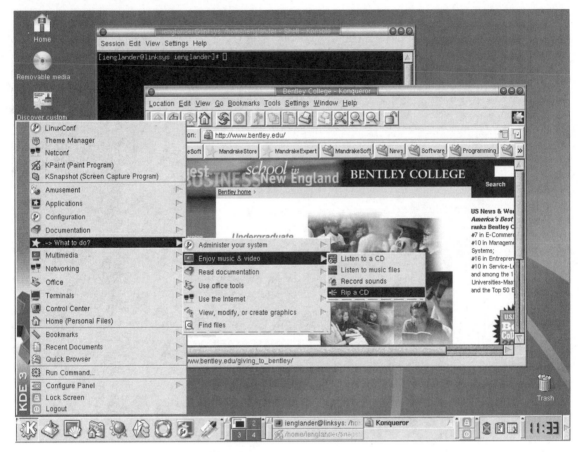

each window has its own menu bar. Each item on the menu bar can be used to activate a hierarchical set of pull-down menus, used for selecting options within the program being executed. Windows and Linux screens also provide a **task bar** for rapid program startup, task switching, and status information.

On many modern systems, Windows can be configured to look and act in different ways. One important option is the "Web interface," which provides the look and feel of a Web browser for all operations within the window.

Many systems allow windows to be iconified, tiled, overlapped, or cascaded. Iconifying a window means reducing it to the size of an icon, even though the window is still open. This allows screen space to be saved. The window is reexpanded by clicking on it. Tiled windows are lined up on the screen in such a way that they do not overlap and use all the available space on the screen. Overlapping windows is the normal situation, with windows located where placed by the system or by the user. Cascaded windows are a version of overlapped windows where the windows are overlapped in such a way that the title bar and one other border of each window can be seen.

On systems that allow multiple screens, a group of windows is attached to a particular screen. Individual screens, together with their associated windows, can be minimized or can be moved forward or behind other screens, but are not usually resizable. When multiple screens are allowed, each screen represents a separate user interface. Four desktops are indicated in the task bar in Figure 14.4.

To the user, the window is a box that is used for the input of text and commands to a program and the graphical or text output resulting. Placing multiple windows on the screen provides a convenient way to implement a multiprogramming interface with separate input and output for each program. At any given time, one window is active, meaning that it will respond to the keyboard and mouse. The color or appearance of the title bar is frequently used to indicate which window on the screen is currently active. On some systems, moving the mouse cursor into a window activates the window. This method is known as **mouse focus.** In other systems, the window must be activated by clicking the mouse while the cursor is inside the window or by opening the window. This is known as **click to focus.**

Depending on the GUI design, data and program files can take the form of text or of graphical symbols called icons. On most systems, icons can be animated. Icons that are in use change shape or color. Icons can be moved around the screen with a mouse. Some systems also allow the use of a light pen or a tablet or a pressure pen for this purpose. Pressure pens are commonly used as the pointing device on personal digital assistants such as the Palm Pilot. The pressure pen itself is just a piece of plastic. The actual pointing signal is produced when the system detects the physical pressure at a particular location on the screen.

Many commands are issued to the operating system by moving the mouse and manipulating a button on the mouse at the appropriate time. For example, a program is initiated by pointing the mouse cursor at the icon for the program and clicking the mouse button twice. A copy command involves holding the mouse button down while the user **drags** the icon from its original position to a position on top of the desired destination directory icon or window, then **drops** it by releasing the button. A delete command is performed by dragging the icon to an icon that represents the picture of a trash can. Other commands use the mouse together with pop-up or pull-down menus.

Both program and data files are stored in folders, and folders may be nested. Double clicking on a folder opens a window that shows the contents of the folder. In other words, folders are equivalent to a file directory structure. The **active window** corresponds to the current directory attachment point.

Requestor boxes can be used for commands that require textual input, such as a new file name. Additional gadgets, such as push buttons and sliders, exist for other types of control of the interface.

Most window-interfaced operating systems also allow the use of special keys on the keyboard to duplicate commands that use the mouse-icon-menu method.

EXAMPLE

The Macintosh OS X interface consists of a single screen known as the **desktop.** The desktop can be used to hold various items, such as a trashcan, folders, and data that is being worked on. A typical Macintosh OS X screen is shown in Figure 14.5. The desktop consists of icons representing each **volume** on the system, a menu bar, the **dock,** and a trash icon. A volume consists of a disk or partition of a disk.

FIGURE 14.5

A Typical Macintosh OS X Screen

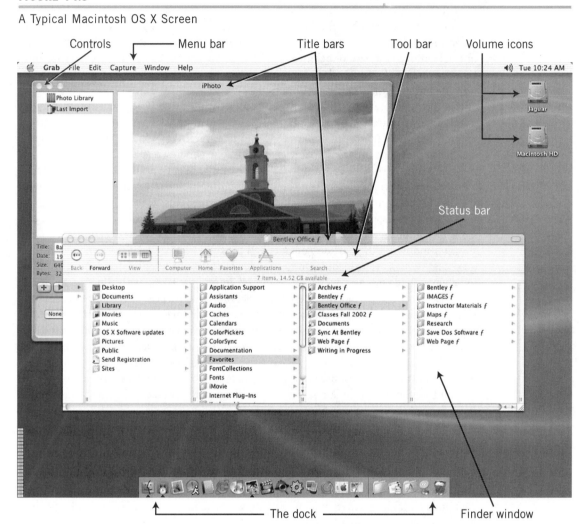

Clicking the mouse on a volume or dock icon opens a window. On the Macintosh, icons can represent folders, applications, and documents. Clicking on an application will **launch** (load and execute) the program. Clicking on a document icon will open the **associated** application program and load the indicated data. Some windows may also be opened from the menu bar.

The dock serves as a convenient receptacle for applications, folder, documents, files, and volumes that are accessed often. It also holds icons for minimized open applications. Mac OS X does not distinguish between applications which are open and minimized from those that are permanently placed on the dock for convenience. If you look at the figure carefully, you will see that the dock is divided by a vertical line into two sections. The left section holds applications. The right side of the dock holds folders, documents, and the like.

Names for the icons on the dock are hidden; they appear when the mouse pointer is positioned on the icon. Some dock icons also sprout pop-up menus. Drag-and-drop is used to add icons to the dock. Icons are removed by dragging them out of the dock. The dock can be hidden, shrunk, or rotated into a new position on the desktop.

Two windows are open in the figure. Windows provide a title bar that contains the usual gadgets, known on the Macintosh as **controls.** These are used to close the window, to expand the window to full screen size, to minimize the window, to resize the window to a desired size, and to provide scrolling left and right, up and down to expose the underlying parts of the window. The mouse can also be used to move the window around the desktop. Some windows also offer a tool bar and a status bar.

The Macintosh desktop uses a single menu bar that is shared by the active window and the desktop. The mouse can be moved over the menu bar to cause pull-down menus to appear. Many of the items on pull-down menus are standard no matter what the user is doing. Those that are inappropriate at a particular time are "grayed out," that is, represented in a lighter color. They do not respond to the mouse. This standardization makes the interface easier to learn and to use. Some menu bar items change to represent possible actions that are unique to a particular situation.

Numerous windows can be open at once, each with its own work, and it is possible to cut or copy and paste data between different windows by marking the desired data using the mouse and using the cut, copy, and paste menu functions. Only one window is active at a time. The user selects the active window by clicking the mouse anywhere inside it. Even though windows can overlap, the active window will always be brought to the front and displayed in full. Once a window is active, the user can manipulate the window and the data within it. During program execution, buttons, dialog boxes, and pull-down menus are used to control the program and to enter data, simplifying interaction between the user and the program.

In the figure, *iPhoto* is an application. The other open window is a special **Finder** window. The Finder window is used to navigate the system. It contains a tool bar that works similarly to a web browser and panels that represent a hierarchy of folders and their contents. The tool bar can be modified for a particular user's preferences. Applications can be launched and documents opened directly from the Finder.

Besides ease of use, what is important about the Macintosh interface is its consistency. Throughout the interface, every operation works the same way. This enhances ease of use and quick learning, as well as user comfort. A powerful library of graphics software routines within the operating system is used to enforce this consistency.

It should be noted that the graphical interface is totally committed to the user end of the user interface. Internally, the commands are executed by the operating system in essentially the same way as that of any other interface. We mention this so that you can see the value of separating the various layers of the operating system conceptually. Modification or change of one layer does not have to affect other layers, as long as the interface between layers is self-consistent.

Trade-offs in the User Interface

It might seem obvious to you that the ease of use of a graphical interface makes this the ideal interface for most users. For the typical end user, the graphical interface is indeed an attractive choice. It is easy to learn and easy to use. Little training is required, and the basic operations are intuitive. It therefore meets the most important criterion of the user interface: it is effective in allowing the user to get work done. The graphical interface has a second, less obvious, advantage as well. With a graphical interface, it is easy to implement a multitasking system in which the user can control every task by placing each executing task in a separate window. Although some command line systems provide a way to execute programs "in the background," the method is much more awkward: switching between tasks is not convenient, displayed output is mixed together, and it is difficult to separate and interact with both programs.

The graphical interface is not without disadvantages, however. The graphical interface is much harder to implement and much more demanding in its hardware and software requirements. This interface works best with a powerful graphic video capability. It requires a lot of memory, just to store the pictures as well as to hold the programs. The software is complex, although visual and object-oriented languages simplify the coding of such programs.

In contrast, the command line interface is simple and straightforward. It is text oriented, and input to the command interpreter can be treated as a simple serial character stream. The CLI is better suited to a multiuser system in which the graphical capability of the different terminals and workstations connected have different standards and characteristics, particularly where the terminals are located remotely from the computer.

The command line interface has more inherent flexibility and power. Many experienced users consider the graphical interface to be slow and clumsy. They prefer to type a command to get their work done. Arguments and operands are easy to use and to specify. It is easier to work with wild card commands when an operation is to be repeated many times or when a specialized search is to take place. It is more difficult to combine commands or to use piping techniques using a graphical interface.

Even though the graphical I/O built into user programs is easy to use, the development of graphical I/O for user programs is more difficult, and the programs are larger and slower, because of the numerous details that must be handled by service routines. It is obviously easier to read and write a stream of text than it is to draw windows, handle menus, and identify mouse movements and actions.

Finally, it is more difficult to combine a series of graphical actions into a working program of commands, especially when branches and loops are required. One of the powers of the command line interface is the ability to "program" the commands.

Despite these difficulties, the graphical user interface is convenient and useful for most users in most circumstances. It is the primary interface on most microcomputer systems and is relatively common on minicomputers and mainframe computers as well.

Gradually, too, the disadvantages of this interface are being solved. Some systems now provide an alternative command line interface, such as the MS-DOS prompt in Windows, for example, for use in situations where the graphical interface is inconvenient or weak. Application programs now exist to help the program developer with the creation of windows and other tasks required for the program interface.

Standards exist that allow different computers and terminals to share the same graphical interface, even though the individual hardware and software is different. Such capability is important in networked and distributed computing environments. A useful development in this regard is **X Window,** which allows various computers that use various forms of UNIX, Linux, and certain other operating systems to work together graphically. X Window provides a language that describes the graphical interface; each individual computer implements the language within its own operating system to produce the desired result. The X Window system was developed at MIT in 1986 and has been accepted by most manufacturers as a way of furthering the idea of a standard graphical interface regardless of hardware. X Window is discussed further in Section 14.4. In many instances, Web browsers can serve in this role, using Java applets, scripting languages, HTML, and XML to create the required display.

Software Considerations

The programs that control the user interface must perform two primary functions.

- Maintain the appearance of the user interface on the screen
- Translate user requests into user services and initiate the programs that will provide those services

Of course, if the interface is a command line, maintaining the appearance of the interface on the screen is trivial, since it is necessary only to print a prompt and wait for a response. The menu system is a bit more complex, because the menu must be reprinted on the screen each time a choice is made. Nonetheless, the process is straightforward and simple. Both CLI and menuing interfaces are text based; therefore, remote display over a network, for example, if necessary, is not a problem.

Similarly, translation of CLI and menu requests into the appropriate services is simple. Each menu request has a defined procedure associated with it, so it's simply a matter of performing the selected procedure. The procedures are defined as part of the command file that makes up the menu program. CLI commands are even easier. It is necessary only to interpret and execute the command as typed by the user. If the command is internal, it is executed within the operating system. If it is external, it is loaded and executed. The operands on the line are passed to the command procedure as arguments.

Windowing interfaces are more difficult. The windowing software is responsible for drawing and maintaining the appearance of the screen; for creating pull-down menus and dialog boxes; for reacting to requests made by the user in the form of mouse clicks; for maintaining the positions of different objects on the screen; for opening, closing, moving, and resizing windows when requested; and for accomplishing many other tasks.

Even a task as conceptually simple as moving an object, say, the cursor or an icon or a window or a slider control, on the screen requires a considerable effort in terms of programming. (Picture trying to write the program to do it using the Little Man Computer machine language!) As the user moves the mouse, the mouse generates interrupts to the CPU. The mouse interrupt program determines the direction and distance that the mouse has moved. It calculates the new X and Y coordinates of the object on the screen by geometrically adding the move to the present position of the object. Then it redraws the object at the new location, by storing a picture of the object in display memory. When it does so, it must also store the shadow of the image stored "behind" the new position of the object and restore the image of whatever was hidden by the object in its previous position. This operation is depicted in Figure 14.6.

In addition to display maintenance and handling, the interface program must also interpret the commands and request the appropriate services. Double-clicking on a document icon, for example, requires the software to identify the icon from its location on the display screen, determine the associated application program, load and execute the application, and load the document data. The command interpreter is thus somewhat more complicated for a windowing system. Note that requesting a service will also require use of the display services, since it will be necessary for the new application to open one or more windows of its own, set up its own menus, and so on.

Overall, you can see that the graphical user interface software is considerably more complex than the corresponding CLI or menu interface software.

FIGURE 14.6

Moving an Object on the Screen

14.4 X WINDOW AND OTHER GRAPHICS DISPLAY METHODOLOGIES

Graphical user interfaces are attractive and convenient when the computer and display are located together, such as in a personal computer or workstation. When the display terminal is separated by a distance from the computer the graphical interface is more difficult to achieve. This is also true if the display and mouse control are taking place over a network. The difficulty is the large amount of data that must be transmitted from one location to the other to transmit graphic images. In Chapter 9 we observed that a single bit-mapped graphical image might contain thousands or millions of bytes of information. Clearly, it is not practical to transmit all this data on a continual basis.

The X Window standard is an attempt to solve this problem. X Window works by separating the software that actually produces the display image on the screen from the application program that creates the image and requests the display. The program that produces the image on the screen is known as a **display server.** In data communications terminology, a server is a program that provides services for other programs. In this case, the server provides display services for one or more client application programs. (We have assumed that the client application programs are running on computer systems located remotely from the display, although, as you will see shortly, this is not a necessary assumption.) The display server is located at the display terminal, computer, or workstation where the image is to appear. The display server can draw and control windows. It provides gadgets, dialog boxes, and pull-down and pop-up menus. It can create and display various fundamental shapes, such as points, rectangles, circles, straight and curved lines, icons, a cursor, and text fonts. In conjunction with a mouse and keyboard located on the same terminal the display server can move, resize, and otherwise control these windows. The mouse can also move the cursor under display server control, that is, local to the terminal. It has only to notify the application as to the final position of the cursor.

Thus, much of the work in creating a graphical window interface is performed local to the display and does not have to be transmitted from the computer system that is running the application program. The application program uses the display services to produce its desired images by interacting with the display server. In data communication terminology, the application program acts as a **client,** requesting display services that it needs from the display server. The program may request that a pull-down menu be displayed, for example; the display server draws the menu on the screen at the appropriate location, as determined by its knowledge of the size and location of the window. If the user at the terminal clicks a mouse on a particular menu entry, the server notifies the application that this event has occurred. Figure 14.7 illustrates the operation of an X Window application with a display server.

Although it is unavoidable that the application must still transmit actual image data to the display, the amount of data to be transmitted is considerably reduced. Essentially, the display server can perform many of the basic display operations with very little communication required. WYSIWYG text, for example, requires only that the choice of font, the display location, and the actual text data be transmitted. The font data is stored at the display server. The server also provides a library of all the basic tools and widgets to draw windows, provide drop-down menus, present control buttons, respond to mouse clicks, and many

FIGURE 14.7

The X Window Client-server Relationship

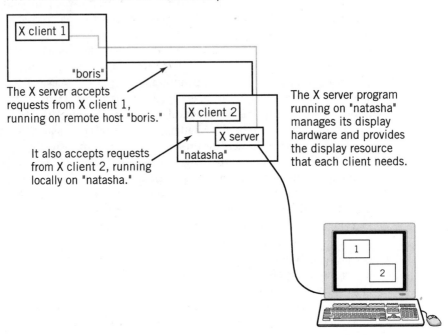

The X server accepts requests from X client 1, running on remote host "boris."

It also accepts requests from X client 2, running locally on "natasha."

The X server program running on "natasha" manages its display hardware and provides the display resource that each client needs.

SOURCE: From *The UNIX Operating System* 3e, K. Christian and S. Richter, copyright © 1994. Reprinted by permission of John Wiley & Sons, Inc.

other functions. This method requires far less data communication between the program and the display than if the transmission of actual text images and windows were required.

X Window places no restrictions on the location of the client application; therefore, the application program could reside on the same computer system as the display server or remotely on a different system. Furthermore, the display server can process requests from several different client applications concurrently, each in its own window. You would expect this to be true, since a graphical user interface can have several open windows at one time. This leads to an interesting and exciting possibility: that different windows on a single display could be communicating with application programs on different machines! Indeed, this is the case. The picture in Figure 14.8 illustrates this situation. The window in the upper-left corner is communicating with a program located on the same PC with the display. The PC is running an X Window server under Microsoft Windows. The other windows on the screen are connected to various systems located remotely: a Digital VAX VMS system connected to a local area network and a Sun UNIX workstation connected via telephone and modem.

As in other windowing systems, the location of the cursor is used to determine the active window.

Notice that the operating system at the display need not be the same as the operating systems where the application programs are running, as long as display server software is

FIGURE 14.8

A Multicomputer X Window Display

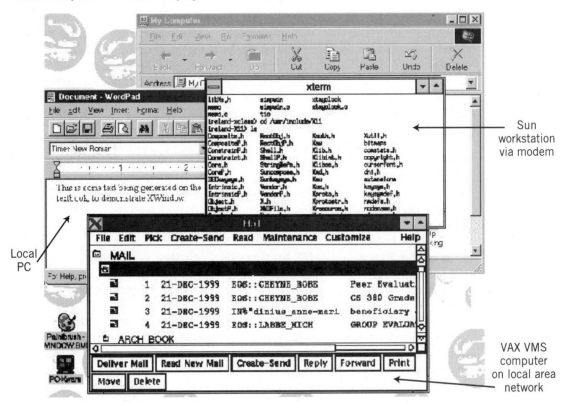

available for the particular operating system in use at the display terminal. X Window display server software is available for most operating systems, including UNIX, Linux, MS-DOS, VAX VMS, the Macintosh OS, and many others. In fact, an X Window server can be built into a terminal and used with a central processor located elsewhere.

Systems similar to the X Window system also exist for public online communication services such as America Online and the Web-based services mentioned previously. Although these systems operate somewhat differently, the concept is quite similar: to produce as much of the display as possible using software located at the display and to minimize the amount of image data to be transmitted. These services provide software for this purpose and also store commonly used images and display features at the display site.

14.5 COMMAND AND SCRIPTING LANGUAGES

In early batch systems it was necessary to submit all pieces of a program at one time, including the data and any other programs that were required as part of the operation. Generally, punched cards were used for this purpose.

Suppose you had a COBOL program that was to be compiled and executed. Your submittal to the computer required the cards that made up the COBOL compiler, the COBOL program itself, perhaps a library of binary math routines that will be called by the program when it is executed, and finally some data for the program. Your submittal also contained commands to the computer telling it what to do with all these cards. (Some of the commands were actually more informational, like "load the following group of cards, which are data for the program that you are running.") The entire submission was known as a *job*.

Later on, the COBOL compiler and math routines became part of the software that was permanently stored on disk within the computer system, but the system still needed to be told what to do, what programs (e.g., the COBOL compiler) to call from the disk, where to find the data, and where to print the results.

As noted, the commands to the computer took the form of punched cards that contained the required information. These cards were called job control cards because they told the computer system how to control the job. The different types of commands made up a sort of language, called **job control language** or, more commonly, **JCL.** In other words, a job consisted of a series of commands in JCL intermixed with the appropriate program and data.

The best known of these languages is IBM zOS/JCL, but you should be aware that other vendors have their own JCL languages. Generally, there is no compatibility between JCL languages from different vendors, and in fact, there are several different incompatible versions of "IBM JCL." (By the way, you might note that the expression "JCL language," which is in common use, is redundant.)

The use of JCL continues to this day. JCL statements are entered into the system with a screen editor and are stored in the system as a file of **card images,** so called because each statement is still laid out as though it were stored on an 80-column card. These card images are usually batched together as a file of commands that is executed in the same way that a program is, except that each line of the "program" is actually a command to the operating system. Operands in each JCL command specify the appropriate files and other details that are required. Both positional and keyword operands are used.

The commands that you use on your computer are not very different from the ones that make up a job control language. After all, a computer is a computer, and the tasks that you do are not really very different from those that are done as part of a batch job. Although you commonly use commands one at a time, you can probably think of times when it would have been convenient to combine a group of commands that you could have called all at once. In fact, you may already be aware that there is a way to do this.

Operating systems provide a way to group commands into a single file that can be executed as if it were a program. The file may itself even contain executable programs. In addition to the usual commands, the operating system provides additional commands that are used specifically for this purpose, commands that allow branching and looping, for example. Figure 14.9 is an example of an MS-DOS command language program that prepares backup for a text file by copying an old version to floppy disk, creating a new backup on hard disk, and then opening the word processor program. The name of the text file is given as an operand when the command file is executed. "%1" is a placeholder for the operand.

Most modern operating systems provide command languages. Perhaps the most elegant implementation of this concept belongs to UNIX. In addition to the usual commands,

FIGURE 14.9

MS-DOS Program DOWP

```
@echo
if '%1' == '' go to error
if exist %1 goto error
if not exist %1.txt goto newtxt
if exist %1.old copy %1.old b:\%.arc
copy %1.txt %1.old
wordproc %1.txt
goto end
:newtxt
echo This is a new file. Opening word processor....
wordproc
goto end
:error
echo proper command format is 'dowp filname'
echo with no extension.
:end
```

the UNIX and Linux shells contain a set of powerful utility commands and other features that allow the creation of very sophisticated command programs. In UNIX, **shell scripts** command programs are the fundamental way of getting work done.

Shell scripts can be executed just as if they were programs, and in fact, due to the power of the shell script language, it is frequently possible to avoid writing a normal program by using a shell script instead.

You've already seen an example of an MS-DOS command language program that assists the user in performing a routine computer task. Shell scripts for similar tasks in UNIX will look fairly similar. Figure 14.10 is an example of how UNIX shell scripts can be used in place of a conventional program. This example is a Bourne shell program that determines the nearest major airport to an arbitrary city entered by the user.

Scripting languages are expanded forms of command languages, often encompassing features well beyond those found in a standard command language. Some scripting languages even provide portability between different operating systems. Perl, Javascript, PHP, and Python are examples of portable scripting languages.

The Elements of a Command Language

Like any programming language, there are certain elements in a command language that affect the usefulness of the language. The choice of commands and utilities is an important consideration, but it is not the only consideration. There are other features that enhance the value of a language. These are some of the most important features of a command language:

- The ability to print messages on the screen and to accept input from the user into the program.
- The ability to specify variables and a method to assign and change the value for those variables.

FIGURE 14.10

The UNIX Airport Distance Shell Script

```
export city state lat long port
grep -i "$1 $2" townfile | read city state lat long port
if [ -z "$city" ] then
    echo "this city is not in the file"
elif [ "$port" = "y" ] then
    echo " $city $state has its own airport"
else
    awk '
    BEGIN {close = 10000}
    $5 == "y" {dist = ($3 - '$lat')*($3 - $lat')+($4 - '$long')*($4 - '$long')
            if (dist < close) {
                close = dist
                ccity = $1
                cstate = $2 } }
    END   {print ( "the nearest airport is in " ccity, cstate)
            print ( " approximate distance is " 60* sqrt (close) " miles")
            } ' townfile
fi
```

A typical line in townfile:

```
Boston MA 42.3333 71.083 y
```

- The ability to branch and loop. Notice that the ability to change variable values is important as a means of controlling branches and ending loops.

- The ability to specify arguments with the command that executes the program and to transfer those arguments into parameters and variables within the program. The command program in Figure 14.9 uses this technique to allow the user to specify the name of the file to be backed up.

- The ability to detect an error that results from a command and recover from it in a graceful way. If the operating system attaches numerical values to its errors, the command program can make decisions and branch based on the level of error. This could be used to determine if a particular file or a particular hardware component exists, for example.

A common use for command languages is to create a single command program that compiles, loads, and executes a program written in COBOL or some other high-level language. The error detection ability can be used to stop the loading and execution commands when the compile step has failed. The OpenVMS DCL (Digital Command Language) command program in Figure 14.11 branches to a path that issues a message to the user, prints the error file on the screen, then opens an editor for the user to correct any errors.

If the primary mode of user operation is graphical, it is also important to be able to create an icon that will execute the command program. This is a surprising absence in some operating system command languages.

FIGURE 14.11

DCL COMPILE and EXECUTE Program

```
>>>>>>>>>>>>>>>>>>>>>>>>>>>>>>>>>>>>>>>>>>>>>>>>>>>>>>>>>>>>>>>>>>>>>>>>>>>>>>
$
!*****************************************************************************
$ !  PROGRAM NAME: CPROGUTIL.COM
$ !         TITLE: C Programming Utility
$ !      LANGUAGE: Digital Command Language
$ !        AUTHOR: James Proia, Bentley College
$ !  DATE WRITTEN: 11/07/94
$ !
$
!*****************************************************************************
$ ! REMARKS: This utility compiles, loads, and executes a program written
$ ! in the C programming language. DCL's error detection ability is used
$ ! to stop the loading and execution commands when the compile step has failed.
$ ! This program will branch to a path that issues a message to the user,
$ ! prints the error file on the screen and then opens the EVE editor for the
$ ! user to fix his/her error.
$
!*****************************************************************************
$ CLS
$ DEFINE/NOLOG SYS$INPUT SYS$COMMAND
$ WRITE SYS$OUTPUT "C Programming Utility Starting..."
$ ON ERROR THEN GOTO PGM_ERROR
$ INQUIRE PROGFILE
$ SOURCEFILE = PROGFILE + ".C"
$ LISTFILE = PROGFILE + ".LIS"
$ TRY_AGAIN:
$ CC 'SOURCEFILE' /LIS='LISTFILE'
$ LINK 'PROGFILE'
$ RUN 'PROGFILE'
$ GOTO PGM_END
$ PGM_ERROR:
$ ERRORLINE = "Program Error encountered in " + SOURCEFILE
$ WRITE SYS$OUTPUT 'ERRORLINE'
$ E 'LISTFILE'
$ E 'SOURCEFILE'
$ GOTO TRY_AGAIN
$ PGM_END:
$ WRITE SYS$OUTPUT "C Programming Utility Ending"
$ EXIT
```

The Command Language Start-up Sequence Files

A major use for a command language is the system start-up file. Most modern operating systems allow the execution of specific command files at system start-up and also when a user logs in to the system. Two types of start-up files exist. One type is used to configure the basic operating system, as we discussed in Chapter 13. Start-up configuration files are only modified by the system administrator.

The second type of start-up file is used to tailor the system to the user's preferences. User start-up commands can be used to set various parameters, such as the preferred places to look for files, the type of terminal that the user is working with, the selection of a **command shell,** and the appearance of the command line prompt. On a multitasking system, the user start-up command file can be tailored to each individual user. It is executed whenever a user logs in. Login start-up files for a UNIX system depend on the default shell being used for the system. The Bourne shell start-up script is called *.login;* the C-shell script is called *.cshrc.* Since these files are text files, they can be easily communicated across a network to provide uniform capability to all users on the network. This allows a system administrator to change every user's profile with the modification of a single file.

14.6 SERVICES TO PROGRAMS

Most of the discussion in this chapter has centered around the user interface and methods of controlling and using the interface, but we would be remiss if we did not say a few additional words about services provided by the operating system to application programs that support and affect the user interface. As we noted in Chapter 14, operating systems have long provided services to application programs in the areas of file management, I/O processing, and system resource management. A few operating systems, particularly the Macintosh OS, have provided services such as the ToolBox that extend these capabilities to include the graphical user interface. Services outside the operating system, but not quite applications either, such as X Window, extend graphical capabilities to other systems.

Windows provides similar services through the Win32 API. These services reflect the trend to expand the role of the operating system generally to include services and support to application programs and users that provide many capabilities that were formerly within the applications themselves. These services enable the system to provide a standard look and feel for different applications extending, even, to the Web interface. They simplify and extend the graphic capabilities of application programs, they improve the capability of programs to communicate with each other and to pass data from one application to another, they provide the ability to launch an application program from within another, they provide e-mail and other communication capabilities, and they provide document and graphical storage services at a more sophisticated level than is found in traditional OS file management facilities.

These concepts form the foundation of the docucentric approach to user interface design. By integrating these capabilities into the operating system, the system can assure that every application program responds in similar ways to user actions. Integration also provides smooth and seamless interaction between the different applications. Just as the file manager assures a consistent representation and interface for file manipulation across different devices, so these new services provide the user with a more powerful and easier to use way to access his program applications. The overall effect is an increased emphasis on the user interface and new ways of working that are more oriented toward the work to be accomplished and less to the launching and manipulation of application programs. Although many of these tools are found in a "shell," they are more tightly integrated into the operating system than was true of previous shells.

The addition of new operating system services is intimately tied to improved programming methods, particularly object-oriented programming. These services commonly take the form of libraries of objects that application programs request via the usual call mechanisms. Several standards continue to evolve for these services. Standards are necessary so that applications may be developed with the assurance that the services required will be available. The most important of these standards include DCOM, .NET, and CORBA.

The dividing line between the operating system and the application programs has become increasingly unclear, as the operating system moves into a realm that has traditionally been part of the application programs themselves. Windows has already integrated the Web browser into its user interface to provide a common look and feel that extends all the way from local file management to the services of the Web. Perhaps these services will be considered part of a new OS layer, called application program services, or perhaps the operating system itself will be divided differently, into user services and a kernel that provides the basic internal services. Some researchers and operating system designers envision a model consisting of a small operating system extended by objects that support the user's applications. This approach suggests the growing operating system emphasis on the user environment and on application integration.

Overall, the effect on the user's interaction with the computer promises to be profound. Presently, the user performs her work by opening applications and working within those applications. The concepts of *suites* of applications, at the application program level, and of object linking, at the system level, extend this capability to allow the applications to communicate, to share data, and to perform operations within an application by launching another application. The additional capabilities envisioned for software at the system level, whether considered part of the operating system or another type of interface shell, will expand this process and ultimately can be expected to shift the user's focus to the document, data set, or other work entity, with applications launched invisibly as they are required to accomplish a particular task.

SUMMARY AND REVIEW

Modern operating systems provide an interface that is used by programs and by the user to interact with the system. The interface provides a variety of user and program services, including a user interface with command capability, program execution and control capability, I/O and file services for programs and for users, command languages for building programs of commands, system information, security features, and interuser communication and file sharing capability. An application programming interface (API) provides a standard set of services that application programs use to access the operating system and to provide a common look-and-feel to their user interfaces. In this chapter we considered each of these services.

Most systems are primarily interactive. For this purpose there are currently two primary types of user interface, the command line interface and the graphical user interface, each with its own advantages and disadvantages. Similar operations can be performed with each, although the method employed is different for each.

X Window is an important graphical display methodology, particularly in networked and distributed environments. X Window is an attempt to provide windowing capability while partially solving the difficulty of transmitting large quantities of graphical data from one location to another. X Window is built around a client-server architecture.

Command languages allow a user to build more powerful functions out of the command set. Most command languages provide looping and selection capability, as well as interactive input and output. Some command languages are intended for batch processing. IBM's zOS/JCL is an important example of a batch language.

KEY CONCEPTS AND TERMS

access control list (ACL)
active window
application association
application program interface (API)
batch file
batch program
card image
click to focus
client
command language
command line interface (CLI)
command shell
common look and feel
controls
CORBA (Common Object-Request Broker Architecture)
cursor

DCOM (Distributed Component Object Model)
desktop
display server
dock
docucentric approach
drag-and-drop
Finder
gadget
graphical user interface (GUI)
icon
intranet
job control language (JCL)
keyword operand
launch
menu bar
menu-driven interface
modifier

mount a device
mouse focus
.NET
operand
positional operand
remote procedure call (RPC)
screen
scripting language
(shell) script
switch
title bar
unmount a device
volume
widget
wild card
window
X Window

FOR FURTHER READING

A general book that discusses the user interface in great detail is Preece [PRE94]. Marcus and colleagues [MARC95] provide an easy-to-read discussion and comparison of graphical user interfaces. There are several others listed in the references. The general operating system aspects of the user interface and program services can be found in any of the operating system texts identified in Chapter 13. The X Window system is introduced well in Christian and Richter [CHR94] and presented in much more detail in many books, including Mansfield [MANS93] or Jones [JON00]].

EXERCISES

14.1 List and explain some definite advantages to the use of a command line interface over other types of interfaces. Do the same for a graphical user interface. Do the same for a menuing interface. What is the target audience for each type of interface?

14.2 Discuss the advantages and disadvantages of providing the user interface as a separate shell, rather than as an integral part of the operating system.

14.3 If you have access to two or more command line interface systems, such as VMS and MS-DOS or MS-DOS and Linux, compare the major commands that are available on each. Note the similarities and differences between them, particularly in their capabilities and in the way the command task is performed.

14.4 Consider the major commands in a command line interface system such as MS-DOS or UNIX. Explain how each task would be performed on a graphical user interface system such as the Macintosh.

14.5 There are some capabilities that are easy to achieve with a GUI, but much more difficult with a CLI. Describe a few of these capabilities.

14.6 Explain piping.

14.7 Explain the concept of redirection.

14.8 What purpose do arguments serve in a batch file or shell script?

14.9 If you have access to a graphical user interface, identify the name and purpose of each of the components of the GUI.

14.10 Use the batch file or shell script capability of your system to build a menuing interface that implements the most common commands.

14.11 Describe the difficulties that exist in providing a GUI at a location remote from the computer that is creating the display. Describe the methods used by X Window to partially overcome these difficulties. Why is it not possible for X Window to totally solve these problems?

14.12 Discuss the advantages that result from the client-server architecture of the X Window system.

14.13 When people describe client-server architecture, they are usually referring to a system in which a large server is serving a client on a PC. With X Window, the reverse is frequently the case. Explain.

14.14 The designers of the UNIX operating system described the ideal shell command language as one that is made up of a large set of simple commands, each designed to perform one specialized task well. They also provided various means to combine these simple commands to form more powerful commands.

    a. What tools are provided to combine the commands?

    b. What are the advantages of this approach over providing a smaller set of much more powerful commands? What are the disadvantages?

    c. If you know something about the UNIX or Linux command set, discuss the characteristics of UNIX/Linux commands that make it easier to combine these commands powerfully.

14.15 If you could design a "wild card" system with features beyond those normally provided in a CLI, what features would you add?

CHAPTER 15

THE INTERNAL OPERATING SYSTEM

Thomas Sperling

15.0 INTRODUCTION

In Chapter 13 we observed that it is possible to represent the architecture of the operating system by a hierarchical target model, consisting of several layers of programs that interact with each other to handle the routine tasks of command processing, file management, I/O, resource management, communication, and scheduling. As you saw in Chapter 14, the outer layers of the model exist primarily to serve the user.

The file management system layer converts the logical representation of files as seen by the user or the user's programs to the physical representation stored and manipulated within the computer. Its function is so important that it will be dealt with separately in the next chapter.

The remaining inner layers are designed primarily to manage the hardware and software resources of the computer and its interactions with other computers. In this chapter, we will look at how these internal operations are performed; we will consider how the operating system programs manage the various hardware resources, including memory, for the convenience, security, and efficiency of the users.

The complexity of the operating system depends on the fundamental type and goals of the operating system, on the number of tasks to be performed concurrently, and on the number of users sharing the system. In this chapter we briefly review the concepts from Chapter 13 first. Then we expand our focus to look at the various components of more advanced operating systems.

Expanding the operating system to allow the processing of multiple programs concurrently has the effect of increasing the size and complexity of the system tremendously. The expanded system must have the means to decide which programs are to be admitted into memory and when, where programs should reside in memory, how CPU time is to be allocated to the various programs, how to resolve conflicting requirements for I/O services, and how to share programs and yet maintain security and program and data integrity and to address many other questions. It is not uncommon for the operating system to require several tens of megabytes of memory just for itself. To solve some of the more challenging operating system problems, the concept of a computer has expanded to include special CPU hardware that works in coordination with the operating system software to form a well-integrated computer system. Virtual storage, first introduced in Chapter 8, is the most important of these advances. Virtual storage is a powerful technique for solving some of the difficulties of memory management. The layering of the instruction set to include protected instructions and memory limit checking are other features built into the hardware to support operating system functions, in this case security. Integration of the CPU hardware and operating system software is characteristic of modern computer systems.

The subject of operating systems can easily fill a large textbook and an entire course all by itself. There are many interesting questions and problems related to operating systems and many different solutions to the problem of creating a useful and efficient operating system.

Obviously, we won't be able to cover this subject in a great amount of detail, but at least you'll get a feeling for some of the more important and interesting aspects of how operating systems work. We will introduce individually the various tasks that are to be performed by the operating system and consider some of the methods used to perform these tasks in an effective manner. We'll show you a simple example in which the different pieces have been put together to form a complete system.

The many tasks that a modern operating system is expected to perform also expand the overhead required by the operating system, both in terms of memory and in the time required to perform the different functions. We will also look at some of the measures that are used to determine the effectiveness of an operating system. Finally, you'll have a chance to read about a few of the more interesting problems, especially those that can have a significant effect on the user.

15.1 A BRIEF REVIEW OF THE TARGET MODEL

Always keep in mind that the fundamental purpose of any operating system is to load and execute programs. This is true regardless of the specific goals, design features, and complexity of the particular operating system that you happen to be looking at.

With this fundamental idea in mind, look again at the various functions that are provided within the operating system target model, shown again for your convenience in Figure 15.1.

FIGURE 15.1

Target Model of an OS

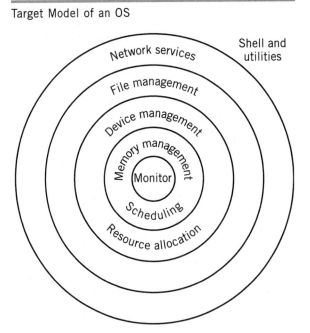

To load and execute a program, the system must provide a method of getting the program from its storage location on some I/O device, such as disk, into memory; it must provide a location in memory for the program and its data; it must provide CPU time for the program to execute; and it must provide access to the I/O facilities that the program needs during its execution. When multiple programs are sharing the system and its resources, it must do all this in a way that is fair and meets the sometimes conflicting requirements of the different programs.

The inner layers of the target model provide programs that fulfill these requirements. The file manager layer translates logical file requests from the command shell or the user's programs into specific physical I/O requests that are then performed by the appropriate I/O device management programs. Resource allocation management is also provided in this layer to resolve conflicts between different programs that may require I/O services at the same time. The I/O device management and resource allocation programs are sometimes known collectively as an I/O control system, or more commonly, IOCS.

The memory management and scheduling layer determines if it is possible to load programs and data into memory, and, if so, where in memory the program is to be loaded. Once the program is in memory, the scheduler allocates time for the program to execute. If there are multiple programs in memory, the scheduler attempts to allocate time for each of them in some fair way.

The monitor program, when included, provides overall control of the system. It establishes guidelines for the general management of the system based on goals provided by the human manager of the system. It watches for conflicts, breakdowns, and problems and attempts to take appropriate action to ensure smooth and efficient system operation. Some monitors can even reconfigure and reassign resources dynamically to optimize performance, particularly in clustered systems. These roles are handled by other operating system components in some systems.

To increase security, many operating systems construct these programs as a hierarchy in which each layer of programs in the model requests services from the next innermost layer, using an established calling procedure. Most modern computers provide special protected hardware instructions for this purpose. Recall from Chapter 13 that this is not the only possible architecture for an operating system. At the very least, the critical parts of the operating system will execute in a protected mode while other programs will execute in user mode. A well-designed operating system will repel attempts to penetrate the internal layers of the system by means other than the established calling procedure.

15.2 FUNDAMENTAL OS REQUIREMENTS

The fundamental concept of the operating system is simple. The operating system must divide up the space in memory, load one or more programs into that space, and then execute those programs, giving each program sufficient time to complete. It also provides file, I/O, and other services to each of the programs. When not providing services, it sits idle.

The challenge comes from the fact that multiple programs are each sharing resources—memory, I/O, and CPU time—that are inherently designed to do one thing at a time. Thus, the operating system must provide additional support functions that allocate each program its fair share of memory, CPU time, and I/O resource time when it is needed.

It must also isolate and protect each program, yet allow the programs to share data and communicate, when required.

There are many different ways of performing each of these functions, each with advantages and disadvantages. The trade-offs selected reflect the design goals of the particular system. To give you a simple example, a computer that operates strictly in a batch mode might use a simple CPU scheduling algorithm that allows each program to run without interruption as long as the program does not have to stop processing to wait for I/O. This strategy would not be acceptable on an interactive system that requires fast screen response when a user clicks the mouse or types something into the keyboard. In the latter case, a more sophisticated scheduling algorithm is clearly required.

Before we continue with discussions of the individual resource managers, you should be aware that these managers are not totally independent of each other. For example, if there are more programs in the memory of an interactive system, the scheduler must give each program a shorter period of time if satisfactory user response is to be achieved. Similarly, more programs in memory will increase the workload on a disk manager, making it more likely that there will be several programs waiting for disk I/O at the same time. Conversely, fewer programs in memory may result in periods of time in which no useful work is being performed by the system, perhaps because the various users are all sitting at their keyboards thinking.

Before proceeding to detailed discussions of each of the major modules in a multitasking operating system, it may provide some insight to introduce you to a simple example of a system, a sort of "Little Man multitasking operating system" if you will. The system discussed here does not run on the Little Man Computer, however. It was designed for a real, working computer system. This example illustrates many of the important requirements and operations of a multitasking system.

Example: A Simple Multitasking Operating System

The miniature operating system (hereafter referred to as MINOS) is an extremely small and simple multitasking system with many of the important internal features of larger systems. It is based on a real operating system that was developed by the author in the 1970s for a very early and primitive microcomputer that was used primarily to measure data in remote rural locations. Calculations were performed on the data and the results telecommunicated back to a larger computer for further processing. The original goals of the design were

- First and foremost, simplicity. Memory was very expensive in those days, so we didn't want to use much for the operating system. There was only 8 kilobytes (KB) of memory in the machine.
- Real-time support for one very important program that was run frequently and had to operate very fast. This was the data measurement program. The system therefore features a priority scheduling system in choosing which program is to run.

The internal design of MINOS was of more interest and importance to the designers than the user interface or the file system. There was no disk on this computer, only an audiocassette tape recorder, modified to hold computer data, so the file system was simple. (Disks were too expensive, too large, and too fragile for this type of system, back then!) There was a keyboard/printer user interface, but no CRT display interface. Security was not a concern.

The features of particular interest to us here are the operation of memory management, process scheduling, and dispatching. Despite their simplicity, the design of these modules is characteristic of the way current operating systems work.

These are the important specifications for MINOS:

- Keyboard/printer command line user interface. To keep things simple, there are only a few commands, most of which could be entered by typing a single character. For example, the letter "l" was used to load a program from tape, the letter "s" to save a program to tape.

- Memory is divided into six fixed partitions of different sizes. A memory map is shown in Figure 15.2. One partition is reserved for MINOS, which is entirely memory resident. Partition P-1 is reserved for high-priority programs, most commonly the data retrieval program, since it must retrieve data in real time. Partitions P-2, P-3, and P-4 are of different sizes, but all share equal, middle priority. Partition P-5 is a low-priority area, which is used for background tasks, mostly internal system checking, but there is a simple binary editor available that can be loaded into the low-priority partition for debugging and modifying programs.

- The operating system is divided into three levels: the command interface; the I/O subsystem; and the kernel, which contains the memory manager, the communication interface, and the scheduler. The operating system kernel has the highest priority by default, since it must respond to user commands and provide dispatching services. It can interrupt and preempt other programs. However, routine operations such as program loading are processed at the lowest priority level. A block diagram of MINOS appears in Figure 15.3.

Note again that MINOS does not support a file system or most other user amenities; it is primarily oriented toward program loading and execution. This limitation does not concern us, since the primary focus of this discussion is the internal operation of the system. The two major components of the kernel are the process scheduler/memory manager and the dispatcher.

MINOS is capable of manipulating up to five user programs at a time. The process scheduler handles requests for program loading. The header for a program to be loaded specifies a priority level and a memory size requirement. Programs are loaded into the smallest available memory space of correct priority level that will fit the program. Of course, there is only a single memory area available each for programs of the highest and lowest priorities. If space is not available, the process scheduler notifies the user; it is up to the user to determine which program, if any, should be unloaded to make room.

FIGURE 15.2

The MINOS Memory Map

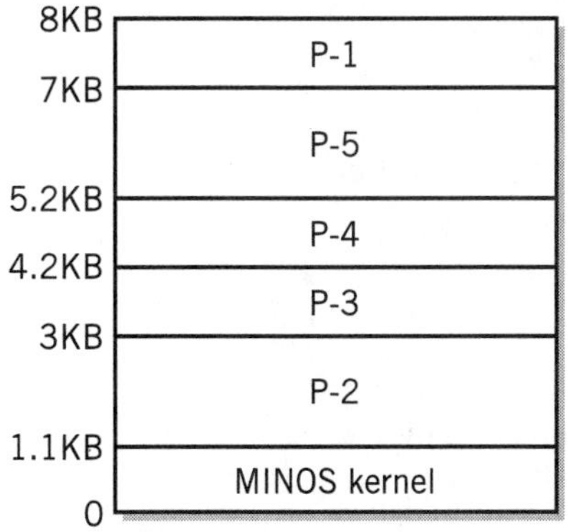

FIGURE 15.3

Block Diagram, MINOS

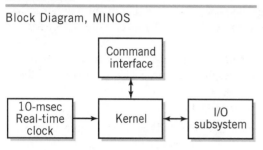

For each program in memory, there is an entry in a process control table, shown in Figure 15.4. Recall from Chapter 13 that at any instant in time, one process is running, while the others are ready to run or waiting for an event, such as I/O completion, to occur. The process control table shows the status of each program and the program counter location where the program will restart when it is next run. It also contains locations for storage and restoration of each of the two registers that are present in the microcomputer that was used. There is also one additional register that keeps track of which midpriority process, partition 2, partition 3, or partition 4, was run most recently. We called this register the mid-priority process run last, or MPRL, register. Since there is one entry in the process table for each partition, the priority value for each program is already known by the operating system.

The most interesting part of MINOS is the program dispatcher. A real-time clock in the computer interrupts the computer every 1/100th of a second and returns control to the dispatcher. The dispatcher goes through the process control table in order of priority and checks the status of each active entry. (An inactive entry is one in which there is no program loaded into the space, or in which the program in the space has completed execution and is not running.) If the entry is blocked because it is waiting for I/O to be completed, it is not available to run and is passed by. The highest-priority ready program is selected and control passed to it. If there are two or three ready programs of the same priority, they

FIGURE 15.4

MINOS Process Dispatch

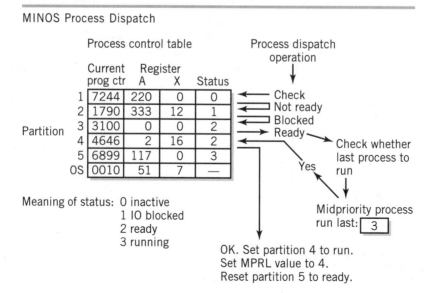

will be selected in a round-robin fashion (program 2, program 3, program 4, program 2, program 3, ...), so that each will get a turn. The MPRL register is used for this purpose.

The MINOS dispatching algorithm guarantees that the high-priority real-time program will always get first shot at the CPU and that the maximum delay before it can execute is 1/100th of a second. The ready bit for this program is actually set by a small interrupt routine controlled by the measuring device. Figure 15.4 illustrates the dispatching process.

The background task represents the lowest priority. Usually, this partition contains software routines for testing various aspects of the hardware. Thus, when no other program is selected, MINOS defaults to the hardware diagnostic routines.

With MINOS as a background, the next five sections of Chapter 15 consider various aspects of a multitasking operating system in more detail. You may also wish to review Section 13.5 of Chapter 13, which introduces the various services and modules present in a multitasking system, before proceeding.

15.3 PROCESSES AND THREADS

When considering a multitasking system, it is easiest to think of each executing task as a program. This representation is not inaccurate, but it is not sufficiently inclusive, precise, or general to explain all the different situations that can occur within a computer system. Instead, we may define each executing task more usefully as a process. A **process** is defined to include a program, together with all the resources that are associated with that program as it is executed. Those resources may include I/O devices that have been assigned to the particular process, keyboard input data, files that have been opened, memory that has been assigned as a buffer for I/O data or as a stack, memory assigned to the program, CPU time, and many other possibilities.

Another way of viewing a process is to consider it as a program in execution. A program is viewed passively: it's a file or a listing, for example. A process is viewed actively: it is being processed or executed.

In batch systems, a different terminology is sometimes used. A user submits a **job** to the system for processing; the job is made up of **job steps,** each of which represents a single **task.** It is not difficult to see the relationship among jobs, tasks, and processes. When the job is admitted to the system, a process is created for the job. Each of the tasks within the job also represent processes, specifically, processes that will be created as each step in the job is executed. In this book we tend to use the words job and process interchangeably.

The difference between a program and a process is not usually important in normal conversation, but from the perspective of the operating system the difference may be quite significant and profound. For example, many multiuser operating systems have the capability of sharing a single copy of a program such as an editor among many users concurrently. Each user has his or her own files and data. This practice can save memory space, since only a single copy of the program is required, instead of many; thus, this technique increases system capability. Crucial to this concept, however, is the understanding that each user may be operating in a different part of the program; therefore, each user maintains a different program counter value during his or her execution time, as well as different data. This concept is illustrated in Figure 15.5. By maintaining a separate process for each user, the operating system can keep track of each user's requirements in a straightforward manner.

FIGURE 15.5

Two Processes Sharing a Single Program

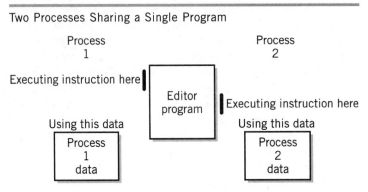

Even in a single-user system, multiple processes may share program code. For example, the program code that produces the Windows interface will be shared by all the processes with open windows on a screen. Each process will have its own data: the coordinates of the window, pointers to the menu structure for that window, and so forth.

To the operating system, the basic unit of work is a process. When a process is admitted to the system, the operating system is responsible for every aspect of its operation. The OS must allocate initial memory for it and must continue to assure that memory is available to the process as it is needed. It must assign the necessary files and I/O devices and provide stack memory and buffers. It must schedule CPU execution time for the process and perform context switching between the various executing processes. The OS must maintain the integrity of the process. Finally, when the process is completed, it terminates the process in an orderly way and restores the system facilities and resources to make them available to other processes.

Processes that do not need to interact with any other processes are known as **independent processes.** In modern systems, many processes will work together. They will share information and files. A large task will often be modularized by splitting it into subtasks, so that each process will only handle one aspect of the task. Processes that work together are known as **cooperating processes.** The operating system provides mechanisms for synchronizing and communicating between processes that are related in some way. (If one process needs the result from another, for example, it must know when the result is available so that it can proceed. This is known as synchronization. It must also be able to receive the result from the other process. This is communication.) The operating system acts as the manager and conduit for these interprocess events.

To keep track of each of the different processes that are executing concurrently in memory, the operating system creates and maintains a block of data for each process in the system. This data block is known as a **process control block,** frequently abbreviated as **PCB.** The process control block contains all relevant information about the process. It is the central resource used by the various operating system modules as they perform their process-related functions.

In MINOS, the process control block is simple. It is only necessary to keep track of the program counter and a pair of register values so that processes may be suspended and restarted, plus the status and priority of the program. Since MINOS divides memory into partitions of fixed size, there is exactly one process and therefore one PCB, per partition, so it is not even necessary for the operating system to keep track of the memory limits of a process.

In a larger system, process control is considerably more complex. There may be many more processes. Contention for the available memory and for various I/O resources is more likely. There may be requirements for communication between different processes. Scheduling and dispatch are more difficult. The complexity of the system requires the storing of much additional information about the process, as well as more formal control of process operations.

The contents of a typical process control block are shown in Figure 15.6. Different system PCBs present this information in different order and with some differences in the information stored, but these differences are not important for the purposes of this discussion.

Each process control block in Figure 15.6 contains a process identification name or number that uniquely identifies the block. In Linux, for example, the process identification number is known as a **process identifier,** or more commonly, a **PID.** Active processes are readily observable on the Linux system using the *ps* command.

Next, the PCB contains pointers to other, related processes. This issue is related to the way in which new processes are created. It is discussed in the next section. The presence of this area simplifies communication between related processes. Following the pointer area is an indicator of the process state. In MINOS, four **process states** were possible: inactive, ready, blocked, and running. In larger systems, there are other possible states; processor states are discussed later in this section. The program counter and register save areas are used to save and restore the exact context the CPU when the process gives up and regains the CPU.

Memory limits establish the legal areas of memory that the process may access. The presence of this data simplifies the task of security for the operating system. Similarly, priority and accounting information is used by the operating system for scheduling and for billing purposes.

Finally, the process control block often contains pointers to shared program code and data, open files, and other resources that the process uses. This simplifies the tasks of the I/O and file management systems.

FIGURE 15.6

A Typical Process Control Block

Process ID
Pointer to parent process
Pointer area to child processes   ...
Process state
Program counter
Register save area   ...
Memory pointers
Priority information
Accounting information
Pointers to shared memory areas, shared processes and libraries, files, and other I/O resources

Process Creation

A little thought should make it clear to you that a process is created when you type a command that requests execution of a program. There are also many other ways in which a process is created. Particularly on interactive systems, process creation is one of the fundamental tasks performed by the operating system. Processes in a computer system are continually being created and destroyed.

Since *any* executing program is a process, almost any command that you type into a multitasking interactive system normally creates a process. Even logging in creates a process, since logging in requires providing a program that serves as your interface, giving you a prompt or GUI, monitoring your keystrokes, and responding to your requests. In many systems, this is known as a **user process.** In some systems, all processes that are not modules of the operating system are known as user processes.

It should also be remembered that the operating system itself is made up of program modules. These modules, too, must share the use of the CPU to perform their duties. Thus, the active parts of the operating system are, themselves, processes. When a process requests I/O or operating system services, for example, processes are created for the various operating system program modules that will service the request, as well as for any additional processes resulting from the request. These processes are sometimes known as **system processes.**

In batch systems, jobs are submitted to the system for processing. Often, there are more jobs submitted than can be executed immediately. These jobs are copied, or spooled, to a disk and placed in a queue to await admission to the system. A long-term scheduler in the operating system, discussed in Section 16.5, selects jobs as resources become available and loads them into memory for execution. A process is created when the long-term scheduler determines that it is able to accept a batch job and admits it to the system.

For convenience, operating systems generally associate processes with the process that created them. Creating a new process from an older one is commonly called **forking** or **spawning.** The spawning process is called a **parent.** The spawned process is known as a **child.** Many systems simply assign priorities, resources, and other characteristics to the child process by **cloning** the parent process. This means creating a process control block that is a duplicate of itself. Once the child process begins to execute, it goes by way of its own path. It can request its own resources and change whatever characteristics it needs to.

As an example of process creation, a C++ program compiler might create child processes that perform the different stages of compilation, editing, and debugging. Each child process is created when the specific task is needed and killed when the task is complete. Incidentally, note the synchronization between processes that is suggested by this example. If the compile process encounters an error, for example, the parent is notified so that it can activate an editor process. A successful compile will result in a load process that will load the new program for execution. And so on.

Removing a parent process usually kills all the child processes associated with it. Since a child process can itself have children, the actual process structure may be several generations deep. Pointers are used within the process control block to help keep track of the relationships between different processes.

When the process is created, the operating system gives it a unique name or identification number, creates a process control block for it, allocates the memory and other initial resources that the process needs, and performs other operating system bookkeeping functions. When the process exits, its resources are returned to the system pool, and its PCB is removed from the process table.

Process States

Most operating systems define three primary operating states for a process. These are known as the **ready state,** the **running state,** and the **blocked state.** The relationship between the different process states is shown in Figure 15.7.

FIGURE 15.7

The Major Process States

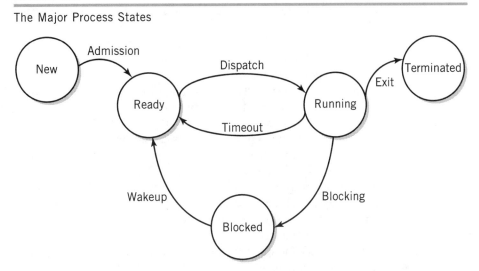

Once a process has been created and admitted to the system for execution, it is brought into the *ready* state, where it must compete with all other processes in the *ready* state for CPU execution time. Being in the *ready* state simply means that a process is capable of execution if given access to the CPU.

At some point in time, presumably, the process will be given time for execution. The process is moved from the *ready* state to the *running* state. Moving from the *ready* state to the *running* state is called **dispatching** the process. During the time that the process is in the *running* state, the program has control of the CPU and is able to execute instructions. Of course, only one process can be in the *running* state at a time for a uniprocessor system. If there are multiple processors or a cluster under the OS's control, the OS is responsible for dispatching a process to run in each available CPU. In a typical multitasking system, there may be many processes in *blocked* or *ready* states at any given time.

When I/O or other services are required for the continuation of program execution, the running process can no longer do any further useful work until its requirement is satisfied. Some operating systems will suspend the program when this occurs; others will allow the program to remain in the *running* state, even though the program is unable to proceed. In the latter case, most well designed programs will suspend themselves, unless the interruption is expected to be extremely brief. This state transition is known as **blocking,** and the process remains in a *blocked* state until its I/O requirement is complete. When the I/O operation is complete, the operating system moves the process from the *blocked* state back to the *ready* state. This state transition is frequently called **wake-up.** Blocking can also occur when a process is waiting for some event other than I/O to occur, for example, a completion signal or a data result from another process.

Nonpreemptive systems will allow a running process to continue running until it is completed or blocked. **Preemptive systems** will limit the time that the program remains in the *running* state to a fixed length of time corresponding to one or more quanta. If the process remains in the *running* state when its time limit has occurred, the operating system will return the process to the *ready* state to await further time for processing. The transition from the *running* state to the *ready* state is known as **time-out.**

When the process completes execution, control returns to the operating system, and the process is *destroyed* or *killed* or *terminated.*

Some operating systems provide one or more additional states, which are used to improve the efficiency of the computer system. Some processes make heavy demands on particular resources, say, a disk drive or a printer, or even the CPU, in such a way that other processes are unable to complete their work in an efficient manner. In this case the operating system may place a process in a **suspended state** until the required resources can be made available. When this occurs, the process is returned to a *ready* state. The transition from the *suspended* state to the *ready* state is known as **resumption.** Some operating systems also allow a user to suspend a process. On UNIX systems, for example, typing Control-"Z" is one way in which to suspend a process. The process may be resumed by issuing the command *fg,* together with the process identification number of the process. Some operating systems will also swap out a suspended process from memory to secondary storage when the system becomes overloaded and will swap it back in when the load is lighter. Particularly in small systems, the use of **swap files** for this purpose is common. Even in large computer systems, transaction processing software often contains interactive processes that are used infrequently. These processes are often swapped out when they are not being used and returned to memory when they are activated by a user request. This technique is called **roll-out, roll-in.** The *suspend, resume,* and *swap* states have been left off the diagram for clarity.

Threads

It is common in modern systems to provide capability for a sort of miniprocess, known as a thread. A thread represents a piece of a process that can be executed independently of other parts of the process. Each thread has its own context, consisting of a program counter value, register set, and stack space, but shares program code, and data, and other system resources such as open files with the other member threads in the process. Threads can operate concurrently. Like processes, threads can be created and destroyed and can be in ready, running, and blocked states. Context switching among threads is easier for the operating system to manage because there is no need to manage memory, files, and other resources and no need for synchronization or communication within the process, since this is handled within the process itself. This advantage suggests, however, that more care needs to be taken when the program is written, to assure that threads do not interact with each other in subtle ways that can create conditions that cause the program to fail. Note that there is no protection among the threads of a process, since all the threads are using the same program code and data space.

Some systems even provide a mechanism for context switching of threads independent of the process switching mechanism. This means that in these systems threads can be switched without the involvement of the operating system kernel. If a process becomes I/O blocked, it cannot proceed until the block is resolved. On the other hand, if a thread becomes blocked, other threads in the process may be able to continue execution within the process's allotted time, resulting in more rapid execution. Because the inner layers of the operating system are not even aware of thread context switching in these systems, thread switching is extremely rapid and efficient. Threads in these systems are commonly known as **user-level threads.**

Threads came about as a result of the advent of **event-driven programs.** In a traditional program, there is a single flow of control. Event-driven programs differ in that the flow of control depends in a much more dramatic way on user input. With a modern graphical user interface, a user can pull down a menu and select an action to be performed at almost any time. Selecting an item from a menu or clicking a mouse in a particular place in a particular way is known as an **event.** The program must be able to respond to a variety of different events, at unknown times, and in unknown order of request.

Such events are usually too small to justify creation of a new process. Instead, the action for each event is treated as a thread. The thread can be executed independently, but without the overhead of a process. There is no control block, no separate memory, no separate resources. The primary requirement for a thread is an area to store the program counter and registers. Threads are processed in much the same way as processes.

15.4 CPU SCHEDULING

CPU scheduling provides mechanisms for the acceptance of processes into the system and for the actual allocation of CPU time to execute those processes. A fundamental objective of multitasking is to optimize use of the computer system resources, both CPU and I/O, by allowing multiple processes to execute concurrently. CPU scheduling is the means for meeting this objective. There are many different algorithms that can be used for CPU scheduling. The selection of a CPU scheduling algorithm can have a major effect on the performance of the system.

As a way to optimize system performance, the CPU scheduling task is separated into two different phases. The **high-level,** or **long-term, scheduler** is responsible for admitting processes to the system. The **dispatcher** provides short-term scheduling, specifically, the instant-by-instant decision as to which one of the processes that are ready should be given CPU execution time. The dispatcher also performs context switching. Some systems also include a third, middle-level scheduler, which monitors system performance. When present, the middle-level scheduler can suspend, or **swap out,** a process by removing it from memory temporarily and replace it with another waiting process. This operation is known as **swapping.** Swapping is done to improve overall system performance. It would be used if a particular process were hogging a resource in such a way as to prevent other processes from executing.

High-Level Scheduler

The high-level scheduler determines which processes are to be admitted to the system. The role of the high-level scheduler is minimal for processes created in an interactive environment. Such processes are usually admitted to the system automatically. If a user requests a service that requires the creation of a new process, the high-level scheduler *will* attempt to do so unless the system is seriously overloaded. To refuse the user in the middle of her or his work would be undesirable. The high-level scheduler will refuse a login process, however, if it appears that doing so would overload the system. The high-level scheduler will refuse admission to the system if there is no place to put the program in memory or if other resources are unattainable. If the request is a user login request, the user will have to wait until later to try again. Otherwise, requests are usually accepted, even though it may slow down the system. You may have experienced such slowdowns when working with Windows. You may have even gotten an "out-of-memory" message if you tried to do too many things at once!

For batch processes, the high-level scheduler has a much more important role. With small systems with limited memory, the high-level scheduler is essential. With batch processes, a delay in processing is less noticeable to the user; therefore, the high-level scheduler has more flexibility in deciding when to admit the process to the system. The high-level scheduler can use its power to balance system resource use as an attempt to maximize the efficiency of the system. Since most modern systems are predominately interactive, the high-level scheduler is of minimal importance for most system use today.

Summing up the activity of the high-level scheduler, the criteria for admission of processes to a batch system are usually based primarily on priorities and secondarily on the balancing of resources, although some systems use a first-come, first-served algorithm. Admission is also dependent on the availability of memory space. In a system with fixed partitions, like MINOS, the high-level scheduler may set up separate queues for each memory partition. Admission in an interactive system is usually based only on available memory and system load.

Dispatching

Conceptually, the dispatching process is simple. Whenever a process or thread gives up the CPU, the dispatcher selects another candidate that is ready to run, performs a context switch, and sets the program counter to the program counter value stored in the process control block to start execution. In reality, dispatching is much more complex than it first appears. There are a number of different conditions that might cause a process to give up the CPU, some voluntary and some involuntary, as established by the operating system. Presumably, the goal of the dispatcher is to select the next candidate in such a way as to optimize system use. But, in fact, there are a number of different measurement criteria that can be used to define "optimum" system performance. Frequently, these criteria are in conflict with each other, and the characteristics of the candidates in contention as well as different conditions within the system can also affect the selection of a particular candidate for CPU execution at any given time.

Similarly, processes vary in their requirements. Processes can be long or short in their requirement for CPU execution time, they can require many resources, or just a few, and they can vary in their ratio of CPU to I/O execution time. Different scheduling algorithms favor different types of processes or threads and meet different optimization criteria. For example, an algorithm that maximizes throughput by consistently placing short jobs at the front of the queue is clearly not fair to a longer job that keeps getting delayed.

As a result, there are a number of different scheduling algorithms that can be used. The choice of scheduling algorithm then depends on the optimization objective(s) chosen, along with the expected mix of process types. Analysis requires consideration of a wide variety of process mix possibilities and dynamic situations. Some of the objectives considered are shown in the table in Figure 15.8. Of the various objectives in the table, the prevention of starvation is particularly noticeable. Some algorithms with otherwise desirable properties have a potential to cause starvation under certain conditions. It is particularly important that the algorithm selected not permit starvation to occur.

With operating systems that support threads, dispatching normally takes place at the thread level. As an additional criterion, the candidate selection decision can be made at either the process or thread level. Some systems will select a candidate that meets criteria measured at the process level. A process is selected, then a thread within that process is dispatched. Other systems will select a thread for dispatch based on thread performance criteria without regard to the process to which they belong.

Some systems implement only a single algorithm, selected by the original system designers. Others provide options that can be selected by the administrator of the particular system installation. Other than preventing starvation, the most important consideration in selecting a scheduling algorithm is to determine the conditions under which dispatching is to be performed preemptively or nonpreemptively.

FIGURE 15.8

System Dispatching Objectives

Ensure fairness	The scheduler should treat every process equally. This means that every process should get a fair share of the CPU time.
Maximize throughout	The scheduler should attempt to maximize the number of jobs completed in any given time period.
Minimize turnaround time	The scheduler should minimize the time between submission of a job and its completion.
Maximize CPU utilization	The scheduler should attempt to keep the CPU busy as close to 100% of the time as possible.
Maximize resource allocation	The scheduler should attempt to maximize the use of all resources by balancing processes that require heavy CPU time with those emphasizing I/O.
Promote graceful degradation	This objective states that as the system load becomes heavy, it should degrade gradually in performance. This objective is based on the assumption that users expect a heavily loaded system to respond more slowly, but not radically or suddenly so.
Minimize response time	This objective is particularly important in interactive systems. Processes should complete as quickly as possible.
Provide consistent response time	Users expect long jobs to require more actual time than short jobs. They also expect a job to take about the same amount of time each time it is executed. An algorithm that allows a large variation in the response time may not be considered acceptable to users.
Prevent starvation	Processes should not be allowed to starve. **Starvation** is a situation that occurs when a process is never given the CPU time that it needs to execute. Starvation is also called **indefinite postponement.**

Early batch systems were predominately nonpreemptive. In a nonpreemptive system, the process assigned to the CPU by the dispatcher is allowed to run to completion, or until it voluntarily gives up the CPU. Nonpreemptive dispatching is efficient. The overhead required for the dispatcher to select a candidate and perform context switching in a preemptive system, particularly if the quantum time is short, becomes a substantial percentage of the overall CPU time available.

Nonpreemptive dispatching does not quite work in modern interactive systems. Some interrupts, particularly user keystrokes and mouse movements, demand immediate attention. **Response time** is an important criterion to a user sitting at a terminal waiting for a result. A long process executing nonpreemptively can cause the system to "hang" for a while. An additional disadvantage of nonpreemptive processing is that a buggy program with an infinite loop can hang the system indefinitely. Most nonpreemptive systems actually have a time-out built in for this purpose. A compromise position uses nonpreemptive processing for executing processes that do not require immediate responses, but allows critical processes to interrupt temporarily, always returning control to the nonpreemptive process. Earlier versions of Windows, through Version 3.1, presented another compromise that is dependent on the cooperation of the processes themselves. This position assumes that processes will voluntarily relinquish control on a regular basis, to allow other processes a chance to execute. To a large measure, this approach worked, although less well than true preemptive multitasking; however, it is subject to errors that may occur in individual processes that can prevent the execution of other processes.

The next section introduces a few typical examples of dispatching algorithms. There are many other possibilities, including algorithms that use combinations of these examples.

Nonpreemptive Dispatch Algorithms

FIRST-IN, FIRST-OUT   Probably the simplest possible dispatch algorithm, **first-in, first-out (FIFO)** simply assumes that processes will be executed as they arrive, in order. Starvation cannot occur with this method, and the method is certainly fair in a general sense; however, it fails to meet other objectives. In particular, FIFO penalizes short jobs and I/O-bound jobs, and often results in underutilized resources. As an illustration of the subtle difficulties presented when analyzing the behavior of an algorithm, consider what happens when one or more short, primarily I/O-based jobs are next in line behind a very long CPU-bound job in a FIFO queue. We assume that the scheduler is nonpreemptive but that it will allow another job to have the CPU when the executing job blocks for I/O. This assumption is essential to the full utilization of the CPU.

At the start of our observation, the long job is executing. While this happens, the short job(s) must sit and wait, unable to do anything. Eventually, the long job requires I/O and blocks. This finally allows the short jobs access to the CPU. Because they are predominately I/O-based jobs, they execute quickly and block, waiting to do I/O. Now, the short jobs must wait again, because the long job is using the I/O resources. Meanwhile, the CPU is idle, because the long job is doing I/O, and the short jobs are also idle, waiting to do I/O. Thus, FIFO can result in long waits and poorly balanced use of resources, both CPU and I/O.

SHORTEST JOB FIRST   The **shortest job first (SJF)** method will maximize throughput by selecting jobs that require only a small amount of CPU time. The dispatcher uses as its basis time estimates provided with the jobs when they are submitted. To prevent the user from lying, systems that use this algorithm generally inflict a severe penalty on jobs that run more than a small percentage over their estimate. Since short jobs will be pushed ahead of longer jobs, starvation is possible. When SJF is implemented, it generally includes a dynamic priority factor that raises the priority of jobs as they wait, until they reach a priority where they will be processed next regardless of length. Although SJF maximizes throughput, you might note that its **turnaround time** is particularly inconsistent, since the time required to complete a job depends entirely on the mix of the jobs submitted both before it, and possibly after it.

PRIORITY SCHEDULING   **Priority scheduling** assumes that each job has a priority assigned to it. The dispatcher will assign the CPU to the job with the highest priority. If there are multiple jobs with the same priority, the dispatcher will select among them on a FIFO basis.

Priorities can be assigned in different ways. On some systems that charge their users for CPU time, users select the priority. The fee is scaled to the priority, so that higher priorities cost more. In other systems, the priority is assigned by the system. Many factors can be used to affect performance, and the priorities may be assigned statically or dynamically. For example, a system may assign priority on the basis of the resources that the process is requesting. If the system is presently CPU bound, it can assign an I/O-bound process a high priority to equalize the system.

Another variation on priority scheduling is basically nonpreemptive, but adds a preemptive element. As the process executes, it is periodically interrupted by the dispatcher, which reduces its priority, a little at a time, based on its CPU time used. If its priority falls below that of a waiting process, it is replaced by the higher-priority process.

Preemptive Dispatch Algorithms

ROUND ROBIN   The simplest preemptive algorithm, **round robin** gives each process a quantum of CPU time. If the process is not completed within its quantum, it is returned to the back of the ready queue to await another turn. The round-robin algorithm is simple and inherently fair. Since shorter jobs get processed quickly, it is reasonably good on maximizing throughput. Round robin does not attempt to balance the system resources and, in fact, penalizes processes when they use I/O resources, by forcing them to reenter the ready queue. A variation on round robin that is used by some UNIX systems calculates a dynamic priority based on the ratio of CPU time to total time that the process has been in the system. The smallest ratio is treated as the highest priority and is assigned the CPU next. If no process is using I/O, this algorithm reduces back to round robin, since the process that had the CPU most recently will have the lowest priority, and the priority will climb as it waits. The round-robin technique is illustrated in Figure 15.9.

MULTILEVEL FEEDBACK QUEUES   The **multilevel feedback queue algorithm** attempts to combine some of the best features of several different algorithms. This algorithm favors short jobs by providing jobs brief, but almost immediate, access to the system. It favors I/O-bound jobs, resulting in good resource utilization. It provides high throughput, with reasonably consistent response time. The technique is shown in Figure 15.10. The dispatcher provides a number of queues. The illustration shows three. A process initially

FIGURE 15.9

Round-robin Scheduling

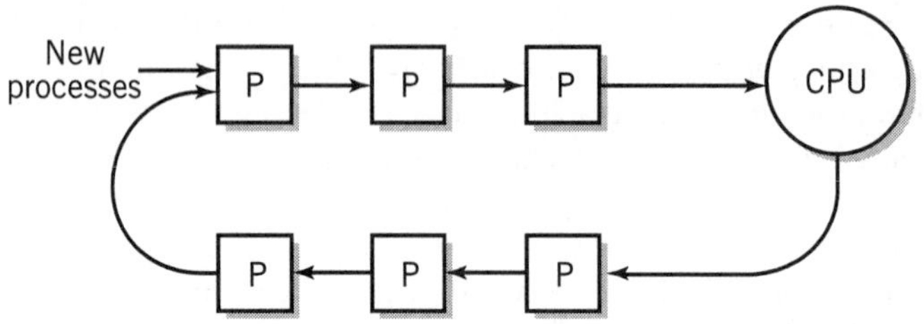

enters the queue at the top level. The queue at the top level has top priority, so a new process will quickly receive a quantum of CPU time. Short processes will complete at this point. Since I/O-bound processes often require just a short amount of initialization to establish their I/O needs, many I/O-bound processes will be quickly initialized and sent off for I/O.

Processes that are not completed are sent to a second-level queue. Processes in the second-level queue receive time only when the first-level queue is empty. Although starvation is possible, it is unlikely, because new processes pass through the first queue so quickly. When processes in the second-level reach the CPU, they generally receive more time. A rule of thumb doubles the number of quanta issued at each succeeding level. Thus, CPU-bound processes eventually receive longer time slots in which to complete execution. This method continues for as many levels as the system provides.

The final level is a round robin, which will continue to provide time until the process is complete. Some multilevel feedback queues provide a good behavior upgrade to processes that meet certain criteria.

DYNAMIC PRIORITY SCHEDULING As noted above, the technique of dynamic priority recalculation can also be used as a preemptive dispatching technique. Both Windows

FIGURE 15.10

Multilevel Feedback Queue

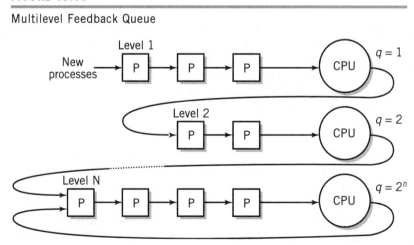

2000 and Linux use a dynamic priority algorithm as their primary criterion for dispatch selection. The algorithms on both systems adjust priority based on their use of resources. Details of the Windows and Linux dispatch algorithms are presented in Chapter 18.

15.5 MEMORY MANAGEMENT

Memory management is the planned organization of programs and data into memory. The goal of memory management is to make it as simple as possible for programs to find space, so that they may be loaded and executed. A secondary and related goal is to maximize the use of memory, that is, to waste as little memory as possible.

Until the advent of virtual storage, this was a difficult problem. There may be more programs than can possibly fit into the given amount of physical memory space. Even a single program may be too large to fit the amount of memory provided. Compounding the difficulty, recall that most programs are written to be loaded contiguously into a single space, so that each of the spaces must be large enough to hold its respective program. Fitting multiple programs into the available physical memory would require considerable juggling by the memory management module.

In passing, we point out to you that there is also a potential relationship between scheduling and memory management. The amount of memory limits the number of programs that can be scheduled and dispatched. As an extreme example, if the memory is only large enough to hold a single program, then the dispatch algorithm is reduced to single tasking, simply because there is no other program available in memory to run. As more programs can be fit into memory, the system efficiency increases. More programs get executed, concurrently, in the same period of time, since the time that would be wasted when programs are blocked is now used productively. As the number of programs increases still further, beyond a certain point, the resident time of each program starts to increase, because the available CPU time is being divided among programs that can all use it, and new programs are continually being added, and demanding CPU time.

Nonetheless, within reason, it is considered desirable to be able to load new processes as they occur, particularly in interactive systems. A slight slowdown is usually considered preferable to a user being told that no resources are available to continue his or her work.

As we have hinted a number of times, virtual storage provides an effective and worthwhile solution to the problem of memory management, albeit at the cost of additional hardware, program execution speed, disk usage, and operating system complexity. Before we explain the process of memory management using virtual storage, however, it is useful to offer a brief introduction to traditional memory management techniques to set the issues of memory management in perspective.

Memory Partitioning

The simplest form of memory management divides the memory space into a number of separate partitions. This was the method used prior to the introduction of virtual storage. Each partition is used for a separate program. For a single-tasking system, a single partition would occupy the entire memory space. Otherwise, multiple partitions are created.

Two different forms of memory partitioning can be used. **Fixed partitioning** divides memory into fixed spaces. The MINOS memory was managed using fixed partitioning. **Variable partitioning** loads programs wherever enough memory space is available, using a **best-fit, first-fit,** or **largest-fit algorithm.** The best-fit algorithm uses the smallest space that will fit the program. The first-fit algorithm simply grabs the first space available that fits the program. The largest-fit algorithm, sometimes called **worst-fit,** uses the largest space available, on the theory that this will leave the maximum possible space for another program. Figure 15.11 shows variable partitioning at work. Note that the starting positions of programs shift as space becomes available for new programs.

No matter which method is used, memory partitioning results in **fragmentation** of memory. This is seen in Figure 15.11. Fragmentation means that memory is being used in such a way that there are small pieces of memory available that, if pushed together, would be sufficient to load one or more additional programs. **Internal fragmentation** means that there is memory that has been assigned to a program that does not need it, but can't be used elsewhere. Fixed partitioning results in internal fragmentation. **External fragmentation** means that there is memory that is not assigned, but is too small to use. Variable partitioning will, after a while, result in external fragmentation, since the replacement of one program in an available space with another will almost always result in a bit of space left over. Eventually, it may be necessary to have the memory manager move programs around to reclaim the space. As you will see in Chapter 16, similar fragmentation and partitioning problems occur in the storage of files on disk. Internal and external fragmentation are shown in Figure 15.12.

Overlays

If a program does not fit into any available partition, it must be divided into small logical pieces for execution. Each piece must be smaller than the allocated memory space. Most systems do not allow the use of multiple partitions by a single program, so an alternative is to load individual pieces as they are actually needed for execution.

FIGURE 15.11

Variable Partitioning of Memory at Three Different Times

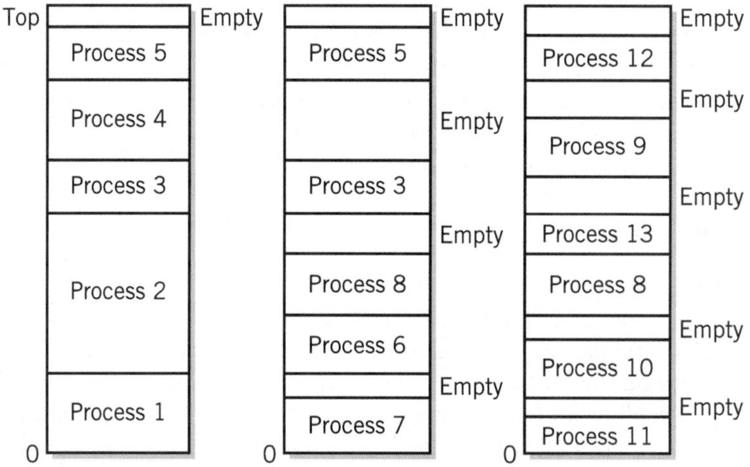

FIGURE 15.12

The Use of Overlays

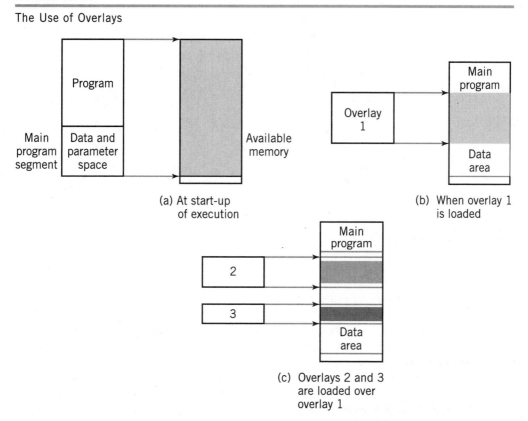

(a) At start-up
of execution

(b) When overlay 1
is loaded

(c) Overlays 2 and 3
are loaded over
overlay 1

The **overlay** technique is illustrated in Figure 15.13. At execution time, the main program is loaded. This is shown in Figure 15.13a. The main program will also include a space that holds data that will be needed by different parts of the program, plus a space that can be used for passing parameters between different parts of the program. When overlay 1 is needed, perhaps in response to a user request for a particular function, it is loaded over the main program. The data and parameter area, and if necessary, part of the main program, are preserved. This is shown in Figure 15.13b.

Further overlays are added as necessary. Two more overlays are added in Figure 15.13c. Note that the system could be designed to preserve part of overlay 1 if necessary.

Most operating systems have never provided much, if any, support for overlays, so the programmers must provide their own overlay management within the program itself. Overlay design requires a lot of skill and care. Still, overlays have been used successfully to solve the problem of fitting a large program into a small amount of memory. Most early word processing and spreadsheet programs made extensive use of overlays. .OVL files were very common in the early days of MS-DOS and Windows!

A disadvantage of the overlay technique is that it cannot take advantage of more memory if it is available, since the overlays are designed to fit into a specific, given amount of memory. We will show you a better alternative when we discuss virtual storage.

FIGURE 15.13

Internal and External Fragmentation

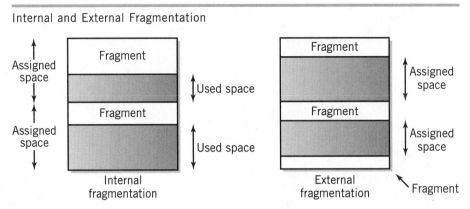

Memory Relocation Procedures

Another difficulty with partitioning is that the final location in memory where a program will be loaded for execution is not known. During loading, addresses within the program have to be adjusted, so that data references actually point to the data and references for jumps and the like will cause the program to flow correctly. With relative addressing, very little readjustment has to be done. With base addressing, the base register can be used by the operating system to set a base location that corresponds to the starting location of the program. Other addressing methods require more effort.

To solve this problem, the assemblers and compilers used with a particular computer system maintain records of the addresses that need to be adjusted during program loading, and the system loader adjusts all the required addresses as part of the loading procedure.

15.6 VIRTUAL STORAGE

Review

As we have already suggested, virtual storage solves many of the problems inherent in memory management. Virtual memory is an important technique for the effective use of memory in a multitasking system.

The basic hardware mechanics of virtual storage were introduced to you in Chapter 8. You may want to look over Section 8.2 again. Reviewing briefly, you learned that the instruction and data references to memory produced by programs within the CPU could be isolated from physical memory references using mapping procedures called paging and/or segmentation. (For ease of discussion, we will assume that virtual storage is implemented with paging. The minor differences between paging and segmentation will not concern us here.) We referred to the program instruction and data memory references as "logical" or "virtual" memory references, as opposed to the physical memory references that actually go out to memory and store and retrieve instructions and data. The words *logical* and *virtual* are used interchangeably.

To translate a virtual address to a physical address with paging, for example, the virtual address is separated into a page number and an offset; a lookup in a page table translates, or *maps,* the virtual memory reference into a physical memory location consisting of a corresponding frame number and the same offset. Every memory reference in a fetch-execute cycle goes through the same translation process, which is known as **dynamic address translation (DAT).** The address that would normally be sent to the memory address register (MAR) is mapped through the page table and *then* sent to the MAR.

The advantage of virtual storage for memory management relies on this separation of logical and physical memory and the realization that logical memory and physical memory do not have to be of the same size. The size of logical memory is established by the number of bits in the address space of an instruction word. The size of physical memory is theoretically determined by the size of the memory address register and the size of the word in the page table; practically, it is determined by the amount of installed memory. This concept is illustrated in Figure 15.14.

As an example, suppose that a Little Man memory consisted of 10010 mailboxes, divided into 10 frames, each of size 10. The frames would be numbered from 0 to 9, and the offset for a particular address on a particular frame would also range from 0 to 9. Then, location 16 in memory would be in frame 1 and would be offset by 6 from location 10, which is the starting point for frame 1.

Perhaps you've already observed that there is a simple relationship between the original address and the page/offset way of expressing the address. The page number and offset in this example can be determined by splitting the address into two parts. The first digit is the page number, and the second digit is the offset. This occurred because we chose the page size to correspond to an integral power of the base, in this example, 10^1.

Page and frame sizes in binary computer systems are selected similarly, for similar reason. A 4KB page size, for example, will require exactly 12 bits of address to express the offset. The remainder of an address will specify the page number. Figure 15.15 illustrates the makeup of an address. This technique allows the system to get the page number and offset from an address without any special effort.

Now let us return to the concept of the translation table, in this case, known as a **page table.** Because the frames and pages are the same size, any logical page can be placed in any physical frame of memory. There will be one entry in the page table for each page in the program. To perform the mapping, the memory management unit splits the logical address into page number and offset. It finds the row in the page table that corresponds to the page number and looks up the frame that the page is mapped into. It then combines the *frame* number with the original offset to form the physical memory address. Figure 8.9, repeated here as

FIGURE 15.14

Frames and Pages

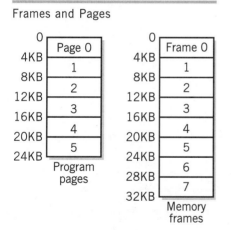

FIGURE 15.15

Composition of an Address for Paging

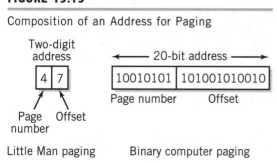

Figure 15.16, shows the translation process. The addresses in this example are shown in hexadecimal. The example uses a 20-bit address space for the logical address and a 32-bit address space for the physical memory address, showing that there is no requirement that the logical and physical address spaces be same the size.

Note, incidentally, that virtual storage would allow expansion of the Little Man's memory to 1000 or even 10,000 locations, but because of the two-digit address space provided in the instruction set, the program would still be limited to 100 locations within that larger space. The illustration in Figure 15.17 shows this condition. This illustration also shows that

FIGURE 15.16

The Page Translation Process

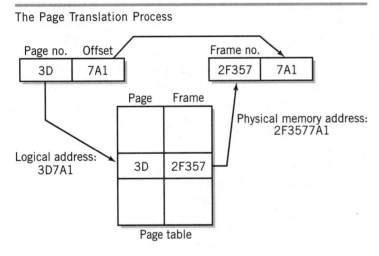

FIGURE 15.17

A Little Man Page Table with a Large Physical Memory Space

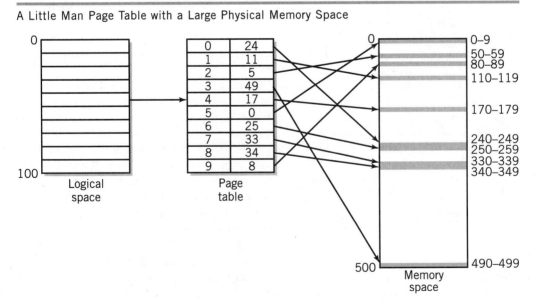

it is possible to locate those one hundred locations as ten blocks of ten locations anywhere in memory. The one hundred locations addressable within a program are spread across five hundred locations of physical memory. Note, also, the zeroth and sixth pages as well as the seventh and eighth pages. This example shows that even when blocks are consecutively located in physical memory, they may or may not represent consecutive blocks in logical memory.

With virtual storage, each process in a multitasking system has its own virtual memory, and its own page table. Physical memory is shared among the different processes. Since all the pages are the same size, any frame may be placed anywhere in memory. The pages selected do not have to be contiguous. Figure 15.18 shows a mapping for three programs located in memory. Note that each program is written as though it will load starting from address 0. Since each program's page table points to a different area of physical memory, there is no conflict between different programs that use the same virtual addresses.

As we noted before, the major challenge for memory management is the limited quantity of physical memory available. Even many megabytes of memory can only hold a few programs. The concept of virtual memory allows the system to extend the address space far beyond the actual physical memory that exists. As you will see, the additional address space required to store a large number of programs is actually provided in an auxiliary form of storage, usually disk, although some large mainframe systems provide a large quantity of slower, secondary RAM. At the same time, you've already seen that virtual memory eliminates the need for overlay techniques, contiguous program loading, and address relocation procedures.

To complete this discussion, we must answer two questions that may have occurred to you:

- Where do the page tables reside and how are they accessed by the hardware for address translation?
- How are memory frames managed and assigned to pages?

The simple answer to the first question is that page tables reside in memory, just like any other program or data. A page table address register holds a pointer to the address in

FIGURE 15.18

Mapping for Three Processes

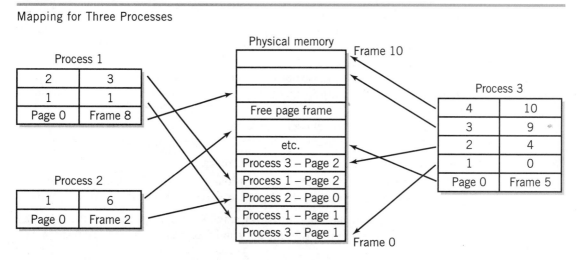

memory where the page table is located. The pointer is stored as part of the process control block; the address of the page table for the current process is loaded into the register as part of the context switching mechanism.

Although this answer is accurate, it is not quite complete. There are a few bells and whistles that improve performance, to be discussed later in this section under the paragraph title *Page Table Implementation.*

Memory frame management is discussed in the next section.

Memory Frame Allocation

Physical memory is shared among all of the active processes in a system. Since each process has its own page table, it is not practical to identify available memory frames by accumulating data from all of the tables. Rather, there must be a single resource that identifies the entire pool of available memory frames from which the memory manager may draw, when required.

There are two common approaches in use. One is to provide an *inverted page table*, which lists every memory frame with its associated process and page. This table shows the actual use of physical memory at every instant. Any frame without an associated page entry is available for allocation. Although the center block in Figure 15.18 was intended to represent memory, it could also be interpreted as an inverted page table.

A second method maintains a list of available frames, usually as a simple linked list. When a process needs frames, it takes them from the top of the list. When a process exits, its frames are added to the end of the list. Since frame contiguity is unimportant, this is an effective way to manage the free frame pool.

Page Faults

So you can see that virtual storage simplifies the problem of memory management, since it is no longer necessary to find memory partitions large enough to fit a program contiguously. But, as the TV infomercials say, there's still more!

So far we have assumed that all the pages of an executing program are located in frames somewhere in physical memory. Suppose that this were not the case—that there are not enough frames available to populate the page table. Instead, some pages of the program are present in physical memory, and an exact, page-by-page image of the program is also stored in a known auxiliary storage location. Page table entries without a corresponding frame are simply left empty.

The auxiliary storage area is known as a **backing store** or, sometimes, as **swap space.** It is usually on disk. Also assume that the page size and physical block size are integrally related, so that a page within the image can be rapidly identified, located, and transferred between the auxiliary storage and a frame in memory.

To execute a program instruction or access data, two requirements must be met:

- The instruction or data must be in memory.
- The page table for that program must contain an entry that maps the virtual address being accessed to the physical location containing the instruction or data.

These two requirements are related. The existence of a page listing in the page table implies that the required value is in memory and vice versa. The memory management software maintains the page tables for each program. If a page table entry is missing when the memory management hardware attempts to access it, the fetch-execute cycle will not be able to complete. In this case, the CPU hardware causes a special type of interrupt called a **page fault** or a **page fault trap.** This situation sounds like an error, but actually it isn't. The page fault concept is part of the overall design of virtual storage.

The operating system memory manager answers this interrupt. And now the important relationship between the hardware and the operating system software becomes clearer. When a page fault occurs, the memory management software selects a memory frame in which to place the required page. It then loads the page from its program image in auxiliary storage. If every memory frame is already in use, the software must pick a page in memory to be replaced. If the page being replaced has been altered, it must first be stored back into its own image, before the new page can be loaded. Page replacement algorithms are discussed later in this section. The process of page replacement is also known as **page swapping.** The steps involved in handling a page fault are shown in Figure 15.19.

Most systems perform page swapping only when it is required as a result of a page fault. This procedure is called **demand paging.** A few systems attempt to anticipate page needs before they occur, so that a page is swapped in before it is needed. This technique is called **prepaging.** To date, prepaging algorithms have not been very successful at predicting accurately the future page needs of programs.

When the page swap is complete, the process may be started again where it left off. Most systems return to the beginning of the fetch-execute cycle where the page fault occurred, but a few systems restart the instruction in the middle of its cycle. Regardless of which way is used, the required page is now present, and the instruction can be completed.

The importance of page swapping is that it means that a program does not have to be loaded into memory in its entirety to execute. In fact, the number of pages that must be loaded into memory to execute a process is quite small. This issue is discussed further in the next section.

Therefore, virtual storage can be used to store a large number of programs in a small amount of physical memory and makes it appear that the computer has more memory than is physically present. Parts of each program are loaded into memory. Page swapping handles the situations when required pages are not physically present. Since the virtual memory mapping assures that any program page can be loaded anywhere into memory, there is no need to be concerned about allocating particular locations in memory. Any free frame will do. We note in passing that virtual storage also eliminates the problem of address relocation. Finally, it also eliminates the need for overlays for large programs, since the virtual storage system can allocate space for the program as it is required.

Working Sets and the Concept of Locality

How many pages should be assigned to a new process just entering the system? It would seem that the more pages that are initially assigned to a process, the less likely it would be that a page fault would occur during execution of the process. Conversely, the more pages assigned to a process, the fewer the number of processes that will fit into memory.

There is a lower limit on the number of pages to be assigned, which is determined by the instruction addressing modes used by the particular computer. Executing a single instruction in an indirect addressing machine, for example, requires at least three pages,

FIGURE 15.19

Steps in Handling a Page Fault

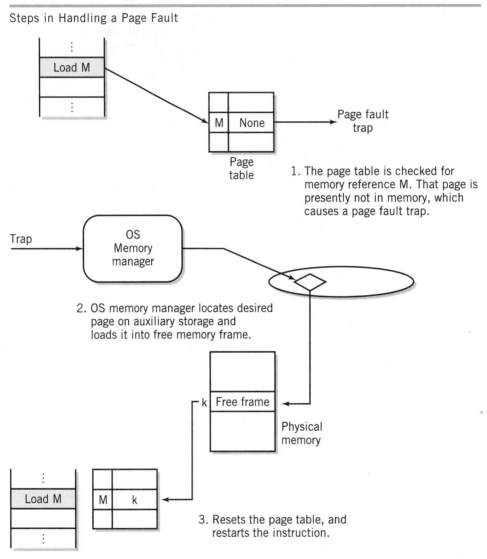

1. The page table is checked for memory reference M. That page is presently not in memory, which causes a page fault trap.

2. OS memory manager locates desired page on auxiliary storage and loads it into free memory frame.

3. Resets the page table, and restarts the instruction.

the page where the instruction resides, the page where the indirect address is stored, and the page where the data is found. This assumes that each item is on a different page, but it is necessary to make the worst-case assumption to prevent instructions from failing in this way. Other instruction sets can be analyzed similarly.

More practically, experimentation performed in the early 1970s showed that during execution programs exhibit a tendency to stay within small areas of memory during any given period of time. Although the areas themselves change over time, the property continues to hold throughout the execution of the program. This property is called the **concept of locality.** An illustration of the concept at work is shown in Figure 15.20. The concept of locality

FIGURE 15.20

Memory Use with Time, Exhibiting Locality

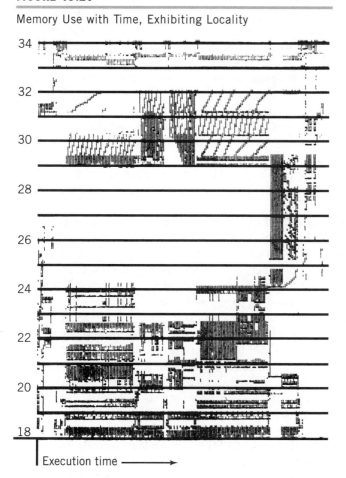

Execution time ⟶

Source: Operating Systems 2/e by Stallings, W. © 1995. Reprinted by permission of Prentice-Hall, Upper Saddle River, NJ.

makes sense intuitively. Most well-written programs are written modularly. During the initial phase of execution of a program, a small part of the program initializes variables and generally gets the program going. During the main body of the program, the likely operations consist of small loops and subroutine calls. These represent the different area of memory being executed at different times.

An effective compromise would allocate a sufficient number of pages to satisfy the locality of a particular program. This number of pages would be sufficient to run the program normally. Page faults would only occur when the local area being used by the program moves. The number of pages that meets the requirement of locality is called a **working set.** It differs somewhat from program to program, but it is possible to establish a reasonable page quantity that meets the needs of most programs without an undue number of page faults. Some systems go further and monitor the number of page faults that actually occur for each process. They then dynamically adjust the size of the working set for each process to try to meet its needs.

Page Sharing

An additional feature of virtual storage is the ability to share pages among different processes that are executing the same program. As long as the code is not modified, that is, the code is pure, there is no need to have duplicate program code stored in memory. Instead, each process shares the same program code page frames and provides its own work space for data. The page tables for each process will simply point to the same physical memory frames. This simplifies the management of multiple processes executing the same program.

Page Replacement Algorithms

There will be times on a heavily loaded system when every available page in memory is in use. When a page fault occurs, the memory manager must pick a page to be eliminated from memory to make room for the new page that is needed. The goal, of course, is to replace a page that will not be needed in the near future. There are a number of different algorithms that are used. As usual with operating system algorithms, each has advantages and disadvantages, so selecting an algorithm is a matter of trade-offs. Some systems select pages to be replaced from the same process. Others allow replacement from any process in the system. The former is known as **local page replacement;** the latter is called **global page replacement.** Global page replacement is more flexible, since there are a much larger number of pages to choose from. However, global page replacement affects the working set size of different processes and must be managed carefully.

As an additional consideration, some pages must never be removed from memory because doing so could eventually make the system inoperable. For example, removing the disk driver would make it impossible to swap in any new pages, *including the disk driver!* To prevent this situation, the frames corresponding to critical pages are locked into memory. These frames are called **locked frames.** An additional bit in each row of the page table is set to indicate that a frame is locked. Locked frames are never eligible for replacement.

FIRST-IN, FIRST-OUT PAGE REPLACEMENT The simplest **page replacement algorithm** is a first-in, first-out algorithm. The oldest page remaining in the page table is selected for replacement. FIFO does not take into account usage of the page. Logically, a page that has been in memory for a long period of time is probably there because it is heavily used. The page being removed may be in current use, which would result in a second page fault and force the system to reload the page almost immediately. FIFO has a second, interesting deficiency. You would assume that increasing the number of pages available to a process would reduce the number of page faults for that process. However, it has been shown that under certain conditions, use of the FIFO page replacement algorithm results in more page faults with an increased number of pages, instead of fewer. This condition is known as **Belady's anomaly.** If you're interested, examples of Belady's anomaly can be found in the references by Deitel [DEIT90] and Silberschatz, et. al. [SILB01].

For these reasons, FIFO is not considered a good page replacement algorithm.

LEAST RECENTLY USED PAGE REPLACEMENT The **least recently used (LRU) algorithm** replaces the page that has not been used for the longest time, on the assumption that the page probably will not be needed again. This algorithm performs fairly well, but requires a considerable amount of overhead. To implement the LRU algorithm, the page tables must record the time every time the page is referenced. Then, when page replacement is required, every page must be checked to find the page with the oldest recorded time. If the number of pages is large, this can take a considerable amount of time.

LEAST FREQUENTLY USED PAGE REPLACEMENT Another possibility is to select the page that has been used the least frequently. Intuitively, this algorithm has appeal, since it would seem that a page not used much is more replaceable than one that has received a lot of use. The flaw with this algorithm is that a page that has just been brought into memory has not been used much, compared to a page that has been in memory for a while. Still, the new page was brought into memory because it was needed, and it is likely that it will be needed again.

NOT USED RECENTLY PAGE REPLACEMENT The **not used recently (NUR) algorithm** is a simplification of the least recently used algorithm. In this method, the computer system hardware provides two additional bits for each entry in the page tables. One bit is set whenever the page is referenced (*used.*) The other bit is set whenever the data on the page is modified, that is, written to. This second bit is called a **dirty bit.** Periodically, the system resets all the reference bits.

The memory manager will attempt to find a page with both bits set to 0. Presumably, this is a page that has not been used for a while. Furthermore, it is a page that has not been modified, so it is necessary only to write the new page over it. The page being replaced does not have to be saved back to the backing store, since it has not been modified.

The second choice will be a page whose dirty bit is set, but whose reference bit is unset. This situation can occur if the page has not been accessed for a while, but was modified when it was accessed, prior to the resetting of the reference bits. This page must be written back to the backing store before a new frame can be read into its spot.

Third choice will be a page that has been referenced, but not modified. And finally, least desirable will be a page that has been recently referenced and modified. This is a commonly used algorithm.

One difficulty with this algorithm is that gradually all the *used* bits "fill up", making selection difficult or impossible. There are a number of variations on this algorithm that solve this problem by selectively resetting *used* bits at regular intervals or each time a page replacement occurs. The most common approach pictures the process pages as numerals on a clock. When a page replacement must be found, the clock hand moves until it finds an unset *used* bit and the corresponding page is replaced. Pages with set *used* bits that the hand passes over are reset. The hand remains at the found replacement page awaiting the next replacement requirement. This variation on NUR is called the **clock page replacement** algorithm.

SECOND CHANCE PAGE REPLACEMENT ALGORITHMS   One second chance algorithm uses an interesting variation on FIFO, using a referenced bit similar to that of NUR. When the oldest page is selected for replacement, its referenced bit is checked. If the referenced bit is set, the bit is reset, and the time is upgraded, as though the page had just entered memory. This gives the page a second pass through the list of pages. If the referenced bit is not set, then the page is replaced, since it is safe to assume that it has not been referenced in some time.

Another second chance algorithm keeps a small pool of free pages that are not assigned. When a page is replaced, it is not removed from memory but, instead, is moved into the free pool. The oldest page in the free pool is removed to make room. If the page is accessed while in the free pool, it is moved out of the free pool and back into the active pages by replacing another page.

Both second chance algorithms reduce the number of disk swaps by keeping what would otherwise be swapped-out pages in memory. However, the first of these algorithms has the potential of keeping a page beyond its usefulness, and the second decreases the number of possible pages in memory by using some of those pages for the free pool.

Thrashing

A condition that can arise when a system is heavily loaded is called **thrashing.** Thrashing is every system administrator's nightmare. Thrashing occurs when every frame of memory is in use, and programs are allocated just enough pages to meet their minimum require-ment. A page fault occurs in a program, and the page is replaced by another page that will itself be needed for replacement almost immediately. Thrashing is most serious when global page replacement is used. In this case, the stolen page may come from another pro-gram. When the second program tries to execute, it is immediately faced with its own page fault. Unfortunately, the time required to swap a page from the disk is long compared to CPU execution time, and as the page fault is passed around from program to program, no program is able to execute, and the system as a whole slows to a crawl or crashes. The pro-grams simply continue to steal pages from each other. With local page replacement, the number of thrashing programs is more limited, but thrashing can still have a serious effect on system performance.

Page Table Implementation

As we mentioned previously, the data in the page table must be stored in memory. You should realize that data in the page table must be accessed during the fetch-execute cycle, possibly sev-eral times, if the fetch-execute cycle is executing an instruction with a complex addressing mode. Thus, it is important that the page table be accessed as quickly as possible, since the use of paging can negatively affect the performance of the system in a major way otherwise.

To improve access, many systems provide a small amount of a special type of mem-ory called **associative memory.** Associative memory differs from regular memory in that the addresses in associative memory are not consecutive. Instead, the addresses in associa-tive memory are assigned to each location as labels. When associative memory is accessed, every address is checked at the same time, but only the location whose address label matches the address to be accessed is activated. Then the data at that location can be read or written. (Cache memory lines are accessed similarly.)

A mailbox analogy might be useful in helping you to understand associative memory. Instead of having mailboxes that are numbered consecutively, picture mailboxes that have those little brass inserts that you slide a paper label into. On each label is written the address of that particular box. By looking at all the boxes, you can find the one that contains your mail. For a human, this technique would be slower than going directly to a mailbox in a known location. The computer, however, is able to look at every address label simultaneously.

Suppose, then, that the most frequently used pages are stored in this associative mem-ory. They may be stored in any order, since the address labels of all locations are checked simultaneously. The page number is used as the address label that is being accessed. Then, the only frame number that will be read is the one that corresponds to that page. A page table that is constructed this way is known as a **translation lookaside buffer,** or **TLB,** table.

The number of locations available in a TLB table is small because associative memory is expensive. There must be a second, larger, page table that contains all the page entries for the program. When the desired page is found in the TLB table, known as a **hit,** the frame can be used without further delay. When the desired page is not found in the TLB table, called a **miss,** the memory management unit defaults to conventional memory, where the larger page table is stored. Access to the table in memory does, in fact, require an extra memory access, which will significantly slow down the fetch-execute cycle, but that can't be helped.

To locate the correct entry in the larger page table, most computers provide a special register in the memory management unit that stores the address of the origin of the page table in memory. Then, the nth page can be located quickly, since its address in memory is the address of the origin plus the offset. The process of page table lookup is shown in Figure 15.21. Figure 15.21a shows how the page is accessed when the page is found in associative memory; Figure 15.21b shows the procedure when the TLB does not contain the desired page.

The size of a page is determined by the computer system designers, as a fundamental characteristic of the system. It is not changeable. There are several trade-offs in the determination of page size. The page table for a program must contain an entry for every page

FIGURE 15.21

Frame Lookup Procedures: (a) Page in TLB, (b) Page Not in TLB

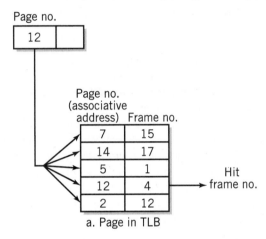

a. Page in TLB

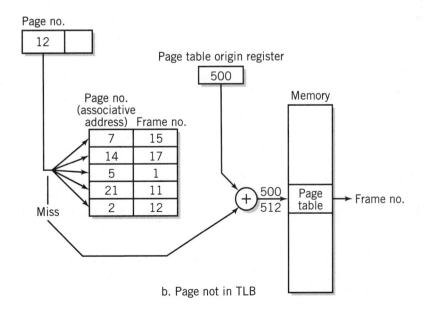

b. Page not in TLB

in the program. The number of pages is inversely proportional to the page size, so as the page size is decreased, the number of entries required increases. On the other hand, we have assumed that the size of the program corresponds exactly to the amount of memory occupied by the pages required for the program. This is not usually true. More commonly, the last page is partly empty. The wasted space is internal fragmentation. The larger the page size, the more internal fragmentation. An example is shown in Figure 15.22.

Also, if the pages are small, memory will consist of more pages, which allows more programs to be resident. Conversely, smaller pages will require more swapping, since each program will have less code and data available to it at any given time. Experimentally, designers have determined that 2KB or 4KB pages seem to optimize overall performance.

Page tables on large machines can, themselves, require considerable memory space. One solution is to store the page tables in virtual memory. Page tables, or portions of page tables, in current use will occupy frames, as usual. Other portions or tables will reside only in virtual memory until needed.

SEGMENTATION   Segmentation is essentially similar to paging conceptually, but differs in many details. A segment is usually defined as a logically self-contained part of a program, as determined by a programmer or by a compiler translation program. Thus, in most systems, segments can be variable in size. (A few systems define segments instead as large pages, of fixed size, but of 1MB, 2MB, or 4MB, or even more. This definition does not interest us here, since the previous discussion of paging applies in this case. When a fixed size segment is further divided into pages, the program address is divided into three parts, a segment, a page, and an offset, and the mapping process takes place in two steps, but the procedure is otherwise identical to our previous discussion.)

Program segments can represent parts of a program such as main routines and subroutines or functions, or they can represent program code and data, even separate data tables. The crucial difference between segments and pages is that due to their variability in size, the boundaries between segments do not fall on natural borders, as pages do. Therefore, in the **segment table,** it is necessary to provide the entire physical address for the start of the segment instead of just a page number. It is also necessary to record the size or upper limit location of the segment, so that the system can check to make sure that the requested location does not fall outside the limit of the segment. Otherwise, it would be possible to read or write data to a location belonging to another segment, which would compromise the integrity of the system. This is not a problem with paging, since it is impossible for the offset to exceed the size of a page.

The program segment numbers are stored with each segment and are treated similarly to page numbers. For each segment number, there is an entry in the

FIGURE 15.22

Internal Fragmentation

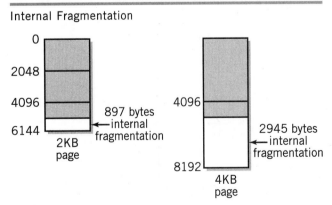

Program size: 5247 bytes

segment table containing the starting location of the segment in physical memory plus the limit of the segment. The physical address is calculated by adding the program segment offset from the start of the segment to the memory starting location and checking this value against the limit.

As with the page table, part of the segment table can be stored in associative memory for faster access. When segmentation and paging are both provided, there may be two TLB tables, one for each. When both are provided, the translation process performs its mapping in two steps. First, the segment table is used to determine the location of the pages that make up the segment. Then, the page table locates the desired frame.

Since the programmer establishes the segments, segmentation is less invisible to the programmer than paging, even though during operation it is still invisible. This provides a few advantages to the programmer, stemming from the fact that each segment can be treated independently. This means that a particular segment could be shared among different programs, for example. Nonetheless, segmentation is harder to operate and maintain than paging and has rapidly fallen out of favor as a virtual storage technique.

Process Separation

The use of virtual storage offers one additional benefit that should be mentioned. Under normal program execution without virtual storage, every memory access has the potential to address a portion of memory that belongs to a different process. This would violate system security and data integrity; for example, a program in a partitioned memory could access data belonging to another process simply by overflowing an array. Prior to virtual storage memory management, this was a difficult problem. It was necessary to implement memory access limits for each process in hardware, because there is no way for operating system software to check every attempted memory access while a program is executing.

With virtual storage, every memory access request points to a logical address, not a physical one. Since the logical address is within the space of the process itself, the translation process assures that it is not possible to point to a physical address belonging to another process, unless the page tables have been set up intentionally to share frames between the processes. Thus, virtual storage provides simple, effective separation protection between processes.

15.7 SECONDARY STORAGE SCHEDULING

On a busy system, it is common to have a number of disk requests pending at any given time. The operating system software will attempt to process these requests in a way that enhances the performance of the system. As you might expect by now, there are several different disk scheduling algorithms in use.

First-Come, First-Served Scheduling

First-come, first-served (FCFS) scheduling is the simplest algorithm. As requests arrive, they are placed in a queue and are satisfied in order. Although this may seem like a fair algorithm, its inefficiency may result in poorer service to every request in the queue.

The problem is that seek time on a disk is long and somewhat proportional to the distance that the head has to move. With FCFS, one can expect the head to move all over the disk to satisfy requests. It would be preferable to use an algorithm that minimizes seek distances. This would suggest processing requests that are on nearby tracks first. The other algorithms in use attempt to do so.

Shortest Distance First Scheduling

The **shortest distance first (SDF) scheduling** algorithm looks at all the requests in the queue and processes the one nearest to the current location of the head. This algorithm suffers from the possibility of **indefinite postponement.** If the head is near the middle track on the disk, a request near the edge of the disk may never get serviced if requests continue to join the queue.

Scan Scheduling

The **scan scheduling** algorithm attempts to satisfy the limitation of SDF scheduling. The head scans back and forth across the disk surface, processing requests as it goes. Although this method is fairer than SDF, it suffers from a different limitation, namely, that blocks near the middle tracks are processed twice as often as blocks near the edge. To see this more clearly, consider the diagram in Figure 15.23.

FIGURE 15.23

Scan Scheduling Algorithm

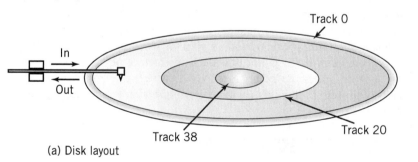

(a) Disk layout

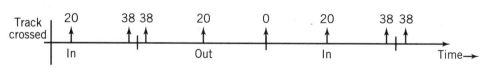

(b) Timing chart

Consider the head moving smoothly back and forth across the disk at a constant speed. The diagram shows the time at which the head crosses various tracks. Note that the middle track is crossed in both directions, at about equal intervals. Tracks near either the inside or outside track, however, are crossed twice in quick succession. Then there is a long interval in which they are not touched. A track at the very edge, inside or outside, is touched only once for every two times that a track in the middle is touched.

N-STEP C-SCAN Scheduling

Two changes improve the *n*-step c-scan scheduling algorithm. One is to cycle in only one direction, then return to the other end before accessing blocks again. This assures that each block is treated equally, even though a bit of time is wasted returning the head to its original position. The other change is to maintain two separate queues. Once the head has started to traverse the disk, it will read only blocks that were already waiting when the traverse started. This prevents block requests that are just ahead of the head from jumping into the queue. Instead, such a block would be placed in the alternate queue to wait for the next pass. This approach is fairer to requests that have already been waiting. Practically, there is no reason to move the head beyond the last block sought, and reversal will take place at that time. Some writers refer to this as c-look scheduling.

Figure 15.24 compares the head movement for different scheduling algorithms. These drawings, based on an example and drawings by Silberschatz, et. al. [SILB01], assume a disk queue containing blocks in tracks 98, 183, 37, 122, 14, 124, 65, and 67. The head starts at track 53.

15.8 NETWORK OPERATING SYSTEM SERVICES

It is possible to implement the simplest forms of data communication with no operating system support, except for a serial port I/O driver. While this might be adequate to establish communications between a car's computer, and a garage diagnostic computer, it is inadequate for modern data communication.

To take advantage of networking, the operating system must include services that support networking and provide the features offered by networking capability. These services include implementation of network software protocols, augmentation of the file system to support the transfer and use of files from other locations, remote login capability, and additional utilities and tools. Modern operating systems include networking facilities as part of the base system.

Transmission Protocols and Data Transmission Formats

Suppose that two or more computers are to communicate via a communication channel. What are the requirements for them to communicate successfully? Obviously, they must agree on the signaling methods and medium-access control protocols used to access the connecting channel, but in addition there is much more. They must agree on the format of the messages. How long is the message? Which part of the message is actual data and which part is overhead information such as the address? How are errors to be detected by the receiver, and what will be done about them? How does the receiver know that it has

FIGURE 15.24

Comparison of Different Disk Algorithms

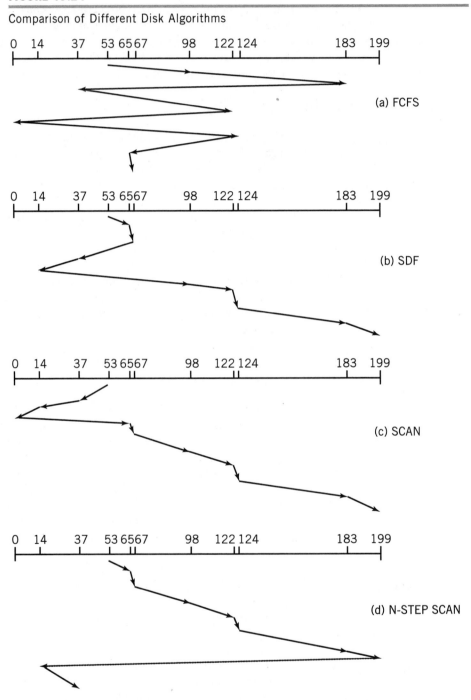

Source: A. Silberschatz, J. Peterson, P. Galvin, *Operating Systems Concepts*, 5/e. © 1998 by John Wiley & Sons, Inc
Reprinted by permission of John Wiley & Sons, Inc.

received a complete message, and how does it reassemble a message that was sent in parts, possibly with the parts arriving in the wrong order? At a higher level, each end of the communication must recognize the commands and requests of the other and be able to respond in a reasonable way. For example, if one computer speaks ASCII and the other speaks Unicode or some other code, successful communication will not occur unless they are aware of the difference and are prepared to perform the translations back and forth. E-mail messages will become garbled or not reach their destination if there isn't agreement on the meaning of the name and address on the "envelope."

There are many more such issues, and it's easy to see that communication is not trivial. Indeed, a substantial number of ground rules are required to satisfy all the conditions necessary to communicate successfully.

When a multicomputer system is designed in such a way that all the different connected computers can communicate successfully at all relevant levels, we refer to the system as an open system. Totally open systems are still difficult to achieve, although the industry is getting closer, and it is possible to implement a reasonably open system with careful selection of system components.

The key to successful communication is a set of protocol standards that agree upon hardware and software rules that will allow computers to establish and maintain useful communication at various levels. International protocols exist for communication by modem, for local area networks, for connection between local area and wide area networks, for Internet and other wide area network communications, and for many other purposes.

The collection of protocols that are designed to work together and guide all aspects of network communications is called the TCP/IP **protocol suite,** although the suite includes much more than TCP and IP. Separating the tasks involved in communication adds flexibility, simplifies design of the protocols, and allows a system to select only the protocols that it needs for a particular application.

One of the most important functions of protocols is to establish agreement on the format of the data being sent across a communication channel. Data is literally passed through a communication channel as a stream of bits, but the meaning of the bits is established by protocol. The bits may be passed a byte or character at a time, as an entire message, or as a message divided into smaller pieces and encapsulated into units called **packets,** and **frames.**[1]

In fact, packets and frames are used for most data communications. A packet is equivalent to an envelope containing pages of data. Like envelopes, packets come in different shapes and sizes. A description of the packet, the designated receiver and source addresses, and information about the data enclosed is provided in a **preamble** or **header,** followed by the data. The amount of data depends on the design of the packet and the requirements of the channel. Some packets require a fixed amount of data, others allow a variable amount. Some packet designs also include a trailer or footer at the end of the packet. The packet design used for a communication installation reflects the protocol suite in use.

Frames are packets that have been divided into units suitable to meet the requirements of the medium access control hardware protocol for a particular channel connection. The Ethernet frame was shown to you in Figure 11.11 Packets are organized similarly, but do not necessarily conform to a specific MAC protocol.

---

[1] Network frames are totally unrelated to the memory frames used for virtual storage.

The use of packets simplifies operations and increases communication efficiency:

- It reduces communication overhead by making it possible to transmit a large block of data while requiring only a single block of overhead information to identify the destination and meaning of the enclosed data.

- It represents a reasonable unit for the routing of data. This factor is particularly important in wide area networks, where a packet of data may be passed through many different networks and communication channels before it reaches its destination.

- Packets offer an alternative to dedicating a channel for the entire length of a message. This increases utilization and availability of a channel by allowing packets from several sources to access and share a single channel.

- It presents a productive way to use a communication channel. A channel can be switched to route data packets to different destinations in such a way that each sender-receiver pair appears to have a channel to itself.

- The receiving computer is able to process a block of data all at once, instead of a character or a byte at a time. Furthermore, it is usually easier to organize the data, since there are fewer individual blocks of data to deal with.

- It simplifies synchronization of the sending and receiving systems by providing a clearly delineated burst of data, with an identifiable start and stop point.

In addition to data transmission, packets can also be used for control of the network itself. To do so, the data is replaced by control messages that specify the action to be taken.

THE OSI REFERENCE MODEL   From a conceptual perspective, the **Open Systems Interconnection Reference Model** or, more familiarly, the **OSI model**, represents an important attempt to present a complete protocol standard. The OSI model identifies all the factors that must be standardized in order for two computers to communicate completely and successfully at every possible level. The OSI standard was created by the International Standards Organization (ISO) after many years of study.

The model consists of seven layers. Each layer represents an attempt to isolate a single factor that is relevant to communication between computers. Originally, the intention was to create a single protocol standard that would be used internationally for all computer communication. Standard protocol components were implemented for several of the layers, but, for various reasons, general acceptance of the OSI implementation has been limited. Although the protocol itself has not been widely accepted and used, the model is considered conceptually important as a means of identifying the factors and comparing the performance and capabilities of different protocols.

Figure 15.25 identifies the seven layers in the model. Operation of the model is hierarchical. Each layer of the model is implemented to fulfill a specific function in the communication process. Each layer at the sending end performs its services, and adds additional data to the message, usually in the form of a header that encapsulates the data from above. (Some layers also require a trailer.) The result is then passed to the next lower layer. This is also shown in the diagram. Each layer relies on the layers below it to provide all the additional functionality necessary to fulfill the communication function. At the receiving end, the matching, or peer, layer interprets and removes the information provided for it by the sender.

FIGURE 15.25

The Layers of the OSI Model

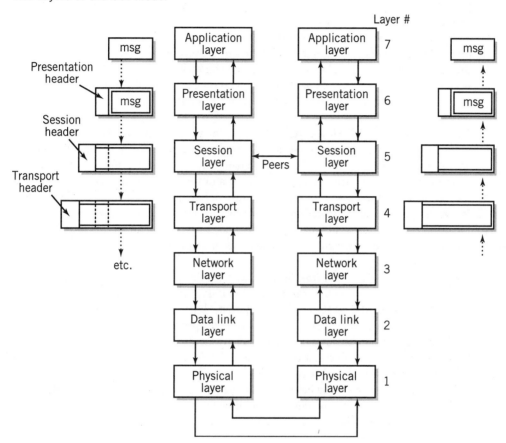

The independence of each layer means that an individual layer needs to be concerned only with the interfaces of the layers immediately above it and below it. Ideally, the operation of a particular layer is transparent to other layers and could be modified without affecting other layers, provided that the layer continues to provide its required services to the communication process and that there is agreement between the equivalent, or peer, layers at the sender and receiver.

Not surprisingly, the message to be sent through the communication channel gets larger and larger as it passes down the chain, since each layer in the sender must add its own component to the previous message. There is an obvious advantage in eliminating layers, whenever they are not needed, to reduce message traffic and overhead. If a message is being sent point-to-point directly between a sender and the ultimate user of a message (i.e., the message is not being forwarded), for example, there is no reason to specify an address for the receiver. Therefore, the seven layers specified in the OSI protocol actually represent a maximum.

Fitzgerald [FITZ01] likens the OSI model to a pair of seven-story office buildings, where the people on each floor are responsible for a specific set of business tasks. The people on the seventh floor of one building put a message for the other building into an envelope, seal the envelope, and send it down to the sixth floor. Each floor adds its own message and puts the previous envelope plus the new message into another, somewhat larger, envelope. When the package reaches the first floor, a messenger person carries the package across the street to the other building, where the people on each floor retrieve their messages and pass the remaining envelopes up, until the final message reaches the seventh floor.

Now consider the function of each layer in the model.

Physical Layer   The **physical layer** is the layer at which communication actually takes place. Communication at the physical layer consists of a bare stream of bits. The physical access protocol includes the medium, the signaling method and specific signal parameters, voltages, carrier frequencies, lengths of pulses, and the like; synchronization and timing issues; and the method used to connect the computer to the medium. An example of a physical access protocol is the specification describing communication between two modems. Physical communication between computers takes place only at the physical layer. The physical layer is implemented primarily in hardware, by a network interface unit (NIU).

Data Link Layer   The **data link layer** is responsible for the reliable transmission and reception of frames across the communication link. Frames are sized by the data link for compatibility with the MAC protocol. The data link layer provides appropriate error detection for each frame. Most data link protocols provide a means for requesting and retransmitting a frame that has not been received successfully. Since some communication conditions make it possible that frames will be received in the wrong order, the data link layer also numbers the frames and reorders the received frames if necessary to recreate the original message. Frames may be received in the wrong order if they are separately routed over communication paths of significantly different path lengths (it takes longer to get a message from Los Angeles to San Diego if it is routed via Alaska and Hawaii, for example) or if a frame has to be resent due to an error.

Most data communication practitioners divide the data link layer into two separate sublayers, the hardware **medium-access control** sublayer, which defines procedures for accessing the channel and detecting errors, and a software **logical link control** sublayer, which provides error correction and manages packet/frame conversions, retransmission, and packet reconstruction.

Network Layer   The **network layer** is responsible for the addressing and routing of messages to their proper final destination. It is also responsible for breaking messages that are too large for the network into packets of manageable size.

For messages confined to a local area network, this task is usually simple. The network layer software simply divides the message into packets of appropriate size, appends an address to each packet, and passes the packets on to the data link layer. There is no routing to do, since all the nodes on a local area network are connected together and directly addressable. If the message address is in symbolic form, the software looks up the physical address in a table.

When the message is being sent to a node outside a local network, for example, to the Internet, addressing is somewhat more difficult. It is not possible to store the address of every location at each node. Instead, the network layer has access to tables at various sites that assist in routing the message.

Transport Layer   The **transport layer** provides services that support reliable end-to-end communications. In a wide area network, a message is passed from node to node to get from its source to its destination. The message will often pass through a large number of intermediate nodes. In effect, each node forwards the message to the next. The three lower layers provide communication services between nodes that are immediate neighbors. The transport layer is fully responsible for generating the final address of the destination and for all end-to-end communication facilities, including establishing a connection, flow control, data assurance and error recovery, and termination of the connection.

We note that although the network layer is responsible for routing of packets, the ultimate destination address is established at the transport layer. The message headers and control messages of the upper four layers make it possible for end nodes to communicate fully without regard or concern for the nature of the intermediate nodes, and conversely, the end-to-end communication is essentially transparent to the intermediate nodes.

Figure 15.26 illustrates an end-to-end communication with an intermediate node. On large networks, the primary purpose of the intermediate node may be routing, and it is sometimes referred to as a **router.** The transport layer controls the flow of packets from the source to the destination. For each link, the network, data link, and physical layers are established according to the rules for the immediate communication. At the intermediate node, the lower three layers are stripped from the message-at-large and recreated according to the rules for the next link. The upper layers, encapsulated in the transport packet,

FIGURE 15.26

Passing a Message Through an Intermediate Node

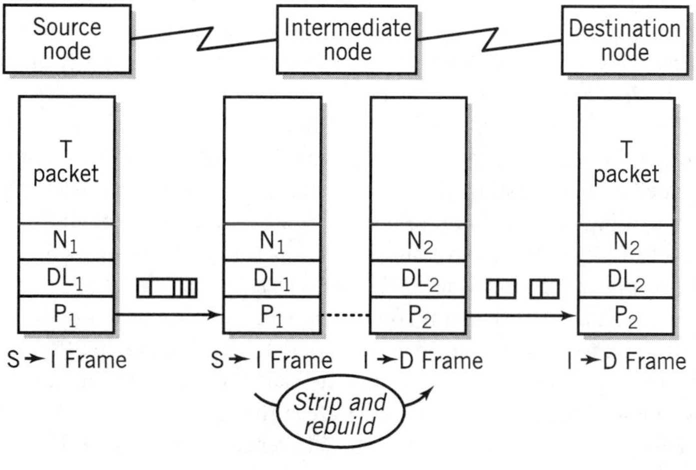

pass through unchanged until the message reaches its destination. The transport layer assures that all the pieces of the transport packet are reassembled correctly.

Session Layer   The upper three layers assume that a successful end-to-end connection is established and maintained at the transport layer. These layers are concerned with the flow of data and control between applications on the communicating nodes.

A session is the dialogue between two cooperating applications or processes at the ends of the communication link. The **session layer** is responsible for establishing the session between the applications, controlling the dialogue, and terminating the session. Remote login and spooling operations would use the services of the session layer to assure successful login and to control the flow of data to the remote printer, for example.

Presentation Layer   The **presentation layer** provides common data conversions and transformations that allow systems with different standards to communicate. The presentation layer includes services such as data compression and restoration, encryption and decryption, ASCII-Unicode conversion, data reformatting, and the like. The fundamental purpose of the presentation layer is to present data at the destination with the same meaning and appearance as it would have at the source.

Application Layer   The **application layer** provides utilities and tools for application programs and users.

TCP/IP   There are a number of different protocol suites in use that operate similarly to the OSI reference model, or implement parts of it. These include the IBM Systems Network Architecture (SNA), Novell IPX/SPX, and Appletalk, among others. In the past few years, the **TCP/IP** protocol suite has become the network connectivity protocol of choice for a large number of installations. TCP/IP has been closely associated with UNIX and with connection to the Internet in people's minds. While the association is accurate, TCP/IP is also popular for general communication at all levels of network connection, from the smallest local area networks to the largest wide area networks, even for modem connections to networks through the telephone system. (**PPP, Point-to-Point Protocol** may be familiar to you, as it is used for dial-up modem, DSL, and cable access to the Internet.) TCP/IP is included or available inexpensively for most modern operating systems. TCP/IP is reliable and mature.

The name TCP/IP stands for *Transmission Control Protocol/Internet Protocol*. Although the name suggests two protocols, TCP/IP is actually a name encompassing an integrated suite consisting of protocols that control various aspects of data communication, including modem communication, communication through a gateway, error reporting, address resolution, and many other functions. There are also a number of perhaps familiar application protocols, including *telnet, ftp,* and *finger*.

Figure 15.27 is a diagram comparing some of the more important protocols in the TCP/IP suite to the OSI reference layer model. Actually, the TCP/IP protocol suite is quite large, encompassing security, file access, e-mail, Web services, and more. The diagram only shows a few of the protocols that are part of the suite.

There are a number of important differences between TCP/IP and OSI that reflect a somewhat different design philosophy on the part of the original TCP/IP designers. The

FIGURE 15.27

A Comparison of OSI and TCP/IP

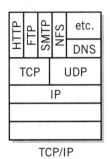

OSI   TCP/IP

intention was to provide universal connectivity, with connection-independent protocols at the network layer. Thus, TCP/IP does not address the data link and physical layers at all. As we noted earlier, these layers are generally addressed by hardware or a mixture of hardware and software that is directly tied to the needs of each particular type of communication channel.

The Internet Protocol is approximately equivalent to the OSI network layer. In a wide area network, IP is present on every node in the network. The role of IP is to segment messages into packets and then route and pass the packets from one node to another until they reach their destination. IP packets are called **datagrams.** An IP datagram is limited to 65,535 bytes.

IP uses dynamic routing with packet switching as its fundamental algorithm. All linkages outside of local area networks pass through internetwork nodes called routers. Thus, a message is passed from router to router, one datagram at a time, until it reaches its destination. Dynamic routing means that each datagram may be routed differently to compensate for failures and tie-ups. Packet switching means that a router can handle datagrams from many different sources and pass them out in different directions. The Internet Protocol provides flexibility in the route chosen, but it also requires unique global addresses for every interconnected computer network or individual nonnetworked computer. IP routes datagrams to their destination network, but final delivery is left to TCP.

The Transmission Control Protocol fulfills the role of the OSI transport layer, plus some of the functionality of the session layer. Like the equivalent OSI transport layer, it is designed to provide reliable end-to-end connectivity. TCP is not required for datagram routing, so it is not included on gateways. TCP requires that acknowledgment messages be sent from destinations back to the sender to verify receipt of the datagrams that make up a message. An alternative protocol that is part of the TCP/IP suite, UDP, for User Datagram Protocol, is sometimes used instead of TCP. UDP is faster and simpler, but does not guarantee receipt.

The TCP/IP protocol suite does not provide separate application, presentation, and session layers. Instead, it bundles all these functions into a single application layer.

OS Protocol Support and Other Services

The operating system implements the protocols that are required for network communication and provides a variety of additional services to the user and to application programs. Most operating systems recognize and support a number of different protocols. This contributes to open system connectivity, since the network can then pass packets with less concern for the protocols available on the network stations.

A modern operating system may provide support for several different protocols. Because of the layered nature of communication protocols, operating system specialists refer to these as **stacks,** for example, a TCP/IP stack or an IPX/SPX stack. You can see the similarity between the behavior of a protocol stack and the last-in, first-out nature of other types of computer stacks that we have already discussed.

In addition to standard communication protocol support, the operating system commonly provides some or all of the following services. Many modern operating systems also make it easy to add to the communication services that they provide using a facility called **sockets.** The concept of sockets originated with BSD UNIX. Sockets allow a user to "plug in" software that provides additional services. Both Windows and UNIX/Linux provide sockets for adding network protocols and services to those already built into the operating system. Sockets provide a means for keeping the operating system current in its offerings, and also offer a simple way for applications to "plug in" to the communication services available from the system.

- ■ File services transfer programs and data files from one computer on the network to another. Network file services require that identification of the network node occur ahead of the file manager in the operating system hierarchy. This allows file requests to be directed to the appropriate file manager. Local requests are passed on to the local file manager; other requests go to the network for service by the file manager on the machine where the file resides. This concept is shown in Figure 15.28.

  - ▪ Some file services require a logical name for the machine to be included on network file requests. For example, Windows assigns pseudodrive letters to file systems accessible through the network. To the user, a file might reside on drive "M:." Although this system is simple, it has one potential shortcoming: different computers on the network might access the same drive by different letters if care isn't taken to prevent this situation. This can make it difficult for users to find their network-based files when they move between computers. Other systems allow the network administrator to assign names to each machine. The machines at Bentley College, for example, are all named after Greek gods. To access a file on the "zeus" computer, the user types "zeus::" ahead of the file path name.

  - ▪ Some operating systems provide transparent access to files on the network. On these systems, network files are mounted to the file system in such a way that network files simply appear in the directory structure like any other file. The operating system uses whatever method is appropriate, local

FIGURE 15.28

The Access for a Networked Operating System

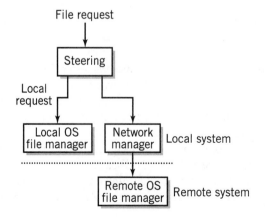

or network, to access the requested files. The user need not know the actual location of the file.

- Print services work similarly to file services. Print requests are redirected by the operating system to the network station that manages the requested printer. This allows users to share expensive printer resources.

  - Other peripherals and facilities can also be managed as network services. System-intensive operations, such as data base services, can be processed on large computers with the capability and then passed over the network to other computers. This technique places the processing burden on the system that is most qualified to handle it and has the additional benefit of making the data available wherever it is needed.

- Web services accept requests from the network connections and return answers in the form of HTML files, image files, and more. Frequently, Web pages require data processing on the server to prepare dynamically created pages. Operating system scripts and servers are often used for this purpose. The common gateway interface (CGI) protocol provides a standard connection between the Web server and the scripts and operating system services.

- Messaging services allow users and application programs to pass messages from one to another. The most familiar application of messaging services is e-mail and chat facilities. The network operating system not only passes these messages, it also formats them for display on different systems.

- Application program interface services allow a program to access network services. Some network operating systems also provide access to services on remote machines that might not be available locally. These services are called **remote procedure calls,** or **RPCs.** RPCs can be used to implement distributed computing.

- Security and network management services provide security across the network and allow users to manage and control the network from computers on the network. These services also include protection against data loss that can occur when multiple computers access data simultaneously.

- Remote processing services allow a user or application to log in to another system on the network and use its facilities for processing. Thus, the processing workload can be distributed among computers on the network, and users have access to remote computers from their own system. The most familiar service of this type is probably *telnet,* which is included in the UNIX TCP/IP protocol suite software, and which is available on many other systems as well.

When considered together, the network services provided by a powerful network operating system transform a user's computer into a **distributed system.** Tanenbaum [TAN95] defines a distributed system as follows:

A distributed system is a collection of independent computers that appear to the users of the system as a single computer.

Network operating systems are characterized by the distribution of control that they provide. **Client-server systems** centralize control in the server computer. Client computers have their network access limited to services provided by the server(s). Novell NetWare is an example of a client-server system. The operating system software on the server can communicate with every computer on the network, but client software communicates only with the server. In contrast, **peer-to-peer** network software permits communication between any two computers on the network, within security constraints, of course.

15.9 OTHER OPERATING SYSTEM ISSUES

There are many challenges in the design of an operating system. In this section we make a few comments about one of the more interesting operating system issues, deadlock.

Deadlock

It is not unusual for more than one process to need the same computer resource. If the resource is capable of handling multiple concurrent requests, then there is no problem. However, some resources can operate with only one process at a time. A printer is one example. If one process is printing, it is not acceptable to allow other processes access to the printer at that time.

When one process has a resource that another process needs to proceed, and the other process has a resource that the first process needs, then both are waiting for an event that can never occur, namely, the release by the other process of the needed resource. This situation can be extended to any number of processes, arranged in a circle.

This situation is called **deadlock,** and it is not unfamiliar to you in other forms. The most familiar example is the automobile gridlock situation depicted in Figure 15.29. Each vehicle is waiting for the one to its right to move, but of course no one can move.

FIGURE 15.29

A Familiar Deadlock Situation

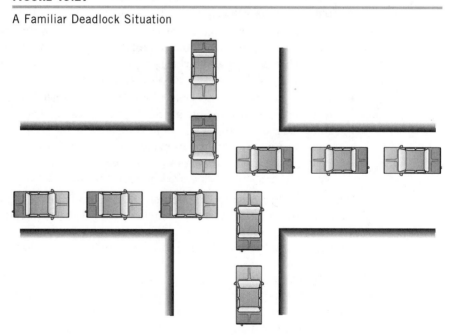

In a computer system, deadlock is a serious problem. Much theoretical study has been done on deadlock. This has resulted in three basic ways in which deadlock is managed. These are **deadlock prevention, deadlock avoidance,** and **deadlock detection and recovery.**

Deadlock prevention is the safest method; however, it also has the most severe effect on system performance. Deadlock prevention works by eliminating in general any condition that could create a deadlock. It is equivalent to closing one of the streets.

Deadlock avoidance provides a somewhat weaker form of protection. It works by continually monitoring the resource requirements, looking for situations in which a deadlock potential exists and then not allowing that situation to occur. If the fourth car is not allowed into the street because there are three other cars already in the intersection, that is deadlock avoidance. In a computer system, the equivalent would be a refusal by the operating system to allocate a resource because doing so would have a potential to cause deadlock.

Deadlock detection and recovery is the simplest method to implement, but the most costly when things go wrong. This methodology allows deadlocks to occur. The OS monitors the resources. If everything stops, it assumes that a deadlock has occurred. It may take some time to notice the condition, time that is lost to productive system work. Recovery techniques include terminating processes and preempting resources. Terminated processes must be rerun. Much work could be lost and require re-creation. Deadlock recovery is generally considered the least satisfactory solution. To drivers too!

Other Issues

There are other issues that must be considered in the design of an operating system. Operating systems require a method for communication between processes. In some systems, interprocess communication may be as simple as sharing variables in a special pool or sending semaphore messages that indicate completion of a task. In others, there may be a complex message passing arrangement, with mailboxes set up for each process. Interprocess communication has increased in importance over the past few years, due to the desire to move data and program execution more easily from one application to another.

One form of communication that is sometimes very important is the ability to synchronize processes with each other. Two or more processes may be cooperating on the solution of a complex problem, and one may be dependent on the solution provided by another. Furthermore, both may be required to access the same data, the order and timing in which access takes place can be critical, and these conditions can affect the overall results. This requires a solution to the problem of **process synchronization.**

As a simple example, consider an address card file shared by you and your roommate or partner. A friend calls to tell you that she has moved and to give you her new phone number. You place a new card with this information in the card file box. Meanwhile, your roommate has taken the old card from the box and has used it to write a letter. He returns to the box, sees the new card, figures that it must be obsolete, and so throws it away and replaces it with the original. The new data is now lost. Similar situations can occur with data being shared by more than one process.

As another simple example, consider two processes, with the goal to produce the result c, where process 1 solves the program statement

```
a = a + b;
```

with initial values $a = 2$ and $b = 3$.

The second process solves the statement

```
c = a + 5;
```

where the value of a is to be taken from the first process.

Clearly, it is important that the first process complete before the value of a is used by process 2. If process 2 looks at the value of a too early, the result, c, will be $2 + 5 = 7$. The correct value is $5 + 5 = 10$. The solutions to the problems of interprocess communication and process synchronization are beyond the scope of this textbook. They are both difficult and interesting. Various books, such as Stallings [STAL01], Silberschatz, et. al. [SILB01], and Tanenbaum [TAN92], discuss these issues at length.

15.10 THE CONCEPT OF A VIRTUAL MACHINE

The operating system creates an important illusion. Particularly in the case of a multiuser system, the operating system makes it appear that each user has the computer system entirely to himself or herself. The operating system allocates resources on a shared basis, processes can communicate with each other, and there is a common set of interrupt routines, controlled by the operating system. Some modern operating systems, including IBM VM (virtual machine) and Windows 95, carry this illusion one step further and create a **virtual machine (VM).**

In this scheme, each virtual machine is an exact duplicate of the system hardware, providing, in effect, multiple machines, each the equivalent of a separate, fully configured system. The virtual machines can execute any operating system software that is compatible with the hardware. Each virtual machine supports its own operating system, isolated both from the actual hardware and from other virtual machines. The virtual machine mechanism is invisible to the software executing on a virtual machine.

As an example, the IBM VM operating system simulates multiple copies of all the hardware resources of the IBM mainframe computer, registers, program counter, interrupts, I/O, and all. This allows the system to load and run one or more operating systems on top of VM, including, even, other copies of VM. The loaded operating systems each think that they are interacting with the hardware, but actually they are interacting with VM. VM isolates the hardware completely. Effectively, each operating system is interacting with a separate virtual machine. Processes on different virtual machines are also isolated from each other.

This design allows different users to use different operating systems on the same machine concurrently. It also allows the system to serve more users concurrently than any single operating system would normally allow, since each virtual machine appears to be a complete machine to its own operating system.

In the previous description, the words "virtual machine" describe an entity that, to a user, takes on the appearance of a computer, but which in actuality is an illusion created by a computer's operating system. The programming language Java executes on a different type of virtual machine, the **Java Virtual Machine** (JVM), which is also an illusion created by an operating system.

The goal of the Java Virtual Machine is to create a standardized computer platform for the execution of binary programs, regardless of the actual architecture of the computer being utilized. Programs written in Java are compiled into a standard binary machine language, called bytecode, similar to the machine languages that you studied in the early chapters of this book, but not representative of an actual physical computer. Instead, when the ersatz machine language is transmitted to a computer where the program is to be executed, an interpreter in the operating system translates the code, one instruction at a time, into the native machine language of the actual computer executing the program. The method is shown in Figure 15.30. The interpreter acts as a virtual processor; it is invisible to the user. To all appearances, the JVM binary language is actually being executed on the target machine. JVM can execute on any machine whose operating system provides a JVM interpreter. In fact, the target machine does not even have to be a computer at all. Nearly every modern operating system provides a JVM interpreter. Thus, under the standards, a Java program should execute almost identically on any computer. Or on any other piece of equipment that provides a JVM interpreter.

Although it would be possible to build a computer in which the Java bytecode is the native language of the machine (a Java Real Machine?), it is not necessary in order to achieve the goal.

SUMMARY AND REVIEW

An operating system is quite complex internally. This chapter has considered some of the more important components of the operating system in some detail. After a brief discussion of a single-tasking system, we explored the critical components of a simple multitasking system, particularly scheduling and memory management.

Turning our attention to more general multitasking systems, we discussed the concepts of processes and threads. We showed you how the operating system creates and manages processes, including description of the standard process states. Threads are important in current systems, and we discussed threads as simplified processes, without the overhead.

Next, we introduced the two, and sometimes three, types of CPU scheduling. We described the difference between preemptive and nonpreemptive multitasking, described the different objectives that can be used to measure performance, and introduced several CPU dispatching algorithms, comparing the way in which these met different objectives.

FIGURE 15.30

Java Virtual Machine

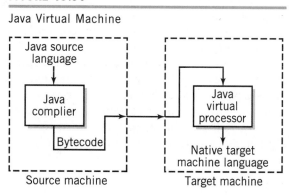

The focus of memory management is to load programs in such a way as to enhance system performance. We discussed the shortcomings of overlay systems and partitioning methods. Next, we reintroduced virtual storage. The emphasis in this chapter is on the symbiosis between the hardware and the operating system to provide a memory management technique that addresses many of the shortcomings of other memory management techniques. The virtual storage methodology eliminates the requirement that the sum of programs to be loaded as a whole must fit all at once into available memory; instead, the active parts of each program are sufficient. It allows each program to exist in the same virtual memory space. It allows programs to be loaded anywhere in memory, and noncontiguously. And it eliminates the need for relocation procedures.

We explained the page fault procedure and discussed several page replacement algorithms. We considered the number of pages that are required to execute a program successfully and efficiently, and we considered the problem of thrashing.

Next, we discussed the algorithms used for secondary storage. Following that, we presented the operating system components that support networking. In particular, we introduced the OSI and TCP/IP protocol suites. For computers to communicate, agreement between computers at a number of different levels is required. In this chapter we introduced a multilayered protocol model called OSI that makes it possible to separate different components of the requirement. The protocol defines communication at both the station to-station level and end-to-end level.

Typically, communication between two computers is done using a data packet format. A data packet consists of a message to be transmitted from a sender to a receiver. The message is encapsulated in a series of "envelopes" by the sender. Each layer of the protocol contributes another envelope. An envelope consists of a preamble and possibly a trailer containing information that will allow the peer level at the receiver to interpret the aspects of the data packet that are relevant to that level. Actual communication takes place only at the physical level. The protocol at the physical level is specific to the characteristics and requirements of the communication channel.

The most important protocol suite at present is TCP/IP. TCP/IP provides communication capability for a wide range of local and remote communications and is provided as a component of many modern operating systems. The TCP/IP protocol suite provides a number of useful and popular communication applications, as well as means for communication over different types of networks and links. For flexibility TCP/IP does not define the lower layers of the OSI model but, instead, interfaces with the data link layer that is dictated by a particular installation.

We next introduced briefly the issues of deadlock, process synchronization, and interprocess communication. These issues are representative of some of the more complex problems that must be faced by operating system designers and administrators.

Finally, we introduced the concept of a virtual machine, and showed two different applications of the concept. The VM operating system provides virtual machines that can be treated as independent machines, each with its own operating system, applications, and users. The Java Virtual Machine provides a standardized architecture for the execution of Java programs, regardless of the underlying architecture of the actual machine being used.

KEY CONCEPTS AND TERMS

application layer
associative memory
backing store
Belady's anomaly
best-fit algorithm
blocked state
blocking store
child process
client-server system
clock page replacement algo-
    rithm
cloning
concept of locality
cooperating processes
data link layer
datagram
deadlock
deadlock avoidance
deadlock detection and
    recovery
deadlock prevention
demand paging
dirty bit
dispatcher
dispatching
distributed system
dynamic address
    translation (DAT)
dynamic priority
event
event-driven program
external fragmentation
first-come, first-served
    (FCFS) disk scheduling
first-fit algorithm
first-in, first-out (FIFO)
fixed partitioning
fixed memory partitioning
footer
forking
fragmentation
frame (memory)
frame (network)
global page replacement
header

high-level, or long-term,
    scheduler
indefinite postponement
independent processes
internal fragmentation
Java Virtual Machine
job
job steps
largest-fit algorithm
least recently used (LRU)
    page replacement
    algorithm
local page replacement
locked frame
logical link control
multilevel feedback queue
    algorithm
n-step c-scan scheduling
    algorithm
network layer
nonpreemptive systems
not used recently (NUR)
    page replacement
    algorithm
Open Systems
    Interconnection
    Reference Model
overlay
packet
page fault
page fault trap
page swapping
page replacement algorithm
page table
parent process
peer-to-peer
physical layer
PPP (point-to-point
    protocol)
preamble
preemptive systems
prepaging
presentation layer
priority scheduling
process

process control block (PCB)
process identifier (PID)
process state
process synchronization
ready state
remote procedure call (RPC)
response time
resumption
roll-out, roll-in
round robin
router
running state
scan disk scheduling
segment table
session layer
shortest job first (SJF)
shortest distance first (SDF)
    disk scheduling
socket
spawn
stack
starvation
suspended state
swap file
swap out
swap space
swapping
system process
task
TCP/IP protocol suite
thrashing
threads
time-out
trailer
translation lookaside buffer
    (TLB)
transport layer
turnaround time
user process
variable memory partition
variable partitioning
virtual machine (VM)
wake-up
working set
worst-fit algorithm

FOR FURTHER READING

Any of the references mentioned in the For Further Reading section of Chapter 14 also address the topics in this chapter. If you have become intrigued by operating systems and would like to know more, there are a large number of interesting problems and algorithms with intriguing names like "the dining philosophers problem." We have only barely touched upon the surface of operating system design and operation, especially in the areas of deadlock, process synchronization, and interprocess communication. We highly recommend the textbooks by Deitel [DEIT90], Tanenbaum [TAN92], Silberschatz, et. al. [SILB01], and Stallings [STAL00] for thorough and detailed treatment of these and other topics.

Information about network and distributed operating systems can be found in Tanenbaum [TAN95, TAN92] and in most recent operating systems and networking texts. Hunter [HUNT95] discusses network operating systems from a business perspective. Miller [MILL95] addresses all aspects of LAN-to-LAN connections and wide area networking. There are a number of books devoted to TCP/IP. Appropriate choices include Comer [COM00] and Martin and Leben [MART94a]. Parker [PARK96] presents TCP/IP in a very straightforward, self-teaching way. The specifics of ATM are discussed in great depth in a special issue of the Communications of the ACM for February, 1995. Information on specific networking operating systems can be found in most UNIX, IBM S/390, and Windows 9x references. King [KING94] presents a clear description of network operating system components in the context of Windows 95. See the For Further Reading section in Chapter 13 for additional references. The Java Virtual Machine is clearly explained in [MEY97].

EXERCISES

15.1 Describe in step-by-step form the procedure that the operating system would use to switch from one user to another in a multiuser time sharing system.

15.2 Discuss the steps that take place when a process is moved (a) from ready state to running state, (b) from running state to blocked state, (c) from running state to ready state, (d) from blocked state to ready state.

15.3 Why is there no path on the process diagram from blocked state to running state?

15.4 Describe what occurs when a user types a keystroke on a terminal connected to a multiuser system. Does the system respond differently for a preemptive or nonpreemptive system? Why or why not?

15.5 The multilevel feedback queue scheduling method looks like FIFO at the upper levels and like round robin at the lowest level, yet it frequently behaves better than either in terms of the performance objectives mentioned in the text. Why is this so?

15.6 Discuss the shortest-job-first scheduling method in terms of the various objectives given in the text.

15.7 A VSOS (very simple operating system) uses a very simple approach to scheduling. Scheduling is done on a straight round-robin basis, where each job is given a time quantum sufficient to complete very short jobs. Upon completion by a job, another job is admitted to the system and immediately given one quantum. Thereafter, it enters the round-robin queue. Consider the scheduling objectives given in the text. Discuss the VSOS scheduling approach in terms of these objectives.

15.8   Earlier versions of Windows use an essentially nonpreemptive dispatching technique that Microsoft calls "cooperative multitasking." In cooperative multitasking, each program is expected to voluntarily give up the CPU periodically to give other processes a chance to execute. Discuss. What potential difficulties can this method cause?

15.9   Why is program relocation unnecessary when virtual storage is used for memory management?

15.10   What are the advantages of virtual storage over the overlay method of managing memory?

15.11   Discuss the impact of virtual storage on the design of an operating system. Consider the tasks that must be performed, the various methods of performing those tasks, and the resulting effect on system performance.

15.12   Develop an example that explains thrashing clearly.

15.13   What kind of fragmentation would you find in virtual storage? Is this a serious problem? Justify your answer. Discuss the relationship between fragmentation and page size.

15.14   Explain why page sharing can reduce the number of page faults that occur in a system.

15.15   The manual for a popular operating system points out that the number of concurrent users on the system can be increased if the users are sharing programs, such as editors, mail readers, or compilers. What characteristics of virtual storage make this possible?

15.16   Explain deadlocking. Why doesn't deadlocking occur in MS-DOS?

15.17   The CPU scheduling algorithm (in UNIX) is a simple priority algorithm. The priority for a process is computed as the ratio of the CPU time actually used by the process to the real time that has passed. The lower the figure, the higher the priority. Priorities are recalculated every tenth of a second.

    a.   What kind of jobs are favored by this type of algorithm?

    b.   If there is no I/O being performed, this algorithm reduces to a round-robin algorithm. Explain.

    c.   Discuss this algorithm in terms of the scheduling objectives given in the text.

15.18   Explain the working set concept. What is the relationship between the working set concept and the principle of locality?

15.19   Why is the working set concept much more effective if it is implemented dynamically, that is, recalculated while a process is executing?

15.20   What are the differences, trade-offs, advantages, and disadvantages between an OS that implements deadlock prevention versus deadlock avoidance versus deadlock detection and recovery?

15.21   The accompanying graph shows that, for a given process, the page fault rate in a virtual storage system increases as the page size is increased and then decreases to 0 as the page size approaches P, the size of the process. Explain the various parts of the curve.

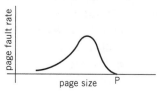

15.22 Assume that you have a program to run on a Little Man–type computer that provides virtual storage paging. Each page holds ten locations (in other words, one digit). The system can support up to one hundred pages of memory. As shown below, your program is sixty-five instructions long. The available frames in physical memory are shown in the other diagram. All blocked-in areas are already occupied by other programs that are sharing the use of the Little Man.

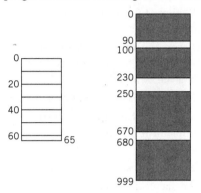

a. Create a starting page table for your program. Assume that your program will start executing at its location 0.

b. Suppose a page fault occurs in your program. The OS has to decide whether to swap out one of your older pages, or one of somebody else's pages. Which strategy is less likely to cause thrashing? Why?

15.23 What is a real-time system? Discuss the impact of a real-time system on the design of the operating systems, paying particular note to the various components and algorithms to be used.

15.24 Consider the operation of a jukebox. Each table has a terminal where customers can feed coins to play songs (50 cents apiece, three for a dollar). Needless to say, in a busy restaurant, the queue to hear your songs can be quite long, sometimes longer than the average dining time, in fact.

Discuss the various disk scheduling algorithms as methods of selecting the order in which to play the requested songs. Be sure to consider the advantages and disadvantages of each method in terms of fairness, probability that each diner will get to hear their songs, ease of implementation, and any other important issues that you feel should be considered. You might note that multiple diners will sometimes request the same song.

15.25 Tanenbaum [TAN92] notes that the problem of scheduling an elevator in a tall building is similar to that of scheduling a disk arm. Requests come in continuously calling the elevator to floors at random. One difference is that once inside, riders request that the elevator move to a different floor. Discuss the various disk scheduling algorithms as options for scheduling the elevator in terms of fairness, service, and ease of implementation.

15.26 Discuss possible tape scheduling algorithms for a tape controller. Assume that files are stored contiguously on tape. What effect would noncontiguous, linked files have on your algorithm?

15.27 You may have noticed a number of similarities between virtual storage paging and cache memory paging. One major difference, of course, is that main memory is much faster than disk access.

Consider the applicability and performance of the various paging algorithms in a memory caching system, and discuss the advantages and disadvantages of each.

15.28 Discuss the major methods of allocation of file space on a disk in terms of the advantages and disadvantages of each.

15.29 The designer of a new operating system to be used especially for real-time applications has proposed the use of virtual storage memory management, so that the system can handle programs too large to fit in the limited memory space sometimes provided on real-time systems. What are the implications of this decision in terms of the way that virtual storage works?

15.30 The manager of your computer system has informed you that the new OS that you are designing will operate fundamentally as a FIFO system for scheduling. Given this position, discuss the implications of choosing a preemptive or nonpreemptive scheduling scheme to implement her decision.

15.31 Discuss the various trade-offs and decisions involved in task dispatching and the options and methods used for implementing those trade-offs and decisions.

15.32 A system status report for a virtual storage operating system shows that between 2 P.M. and 4 P.M. CPU usage and I/O usage both climbed steadily. At 4 p.m., the I/O usage reached 100 percent, but continued to increase. After 4 p.m., the CPU usage, however, dropped off dramatically. What is the explanation for this behavior?

15.33 Discuss the network features and services provided in an operating system. Which services are mandatory? Why?

15.34 Describe clearly, step by step, and layer by layer, the operation that takes place when passing a datagram through an intermediate node in a switching network.

15.35 The chapter notes that the physical layer is only concerned with the transmission of a sequence of bits from one point to another. Suppose that the sequence 110010011 is used as a synchronization sequence preamble to a data packet. Propose a method that can be used to allow the channel to distinguish the synchronization sequence from an identical data sequence within the packet. In what layer of the OSI model would you implement your solution? Why?

15.36 Is it possible to build a network that can recognize more than one protocol? If so, explain how this could be done.

15.37 The TCP/IP protocol suite appears to have no equivalents to the OSI session and presentation layers. How are the services provided by those layers handled in TCP/IP? Be as specific as you can when you refer to the particular services provided by those layers.

15.38 Find a good reference on the Java Virtual Machine. Describe the architecture and machine language of the virtual machine. How does it compare with the languages you studied in previous chapters?

CHAPTER 16

FILE MANAGEMENT

Thomas Sperling

16.0 INTRODUCTION

Most direct interactions between the user and the computer involve significant use of the file management system layer of the operating system. From the perspective of the user, the file management system is one of the most important and visible features of the operating system. Most user commands, whether typed into a command line interface (CLI), or selected from a menu, or activated with a mouse, are operations on files. Many interactions between programs and the operating system are file requests. When a user retrieves a document file using the drop-down file menu in a word processor, the word processor program is using the services of the operating system file manager to retrieve the document file. Even the data base management application software requires the services of the file management system to perform its file storage and retrieval operations. It is the file management system software that allows users and programs to store, retrieve, and manipulate files as logical entities, instead of as physical blocks of binary data. Because of its importance and visibility to the user, we have chosen to discuss the file management system separately from the rest of the operating system.

We begin this chapter by reviewing the differences between the logical, or user, view of a file and the physical requirements of its storage and retrieval. Next, we show how the file management system accomplishes its mission of providing a logical file view to the user and the user's programs. You will see how logical file system requests are mapped to physical files. You will see how files are physically stored and retrieved, and how the logical file commands that you issue to the operating system are implemented. You will see some of the trade-offs that must be made as a result of specific user and program requirements and the limitations of different file storage methods. You will understand how a directory system works and read about some of the different methods that are used by file systems to keep track of and locate files and directories. You will see how the file manager finds and allocates space for files, and how it reclaims and keeps track of space vacated when a file is moved or deleted.

It is hoped that, as a result of the discussion in this chapter, you will be able to use and manage computer file systems more effectively.

16.1 THE LOGICAL AND PHYSICAL VIEW OF FILES

Whether on computer or paper, a file is an organized collection of data. The organization of the file depends on the use of the data and is determined by the program or user who created the file. Similarly, the meaning of the data in the file is established by the program or user. A computer file may be as simple as a single data stream that represents an entire program to be loaded at one time or a collection of text data read sequentially, or as complex as a database made up of individual records, each with many fields and subfields, to be retrieved one or a few records at a time in some random order.

Nearly all data in the computer is stored and retrieved as files. Thus, files may take many different forms. Here are a few examples of common forms files might take:

- A program file, consisting of binary data; the bytes of data in the file represent the sequence of instructions that make up a program. The file is stored on a device such as disk and is loaded sequentially into succeeding locations in memory for execution.
- A data file consisting of alphanumeric Unicode text that represents a program in source code form and will serve as "data" input to a C++ compiler.
- A data file consisting of a sequence of numbers stored in ASCII form and separated by delimiters that will be used as input to a C program that does data analysis.
- A data file consisting of a mixture of alphanumeric ASCII characters and special binary codes that represents a text file for a word processor or spreadsheet.
- A data file consisting of alphanumeric Unicode characters representing records made up of names, addresses, and accounting information applicable to a business database.
- A data file configured in some special way to represent an image, sound, or other object. Several examples of these types of files were illustrated in Chapter 3.
- A directory file consisting of information about other files.

One common file representation views a file **logically** as a collection of **records,** each made up of a number of **fields.** A typical record-oriented file is shown in Figure 16.1. In this illustration, each record is made up of the same fields, and each field is the same fixed length for all records, but these restrictions are not necessarily valid in all cases. Some fields may not be required for certain records. The company personnel file shown in Figure 16.2 does not require the salary field for retired employees. This file also uses a field of comments. The comments field is a variable length field, so that more comments can be added when necessary. This figure also shows that the file may appear differently, without affecting the record structure underneath. The layout shown in Figure 16.1 is sometimes called a **table image,** while the layout in Figure 16.2 is referred to as a **form image.**

Describing a file by its records and fields represents the file logically; that is, it represents the file the way the user views it. The logical view may or may not be related to the

FIGURE 16.1

A Typical File

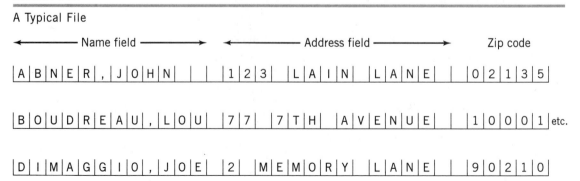

FIGURE 16.2

An Alternative Typical File

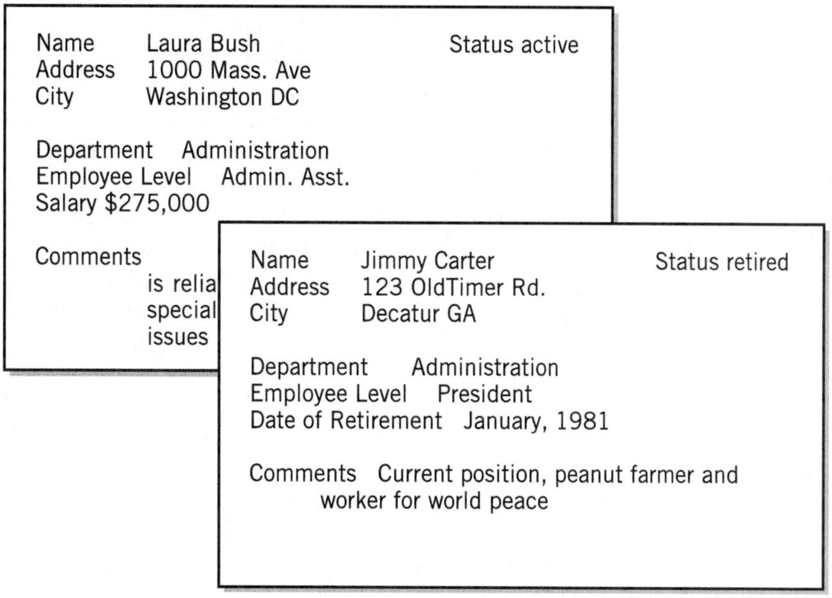

```
Name        Laura Bush                    Status active
Address     1000 Mass. Ave
City        Washington DC

Department   Administration
Employee Level   Admin. Asst.
Salary $275,000

Comments
         is relia    Name        Jimmy Carter              Status retired
         special     Address     123 OldTimer Rd.
         issues      City        Decatur GA

                     Department     Administration
                     Employee Level    President
                     Date of Retirement   January, 1981

                     Comments   Current position, peanut farmer and
                                worker for world peace
```

physical view of the file, the way in which the data is actually stored. Most commonly, the data is stored in physical **blocks** on a disk. The blocks are of fixed size, say, 512 bytes. Just as there is no reason to assume that a paper record will fit exactly on a single sheet of paper, there is no reason to assume that the size of the logical records within the computer file corresponds to the physical in any particular way, although on some computer systems it may. This is an issue to which we shall return shortly.

Consider again, for example, the file shown in Figure 16.1. Another representation of this file, more akin to the means used physically for its storage, is shown in Figure 16.3. As another example, the program file mentioned earlier could be interpreted as a single-record, single-field logical file, with one long variable field in the record. Physically, the file might be stored as a sequence of physical blocks, accessed one after another to retrieve the program. Many word processors also treat files this way. Files of these types are frequently loaded entirely into memory as a single unit.

Different file management systems exhibit a range of capabilities in the ways in which they represent files logically. Some operating systems recognize and manipulate several different

FIGURE 16.3

Yet Another File Representation

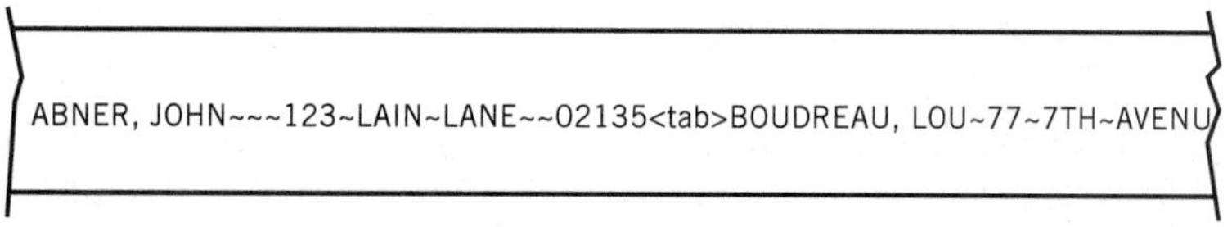

```
ABNER, JOHN~~~123~LAIN~LANE~~02135<tab>BOUDREAU, LOU~77~7TH~AVENU
```

types of files and record structures, while others simply treat all files as streams of bytes and leave it to utility and application programs to determine the meaning of the data within the file. The file managers in UNIX and Windows, for example, differentiate only between directories and byte stream files. On these systems, program and data files are treated identically by the file manager. You may have seen this as a result of using a command that displays the contents of a file on the screen, such as *cat* or TYPE or MORE, with a program file. Since the program file can contain any combination of bytes, including control characters, the result on the screen is gibberish. IBM z/OS represents the opposite extreme, providing detailed record management within its file management system.

There are good arguments for either approach. It would certainly be reasonable to interpret the program and word processing files mentioned above as a single stream of bytes, for example. Furthermore, we note that the structure of files can be complex, and every one is different. Treating all files in a similar way simplifies the file management programs, while at the same time adding flexibility to the application programs and utilities, since each application program can define the contents of its files in any way convenient to meet its own needs. Input and output redirection is simplified, since all data is treated in the same way, as a stream of bytes. The same is true for the use of program pipes, as described in Chapter 14.

Conversely, treating all files as a stream of bytes requires significantly more effort on the design of application and utility programs. Retrieval of data in the "middle of the stream," for example, is more difficult when the application program must keep track of its position in the file. A file management system that imposes well-designed standards on its files can simplify data storage and retrieval and simplify application program design, without severely limiting application flexibility.

As a practical matter, much of the data that is useful to a user is logically represented in record form. Data files whose records are always retrieved in sequence from the beginning of the file are known as **sequential files.** Some applications require that records be retrievable from anywhere in the file in a random sequence. These are known as **random access files,** or sometimes as **relative access files,** since the location is frequently specified relative to the beginning of the file. (We want the twenty-fifth record, for example.) One common method for retrieving records randomly from a file uses one field, known as the **key field,** as an index to identify the proper record. The key field in Figure 16.2 might be employee's name, since the file is alphabetized by name.

There are other methods of retrieving particular records from within a file. Some of these are discussed in Section 16.3. For now, it is only important that you be aware that, for certain types of files, it is necessary for either the file management system or the application program to be able to locate and access individual records from within the file.

In addition to the data within the file, it is convenient to attach attributes to the file that identify and characterize the file. The most important file attribute, obviously, is its name. The name itself may be specified in such a way as to allow identification with a particular type of file (usually known as a **file extension**); it may also be expanded to identify the file with a particular group of files or a particular storage device. In Windows, for example, the expanded name

```
B:\GROUPA\PROG31.CPP
```

identifies the file (if the user chose an appropriate name!) as a C++ program named PROG31, stored together in a group of files known as GROUPA, and located on the floppy disk inserted into disk drive B. The file extension may be important only to the user, or it may be required by the operating system or by an application program, to activate the correct application programs, for example. The extension .EXE, for example, notifies Windows that the file is an executable file. Similarly, the file extension may or may not be relevant to the file management system.

In addition to the name, the file can be characterized in various other useful ways. A file may be executable, as a program, or readable, as data. A file may be considered to be either binary or alphanumeric (although, of course, even alphanumeric characters are actually stored in binary form). The file may be characterized by the way data is to be retrieved. A file might be temporary or permanent. A file might be writeable or write-protected. There are other possibilities.

Files may also have such attributes as the date of origination, the most recent update, and information about who has the right to access, update, and delete the file. Some systems allow a data file to specify the program it is to be used with. This property is called an **association.** In such a case, calling the data file automatically loads and starts the associated program file. For example, Windows uses the file extension to create the necessary association. Other operating systems may store the association as a property of the data file.

The previous discussion has focused on the logical view of a file, the meaning of its contents and its attributes, as viewed by the user, operating system utilities, and application programs. All the files, plus all the attributes and information describing those files, are stored, controlled, and manipulated by the file management system.

The **physical view** of a file is the way in which the file is actually stored within the computer system. We have already indicated that the physical view of a file may look very different from the file's logical view.

Physically, the file on nearly every system is stored and manipulated as a group of blocks. The blocks on a disk are normally of fixed size, typically 256, 512, or 1024 bytes. Some systems refer to a group of one or more blocks as a **cluster.**[1] The block or cluster will correspond to one or more sectors on a single track or cylinder. The block or cluster is the smallest unit that the file management system can store or retrieve in a single read or write operation.

There is, of course, no direct correlation between the logical size of a record and the physical block or cluster—the logical record size is designed by the programmer or user for the particular application and may actually be of variable size; the physical block is fixed as a part of the computer system design.

A file may fit entirely within a single physical block or cluster, or it may require several blocks or clusters. The file management system may pack the file into physical blocks without regard to the logical records, as shown in Figure 16.4a, or it may attempt to maintain some relationship between the logical records and physical blocks, as shown in Figure 16.4b. Logical records may be packed several to a physical record, or may be larger than a physical record and require several physical records for each logical record.

A minimum of one full block is required for a file, even if the file only contains a single byte of data. Depending on the file management system design, and perhaps on attributes of the file, the blocks that hold a particular file may be **contiguous,** that is, stored together, or may be scattered all over the disk or tape, **noncontiguously.**

---

[1] Note that a disk cluster is not related to a computer system cluster. Same word, totally different meaning.

FIGURE 16.4

The Relationship Between Logical and Physical Records

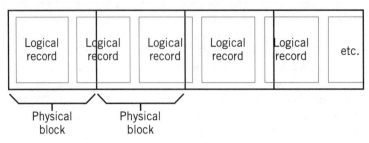

a. Logical records and physical blocks unrelated

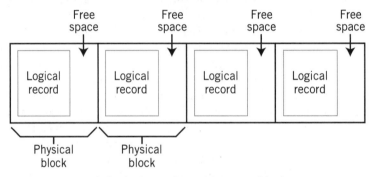

b. Logical records stored one to a block

The physical block or cluster size is a compromise between file access speed and wasted space. If the blocks are too small, then most files will require several disk reads or writes to retrieve or store the data, as well as considerable space to keep track of usage of each block. Conversely, if the block size is too large, there will be a large amount of unused space at the end of many, perhaps most, blocks.

Note that it is the logical view that gives the data in a file meaning. Physically, the file is simply a collection of bits stored in blocks. It is the file management system that establishes the connection between the logical and physical representations of the file.

Tape organization is somewhat different. Most tape systems use a variable size block, so it is possible to store a file exactly, with no internal fragmentation. Furthermore, some file management systems separate logical records into different blocks, making it possible to record individual records on tape.

16.2 THE ROLE OF THE FILE MANAGEMENT SYSTEM

The file management system is commonly called the **file manager.** In this text, we will primarily use the term "file manager," so please remember we are talking about a software program, *not a person!* The file manager acts as a transparent interface between the user's logical view of the file system and the computer's physical reality of disk sectors, tracks, and clusters, tape blocks, and other I/O vagaries. It provides a consistent set of commands and a consistent view of files to the user regardless of the file type, file characteristics, choice of physical device, or physical storage requirements. It translates those commands to a form appropriate for the device and carries out the required operation. To do so, it maintains **directory** structures for each device. These, too, are presented in logical form to the user and to the user's programs.

User file commands and program file requests are interpreted by the command shell, then passed in logical form as requests to the file manager. Program requests are made directly to the file manager. These requests commonly take the form of OPEN, READ, WRITE, MOVE FILE POINTER, RESET POINTER TO BEGINNING OF FILE, or CLOSE, and other similar procedure calls.

The file manager checks the validity of the requests and then translates the requests into the appropriate physical course of action. The directory system assists in the location and organization of the file. When required, the file manager makes specific I/O data transfer requests to the I/O device handler layer for execution of the transfer. Upon completion of the request, the directory is updated, if necessary, and control is returned to the command shell or program. The process is illustrated in Figure 16.5.

As a specific example of this process, consider what occurs within the operating system when the user of a typical system types the command

FIGURE 16.5

File Manager Request Handling

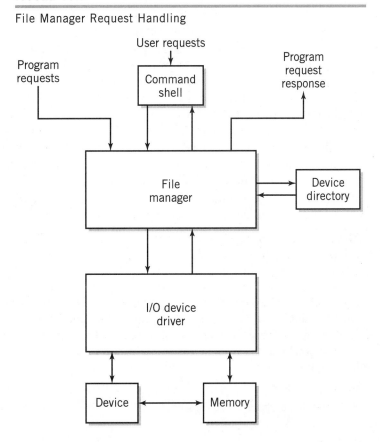

```
COPY A:FILEX TO C:
```

(or moves the FILEX icon with a mouse to the C: drawer on a system with a graphical command interface—the operation is the same).

The following sequence of steps takes place. (Although this description seems long, the steps are reasonable and should not be too difficult to follow.):

1. The command interface interprets the command and determines that a copy of FILEX on device A: is to be made and stored on device C:. The Command shell passes the request to the file manager. Typically, the shell will request that the file manager open FILEX on A: and create FILEX on C:.

2. The file manager looks in the directory for device A: to find a file named FILEX. If it succeeds, the file manager reserves a block of space in memory, called a memory buffer, large enough to hold one or more physical blocks of data from the file.

3. Next, the file manager looks in the device C: directory to determine if there is enough free space to fit the file. If there is, the file manager adds FILEX to the directory and assigns enough blocks to the file for storage of the file.

4. The shell is informed that these requests succeeded. It now requests that the file manager read a block from A:FILEX. The file manager requests that the data from the first block or group of blocks from FILEX be read into the memory buffer. This request is addressed to the I/O device handler for device A:.

5. The device A: I/O device handler completes the transfer and notifies the file manager that the requested data is in the memory buffer.

6. The file manager now passes on a request that the data in the memory buffer be transferred to the first block or group of blocks that it assigned to C:FILEX. This request is addressed to the I/O device handler for device C:. (If device A: and device C: are the same type of device, both disks, for example, the same I/O handler may service both devices.)

7. The last three steps are repeated until the file copy is complete. Some systems allow the user to specify the size of the memory buffer. Note that the use of a larger memory buffer can make the copy operation for a large file much faster by limiting the number of individual I/O transfers.

8. The file manager returns control to the command interface with an internal message to indicate that the copy was successful.

The COPY operation is typical of requests made to the file manager. You are probably familiar with many others. Most user commands to the operating system are actually requests to the file manager.

Consider the operations on a file that a file management system would perform. These operations can be divided into three different categories of operations: those that work on the entire file, those that operate on data within the file, and those that actually manipulate the directory of the file without actually accessing the file itself.

The following examples of operations that work on the file as a whole are likely to be familiar to you as a user:

- Copy a file.
- Load and execute a (program) file.

- Move a file (assuming the move is to a different device).
- List or print a file.
- Load a file into memory.
- Store a file from memory.
- Compile or assemble a file.
- Append data from memory to a file.

Fundamental to every file manager, both stream- and record-based, is the ability to manipulate the data within the file itself. The file manager provides a basic set of operations that are used for this purpose. These operations probably seem less familiar to you as a user. That is because they are usually requested by a program, rather than directly by the user.

- Open a file for reading or writing. This procedure provides a buffer for holding the data as it is read or written and also creates a pointer that moves through the data as it is read or written.
- Read a number of bytes from the file. The number of bytes can be specified as part of the request, or it may be indicated by a delimiter, such as a carriage return or comma, depending on the system.
- Write a number of bytes to the file.
- Move the file pointer a distance forward or backward.
- "Rewind" the pointer to the beginning of the file.
- Close the file.

A file management system that provides support for individual record storage and retrieval includes additional operations. The following are examples of record-based operations. These operations can be performed either sequentially or randomly, depending on the nature of the file, the capabilities of the file manager, and the particular application:

- Read (retrieve) a record.
- Write (store) a record.
- Add a record to a file.
- Delete a record from a file.
- Change the contents of a record.

These operations manipulate the file directory, rather than the file itself:

- Delete a file.
- Rename a file.
- Append one file to another (known as concatenation).
- Create a new (empty) file. On some systems this operation will assign a block to the file even though the file is empty.
- Move a file from one directory to another on the same physical device.

It is often convenient to operate on a group of files together, for example, to copy all the files whose names begin with *assign* from your hard drive to a floppy disk for backup purposes. One way to do this is to organize your files in such a way that they are grouped into different areas of the disk. As we will discuss later, most systems provide a subdirectory structure for doing this.

An alternative method provided by most systems is the use of **wild cards** to identify a group of files. Wild cards are replacements for letters or groups of letters in a file name. When used with a command, they can identify a group of files whose names qualify when the wild card is substituted for some of the letters in the name. The most common wild cards in use are "?," which replaces any single letter in a file name, and "*," which replaces a group of zero or more letters that can be any letters that are legal in a file name. With one exception, the examples that follow work the same in UNIX or at a Windows command line prompt.

EXAMPLE

ASSIGN?.DAT will find files ASSIGN1.DAT and ASSIGNX.DAT, but will ignore ASSIGN.DAT, ASSIGN1.TXT, and ASSIGN12.DAT.

ASSIGN*.DAT will find ASSIGN.DAT, ASSIGNXQ.DAT, and ASSIGN12.DAT, but not ASSIGN2.TXT.

DE.DAT will find HOWDEDOO.DAT, ADAMBEDE.DAT, and DESIREE.DAT.

. will find every Windows file, even if there is no extension. It will find the UNIX file *textfile.*, but not the file *textfile,* because the latter has no dot in it.

UNIX provides an additional wild card form, "[choices]." For example, [aeiou] would look for a file name with a single letter a, e, i, o, or u in the given position. [a-zA-Z]* would accept zero or more uppercase or lowercase letters, but no numbers, in the given position.

In addition, many systems provide file utilities within the command structure that call upon the file management system for support. Sort utilities sort the records within a file by key field or by some other positional indicator. Some sort utilities load the entire file into memory, while others retrieve and store records one by one. In both cases, the file management system is used to perform the actual file and record retrieval and storage. Other examples of utilities commonly provided include utilities to merge two files record by record and to compare two files record by record.

The file management system is directly responsible for all aspects of the maintenance of the file system. This requires the file system to perform five major functions:

- The file management system provides the connection between the logical file system with its physical implementation, allowing the physical view to remain essentially invisible. It creates a logical view for the user, masks the physical view, and provides the mapping between the two views. Stating this more informally, the user requests a file by name, and the file is retrieved; the user does not know where the file is actually stored, nor does he or she care.

- The file management system maintains the directory structure for each I/O device in use. It also maintains a record of available space for each device and assigns and reclaims physical space as required to meet the needs of file storage.

- The file management system supports manipulation of the data within the file. For some systems, it can identify, locate, and manipulate individual records or individual blocks within a file, possibly for several different methods of file access. For others, the manipulation is limited to reads, writes, and the movement of a pointer.

- The file management system acts as an interface for the transfer of data to and from the various I/O devices by requesting transfers from the I/O device driver level of the operating system. It also assigns buffer spaces in memory to hold the data being transferred. The actual transfer, and the interface between the physical device and the operating system, is handled by the appropriate I/O device driver.

■ The file system manages file security and protection. It attempts to protect the integrity of files and prevent corruption. It provides a mechanism to control access to files. There are several different types of access control in use. These are discussed in Section 16.7.

Summing up the operation, the file manager receives requests from the utility/command layer of the operating system or from application programs, determines the course of action, and attempts to fulfill the request. In those cases that require data transfer to or from an I/O device, the file manager will issue a request to the appropriate I/O device driver in the next inner layer to perform the actual I/O transfer. The file manager specifies the physical block to be transferred, the direction of the transfer, and the memory location to be used, but the actual transfer is performed by the I/O device driver.

There are two powerful advantages in separating the file and I/O functions into different tasks.

1. When new I/O devices are added, or the device is changed, it is necessary only to replace the I/O driver for that device. The file system remains unchanged. The idea of changing an I/O device driver is familiar to you if you have ever installed a new printer, video card, or disk drive for your PC.

2. A command request to redirect data is easy to implement, since the file manager controls the file. The file manager simply directs the binary data to a different I/O driver.

In general, the file manager is responsible for, and assumes the chore of, organizing, locating, accessing, and manipulating files and file data and managing space for different devices and file types. The file manager takes requests as its input, selects the device, determines the appropriate format, and handles the request. It uses the services of the I/O device layer to perform actual transfers of data between the devices and memory.

16.3 LOGICAL FILE ACCESS METHODS

There are a number of different ways in which to access the data in a file. The method used reflects both the structure of the file and the way in which the data is to be used. For example, a program file made up of executable code will be read as a whole into memory. A file made up of inventory data records will often be accessed one record at a time, in some random order queries to the system. As we have already said, some file management systems support a number of different formats, while others leave the structuring and formatting of data within a file to the application programs and utilities that use the file.

It is beyond the scope of this textbook to discuss file access methods in any detail. That material is better left to a file and data structures text. To an extent, however, the access method used affects the ways in which the file may be stored physically. For example, a file in which variable-sized records must be accessed in random order is not conveniently stored on tape, where the system must wind from the beginning of the tape to find the desired record. An overview of file access methods will serve to pinpoint the requirements of physical file storage.

Sequential File Access

Nearly every file management system supports **sequential file access.** Files that are accessed sequentially represent the great majority of all files. Sequential files include programs in both source and binary form, text files, and many data files. Information in a sequential file is simply processed in order of storage. If the file is record-oriented, records are processed as they are stored. A file pointer maintains the current position in the file. For read operations, the data is read into a buffer, and the pointer is moved forward into position for the next read. For write operations, the new data is appended to the end of the file. The pointer always points to the end. Most systems allow resetting the pointer to the beginning of the file. This operation is often referred to as *rewind,* because of its similarity to a tape operation. Some systems also allow the pointer to be moved a fixed amount. This operation is sometimes called seek. Sequential access is based on a tape model, since files on tape can only be read sequentially.

A file that is always read in its entirety is clearly accessed sequentially. Sequential access is fast, since no seek is required to find each succeeding record. Appending new records to the end of the file is also easy. On the other hand, it is not possible to add a record in the middle of a file accessed sequentially without rewriting at least all the succeeding records. This is a severe disadvantage in some situations.

Random Access

Random access assumes that a file is made up of fixed length logical records. The file manager can go directly to any record, in any order, and can read or write records in place without affecting any other record.

Some systems rely on the application to determine the logical block number where data is to be accessed. Others provide mechanisms for selecting locations based on a number of different possible criteria: for example, sequenced alphabetically on a key, sequenced in order of the time of entry, or calculated mathematically from the data itself. The most common method used is called **hashing.** Hashing is based on some simple mathematical algorithm that calculates a logical record number somewhere within the permissible range of record numbers. The range is based on the anticipated number of records in the file.

Hashing is very effective when the number of records is relatively small compared to the overall capacity of the file. However, hashing depends on the idea that the algorithm will result in a unique record number for each record. As the file fills, this becomes less and less probable. A **collision** occurs when two different records calculate to the same logical record number. Collisions must be detected by the file manager to prevent erroneous results. This is done by comparing the key used for hashing with that stored in the file. When a collision occurs, the system stores the additional record in an **overflow** area that is reserved for this purpose.

Once the logical record number is known, the file manager can locate the corresponding physical record relative to the start of the file. If there is an integer-to-one relationship between the logical and physical blocks, this calculation is almost trivial. Even at its most difficult, the translation requires nothing more than the use of a simple mathematical formula

$$P = \text{int} (L * S_L / S_P)$$

Where

P = the relative physical block number

L = the relative logical block number

S_L = the size in bytes of a logical block

S_P = the size in bytes of a physical block

Once the relative physical record is known, the actual physical location is located using information stored with the directory. Because physical records must be accessed a block at a time, the file manager provides a memory buffer large enough to hold the physical record or records that contain at least a single logical record. It then extracts the logical record from the buffer and moves it to the data area for the program requesting access.

Random access is also known as relative access, because the record number to be accessed is expressed relative to the start of the file. Most modern file management systems provide a way for an application to access files randomly. It is easy to simulate sequential access in a system that supports random access. The system simply reads the records in order. The reverse is not true. It is possible, but difficult, to simulate a random access file using sequential access. Random access is based on a disk model; the head on a disk can be moved immediately to any desired block.

Indexed Access

Indexes provide an additional means for accessing specific records in a file. A file may have multiple indexes, each representing a different way of viewing the data. A telephone list could be indexed by address, by name, and by phone number, for example. The index provides pointers that can immediately locate a particular logical record. Furthermore, an index is often small enough that it can be kept in memory for even faster access. Indexes are generally used in combination with sequential and random access methods to provide more powerful access methods.

Simple systems normally provide sequential and random access at the file manager level and rely on application programs to create more complex methods of access. Large systems provide additional access methods. The most common of these is the **indexed sequential access method (ISAM)**. ISAM files are kept sorted in order of a key field. One or more additional index files are used to determine the block that contains the desired record for random access.

The IBM mainframe operating system z/OS provides six different access methods, and one of these, VSAM, is further divided into three different submethods. All these additional methods are built upon either random or sequential access or a mix of the two and use index files to expand their capability.

16.4 PHYSICAL FILE STORAGE

The file manager allocates storage based on the type of I/O device, the file access method to be used for the particular file, and the particular design of the file manager. There are three primary file storage methods used for random access devices, such as disks. For sequential access devices, particularly tape, the options are somewhat more limited. We shall deal with each type of device separately.

Consider the disk first. As you are already aware, disk files are stored in small, fixed-size blocks. This gives disk the important advantage that individual blocks can be read and written *in place,* without affecting other parts of the file. Many files require several blocks of storage. If the file is larger than a block, then the system needs to be concerned about an efficient storage method that allows for efficient retrieval of the file. If the file is accessed sequentially, then the file manager must be able to access all of it quickly. If the file is accessed randomly, the file manager must be able to get to the correct block quickly. As you will see, the methods that are most convenient for storage are not necessarily consistent with these requirements. There is no ideal solution to this problem. The physical allocation method chosen may depend on the way in which the file is to be logically retrieved. In particular, you will see that there is more flexibility in the physical storage method if the file is to be retrieved sequentially than if random access capability is required.

Three methods are commonly used to allocate blocks of storage for files. These are commonly known as **contiguous, linked,** and **indexed storage allocation.**

Contiguous Storage Allocation

The simplest method to allocate storage is to assign contiguous blocks sufficient to hold the file. Figure 16.6 shows a group of files of different sizes assigned using contiguous storage.

FIGURE 16.6

Contiguous Storage Allocation

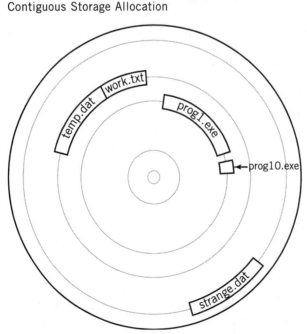

On the surface, this seems like the obvious way to allocate storage. Only a single directory pointer is required to locate the entire file. Since the file is contiguous, file recovery is quite easy. Retrieval is straightforward: the file manager can simply request a multiblock read and read the entire file in one pass. Relative file access is also straightforward: the correct block can be determined easily from the formula shown in Section 16.3 and then added to the pointer value that locates the beginning of the file.

There are some important difficulties with contiguous storage allocation, however.

- The file system must find a space large enough to hold the file plus its anticipated growth.
- Unless sufficient space is allocated initially, the file may grow to exceed the capacity of its storage allocation. In this case, the file may have to be moved to another area, or other files rearranged to make expanded room for the enlarged file.
- The use of contiguous storage allocation eventually leads to fragmentation of the disk. As files come and go there will occur small block areas between files, but none large enough to hold a new file unless the new file is small.

Fragmentation also occurs when a file is deleted or moved. Unless the space can be filled with a new file of the same size, there will be a space left over. Finding an exact replacement is unlikely: files are rarely exactly the same size, file space may be limited, a new, smaller file needs to be stored, and there is no alternative space available, so the space is used.

Allocation strategies can be used to try to minimize fragmentation. The **first-fit strategy** simply places the file into the first available space that the system finds. The **best-fit strategy** looks for the space that will most closely fit the file, thereby minimizing the external fragmentation. (At one time there was also a worst-fit strategy, which allocated file space from the largest available cluster. The idea was to leave as much room for another file as possible, but studies showed that it didn't work any better than the others.)

Ultimately, it becomes necessary to reorganize the space periodically to eliminate the fragments by collecting them together to form one new, usable space. This operation is called **defragmentation,** usually shortened to **defragging.** It is also sometimes called *compaction.* The time and effort required to defrag a disk is large, but pays off in faster disk access.

Noncontiguous Storage Allocation

A file system will normally attempt to allocate file storage space contiguously. When this is not possible, the file must be stored **noncontiguously** in whatever blocks are available. With noncontiguous storage, new blocks do not have to be assigned until they are actually needed. Fragmentation of the storage space cannot occur, although defragmentation may still be used to reduce the number of file accesses by maximizing the contiguous use of space.

The use of noncontiguous space requires that the file system maintain a detailed, ordered list of assigned blocks for each file in the system, as well as a list of free blocks available for assignment. For consistency, the file system will maintain ordered lists for all files, contiguous and noncontiguous.

There are two basic approaches to maintaining the lists of blocks allocated to each file:

1. The block numbers for a file may be stored as a linked list, using pointers from one block to the next. This method is known as a **linked allocation.**

2. The block numbers for each file may be stored in a table. This method is known as **indexed allocation.** Commonly, there is a separate table for each file.

LINKED ALLOCATION AND THE FILE ALLOCATION TABLE METHOD   At first it would seem that the system could simply place link pointers to the next block at the end of every file block. However, placing link pointers within the file blocks themselves is impractical, because it would be necessary to read each block from the beginning of the file, in sequence, to obtain the location of its succeeding block. This method would therefore be slow, awkward, and unsuitable for relative access files, where it is desirable to read or write *only* blocks containing relevant data.

A more practical method is to store the pointers as linked lists within a table. Windows, MS-DOS, and OS/2 use a single table for each disk (or disk partition, since these systems allow a disk to be divided into partitions) on the system. This table is called a **file allocation table** or **FAT.** Each file allocation table holds the link pointers for every file stored on the particular disk or disk partition. All file allocation tables are copied to memory at system boot time, and remain in memory as long as the system is active.

The directory for each file contains an entry that points to the first block of the file. Each entry in the FAT corresponds to a block or cluster on the disk. Each entry contains the link pointer that points to the next block in the file. A special value is used to indicate the end of a file. Any 0 entry in the FAT represents a block that is not in use. Therefore, it is easy for the system to locate free space when it is needed. To locate a particular block in a particular file, the file manager goes to the directory entry and finds the starting block for the file. It then follows the links through the FAT until the desired block is reached. Since the FAT is stored in memory, access to a particular block is fast. The FAT method is illustrated in Figure 16.7.

For example, for the file STRANGE.DAT shown in Figure 16.7, the directory entry indicates that the first block of the file is stored in block number 42. Successive blocks of this file are stored in blocks 48, 70, and 16. Confirm your understanding of the FAT method by finding the third block of the file WORK.TXT in the figure.

The file allocation table can be stored in memory for faster access, but this requires the use of large clusters to minimize the amount of memory space required. Using an 8 KB cluster, an FAT with 64KB entries can support a 512 MB disk. To support sixty-four thousand clusters requires that each entry be 2 bytes. Thus, 128KB of memory is required for the FAT.

One disadvantage of the FAT approach is that it becomes inefficient for large disks, because the FAT itself requires a large amount of memory. If the disk is broken into 2^{16}, or 65,536 clusters, with a corresponding 2 byte entry for each cluster, the FAT will require 128 KB of memory. For this table, a 1 GB disk would require a cluster size of 16 KB. If most of the files on the disk are small, then much of the capacity of the disk is wasted. A 1 KB file stored in a single cluster would waste more than 90 percent of the capacity of the cluster.

Alternatively, the number of blocks in the table can be increased with a corresponding increase in the memory requirements to hold the table. FAT32 allows as many as 2^{28} or 256 million clusters. Each entry requires 4 bytes of storage. Of course, the actual number of clusters is set much smaller than that, because the size of such a table would require an outrageous amount of memory.

Neither of the above solutions is desirable. The FAT technique also has a number of other disadvantages and would appear to be nearing the end of its useful life, at least for large disk storage.

FIGURE 16.7

File Allocation Table

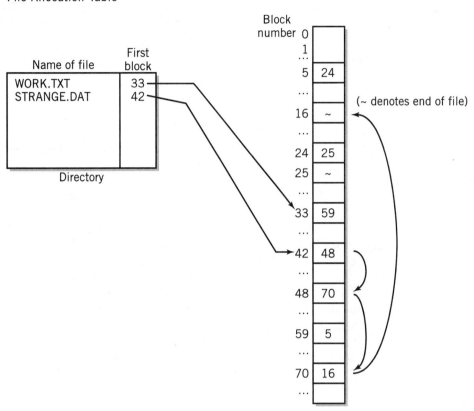

Indexed Allocation

Indexed allocation is similar to linked allocation, with one major difference: the link pointers are all stored together in one block, called an **index block.** There is an index block for each file. Loading the index block into memory when the file is opened makes the link pointers available at all times for random access. Assuming the same linkages shown in Figure 16.7, the index blocks would look like those in Figure 16.8.

Since the only index blocks in memory are those for open files, indexed allocation represents a more efficient use of memory.

One method used by some systems, including Windows 2000, to reduce memory usage even further is to allocate storage in groups of contiguous blocks as much as possible. Rather than store individual block links, this method allows the system to store a single link to the starting block of each group, together with a count of the number of blocks in the group. Obviously it is desirable to make the groups as large as possible. For files that grow in size gradually this may not be a useful strategy, but for a file of known size that is to be stored on a disk that does not have a single contiguous space that is sufficient for the

FIGURE 16.8

Index Blocks for Indexed Allocation of
Linked Files Shown in Figure 16.7

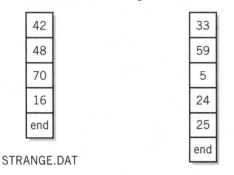

STRANGE.DAT

WORK.TXT

entire file, it may be possible to store the file in a small number of groups.

There are several possible options as to where the index block should be placed. As you will see in Section 16.5, the file management system maintains a directory structure that identifies and locates each file by name. Directory entries also store the attributes of the file that we mentioned earlier. Some systems store a single pointer to the index block in the directory entry as a way of locating the file. Other systems store link pointers in the directory entry itself.

The following examples show two of the most common approaches, the UNIX I-node method and the NTFS method.

UNIX and Linux use an indexed file allocation method, as shown in Figure 16.9. The directory entries in a UNIX system each contain just the name of the file plus a single pointer to an index block called an **i-node.** The i-node for a file contains the index pointers, and also the attributes of the file.

A typical i-node design allocates thirteen index pointers. The first ten pointers are links, just as we have described. This is adequate for small files. In fact, the needs of most of the files on the system are met this way. The last three entries in the table serve a special purpose. These are called the **single indirect, double indirect,** and **triple indirect block pointers.** The single indirect block pointer points to another index block. Additional links are found in that block. The number of links is determined solely by the size of a standard

FIGURE 16.9

UNIX i-node File Storage Allocation

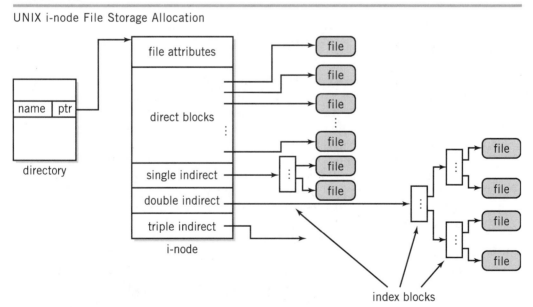

disk block. The double and triple indirect blocks are two and three steps removed, respectively. We have shown the single and double indirect blocks on the diagram. Using 4KB clusters, this scheme is sufficient to access files in the hundreds of gigabytes. Actually, the limiting factor turns out to be the number of bits in each pointer.

WINDOWS NTFS FILE SYSTEM   The **Windows NT File System (NTFS)** was originally created to solve the shortcomings of the FAT file system, specifically to support large files and large disks, to provide file security, to reduce access times, and to provide recovery capability.

NTFS operates on volumes. In Windows NT volumes were determined by logical disk partitions. A Volume in Windows NT is created by creating logical disk partitions, using the Windows NT Fault-tolerant disk manager. Volumes in Windows NT may occupy part of a disk or an entire disk or may span multiple disks. Windows 2000 continues to support the Windows NT disk manager for legacy volumes, but new volumes in Windows 2000 are created and managed by a Logical Disk Manager, which allows the creation of volumes dynamically. Windows 2000 volumes need not correspond to logical disk partitions. Dynamic volumes can be expanded or contracted to meet changing user needs while the system is on-line.

Like other systems, the NTFS volume allocates space in clusters. Each cluster is made up of a contiguous group of sectors. The NTFS cluster size is set when the volume is created. The default cluster size is generally 4 KB or less, even for large disks.

Figure 16.10 shows the layout for an NTFS volume. The core of each volume is a single file called the **master file table (MFT).** The master table is configured as an array of file records. Each record is 1 KB in size, regardless of the volume cluster size. The number of rows is set at volume creation time. The array contains one row for each file in the volume. The first sixteen rows contain metadata files: files that describe the volume. The first record stores attributes of the MFT itself. The second record points to another location in the middle of the disk that contains a duplicate of the metadata, for disk recovery.

NTFS file records are made up of **attributes.** An attribute is a stream of bytes that describes some aspect of the file. Standard attributes include the file name, its security descriptor, time stamps, read-only and archive flags, links, and data. Directory files have attributes that index the directory. Each attribute has a name or number plus a byte stream representing the value of the attribute. The primary data stream is unnamed, but it is possible to have named data streams in addition. Thus, there may be multiple data streams in a single file record.

Small files may fit within the MFT record itself. For larger files, the MFT record will contain pointers to clusters in an area of the disk outside the MFT. Attributes that extend beyond the MFT are called *nonresident attributes* (usually the data attribute, obviously). Nonresident clusters are called runs. If the attribute outgrows its space, the file system continues to allocate runs as needed.

Free Space Management

To allocate new blocks as they are required, the file management system must keep a list of the free available space on a disk. To create a new file or add blocks to an existing file, the file manager takes space from the free space list. When a file is deleted, its space is returned to the free space list. There are two methods commonly used for this purpose.

FIGURE 16.10

NTFS Volume Layout

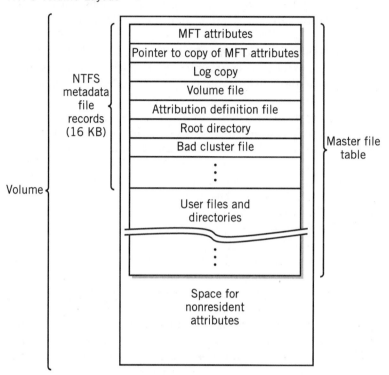

Source: Adapted from D. A. Solomon, *Inside Windows NT,* 2nd ed. (Redmond, WA: Microsoft Press, 1998).

BITMAP METHOD One method of maintaining a free space list is to provide a table with one bit for each block on the disk. The bit for a particular block is set to 1 if the block is in use and to 0 if the block is free. (Many systems also set defective blocks to 1 permanently to prevent their use.) This table is known as a **free space bitmap** or, sometimes, as a table of **bit vectors**. A **bitmap** is illustrated in Figure 16.11. A bitmap is usually kept in memory for fast access.

The bitmap method is an economical way of keeping track of free space, since only one bit is needed for each block on the disk. It has the further advantage that it is easy for the file manager to locate contiguous blocks or blocks that are nearby to those already allocated to a file. This allows the file manager to maintain files in a way that can minimize disk seeks during file access.

Although the bitmap must be stored eight bits to a byte, most CPU instruction sets provide bit manipulation instructions that allow efficient use of the bitmap. One disadvantage of the bitmap method is that there is some processing overhead in returning space from a large file with many blocks to the free space list. A second disadvantage is that once space has been returned to the bitmap, it may be immediately reassigned. There is no way of determining the order in which the space was returned.

FIGURE 16.11

Free Space Bit Map

Block numbers

0–15	1001010110101001
16–31	0111101101100000
32–47	1110000111011100
48–63	0101000111010110
...	...

Therefore, the space used by a deleted file may be reused again immediately, eliminating the chance for file recovery.

LINKED LIST METHOD   An alternative method maintains all the free space on the disk in a **linked list.** A pointer to the first free block is kept in a special location on disk and also in memory. Each free block is then linked to the next. The file manager allocates blocks from the beginning of the list. The blocks from deleted files are added to the end of the list.

This method has considerable overhead in disk seeks if a large number of blocks are to be allocated, but is simple and efficient for small numbers of blocks. It is not practical with this method to identify blocks in particular locations for optimizing allocation to an individual file.

One advantage of the linked list method is that file recovery is enhanced. The blocks in a linked free space list are stored in the order in which files are deleted. Since deleted files are placed at the end of the list, the data on those blocks will be recoverable until the blocks are needed for reuse.

The FAT method makes a free space linked list very convenient, since the free space linked list can be stored in the same FAT as any file.

Note that the data in deleted files is not truly deleted from disk unless special effort is made to clear or scramble all the bits in the blocks used by the file. This is a potential security risk. Special software, called **shredder software,** is available for the purpose of truly deleting files from disk in a way that they cannot be recovered.

Tape Allocation

Tape allocation is simpler than disk allocation. The size of a block can be varied to fit the logical requirements of the file. It is usually not practical to reallocate space in the middle of a tape, so files that grow must be rewritten. If necessary, the tape can be compacted, but it is usually easier to do so by copying the tape to a new tape. Tape blocks can be linked, but, in general, files are stored contiguously whenever possible.

Tape is convenient for sequential access, but not practical for random access. Random access files that are stored on tape are normally moved to disk as a whole before use.

CD-ROM and DVD-ROM Allocation

In Chapter 10, we described the block system used for CD-ROMs. We noted that a disk contains approximately 270,000 2KB fixed-size physical data blocks. The CD-ROM file system is similar to those found on hard disks. It allows up to eight levels of subdirectories, with subdirectories stored as files on the disk. The directory format is similar to that used on MS-DOS (see the next section), although there are extensions that allow the use of longer file names and deeper subdirectory levels. Files can be stored noncontiguously on a CD-ROM. There are also extensions that make it possible to store a mixture of data, audio, and images on the same disk. The same type of file system is also used on DVD-ROMs.

16.5 THE DIRECTORY STRUCTURE

A computer system may store hundreds or even thousands of files. The directory system provides a means of organization so that files may be located easily and efficiently. The directory structure provides the linkages between logical files identified by their names and their corresponding physical storage. Every stored file on a device is represented in the directory for that device. The directory system serves as the basis for all the other file operations that we have already discussed. It also maintains records of the attributes for each file. Some of the important attributes for a file that are commonly found in a directory (or in the UNIX i-node) are shown in Figure 16.12.

A file system may support many different devices, including, often, multiple disks, as well as tapes, CD-ROMs, and devices elsewhere on a network. In many systems, the directory system conceals the physical differences from the user, providing logical consistency throughout the system. To the user, a different device may be nothing more than a letter change preceding the file name, F: for the CD-ROM on a Windows system, perhaps, and M: for the network file server. On a system with a graphical interface, different devices may simply be represented by different disk or folder icons.

Many systems also provide a means for dividing the physical devices differently from the logical layout of the file system. Thus, a disk drive may be divided into independent sections called **partitions,** each with their own directory structure. Partitions can also extend over the physical disk drive boundaries to include parts of two or more physically separate disk drives. Partitions are also known as **minidisks** in IBM mainframes. On many systems, only one partition is active at a time. When one partition is active, files located on other partitions are invisible to the system. Each partition in a Windows system, for example, is

FIGURE 16.12

Typical File Attributes

Name and extension	Name and extension, if any, stored in ASCII or Unicode form
Type	Needed if system supports different file types; also used for special attributes, such as system, hidden, archive; alphanumeric character or binary; sequential or random access required; and so on.
Size	Size of file in bytes, words, or blocks
Maximum allowable size	Size file will be allowed to grow to
Location	Pointer to device and to location of starting file block on device, or pointer to index block, if stored separate from file, or pointer to entry in FAT table
Protection	Access control data limiting who has access to file, possibly a password
Name of owner	User ID for owner of file; used for protection
Name of group	Name of group with privileges, in some protection systems
Date of creation	Time and date when file was created
Date of modification	Time and date of most recent modification to file; sometimes user identification is also maintained for audit purposes
Date of last use	Time and date of most recent use of file; sometimes user ID

assigned a different letter and has its own file system. From a prompt, a partition is selected by specifying the letter of the desired file system, followed by a colon.

The partition concept can be extended to providing separate operating system facilities on different partitions, so that each partition may have its own bootstrap loader, operating system, and file system. When this is the case, the file systems on different partitions may be incompatible with each other, so that it is not possible for one file system to read the directory or load the files from a different partition, even on the same physical disk.

OS/2 and some versions of UNIX take advantage of partitioning as a way to provide different types of file systems, each with different capabilities, on the same machine, offering additional flexibility for the user. OS/2, for example, allows the use of two different file systems, the OS/2 native file system, called HPFS, for high-performance file system, and MS-DOS compatible FAT. The FAT system is used when files are to be used with software that is MS-DOS- and Windows-based. The FAT system also uses MS-DOS's limited naming conventions. HPFS provides longer file names and faster file access, at the expense of MS-DOS compatibility. The user can switch between the two file systems by changing from one partition to another.

The file system must maintain a directory structure for each device or partition. In most cases, the directory for a device is stored on the device itself. In many computer systems, the file system for each partition or device is called a **volume.** On some of these systems, the directory is called a **volume table of contents.**

Also, on many systems, it is necessary to mount a volume, device, or partition before it can be used. Mounting a volume means that the directory structure for the volume is merged into an overall file structure for the system by attaching the directory structure of the volume to some point in the overall file structure. This point is known as the **mount point.** In some systems mounting is automatic. In others, mounting must be performed manually, using a mount command. Volumes in the Macintosh system, for example, are mounted automatically if they are present when the system is booted. Diskettes are also mounted automatically when they are inserted into the drive. Other devices must be mounted manually. On a UNIX system, all directories are mounted manually. Thus, it is necessary for the user to issue a mount command when a diskette is changed on a UNIX workstation. The mount point also depends on the system. On a Macintosh, all volumes are mounted on the desktop; on a UNIX system, a volume can be mounted anywhere on the directory structure. The Linux file system design allows the mounting of multiple file system types for transparent access across partitions and, even, across networks.

There are a number of possible ways in which a directory can be organized. The simplest directory structure is just a list. It is also known as a single-level, or flat, directory. All the files stored in the system, including system files, application programs, and user files, are listed together in a single directory. The single-level directory system has some obvious disadvantages:

- There is no way for a user to organize his work into logical categories as all the files are of equal status in the directory.
- It is possible to destroy a file by mistake if the user isn't careful when naming files. This is particularly true because many of the files in the directory, notably the system and application program files, were not originally created and named by the user. There is even potential naming conflict between different commercial software packages. Installation of a software package could cause

another package to fail at a later date, and it would be difficult to track down the problem.

- The single-level directory is unsuitable for a system with multiple users. There would be no way to differentiate which files belong to which user. Naming of files by the users would have to be done extremely carefully to prevent destroying another user's work. (How often have you named a program assignment "PROG1.JSP" or "ASSIGN3.C"? How many other students in your class would you guess also did so?)

- Implementation of a single-level directory system is simple. However, as the directory grows, the list will expand beyond its original space allocation and it will be necessary for the system to allocate additional space, with pointers to move between the spaces. Although this is also true of other directory systems, the single-level directory system does not provide any organization that will make it easier to locate file entries when the files are to be retrieved, so the search procedure must follow all the pointers until the file is located. This is somewhat akin to searching an unalphabetized address book from the beginning to find the name you want. On a large system, with many files, an undirected search of this kind could take a considerable amount of time.

As a result of these disadvantages, it is rare to see a single-level directory system in use today.

Tree-Structured Directories

A tree structure satisfies most file directory requirements and is in common use in modern computer systems. The directory in MS-DOS and older versions of Windows is a **tree-structured directory.** A variation on a tree-structured directory, the **acyclic-graph directory** structure is even more powerful, but introduces some difficulties in implementation. UNIX, Windows 2000 and XP, and Macintosh systems support an acyclic-graph directory structure. Nearly all modern computer systems provide one of these two structures.

An example showing part of a tree-structured directory, also known as a **hierarchical directory,** is represented in Figure 16.13. The tree structure is characterized by a root directory, from which all other directories stem. On most systems, the root directory contains few, if any, files. In this illustration, two files, AUTOEXEC.BAT and CONFIG.SYS, are found in the root directory. All other entries in the root directory are themselves directories, sometimes called **subdirectories** for clarity. The root directory and all its subordinate directories can contain files or other directories. Additional branches can stem from any directory. The root directory is stored in a particular location, known to the file system. Other directories are themselves stored as files, albeit files with a special purpose. This means that directories can be manipulated by the system like any other file.

The root directory, other directories, and files are all identified by names. Duplicates within a particular directory are not legal, but use of the same name in different directories is acceptable. Every file in the system can be uniquely identified by its **path name.** The path name for a file is the complete list of names along the path starting from the root and ending at the particular file. A **separator** symbol separates each name along the path. In many systems, the separator symbol is the same as the name of the root directory. This is true both for Windows, with a root named "\," and for UNIX, "/".

FIGURE 16.13

Part of a Tree-Structured Directory

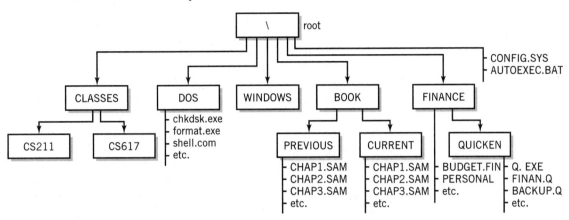

Although it looks considerably different, graphical interface systems support a similar structure. Folders have a one-to-one correspondence to directories. Starting from the desktop, you move through the tree structure by opening folders until you reach the folder containing the desired files.

On single-user systems, the hierarchy is established by the user, usually in response to a logical arrangement of his or her work. On systems that support multiple users, the main part of the hierarchy is established by the system administrator, usually in an arrangement that is consistent with a standard layout for the particular type of system. This makes it easier for users who must move between multiple machines. Generally, the system has a particular subdirectory that serves as the account directory for everyone on the system. Each user is assigned a tree branch that can be expanded below that subdirectory and a starting point, known as the initial **working directory.** On a single-user system, the initial working directory is established by the system. In Windows, it is the root. In OS/2 and the Macintosh, it is a subdirectory just below the root called the *desktop.*

From the current directory, the user can access files anywhere in the system. The file name or new working directory can be specified relative to the current working directory, or absolutely, from the root, by using a **relative** or **absolute path name,** respectively. The difference is easily determined by the system, since absolute path names begin with the root name or symbol and relative path names don't. In Figure 16.13, the file called BACKUP.Q can be specified absolutely as \FINANCE\QUICKEN\BACKUP.Q. If the current working directory is FINANCE, then the file can be accessed relatively as QUICKEN\BACKUP.Q. Most systems do not allow the use of a relative path name above the current directory. To access files above the current directory or on a different branch of the tree requires the use of the absolute path name. Thus, to open the file CHAP1.SAM in the directory CURRENT from a current working directory of PREVIOUS, you must specify the file as \BOOK\CURRENT\CHAP1.SAM. It is often desirable to address a file relative to the level just above the current working directory, so these systems provide a special name that can be used for the node at the next level above the current working directory. In both Windows and Linux, this name is "." (double dot). Thus, the same file can also be accessed relatively as ..\CURRENT\CHAP1.SAM.

When a user requests a file from the system, the system looks for the file in the user's current working directory, or in the location specified by the path name. Most systems also provide an **environmental variable** called *path* that allows the user to specify other path locations that are to be searched for the file if a path name is not given and if the file is not found in the current working directory. There is a specified order to the search so that if there is more than one file that qualifies, only the first file found is accessed.

The user can also change his or her current working directory. The user moves around the tree using a CHANGE DIRECTORY command. An absolute or relative path name can be used. To change the current working directory from directory PREVIOUS to directory CURRENT in the figure, for example, one could issue a CD ..\CURRENT command or one could use the full path name, CD \BOOK\CURRENT. On systems that do not allow relative path names above the current directory, the CD .. command provides a convenient way to move upward to the next-level node. The user can also add and remove branches from the tree with MAKE DIRECTORY and REMOVE DIRECTORY commands to provide a file organization that meets the user's requirements and desires.

In a graphical interface system, the current working directory is the folder that is currently open. Folders can be created and deleted, which is equivalent to adding and removing branches to the tree structure. Since there may be many folders open on the screen, it is easy to move from one current working directory to another on a graphical interface system.

The tree-structured directory system provides solutions to the problems described at the beginning of this section. The tree structure provides flexibility that allows users to organize files in whatever way they wish. The tree structure solves the problem of organization for a system with a large number of files. It also solves the problem of growth, since there is essentially no limit on the number of directories that the system can support. It also solves the problem of accessing files in an efficient manner. A directory is located by following the path name from the current directory or from the root, one directory file at a time. One negative consequence of this method is that it may require retrieval of several directory files from different parts of the disk, with the corresponding disk seek times, but at least the path is known, so extensive searching is not necessary.

Since duplicate names in a tree structure use different paths there is no confusion between identical file names, because each has a different path name. For this textbook, for example, the author has two different sets of files named CHAP1.SAM, CHAP2.SAM, and so on. One set is located in a directory with the path name BOOK\CURRENT. The other set is in a directory called BOOK\PREVIOUS. This provides protection for the author in case of a disk error. Similarly, each user on a multiuser system starts from a different path name, so the use of similar file names by different users is not a problem.

Acyclic-Graph Directories

The acyclic-graph directory is a generalization of a tree-structure directory, expanded to include **links** between separate branch structures on the tree. The links appear in the directory structure as though they were ordinary file or directory entries. In actuality, they serve as pseudonyms for the original file name. The link provides an alternative path to a directory or file. An example is shown in Figure 16.14. In this diagram there are two links, shown in heavy print.

There is a link between the directory CURRENT, belonging to user imwoman, and the directory 2002, belonging to user theboss. This makes all the files in directory 2002 available to imwoman. There is also a link between directory MYSTUFF, belonging to user jgoodguy, and the file PROJ1.TXT. (Apparently, jgoodguy is working only on this one project.) The file PROJ1.TXT can be accessed by theboss from her current directory by using the path name PROJECTS/2002/PROJ1.TXT. jgoodguy can access the same file using path name MYSTUFF/PROJ1.TXT. imwoman uses path name CURRENT/2002/PROJ1.TXT to reach the file. Note that it is also possible for imwoman to change her current directory to 2002 as a result of the link.

The ability to add links between branch structures in a tree makes it possible to create multiple paths, and path names, that lead to a single directory or file. From the perspective of users on the system, this adds the powerful capability of being able to share files among users. Each user has his path to the file with its own path name. For a group collaborating on a document, for example, a subdirectory could be created with all the pertinent files and then linked to the working directories of each of the users. An individual user can even create multiple paths to a file, if so desired. This capability could be useful if the file is associated with two different directories, and the user would like to place it as an entry in both for more convenient access.

One difficulty with implementation of an acyclic-graph directory is assuring that the links do not connect in such a way that it is possible to **cycle** through a path more than once when tracing out the path to a file. Consider the situation in Figure 16.15. The links

FIGURE 16.14

An Acyclic-Graph Directory

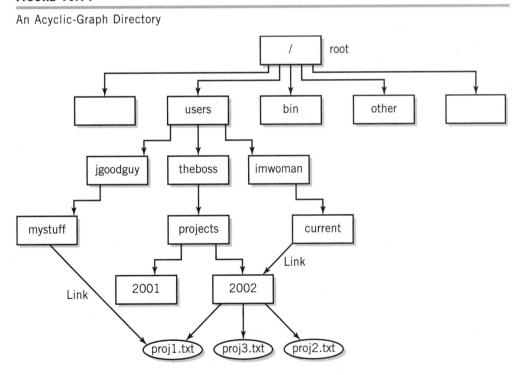

between current and project and between projects and imwoman complete a cycle. Thus, the file name PROJ1.TXT can be reached by an infinite number of paths, including

```
IMWOMAN/CURRENT/PROJECTS/2002/PROJ1.TXT
IMWOMAN/CURRENT/PROJECTS/IMWOMAN/
CURRENT/PROJECTS/2002/PROJ1.TXT
IMWOMAN/CURRENT/PROJECTS/IMWOMAN/
CURRENT/PROJECTS/IMWOMAN/CURRENT/PROJECTS/...
```

and so on. This is obviously an unsatisfactory situation. When the file system is searching for files, it will encounter an infinite number of paths that it believes must be checked. The system must assure that the addition of a link does not create a cycle.

An additional difficulty is establishing a policy for the deletion of files that have multiple links. Removing a file without removing the links leaves **dangling links,** links that point to nowhere. It is also possible on some systems to remove all links to the file, leaving file space that can't be reclaimed by the system.

There is also the necessity for setting rules about the modification of a file that is open by two different users at the same time. As an example, suppose that users 1 and 2 are both working on the same file. User 1 makes some modifications and saves the file with his changes. Then, user 2 makes other modifications and saves the file with her changes. Under certain conditions, the changes made by user 2 will destroy the changes made by user 1. A

FIGURE 16.15

A Graph with a Cycle

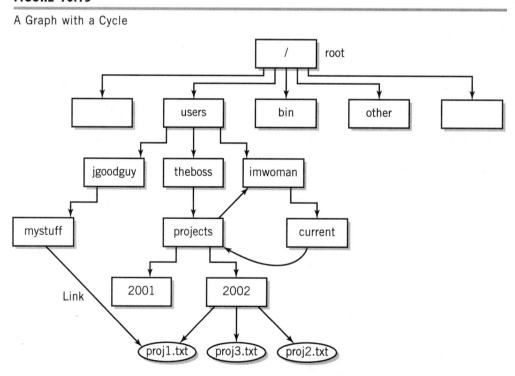

Source: Adapted from [CHR94]. Reprinted by permission of John Wiley & Sons, Inc.

system for **locking** the file temporarily to prevent this type of error is required. Further discussion of locking is outside the scope of this textbook.

As you can see, there are difficulties and dangers in providing and using acyclic-graph directories. Many system designers feel that the advantages outweigh the disadvantages, however.

UNIX and the Macintosh both support acyclic-graph directories. Macintosh links are called **aliases.** The Macintosh uses a simple implementation. An alias is a **hard-coded link** that points to the original file. If the original file is moved or deleted, use of the link will cause an error. The Macintosh does not check for the presence of cycles; however, the visual nature of the Macintosh interface makes cycles less likely to occur and less problematic. The search operations that can cause loops are instead performed visually, and there is no reason for the user to continue opening folders beyond a point of usefulness. Windows implements links similarly with **shortcuts.**

UNIX provides two different kinds of links. The difference between them is shown in Figure 16.16. A hard link points from a new directory entry to the same i-node as another directory entry somewhere in the file system. Since both entries point to the same i-node, any changes made in the file are automatically reflected to both. The i-node has a field that keeps track of the number of directory entries pointing to it. Anytime a link is added, the counter is increased by one. When a file is "deleted," the count is reduced by one. The file is not actually deleted until the count is zero. A major disadvantage of hard links is that some programs, such as editors, update files by creating a new file, then renaming it with

FIGURE 16.16

The Difference Between Hard and Symbolic Links

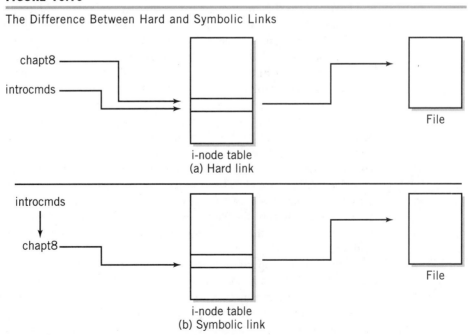

i-node table
(a) Hard link

i-node table
(b) Symbolic link

Source: Adapted from K. Christian and S. Richter, *The UNIX Operating System,* 3rd ed. New York: John Wiley, 1994.

the original name. Since the file creation results in a new i-node, the links now point to different i-nodes and different versions of the original file. In other words, the link is broken.

Symbolic links work differently. With a symbolic link, the new directory entry creates a file that holds a pointer to the original file's path name. Then, when accessing the new entry, the symbolic link uses this file to identify the original path name. Even if the original file is physically moved, the link is maintained as long as the original path name exists. Of course, the link is broken if the original file is logically moved to a different directory, deleted, or renamed. In this case, an attempt to reference the file specified by the link will cause an error. UNIX does not attempt to keep track of symbolic links, as it does with hard links. An additional minor disadvantage of symbolic links is that the symbolic link also requires the existence of an additional file to hold the link pointer.

The UNIX system does not attempt to avoid cycles. Instead, it restricts access to the linking capability of the system. Normal users may only create hard links to files, but not to directories. This prevents the normal users from inadvertently creating cycles. Only the system administrators can create links between directories. It is their responsibility to assure that they do not create cycles.

16.6 NETWORK FILE ACCESS

One of the primary capabilities provided by networks is the access to files on other systems connected to the network. Depending on the method used, files may be copied from one system to another or may be accessed directly on the system holding the file.

For the transfer of files from one system to another, the TCP/IP protocol family includes **ftp,** a standard file transfer protocol. ftp is implemented as a series of commands that can be used to move around and view directories on a remote system and to upload or download a file or group of files residing on that system. However, ftp does not include a facility for accessing and using the file remotely. It must be copied to the local system for use.

For more general use, most operating systems provide a facility for using files at their remote locations, without copying them onto the local system. There are two different approaches. One technique, used by Microsoft and others, is to identify with a name a connection point on each system that allows access, and to alias a local drive letter to that name. Files may then be manipulated using the drive letter as though the files were stored locally. For example, files stored in the USER/STUDENT/YOURNAME directory on the Icarus system might be aliased to drive letter M: on your personal computer. Then, you could perform any file or directory operation as though the files and directories were stored locally on drive M:. The M: drive icon would appear in your "My Computer" window, for example, if you were using Windows 9x , NT, or 2000, for example. Notice that it is not necessary to copy the file to your local system to read or write it, but that you can do so if you wish, using the usual copy command or by dragging-and-dropping the file icon with the mouse.

The alternative approach is to use the **Network File System (NFS),** originally created by Sun. With NFS, a remote directory is mounted to a mount point on the local system. Remote files and directories are then used transparently in the same way as local files. In fact, if the mount procedure was performed by the system as part of the network connection procedure, the user might not even be aware of which files and directories are local and which are remote. The NFS client/server manager is built into the operating system kernel, and operates as an alternative to the local file system manager, using the RPC (Remote Procedure Call) protocol. A typical NFS connection is shown in Figure 16.17.

More recently, steps have been taken to provide more generalized, distributed network directory services. These would be used for locating other types of information, in addition to file services. Such generalized services could identify the configuration of a system, or information about employees in a business, for example. These systems are based on generalized naming schemes, such as the Internet Domain Name Service, and are designed to locate files and information uniquely wherever the information is located. A standard protocol, **LDAP (Lightweight Directory Access Protocol),** exists for this purpose. Two examples of generalized network directory services are ActiveDirectory, supported by Microsoft, and Novell Directory Services.

16.7 FILE PROTECTION

Except in small, single-user systems, the system must provide file protection to limit file access to those who have authorization to use the file. File protection is provided on an individual file-by-file basis. There are several different forms that file protection might take. A user might be allowed to execute a file but not copy it, for example, or may be able to read it but not modify it. A file might be shared by a group of individuals, and the file protection system should make it convenient for group members to access the file, while protecting the file from others.

FIGURE 16.17

Typical NFS Configuration

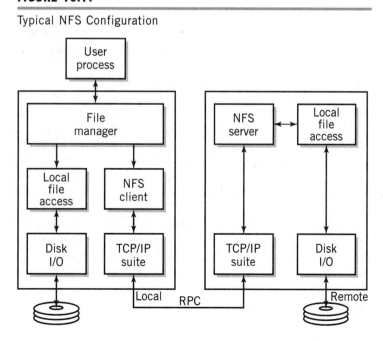

Although some systems provide additional forms of protection, most systems provide three types of protection on files:

- A file may be read or not be readable (**read protection**).
- A file may be written to or not accessible for writing (**write protection**).
- A file may be executed or not be executable (**execution protection**).

Although there are other, more specific, possibilities, these restrictions are sufficient for nearly every purpose and represent a good compromise for implementation purposes. For example, it might be important that a particular user not be able to delete a file. Write protection, although more restrictive, prevents deletion. If the user needs to modify such a file, the user can copy the file, provided he or she has read rights, and modify the copy.

The ideal form of protection on a multiuser or server-based system would provide each file with an **access control list (ACL)** of users that may access the file for each of the three forms of protection. The list for a particular file would be maintained by the owner of the file. The amount of overhead required to maintain and use ACLs is tremendous. The system must provide utilities for maintaining the lists, storage space for the lists, and the mechanisms to check the lists whenever a file is accessed. If the number of users on the system is large, the ACL for each file might require a large amount of storage space. Since the system administrator is effectively the owner of all the system files, there is a tremendous responsibility on one person to maintain a large number of ACLs. Nonetheless, some systems do provide ACL protection.

A simpler, but more practical, protection method divides the user base of the system into three categories. For each file, the system defines an **owner,** a **group** associated with the file, and a **universe** that consists of everyone else. The file system maintains lists of groups. Each group has a name, and a user can be a member of more than one group. Generally, groups are administered by the system administrator, but on some systems, a group can be created by the owner of a file.

Under this protection method, each file provides nine protection flags, specifically, read, write, and execute permission for each of the three categories—owner, group, and universe. When a file is created, the system sets a default protection established by the system administrator. The owner of the file can then determine and set the protection differently, if so desired. In UNIX, there is a CHMOD command for this purpose. The nine protection flags can be stored in a single word within the directory. Figure 16.18 shows a typical UNIX directory listing. The leftmost flag in the listing simply indicates whether a file is a directory (*d*), a symbolic link (*l*), or an ordinary file (-). The next nine flags represent read, write, and execute privileges for owners, groups, and universe, respectively. The presence of a hyphen in the listing indicates that the privilege is turned off. The number of links to the file is next, then the name of the owner and the name of the group. The remainder of each row gives the name of the file and various file attributes.

Since directories are, themselves, files, most systems, including UNIX, provide similar protection for directories. You'll notice the same protection pattern listings for directories in Figure 16.18. A read-protected directory, for example, could not be listed by a user with no read access. It is not possible to save a file or delete a file to a write-protected directory. And a user without execute permission cannot change his or her current directory to an execute-protected directory.

FIGURE 16.18

File Directory Showing Protection

```
$ls -lF
drwx------ 1 iengland csdept 36005 Feb 15 12:02 bookchapters/
-rw-r--r-- 1 iengland csdept   370 Sep 17  1:02 assignment1.txt
--wx--x--- 2 iengland csdept  1104 Mar 5 17:35 littleman*
-rwxrwx--- 1 iengland csdept  2933 May 22  5:15 airport shell*
drwxr--r-- 1 iengland csdept  5343 Dec 3 12:34 class syllabi/
```

A few systems provide an alternative form of file protection by assigning passwords to every file or to every directory. This method puts a burden on the user to remember the different passwords attached to each file or each directory.

No matter how file protection is implemented, file protection adds considerable overhead for the system, but file protection is an essential part of the system.

In addition to the file protection provided by limiting file access to authorized users, most modern systems also provide file encryption capability, either for individual files and directories or to the file system as a whole. This additional layer of protection is particularly useful when the file is exposed to users (and, potentially, system invaders) on a network.

16.8 JOURNALING FILE SYSTEMS

For many business applications, the integrity of the file system is critical to the health of the business. Of course, the first line of defense against the file system failure is a well-defined set of proper system backup and file maintenance procedures. **Journaling file systems** extend this protection to include automated file recovery procedures in the event of a disk crash or system failure during file access operations.

Journaling systems provide a log file that records every system transaction that requires a write access to the file system. Before a file write operation actually occurs, the logging system reads the affected file blocks and copies them to the log, which is stored as a separate file. If a system fault occurs during the write operation, the journaling file system log provides the information necessary to reconstruct the file. Of course, there is a performance cost for journaling, due to the extra file block reads and writes that are necessary to support the log file.

Journaling file systems provide two levels of capability. Simple journaling file systems protect the integrity of the file system structure, but cannot guarantee the integrity of data that has not yet been written to the disk. The disk is simply restored to its pre-failure configuration. The Windows NTFS file system is a simple journaling file system. It is able to recover all of the file system metadata, but does not recover current data that had not yet been saved when the failure occurred.

A full journaling file system provides the additional ability to recover unsaved data and to write it to the proper file location, guaranteeing data integrity as well as file system integrity.

Current full journaling file systems include IBM JFS, Silicon Graphics XFS, and Linux Reiserfs.

SUMMARY AND REVIEW

The file management system makes it possible for the user, and for programs, to operate with files as logical entities, without concern for the physical details of file storage and handling. The file system opens and closes files, provides the mechanism for all file transfers, and maintains the directory system.

File systems vary in complexity and capability from the very simple, where all file data is treated as a stream and just a few operations are provided, to the very sophisticated, with many file types and operations. The simpler file systems require more effort within each program but, in trade, provide additional flexibility.

Files are accessed sequentially, randomly, or some combination of the two. More complex file accesses generally involve the use of indexes. To some extent, the method of storage depends on the required forms of access. Files may be stored contiguously or noncontiguously. Each has advantages and disadvantages. The pointers to the various blocks that allow noncontiguous access can be stored as links in the blocks themselves or in an index table provided for that purpose. Often the index tables are associated with individual files, but some systems store the indexes for every file in a single table, called a file allocation table. The file system also maintains a record of available free space, either as a bitmap or in linked form.

The directory structure provides mapping between the logical file name and the physical storage of the file. It also maintains attributes about the files. Most modern file systems provide a hierarchical directory structure, either in tree form or as an acyclic graph. The hierarchical file structure makes it possible for the user to organize files in whatever way seems appropriate. The acyclic-graph structure adds file-sharing capability, at the expense of more difficult maintenance of the structure.

The file system also provides file protection. Some file systems maintain access lists, which can establish privileges for any user on a file-by-file basis. Most systems provide a simpler form of security that divides users into three categories and affords protection based on category.

KEY CONCEPTS AND TERMS

absolute path name	contiguous storage alloca-	execution protection
access control list (ACL)	tion	fields
acyclic-graph directory	cycle	file allocation table (FAT)
alias	dangling link	file extension
association	defragmentation (defrag-	file manager
best-fit strategy	ging)	file owner
bitmap	directory	first-fit strategy
bit vectors	disk partition	form image
block	double indirect block	free space bit map
cluster	pointers	free space management
collision	environmental variable	group

FOR FURTHER READING

General discussions of file management systems will be found in any of the operating systems texts that we have mentioned in previous chapters. Details about the file systems for particular operating systems can be found in books that describe the operating system innards for the particular system. For MS-DOS, for example, Jamsa [JAMS93] is effective. Glass [GLAS99] and Christian and Richter [CHR94] describe the UNIX file systems. There are many good books on file management. Among the best are those of Weiderhold [WEID87], Grosshans [GROS86], and Livadas [LIV90].

EXERCISES

16.1   You have noticed that loading the programs from one of your floppy disks seems to take longer than it used to. A friend suggests copying the files from your disk, one at a time, to a new disk. You do so and discover that the programs load much faster now. What happened?

16.2   Explain why a MOVE operation from one device to another requires manipulation of the file itself, whereas a MOVE operation from one place to another on the same device involves manipulation only of the directory.

16.3   In many systems, the operations that work on a file as a whole are made up by combining the operations that manipulate the internal file data. Explain how you would copy a file from one location to another using the internal file operations. Does this method seem consistent with your experience of what happens when you copy a large file from one disk drive to another on your PC?

16.4   Show that the physical block number for a random access file can be calculated from the formula

$$P = \text{int } (L * S_L / S_P)$$

16.5   From an MS-DOS or OS/2 C:\ prompt, do a DIR command. Carefully note how much space remains on your disk. Now open up your favorite editor, or use EDIT, and create a new file containing just a period with a carriage return. Call this file PROB165.TXT and return to DOS or OS/2. Do a DIR PROB165.txt command. How much space does your new file take up? How much space remains on your disk? Explain what happened.

16.6   Refer to the discussion in Section 16.5 concerning the directory format used by MS-DOS and Windows. Why does Microsoft suggest that the use of long file names be limited at the root level of the directory?

16.7   List a number of types of files that you would expect to be accessed sequentially. Do the same for files that you would expect would require random access.

16.8   List the directory for the files on your PC. For each file, determine how many blocks would be required if the block size were to be 1 KB, 4 KB, and 8 KB. Calculate the internal fragmentation for each file and for each block size. How much disk space on your PC is wasted for each block size? Also give the answer as a percentage of the total block space used.

16.9   Explain the trade-offs between contiguous, noncontiguous linked, and noncontiguous indexed file allocation. In particular, note the effect on sequential and random access methods.

16.10   Assume a UNIX i-node requires a block of 60 bytes. How many disk blocks can be accessed using just direct, single, and double indirect indexing, as shown in Figure 16.9?

16.11   What are the advantages of partitioning a disk, rather than using the entire disk as one partition?

16.12   What does it mean to mount a disk?

16.13   What role does a path serve?

16.14   Describe the file privileges for each file in Figure 16.18.

16.15   The access control list for a file specifies which users can access that file, and how. Some researchers have indicated that an attractive alternative would be a user control list, which would specify which files a user could access, and how. Discuss the trade-offs of such an approach in terms of space required for the lists, and the steps required to determine whether a particular file operation is permitted.

16.16   What is the purpose of the open and close operations?

16.17   Discuss the advantages and disadvantages of "long file names." Also consider the effect of spaces in file names.

16.18   **a.**   Disk caching is a technique that is used to speed up disk access, by holding blocks of disk in memory. Discuss strategies that could be used to improve system performance with disk caching.

b. The time of write back for files that have been altered depends on the system. Some systems write back a file immediately when it has been altered. Others wait until the file is closed or until the system is not busy or until activity on the particular file has stopped for a given period of time. Discuss the trade-offs between these different approaches.

16.19 Consider a file that has just grown beyond its present space on disk. Describe what steps will be taken next for a contiguous file, for a linked noncontiguous file, and for an indexed file.

CHAPTER 17

PROGRAMMING TOOLS

"I didn't understand all that stuff he said between 'Good Morning, Class' and 'That concludes my lecture for today'."

Adapted, courtesy of David Ahl, Creative Computing

17.0 INTRODUCTION

Although the computer executes programs made up of binary instructions, it would be too difficult and time consuming to write programs in binary form.

Instead, programmers write their programs in languages such as assembly language or C or Java and use the facilities of the computer itself to provide translation of these "higher-level" languages into the binary instructions that the machine can understand and execute. Figure 17.1 illustrates the process.

Programming tools give programmers the facilities they need to prepare programs for use on the computer. These tools include **editors** for entering and modifying a program in text form into the computer; **assemblers, interpreters,** and **compilers** for translating a program into binary machine language; **linking loaders** that create an executable program by linking a machine language program with other separately translated binary program modules and built-in function libraries; and **debuggers** to aid in tracing and debugging a program as it is executed.

In a modern system, many of these functions are combined into an **integrated development environment (IDE).** Visual Basic, for example, contains an editor, an interpreter, a compiler, an object browser, a linking loader, and a debugger, all in a single, integrated package that allows the programmer to switch rapidly among the different functions. Thus, an error found during compilation will switch the programmer into the editor module with a pointer to the error on the screen. This allows the programmer to fix the error in a more efficient fashion than if the modules were separate. A block diagram for Visual Basic is shown in Figure 17.2.

More traditionally, these various tools have been independent of each other; in older systems that is still the case. There is some minor advantage to the use of separate tools: the programmer can mix and choose the tools to maximize his own productivity. A programmer might, for example, have a particular favorite editor that contains features important to the way that programmer works. Or a particular compiler might generate code that executes more quickly and uses less memory.

Today, programming tools are usually purchased separately from the operating system, since many computer purchasers have no need to write any programs; more traditionally, many of these tools were provided as a part of the operating system. Most operating systems, for example, still include some sort of editor as part of the operating system; UNIX even provides a C++ compiler and all of its related tools. As you would expect, the built-in utilities are often far inferior to those separately purchased. Notepad, the editor provided with Windows, for example, is not considered useful by most programmers for serious work. There are also some excellent programming tools available as free public domain software. EMACS is a popular editor that falls into this category.

Modern object-oriented and event-driven languages with graphical interfaces require the additional support and convenience provided by an integrated development

FIGURE 17.1

The Program Translation Process

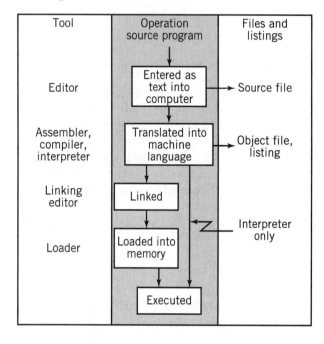

FIGURE 17.2

Visual Basic Block Diagram

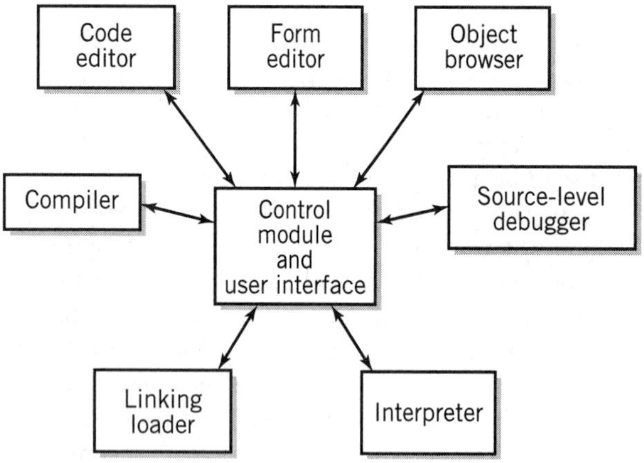

environment such as Visual Basic. The integrated forms editors and object browsers found in modern programming environments ease the task of creating the interface and managing objects. Designing object properties, determining the programming response to system events, such as a mouse click or menu activation, and building methods are all simplified with a set of tools and built-in objects that work together to support program creation. Execution and debugging modules provide rapid feedback to the programmer to aid in testing program correctness.

Overall, the modern IDE provides positive benefits to the programmer that more than offset the advantages of using individual tools. Nonetheless, the required outcome is the same: a program that will ultimately consist of sequences of binary instructions to be executed by the computer. Even the "objects" of object-oriented programming are made up of data and methods; the methods are procedures to be executed like any other procedure or function. The tools in an IDE may look more elegant and be easier to use, but the jobs they perform are essentially similar to separate tools that provide individual pieces of the editing, compilation, and debugging process.

In this chapter, we shall discuss some of the more important tools individually and attempt to show how these tools fit into the overall context of the computer system. As has been the case throughout the textbook, our emphasis is on the fundamental principles of operation rather than on the features of individual tools.

As a final comment before we begin, we remind you again that these tools are, in fact, programs. Like other programs, they process *input data* and produce *output data*. Input data to a text editor is text from the keyboard or a file and commands from the keyboard. The editor processes this input to produce an output data file of program text. The compiler accepts a program text file as input data and produces a file of binary machine code as output data. To the compiler, the machine code that the compiler produces is output data, even though that machine code will eventually be executed as a *program* with its own input and output data.

It is useful to keep this idea in mind as you read this chapter. It will allow you to think of these tools in programming terms—as programs that with some effort you could produce.

17.1 PROGRAM EDITORS

In the early days of computing, most high-level language (HLL) programs were entered into the computer with punched cards. (You can see an example of a punched card in Exercise 3.5.) Each card held one line of up to 80 characters of a program. A COBOL program 1000 lines long would require 1000 cards (and very careful handling not to drop the cards!). Today, most programs are entered directly into the computer with a keyboard, a mouse, and an interactive editor. The editor accepts input from the keyboard, and from various file sources, and outputs the result as a file of text.

In many respects, modern program editors are similar to word processors. The editor has many of the normal features one would expect from a word processor, such as cursor control, text search, block operations, and cut and paste, but there are some differences. Since most programming languages are formatted line by line, rather than paragraph by paragraph, word wrap is not required (or wanted), for example. Also, some program editors separate a "command mode" from the more familiar word processor text insertion mode; they also provide commands for switching between modes. In *vi*, a popular UNIX program editor, for example, you can type the letter *i* or the letter *a* to switch from command mode to insert mode; the escape key returns you to command mode. Typing the letter *i* or *a* in insert mode would simply place that letter within the text. Thus, the same alphanumeric keys have different meanings in each mode. *vi*'s command mode, for example, allows the use of the letters *h, j, k,* and *l* as cursor movement keys so that *vi* can be used with any keyboard, even if the keyboard has no special cursor movement keys. Other program editors, the Visual Basic editor, for example, work more like word processors, using mouse movements, drop-down menus, cursor keys, and special key combinations for commands.

Many program editors also contain features that reflect their special purpose. Since most programs are tabbed to reflect the structure of the program, for example, the program editor may automatically start each line at the tab position of the previous line. Some program editors are even capable of formatting the program text according to the particular language being used and can detect missing "END" statements and punctuation. The Visual Basic editor even color-codes keywords, detects misspelled keywords, and completes partially typed object and variable names.

Another difference between word processors and editors is that most word processors use special characters as a way of internally keeping track of the formatting for the document. Files built with an editor are generally stored in text form, using only the standard characters found in the ASCII, Unicode, or EBCDIC character set.

Again we remind you that the program editor is itself a program. It was probably written in some high-level language, such as C, and was compiled into an executable binary program in the same way that you compiled the programs in your programming language courses. As an example of how the editor might be implemented, consider the following:

A simple program editor might hold the text as a table of characters in memory. A variable points to the "current location" in the table, where the user is working. A command to insert new text could then be implemented by moving the text following the current location out of the way temporarily, placing newly typed text into the table at that point and then moving the later text back into the table, following the new text. Other operations are similarly straightforward.

Actually, the design and implementation of a program editor are more difficult in remembering all the details than in the design itself. A particularly interesting and challenging programming problem is the maintenance of the display in a scrolling screen editor.

Exercise 17.1 gives you the opportunity to implement some of the commands in a simple screen editor.

17.2 THE CONCEPT OF PROGRAM TRANSLATION

On the very earliest computers programs were written and entered in binary form. In fact, data entry on some of these machines required the program to be entered one binary word at a time, using switches on the front panel of the computer, one switch for each bit in the word. Naturally, this process severely limited the size and complexity of these programs. Debugging was a formidable task, since errors in bit entry were common. Programmers had to debug their programs very carefully by hand *before* the program was entered into the computer, since each modification of the program required reconstruction and reentry of much of the code. Addition of a single word early in the program would necessitate reentering every line following, since each succeeding word would have to be moved forward by one location in memory! Worse yet, *every* instruction would have to be checked, since references to later instructions and data, such as forward jump instructions, would also have to be modified.

The Little Man program shown in Figure 17.3a is supposed to find the positive difference (absolute value) of two numbers, but we forgot an instruction. Adding a new instruction to location 03 requires us to move every instruction following. It also requires us to modify every instruction that references data (e.g., instructions 01 or 03) or branches forward (instructions 04 and 05). The modified program, with the moved instructions shown in italics and the referencing modifications boldfaced, is shown in Figure 17.3b. Notice that many instructions require both types of changes. You can just imagine the effort that would be required to modify a large program!

The important concept of *using the computer itself to ease the programmer's work* occurred quite early in the history of digital computing. People realized that the computer could be used to translate programs from a more human-readable form into executable binary code.

This concept resulted in the development of two types of programming languages. Machine-oriented programming languages allowed programmers to write programs that performed the machine's instructions but could be read by humans. The translator programs were known as assemblers, because they simply assembled the individual parts of each instruction into a corresponding machine instruction. Assemblers were available for IBM computers as early as 1953 or 1954.

Function-oriented programming languages attempted to free the programmer from the details of the machine's instructions. As you are aware, these languages became known as **high-level languages;** they are also sometimes called **procedural languages,** because the function is defined by a particular procedure that is to be followed. Not surprisingly,

FIGURE 17.3

The Result of a Programming Error

00	INPUT		00	INPUT
01	STA 10		01	STA **11**
02	INPUT		02	INPUT
03	SUB 10	← ⌐ Missing →	03	STA **12**
04	BRP 06	instruction	04	*SUB 11*
05	BR 08		05	BRP **07**
06	LDA 09		06	*BR 09*
07	SUB 10		07	*LDA 10*
08	OUT		08	*SUB 11*
09	COB		09	*OUT*
10	(used for data)		10	*COB*
11	(used for data)		11	(used for data)
			12	(used for data)
	(a)			(b)

development of the first high-level languages took longer than the development of assemblers, due to the additional complexity of these languages. The first true high-level language translators, known as compilers, for FORTRAN, Algol, and COBOL, appeared in 1954–56, 1958, and 1959, respectively. A somewhat different type of high-level language translator, known as an **interpreter,** appeared for Lisp around 1959.

Today there are hundreds of so-called "third-generation" high-level programming languages. Interestingly, COBOL and FORTRAN, in somewhat modernized form, are still among the most popular. Also well known are C, Pascal, BASIC, and many others. A large computer system may have dozens of assemblers, compilers, and interpreters built in to the system.

More recently, the concept of function-oriented languages has been extended even further to include various types of languages where the functions are defined in such a way that the procedures can be determined within the language itself, rather than explicitly by the programmer. These languages include **fourth-generation** or **nonprocedural languages,** and **natural languages.**

Fourth-generation languages require a different type of translator, since the translator has to generate the appropriate procedure as a major element of the translation. Translators for fourth-generation languages are usually called **program generators.** A discussion of program generators is beyond the scope of this textbook.

Natural languages attempt to translate English-like sentences into requests that can then be processed using other languages. Natural language translators are very difficult to develop because English is such a complex language. Sentences in English frequently have ambiguous or indefinite meaning that is clarified only within the context of the situation. For those interested in nonprocedural and natural translation processes, the For Further Reading section at the end of the chapter suggests appropriate reading material.

Object-oriented languages represent a significant conceptual advance over procedural languages. Nonetheless, the program code is an outgrowth of procedural language code. As such, programs written in object-oriented languages can be translated using extensions to conventional compilers. The objects themselves are provided as libraries that can be called from the compiled code using the linking techniques discussed in Section 17.5. For some object-oriented languages the extended language is actually translated first into a third-generation language, using a translation tool known as a **preprocessor.** Then a conventional compiler is used for the subsequent translation into machine language. This is the method used by many C++ compilers, for example.

Regardless of type—assembler, compiler, interpreter, preprocessor, natural language translator, or fourth-generation program generator—the purpose of programming language translators is to use the computer itself to change programs from a form convenient to humans into a form the machine can understand.

17.3 ASSEMBLY LANGUAGE AND THE ASSEMBLER

Assembly language is a computer language that substitutes simple alphanumeric names or mnemonics for the op codes and addresses found in machine language instructions. An assembler is a computer utility that translates assembly language program code, known as **source code,** line by line, into executable binary code. Each line of assembly language code corresponds to a single machine instruction. The assembler is the simplest form of human-readable-to-machine-usable program translator. Since assembly language is simply a direct substitution for machine language, the code generated by an assembler can be expected to run only on a single type or family of machine.

You have already seen, in Chapter 7, the advantage of representing the Little Man op codes by short mnemonic names such as ADD or LDA. Doing so made the programs much easier to read and write. When the code is binary and made up of a complicated instruction set, the need is even more obvious. (In case you have any doubt, Figure 17.4 is an example of part of a *binary dump,* the listing of a binary program and data, produced on an IBM S/370 computer.) The simplest form of assembler would simply translate the mnemonic op codes into machine language, using a lookup table to do the translation. Additional addressing modes could also be included in the table.

In practice, the example of Figure 17.3 shows a limitation of such a simple assembler: a major concern of programmers is *locating* the particular address where data is to be found or the target address of a BRANCH instruction; changing the program forces the programmer to find and recalculate all these addresses. The problem is much worse where the instructions and data are of different sizes.

The idea of using simple names to represent numbers can be extended to give alphanumeric names to important addresses within the program, for example, the targets of jump instructions and the locations of data elements. In fact this technique is probably consistent with the way you initially laid out your Little Man program assignments. Most likely you used arrows to point your jumps to the correct location, or you used names to identify the data you were working with (e.g., ADD first-number) Thus, instead of writing

```
LDA 57
```

to represent the loading of data from memory location 57, the programmer could write

```
LDA BOO
```

where the name BOO is equivalent to memory location 57.

Of course, the assembler must be told somehow that the name BOO is equivalent to memory location 57. The programmer will do this by putting a **label** at location 57, indicating that the name BOO has been assigned to that location:

```
(57) BOO: <instruction or data>
```

The names chosen to represent particular addresses are chosen by the programmer. Like high-level language variables, the names are often chosen to have some meaning to the programmer (although, for some reason, meaningless names like BOO get used a lot!).

FIGURE 17.4

Part of an IBM S/370 Binary Dump

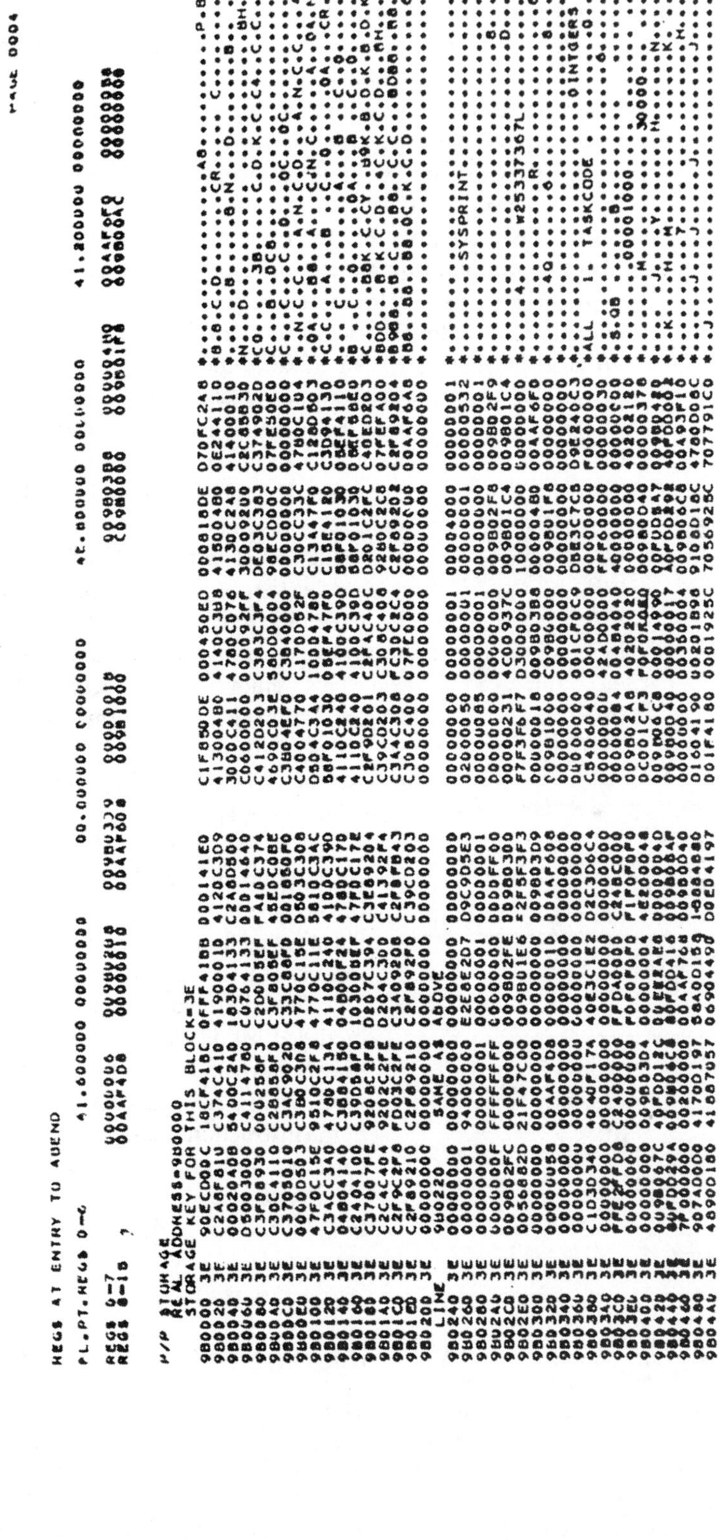

Consider, as an extremely simple example of the use of labels, the program from Chapter 6 shown in Figure 17.5. (The actual memory location addresses are also included so that you can see the relationship between the labels and their equivalent memory addresses.)

As noted earlier, assembly language is characterized by the fact that each line of program text represents a single instruction. In the Little Man Computer, one line of assembly language code corresponds to exactly one memory location, since every instruction in the Little Man Computer occupies a single memory location.

(As you have seen, this is not necessarily true in real-world computers, where a single instruction may occupy more than one memory location and, in particular, where the number of locations required for an instruction varies from instruction to instruction. This can make the hand calculation of a particular memory address difficult, and provides additional incentive for the use of labels to identify memory addresses.)

It takes only a moment's perusal of the program in Figure 17.5 to see that this program can be translated into machine code by translating the op code mnemonics and then substituting the address 06 for the name FIRST in instructions 01 and 03. Note, incidentally, that the program, written in this form, is much easier to read than the corresponding machine code.

Using names to represent addresses not only makes the program easier to read, it also simplifies the programmer's task, since the assembler program itself can calculate the correct memory address to substitute for the name when it performs the translation. This removes the difficulty of locating the appropriate addresses from the programmer. As a more significant example, consider again the sample program given in Figure 17.3a rewritten in assembly language, using simple names for the addresses, shown in Figure 17.6.

Since each line of the listing corresponds to a single memory location, the labels DOOUT, FIRST, and SECOND naturally line up to memory locations 08, 10, and 11, respectively. Substituting these values for the names in the program instructions recreates exactly the program listing in Figure 17.3a.

The additional instruction at location 03 results in the modified listing shown in Figure 17.7. Note that the labels DOOUT, FIRST, and SECOND are now each shifted by one to make room for the new instruction. Substituting these new values in the instructions automatically results in the corrected code corresponding to Figure 17.3b.

When we use labels for the various addresses, retranslation by the assembler will automatically produce the corrected code, making modification of the program much easier for the programmer.

Operation of the Assembler

The operation of an assembler is relatively straightforward. Consider the process that you would use if you were translating

FIGURE 17.5

Simple Program

(00)	START:	INP	
(01)		STA	FIRST
(02)		INP	
(03)		ADD	FIRST
(04)		OUT	
(05)		COB	
(06)	FIRST:		

FIGURE 17.6

Assembly Language Version of Figure 17.3a

(00)	START:	INP
(01)		STA FIRST
(02)		INP
(03)		SUB FIRST
(04)		BRP GOON
(05)		BR DOOUT
(06)	GOON:	LDA FIRST
(07)		SUB SECOND
(08)	DOOUT:	OUT
(09)		COB
(10)	FIRST:	(used for data)
(11)	SECOND:	(used for data)

FIGURE 17.7

Assembly Language Version of Figure 17.3b

(00)	START:	INP
(01)		STA FIRST
(02)		INP
(03)		STA SECOND
(04)		SUB FIRST
(05)		BRP GOON
(06)		BR DOOUT
(07)	GOON:	LDA FIRST
(08)		SUB SECOND
(09)	DOOUT:	OUT
(10)		COB
(11)	FIRST:	(used for data)
(12)	SECOND:	(used for data)

FIGURE 17.8

Little Man Computer Operations Table

Mnemonic	OP code	Number of operands
ADD	1	1
SUB	2	1
STA	3	1
LDA	5	1
BR	6	1
BRZ	7	1
BRP	8	1
INP	901	0
OUT	902	0
COB	0	0

an assembly language program by hand. As an example, look again at the program in Figure 17.6.

You would start at the top of the program, working through each instruction, a line at a time. For each line, you would determine the type of instruction from the mnemonic, and thus you would know the number of memory locations required for that instruction. This information is stored in an **operations table.**

The operations table contains the mnemonics for each instruction together with the corresponding binary op code, the number of operands, and other format information required in order to translate the instruction. Since the characteristics for a particular instruction do not change, the operations table is built right into the assembler program.

Figure 17.8 provides an example of an operations table for the Little Man Computer. This is a particularly simple table, since the format rules for every instruction are identical; every instruction requires exactly one memory location, and the decimal code for every instruction is calculated from a single translation rule:

```
code = 100 × op code + operand (if used)
```

Providing the expected number of operands in the table allows the Little Man assembler to check for errors in the source code.

In computers with many different addressing modes, different numbers of operands, different numbers of memory allocation formats, and different translation rules, the operations table will obviously be more complex. Nonetheless, the principle is identical: locate the correct mnemonic (and format, if there is more than one format for a particular mnemonic) in the table. The information in that data entry is then used to check the source code format and to allocate the required number of memory locations for the instruction.

Continuing this line-by-line process for each instruction will allow you to verify the format of each instruction—and to determine the correct memory location that corresponds to each instruction and to each label name present in the source code program.

For example, reading the first line in the program in Figure 17.6 verifies that the instruction has a correct format, with no operands. Furthermore, you now know that the label name START corresponds to memory location 00. You will store the name START in a separate table in case it is needed as an address later. This table will be called a **symbol table.** It is specific to the particular program, and it is used during the final translation to look up any symbols that are not located in the operations table.

When you now move to line 01 in the program and perform the same process, you realize that the address for FIRST is not yet known, because line 10 has not yet been processed. Thus, it will not be possible to complete the translation of this instruction at this time. It is not practical to look ahead, because looking ahead requires identifying the memory needs of each instruction prior to the line with the desired label, which effectively duplicates the effort of analyzing each instruction in turn.

Furthermore, the situation in which an address name is identified in the program after it is referred to is one that will occur often in assembly language programs. Instead of attempting to look ahead each time, it makes more sense to continue processing each line, in order, until the end of the program is reached. A second pass through the program will be used to complete the translation process.

That a second pass will be required for many instructions suggests that it is not useful to translate any instructions on the first pass through the program. Instead, you will use this pass to check each instruction for validity (legal op code, correct number of operands, etc.) and to determine the memory address that corresponds to each label. At the end of the pass, you will have created a symbol table containing each label name that appears in the program, together with the memory address corresponding to that label name. The symbol table for our example appears in Figure 17.9.

Together, the operations table and the completed symbol table now provide everything that is required to complete the translation of every instruction. On the second pass through the program, you complete the translation by looking up the op code in the operations table and, if necessary, the address in the symbol table. Any referenced address that is not found in the symbol table has no matching label, which is clearly to be flagged as an error condition.

This completes the discussion of how you would perform an assembly by hand. As you would expect, the computer assembler operates in a similar way. It starts at the top of the program and reads each line of text, one character at a time, searching for the groups of characters that form labels, op codes, and operands for the instruction being analyzed. This process is known as **scanning.** As this occurs, the constituents of the line (label, op code, operands) are identified. Formally, the identification process is known as **parsing;** it is similar to the grammar parsing that you probably were forced to do on English sentences in junior high school. At the risk of losing many readers, there is a reminder of English grammar parsing in Figure 17.10. (We will return to the subject of English grammar again in the next section.) Since assembly language statements have a fairly rigid format, the parsing is simple, so scanning and parsing usually take place simultaneously in the assembler. A parsed line of Little Man assembly code appears in Figure 17.11.

Now, the parsed instruction can be looked up in the operations table. A counter variable within the assembler program is used to keep track of the corresponding memory location for each instruction. Initially, the counter is set to zero, since the top line of the program will presumably be loaded into memory location zero. Each time a line of assembler code is parsed, the counter variable is incremented by the

FIGURE 17.9

Symbol Table for Program in Figure 17.6

START	00
GOON	06
DOOUT	08
FIRST	10
SECOND	11

FIGURE 17.10

A Parsed English Language Sentence

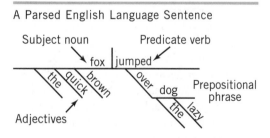

FIGURE 17.11

Parsed Assembly Language

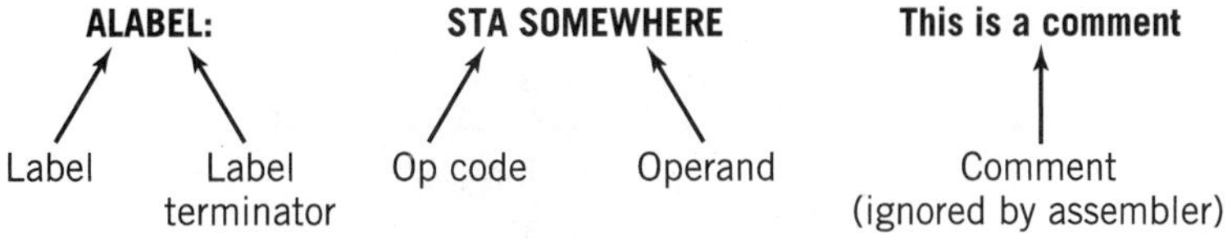

ALABEL: **STA SOMEWHERE**   **This is a comment**

Label   Label   Op code   Operand   Comment
terminator   (ignored by assembler)

number of memory locations required for the particular instruction, as determined from the operations table. This will set the memory location for each instruction.

If the line of text contains a label, the address of that label will correspond to the number in the counter. The name of the label will be stored in the symbol table together with the memory address that has just been determined.

Since the op code on many computers affects the number of memory locations required for the instruction, any op code not found in the operations table makes it impossible to determine the memory address of future instructions, and the program line with the illegal op code is flagged as a first-pass error. Most assemblers will attempt to complete the first pass in order to determine any other op code and format errors, but the second pass will not be performed.

On the second pass, the assembler again scans and parses the code one line at a time. The operation table is used to determine the op code and the translation rule for the instruction; required addresses are looked up in the symbol table. Finally, the various components are combined according to the translation rule to produce binary machine code.

In addition to the binary code, the assembler also produces a listing that shows both the source code and the binary code, complete with memory assignments for each instruction.

Most assemblers work pretty much as we have described. It is possible to build a one-pass assembler by keeping track of the instructions that are missing symbol table addresses and then going back and fixing them when the address is known, but most assembler designers don't consider the slight assembly time savings worth the effort.

Assembly Language Formats

The assembly language format for a particular computer naturally depends on the instruction set for that computer. And, of course, the use of several different instruction formats within a computer will require slightly different assembly language formats for each instruction type. Within these constraints, there is surprising similarity between the assemblers on different computers.

Snippets of assembly language source code from three typical computers appear in Figure 17.12. It is not important that you understand the code. But note the formats of the various instructions. Note the similarities in format, in instruction design, and in layout between the three samples.

The first example, in Figure 17.12a, is taken from a single-accumulator, single-address machine, very similar in concept and programming form to the Little Man Computer. In

FIGURE 17.12

Three Assembler Examples: (a) PDP-8, (b) 80386 assembler, (c) VAX assembler

			(a) PDP-8 Assembler
			/multiply by shift and add
	CLA	CLL	/clear accumulator and link flag
	TAD	NUM1	/get NUM1 (multiplier)
	DCA	A	/deposit (store) in var.A, clear accum
	TAD	NUM2	
	DCA	B	
	DCA	PROD	
START,	CLL		
	TAD	A	/get multiplier
	RAR		/rotate right one bit thru link
	DCA	A	
	SNL		/skip if link is 1
	JMP	SHIFT	/jump to shift if link is 0
	TAD	B	
	TAD	PROD	/fetch multiplicand and add to total
	DCA	PROD	/return to prod
SHIFT,	CLL		
	TAD	B	
	RAL		
	DCA	B	/fetch multiplicand, shift L, return to b
	ISZ	COUNT	/increment count, test for end
	JMP	START	
	HLT		
PROD,	0000		
A,	0000		
B,	0000		
COUNT,	7764		/-14 octal

SOURCE: J.C. Cluley, Programming for Minicomputers, © 1978, Crane, Russak, and Co.

(continued)

this case, the computer is the Digital PDP-8, a now obsolete, but once very popular, minicomputer in its heyday.

The second example, in Figure 17.12b, is taken from a two-address, multiregister machine, in this case the Intel x86 microcomputer used in the PC.

The third example, in Figure 17.12c, is from the VAX computer, a machine with many different instruction types and addressing modes.

Many other machines could have been selected to make the point just as easily. The differences between these machines are more a matter of detail than of real substance.

All three machines use a basic four-field layout to describe each instruction. The fields are separated by spaces or tabs. The first field holds an optional label; if the label is not

FIGURE 17.12

Three Assembler Examples: (a) PDP-8, (b) 80386 assembler,
(c) VAX assembler (continued)

(b) X86 Assembler			
			/convert 16 bit binary to ascii
dec 16out	proc	far	
	mov	ax,datas	
	mov	ds,ax	
;number is in dx..put the digits in a buffer			
;			
	mov	cx,0	;initialize counter
	lea	di,tbuff	;point to buffer
dec16out1:	push cx		;save cx
	mov	ax,dx	
	mov	dx,0	
	mov	cx,10	;set divisor of 10
	div	cx	
	xchg	ax,dx	
	add	al,30h	;add 30 hex for ascii
	move	[di],al	;save in buffer
	pop	cx	
	inc	cx	
	cmp	dx,0	;done?
	jnz	dec16out1	

(c) VAX Assembler			
MINABC:	CMPL	A,B	;minone = min(a,b,c)
	BLSS	10$	;branch if a is smaller
	MOVL	B,MINONE	;b is smaller
	BRB	20$	
10$:	MOVL	A,MINONE	
20$:	CMPL	C.MINONE;	do again for c
	BGTR 30$		
	MOVL	C,MINONE	
30$:	END		

present, the line starts with a space or tab. The second field holds the op code. Operands appear in the third field. The addressing mode is usually specified as part of the operand field, as is the case in these three examples, but a few older assemblers place the addressing mode at the end of the op code field.

The contents of the operand field shows the largest variation, since the operands depend on the nature of the instruction. Registers, addresses, addressing modes, and condition codes, in various combinations, will appear in this field. There may be a large variation even within a single machine. Of course, for some instructions, the operand field does not even exist!

Even in an architecture as simple as the Little Man Computer, there is variation in this field. Although most instructions in the LMC use this field for a single address, the INP and OUT instructions use the operand as a device address, and the COB instruction does not use the field at all.

Some assemblers even allow the use of simple arithmetic operators within the operand field to indicate that an address is actually offset from the label. Thus, LDA BOO+2 means to load data from an address that is found two memory locations beyond BOO. (Note that the arithmetic is actually a command to the assembler, *not* an arithmetic instruction.) In most assemblers, the entire field of operands must be written without spaces.

The fourth field is usually a comment field, which is ignored by the assembler, except to print out on the assembler listing. Most assemblers also provide a special symbol that can be used to place a comment at the beginning of a line. A few assemblers even provide a symbol to allow comments to appear in the middle of a line. The comment field is strictly for the use of the programmer, to clarify the flow of the program to someone attempting to understand the program. For translation purposes, everything after the operand field is ignored.

Features and Extensions

Although the fundamental format is determined by the design of the computer, most assemblers provide additional features for the flexibility and convenience of the programmer. From the examples given, you have already seen that nearly every assembler provides a method for inserting comments into the code.

It is also common to provide special op codes that are not part of the language but, instead, are *special instructions to the assembler itself.* These instructions are known as **directives,** or **pseudo-op codes,** or simply **pseudo-ops.** Figure 17.13 shows a few typical directives that are commonly provided. Of course the actual pseudo-op code will vary on different machines. Some directives, particularly DATA, actually generate binary code (loading a particular value into memory), but most do not. Of course these pseudo-ops must be included in the operations table, so that the assembler knows what to do with them.

Some assemblers also allow the programmer to give a name to a group of instructions that will be used more than once within a program. This name can then be used as though it were an op code to indicate that the entire group of instructions is to be placed at that location in the code. The group of instructions is known as a **macro,** and assemblers with this facility are known as **macro assemblers.** Some macro assemblers will even allow the programmer to specify arguments that are substituted into the code each time the code is used.

Finally, it should be noted that nothing in our discussion requires that the binary code generated by an assembler must be executable on the same computer where the assembly translation takes place. It is entirely possible that the assembler is intended to generate binary code that will be executed on a different type of computer. For example, we might be using a VAX computer to generate binary code for an IBM PC.

Since the assembler is itself a program, it can be designed to execute on any particular computer—it is not necessarily limited to the machine where execution of the program will occur. The requirement for such an assembler is the same as that for any assembler,

FIGURE 17.13

Some Typical Assembler Directives

START	Tells the assembler where to start assembling. Sometimes an address field is used to specify the memory address where the program is to be located.
END	Tells the assembler where to stop assembling. Any source code beyond this point is ignored.
DATA	Tells the assembler that this memory location contains data. The data to be stored initially at this location can be specified in the operand field. Many assemblers have several different DATA directives for different types of data, including bytes, words, ASCII text, and a blank block of storage.
ORG	(For ORiGin) tells the assembler that the code following this directive is to be assembled starting at the memory address specified in the operand field of this directive.
EQU	Typically appears with the format label EQU value This directive can be used to give a name to a value when the address field is actually a value rather than an address, for example, when using immediate addressing or specifying a condition. The directive THREE: EQU 03 might be used to clarify an assembly program by allowing the programmer to write "THREE" any time the value 3 is used in a statement. Effectively, this directive tells the assembler to add the label and corresponding value to the symbol table.
EXTRN	Followed by a list of labels, tells the assembler to assume that these addresses reside in another, separately assembled module. The linking loader will be used to tie the two modules together later.

namely, that the source code formats, op code mnemonics, and instruction translation tables for that assembler must correspond to those of the target machine—that machine where execution is to take place.

An assembler that assembles code on one type of machine for use on a different type of machine is known as a **cross-assembler.** A cross-assembler might be useful to a programmer who wants to use a well-equipped computer facility to develop programs for a less fancy system or a new system under development, but not yet existent.

Relocatability

One remaining issue that we have not yet considered—the output from the assembler generally assumes a fixed program starting point, most commonly, memory location 0. Most modern operating systems do not assign programs to a particular location; rather, the operating system assumes that the program is relocatable and assigns it a location that is convenient under the particular circumstances at the load time. For most modern instruction sets, relocation is not difficult. With base mode addressing, relocation can be achieved simply by loading the correct value into a base register. Relative addressing is even easier: any address specified relative to the current address is relocated automatically. Of course, with virtual storage systems, relocation is handled automatically, since the dynamic address translation process converts from logical to physical storage without any additional requirement.

There are some instances when absolute addressing is required, however. Sometimes a relative instruction must point to a fixed location, perhaps to interface with the operating system for an interrupt call, and the relative distance must be adjusted if the program is relocated. Some instructions require absolute addressing. Whatever the reason, the assembler can provide for relocation by including an additional table that specifies which locations must be adjusted at the time that the program is actually loaded into memory for execution. This table will stay with the executable program and will be used by the loader to make the appropriate corrections at load time.

17.4 PROGRAM LANGUAGE DESCRIPTIONS AND RULES

The procedure that we used for assembling a program was essentially simple enough that we did not attempt to formalize the methodology in our discussion. Nonetheless, all the essential elements required for any form of program translation were present in the assembler process: first we scanned the program to divide the input text into recognizable components, then we parsed the components to identify the various syntactic constituents by matching the components against known format rules, and finally we generated code corresponding to each constituent piece. An operation table helped to identify the legal components to generate the code; a symbol table identified the individual components used in the translation. Similar elements will be used for the compilation process.

High-level procedural languages are translated into binary code by compilers and interpreters. The method is similar to that used by assemblers, but the actual process is a good deal more difficult and complex. There are three primary reasons why this is the case:

1. Each instruction in assembly language translates to a single machine code instruction. In a high-level language, even a simple assignment statement may translate to a large number of machine code instructions.

2. There is a tremendous amount of flexibility in each high-level language statement type. An assembly language op code has a limited number of possible operand types, thus the instruction is easily determined. In contrast, a statement in the high-level language may vary in an infinite number of ways. A simple IF-THEN-ELSE statement, for example, might contain within itself any number of other statements, *including, even, other IF-THEN-ELSE statements*. An assignment statement can contain many different types of arithmetic operations, involving a mixture of integer and real data types.

   This flexibility means that the compiler must be capable of creating code that correctly follows the flow of a wide range of statement possibilities.

3. There are potential ambiguities in high-level languages that must be satisfactorily resolved as part of the translation process. As an example, consider just a

few of the issues that must be resolved when analyzing the following simple assignment statement:

```
avar = bvar + cvar * (dvar - 1);
```

a. During execution, the machine code must be designed to process the substatement in parentheses first and must create a temporary storage location for the result. The compiler must know that it should analyze the substatement first.

b. The machine code must reflect the correct precedence rules, in this case, multiplication before division.

c. The mathematical signs, +, −, *, have different meaning if the variables being added are real than if they are integer. Furthermore, type conversions may have to be included in the code.

You can see the difficulties that arise even in simple examples. Because of the additional complexity, a more formal approach to the compilation process is necessary. It will not be possible in this chapter to explain the operation of a compiler in all its details. The subject of compiler design is very theoretical and intricate. It is hoped, though, that this discussion will give you at least a fundamental understanding of the principles upon which the compiler operates.

A Description of Written English

Before we attempt to describe the translation process for a programming language, it is helpful to understand the design and specification of the language. This description will ultimately be useful as a road map to the translation process.

In many respects, computer languages are defined similarly to spoken and written languages such as English. It will help you to understand the steps that a compiler must use to process a programming language if we spend a few moments looking at the way English sentences are constructed and analyzed, and the way in which meaning is conveyed to those sentences. You will see shortly how closely related the analysis of an English sentence and the analysis of a computer program really are!

Written languages such as English are defined primarily by three interrelated components:

1. **The lexical component.** The lexicon is the list of all legal words in the language, together with information about the words. Information about a word includes its meaning and its syntactic type (verb, noun, preposition, etc.). Words also form other classes that define their usage in terms of meaning, known as *semantic terms.* For example, the word "green" is a member of the class "colors." The sentence "The tree is green." makes sense, because trees possess color. The sentence "The tree is happy." does not make sense, because the class of words that includes "happy"—*emotions,* perhaps—does not pertain to trees. Some of the words in a language are fundamental to the syntax of the language. In a sense, they are keywords. For example, the word "over" in the phrase "over my head" defines the phrase syntactically as prepositional.

2. **The syntactic component.** Syntax defines the form and structure of a language. In English, syntax includes definition of the various component types and the

rules that determine how these component types interact to form legal sentences. Together, the syntax rules for a language are known as a **grammar** for the language.

For example, in English, a sentence can be defined by a set of English grammar rules. A few typical rules are

- Verbs are words that define actions or states of being.
- Nouns are words that identify people, places, things, and ideas.
- A sentence may be simple, compound, complex, or compound-complex.
- A simple sentence contains one independent clause and no subordinate clauses. It may contain a compound subject or a compound predicate and any number of modifiers other than a subordinate clause.
- A clause is a group of related words that contains both a subject and a predicate and that functions as part of a sentence. A clause may be *main* (independent) or *subordinate* (dependent).
- A subordinate clause is a clause whose function is to modify part of another clause or to form a single syntactic unit with another clause.
- A phrase is a group of related words without both a subject and a predicate.
- A subject is a noun or noun phrase that defines the topic of the clause or sentence.
- A predicate is a word or words that make a statement about the clause or sentence. A predicate may be a verb or verbal phrase, with or without a required complementary phrase or clause (e.g., the object of a transitive verb).
- The subject and predicate of a clause or sentence must agree in number, gender, and person.

Obviously, these rules represent only a small portion of the syntax rules for English. What is noticeable from the sample just given, however, is that the first rules are very general rules for defining a sentence. Each subsequent rule clarifies a term used in a previous rule. Combining these rules in various appropriate ways determines whether a sentence is syntactically or grammatically correct.

Given these rules, we can identify the English sentence

Elephants eat peanuts.

as a legitimate sentence in the language. The sentence is simple, since it contains one independent clause and no subordinate clauses. We know that it contains a clause, because it has both a subject and predicate, and we know that it is independent because it is the *only* clause in the sentence. The subject, "elephants," is a noun, and the predicate "eat peanuts" is a *transitive verb* with its *direct object*. (We could have gone further and defined transitive verb and direct object, but this is enough for now.)

On the other hand, the sentence

Elephant eat peanuts.

is not legal, because of the last rule: "elephant" is singular, and "eat" is plural. Therefore, the subject and predicate do not agree in number. Such details make natural language difficult to analyze.

(Incidentally, another difficulty of natural language translation is the number of special cases that arise: the sentences "Eat your breakfast!" and "Get ready to party!" seemingly violate the clause rule. In each of these sentences, the subject "you" is implied, but not actually stated.)

3. **The semantic component.** The **semantic component** of a language deals with the meaning of sentences as a whole, that is, the meaning of the words of a sentence when they are combined into a sentence. It is particularly important to notice that the syntax rules contribute to, but do not in themselves establish, a meaning for the sentence. The syntax rules establish only that the sentence is correct grammatically. It is semantics that establish the way the words combine to form a given meaning for the sentence, given the meaning of the individual words and the particular syntactic construction for the sentence. The word "snow" in the sentence "I like to play in the snow." is part of a prepositional phrase and has a different meaning and importance within the sentence than the word "snow" that forms the subject in the sentence "The snow is white."

In each of the previous sentences, the word "snow" is a noun. You can see the interrelationship between syntax and semantics clearly if you look at the sentence "It will snow tomorrow." Now the word "snow" is a verb; the syntax for the sentence must be established for the semantic meaning to be understood.

The field of semantics is relatively new, and, so far, it has not been possible to codify semantics into a set of formal rules. Instead, semantics are often defined descriptively.

As an example of a semantic consideration in English, consider the sentence

    Peanuts eat elephants.

Although this sentence is grammatically correct, it clearly does not have reasonable meaning. The problem is one of semantics. The subject of the sentence, "peanuts" is inanimate. We have used the verb "eat" in a way that requires the subject to be a member of a class of animate nouns. But note the difficulty in assigning semantic rules: the sentence

    Rust eats metal.

is perfectly reasonable because the word "eats" is now being used with the meaning "corrodes" rather than "consumes for nutrition," and the subject is now a member of a different class, perhaps that of objects that are susceptible to corrosion.

This example shows that ambiguity and differences of word meaning add an additional dimension of difficulty to the semantic interpretation of sentences. As you will see, computer languages share this difficulty. Extreme care is taken in the design of computer languages to create syntactical constructions in such a way as to prevent such semantic ambiguities from arising.

As a further example, consider the semantic problem that arises from the different meanings of the word "just" in the two sentences "Life is just" and "Life just is." The difficulties inherent in natural language processing should be quite obvious by now!

There is a fourth factor in the meaning of English sentences that the definition of a language does not handle. That is the situation in which a sentence contains an error of logic, or fact. The sentence

> Elephants eat fish.

is both syntactically and semantically correct. It just happens to be untrue. There is no practical way for a definition of the language to handle this situation. The same is true of programming languages, of course. A compiler will obviously translate the assignment statement supposedly representing the area of a circle

```
area = pi * radius;
```

correctly, but the result of execution will be incorrect, because the formula for the area of a circle is obviously area = pi * radius^2. There is no way to design a programming language to detect logical errors on the part of the programmer.

Programming Language Rules

Just as English is defined by the syntax rules that make up its grammar, so, too, are programming languages. The grammar of a programming language is specified as a set of rules that completely define the language. In addition, there are precise definitions for the meanings of the individual words that make up the lexicon of the language. Again, as in English, the syntax defines the form of a programming language, not its specific "meaning." Obviously, in this case, the "meaning" of the program is the series of actions that the program is to perform. Stated differently, if we are given a particular program that a programmer has written, we can use the syntax of the language to determine if the program is grammatically correct, but the meanings of the individual words and symbols that make up the program must be further analyzed to determine exactly what the program is going to do.

Fortunately, the rules of a programming language are far more restricted than a natural language such as English. Since programming languages are designed by individuals or small groups of individuals, the design can be tightly controlled and standardized. Changes to the language can be made to occur in an orderly fashion, rather than just growing topsy-turvy. Words and symbols are given narrow definitions. Care can be taken to avoid problems of semantic ambiguities. Attempts are made to design the language so that particular syntactic constructions have single, well-defined semantic meaning. Even so, as you shall see, semantic ambiguities do unavoidably creep into the design. Fortunately, these ambiguities can be handled by simple semantic rules.

As in English, the lexical, syntactical, and semantical components of the language are interrelated. By design, however, the interrelations in a programming language are designed to aid in the analysis of the source program, as well as to generate correct, unambiguous code. Parsing a program syntactically, together with some simple semantic conditions, will be sufficient to break the program into small individual pieces that can be translated into snippets of machine code. Furthermore, the parsing will establish the patterns required to glue those individual snippets of machine code together, to form a machine program that matches the source program.

Although the foregoing discussion sounds very abstract, we can illustrate the concepts of program generation with a simple informal example from our previous consideration of the operation of the Little Man assembler.

EXAMPLE

The syntax for a Little Man assembly language program can be described informally by a few simple rules:

1. A program is made up of *lines of code.* Each *line of code* is either a *program line* or a *comment line,* followed by a carriage return.

2. A *program line* consists of an optional label symbol, an op code-dependent address field, and an optional comment. Fields within a *program line* are separated by "white space" (one or more spaces or tabs).

3. A comment line contains nothing but a comment.

4. All labels are followed by a colon (:). All comments are preceded by a slash mark (/).

5. For op codes that take an address, the address field consists of a symbol or number. For other op codes, the address field is blank.

The lexical analysis for a line of assembly language consists of scanning each *program line* and separating it into individual components, known as **tokens.** Since comments are not relevant to code generation, they may be discarded immediately. There are only three types of tokens remaining: op codes, symbols, and the colon that identifies a label field.

The syntactical analysis, or parsing, procedure matches the patterns of tokens against the syntax rules. For example, if the parser expects to see an op code token and sees a symbol instead, it knows that there is a syntax error. The assembly notifies the programmer of the error, no program code is generated.

Because of the simplicity of Little Man assembler language, the only semantic analysis required is that needed to match an address with each symbol token identified during the scanning operation. The assembler is now ready to generate program code. The program code is built by applying code for the appropriate syntax rules (rules 2 and 5, in this case), symbol tokens, and op code tokens to each line of assembly language.

Now let us consider ways to specify the syntax rules for a typical programming language. Understanding the grammar of the language will serve two primary purposes in the compilation process:

1. The grammar defines the language. Just as in English, the rules define every legal sentence in the language. (Of course, in this case legal sentences are actually program statements.) Thus, the syntax rules become the tool of choice to detect errors in a program by determining the points in the program that deviate from the rules.

2. When we analyzed a simple English sentence by applying a sequence of syntax rules to it, we were effectively parsing the sentence into its different components. Similarly, as the previous example shows, parsing source program code is a crucial step in the program translation process. The parsing process essentially

consists of determining which rule applies in a particular instance as we trace through the sentence. Again, each syntax rule corresponds to a particular segment of program code. The way in which the various syntax rules combine therefore establishes the particular groups of code and their organization. Thus, identifying the rules that make up a particular program will allow the compiler to produce the corresponding machine code.

Specifying a language formally also helps the designer(s) of the language to determine the areas of their language that are too complex or require clarification, to locate ambiguities in the language, to aid in the design of their compilers, and to evaluate the performance of their compilers.

Computer Language Descriptions

There are many different ways of expressing the grammar of a high-level computer programming language. These range from informal narrative descriptions of the language to extremely formal and precise syntax specifications.

INFORMAL NARRATIVE DESCRIPTION   One obvious method of describing a programming language is in narrative fashion. You are certainly familiar with the idea of describing a programming language narratively, since this is the primary method used by programming textbooks. Similarly, we used a narrative description in the previous example to define the grammar for the Little Man assembly language. The narrative description of a language has the appealing advantage that it is easily understandable by a competent programmer. It is therefore useful as a reference source. For example, C might be partially described by the narrative shown in Figure 17.14.

This method of description is useful to the programmer, but it would be difficult to implement in a compiler because it is too wordy and insufficiently precise. (The Java narrative description is nearly 450 pages long!) It would be nearly impossible to provide the degree of organization, precision, conciseness, and level of detail that would be required to include all possible situations, yet the compiler must be capable of handling every possible situation that arises. Therefore, we turn to another, more formal method for describing the language.

SYNTAX DIAGRAMS   Syntax diagrams provide a more formal definition of grammar. You may have noticed that within the grammar, each English grammar rule defines a syntactic construction in terms of other syntactic entities, some of which are previously known or defined, and some of which are yet to be defined. We use the rules by continually substituting the unknown parts until everything is known. Thus, a sentence is defined as a subject and an object, a subject is defined as a noun phrase, a noun phrase is defined as a noun or an adjective and a noun, and so on.

This is also the approach that is used to define the grammar for a programming language. The first question that we need to answer is: "How far should we go to break down the text stream we're working with?" Grammars are defined in terms of **terminal symbols** and **nonterminal symbols.** Theoretically, the terminal symbols consist of individual characters and digits and punctuation marks that make up a language. Nonterminal symbols are then defined as any collection of symbols that may be broken down further into the

FIGURE 17.14

Partial Narrative Description of C

Basic Structure

C is written free form, with no required layout. Tokens are separated by "white space": spaces, tabs, carriage returns, or comments. Conventionally, however, C is written so that blocks and nested statements are indented.

The basic C structure is the *block.* A block consists of some of the following components, enclosed with braces:

> *label declarations*
>
> *constant definitions*
>
> *type definitions*
>
> *variable declarations*
>
> *function declarations*
>
> *program statements*

C is constructed of one main function block. Additional function blocks may be nested inside the main block as part of the function declarations. A C program consists of special headers, the return data types, the main function identifiers, and the **main function block:**

> **int** main (optional parameters);
> {   main function block
> }

Data Types

C supports various primitive types, including **void, byte, int, short, long, float, double,** and **char.**

Additional types may be defined and declared as *enumerated types.* These are simple, indivisible types.

C also supports the following structured types: arrays, structures, sets, and files. Arrays are *n*-dimensional tables of values of any single type, simple, structured, or pointer, indexed by a simple type. Structures are organizations made up of fields of primitive and structured types, as defined by the programmer, and accessed by field name. Sets are groups of similar type used during special operations. Files are sequentially accessible collections of any type. Finally, C supports pointer types. A pointer variable points to a dynamically allocated variable of any type.

Statements

C supports the following types of statements. All statements conclude with a semicolon (;):

> *assignment statements*
>
> *compound statements*
>
> *program flow statements*

...and so on.

terminal symbol set. It would not be hard to define programming language symbols in these terms if we wish. For example, the nonterminal symbol variable could be defined by the following set of syntax rules:

1. *variable* is defined by *letter* followed by 0 or more instances of letter or *number-digit* or *underscore-symbol.*

2. *letter* is defined by a or b or c or d or ... or z.

3. *number-digit* is defined by 0 or 1 or 2 or 3 or ... or 9.

In this example, *variable, letter,* and *number-digit* are nonterminal symbols. In each case, the rule defines a nonterminal symbol in terms of terminal symbols and nonterminal symbols.

This is the approach we're going to take, but we're going to loosen up the definitions a bit. For our purposes, we will define a **token** as the smallest group of character symbols that has a specific meaning within the language and that would not normally be broken down further. Thus, in C, the single characters +, -, =, <, {, and ; are examples of tokens. So are the multiple character symbols +=, !=, and &&. Keywords such as while, int, and static are also tokens. Many authors also use these tokens as though they were terminal symbols. We shall do the same.

We will also consider legal identifiers such as labels, variables, constants, procedure names, and the like to be tokens, since there is no practical reason to break them down any further once they are identified as such. Although these identifiers are technically nonterminal symbols, we will not usually attempt to break them down any further.

Finally, we will proceed to give names to recognizable syntactic constructions (that is, particular combinations of tokens) within the language. These names will be known as *nonterminals* or *nonterminal symbols. if-else-statement* and *boolean-expression* are examples of nonterminals. As we have already hinted, each syntax rule will define one nonterminal symbol in terms of tokens and nonterminal symbols. Each rule is known as a **production.** All possible instances of the language (i.e., every possible legitimate sentence) can be produced by combining the productions in appropriate ways. One production, usually the first one listed, is known as the **starting production.** The grammar as a whole starts from this production. It is also useful to remember that these productions operate on strings of alphanumeric and punctuation characters, just as in English.

Now we will represent these productions as a set of diagrams known as **syntax diagram.** These diagrams are also sometimes known as **railroad diagrams** because of their similarity to railroad tracks. On the diagrams, tokens are identified by being enclosed in a circle. Nonterminals are enclosed in rectangles. Arrows specify the direction of flow. Splits in the flow indicate that either path may be taken, and flows that circle back upon themselves can be repeated as many times as necessary.

Each diagram has an entrance label that consists of a nonterminal symbol. Following the diagram from entrance to exit defines the particular nonterminal. In fact, every possible legal definition for the nonterminal symbol may be determined by tracing every possible path through the diagram. (Of course, there may be an infinite number of possibilities!) More importantly, we (or a compiler program) can establish the legality of a code fragment by finding a path from entrance to exit that matches the fragment.

As a simple example, reconsider the grammar rules that define a line of Little Man assembly language code, shown, this time, as a set of syntax diagrams. (As an exercise, you might choose to reduce these diagrams to a single diagram that represents the entire grammar identically.)

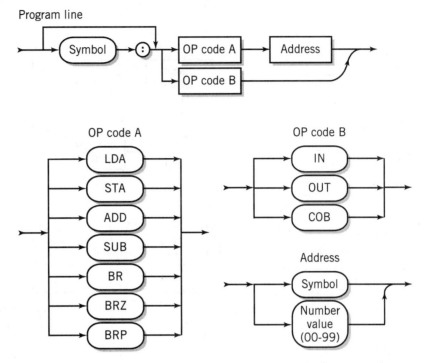

As another example, here is the diagram for the Java nonterminal symbol *if-else-statement:*

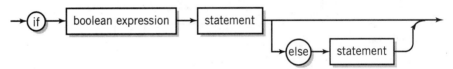

Following the arrows, you can see that an if-then-else statement starts with the keyword token **if.** A nonterminal, *boolean-expression,* follows. The path next leads us to the nonterminal *statement.* At this point, we can follow one path directly to the exit, or the other path, which includes the **else** token and the *statement* nonterminal. This shows that the else-clause is optional.

A small portion of the production set of Java railroad diagrams is shown in Figure 17.15. The starting production is the one entitled *CompilationUnit.* You should trace through some of these to assure that you understand how the railroad diagrams work.

Incidentally, you should notice that the productions are inherently recursive. The production for an if-else statement includes the nonterminal symbol statement. But the production for a statement includes *if-else-statement* as one of its options.

Obviously you couldn't do so, but at least you should be able to see that tracing every possible path of a grammar beginning from the start production will describe every legal instance of the language. Stated differently, if you can't trace the path of a particular program using the appropriate production rules, then the program *can't* be legal because it

FIGURE 17.15

Partial Set of Java Railroad Diagram Productions

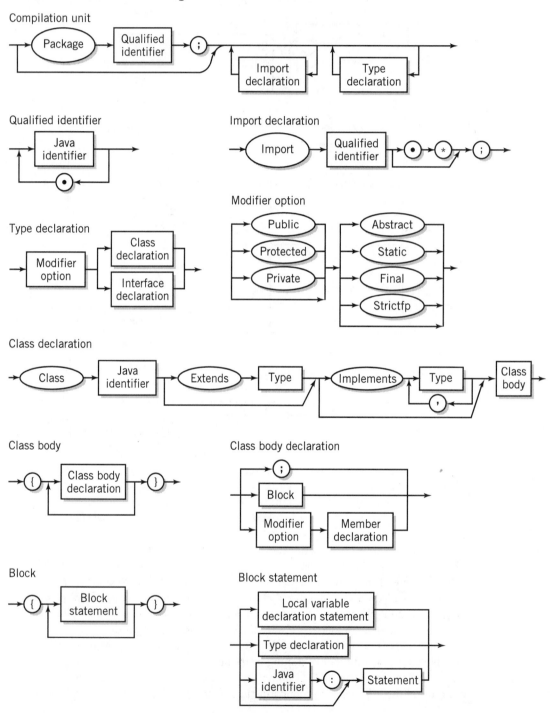

FIGURE 17.15

Partial Set of Java Railroad Diagram Productions (continued)

Statement

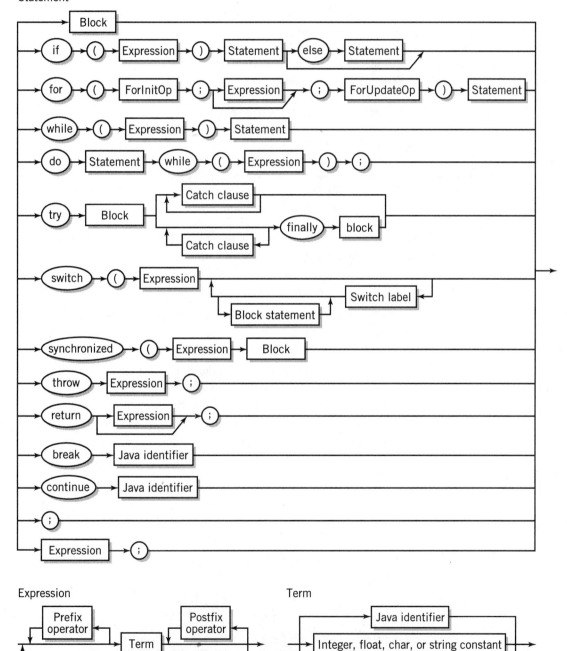

Expression

Term

does not follow the syntax rules for the language. In a few cases, the converse is not true. Semantic rules must also be applied to the code. Semantically, certain combinations are not possible. Also, some rules must be applied in a particular order.

Each of the production rules can be reduced to some machine language code. The goal of the compiler is to reduce a program by substituting appropriate productions for nonterminals until only tokens remain, then noticing which productions were used in the reduction, and in what order. Then, binary program code can be substituted for each production. This process, called parsing, is similar to the English language parsing that we discussed earlier. Parsing is discussed more a bit later in this section.

BACKUS-NAUR FORM   The third, and most precise, common method for describing the grammar of a computer language is known as the **Backus-Naur form** of description, or **BNF.** BNF is also known as context-free grammar.

Again, the rules of the language are defined by terminal (or token) and nonterminal symbols. Again the syntax of the language is made up of productions that define each nonterminal symbol as a combination of terminal and nonterminal symbols. And, again, the BNF productions are used by replacing each nonterminal symbol by its definition until only terminal symbols remain.

There are several slightly different notations used for BNF productions. Here are the definitions for the notation that we have adopted:

the symbol	means:
—>	is defined, or, is replaced by
|	or. For example, A | B means select either A or B
<name>	nonterminal symbol
symbols	terminal symbols reproduced exactly as is
[symbols]	symbols within [ ] are optional. For example, [*<name>*] means that the nonterminal symbol *name* is optional
{symbols}	the symbols within the { } are repeated 0 or more times

Figure 17.16 shows a few of the BNF productions that define Java. Again, you should trace through some of the productions to assure that you understand how the BNF works.

FIGURE 17.16

Typical BNF Rules for Java

```
<compilation-unit> —>[package <qualified-identifier> ; ] {import-declaration}{type-declaration} .
<qualified-identifier —> <Java-identifier> { . <Java-identifier> } .
<import-declaration —>import <qualified-identifier> [ . * ] .
<Java-identifier> —> <J Letter>{<J Letter>|<digit>} .
<J Letter> —> A | B | C.. | Y | Z | a | b | c.. | z | _ | $ .
<digit> —> 0 | 1 | 2 | 3 | 4 | 5 | 6 | 7 | 8 | 9 .
<type-declaration> –><modifier-option> <class-declaration>|<interface-declaration> .
```

There are 82 productions in all listed for Java. If you are interested, you can find the complete set in [GOSL00]. (The list in [GOSL00] is *almost* complete. It is known to be missing some productions, and has some errors as well.)

SEMANTIC ISSUES   Even in cases where the syntax can be described precisely, there are issues that require additional description. Some of these could be interpreted as semantic rules, and some as lexical rules, but all reflect the interrelationship between the three. For example, the length of a variable is usually interpreted as a lexical rule, but the compiler must, at some point, check to assure that the rule has been met. Semantic rules include the fact that a variable must be declared (in many languages) before being used; establish which operation (real or integer) to use in the case of arithmetic expression evaluations; determine type casting requirements; establish the order of evaluation in expressions, including establishing shortcutting priorities and rules for expressions connected by Boolean logic; make sure an array isn't addressed by a real subscript; resolve ambiguities in if-else statements; and so on. Note, too, that tokens have different meanings depending on their context: the period token can mean the end of a program or a decimal point, the = symbol can stand alone or joined to other symbols and can mean assignment or comparison. Again, notice the similarity to the different meanings of words in English.

Generally, it is much more difficult to specify the semantics of a language in a precise form than it is to specify the syntax. Semantic rules are usually described in English. Well-designed third-generation languages avoid the problem that this causes by defining the semantics very narrowly, so that a syntactically correct program can be easily tested for semantic correctness by applying a small number of rules. Natural languages and program-generating languages suffer much more from this difficulty because they require interpretation of a broad group of English-based semantic rules.

The Compilation Process

The compilation process is normally broken down into four major steps. These steps are similar to, but considerably more complex and difficult than the steps used in the assembly process. The compilation process is the subject of much advanced research, and it is not the intention of this book to explore compilation in detail. There are many excellent references available for that purpose. For our purposes a basic overview is sufficient.

Figure 17.17 shows a block diagram for the compilation process. As in the assembler, the source program is considered as a stream of text characters. As a first step, the source program character stream is scanned. This step is known as **lexical analysis** or *scanning*. In this step, the text is broken down into the smallest possible meaningful language components. These will consist of the terminal symbols of the particular programming language, number constants, and identifiers

FIGURE 17.17

The Compilation Process

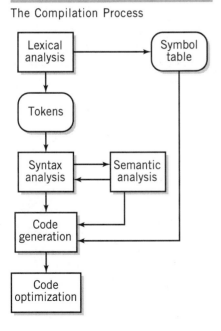

such as labels and variable names. A symbol table will be built of the various identifiers used in the program. The various tokens will be stored as a compact replacement for the original text.

As an example, consider the following snippet of Java source code:

```
if (y == (x + 5)) {
    a = b + (c/d - 18);
    if (q)
            a = b - (c/d - 18);
}
```

The lexical analyzer will reduce this code to a sequence of tokens

```
if-token - (-token - variable token [y] - comparative token
[==] etc.
```

and a symbol table that defines the variable tokens *a, b ,c, d, q, x,* and *y,* as well as comparative tokens, algebraic tokens, and the like.

Once lexical analysis is complete, the compiler moves to the syntax analysis stage. The purpose of the syntax analysis stage is to parse the result of the lexical analysis into its individual productions. There are various methods for parsing in use. One well-established technique is called **recursive descent.** This technique is easily illustrated using railroad diagrams. Part of the parsing for the code snippet, for example, is shown in Figure 17.18. The procedure begins at the beginning of the program code. Each time a rectangular block is encountered, the technique descends a level and attempts to match the block, using its diagram. When there are multiple alternative possibilities, the technique selects one. It is sometimes necessary to back up and try a different path. Syntax analysis is the most difficult part of the compilation process. Further discussion of parsing techniques is beyond the scope of this textbook. It will help clarify your understanding if you trace the parsing in Figure 17.18 with Figure 17.16 as your guide.

Figure 17.17 shows that the semantic analysis stage is usually coactive at the time of the syntax analysis. This means, for example, that in our snippet of Java, the syntax analyzer can verify that *q* is, indeed, declared to be a Boolean variable and that there are no data type inconsistencies within the assignment statements.

FIGURE 17.18

Recursive Descent Parsing

Statement

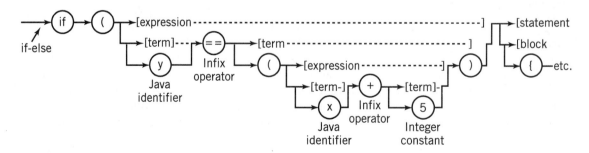

Parsing in the face of programming errors can be very difficult. A programming error can cause the parser to wander into an incorrect production and become confused. This can cause the compiler to generate a large number of errors, where, in fact, only a single error exists. Some compilers, including Visual C++ and others, stop when they encounter an error and require that the error be fixed before proceeding. Other compilers attempt to parse the remainder of the program, using familiar keywords as places to return to the correct production path. Although these compilers may generate many spurious errors, with careful interpretation, they can sometimes allow the programmer to fix several actual errors at one time, thereby speeding up the debugging process.

During the **code generation** step, memory locations and registers will be assigned to the various data objects, that is, the various variables, arrays, and other items of data, and code will be generated for each of the productions identified during the syntax and semantic steps. The code will include necessary run-time support routines for performing such run-time operations as range checking on array subscripts, and so on.

Finally, most compilers will perform one or more **optimization** steps, in which the code is analyzed to determine if there are ways to reduce the amount of code, to eliminate repeated operations, to reorganize parts of the program to execute faster and more efficiently, and to use the computer's resources more effectively. We could give many examples here, but a particularly simple example is the case of a calculation that is repeated within the body of a loop that does not use any value that is modified by the loop. The optimizer would move the code outside of the loop and execute it once. There are many other examples.

Optimization steps are of particular importance in modern CPUs, where pipelining and instruction design can affect the order in which instructions are performed. For example, if the instructions are in a pipeline, the compiler would attempt to perform the instructions in such a way that a later one does not need to wait for data from a previous one. By separating the instructions, the pipeline can be made more effective. With RISC and superscalar computers, in particular, the optimizing compiler becomes essential to the performance of the system. With these CPUs, certain combinations of instructions can cause delays that require special care or, even, errors. In Chapter 8, we noted that the Transmeta Crusoe and Intel Itanium *require* that the binary code meet processor guidelines to assure correct results. The optimizing compiler is specifically designed to prevent and eliminate these trouble spots.

The parsing technique, code generation process, and quality of optimization performed by a compiler can have a major effect on the size and execution speed of the resulting machine language program code. Different compilers may produce very different results. The careful selection of a compiler is an important consideration in the system development process.

Interpreters

High-level procedural languages may be compiled, or they may be interpreted. A compiler operates on the entire program, translating it in its entirety and providing a permanent binary module representing the program. Once compiled, the program may be executed directly and repeatedly from the binary program. The program would be recompiled only if the source code is modified. An interpreter translates source code and executes it, one source code program line at a time. Thus, if a program contains an assignment statement within a loop, and the loop is executed 300 times, the assignment statement will be translated (and executed) 300 times. Obviously, this is less efficient than translating the statement once, and the additional translation process will cause interpreted code to execute much more slowly than compiled code.

There is an important advantage to interpretation, however. When a program is to be executed only once or twice, or when a program is frequently modified, it is easier and faster not to have to perform the compilation process in order to run the program. It is also a useful way to "try out" source program code quickly when building a new program.

There are two special considerations that apply to interpreted languages that differ from compiled languages.

1. The grammars for interpreters must be designed in such a way that each line may be translated and executed independently of other lines in the program. This places important restrictions on the design of the language, including simplified syntax requirements and additional rules, such as layout rules that specify which components of multipart statements like **if-then-else** statements are to be placed on different lines, or at least clearly separated into individual clauses.

EXAMPLE

In many versions of Basic, an **if-then-else** statement must be divided up as follows:

```
if condition1 then             line 1
    [statementblock-1]         lines 2..k
[elseif condition2 then        line k+1
    [statementblock-2]...]     lines (k+2)..m
[else                          line m+1
    [statementblock-n]         lines m..(n-1)
endif                          line n
```

The statement components within brackets [ ] are optional. (Alternatively, the entire statement may be placed on a single line.)

This placement allows the interpreter to determine easily the start of each statement block. If the condition is false, for example, the interpreter simply skips lines until it encounters a line that begins with **elseif, else,** or **endif.** Note, too, that the **endif** token explicitly separates the **if-then-else** statement from following statements in the program.

As a further restriction, notice that the individual statements that make up a statement block are located on separate lines, or separated by colons, and thus are easily separable and identifiable.

Finally, notice that the condition clauses are explicitly terminated by a **then** token that simplifies evaluation of the condition.

This example shows clearly how the language is designed to separate the statements of the language into manageable clauses for interpretation.

---

2. The translation process for interpreters is simplified, since the code does not need to be generalized for different possible conditions. Assignment statements can be executed more simply, for example, because the actual numeric values of the various variable identifiers are known at the time of translation and can be calculated as though they were numeric constants.

In the preceding example, for instance, there is no need to translate the statements within the statement blocks that are bypassed during the **if-then-else** operation, since the condition has already been evaluated, and its results are known.

Together, these two considerations mean that the formal translation procedures required for compilation are not required for interpretation. Instead, a simplified line-by-line combination translator/executor is provided. We will not consider the interpreter further in this chapter, but you should be able to picture simplified versions of the compilation process that would perform the required interpretation steps.

Just-in-Time Compilation

Just-in-time compilation is a technique that attempts to combine the best features of the interpreter with those of the compiler.

Like an interpreter, the just-in-time compiler springs into action at the time the program is presented for execution. However, instead of line-by-line interpretation, the JIT compiler creates binary code on the fly, and saves it, so that code does need to be re-created each time a section of code is executed.

Better still, as the code executes, the JIT compiler attempts to optimize the code so that it will execute faster as it runs. The optimized code can be saved for future use.

JIT compilation is a recent development that requires the processing power of modern computers to be effective.

17.5 LINKING AND LOADING

Although student programs can often be compiled as a single module, most real-world programs are large and must be compiled in several separate pieces. For example, a program might be written as a collection of objects and compiled separately by different programmers. In fact, the Java productions illustration in Figure 17.15 started with the production *Compilation Unit*. A Java program might contain numerous compilation units. Ultimately, the binary code for each piece must be tied together to form a single executable program.

Virtually every program also requires the use of **libraries,** collections of prewritten functions and subroutines that are made available to perform commonly required activities. These library functions perform such common tasks as keyboard entry and display routines, file input and output, type conversions, common mathematical functions, run-time support, and many other activities. Even a simple program that prints "Hello, World" requires a library routine to perform the screen display!

Expected growth in the use of distributed objects and components requires the capability to load and integrate these objects to form executable programs, whether the objects are executed locally or remotely.

This means that at the completion of the translation process, the binary code for any useful program is not executable, because there are references to external subroutines and functions that are unresolved. Each of the various program pieces is known as an **object module.** The task of collecting together the object modules and combining them into an executable program is known as **linking** or, sometimes, as **binding.** In addition to assigning memory space to each of the required program pieces, linking also ties together the required subroutine, function, and object method calls and their returns, and variable and other symbol references.

There are four different times at which linking operations may take place.

- At the conclusion of program development.

    In this case, the programmer or programming team combine all of the program modules in source form into a single unit, then compile or assemble them together directly into a binary executable program. There is no linking operation, per se.

    Although this method creates highly efficient executable programs, it is impractical except for small programs, preferably written in assembly language. Any libraries and other outside routines to be included must be available in source code form, which is often not the case. Large programs written in high-level languages would require considerable compilation time, and the entire process would have to be repeated each time a modification or bug fix takes place.

    This technique is rarely used today except, occasionally, by hot-shot programmers for small utility programs.

- At compile or assembly time.

    This procedure takes all of the required object modules and required object libraries and links them into an executable binary program. A separate **linking editor** is used for this purpose.

    The linking operation is fairly straightforward. Output from the translation program for each module includes a symbol table of known locations within the module and a table of unresolved external references for that module, commonly known as a *patch list*. These external references may consist of subroutine or function calls and returns or references to data to be found in another module. Some systems may also include branches to points in other modules. The linkage process consists of merging the programs and data spaces of the various modules into a single *load module* and then patching the program to connect the required points, using the patch lists and symbol tables from the various modules to identify and locate the required connections. In addition, the addresses of various instructions must be adjusted to compensate for the relative location of each module in the merged program. The result is a **static** executable program, so called because the final form of the binary code is completely established before it is loaded and executed. This procedure is also known as **early binding.**

    Linking at compile time results in an efficient executable program. There are certain potential drawbacks, however. First, the libraries and outside objects must be available as object modules at link time. This is commonly the case if the program is being linked on the machine where it will eventually be executed. However, early binding prevents any modifications at load-and-execute time. In particular, the program is designed to work with a specific set of I/O device drivers, using the libraries available on a particular system. If the program is to be run on different machines with different system characteristics, or even with different I/O devices on the same machine, the procedure yields unsuitable results. To compensate for this shortcoming, a **program installation** procedure can be used to create new linkages when the program is moved to different machines. For programs that will be used regularly under steady-state conditions, this method is highly suitable.

■ At **run time.**

In this case, the linking and loading operations are combined into a single program tool known as a **linking loader,** which loads each module, links them, and starts program execution. The obvious advantage of this method is the flexibility gained. Linkages are made to the appropriate libraries, I/O drivers, and other objects at the time the program is to be executed. Furthermore, the objects can be shared with other programs. The linkages can be made to point to the object already in memory, lessening memory usage. This technique is known as **late binding.**

There are two potential drawbacks to this method. First, a missing or incompatible version of an object will prevent the program from executing. Second, the time required to create the executable program will cause the program to load more slowly, particularly if the program is large. This can be an annoyance for the users.

■ During program execution, as each object is required.

This method is most flexible. It allows objects to be selected and used during the course of program execution. For example, a user print request can be directed to whichever printer the user selects. If already present in memory, objects can be shared. If not, they can be loaded as needed. They can even be accessed across a network. The executable program is loaded in parts and linked **dynamically.** Memory is only required for those parts of the program actually being used. Of course, this process offers binding at the latest possible moment. Many current operating systems offer their API services as **dynamic load libraries,** or DLLs. Additionally, a program may provide its own DLL files. The initial installation process places the program and its DLLs into appropriate file directories and confirms the presence and location of other DLLs that may be required for program execution.

The downside to dynamic linking is program execution speed. At run time, and whenever a new module must be loaded, the user will have to wait until the process is completed to continue her work. Nonetheless, this method is preferred for most modern applications, because of the flexibility.

A slight complicating factor in the linkage process is the necessity for providing a standardized method to pass function and subroutine arguments between different modules, especially when the modules are accessed across a network. Most programming systems conform to a standard method for argument passing that is used by the various compilers and libraries included with the system. The compilers then provide the necessary programming code to handle this situation automatically during translation. Assembly language programmers must provide the required code explicitly as part of their programs in order for the linkages to perform properly during execution. Initiatives such as .NET, .DCOM, and CORBA attempt to provide uniform standards between different systems on a network.

During loading, the loader module may be required to perform a **relocation** operation on some instructions. You have already seen that the location of a program in memory is normally determined by the operating system at load time, and can change each time the program is executed. This makes it necessary to adjust the addresses within instructions, so that they properly point to data and to branch locations. In instruction sets with relative addressing, and when virtual memory is used, there is very little or no relocation required. Absolute addresses, on the other hand, almost always need relocation adjustment. The symbol table for an object module contains additional information identifying the instructions that must be adjusted. Adjustment is part of the object loading process.

Donovan [DON75] identifies four basic steps in the operation of a linking loader:

1. Allocate space in memory for the programs (allocation).
2. Resolve symbolic references between objects (linking).
3. Adjust all address dependent locations to correspond to their allocated spaces (relocation).
4. Physically place the machine instructions and data into memory (loading).

17.6 DEBUGGERS

The final component required for program development is the debugger. Debugger programs can read the symbol table of the program being debugged and can, thus, identify object entry and exit points, the location of variables, and the like. Some debugger programs work only with machine or assembly language. To use these with a program written in high-level language, the user must understand the relationship between the original language and the code generated by its compiler. A low-level debugger allows the user to run her program a step at a time, to set breakpoints that will suspend the program when a particular line of code is executed, to change the values in registers and memory locations, and to perform many other functions, but the user must understand the code in assembly language form.

Most modern debuggers are called **source-level debuggers** because they are capable of identifying the code that corresponds to high-level language statements, making it unnecessary for the user to work with the underlying machine code. Source-level debugger programs provide similar functions as the machine-level debugger, except that the programmer works with source code. They can track and print the values of variables. They can step through a program, one source line at a time, or they can suspend execution of the program when a particular statement is executed or when a particular variable is accessed, or even when a variable takes on a value within a particular range of values. Control is then returned to the programmer. The programmer can look at and modify variable values, can restart the program where it was suspended, and can perform many other functions that aid the programmer in assuring the correct operation of the program.

SUMMARY AND REVIEW

Programs are developed using a set of program development tools. The primary tools are editors, assemblers, compilers, interpreters, linking loaders or link editors, and debuggers. Program editors are similar to word processors, but focus more directly on the needs of a programmer to enter program source code. There are both line and screen editors available.

Almost no one writes program code in machine language today. Assembly language is close to machine language, but it allows more readability and more flexibility when making corrections. Assembly language substitutes symbolic names for both op codes and addresses. The assembler converts assembly language to machine language. Even assembly language is fairly rare today.

Most programs today are written in high-level languages. High-level languages have many similarities to written and spoken languages, such as English. HLLs have syntactic and semantic rules and can be described by a grammar. Description grammars include railroad diagrams, BNF, and narrative descriptions.

Compilers and interpreters convert high-level language to machine language, using a process that parses the source code, then analyzes it syntactically and semantically in order to generate appropriate machine language. Compilers translate an entire program at once, whereas interpreters translate and execute on a line-by-line basis. Many compilers also attempt to optimize the code for performance.

Debuggers allow the programmer to execute the code in such a way as to determine where errors have occurred. Some debuggers operate on the machine language code, but most debuggers today can work with the original source code.

KEY CONCEPTS AND TERMS

assembler
assembler directive
assembly language
Backus-Naur form (BNF)
binary dump
compilers
cross-assembler
debugger
dynamic (executable)
dynamic load library
  (DLL)
early binding
editor
fourth-generation
  language
grammar
grampa
high-level languages
integrated development
  environment (IDE)

interpreter
just-in-time compilation
label
late binding
lexical analysis
library
linking
linking editor
linking loader
loader
macro
macro-assembler
natural languages
nonprocedural languages
nonterminal symbol
object module
operations table
parsing
preprocessor
procedural language

production
program generator
pseudo-op codes
railroad diagram
recursive descent
relocation
run time
scanning
semantic analysis
source code
static (executable)
symbol table
syntactic analysis
syntax
syntax diagram
terminal symbols
token

FOR FURTHER READING

The material in this chapter is discussed in books and articles representing a number of different areas of computing, including books on computer science, programming languages, system software, compiler theory, as well as linguistics, and, yes, English grammar. A simple introduction to program translation in general can be found in Decker and Hirshfield [DECK98]. MacCabe [MACC93] deals with the assembly, linking, and loading process in quite some detail. Marcellus [MARC84] and Ellzey [ELLZ87] provide excellent, in-depth, treatments of all aspects of system programming. A thorough description of Java can be found in Gosling [GOSL00]. Cooper [COOP83] and Jensen and Wirth [JENS74] describe Pascal syntax and semantics and show both the BNF and railroad diagrams for that language. In addition, there are many books that treat assembly language and the assembler process from the point of view of particular machines. These include Bailes and Riser [BAIL87] for the IBM 370 series, Kapps and Stafford [KAPP85], and Brumm and Brumm [BRUM89] among others. These books provide an understanding of architecture as well as of assembly language. Arguably the classic description of compilers is found in the book by Aho, Sethi, and Ullman [AHO86], known lovingly by generations of students as "the Dragon Book." A new edition is scheduled for mid-2003.

EXERCISES

17.1 Using your favorite Visual programming language, write a simple screen editor. Your editor will allow the user to enter, print, and modify text, using the following commands:

Clicking the mouse inserts text at the current location. Note that every line ends with a carriage return. No wraparound is provided.

A menu option quits the editor, and saves and loads files in text form. (No special characters.)

17.2 Describe the major differences between program screen editors and word processors, and explain the reason for each difference.

17.3 Suppose you were going to design an editor special for the writing of programs in your favorite language. What features would you include in this editor that would ease the entry and checking of the code?

17.4 The UNIX operating system provides an editor in which editing operations are performed without user interaction. Input text for the editor generally comes from a file or is piped from another program. The output is either shown on the screen or returned to a file. We emphasize that there is no user interaction with this editor while it is operating. Instead, the editor just "does its thing." Such an editor is known in UNIX as a stream editor, because it operates on a stream of text. Describe situations for which a stream editor would be a useful tool.

17.5 *vi* is a fairly primitive UNIX editor, and yet some users have a strong preference for it over other, easier-to-use editors. Can you think of some reasons why this might be the case, other than it's what they're used to?

17.6   Assemble by hand the following Little Man assembly program. Show both the code and the symbol table:

```
START:    INP
          STA    COUNT
          LDA    ZERO
          STA    SUM
AGAIN:    INP
          ADD    SUM
          STA    SUM
          LDA    COUNT
          SUB    ONE
          STA    COUNT
          BRZ    DONE
          BR     AGAIN
DONE:     OUT
          COB
ONE:      DAT    1
ZERO:     DAT    0
COUNT:
SUM:
```

17.7   The PDP-8 computer used an instruction that was 12 bits long, with a 3-bit op code and a 9-bit address. Every instruction was a single 12-bit word long. Assume the following op code table for the PDP-8 (Codes and addresses are expressed in octal.):

```
op code                            instruction
    0      AND
    1      TAD
    2      ISZ
    3      DCA
    4      JMS
    5      JMP
    6      IOT
    7      conditionals. Where more than one is specified, the
           address codes are added to get the result.
           Therefore, rar cll would have a code of 010 + 200 =
           7210.
           CLA   7100 clear accumulator
           CLL   7200 clear link flag
           RAL   7004 rotate accumulator left one bit
           RAR   7010 rotate accumulator right one bit
           HLT   7402 halt
           SNL   7420 skip if link is set (nonzero link)
```

Assemble by hand the PDP-8 code shown in Figure 17.12. Show the machine code and the symbol table. Is there something missing in the code? Make a reasonable assumption in order to complete the assignment. Assume that the code will load at location 0.

17.8   This problem illustrates the steps involved in parsing and code generation. Assume that you are given the simplified C or Java railroad diagrams shown here:

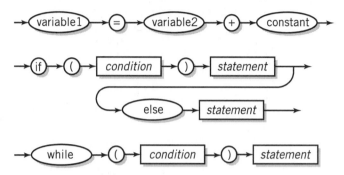

a.   Create Little Man code that will satisfy each of these simplified Pascal railroad diagrams. Assume that the value "1" represents the condition true and "0" is false. When you generate the code, leave space for rectangular blocks to be filled in later. Remember that a while loop checks the condition first and then performs the loop body before checking again.

b.   Now parse the following program snippet, and create the Little Man code that will represent the program snippet.

```
value = 5;
test = true;
while (test = true) {
   value = value - 2;
   if (value < 0)
           test = false;
};
```

17.9   a.   You are given the following railroad diagram. Describe in English the ground rules for an identifier in this language. You may assume that a letter is A–Z and a number is 0–9.

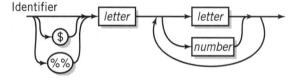

b.   Show the BNF rules for this type of identifier.

17.10   Using the railroad diagram as a starting point, generate the BNF rules for an assignment statement.

17.11   The railroad syntax diagrams in Figure E17.1 partially describe a language similar to, but definitely not the same as Pascal. For each of the code snippets presented, either indicate that the snippet will compile correctly, or identify the token in the snippet where the failure occurs. Spaces and carriage returns are ignored by the compiler and are included just for clarity.

FIGURE E17.1

Railroad Syntax Diagrams for Exercise 17.11

statement:

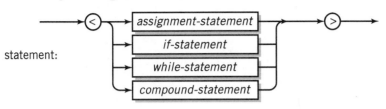

assignment-statement:

if-statement:

while-statement:

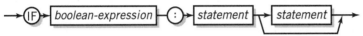

compound-statement:

arithmetic-expression:

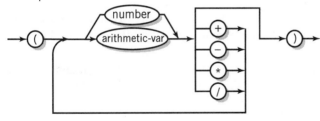

boolean-expression:

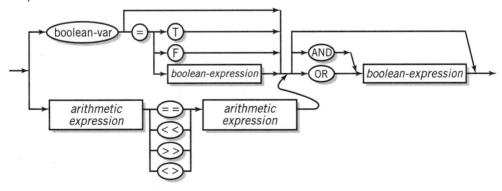

a. `< NUMVAR1 =: (NUM5 + NUM6)>`
   `<NUMVAR2 =: (NUM12/ (NUM15 + 5))>`

b. `< IF BOOL1:`
   `<< NUM1 =: (25)>`
   `< IF BOOL2 = F:`
   `< NUM2 =: (15 + NUM5) >>>`
   `< NUM3 =: (15 * NUM4) >`

c. `< WHILE (NUM + 2) < (0) OR BOOL2 = T:`
   `NUMB =: NUMB + 1 >`

17.12 a. What advantages do assembly language programs have over those written in a high-level language?

b. Suppose you could write a program using a mixture of high level and assembly language. Which segments of your program would you choose to write in assembly language? Why?

17.13 a. Under what conditions would you choose to use a high-level language interpreter rather than a compiler?

b. Under what conditions would you select a compiler over an interpreter?

c. Suppose you are involved in a major program development project and have available both a compiler and an interpreter for the language you are using. Describe a reasonable development procedure that would take advantage of the fact that both tools are available.

17.14 Relocate the program in Exercise 17.6 so that it loads starting at location 50. Indicate which instructions must change, and show their new values.

17.15 Consider the steps that you go through in order to debug a Java (or other language) program. What features would you consider important in a source-level debugger?

17.16 Suppose you had a system that could link different objects at different binding times. What types of objects might you bind early? Which at load time? Which during execution?

THREE OPERATING SYSTEMS

DILBERT reprinted by permission of United Feature Syndicate, Inc.

18.0 INTRODUCTION

The design of an operating system reflects the nature of the system, the philosophy and goals of its designers, the architecture of the hardware, and the needs of its users. As you have seen in the previous five chapters, there are many different types of operating systems.

Along the way we have used the features of several operating systems to illustrate many of the concepts that we introduced. In this chapter we conclude our discussion of operating systems with more substantial examples, representing three very different approaches to operating system design. Each of these systems was designed for a different purpose, to meet different goals and user needs. Each is important within its own type of computing environment.

Microsoft Windows 2000 and Windows XP are the current implementations of the Microsoft Windows professional operating system environment. They are intended to support the needs of a wide range of users, from the individual user working with simple productivity tools on a personal computer to the large enterprise requiring the varied network services, Web services, transaction processing, database, and other corporate information needs supplied by a powerful processing facility. Windows 2000 and Windows XP provide a graphical user interface, graphical tools, networking capability, and a powerful set of API functions, all supported by a highly reliable and secure environment. Windows 2000 and Windows XP run on X86 hardware platforms with Pentium-level and higher CPUs. We selected Windows as an example, not simply because of the predominance of Windows in the marketplace, but also because it implements most of the features that we have discussed in the last several chapters.

UNIX is a powerful, multitasking operating system. It combines powerful, flexible user tools and commands with built-in capability for networking, distributed processing, multiuser time sharing, and groupwork processing. Programming and text processing tools are integrated into the user interface of the system. All of this power and versatility make it the system of first choice for many programmers and knowledgeable computer users, even though a UNIX system is initially more difficult to learn and use than a Macintosh or Windows system.

The UNIX name itself is a registered product of the Open Group, which specifies a UNIX standard, and tests for conformance to that standard. The Open Group is an organization supported by a large group of major computer manufacturers. Hewlett-Packard HP-UX, IBM AIX, and Sun Solaris are among many products that conform to the UNIX specification. As a result of this effort, UNIX is the closest thing we have to a universal portable operating system. In addition, there are a number of UNIX "clones." Linux and FreeBSD are the best known of these.

All these factors—compatibility and portability between different systems, useful productivity tools, built-in groupwork features, reliable, effortless networking, long-term stability, interactive multiuser capability, and powerful scalability—provide important advantages to business, especially in the era of e-business and intercorporate connectivity. The use of UNIX has continued to grow, even though the basic system is more than thirty years old. We selected UNIX to illustrate the factors and features that are representative of a powerful, flexible, and well-rounded operating system. Because of its growing importance in the business environment, particularly for Web-based services, we have chosen to focus on Linux as a specific implementation of UNIX-based systems.

z/OS, from IBM, is our third example. As the premier operating system for IBM mainframe computers, it is arguably the most important example of an operating system intended for the support of large complex computer systems. It provides myriad features, as well as powerful support for the wide variety of I/O facilities, CPU multiprocessing, and system interconnection capabilities found on large IBM systems. z/OS evolved from an era in which most computer processing was batch oriented, and has been continually upgraded and adapted to meet the requirements for modern large-scale business processing. Although z/OS provides powerful support for the execution of batch programs, transaction-processing systems, and large database services on large and complex computer systems, it is not well suited for casual interactive personal productivity use at the operating system level. z/OS-based systems require a substantial staff of programmers and operators to be used effectively.

For each example, we present an overview of the system; introduce the design goals, philosophy, and history of the system; discuss the environment provided by the system to its users; and consider the important features, internal architecture, and operating methods of the operating system itself.

It is probably already apparent to you that the systems that we have chosen as examples differ significantly in purpose and approach. Nonetheless, as you read about each of the operating systems discussed in this chapter, it is useful to notice the fundamental similarities between these three very different systems. Each supports multitasking, and each attempts to schedule tasks and manage memory and I/O resources efficiently. Each provides a logical file system and interrupt-based I/O support for the hardware. Each offers dynamic address translation and demand paging for virtual storage. Each provides a multitude of services to application programs and a user interface appropriate to its purpose. For more, read on!

18.1 MICROSOFT WINDOWS 2000 AND WINDOWS XP

Overview, Design Philosophy, and History

Windows XP is the most recent implementation of the predominant operating system for X86-based personal computers. Together, Windows XP and Windows 2000 are a family of powerful, multitasking operating systems with an integrated graphical user interface that operate on high-end Pentium-class personal computer systems. Currently, there are four different levels, or versions, of Windows 2000, each focused on a different user base, plus two levels of Windows XP. All six share a common kernel and set of system services, but each level adds capability not found at lower levels. In comparison with Windows 2000, Windows XP offers an improved user interface, plus new tools, but is essentially similar otherwise. For this discussion, we shall refer to both together as Windows 2000/XP.

Every version of Windows 2000/XP provides a versatile graphical user interface with a rich set of features for users at many different levels of experience, preemptive multitasking, virtual storage support, a file system that supports a number of different file formats, each with its own features and capabilities, powerful network support, access to a large, linear memory space, robust security, and a wide range of API services and support for 32-bit application programs, all of this while maintaining compatibility support for most older 16-bit application programs that were originally written to run under MS-DOS and Windows 3.1.

Windows 2000/XP is ultimately intended to replace two separate lines of operating systems, Windows 9x and Windows NT, which both evolved independently from Windows 3.1, and ultimately from MS-DOS. MS-DOS was originally released to coincide with the introduction of the first IBM PC in 1981. MS-DOS initially was designed for the 8088 and 8086 microprocessor CPUs. The design goals were to provide I/O services and support for standard hardware, a logical file system, and a simple interactive command interface for a single user working at a personal computer.

The limitations of MS-DOS are well known. Its usable address space is limited. It is designed to run in X86 real mode only (you may wish to review the different X86 addressing modes in Chapter 12), and it is limited to single-tasking, 16-bit, operation. It provides no scheduling facility and next-to-no memory management. The user interface has many limitations: file names too short to be descriptive, a command language with little support for batch program operations, and commands that are difficult for the inexperienced user. Each version of MS-DOS added features and capabilities, but many of the original limitations remained until MS-DOS was ultimately retired as a separate operating system in the mid-1990s.

The first release of Windows appeared in 1985. It provided a primitive graphical user interface and attempted to overcome some of the limitations of MS-DOS. However, Windows ran as a shell over MS-DOS, so it was constrained in the services it could provide by 16-bit processing limitations, by the lack of support for memory addresses above 1 megabyte (MB), and by the file system. Since MS-DOS provided no basis for preemptive scheduling, the Windows shell depended upon the cooperation of its application programs to provide limited multitasking capability. If you are familiar with Windows 3.1, you are undoubtedly aware of situations in which you have had to wait some length of time for an "hourglass" operation to complete before the system would even respond to a mouse click. This results from the inability or unwillingness of a program to cede control to Windows. Windows 1.0 was not very popular.

Successive versions of Windows improved the user interface and provided as many amenities as the MS-DOS kernel would allow, including limited use of protected mode addressing, but they were always limited by MS-DOS. Nonetheless, the improvements were sufficient that Windows 3.0 attained huge success and popularity.

Windows 95 was a significant step forward in the evolution of Windows. Most important, it replaced the majority of the MS-DOS backbone with its own integrated operating system kernel. This enabled full access to the range of features available on modern X86 systems, including preemptive multitasking, resource management, scheduling, virtual storage, large memory space, and 32-bit register, operand data, and addressing capability. It also provided a much-improved user interface, plug-and-play hardware installation capability, and long-name file handling. Even so, Windows 9x continued to provide means for the support of earlier MS-DOS and 16-bit Windows application programs. Since there were millions of older application programs in use, this compatibility was an important design goal; however, it was provided at the expense of some awkward compromises in operation and performance.

Windows 98 and Windows ME added a number of features, particularly, improvements to the graphical user interface, support for plug-and-play I/O devices and other new hardware, improved system management tools, and better multimedia performance.

In 1993, Microsoft released two versions of Windows NT 3.1, the first members of a new line of personal computer operating systems targeted for a more sophisticated market. From the outset, Microsoft intended that Windows NT would find application as a network server as well as a personal productivity system. There were two versions of Windows NT 3.1: Windows NT 3.1 and Windows NT 3.1 Advanced Server. Windows NT 3.1 featured the same user interface as that found on Windows 3.1, but offered a completely new 32-bit operating system in place of the MS-DOS-based kernel of Windows 3.1, a new file system called NTFS, intended to meet the stringent requirements of business for reliable, secure file storage, networking support, and many other features required to meet the demands of business. Subsequent releases of Windows NT added a Windows 95-style GUI, improved networking and I/O, added new API services, and increased the overall processing power and stability of the system. The fundamental kernel and executive system design has remained relatively unchanged through each of the releases. Microsoft continued to improve the Windows NT system management tools and enterprise business applications. It also ported Windows NT to Digital, now Compaq, Alpha-based systems. As a result of these efforts, the use of Windows NT-based computers expanded to include the role of network server to increasingly large and sophisticated networks of computers.

Windows 2000 combined the best features of Windows NT and Windows 98. It offered the features and user interface of Windows 98 with the flexibility, power, security, and stability of Windows NT. It was intended to support a wide variety of users and applications, ranging from individual users of personal computers up to enterprise-wide network servers. Windows XP improved the user interface; it improved system stability and security; and it added and upgraded system tools.

There are currently six members in the Windows 2000/XP family. Windows 2000 and Windows XP Professional are intended primarily for users performing productivity tasks on single user, personal computers. They have limited capabilities for use as a network server, but are more suitable for use as standalone systems or network clients. Windows 2000 Server adds support for two-way symmetric multiprocessing and expands the system capability for use as a network server. Windows 2000 Advanced Server provides four-way SMP capability, and supports simple clustering. The most powerful system, Windows 2000 Datacenter Server, provides 16-way SMP. It is intended for large-scale network server applications, such as data warehousing. Windows XP Home Edition is a slightly limited version of the Professional edition.

The primary design goals for Windows NT, and by extension, Windows 2000 and Windows XP, included:

- **Extensibility.** An object-based modular design was chosen to make additions and modifications to the system easier to install, with less concern about interaction between components.

- *Portability.* Windows NT was written in C and C++ so that it could be ported easily to new CPUs. The hardware specific assembly language code is collected into a single hardware module for easy replacement. Although a number of different CPUs have been supported over Windows NT's lifetime, Windows 2000/XP currently supports only Pentium-class X86 and Itanium processors.

- *Reliability.* Windows NT was designed for business and professional use, where reliability is crucial. The kernel architecture is designed to protect itself and applications from internal errors as well as buggy application programs and attempted infiltration. The NTFS file system has built-in recovery procedures to protect files from system crashes and defective disk sectors. Windows 2000/XP also supports clustering with automatic failover and RAID for nonstop processing.

- *Compatibility.* Windows NT was designed to execute legacy programs written under MS-DOS and previous versions of Windows. Windows 2000/XP continues to support most legacy programs. The Windows 2000/XP API includes all of the services provided by other 32-bit Windows APIs, making migration to Windows 2000/XP reasonably straightforward. Windows 2000/XP also supports the addition of other API subsystems that can execute other types of programs, including those that conform to the POSIX standard.

- *Scalability and Performance.* Windows NT supported symmetric multiprocessing and other features designed to provide high performance. Realistically, however, the decision to provide the features of a large system have, until recently, limited the use of Windows NT to high-end X86 processors. Gradually, the X86 hardware architecture has progressed sufficiently to make Windows 2000/XP performance more scalable to larger systems and networks. In practical terms, Windows 2000 Professional requires a minimum of 64 MB of RAM, 1 GB of free disk space, and a 233 MHz Pentium to run acceptably. This effectively prevents its use on older systems. Even more computer power is suggested for Windows XP.

On a more practical level, Windows 2000/XP provides

- A single-user 32-bit or 64-bit operating system with preemptive multitasking capabilities.

- A powerful, but logical, consistent, and intuitive window-and-mouse-based graphical user interface integrated into the operating system. With its integrated Web browser, the interface behaves consistently and nearly transparently for local, network, and Internet use.

- Ability to execute most MS-DOS and older Windows programs as separate processes without modification, including support for 16-bit preemptive multitasking

- Continued evolutionary progress toward a docucentric, or document-oriented, view of processing, in contrast to the present application program approach. This view is intended to allow the user to focus directly upon a document, instead of upon the individual application programs that must be executed to create the document.

- Support for, and management of, the newest capabilities of Pentium-class X86 and Itanium CPUs, including support for multimedia, plug-and-play hardware installation, electrical power conservation management, and new system hardware.

- A file system that preserves compatibility with older Windows and MS-DOS programs and files, but offers an alternative that is more manageable and more secure, with built-in recoverability options. Windows 2000/XP NTFS allows dynamic soft disk partitioning and tree-mountable directory structures.

- An API that provides a wide range of services to simplify the development of application programs and to provide consistent behavior and style from program to program.

- Built-in networking capability for connection to prevalent types of networks, and simple installation for new types of networks and network services that may appear in the near future. A new distributed file system makes access to multiple network servers easy to manage and essentially transparent to the user. Windows 2000/XP also supports the distributed computing environment standard.

- Network server capabilities that provide all the features required for management and support of large networks, including a new distributed directory system that provides large-scale directory services without user intervention. Tools for the remote deployment, setup, and administration of user client systems are provided, including provision for user profiles, user disk quotas, and group data sharing.

These design features reflect the desire to support a range of activities that formerly were provided by two different families of operating system. For the casual end user, the features that made Windows 95 reasonably easy to use are included and improved. The intention is to provide the user with a system that is easy to use and easy to maintain, with little or no outside help, and minimal special skills and knowledge. It should be possible to install new programs and new hardware with little effort. The user interface should be easy to use, and behave similarly from application to application. For consistency, and to simplify application development, many of the difficult tasks that must be performed within application programs are handled by the more than 2000 user interface, file I/O, memory management, device driver, and other service functions that are defined by the Windows 2000/XP API. In addition, the operating system continues to support older programs, while providing increased capability to newer programs. Network and Internet use is enhanced and transparent. System maintenance is simplified.

At the same time, the tools and facilities required to manage and use Windows 2000/XP to control and serve a large network are provided.

Internally, Windows 2000/XP provides the following major features and facilities:

- A full range of graphically based user services, including window manipulation, drag-and-drop operations, drop-down menus, hierarchical file management, and document-based application execution, as well as application program support for the manipulation and control of windows, various kinds of dialog boxes, and mouse operations, including font support, color control, and drawing tools.

- Process control for multitasking, including process creation, communication between processes, and virtual and physical memory allocation, deallocation, and management. Processes may also be grouped into tasks that work together and share system resources. Windows 2000/XP also provides multithreading capability and support. Applications designed to the Windows 2000/XP API can incorporate multiple threads, so that particular tasks can take place in the background while the application continues to execute. For example, a word processor could perform spell checking in the background while the user continues to enter and edit text. CPU dispatch scheduling is performed at the thread level. The communication facilities between programs include object linking and embedding (OLE) services as well as more traditional message passing services.

- File management services, including support for various network formats, as well as standard disk drive and CD-ROM formats, with expansion capability for other formats.

- I/O device drivers and resource drivers for a wide range of peripherals and management of each resource, including access control for resource sharing (for example, spooling for printers), plug-and-play installation capability, and electrical power management.

The User Environment

In keeping with its design goals, the Windows 2000/XP user operates primarily from a graphical user interface. Although the Microsoft design team refers to the interface as a "shell," it is nonetheless an integral part of the operating system. The user interface is designed for ease of use by a novice, but contains a substantial number of tools and utilities that are designed to simplify operations for advanced users as well. A window with an MS-DOS–like command line interface and the Windows Scripting Host are available to the user for more sophisticated operations. The shell supports icon- and menu-based program execution, file manipulation, system configuration and management, and window control. Network support is built in and is nearly transparent to the user in its operations.

In Chapter 14 we discussed some of the important criteria for a graphical user interface. The Windows 2000/XP interface is designed to fulfill these conditions in a number of ways:

- It is simple to use for a novice, but powerful enough for an advanced user. There are usually a number of different ways to perform a particular operation, to suit different user levels of experience and preferences.

- Tools and operations behave in a consistent manner, as do applications that use the API to its full extent.

- Tools and operations perform as a user would reasonably and intuitively expect.

- There is extensive context-sensitive help available at the touch of a button. Reference to a manual is usually unnecessary. The help system even provides shortcuts to alternative ways to complete an operation.

- System parameters that are important to a user can be modified easily on the fly. For example, a single mouse click allows access to various system and application properties, including the system audio volume control, or to the size and font of text on the command line interface.

- Applications have access to the same services and interface features as those provided directly to the user.

Of course, we would be remiss if we did not at least mention that most of the features in the Windows 2000 interface will be immediately familiar to users of the Apple Macintosh and other window-based systems. Similarly, the Windows XP interface will be recognizable by Macintosh OS X users.

When you boot the computer, the computer opens directly into a desktop-based windowing environment. A typical Windows XP start-up screen appears in Figure 18.1. This start-up screen has icons that provide access to the user's basic facilities and a *start* button that can be used immediately to open folders and documents, launch programs, and locate information. Icons represent various window **objects:**[1] programs, documents, folders, files, even drivers for printers and other specialized operations. Double-clicking the mouse on an icon provides an alternative start-up path to the programs, folders, and documents represented by the icons on the screen. The *My Computer* icon opens a folder with the user's high-level directories, represented as disk drives, plus other resources available to the user, including access to the facilities of the Distributed File System and to the Internet.

FIGURE 18.1

Typical Windows XP Start-up Screen

---

[1] We note that the word "object" has a different meaning here than when used as an object in "object-oriented programming." Although the word "object" is used in each case to represent some identifiable entity, the properties of the objects in the two cases are different.

The start-up screen actually serves as a desktop that can hold icons, windows, and other objects. Any element on the screen is considered to be an object. The user can tailor the desktop to his or her own preferences. Figure 18.2 illustrates some of the features of the Windows 2000 desktop in use. The illustration shows two open windows, *My Computer* and *Data\docs*. The folders and disk symbols in the *My Computer* window are icons that can be opened to reveal files and other folders. Folders represent the directories in a tree-based hierarchical directory structure and can be nested to form whatever groupings are convenient for the user. The user can move from window to window to browse.

Each window provides gadgets for resizing and reshaping, for reducing the window to an icon, for closing the window, and if necessary, for scrolling the information within the window. The title bar can be used to move the window around the screen. Drop-down menus provide control appropriate to the contents of the particular window.

The operating system multitasks between the different open windows. Minimized windows are actually open and are also multitasked. When the mouse is moved into the area of a window, that window becomes active for keyboard input. The desktop also provides a task bar for rapid switching of the active window from task to task. The task bar provides a button for each open window, even if the window is minimized or hidden

FIGURE 18.2

A Typical User Desktop

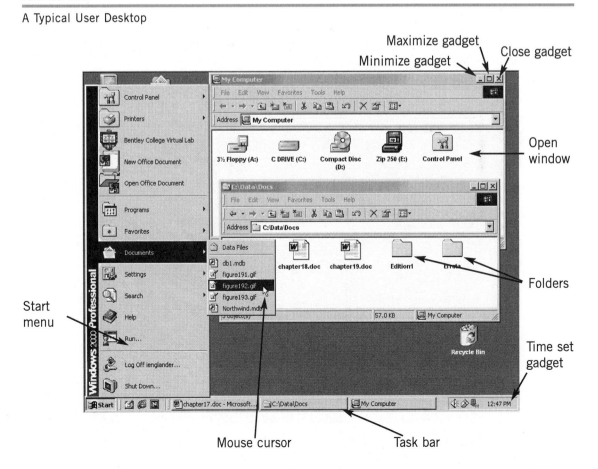

behind other windows. In the illustration just introduced, there are actually three open windows, *My Computer, Data\docs,* and *Microsoft Word,* which is minimized and is not visible in the figure.

At the time that the screenshot in Figure 18.2 was made, the mouse was being used with the start button feature to open a document called *figure192.gif.* Note from the taskbar at the bottom that the operating system associates *Chapter17.doc* with the Microsoft Word word processing application. Clicking on the *Chapter17.doc* icon opens Microsoft Word, and creates an active window with *Chapter17.doc* open and ready to edit.

Windows 2000/XP provides a variety of tools to simplify and standardize operations. The mouse is used with the icons for various purposes. Double-clicking the mouse on an icon is the method commonly used to open windows and start program execution, although Windows 2000/XP also provides menus (and the start button) for this purpose. The mouse is also used to drag-and-drop icons to perform various move and copy operations. Files can be dragged from one folder to another, can be copied to another disk drive, or can be moved to the desktop for convenience. Dropping a file icon on the printer icon will cause the file to be printed. Windows 2000/XP provides a briefcase icon for replicating files between one computer and another, an important feature for business users who must frequently move their work between a desktop and laptop computer. The recycle bin

FIGURE 18.3

Some Useful Windows 2000 Utilities and Capabilities

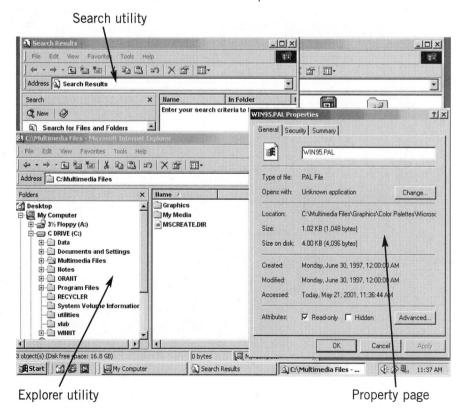

is used to delete files. Clicking the right mouse button on an object brings up a window of information about the object. The system allows users to create "shortcut icons," duplicate icons representing the same object that can be placed in multiple locations for convenience. Shortcut icons represent alternative paths to a particular folder or file.

The system also supports standardized pop-up and drop-down menus, dialog boxes, and various types of controls to simplify the user interface. Controls include sliders, various kinds of selection and ON/OFF buttons, and list-scrolling selectors. An MS-DOS–type command line interface is available for those situations that require special handling.

Windows 2000/XP provides utilities to allow a knowledgeable user to move efficiently around the computer's file system and, indeed, around the file systems of other computers that are connected by a network. The *search* utility allows a user to locate and identify files by partial name, date of modification, or specified text contents. The novice user may choose to start at the *My Computer* icon and open a succession of folder windows to browse through the file system, but the *explorer* utility allows the more advanced user to move quickly around the file system and provides different views of the file system, including tree and icon views. The *quickview* utility allows the user a simple way to inspect the contents of different types of files, even files based on applications that are not installed on the system. There are many other utilities designed to simplify use and management of the computer system. Figure 18.3 illustrates a few of the tools and techniques that we have mentioned here. (The Windows XP interface looks somewhat different, but provides similar capabilities.)

The Windows 2000/XP API includes access to all the tools and utilities supported by the user interface. Thus, application programmers can easily provide the same user capabilities and facilities, dialog boxes, controls, menus, drag-and-drop operations, and the like as those provided by the interface itself. A simplified overview of the relationship between the shell and other system components is shown in Figure 18.4.

FIGURE 18.4

Simplified Overview of Windows 2000

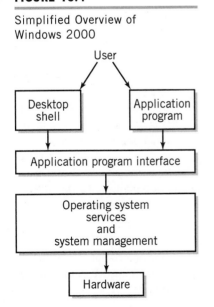

Internal Organization and Operations

The Windows 2000/XP internal organization is based on the model provided by Windows NT. Figure 18.5 shows a block diagram of the Windows 2000/XP architecture. Microsoft describes the architecture as "modified microkernel-based". The Windows 2000/XP kernel provides more services than one normally associates with a microkernel. Also, more auxiliary services execute in the protected mode than is characteristic of a microkernel architecture. Still, the internal organization has many of the characteristics and qualities of a microkernel design, including a client-server approach to system services.

The Windows 2000/XP architecture is divided into three layers executing in a protected mode called **kernel** mode, plus a number of services that execute in user mode. The lowest layer, the **hardware abstraction layer,** provides all direct connections to the system hardware. The hardware abstraction layer is written in assembly language. The hardware abstraction layer presents a standard interface to the remainder of the system, effectively isolating the remainder of the operating system from the hardware.

FIGURE 18.5

Windows 2000/XP System Block Diagram

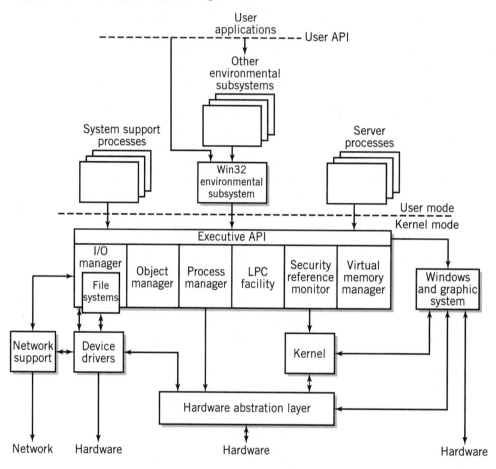

This feature allows architectural independence; and enabled the use of high-level language for nearly all of the remainder of the system, enhancing system portability.

The kernel provides basic services, including interrupt and exception handling, process synchronization, thread scheduling, and interprocess communication. The kernel pages are locked into memory. Kernel code is nonthreaded and nonpreemptible.

The Executive layer of Windows 2000/XP supplies most of the internal services required of an operating system. Although Windows 2000/XP was not developed using object-oriented techniques, its basic design utilizes object concepts throughout. Objects include files, directories, processes and threads, I/O ports, interprocess signals and messages, and so on.

- The *object manager* provides a standardized interface for every object in the system. To use an object, a process makes a request to the object manager, which checks the validity and permissibility of the request, then passes a pointer to the object called a handle for the process to access the object.

- The *process manager* creates, manages, and kills process and thread objects.
- The *virtual memory manager* allocates and manages memory space.
- The *I/O manager* processes all file and I/O requests.
- The *security reference monitor* enforces access validation procedures and audits accesses at the object level. All protected objects, including files, I/O devices, processes, and memory spaces are monitored, using a uniform interface to assure consistency. This is a fundamental element of system security and reliability.
- The *Local Procedure Call (LPC) facility* provides a central point for the control of all service requests and interprocess activities.
- The *Windowing and Graphics System* provides Windows screen interface tools and manages Windows graphics.

In addition to the kernel mode services, there are three groups of operating system processes that operate in user mode.

- *Environmental Subsystems* expose the services of the operating system to user applications through an API. Each environmental subsystem has its own characteristics and personality. There are four subsystems provided with Windows 2000/XP: Win32, POSIX, Win16, and MS-DOS Virtual Machine. Other environmental subsystems are available from third party vendors. Win32 is loaded by default. It supplies the basic personality of Windows 2000/XP and also the basic facilities that support the other subsystems. The other subsystems are loaded only as required to support particular user applications or services.
- *System Support Processes* provide user services such as logon and user session management.
- *Server processes* are upper-level Windows 2000/XP services, such as event logging and high level scheduling. Some add-on server applications, such as Microsoft SQL Server, supplement the server processes with additional components that are placed in this group.

Within each subsystem of Windows 2000/XP, individual functions and services are implemented as separate object processes. This separation of duties allows the replacement of individual services without affecting the stability of the operating system as a whole. All services are implemented as servers. A client, which can be a user application or another module within the operating system, makes a request to the local procedure call facility, which validates and passes the request to the appropriate server. This is the client-server model that was shown to you in Chapter 15. All operating system services follow this same procedure. The object that provides the requested service performs the required operations and passes any required information back to the client, completing the transaction

Memory allocation and paging is performed by the virtual memory manager. Each process is allocated its own 4 GB logical address space. A process logical memory map is shown in Figure 18.6. The first 2 GB of memory, except for the lowest 64 KB and highest 136 KB, are private, reserved for the use of the individual process. The excluded areas serve to hold process and thread control blocks, and to protect the system. The other 2 GB are used by the operating system. The details are beyond the scope of this discussion but may be found in [SOL98].

FIGURE 18.6

Windows 2000/XP Logical Memory Map

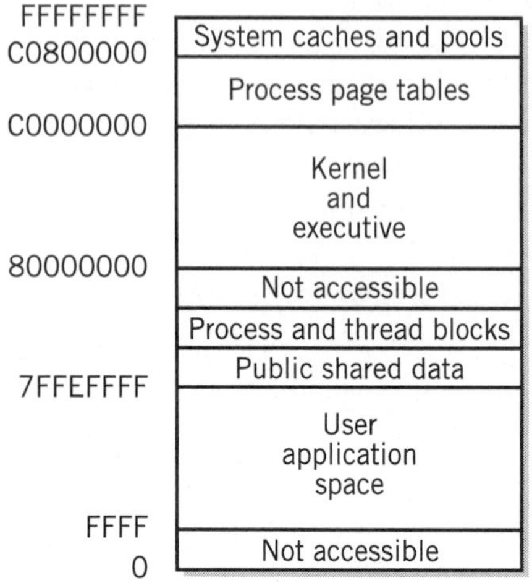

FFFFFFFF	System caches and pools
C0800000	Process page tables
C0000000	Kernel and executive
80000000	Not accessible
	Process and thread blocks
7FFEFFFF	Public shared data
	User application space
FFFF	Not accessible
0	

Windows 2000/XP processes enter the system with a base priority, which is used for thread dispatch. Windows 2000/XP provides thirty-two levels of priority. The highest 16 levels are reserved for use by real-time processes. Normal processes receive a base priority between 1 and 32.

Scheduling dispatch is performed strictly at the thread level, without consideration of the number of threads belonging to a process. Each thread is initially assigned a priority corresponding to its process priority and a quantum number. The quantum number represents the number of clock ticks that the thread will receive. Both the priority and quantum number of normal processes are adjusted dynamically for a number of different situations. For example, a thread that belongs to the process running in the window that has the focus receives a higher quantum number. Threads waiting for I/O receive priority boosts related to the particular device. Real-time priorities are never adjusted. Priority and quantum number adjustments are designed to equalize resource use and to improve the execution of interactive processes.

Thread selection is reevaluated at each clock tick, when a thread requests a system service, when a new thread is created, or when a thread becomes unblocked. The highest priority thread is dispatched. A thread of higher priority will preempt a running thread, even if the running thread has time remaining. Threads of equal priority are dispatched in a round-robin fashion, however a preempted thread that has not completed its time allotment is positioned at the front of its priority level ring.

Without dynamic priority adjustment, the Windows 2000/XP dispatching algorithm could cause starvation, so every 300 clock ticks (3-4 seconds, depending on the CPU) the dispatcher checks threads in the ready queue. Threads that are being starved have their priorities boosted sufficiently to guarantee them run time.

Windows 2000 File System Facilities

Windows 2000 provides support for the FAT and FAT-32 legacy file systems, for CDFS, the legacy CD-ROM file system, for UDF (Universal Disk Format) file system, the successor to CDFS, for NFS, the standard network file system, and for the **Windows NT File System (NTFS).** NTFS is discussed in Chapter 16.

Network and Communications Services

As you would expect, Windows 2000/XP provides an extensive set of network and communications services, including a full TCP/IP suite, with packet filtering, secure data transfer protocols, encryption, authentication, tunneling protocols to support virtual private networks (which are secure pseudo-networks that communicate using the Internet), routing protocols, domain name services, a telephony API, streaming media services, and more. Although discussion of these topics is outside the scope of this textbook, it is worth noting that Windows 2000 is positioned as a powerful network resource.

18.2 UNIX AND LINUX

Overview, Design Philosophy, and History

> UNIX has been around for 25 years and is mature and proven, while the PC operating systems, even the oldest one, DOS, is only 10 years old or so. And it's lousy.
> [VACC95]

This rather strongly worded opinion by James Greene, an analyst at Summit Strategies, Inc., quoted in a *ComputerWorld* article a few years ago, expresses a commonly held view among power users, programmers, and other knowledgeable computer personnel and shows the importance of the workplace environment presented by an operating system to its users.

UNIX is a powerful, high-reliability, multitasking operating system designed primarily for commercial use. Although not truly portable in the sense that binary programs can be carried from one type of machine to another, it is available for a wide variety of hardware platforms. Within the UNIX world, it is relatively easy to transport programs from one system to another using the tools and libraries of services that are included with UNIX.

In reality, there are many different versions of UNIX, each reflecting the capabilities of a particular hardware platform, as well as the interests of the particular implementor. Nonetheless, from the user perspective, the environment and behavior of UNIX operating systems are very similar across UNIX's many implementations. A user can move from one implementation to another and expect the same commands, utilities, and services, and can expect programs to behave in the same way.

UNIX is designed for multiuser time sharing and for server applications, although it is also frequently the operating system of choice for experienced individual users at a workstation or personal computer. A common base of support for networked and distributed computing is built-in, as are facilities that allow users to work together, communicate, and share information in groups. The protection facility explicitly recognizes the concept of a group as an entity. Computer systems with different UNIX implementations can readily communicate with each other. The command set provides an extremely powerful and elegant set of tools for programming, text processing, file manipulation, and system control that support a high degree of flexibility and productivity for knowledgeable users and workgroups.

An additional comment: there are few noticeable differences between Linux and UNIX. Most of the differences occur in the details of implementation. In this discussion, everything said about UNIX also applies to Linux, unless specifically noted otherwise.

The history of UNIX is an important factor in the evolution of modern computing methods. Much of the power and flexibility of modern computer systems, and many of the operating system concepts that we take for granted today, arose directly from the initial philosophy and design goals of the originators and developers of UNIX. A strong argument could be made that the very concept of personal computers with interactive user interfaces might not exist today if it were not for the pioneering work on UNIX.

UNIX was originally created in 1969–70 at Bell System Technical Laboratories by a single programmer, Ken Thompson, for his own personal use. His original purpose was to create a simple interactive system to support his programming and document preparation efforts. (There is a reliable anecdote that indicates that a "Space Travel" game was also involved.) The design was based on previous time-sharing research projects at MIT, particularly a large and innovative, but only partially successful, time-sharing system project called Multics. Multics had been created by a partnership consisting of Bell Laboratories, GE, and MIT, and Thompson had been a researcher on the project. The name UNIX was coined by another Bell Labs researcher, Brian Kernighan, as a multiple pun on the Multics name, and many of the original concepts developed for Multics were incorporated into the UNIX design.

Thompson developed the first version of UNIX on a Digital PDP-7 computer. Because the PDP-7 was a tiny machine (a standard PDP-7 configuration had only 32K words of memory, a 320KB hard disk, and a miniature reel-to-reel tape system for long-term storage), the operating system had to be small and efficient. The primary PDP-7 user interface was a slow and clunky printing terminal, which mandated a user interface that required minimum typing and terse commands. UNIX was written in PDP-7 assembly language.

At that point in time, there was no such concept as "personal computing." Computers were generally difficult to use. Although operating systems for batch system processing on large machines were well developed, small computers had primitive operating systems, if they had any operating system at all, and were not designed for interactive use.

The possibilities for a small, flexible interactive operating system were quickly understood within Bell Laboratories. Within a year, another Bell Laboratories researcher from the Multics project, Dennis Ritchie, had joined with Thompson to further research into UNIX. Ritchie created a new programming language, C, to make the operating system easier to understand and easier to move to other computer systems, a process called **porting.** Together, Thompson and Ritchie ported UNIX to a more modern Digital PDP-11 computer and rewrote the system in C. The original UNIX design had been developed as a single-tasking system for a single user because the PDP-7 computer did not support the features necessary to separate multiple tasks effectively. The PDP-11 design made it possible to incorporate support for multitasking and multiple concurrent users. This capability was quickly added to the design. Document processing and typesetting features were also added as standard features. These additional capabilities made the UNIX system popular within the Bell Laboratories, and soon there were a number of UNIX systems in use, along with support for additional development of the system.

In 1974, Ritchie and Thompson wrote a landmark paper describing their work on UNIX. For their pioneering work, Ritchie and Thompson won the prestigious ACM Turing award in 1983. An interesting personal recollection of the history of UNIX is found in Ritchie [RITC84].

The UNIX features and design goals were consistent with the needs of researchers everywhere, and Digital PDP-11 computers were in widespread use at colleges, universities, and research laboratories. AT&T, the parent company of Bell Labs, was willing to license UNIX to researchers for a modest fee, so the use of UNIX spread, and it became the subject of much research. AT&T made the source code freely available for study and modification. By 1978 there were more than 600 UNIX system installations in use. (Your author even word-processed his doctoral thesis on a UNIX system in 1978.)

In particular, computer gurus at the University of California at Berkeley created an alternative version of UNIX, called **BSD,** for **Berkeley Software Distribution,** with its own shell and its own features. Because UNIX was written mostly in C, it was relatively easy to add features and port UNIX to other machines. The BSD distribution became extremely popular and ultimately helped to establish UNIX as a commercial success through such companies as Sun and Hewlett-Packard. Successive BSD releases introduced many important innovations, including the vi editor, the C shell, the first UNIX support for virtual storage, long file names, many utilities, support for distributed computing environments, and the TCP/IP network protocol that dominates today's networking. FreeBSD is the current implementation of the BSD design.

The design of Linux was begun by Linus Torvalds, a Finnish student, as an exercise to better understand the inner workings of an operating system. His working model was MINIX, a variant of UNIX developed as an educational tool for an operating systems textbook by A. Tanenbaum. By November 1991, Torvalds had a working version of a UNIX-based operating system kernel, which he posted on the Internet under the name Linux. X86 was the hardware platform.

Torvalds invited participation in further development of Linux. Since then, thousands of volunteer participants have contributed to the design, coding, testing, debugging, and documentation of Linux. They have expanded its scope to other CPUs and broadened the availability of critical components, such as device drivers to support a wide range of peripheral devices. Support groups and Usenet forums were organized to help Linux users, both new and experienced, and to aid in new development. A commercial vendor network sprung up to distribute the system and to provide system support and new applications. Although Linux is legitimately available at no cost from a number of sources, commercial distributions of Linux earn money for their suppliers by providing add-on value: easy installation programs, improved user interfaces, technical support, additional features, and new application programs. As a result, Linux is now generally considered a viable operating system for business use, despite the noncommercial basis of its original development.

There have been numerous efforts to merge the different versions of UNIX into a single, standard UNIX operating system, but to this day there are many variants, each with its own enhancements and internal design. Nonetheless, there is sufficient standardization between different UNIX variants that different systems can communicate with each other, that a user will feel comfortable moving from machine to machine, and that programs can usually be moved or ported to different systems without much difficulty. There are millions of UNIX based installations in use all over the world on computers of all types and sizes, from Linux for X86 and FreeBSD-based Mac OS X for Macintosh personal computers, to AIX and Linux for IBM mainframes.

The set of criteria that ultimately determined the design of the original UNIX operating system resulted from Thompson and Ritchie's visions and innovative ideas, at first tempered by the limitations of the PDP-7 computer system and, then, expanded as the system moved to take advantage of the inherent possibilities of newer machines with more advanced technological capabilities. The most important criteria included

- An easy-to-use, interactive, powerful, and flexible interface for the user.
- Powerful programming tools, including built-in compilers, and powerful text and document preparation tools. These would be extra-cost, third-party application programs with most other operating systems.
- The use of small, simple utility programs as tools to perform generic tasks and the ability to combine tools to construct more complex applications. Central to this idea is the concept that the output of any program may become the input to another, as yet unknown, program [MCIL78].

- A small and simple operating system kernel, together with a separate interface shell that can be modified or replaced by the user if something better comes along.

- A logical file system, where files are addressed by name, without regard to their physical storage location. This quickly evolved into the familiar tree-structured file system design that is characteristic of UNIX today.

- Multitasking and multiuser capabilities, together with support for group work. Group work features evolved to include e-mail, group protection features, and the ability to reach files from different user accounts. Of course these capabilities were not possible on the original system, but they were added as soon as the technology was sufficient to support them.

- Simple system portability, resulting from the use of a portable high-level language to build the operating system.

The ideas of a logical file system and e-mail seem so standard today that it is easy to forget that these were radical concepts at the time! In fact, many of the features of computer operating environments that we take for granted today originated with UNIX. These include the way processes are created and controlled, the concept of a separate shell for a user interface, the hierarchical directory file system, the ability to combine small *independent* software modules to accomplish a larger task by passing data from one to another, and even the idea of a command line interface and tools that could be used as a programming language.

More recent developments in computer technology have resulted in many additions and modifications to the original UNIX design. These include support for new I/O devices, support for advances in CPU design such as virtual storage, multiprocessing, strong interprocess communication, built-in networking and distributed processing capabilities and tools, and a graphical user interface. The newest versions of UNIX support multithreading. Still, each of these advances builds upon the original criteria within the context of modern computing needs.

It is interesting to note that the original UNIX design philosophy was sufficiently flexible to support advances that continue to keep the system in tune with the times. Even in many of its implementation details, a modern Linux system differs surprisingly little from early UNIX designs. Indeed, many of the early UNIX techniques and innovations became the basis for features that are standard today on operating systems in general.

Modern UNIX systems are consistent with the UNIX tradition represented by the original design criteria. A UNIX or Linux system today may be described by the following characteristics:

- Support for preemptive multitasking, with multiuser capability and with automatic scheduling and background execution capability for batch processes.

- One or more shells that provide an interactive, user-tailorable interface with simple, but powerful and flexible commands, tools, programming language features, and utilities that can be combined to build programs called shell scripts. The same tools and services are also made available for use by application programs.

- Support for the creation and execution of new processes interactively, with control over process and dispatch scheduling priorities and allocation of memory and other resources. Interprocess support includes the ability to share program code and to communicate with signals and messages.

- A logical, easily maneuvered, tree-based file system that supports both local and network access, with support for file protection at both individual and group levels and file integrity protection for file sharing, with protection capability extending to as little as a single byte. File support for multiple devices is transparent.
- A kernel that provides access to the features of the underlying hardware in simple and elegant fashion, including support for virtual storage and sophisticated resource sharing.
- A powerful set of tools for the use, support, control, and administration of a wide range of network services.

The User Environment

Because UNIX is designed as a multiuser system, it is necessary to log in to the system before you can use it. Booting a UNIX system leaves the system running and ready to accept logins. UNIX maintains a password file, which contains a user profile for each authorized user on the system. The profile contains the user name, his password in encrypted form, and some basic information about the user.

When a user logs in successfully, UNIX executes a start-up file tailored to the individual user and activates the mechanisms needed for system, group, and user protection. The start-up file determines the type of terminal or computer that the user normally logs in on, the location of the user's files, the shell that the user prefers, and other places in the system to look for files. The system maintains a standard file for every user, but users can modify their own start-up routines to suit their own preferences. A user can change the prompt, create alternative names for commands, or select a different user interface shell, for example.

The primary user interface in UNIX is a command line prompt, but the start-up routine in many modern UNIX systems will include a program to start up an X Window system at login time. Still, most knowledgeable UNIX users prefer to do most of their work at a prompt. The UNIX multitasking mechanism actually allows a user to open several windows on their screen, each with its own shell and command line prompt. A user may be doing several tasks at once, each in its own window. The mechanism also allows a user to perform a foreground task and additional background tasks from a single prompt. A **background task** is one that executes noninteractively.

Even more powerfully, UNIX allows a user to login to a remote computer that is accessible by network. A truly busy user might be staring at a video screen with the command prompts from several different systems, each in its own window (or windows). They may be compiling a program in one window, working on a document together with other group members connected to other machines in a second window, and surfing the Web on the Internet in a third!

On a typical system, the user has a choice of several user interface shells. The most common UNIX shells are the Bourne shell, the C shell, and the Korn shell. Linux supplies a set of similar shells, *bash, tcsh,* and *pdksh,* respectively. A user can select a different shell from the command line. There is a basic set of commands that execute similarly in each shell, but each shell also has features and a style of working that is unique to the particular shell. Many users take advantage of this feature. They may prefer to do their interactive work with one shell, for example, but produce shell scripts that execute within a different shell.

In keeping with the basic UNIX system philosophy, there are a large number of system commands and utilities, each designed to perform one simple task. These include file manipulation tools, search and sort tools, text processing tools, programming tools, user and system management tools, communication tools, and a variety of miscellaneous tools. To give you an idea of the range of commands, the table in Figure 18.7 lists a representative sampling of the available UNIX commands. Many commands and utilities provide a number of different options and modifiers, adding capability to each command. Most commands are simply programs that are executed from the command line, so it is simple for a user to add a command, or supersede a command with one tailored to her own preferences.

UNIX commands can be combined in a number of different ways to perform more complex operations. Three important principles fundamental to UNIX provide much of the basis for the flexibility of the UNIX command set:

- I/O streams. UNIX treats *all* input to a process and output from a process as a simple sequences of bytes, which flow much like a stream. This is true whether the input comes from a keyboard, or a file, or as a message from another process. Similarly, the output might go to a printer, or a screen, or a file, or even a network. The operating system imparts no meaning to the sequence. It simply passes the input stream intact on a first-in, first-out basis from wherever it comes to the program that is processing it. For example, the keystrokes that you type into your keyboard are passed as an input stream, one character at a time, to the shell, which similarly echoes them back to the screen as an output stream, one character at a time. When the shell receives the carriage return keystroke, it processes the command.

- All I/O streams are handled in the same way, as though they were flowing from or to sequential files. This is true whether the actual source or destination is a stored file or some character-oriented device, such as a keyboard or printer. The device drivers for actual I/O devices are represented by special device files that are stored as part of the file system; therefore, the operating system is able to treat all I/O streams as file transfers and all file transfers as I/O streams.

- Three conceptual files named *stdin, stdout,* and *stderr* are included as an integral part of the system (conceptual, because they are not actually stored physically as files). These three files represent the standard source of user input to a process, the standard output from a process, and the standard output from a process when an error occurs. By default, *stdin* is assigned to the keyboard. *stdout* and *stderr* are usually assigned to a video screen. The parameters that assign *stdin, stdout,* and *stderr* can be reassigned to different devices by a user. Most user commands and utilities assume the use of *stdin* and *stdout* if alternative operands are not specified. *stdout* and *stderr* are differentiated so that error messages can be separated cleanly from program output when necessary.

EXAMPLE

To illustrate the way these concepts are used in practice, the *ls* command reads the data in a directory file as a stream of characters that represent information about the files in the directory. The command formats the characters according to the options requested by the user and presents the output as a stream of characters, including appropriate tabs and carriage returns, to *stdout,* where it is displayed on the screen.

FIGURE 18.7

A Selection of UNIX Commands

File and directory manipulation

cat	join (concatenate) and display files
cd	change directory
chmod	change file access rights
cp	copy files
cut	select columns from a file
ln	link alias name to a file
ls	list directory contents
mkdir	create a new directory path
mv	move or rename file or directory
paste	merge columns to a file
pwd	print working directory
rm	remove (delete) files
rmdir	remove directories

Search and sort tools

awk	pattern matching language
find	search system for filenames
grep	search files for text patterns
sort	sort or merge files by rows
strings	search binary files for text

Communication

ftp	file transfer between systems
login	login to local system
mail	e-mail
rcp	copy files between systems
rlogin	login to remote system
talk	network phone system
telnet	connect to another system
vacation	return e-mail with vacation message
write	send message to another terminal

Miscellaneous

bc	calculator
cal	calendar
calendar	appointment calendar
man	on-line manual
news	read on-line news

Text and document manipulation

awk	pattern matching language
emacs	screen editor
eqn	equation preprocessor
lp	print text
more	display text one page at a time
nroff	format text for printer or display
pic	line graphics preprocessor
sed	edit stream of text without intervention
spell	spell checker
tbl	table preprocessor
troff	format text for typesetting
vi	screen editor
wc	count words, lines, characters

Programming tools

cb	C source code formatter
cc	C compiler
lint	C source code compatibility checker
make	update files for compiling and linking
sdb	symbolic debugger

File and directory manipulation

at	execute commands at a specified time
cpio	copy archive files in or out
crontab	automate commands
date	display or set date
du	show disk usage
finger	print information about users
kill	terminate running process
nice	reduce a process's priority
nohup	keep a job running after logout
passwd	set password
perl	system programming language
ps	display process information
script	produce transcript of login session
su	login as superuser
tar	tape archiver
who	show lis of logged-on users

I/O streams allow processes to employ the technique of **piping,** which channels the output stream from one process to serve as the input to another. The *stdout* of a command can be piped to serve as the *stdin* for another command, for example. To use piping from a command line, the pipe is typed as a vertical bar (I) between the two commands. A program that normally takes its input stream from *stdin,* processes it, and produces the result to *stdout* is called a **filter.** Filters are commonly used with pipes. Many UNIX commands and utilities serve as filters. For example, in the compound command

```
who | wc -1
```

the *wc -l* command accepts an I/O stream of text from the output of the *who* command that consists of a list of users logged into the system, one user per row, and returns a count of the number of lines to stdout. This command is illustrated in Figure 18.8.

It is possible to reassign *stdin, stdout,* and *stderr* from the command line. The technique is called **redirection.** Redirection allows the user to change the source of data for a command from the keyboard to a file or another device, for example. Note, incidentally, the flexibility that results from treating I/O devices as files. Similarly, the output result may be redirected from the screen to a file. **In-line command execution** is a technique that makes it possible to use the *stdout* results of one command as a data operand for another command. All these features—piping, redirection, and in-line command execution—can be combined on the same command line.

EXAMPLE

As another example, the *cat* command is often used to display a text file on the screen. The form

```
cat filename
```

is used for this purpose. The operand *filename* is used for the input stream; the output stream goes to *stdout.* If the operand is omitted, however, and the output stream is redirected to a file, as follows:

```
cat >fileout
```

the input is redirected to *stdin,* and the output to *fileout.* Then the command can be used as a quick and dirty way to create a text file. In this case the cat command accepts user input from the keyboard, and stores it in *fileout.* This is illustrated in Figure 18.9.

■ ■ ■

FIGURE 18.8

The Use of a Pipe

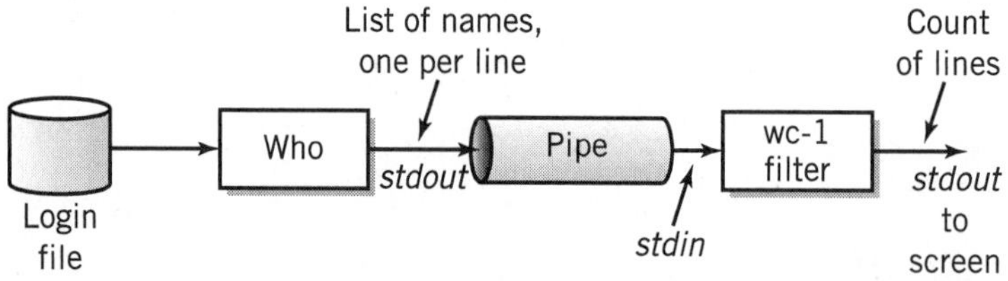

FIGURE 18.9

Redirecting the cat Command

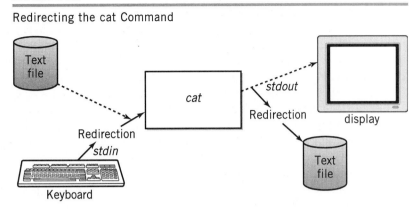

As an example of in-line command execution, the *grep* command can be used to identify the name of a file or files that contains some particular text to be displayed. The "reverse apostrophes" (`) are used to contain the in-line *grep* command:

```
cat `grep -l 'matching text' filepath/* `
```

In this example, the output from the *grep* command is the name or names of files that contain "matching text." This output becomes the filename operand for the cat command, just as though the names had actually been typed on the command line. In this way the cat command operates on the result of a search without any further effort on the part of the user.

In addition, commands can be executed directly from a file, as well as from the keyboard. Each shell provides decision and loop control structure commands that allow a user to create **shell scripts.** Shell scripts can be used to combine commands, and even programs, to automate complex operations and are often a much easier way to accomplish a task than to write a full-fledged program. We illustrated a shell script that located local airports in Figure 14.13. When considered together, all the commands and features built into the UNIX shells provide a control and programming capability of uncommon power and flexibility.

There is a special login name, *su,* for superuser, that is used for management of the UNIX system. The superuser has access to all facilities in the system, without regard to ordinary security restrictions.

Internal Design

There are small differences in the internal organization of different UNIX systems, reflecting the characteristics and requirements of the underlying hardware, as well as the technical features included and the personal style of the implementation designer. Nonetheless, there are clear guiding principles and standard architectural features and methodologies for a UNIX system, particularly in the areas of process control, I/O handling, file management, interprocess and intersystem communication, and device driver organization. UNIX systems are implemented almost entirely in C, making it easy to port UNIX from one system to another, since all that is required is a C compiler for the target machine. The only exception is the hardware-dependent code specific to a particular CPU, which must be implemented in the assembly language of the target machine.

A broad overview of the UNIX system architecture is shown in Figure 18.10. The user normally interacts with a command interface shell. The shell itself is a utility program, as are nearly all of the commands typed by a user. The system is controlled by a relatively small, monolithic, memory resident kernel. The shell and other programs interact with the kernel through a series of system calls. To simplify programming, the system provides a library of functions, which are used to call the system services. The use of a library also makes it possible to add or modify services without affecting the kernel. The kernel is responsible for process control, scheduling, file management, I/O, and memory management operations, including virtual storage management. Other services are loaded dynamically and executed as they are required. The kernel itself is mostly made up of small programs, each designed to handle a particular task. There is no special hierarchy of kernel services as there is in some other systems.

Linux provides an additional feature, called a module, designed to minimize the amount of memory resident kernel code. Modules are kernel functions that can be loaded and linked to the remainder of the system or removed at run-time. A kernel daemon (See page 625) detecting a missing device driver, for example, could load the driver, which then becomes part of the system. Note that the loaded module is not a separate process. This technique allows Linux to load only the device drivers actually needed. File systems are also supplied as modules.

There are five major groups of operations that are executed by the kernel:

- Virtual storage and memory management: page table creation and management, demand paging, and memory protection.
- Process management: creation of processes, memory allocation, device resource allocation and management, process scheduling, swapping, and dispatch, interprocess communication, and servicing of process requests. Some systems also support thread management, and dispatch scheduling is managed at the thread level.
- File management: storage and retrieval of files, directory system management, file location and storage management, free space management, and file protection

FIGURE 18.10

General Organization of a UNIX System

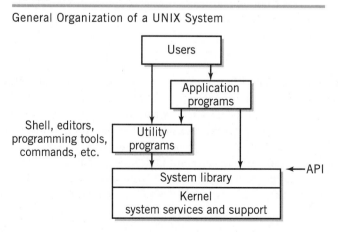

and control. Some file systems provide remote file access to other systems across a network. Remote file access, which is often transparent to the user, makes possible diskless workstations. These services are coordinated with the networking and communication services of the systems at each end of the transaction.

- I/O: management of I/O devices, control of I/O hardware, transfer of data, and I/O interrupt processing
- Networking and communication: hardware and software protocol support to allow login and control of remote systems across a network, data and file transfer, and other services. Many systems also provide support for distributed processing. A few systems, including Linux, also support multiprocessing.

As you can see, the kernel services are limited to the essential services required to control resources and manage processes. Unlike other systems, many of the features that characterize a modern UNIX system, such as e-mail, user shells, and the X Window graphical display system, are *not* an integral part of the system, but are provided outside the kernel by utility programs. This design provides tremendous system flexibility, since the utilities can simply be changed or modified without affecting the underlying kernel.

Kernel services are provided by a library of system calls. These services are available to system and application programs. There is no direct user access to the kernel services. Instead, users access kernel services through the use of shell commands and utility programs. In some cases, a utility exists specifically to support a particular system call. In such a case, the utility and system call may have the same name. UNIX documentation uses a special notation to differentiate the two: the name of a system call has a set of parentheses appended, for example, *someservice()*. System call libraries are relatively standard across different UNIX systems, to enhance the portability of application program source code written in C or other high-level languages. A standard library of user services is defined in the POSIX specification.

PROCESS CREATION AND MANAGEMENT   The fundamental unit of work in UNIX is the process. As in other systems, a process consists of a program in execution, together with its assigned resources. The memory assignment for a UNIX process consists of the program code, known in UNIX jargon as a *text segment,* a separate data area, and a stack area, arranged as shown in Figure 18.11. Normally, the program code is fixed in size, but the memory allocation method provides for the dynamic expansion of the data and stack areas as required by the process during execution. In most modern systems, each process would be assigned its own virtual memory space.

Because the UNIX kernel divides its work into small components, a typical UNIX system has many processes in the system at any given time. When the system is booted, it creates a number of processes. For example, the system provides a process to each terminal on the system for login. The system also provides processes that provide specific services when requested. These processes are known as **daemons.** Some daemons are created at boot time and run forever. Others are created as their services are requested. Each daemon provides a single service and runs as a background process. Typical daemons include the print queue manager, the e-mail handler, the system free-page controller, and various network tools. Many daemons serve specific command and utility requests.

Many of these processes are asleep, waiting in a state of suspension until they are needed. They are activated by a wakeup call from the kernel when their services are

FIGURE 18.11

Virtual Address Space for a Process

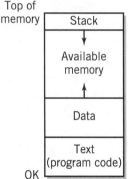

Top of memory

Arrows indicate the direction of expansion when additional memory is needed.

OK

needed. An interprocess communication entity called a **signal** is used for this purpose. The *cron* utility, for example, is a daemon process that is used to manage batch programs. Users specify the time(s) that these programs are to be run. The cron utility acts as an alarm clock. It wakes up once a minute, checks the schedules, activates processes for programs that are to be run, and goes back to sleep. As an example, *cron* could be used to log the number of users on a system over a 24-hour period, by executing the *who*|*wc* command illustrated earlier once a minute and redirecting the results into a file.

The data that represents the context for a process is stored in two tables, a process table and a user table. Together, these tables contain information equivalent to the process control block discussed in Chapter 16. There is a single process table for the entire system that resides permanently in memory whenever the system is in operation. The process table maintains critical data for every process. Each process is identified by a number, called a PID, for Process IDentifier. The process table data includes the location and size of each process, plus the current status of the process. Other relevant process data, including the process context, signal data, and file references, are stored in the user table, which is kept with the data in the memory space of the process itself. There is a separate user table for each process.

Separating the process control information into two tables results in two major benefits:

- It becomes easy to share program code among several processes. Each process has its own text segment area in virtual storage, but every process table points to the same text area in real memory. The data area and stack area for each process is maintained separately.

- On occasion it is necessary for the scheduler to swap an entire process out to disk to make room for other processes. By storing the user table for the process with the process, additional memory can be freed. Note that when a swap occurs, the only process data that must remain in memory are the location and size of the process on disk, along with the fact that the process is not currently in memory.

UNIX provides a simple and elegant technique for creating and managing processes that is well suited to an interactive environment. Any existing process can create another process. The procedure is called **forking.** The technique is illustrated in Figure 18.12. The kernel provides four basic service routines for this purpose. To create a new process, an existing process calls the *fork()* routine. This creates a new process that is an exact copy of the calling process, except that the new process is assigned a different PID. The calling process is called the **parent** process, and the copy is called a **child** process. A parent may have many children, but each child has only a single parent.

Next, the new process calls the *exec()* system routine. The *exec* routine loads new program text and data into the child process from the file named as an argument to the call and makes the new process available for execution. In most cases, the parent process goes to sleep until the child terminates. The parent calls the *wait()* service routine for this purpose. Among other reasons, this makes the terminal available to the child process. The parent process is not required to sleep. It may remain awake and continue processing. In this case, the child process will execute as a background process, and both will process concurrently. The *exit()* call terminates a process.

Except for the processes created during system bootup, the *fork()* service routine is the *only* way to create processes in a UNIX system.

EXAMPLE

The system provides a shell process for every user logged into the system. When a user types a command, the shell process uses the *fork()-exec()-wait()* procedure to create a child process that loads and executes the command. When the command includes pipes, there may be several child processes executing concurrently, including children for each command and for the pipe process itself. When the command is completed, all the children terminate, and the shell process again becomes active. It types a prompt to the *stdout* device and waits for the next command.

FIGURE 18.12

Creating a New Process

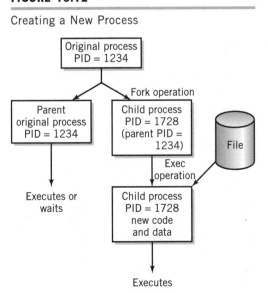

Executes

MEMORY MANAGEMENT AND SCHEDULING

Modern UNIX systems are designed to operate with virtual memory. As noted before, each process operates in a separate virtual space. The UNIX kernel manages paging in whatever manner is required by the particular hardware system in use. Most systems use demand paging with a least recently used algorithm for page replacement. Most UNIX systems allow processes to share memory. This capability allows processes to share data and to pass messages easily and also uses physical memory more efficiently.

As already noted, process creation is normally automatic, so process scheduling is usually not required unless the process table has reached its maximum capacity or the number of free physical pages falls below a predetermined minimum. In that case, the process scheduler may choose to terminate a process or swap a process out of memory to make room for the new process. Generally, processes that have slept for a long period are good candidates for swapout, but on some systems, the scheduler may occasionally swap out a process that is hogging resources to improve system performance. Dispatch scheduling may be done at the process level or, on systems with thread-handling capability, at the thread level. Sun Solaris, in particular, has a powerful thread-handling capability. Linux dispatches at the process level. However, the process memory-sharing capability allows a program designer to build processes to share resources and dispatch in the manner of threads.

UNIX systems generally use a dynamic priority dispatch algorithm to prevent starvation. The Linux scheduling algorithm is typical. Linux provides three types of user-level process scheduling; FIFO, Round Robin, and Other. A process is assigned to a particular type based on its needs. Each process is assigned a baseline priority value based on its scheduling type and various process characteristics. FIFO processes are of the highest priority. A FIFO process will always preempt other running processes and will normally run to completion unless a FIFO process of higher priority occurs. The FIFO level is reserved for real-time processes and other processes that are of extreme importance. The Round Robin level is next in priority; it is intended for processes with above-average speed requirements. Standard User processes are assigned to the Other level. Their baseline priorities are the lowest. In addition, the system provides a utility called nice that allows users or processes to lower the priority within their own level as a favor to other users or processes. When a process enters the system, a counter that will measure the CPU time actually used is set to a value corresponding to its priority value.

Scheduling is controlled by a timer interrupt that occurs every 10 milliseconds. Normally, the only action that occurs is that the counter belonging to the running process is decremented. When the counter value reaches 0, however, the process is preempted, and rescheduling occurs. Rescheduling also occurs when a process is blocked and when certain system events occur. The User process priority levels are designed so that rescheduling will normally occur at least approximately once per second. Rescheduling recalculates the counter value of every process, using the simple formula

```
New counter value = (previous counter value / 2) + priority level.
```

The process with the highest counter value is selected to run. Notice that within a particular scheduling type this method favors processes that have used the least CPU time recently, since their counter values will be highest. To see this more clearly, consider a process of priority 100 that has just used its current time slice. From the formula, successive reschedulings will set its counter to 100, 150, 175, 187, and so on.

Kernel service routines are exempted from scheduling. To protect data structures within the kernel, kernel routines are nonpreemptible, except by interrupt services or by a decision within the kernel routine to block itself while waiting for an event such as an I/O completion to occur. Interrupt services are designed not to affect critical data structures, and the scheduler will always return control to kernel code that is prepared to continue processing. Where necessary, a kernel service can disable interrupts. Thus, the system data integrity of the kernel is protected in a very simple manner.

The UNIX dispatching method is well suited to an interactive system. Interactive processes normally have a very low CPU time/actual time ratio. As a result, they will have high priority and receive fast response. The same is true for I/O-bound and sleeping processes. Conversely, the priority of a CPU hog will drop to make room for other processes. All in all, the system provides a good balance of resources and fast interactive response time under most operating conditions.

UNIX File System Organization

The UNIX file system is responsible for the organization, identification, storage, and retrieval of every file in the system. UNIX defines files very simply. To UNIX, a file consists of a sequence of bytes. This idea is consistent with the I/O stream concept described earlier. The UNIX file system does not impose any structure or meaning to the contents of a file. Instead, interpretation of the bytes within a file is left to the program using the file.

Files are accessed by logical file name. A logical file name consists of a sequence of ASCII characters. The only character that cannot be used within a file name is the forward slash mark (/), which is reserved for use as a separator of path name components in the directory system. It is usually preferable to select names made up of printable characters, but UNIX does not impose such a requirement. All UNIX file systems distinguish at least the first 14 characters of a file name, although most modern systems distinguish many more than 14. The logical file name has no meaning to the file system, although some application programs require a particular file extension (a period followed by a specific sequence of characters) as a correctness check. The C compiler expects *.c* as the file name extension on a C source program, for example.

The only files that are differentiated by the UNIX file system are those that are used for special purposes by the kernel of the operating system. All other files are considered to be ordinary files. Ordinary files can store text for word processing, a program to be executed, database records for an organization, images to be displayed, or any other data that users wish to store in the computer. Ordinary files even hold the shell and most of the utilities and programs that make up the operating system.

The file system provides a means to identify five types of special files that are used by the operating system. These include directory files, symbolic link files, block device files, character device files, and named pipe files. Special files are identified by a single letter that is stored with the protection mechanism for the file. When a user issues a command to list directories the first space in the protection element of the listing identifies the type of file, "-" for ordinary files, "d," "l," "b," "c," or "p" for the special files. Directory files are used to hold directory names and file pointers for the file system. Symbolic link files provide the connection between a symbolic link name and the actual file being referenced. Block and character device files are the device drivers that are used by UNIX programs to access I/O services, including virtual device drivers as well as device drivers that actually provide access to physical hardware. Named pipes are used by the operating system as a means to provide communications between different processes.

The UNIX file system is organized in a hierarchical directory structure. A slightly simplified version of the top part of a typical UNIX file organization is shown in Figure 18.13. In the diagram directories are enclosed in boxes. Other names represent files. The root directory is always named / (slash). The slash character is also used as a delimiter between levels of the tree.

The most important subdirectories shown in the figure and their uses are

- */home* provides the directory structure for users of the system. Each user has her own home subdirectory and creates a structure downward from there to meet her individual needs.
- */bin* holds the shells and most commonly used commands and utilities.
- */etc* holds administrative, configuration, start-up, and other important system files.

FIGURE 18.13

Top of the Typical UNIX Directory Hierarchy

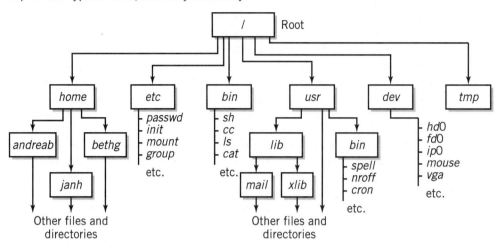

- */usr* is used for a variety of subdirectories that contain libraries and other information used by the system. */usr/bin* also holds commands that are used less frequently. Files in subdirectories of */usr* rarely change.
- */dev* holds the files that represent device drivers.
- */tmp* is used for temporary storage when required by system commands and utilities.

Although the system administrator could configure the system differently, there are strong reasons for providing a standardized structure, so the organization of most UNIX systems would appear similar to that shown in the figure. Consistency between systems makes it easy for users to move from system to system. It also means that system programs and utilities will always be found in the same locations when they are needed.

At any given time, the user is attached to a point on the tree known as the present working directory. From there, the user may access files by specifying a path relative to the present working directory or, absolutely, from the root. A path name consists of the names of each node, each separated by /. A path starting with a / is an absolute path. Normally, a relative path name extends downward from the present working directory, but it is possible to climb the tree, one level at a time, by using the special .. node. As an example, the *nroff* file in Figure 18.13 can be reached relatively from the */usr/lib/mail* directory with the path name *../../bin/nroff*. The user may change the present working directory with the *cd* (change directory) command. Used without arguments, *cd* returns the user to her home directory. The *mkdir* and *rmdir* commands are used to create and remove directories from the tree.

Operationally, UNIX treats the file system as a single entity, independent of the physical devices that the files reside on. The boot process makes available the root file system as configured by the system administrator. To this structure can be added the file systems from other devices or partitions on devices. The **mount** operation attaches the root of an individual device to a specified directory point on the file system as already configured.

Often, the administrator will provide an empty directory for this purpose. The result of the mount operation is an integrated tree structure with new branches corresponding to the additional file system. Path names for the new branches are specified as though the additional branches were always a part of the integrated structure. Thus, the root directory on the mounted device has the path name corresponding to the mount point. Note that this approach is quite different from that used by MS-DOS and Windows, for example, where the file system on each device has a separate identifier, root, and structure.

The UNIX file system was introduced as an example in various sections of Chapter 16. You may recall from that chapter that files are stored noncontiguously in blocks. Directory files contain the file names emanating from that directory, together with pointer to i-node tables. The i-node table stores pertinent information about the file, including the locations of each block in the file. If you don't remember how i-nodes work, you may wish to review the appropriate sections of Chapter 16. The UNIX file protection system, which is based on data included in the i-node table, is also discussed in Chapter 16.

The Linux file system differs slightly. Linux can support multiple native file systems with different features. All are organized similarly, but a user who wants journaling support, for example, would select a file system that supports the journaling feature. Linux also provides file driver support for a number of other file systems, including the Windows FAT and FAT32 system, plus read access for NTFS. This allows Linux to access Windows files stored on the same disk, for example. Alternative file systems are mounted in the same way as any other device file system. To implement these features, Linux adds an additional layer of file management, which it calls a virtual file system. Processes interact with the virtual file system. The virtual file system supplies system calls to the appropriate file system, which then accesses the file in the usual way.

UNIX I/O is relatively simple. I/O operations are managed as part of the file system. There is a device driver file corresponding to every device connected to the system. The device driver files provide standard interrupt-based routines for performing I/O.

Conceptually, I/O is divided into two categories, character I/O and block I/O. Character I/O is used for devices that are inherently stream oriented. Files are read from the disk in blocks. However, the file services provided to programs allow a program to receive as little as a single byte or, conversely, thousands of bytes. The file system provides buffering in memory that can hold many blocks of a file. Data is read into a program from the buffers as it is needed. The file system also attempts to anticipate future needs by reading blocks into buffer storage before they are needed. Blocks of data are moved between physical storage and buffers in the background, invisible to a program. The program interacts only with the buffers. Write operations work similarly. Because the operating system does not impose a structure on files, only five simple API services are required for a program to use a file. *Open()* activates a file and provides buffer space for the file blocks. *Read()* and *write()* read and write a number of bytes between a program and the file buffer. *Seek()* moves a pointer to a different part of the file. *Close()* releases the file's resources.

Networking Services

Data communication capabilities are a fundamental part of UNIX-based systems. Peer-to-Peer networking, using the TCP/IP protocol stack, was designed originally for UNIX. Every UNIX system provides networking capabilities. Many, including Linux, implement networking capabilities using a socket interface. The socket interface serves a role for networking similar to the role played by the Linux Virtual File System in managing files: it directs network requests to the appropriate protocol stack, and ultimately to the proper network device drivers. Conversely, the various protocol stacks use the socket layer to bring in data from the network. Figure 18.14 shows the similarity between the socket interface and the Virtual File System. Linux supports a number of protocols in addition to TCP/IP, including Appletalk and Netware IPX/SPX.

18.3 THE IBM zSERIES z/OS OPERATING SYSTEM

Overview, Design Philosophy, and History

The IBM zSeries can be run under a number of different operating systems, including VM, AIX, VSE, Linux, and z/OS. The z/OS operating system is the most recent version of an operating system whose roots date back more than thirty-five years. z/OS is the most powerful general-purpose operating system available for IBM zSeries mainframe computers. z/OS is designed to provide the stable, reliable, and secure operating environment for large mainframe computer configurations that is required for business processing.

z/OS is descended from OS/360, a family of operating systems from the mid-1960s that provided multiprogrammed batch processing for the System/360 series of computers. The memory of the System/360 was limited to real storage, and the small amount of memory that was practical in the 1960s, usually 1MB or less, further restricted the number of tasks that could be placed in memory for processing at one time. The OS/MVT member of the OS/360 family supported a memory management technique that attempted to maximize the use of memory by placing tasks in separate, variable-sized partitions. OS/MVT

FIGURE 18.14

Comparison of Virtual File System and Socket Layered Structure

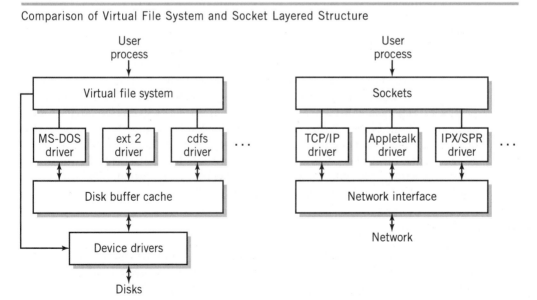

stands for OS/Multiprogramming with a Variable (N)umber of Tasks. We introduced variable partitioning briefly in Chapter 15.

The IBM System/370 computer family added virtual storage capability, which increased the number of tasks that could be processed concurrently. IBM introduced an enhanced version of OS/MVT called OS/VS2 to support virtual storage. OS/VS2 created a single 16MB virtual address space, which was then broken into variable partitions in a manner similar to OS/MVT. Responding to the need for still more space, IBM expanded OS/VS2 to create MVS/370. The name **MVS** is an acronym for **multiple virtual storage,** to indicate support for the separation of tasks into individual virtual spaces.

In Chapter 12, we discussed the evolution of the System/370 architecture through a number of technical advances and improvements. The S/370XA increased the virtual address space to 2GB and provided a more effective I/O channel design. The ESA/370 introduced a number of features, including the use of access registers to create additional address spaces called data spaces. The System/390 introduced ESCON I/O processing and support for the integration of computer resources into a system complex called a parallel sysplex. There have been many other improvements in the continuing evolution from System/370 to System/390.

MVS underwent continual upgrades to support enhancements and growth in the S/370-390 architecture. New versions were renamed to represent the level of hardware support, first, to MVS/XA and, then, to MVS/ESA. In 1996, IBM reconfigured MVS and added a number of major new features, including support for large-scale shared disk clustering and parallel processing, as well as a complete UNIX subsystem, including the UNIX user interface and a complete UNIX-compliant kernel. The reconfiguration included the integration into the base system of many tools that had been MVS add-ons. The new operating system was renamed OS/390. The MVS kernel and support facilities remain at the heart of z/OS.

The most recent versions of z/OS are designed to support the features of the largest zSeries installations. z/OS can support a parallel sysplex consisting of up to 32 or 64 large zSeries computer facilities in a cluster, each with its own symmetric multiprocessing and I/O capabilities. Additional I/O capabilities, normally in the form of RAID subsystems, can be shared transparently between individual facilities.

With the appropriate application software, z/OS can support thousands of users working concurrently with a huge database or Web application. It can also support a large organization by providing Web, database, and transaction services with massive amounts of data across a client-server network

The primary design goal of OS/360 was to maximize the amount of processing that could be performed within the hardware capabilities of a System/360 computer by providing multiprogramming, data management, memory management, I/O services, and operator support for the execution of batch programs, with the additional requirement that the system must be as reliable and secure as possible to meet the critical needs of business. Although z/OS is a much larger operating system, supporting much bigger (although not necessarily in the physical sense!) computer systems, its goals are essentially the same, to provide services that maximize system performance, availability, reliability, and security and minimize operator support effort, in the framework of large computer systems and system complexes. For a long time, IBM has used the acronym RAS to describe the fundamental goals of its most powerful operating systems. RAS stands for reliability, availability, and service.

The most important services provided by z/OS include

- Sophisticated resource allocation services and workload management, to achieve efficient use of the system's large memory, multiple processors, and complex I/O channel structure. These services include dynamic resource allocation based on business priorities, system performance monitoring and analysis, load balancing, and task assignments to different CPUs in a complex, in addition to the more familiar services.
- Data set management services, to allocate, track, and access files and file data. z/OS supports a number of different allocation methods and file structures. In IBM jargon, a file is called a data set. Distributed file services that support Linux, OS2, NFS, and Windows files and directories are also included.
- Job and task entry, scheduling, control, completion, and management.
- Virtual storage operation and management.
- Networking services, including Web services, intrasystem TCP/IP services, and multiple protocols and MAC types.
- Time-sharing support and productivity tools for program development and job entry.
- System resource logging, auditing, and accounting.
- Error detection and recovery, error logging, failure detection and reassignment of tasks and data to other resources.
- System support programs and utilities. These include linkage editing, loading, file and directory manipulation utilities, sort utilities, tracing functions, and many other services.
- Graphical system operator communication services.
- Security services, including cryptography, firewalls, network authentication and certificate services, resource control, VPNs, and more.
- Large-scale cluster support, including data coordination and integrity protection, workload distribution and balancing, time coordination, automatic failover switching, geographically dispersed-cluster support, and dynamic on-line system upgrade and reconfiguration.

The User Environment

USER FACILITIES   z/OS is designed primarily to execute and control batch programs and server applications. z/OS does not provide an interactive user interface with direct access to the operating system in the familiar sense. Instead, the users communicate with z/OS through one of several user environments that are provided as z/OS subsystems or as special programs called application enablers. Communications with the **Base Control Program (BCP)** kernel itself are made with service requests from programs, and with **Job Control Language,** more commonly called simply **JCL.** Programs are submitted to the system for execution. JCL describes in detail the specifications of a program to be executed. JCL is submitted with every program. The most important of the user environments are

- TSO, the Time Sharing Option

- ISPF, the Interactive System Productivity Facility
- JES, the Job Entry Subsystem
- CICS, the Customer Information Control System
- UNIX

Figure 18.15 illustrates the relationship between BCP, the user, and the various subsystems mentioned. Although it is tempting to view the different user environments as akin to the shells that we have considered with other operating systems, there are a number of significant differences. A user logs into a UNIX system. When the user moves from one shell to another in UNIX, it is not necessary to log in to the system again. Furthermore, all of the shells provide similar capabilities. A user selects a particular shell because of her or his preference to perform a task in a particular way.

By contrast, each environment in the z/OS system serves a different purpose. Each environment, including the UNIX environment, serves a different group of users and provides its own features, its own command language, its own login requirement, and its own interface. A knowledgeable system user, such as an application programmer, might use all these environments during the course of a day, at different times.

JES and TSO are subsystems of z/OSOS/390. They are considered part of the base operating system and perform specific functions within the operating system, as well as for the user. Although TSO provides an interactive time-sharing facility, it is not designed for the type of interactive use with application programs that is characteristic of a personal computer. TSO is intended primarily for use by programmers to develop programs and to prepare jobs for execution. TSO provides a command line interface for basic file manipulation capabilities, program listings, an editor, and an assortment of utilities. It also provides access to JES for the submission of jobs. TSO commands can be grouped for execution using a built-in language called CLIST.

JES, as the name suggests, is the mechanism for the submission of jobs to the system for scheduling and execution. A job consists of one or more programs to be executed, together with the JCL code that describes the steps to be taken and the data to be used. More about jobs and JES in the next section.

ISPF is a menu-driven facility that serves as an extension to TSO. ISPF provides a series of menu screens, called panels, that offer most of the functionality of TSO is an easy-to-use form. ISPF also provides a more powerful screen editor.

CICS is an **application enabler.** An application enabler is an application-level program that serves as a stand-in for the operating system, providing services to application programs designed specifically to work with it. It is not part of the MVS operating system, and in fact CICS is available for a number of different operating systems. As an application enabler, CICS provides the capability for the execution of on-line interactive programs that MVS is lacking. CICS

FIGURE 18.15

Relationship of Various User Interfaces

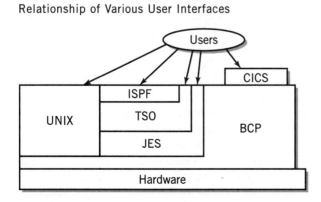

itself has many of the features of an operating system. It can access terminals, it can allocate memory, it provides multiprogramming. It dispatches programs with a scheduling algorithm optimized for interactive processing response. However, it is not used as a programming facility. The interactive programs executed by CICS are developed by programmers using TSO. To z/OS, CICS is simply another batch program, albeit a large one that runs in most installations indefinitely. CICS operates in its own virtual memory space, like any other z/OS application, and allocates memory to its online programs from its own space. It requests other resources from z/OS on behalf of the CICS programs that need them. The CICS programs do not have direct access to z/OS services. CICS is used primarily for transaction processing and for other end user work.

z/OS JOB CONTROL LANGUAGE Jobs are submitted to JES, and from JES to BCP for scheduling and execution. Major system jobs such as CICS are submitted from an operator's console terminal; other jobs are normally submitted through TSO or ISPF, although it is possible to access JES directly from an input device or another system in a sysplex. z/OS JCL provides the means for the user to issue instructions and information to the operating system about the job. A JCL procedure is included with every job. The procedure tells the operating system what programs to execute and where to find them, what data to use, and what to do with the results.

A job is made up of one or more job steps. Job steps are also known as tasks. Each job step consists of one program or one cataloged procedure to execute, plus specification of all of the data requirements for that step. A cataloged procedure is itself a collection of job steps that can be stored on the system to simplify the effort of building jobs for common operations, such as program compilers. JCL is a complicated and arcane language, difficult to learn and use, sensitive to easily made errors, and slightly different for each system installation. Cataloged procedures make it possible for a user to work with a z/OS system with only a minimal knowledge of JCL. A typical JCL procedure is shown in Figure 18.16. This procedure compiles, links, and executes a COBOL source program.

Internal Organization

SYSTEM OVERVIEW z/OS is a large operating system, providing many different functions and services. The design requirements emphasize high performance, reliability, security, and availability. The system must also be highly flexible, to support a wide range of computer models, peripherals, and system configurations. In additional to the usual hardware support, file management, resource management, and process control, z/OS must support multiprocessing, system accounting, failure detection and recovery, and a high level of security. z/OS systems in a parallel sysplex must be able to work together cooperatively, to share workloads and data reliably, and to make alternative CPUs and peripherals available for processing in case a system fails.

Internally, z/OS is organized into a number of subsystems, and many individual component programs, which interact to provide the various functions and services. To meet the design criteria of such a large system, z/OS is organized hierarchically, with several layers of management to assure functionality, reliability, and the best possible integration of components and subsystems. Some subsystems are part of the basic structure; others are optional add-ons. Each version of z/OS has added even more components and more functionality.

FIGURE 18.16

A Typical JCL Procedure

```
//MYPROG JOB (CISDEPT, 18),'I. ENGLANDER',CLASS=A, TIME=(,20)
//*COMPILE STEP
//COMPILE EXEC PGM=IGYCRCTL,REGION=1024K
//SYSIN DD DSN=ENGLNDR.COBPROG(PROG5),UNIT=FACDRIVE,
//   DISP=(OLD,KEEP)
//SYSLIN DD DSN=&&TEMPFILE,DISP=(NEW,PASS),
//   UNIT=SYSDISK,SPACE=(TRK,5)
//SYSPRINT DD SYSOUT=A
//SYSUT1 DD UNIT=SYSDISK,SPACE=(CYL,(1,1))
{there are six more SYSUTn work data sets required by the COBOL compiler}
//*
//* LINKAGE STEP
//LKED EXEC PGM=IEWL,PARM='LIST,XREF',COND=(8,LE,COMPILE)
//SYSLIN DD DSN=&&TEMPFILE,DISP=(OLD,DELETE)
//SYSLIB DD DSN=&LIB,DISP=SHR
//SYSLMOD DD DSN=&&GOSET(GO),DISP=(NEW,PASS),
//   UNIT=SYSDISK,SPACE=(CYL(1,1))
//SYSPRINT DD SYSOUT=A
//SYSUT1 DD UNIT=SYSDISK,SPACE=(CYL(1,1))
//*
//* EXECUTION STEP
//GO EXEC PGM=*.LKED.SYSLMOD,COND=(8,LE,COMPILE),(4,LE,LKED))
//STEPLIB DD DSN=&LIB,DISP=SHR
```

Figure 18.17 presents an overview of the major upper-level subsystems, components, and functions in the form of an organization chart. Like any organization chart, there is substantial interaction between the tasks performed by different components of the chart, so the diagram is only an approximate representation of the system. Not only that—the diagram only shows a few of the most important modules that actually make up the system! As you can see, z/OS is a complex system, with work carefully divided among different modules.

Overall responsibility for the system rests with the base control program. With the assistance of the intelligent resource director, the BCP manages workflow throughout the system. To do so, the BCP keeps track of tasks, controls address spaces, dispatches tasks, and manages interrupt processing. Most of these functions are handled by dispatching the proper modules to perform the required action.

At the next level, z/OS is functionally divided into seven major subsystems: job management, IRD, security services, communication server, data management, and TSO. Job management is responsible for the entry, scheduling, and execution of jobs. The major task for system services is the management of all virtual and physical resources, including memory address space management, control of virtual storage, CPU dispatching, workload balancing and tracking of system facility use, and the loading and execution of programs. Data management organizes, manages, and provides access to data sets and data. TSO is the timesharing facility. There is also a master scheduler that is responsible for setting up the specific parameters and scheduling algorithms of the environment at initial program load

FIGURE 18.17

Overview of MVS Organization

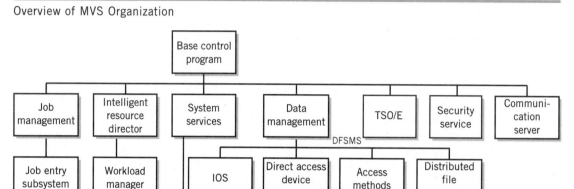

time. During normal operation, the master scheduler serves as an interface to the system operator. The most important operations are considered in the next several subsections.

JOB MANAGEMENT   The component responsible for most aspects of job management is the Job Entry Subsystem, or JES. As already noted, jobs are submitted to JES for scheduling and execution. JES checks the JCL procedure attached to the job for syntax errors and converts it into the form of service requests for other modules to handle. JES categorizes jobs by job class, size, and priority and places them into different execution queues for allocation of address space. When a job gets accepted for execution, job control is turned over to the system resource manager. At the completion of job execution, JES regains control. JES is responsible for spooling output data sets for printing. Once all spooled data sets are printed, the job is purged from the system.

TASK CONTROL AND EXECUTION   Once a job is accepted for execution, the job is turned over to the system resource manager (SRM), which manages jobs during execution. The SRM works with an I/O manager and the workload manager to assigns resource to maximize throughput and to make resources available when and where they are needed. Under SRM management the storage manager makes virtual and real address space available, the program manager locates, loads, and executes the programs that represent job steps, and the data management subsystem provides data access. The workload manager maintains statistics on resource usage and address space, and uses this information together with a set of resource-use algorithms to assist with SRM decisions.

The unit of work in z/OS is an address space. JES creates, and numbers, a separate virtual space for each batch job, TSO session, and system task admitted for execution. The original version of MVS was built around a 16 MB space. Later versions provided a 2GB space and a *Cross-Memory Facility* that allows programs in one virtual space to communicate with programs in another space. For address translation purposes, the virtual space is divided into 1MB fixed-size segments, each of which contains 256 4K pages. The current version of z/OS, further allows a task up to 15 additional 2GB virtual spaces to use for data only. There is a limited support for 16 EB virtual spaces, with full support expected soon. A memory map of the 2 GB virtual space for a task is shown in Figure 18.18. Notice that the space is divided at the 16 MB mark to provide backward compatibility for older programs. One interesting difference between z/OS and UNIX for you to observe is that UNIX isolates the operating system kernel in its own space, whereas z/OS includes the kernel in the space of each task.

Work is dispatched and executed under the control of the task manager, which handles dispatching of the CPU, manipulates task priorities, and creates and deletes subtasks in conjunction with the support policies established by the SRM. There are two types of tasks in z/OS. Regular tasks consist of job steps, utilities executed under TSO, and system tasks. As has been noted, these are identified by their address space. Service requests are tasks that are requested by one address space and executed in another. Service requests are usually shorter and are dispatched with higher priority than regular tasks. Dispatch priorities are established by the data center, according to performance groups that apply to a range of tasks, or more specifically within the JCL procedure for a job. Priorities are adjusted dynamically. Each time a task is passed over for CPU time, its priority is raised.

MEMORY MANAGEMENT   Virtual storage is handled by three components of the storage manager. The *real storage manager* controls real storage and causes pages to be moved between real storage and the paging device, under the guidance of the SRM. It handles page-fault processing, free-page management, and working set size adjustment. The *virtual storage manager* manages the virtual storage for each task. The *auxiliary storage manager* manages storage on the paging device. In addition to normal paging, the SRM can request that a task be swapped out of real memory when the number of free pages is too small. Page replacement is based on the Not Used Recently algorithm.

DATA MANAGEMENT   In IBM terminology, z/OS files are known as **data sets.** The data stored in z/OS data sets is structured into logical records and physical blocks. The structure is initially defined by a JCL data definition when a program creates the file. After that, data within the data set may be accessed from a program by logical record or block,

FIGURE 18.18

Virtual Memory Map for a Task

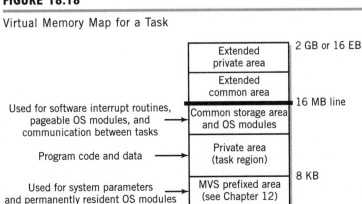

as specified in the data definition. The records in a data set may be organized for sequential access, for random access, or for indexed sequential access. Records may be of fixed or variable size. There is an additional data set type, called partitioned. A **partitioned data set** consists of a directory and a group of independent records called members. Each member has a name, which is stored in the directory together with information about the member and a pointer to the member. Thus, each member is effectively a data set within a data set. Partitioned data sets are useful for organizing data sets of similar type as a collection. Programs are also stored in partitioned data sets called **libraries.**

The data definition for a data set must be provided with the JCL procedure for any job step that uses the data set. This is the method used to make the structure available for program access to the data. The code within programs does not address data by the actual name of the data set. Instead, programs use the name element in the JCL DD statement as a reference. You may recall that the actual data set name is a parameter in the data definition. Thus, the actual data set is linked with the executing program at execution time. This means that a user may reference a different data set from the same program or use the same data set with different programs. However, it also means that the JCL data definition statements must use the names that are expected by the program in the EXEC statement for the job step. Good program documentation is essential when using a z/OS system! Interestingly, the name used within the program is called a file name. Notice that the file name may refer to different data sets by changing the DD parameters in the corresponding JCL statement; files and data sets are *not* the same in z/OS.

As an example, refer again to Figure 18.16. The names used with data definition (DD) statements in this example are not arbitrary. The person submitting a job must know that the COBOL compiler requires data definition statements named SYSIN, SYSLIN, SYSPRINT, and SYSUT1 through SYSUT7, and must know what each data set is to be used for.

Within z/OS, data sets are managed by the Data Facility Storage management subsystem, which includes four major components:

- The data facilities program manages open data sets. It provides device support, catalog access and updating, data access methods, and error recovery. Data access methods are programs that actually access the data in a data set. There are separate access methods for different data set structures. We will discuss access methods in more detail later in this section.

- The hierarchical storage manager program provides data set management facilities for locating data sets, for managing the directory structure, for free space recovery and management, and for other related tasks. It also attempts to balance storage utilization among different devices.

- The data set services program is used to move data rapidly from one device to another. It is also used for high-speed backup and recovery and data set or volume dumps.

- The removable media manager program maintains a system for keeping track of removable disk and tape media and helps locate media required for a job. It also controls the expiration of data sets and manages media reuse.

Newer systems offer a number of other optional components that perform other related services, such as data set management for distributed system environments, including support for other OS file systems. Cross-system access is managed transparently. Other file systems are managed as data sets within the z/OS structure.

Data sets are identified by names that are made up of multiple components called qualifiers. Qualifiers are separated by periods. Each qualifier is a maximum of 8 characters, with a maximum of 44 characters for the entire name. Data sets that are members of a partitioned data sets are additionally identified by the member name in parentheses. An additional 10 characters are allowed for this purpose. A typical partitioned data set name might appear as follows:

```
FACULTY.CISDEPT.ENGLNDR.COBFILES(PROGRAM1)
```

In a sense, the qualifiers correspond to the directories in a standard hierarchical file system. The major difference is that the technique used for accessing the data set in z/OS suggests that minimizing the number of qualifiers to maintain performance is more important than using more qualifiers to improve the organization of the data sets.

Directories in z/OS are called **catalogs.** There is a master catalog for the system. OS/370 catalogs were VSAM catalogs, but newer systems use a special access method called the **Integrated Catalog Facility,** or **ICF,** for catalogs. The master catalog name is known to the system and is not included as a qualifier. The master catalog contains the full catalog entry for important system data sets, such as those used for paging and swap operations, but most entries simply consist of qualifier names and pointers to a set of catalogs called user catalogs. There is a user catalog for each indexed entry in the master catalog. The user catalog has an entry for every data set name that begins with the selected leftmost qualifier. The user catalog pointer specifies the physical I/O channel and device number where the data set is located.

Each DASD (disk) device has a catalog called the **Volume Table of Contents,** or **VTOC** (pronounced vee-tock). The rightmost qualifier corresponds to the VTOC. The VTOC entry contains a pointer to the track where the data set begins, plus additional information about the data set. Of course, partitioned data sets contain their own directory for locating a member. (Notice that in this case only the directory is called a directory. Just another IBMism to keep track of!) Figure 18.19 shows the technique used to search for the data set name that we used as an example.

Space is allocated by the system, but the amount of space must be specified by the user in the JCL statement that creates the data set. Space is specified in tracks, cylinders, or blocks. A minimum of one track is required for a data set stored on DASD.

Physical data access is provided by an access method. z/OS provides a number of different data set access methods, including a sequential access method, a direct access method, an ISAM access method, and a partitioned access method. Many, perhaps most, modern data sets are stored using a single access method, **VSAM,** (pronounced vee-sam) for **virtual storage access method,** which supports both sequential and direct access. VSAM is optimized for use with virtual storage, and provides reliability, speed, integrity, and convenience beyond that of other access methods. VSAM even provides an audit trail to the **System Management Facility** that records changes that are made to a data set. VSAM can access data stored in three different ways:

- Key-sequenced data sets are stored in order and accessed by a key field connected with each record. The order is preserved when new records are added to the data set.

- Entry-sequenced data sets are stored in the order in which records are entered into the data set. New records are appended to the end of the data set. For each entry, VSAM returns a relative address in the data set to the program storing the record.

FIGURE 18.19

The Steps in Location of a Data Set

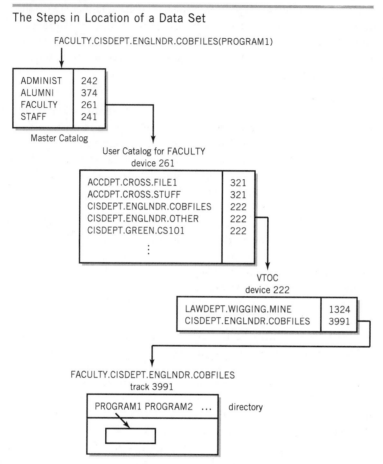

- Relative record data set records are also stored at a relative address in the data set. This mode allows two different options. The relative address may be specified by the program, in which case the record is stored in order relative to other record, similar to key-sequencing. Otherwise, VSAM appends the record to the end, like entry-sequencing.

VSAM can also build and use multiple index tables to increase random access flexibility. VSAM is well suited for large databases and for applications such as CICS.

Although the amount of space for a data set is requested when the data set is created, the other requisite attributes of the space—actual allocation, release, and physical location—are managed by the direct access device manager. Device drivers and physical I/O access resides in the I/O System (IOS).

Additional Features

We have only touched the surface of z/OS. There are many features that we have not discussed. For example, z/OS requires many additional modules to handle multiprocessing and telecommunication. Multiprocessing support, in particular, requires great care, to assure that tasks remain safe and secure when work is being shared between processors or systems. Telecommunication incorporates data and workload sharing across multiple systems, as well as communication between a processor and its remote terminals. Within a single processor, telecommunication is handled primarily by the Communications Server, which includes TCP/IP services, virtual telecommunication access method (VTAM) services, Web services and Web Domain Name support, and peer-to-peer and server-client networking. The distributed computing services offer support for distributed file system services, remote procedure calls, CORBA, enterprise directory services, and more, all at a high level of security.

Finally, we remind the reader that z/OS includes a complete, integrated UNIX system, with standard UNIX features, including UNIX sockets, the Network File System, the Distributed Computing Environment, and shell operations and commands, allowing UNIX users access to the powerful resources of the MVS system without the necessity of understanding MVS methodologies. This, in addition to the availability of Linux as a complete alternative to z/OS. The world is indeed getting smaller!

SUMMARY AND REVIEW

In this chapter we have presented a fairly detailed overview of three operating systems, each with a different set of goals and purposes, a different primary user base, and a different work focus. Each of the systems described satisfies the basic operating system requirements and major features discussed in Chapters 13 through 16. There are many similarities between the three systems, even though there are many important differences in their implementations, differences that support and reflect each system's design goals.

Although you will probably not remember most of the details presented in this chapter for long, we hope that presentation of these three important operating systems will help you to understand operating systems concepts better, the different options that are available to you in a system, and the reasons behind particular system choices.

KEY CONCEPTS AND TERMS

access method
application enabler
application program
   interface (API)
background task
base control program (BCP)
Berkeley Software
   Distribution (BSD)
catalog
child process
Customer Information
   Control System (CICS)
daemon
data set

Data Facility Storage
   Management Subsystem
   (DFSMS)
directory
docucentric processing
dynamic link library (DDL)
explorer utility
file
filter
foreground task
forking
hardware abstraction layer
   (HAL)
I/O stream

indexed sequential access
   method (ISAM)
in-line command execution
installable file system
Integrated Catalog Facility
   (ICF)
Interactive System
   Productivity Facility
   (ISPF)
JCL procedure
JCL statement
job
Job Control Language (JCL)
Job Entry Subsystem (JES)

job management module
kernel mode
library
master catalog
master scheduler
mounting
NT File System (NTFS)
object
object linking and
    embedding (OLE)
parallel sysplex
parent process
partitioned data set
pipe
plug-and-play installation
porting
process identifier (PID)
redirection
sequential access method
    (SAM)

shell script
signal
stderr
stdin
stdout
superuser
supervisor
System Management
    Facility (SMF)
system resource manager
    (SRM)
task
taskbar
Time Sharing Option (TSO)
UNIX
user catalog
user mode
vi editor
virtual file allocation table
    (VFAT)

virtual device driver (VxD)
virtual machine manager
    (VMM)
Volume Table of Contents
    (VTOC)
virtual storage access
    method (VSAM)
virtual telecommunications
    access method (VTAM)
Win16 process
Win32 process
Windows 2000
Windows XP
working directory
workload manager
z/OS

FOR FURTHER READING

There are only a few books that describe the capabilities and design of Windows 2000 or Windows XP in any detail. Northrup [NORT99] and Honeycutt [HON00] are books that describe the features and components of Windows 2000, but the internals are touched upon only lightly. Solomon [SOL00] is an excellent reference on Windows 2000 internals. Most of the internal design is derived directly from Windows NT. Reasonably clear discussions of Windows NT can be found in Bacon [BAC98], Silberschatz and others [SILB00], Stallings [STAL00] and the Microsoft Windows NT Resource Kit [MIC97]. Nearly every issue of the Microsoft Technical Journal features a discussion of some aspect of Windows 2000 or Windows XP. There is also a wealth of material on the Microsoft Web site www.microsoft.com.

The history of UNIX, as well as the design philosophy and fundamental operation, is well documented in a series of papers that were collected together in the Bell System Technical Journals for July–August 1978 and October 1984. These journals were reissued in 1987 as a two volume set entitled UNIX System Readings and Applications [ATT87]. Most of the papers in this set were written by the original UNIX designers. You will find many of the articles separately referenced in the bibliography of this book. There are many excellent text and professional books that introduce UNIX at the knowledgeable user level. My own favorites are books by Sobell [SOB95], Glass and Ables [GLAS99], and Christian and Richter [CHR94]. Each of these books also provides an introduction to the internal organization of UNIX. For the future UNIX guru, Gilly [GILL92] provides a brief but clear description of nearly every UNIX command, including the variations available on different implementations. Finally, Peek and others [PEEK93] is a truly amazing collection of applications and tricks using the UNIX command set.

There are numerous Linux books, as well. The internals of Linux are presented in Beck and others [BECK02] and Card and others [CARD98]. There are numerous Web sites devoted to all aspects of Linux. Check the Web site for this book for current links.

As you've probably noticed, z/OS is a large, sophisticated, and complex operating system. As of this writing, there are no books that discuss z/OS specifically. However, there are a number of books, written at different levels, that discuss MVS, its predecessor, which can ease the process of learning about z/OS. At the simplest level, Hoskins [HOSK94] presents an overview of the System/390, including an introduction to the various operating systems from the business user's perspective. Kirk [KIRK92] and Davis [DAV02] carry the discussion one step further, with straightforward introductions to MVS and its tools. Samson [SAMS96] presents an excellent introduction to OS/390 from the perspective of tuning and managing the system. Davis [DAV02] and Brown [BROW91] offer detailed introductions to the writing and use of MVS/JCL. Janossy and Samuels [JAN95] do the same for CICS. General discussions of the MVS internal organization and functions can be found in Deitel [DEIT90] and Flynn and McHoes [FLYN00]. For a more thorough treatment, the author recommends Johnson [JOHN89], although this book assumes a great deal of prior knowledge and uses a lot of acronyms and jargon. IBM publishes a large number of manuals covering various specific aspects of MVS and z/OS, and two publishers, McGraw-Hill and QED Technical Publishing Group, each have an entire series of books focusing on MVS, its tools, and its environment. IBM manuals are available at www.ibm.com.

The book by DuCharme [DUCH94] introduces UNIX and MVS, plus VMS, VM, and OS/400, from the perspective of a new user trying to get started on a particular system. It is excellent for this purpose.

EXERCISES

18.1   Describe what actions take place from the perspective of a process when you double-click on an icon in Windows 2000 or XP.

18.2   Describe the organization of the Windows 2000 file system in terms of windows and icons.

18.3   What shortcoming of GUIs is solved with the Windows 2000 or XP taskbar?

18.4   Explain how each of the basic components of an operating system that were discussed in Chapter 14 are implemented in Windows 2000 and XP.

18.5   Compare and contrast the way Windows 2000 and XP, UNIX, and z/OS utilize and implement virtual storage.

18.6   Explain the concept of a virtual machine in the context of Windows 2000 or XP.

18.7   What happens if a program tries to address an I/O device directly in Windows 2000 or XP? Why?

18.8   Explain the differences between a FAT and an NTFS file system. Discuss the advantages and disadvantages of each.

18.9   Windows 2000 has a new feature called reparse points, which can be used to shift directories around the directory tree. Compare this feature with the mount capability in UNIX.

18.10 If you have access to a Windows system, demonstrate and explain an operation that uses OLE support.

18.11 What sorts of tasks could you perform easily as a UNIX user that would be extremely difficult in Windows 2000 or XP? Give some examples for which the opposite is true. Beyond the differences that result from the user interfaces, consider also tasks that are more fundamental to the design and philosophy of each system.

18.12 Discuss the features, advantages, disadvantages, and trade-offs between directory look-up in Windows NTFS and UNIX file systems.

18.13 Explain the steps that are required to port a UNIX system from one machine to another.

18.14 If you have access to the IEEE POSIX specifications, discuss which UNIX features are included and which are unique to particular UNIX installations.

18.15 Illustrate a way in which each of the UNIX design criteria are addressed in a UNIX system. Describe the advantages, and perhaps disadvantages, of the effect that each of the design criteria has on a UNIX system in contrast to other operating systems discussed in this chapter or that you are familiar with.

18.16 Discuss the differences, advantages, and disadvantages in the approach taken to process management and control in UNIX, Linux, z/OS, and Windows 2000.

18.17 Consider several different user bases: clerks performing repetitive transaction tasks, such as data entry and customer order processing, end users working with productivity tools such as word processors and spreadsheets, application programmers, and system programmers. Compare and contrast the ways in which z/OS, UNIX, and Windows 2000 simplify or make more difficult work for the particular user base.

18.18 Compare and contrast batch processing in Windows 2000, UNIX, and z/OS.

18.19 Discuss the advantages and disadvantages of the use of application enablers instead of integrating the capabilities of application enablers into the operating system itself.

18.20 What is the value of UNIX shell scripts?

18.21 Clearly explain how the I/O stream concept in UNIX simplifies the implementation of pipes, redirection, and communication between different processes.

18.22 Find a good book on UNIX or Linux and explain how daemons work, and how they are used, and give several examples of daemons that were not included in our text.

18.23 Illustrate some conditions under which swapping in UNIX or z/OS is preferable to paging.

18.24 What is the advantage of treating device drivers as files, as is done in UNIX and Linux?

18.25 Describe the differences in methodology along with the advantages and disadvantages resulting from each in locating and accessing files in UNIX and data sets in z/OS.

CHAPTER 18   THREE OPERATING SYSTEMS   **647**

18.26 Discuss the trade-offs from the perspective of the user, and the user's application programs, in the simple byte approach to files used in UNIX versus the record- and block-structured approach used in z/OS.

18.27 Discuss the trade-offs in automatic mounting, as in Windows 2000, versus manual mounting, as in UNIX. In addition to the user perspective, consider the differences when dealing with removable media such as floppy disks, CD-ROMs, and tapes.

18.28 Describe the various features that are included in UNIX to support group work.

18.29 Explain the advantages and disadvantages of the JCL approach to processing that is used in z/OS.

18.30 The virtual memory map for a z/OS task includes many modules of the operating system, whereas the UNIX memory map isolates the operating system from the virtual memory space assigned to a process. What are the trade-offs in each approach?

18.31 The capabilities of VSAM make it possible to use VSAM in place of the other access methods provided with z/OS. If you have access to Johnson [JOHN89] or a similar book, read about various access methods; then discuss the advantages and disadvantages of VSAM with ISAM, SAM, and direct access storage of data in data sets, and describe the conditions under which one would be preferred over another.

18.32 Assume that you have been assigned the task of selecting an operating system for your business organization. What important questions would you want answered to help to make and support your decision?

18.33 Find a copy of Samson [SAMS97]. Describe the various features of the MVS system resource manager. Which of these features could you perform on a Windows system? How would you do so? Which features would be nearly impossible to perform on a Windows system? What advantages would be gained if you could do so?

AN INTRODUCTION TO DIGITAL COMPUTER LOGIC

"I keep telling you Gwendolyth, you'll never attract today's kids that way."

S1.0 INTRODUCTION

Many students are curious about the inner workings of the computer. Although understanding the computer's circuitry is not essential to working with computers, doing so is satisfying, for it reduces the mystery of computers; it also eliminates any idea that the computer is a "magical box" to be feared and respected. Instead, you get to see that the computer is actually nothing more than a rather simple collection of digital switches—more like a toy for adults to play with!

Computers are built up from integrated circuits. Each integrated circuit in a computer serves a specialized purpose within the computer. For example, there is an integrated circuit that represents the CPU, another that provides an interface to the external bus, another that manages memory, another that manages DMA (see Chapter 9), and so forth.

The integrated circuits themselves are made up of transistors, resistors, capacitors, and other electronic components that are combined into circuits. The primary component of interest to us is the transistor. A single integrated circuit may have thousands, or even millions of transistors. The CPU chip in the Motorola MPC 7400 PowerPC module, shown in Figure S1.1, contains approximately 6.5 million transistors in an area of less than 1/2 square inch.

Transistors can act as amplifiers or switches. The transistors in your television set and stereo are used mostly as amplifiers. Except for a few specialized devices such as modems, virtually all the circuitry in computers is digital in nature: the ON and OFF positions of transistor switches serve to represent the 1's and 0's of binary digital circuits. In the computer, these transistor switches are combined to form **logic gates,** which represent values in Boolean algebra. Boolean algebra is the basis for computer logic design and transistors the means for implementation.

Digital circuits are used to perform arithmetic, to control the movement of data within the computer, to compare values for decision making, and to accomplish many other functions. The digital logic that performs these functions is called **combinatorial logic.** Combinatorial logic is logic in which the results of an operation depend only on the present inputs to the operation. For the same set of inputs, combinatorial logic will always yield the same result. As an example, arithmetic operations are combinatorial. For a given set of inputs and the add operation, the resulting sum will always be the same, regardless of any previous operations that were performed.

Digital circuits can also be used to perform operations that depend on both the inputs to the operation and the result of the previous operation. Digital circuits can store the result or state of an operation and use that result as a factor the next time the operation is performed. Each time the operation is performed, the result will be a function of the present inputs and the previous state of the circuit. Digital logic that is dependent on the previous state of an operation is called **sequential logic.** An example of sequential logic is a counter. Each time the counter operation is performed, the

649

FIGURE S1.1

The Motorola MPC 7400 PowerPC CPU

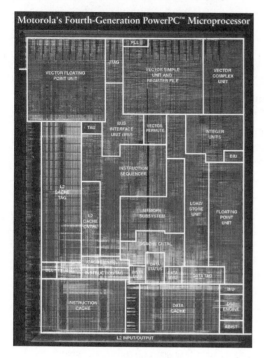

result is the sum of the previous result plus the counting factor. The counter continues to hold the state—in this case, the current count—for use the next time the operation is performed. Computers incorporate both combinatorial and sequential logic.

S1.1 BOOLEAN ALGEBRA

The digital computer is based on **Boolean algebra.** Boolean algebra describes rules that govern constants and variables that can take on two values. These can be represented in many different ways: true or false, on or off, yes or no, 1 or 0, light or dark, water valve open or shut, to indicate a few possible representations. (Yes, there have been attempts to build hydraulic water-based computers!)

The rules that govern the ways in which Boolean constants and variables are combined are called **Boolean logic.** There are a number of logical rules, but these can all be derived from three fundamental operations, the operations of AND, OR, and NOT. Boolean logic rules can be described as a formula, or by a **truth table,** which specifies the result for all possible combinations of inputs. Truth tables are the Boolean equivalent to additions and multiplication tables in arithmetic.

The Boolean AND operation can be stated as follows: The result of an AND operation is TRUE if and only if both (or all, if there are more than two) input operands are TRUE. This is shown in the truth table in Figure S1.2. Arbitrarily, we have assigned the value 0 to FALSE and the value 1 to TRUE. This is a normal way of describing Boolean algebra. If you prefer, you could use the value GREEN for true and RED for false, and note that the AND operation says that you can only go if both lights are green. The Boolean symbol for the AND operation is a center dot: ($\cdot$). The Boolean equation

$$C = A \cdot B$$

states that the Boolean variable C is true if and only if both A and B are true.

The Boolean or operation, or more accurately, INCLUSIVE-OR, is stated as follows. The result of an INCLUSIVE-OR operation is TRUE if the values of *any* (one or more) of the input operands are true. The truth table for the INCLUSIVE-OR operation is shown in Figure S1.3. The Boolean symbol for the OR operation is a plus sign ($+$).

Therefore,

$$C = A + B$$

states that C is true if either A or B or both are true.

The Boolean NOT operation states that the result is TRUE if and only if the single input operand is FALSE. Thus, the state of the result of a NOT operation is always the opposite state from the input operand. Figure S1.4 shows the truth table for the not operation. The symbol for the not operation is a bar over the symbol:

$$C = \overline{A}$$

There is a fourth operation, the EXCLUSIVE-OR. The truth table for the EXCLUSIVE-OR operation is shown in Figure S1.5. The symbol for the EXCLUSIVE-OR operation is a plus sign within a circle:

$$C = A \oplus B$$

The EXCLUSIVE-OR operation is used less frequently than the others. It can be derived from the INCLUSIVE-OR, AND, and NOT operations as follows: the result of the EXCLUSIVE-OR operation is TRUE if either A or B is TRUE, but not both. Two ways to express this equivalence are

$$A \oplus B = (A + B) \cdot (\overline{A \cdot B})$$

which can be read "A or B and not both A and B," or alternatively

FIGURE S1.2

Truth Table for AND Operation

A	B	C
0	0	0
0	1	0
1	0	0
1	1	1

FIGURE S1.3

Truth Table for INCLUSIVE-OR Operation

A	B	C
0	0	0
0	1	1
1	0	1
1	1	1

FIGURE S1.4

Truth Table for NOT Operation

A	C
0	1
1	0

FIGURE S1.5

Truth Table for EXCLUSIVE-OR Operation

A	B	C
0	0	0
0	1	1
1	0	1
1	1	0

$$A \oplus B = (A \cdot \bar{B}) + (B \cdot \bar{A})$$

which reads "either A and not B or B and not A."

It is useful to study this example for practice in the manipulation and reasoning of Boolean algebra.

There are a number of useful laws and identities that help to manipulate Boolean equations. Boolean algebra operations are associative, distributive, and commutative, which means that

$$A + (B + C) = (A + B) + C \qquad \text{(associative)}$$
$$A \cdot (B + C) = A \cdot B + A \cdot C \qquad \text{(distributive)}$$
$$A + B = B + A \qquad \text{(commutative)}$$

These laws are valid for INCLUSIVE-OR, AND, and EXCLUSIVE-OR operations. Perhaps most useful are a pair of theorems called **DeMorgan's theorems,** which state the following:

$$\overline{A + B} = \bar{A} \cdot \bar{B} \text{ and } \overline{A \cdot B} = \bar{A} + \bar{B}$$

These laws and theorems are important because it is frequently necessary or convenient to modify the form of an Boolean equation to make it simpler to understand or to implement.

S1.2 GATES AND COMBINATORIAL LOGIC

Many functions in a computer are defined in terms of their Boolean equations. For example, the sum of two single-digit binary numbers is represented by a pair of truth tables, one for the actual column sum, the other for the carry bit. The truth tables are shown in Figure S1.6. You should recognize the truth table for the sum as the EXCLUSIVE-OR operation and the carry as the AND operation. Similarly, the complement operation that is used in subtraction is just a Boolean NOT operation. These operations are combinatorial. They are true regardless of any previous additions or complements performed.

Complementary Boolean logic in a computer is implemented by using electronic circuits called **gates** or logical gates. Gates are constructed from transistor switches and other electronic components, formed into integrated circuits. A *small-scale* integrated circuit may contain half a dozen gates or so for building special Boolean logic circuits. The gates in a CPU are organized into a **very-large-scale integrated** circuit or **VLSI** chip. The drawn representations for logical gates are shown in Figure S1.7.

FIGURE S1.6

Truth Tables for the Sum of Two Binary Numbers

A	B	S
0	0	0
0	1	1
1	0	1
1	1	0

sum

A	B	C
0	0	0
0	1	0
1	0	0
1	1	1

carry

FIGURE S1.7

Standard Logic Gate Representations

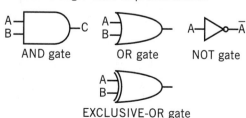

It is not difficult to manipulate the Boolean algebra to show that combinatorial Boolean logic can be implemented entirely with a single type of gate, appropriately combined. Either of the two gates shown in Figure S1.8 will fill the bill. The NAND gate is an AND operation followed by a NOT operation. The NOR operation is an INCLUSIVE-OR operation followed by a NOT operation. The small circle is used to indicate the NOT operation.

We can use DeMorgan's theorem to show that a NAND operation is the same as an or operation performed on inverted inputs. For convenience, the NAND gate may also be drawn in the alternative form shown in the figure. (The same thing can be done with the NOR gate.) The advantage of doing so is shown in Figure S1.9. This logic drawing represents a pair of ANDs followed by an OR. Since two NOTs in succession cancel each other, the pair of circles in succession make it clear what is actually happening. The result in algebraic form is

$$Y = A \cdot B + C \cdot D$$

EXAMPLE

Just for fun, let's consider a practical application for the circuit in Figure S1.9. Figure S1.10 shows the same circuit with one modification: an additional NAND gate has been used to perform a NOT operation, so that only one of the AND gates in the AND-OR combination can be active at a time. If the *select* line is a "1," then the output of the upper NAND gate will reflect the inverse of whatever input is present at A. On the other hand, if the *select* line is a "0," the output of the lower NAND gate will reflect the inverse of whatever is present at B. Since the final NAND gate generates the OR operation of the inverted inputs, only the active AND operation gets passed through to the output. Therefore, Y represents either A or B, depending on the value of the select line.

For obvious reasons, this circuit is called a **selector.** Since it can be used to switch the input back and forth between A and B, it is also sometimes called a **multiplexer.** If we

FIGURE S1.8

NAND and NOR Gate Representations

NAND gate
$C = \overline{A \cdot B}$

NOR gate
$C = \overline{A + B}$

alternative form for
NAND gate
$C = \overline{A} + \overline{B}$

FIGURE S1.9

AND-OR Operation Made up
from NAND Gates

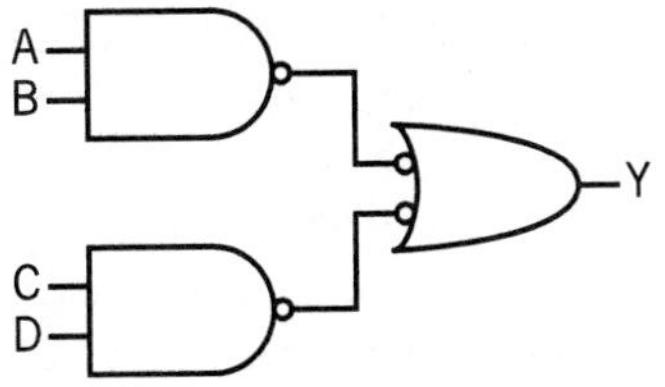

FIGURE S1.10

Selector Circuit

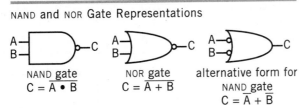

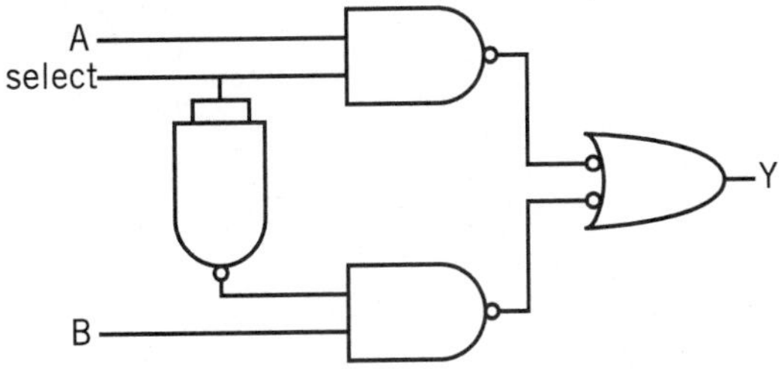

wanted to switch between two bytes of data, we would use eight identical selector circuits, one for each bit. One byte would be placed on the A input, the other on the B input. The same select signal would be connected to the select line on every circuit. What this shows you is that the logic circuits that make up a computer are relatively simple, but they look complicated because so many circuits are required to perform useful work.

■ ■ ■

Another important example of a combinatorial logic circuit is the arithmetic adder. In Figure S1.6 we showed you the truth tables for a simple adder. The NAND logic circuit that produces the desired outputs for a single bit is shown in Figure S1.11. This circuit is called a **half adder.** For practice, you should make sure that you can correlate the circuit to the formulas for a half adder.

The circuit in Figure S1.11 is called a half adder because in most cases a complete adder circuit must also handle a possible carry from the *previous* bit. Figure S1.12 shows a logic circuit for one bit of a **full adder.** To simplify the circuit, we have used the modified half adder enclosed in the dotted line; the use of instead of C reduces the number of gates somewhat. The half adder circuit is represented in Figure S1.12 as a block in this drawing. This approach is a common solution to the problem of making logic drawings readable.

A 32-bit adder would be made up of 32 of these circuits. Because the carry ripples through each of the 32 bits, the adder is called a *ripple adder.* Modern logic designers use some tricks to speed up the adder by reducing the ripple effect of the carry bits, but the basic design of the 32-bit adder in a computer is as you see it here.

S1.3 SEQUENTIAL LOGIC CIRCUITS

Sequential logic circuits are circuits whose output is dependent not only on the input and the configuration of gates that make up the circuit, but on the previous state of the circuit as well. In other words, the state of the circuit is somehow stored within the circuit and used as a factor in determining the new output. The key to sequential logic circuits is the presence of memory within the circuit—not memory as you think of computer memory, but individual bits of memory that form part of the circuit itself. The **state** of the circuit is stored in these memory bits.

The basic memory element in a sequential logic circuit is called a **flip-flop.** The simplest flip-flop is made up of two NAND logic gates connected as shown in Figure S1.13. This circuit is called a set-reset flip-flop. A similar flip-flop can be built from NOR gates.

Suppose that and are both initially set to 1. Can you determine the two outputs? It turns out that you can't. All you can say is that one of them will be a 0 and the other will be a 1. You can see this by assuming the value

FIGURE S1.11

Half Adder

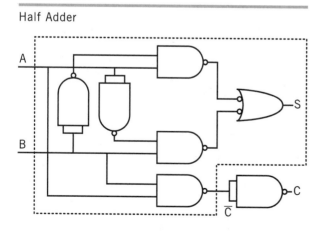

FIGURE S1.12

Full Adder

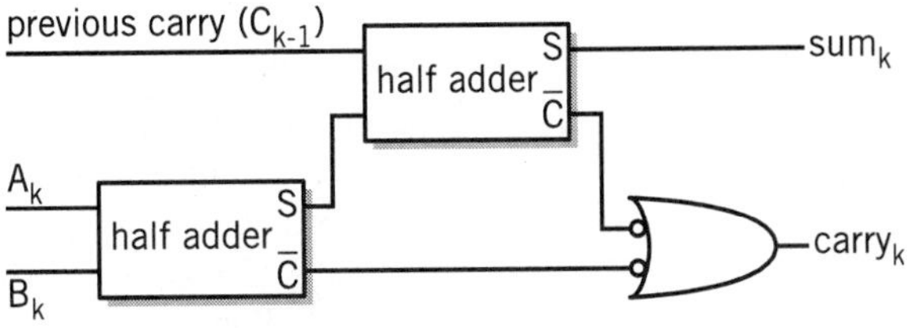

FIGURE S1.13

Set-Reset Flip-flop

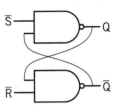

for one output, determining the other output, and then verifying that everything in the circuit is self-consistent.

For example, assume that the upper output in the figure is a 1. Then both inputs for the lower gate are 1's, and the output is a 0. This means that one of the inputs to the upper gate is a 0, which verifies that the upper output is a 1. Everything is self-consistent, and the circuit is stable as long as the and inputs remain at 1. (You might need to review the truth table for the NAND gate to convince yourself that the flip-flop works as we claim.)

Now suppose that the input momentarily becomes a 0. This forces the output of the lower gate to a 1. The two upper inputs are now both 1's, so the Q output becomes a 0. The Q output will hold the lower output at 1, even after the input returns to a 1. The flip-flop has switched states. It is now stable in the alternate state to the one that we began with. In other words, the flip-flop *remembers* which input was momentarily set to 0. (One ground rule: the logic surrounding this flip-flop must avoid situations where both and are 0 at the same time.)

There are other types of flip-flops as well. Some are designed to work on the basis of the 1 and 0 levels at the input. These types of flip-flops are sometimes called *latches*. Other flip-flops work on an input *transition,* called an *edge trigger,* the instantaneous change from 1 to 0 at an input, for example. A D flip-flop has a single data input. When the input marked Ck, for *clock,* is momentarily changed to 0 the Q output will take on the value present at the *D* input. The *preset* (P) and *clear* (Clr) inputs are used to initialize the flip-flop to a known value; they work independently of the D and *clock inputs.* A toggle flip-flop switches states whenever the T input momentarily goes to 0.

The equivalent of a truth table for a sequential circuit is called a **state table** or behavior table. The state table shows the output for all combinations of input and previous states. For edge-triggered flip-flops, the clock acts as a control signal. The new output occurs when the clock is pulsed except for preset and clear inputs, which affect the output immediately. The symbols and state tables for several types of flip-flops are shown in Figure S1.14.

Flip-flops of various types have many uses throughout the computer. Registers are made up of flip flops. They hold the results of intermediate arithmetic and logic operations. Flip-flops are used as counters, for the steps of a fetch-execute cycle, and for the program counter. Flip-flops control the timing of various operations. Flip-flops serve as buffers. Static RAM is also made up of flip flops, although dynamic RAM uses a different storage technique.

EXAMPLE

This example is a simple illustration of the use of both sequential and combinatorial logic in a computer. The text in Chapter 7 points out that the copying of data from one register to

FIGURE S1.14

Several Types of Flip-flops

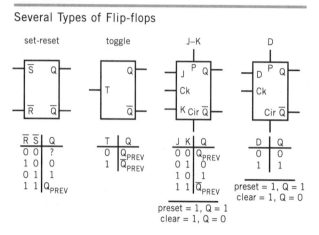

set-reset

$\overline{R}$	$\overline{S}$	Q
0	0	?
1	0	0
0	1	1
1	1	Q_{PREV}

toggle

T	Q
0	Q_{PREV}
1	$\overline{Q}_{PREV}$

J–K

J	K	Q
0	0	Q_{PREV}
0	1	0
1	0	1
1	1	$\overline{Q}_{PREV}$

preset = 1, Q = 1
clear = 1, Q = 0

D

D	Q
0	0
1	1

preset = 1, Q = 1
clear = 1, Q = 0

FIGURE S1.15

Logic to Copy Data from One
Register to Another

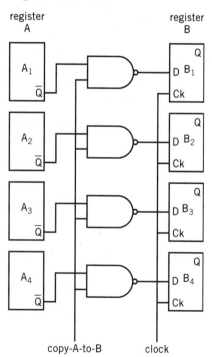

register A   register B

copy-A-to-B   clock

another is an essential operation in the fetch-execute cycle. The logic shown in Figure S1.15 represents the essential part of implementing a register copying operation. Flip-flops A_1 through A_4 represent four bits of a register. Flip-flops B_1 through B_4 represent the corresponding bits of a second register. This circuit can be used to copy the data from register A to register B. If the signal marked *copy-A-to-B* is a 1 when the clock is pulsed, data will be copied from A to B. The *copy-A-to-B* signal would be controlled from a circuit that counts the steps in a particular instruction fetch-execute cycle, then turns on the signal when the copy is required.

To carry this discussion a step further, consider the simplified hardware implementation of a LOAD instruction, shown in Figure S1.16. For this instruction, the clock pulse is directed to four different lines, each of which carries one of the clock pulses, in sequence, controlled by an instruction step counter. The first line, called t_1 in the diagram, closes the switches that transfer the data from the program counter to the memory address register for the first step of the fetch phase. The same pulse is delayed, then used to activate memory for a READ. The next clock pulse, t_2, connects the memory data register to the instruction register, completing the fetch phase.

Lines t_3 and t_4 will perform different operations depending on the instruction. The combination of bits in the op code portion of the instruction register determine the instruction being performed, and these are used together with the clock lines to determine which switches are closed for the execution portion of the instruction. The remainder of the operation can be seen in the diagram. (The incrementing of the program counter has been omitted in the diagram for simplicity.) The last time pulse is also used to reset the instruction step counter for the next instruction.

As you can see, the basic hardware implementation of the CPU is relatively straightforward and simple. Although the addition of pipelining and other features complicates the design, it is possible, with careful design, to implement and produce an extremely fast and efficient CPU at low cost and in large quantities.

FIGURE S1.16

Simplified Implementation of the Steps in a LOAD Instruction

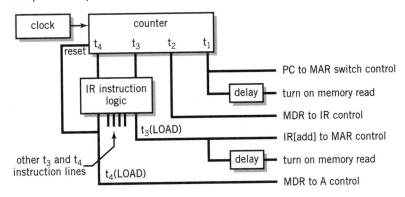

SUMMARY AND REVIEW

The circuitry in a computer is made up of a combination of combinatorial and sequential logic. Computer logic is based on the rules of Boolean algebra, as implemented with logic gates. Sequential logic uses logic gates to provide memory. The output and state of a sequential logic circuit depends on its previous state as well as the current sets of inputs.

KEY CONCEPTS AND TERMS

AND	gates	sequential logic
Boolean algebra	half adder	selector circuit
Boolean logic	INCLUSIVE-OR	state
combinatorial logic	logic gate	state table
DeMorgan's theorems	multiplexer circuit	truth table
EXCLUSIVE-OR	NAND	very-large-scale integrated
flip-flop	NOR	(VLSI) circuit
full adder	NOT	

FOR FURTHER READING

Most general computer architecture textbooks have at least brief discussion of digital logic circuits. Reasonable discussions can be found, for example, in Stallings [STAL02], Patterson and Hennesey [PATT97], and Tanenbaum [TAN99]. More detailed discussions can be found in Lewin [LEW83], Wakerly [WAKE00], Proser and Winkel [PROS87], or Mano [MANO91]. There are many other excellent choices as well.

EXERCISES

S1.1   **a.**   Verify using truth tables that both equivalence equations for the EXCLUSIVE-OR operations are valid.

       b.   Do the same using DeMorgan's theorem.

S1.2   Show the truth table for the following Boolean equation:

$$Y = A + A \cdot B$$

Look at the result. What general rule for reducing Boolean equations can you deduce from the result?

S1.3   Reduce the following equations to a simpler form

       a. $Y = A + 1$

       b. $Y = A + 0$

       c. $Y = A \cdot 1$

       d. $Y = A \cdot 0$

S1.4   Show the truth table for the following Boolean equation:

$$Y = A + A \cdot \overline{B} \cdot C + A \cdot B \cdot \overline{C}$$

S1.5   One easy way to construct a logic gate implementation from a truth table is to recognize that the output is the OR of every row that has a 1 as the result. Each row is the AND of every column that has a 1 in it. Given the following Boolean expression:

$$Y = ((A \cdot \overline{B} + \overline{C}) + B \cdot (\overline{A} \cdot B \cdot C)) \cdot (\overline{B} + C)$$

determine the truth table; then implement the result using NAND gates. You may use three input NAND gates if necessary.

S1.6   Show a selector circuit implementation made up of NOR gates.

S1.7   The sum output from the half adder in Figure S1.11 is implemented from the equation

$$S = A \cdot \overline{B} + \overline{A} \cdot B$$

An alternate representation for the sum is

$$S = \overline{((A \cdot B) + \overline{A}) \cdot ((A \cdot B) + \overline{B})}$$

       a.   Show using either truth tables or algebraic manipulation that these two representations are equivalent.

       b.   Use the latter form to develop a NAND gate implementation that requires only five gates to produce both the sum and carry.

S1.8   A decoder is a combinatorial logic circuit that produces a separate output for every possible combination of inputs. Each output is a 1 only for that particular combination. A decoder with three inputs, A, B, and C, would have eight outputs, for 000, 001, 010, ... Implement a logic decoder circuit for three inputs.

S1.9   Consider the sequential logic circuit shown in the accompanying figure together with an input that consists of an alternating sequence of 0s and 1s as shown. Assume that the initial state of this circuit produces an output that is all 0's. Show the next six output states. In one word, what does this circuit do?

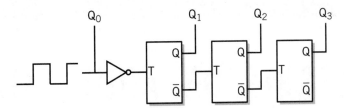

S1.10 Design a circuit that would serve as a four-stage *shift register*. A shift register shifts the input bits one bit at a time, so that the output from each stage represents the previous output from the previous stage.

INSTRUCTION ADDRESSING MODES

"Now go to 15 Front Street, where you'll find a box. In the box, there's another note with a number on it. Add that value to the address of the first house past the vacant lot on the southwest corner of Back and Side Streets. Then go to that address on Campus Road, and you'll find the prize under the third rock in the garden. Unless somebody else got there first."

Irv Englander and Benjamin Reece

S2.0 OVERVIEW

Most of the instructions in a typical program will manipulate data. The data may be variable data, constants, addresses, or even arrays of data. The manipulations consist of movement from one location in the computer to another, calculations, shifts, and various other operations. The data may be stored in memory, or it may be located in various programmer-accessible registers.

Much of the power of the instruction set in real computers comes from the ability to manipulate data quickly, flexibly, and efficiently. In the Little Man Computer, only a single method of addressing memory was provided, and only one register was available to the programmer. The method used in the Little Man Computer is known as **direct, absolute addressing.**

In real computers, instructions address registers and memory locations in a variety of ways. Each of the terms used to describe the Little Man instruction, *direct* and *absolute,* has its own meaning. There are also alternatives to each term. The term direct refers to the fact that the data is reached directly from the address in the instruction. This might suggest to you that there could be an *indirect* mode of addressing— you would be correct in such an assumption. The term absolute means that the address given in the instruction field is the actual memory location being addressed. In other words, if the address in the instruction field is 49, then the data is located at memory location number 49. It would be possible to have an addressing mode in which an offset is added to the specified address, in which case the address specified would actually be relative to the offset. If the offset were 120, for example, and the address in the instruction field were 49, the actual address where the data is to be found would be 120 + 49, or 169.

Although it is possible to program using only direct absolute addressing, it adds convenience and flexibility to have available other modes of addressing. You have already seen that one important reason to provide additional addressing modes is that to do so allows a much larger range of addressable memory while using a reasonable number of bits for the address field. Another important reason is that additional addressing modes also can make it much easier to write certain types of programs, such as loops that use an index to address different entries in a table or array. Finally, as noted before, most modern computers provide a number of programmer-accessible registers. These machines will usually contain instructions that move and manipulate data directly between registers. Register-based instructions execute faster because the time required to access data from memory is eliminated. For these reasons and others, most computers provide several different modes for addressing memory.

S2.1 REGISTER ADDRESSING

Register addressing has the advantage that it is implemented directly as part of the CPU. As shown in Figure S2.1, the fetch-execute cycle for a register-to-register move instruction can be reduced to the four steps shown. The contents of the source register specified in the instruction can be moved directly to the destination register without a memory access. Since the step that adjusts the PC for the next instruction can be performed in parallel with earlier steps, only three time units are required for this instruction. Obviously, instructions that do not require a memory access can execute faster. This suggests that frequently used data could be loaded from memory into a register and left there. The programmer's goal would be to minimize the use of memory referencing instructions and use registers alone for most operations.

This technique can significantly speed up program execution. As noted earlier, RISC machines provide an instruction set made up almost entirely of register operation instructions in order to achieve high program execution speeds. For this purpose, RISC machines are equipped with a larger than usual number of registers.

S2.2 ALTERNATIVES TO ABSOLUTE ADDRESSING

As previously stated, all the addressing in the Little Man Computer is absolute. The address specified in the instruction refers directly to the address of the data. Alternatives to absolute addressing are designed to allow the addressing of large amounts of memory while maintaining a reasonably sized instruction word address field.

Most program code executes within a relatively small area of memory that changes as the program proceeds. This is true because well-written programs tend to be modular, with local variables. Loops and conditional branches are usually confined to a fairly small area of program code; therefore, most program jumps tend to be short. This suggests that a small address field would be adequate, provided that there is a way to move the entire area that the address field references at a given time. This concept is illustrated in Figure S2.2.

There are several different ways of modifying the address in the address field to accomplish implementing a large memory address space with a small instruction address

FIGURE S2.1

Fetch-Execute Cycle for Register-to-Register Move Instruction

```
          PC -► MAR
          MDR -► IR
contents(IR[add1]) -► contents(IR[add2])
          PC + 1 -► PC
```

FIGURE S2.2

Moving the Address Space to Address More Memory

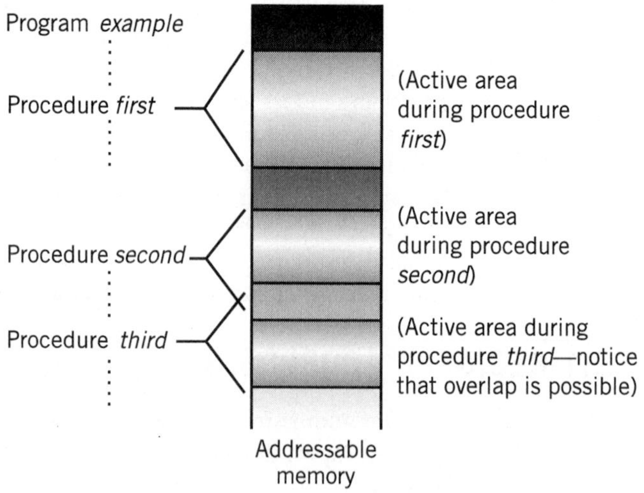

Program *example*

Procedure *first* — (Active area during procedure *first*)

Procedure *second* — (Active area during procedure *second*)

Procedure *third* — (Active area during procedure *third*—notice that overlap is possible)

Addressable memory

field. The most common ways are known as *base offset addressing,* or **base register addressing,** and **relative addressing.**

Effectively, each of these methods works by providing a starting address and an offset, or displacement, from the starting point. The starting address could be stored in a register and the address field of the instruction then becomes the offset. (Note, incidentally, that a different way to look at *absolute* addressing is to recognize it as just the case where the starting address is fixed at zero.)

There is a programming advantage to using one of these movable starting address methods. If all of a program's memory referencing instructions will be specified as displacements rather than as absolute addresses, it will be possible to move the entire program to a different location in memory without changing any of the instructions. This means that a program can be loaded into any part of memory that is convenient. As you will understand when we explore the operating system in Part IV of this book, this feature, known as **relocatability,** is important to the efficient use of the computer.

Base offset addressing is illustrated in Figure S2.3. A *base register* is used to set an initial address value. The final address for each instruction is established by adding the address field of the instruction to the base address. A new block of addresses can be established at any time simply by loading a new value into the base register. On some machines, the base register may be a special, separate register reserved for the purpose of base offset addressing; on others, the general purpose registers can be assigned for this purpose. In either case, the base register is generally quite large, which provides the capability of a large memory space. It is not uncommon to provide memory capacities of several gigabytes using this technique.

EXAMPLE

The IBM zSystem allows use of its 16 64-bit general-purpose registers as base registers. The number of the selected base register is contained in the instruction word along with a 12-bit displacement value. The 12-bit displacement allows a range of 4096 locations from the base value. The displacement value is added to the value in the base register to determine the absolute address of the data. The format used for a load instruction is shown in Figure S2.4.

FIGURE S2.3

Base Register Address Creation

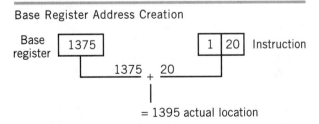

= 1395 actual location

FIGURE S2.4

Load Instruction Format

	op code	reg #	index	base #	displacement

bit 0   7 8   11 12   15 16   19 20   31

In this format the register number is the number of the general-purpose register where the data from memory is to go, and the base number is the number of a different general-purpose register that holds the base address value. For now, we'll ignore the index field and assume that the index value is 0; we'll deal with indexing in the next section of this chapter.

Suppose that general-purpose register 3 is being used as the base value register and that data is to be loaded from memory into register 6. Then if register 3 has the value

$$1 \; C \; 2 \; 5 \; E \; 0_{16}$$

and if the displacement for this instruction is $3 \; 7 \; A_{16}$, the absolute address of the data to be loaded will be

$$
\begin{array}{r}
1 \; C \; 2 \; 5 \; E \; 0_{16} \\
+ \; 3 \; 7 \; A_{16} \\
\hline
= \; 1 \; C \; 2 \; 9 \; 5 \; A_{16}
\end{array}
$$

The instruction word for this example will be

Op code   Base register

| 58 | 6 | 0 | 3 | 37A |

Destination register   Displacement

The Intel X86 architecture offers several different types of base register addressing. One method uses two registers, BX and BP, as base registers. A second method was used in early models of X86 architecture to handle the limitations of a 16-bit address space. This method is still provided in later models of the X86 series, and is now known as **real mode addressing.** Real mode addressing defines a 64KB region of memory as a paragraph. The value stored in a 16-bit *segment register* is shifted left 4 bits and added to the address, providing a 20-bit address. With this method, the programmer can address 1MB of memory, 64K at a time. X86 addressing methods are discussed further in Chapter 12.

Another method for constructing a block of addresses is to create addresses relative to the current instruction being executed. The desired address consists of the value in the address field added to the value in the program counter. This technique is known as relative addressing. As an example, suppose the computer is presently executing the instruction in memory location 46 (i.e., the program counter is set to 46). If the address in the instruction address field is 03, the data would be found 3 locations up from 46 in memory location 49. You might be interested in noticing that *relative addressing* is similar to base offset addressing with the program counter being used as base register.

Notice that in relative addressing the address field must be capable of both positive and negative numbers; otherwise, it would be impossible to jump backward in loops. Thus, the address field must be capable of storing and manipulating complementary numbers. Notice also that the block of addresses created using relative addressing moves with each instruction that is executed, because the program counter changes. When the program counter is 50, the same LOAD RELATIVE 3 instruction now refers to location 53.

Both techniques allow the addressing of more memory with a given address field size than would be possible with absolute addressing. The trade-off is the inability to reach data at distant locations outside the range of the address without modifying the base location or using some alternative to direct addressing. In relative addressing, the base is implied by the location of the instruction itself, and other techniques must be used to extend the range of addressing when the data is outside the range for a particular instruction. Indirect addressing, which is discussed in the next section, is useful for this purpose.

The fetch-execute cycle for each of these address modification techniques is similar. The relative addressed ADD instruction in Figure S2.5 is typical. The only change from the fetch-execute cycles that you have previously seen is the addition of the program counter in step 3. For base displacement addressing, the value in a base register would be used in step 3 of the cycle instead of the value in the program counter.

S2.3 ALTERNATIVES TO DIRECT ADDRESSING

Any of the techniques used to determine the absolute address that we have discussed can be used with direct addressing. With direct addressing the absolute address, as established, becomes the address where the data is to be found. There are also useful alternatives to direct addressing.

Before we explore alternatives to direct addressing, let us consider the features and advantages of direct addressing itself. One important feature and advantage of direct addressing is that it separates the data into a location different from the location of the instruction itself. This provides two major benefits to the programmer:

1. The data can be changed without affecting the instruction itself. This is important since most program data actually represents data variables, which of course change as the program progresses.

2. The data is available to be used by different instructions. This would not be the case if the data were located within the instruction word itself.

These benefits mean that a variable can be assigned to a particular location in memory independent of the various instructions that refer to that data.

You should be particularly aware of an important conceptual difference between the alternatives used to determine an absolute address discussed in the previous section and the address modification operations that will be discussed in this section. Although both groups of addressing techniques alter the final address where data is to be found, the primary objective of alternative techniques that are used to build the absolute address is to allow access to a large memory space in an efficient manner. The operations discussed in this section start from the absolute address previously obtained and modify that address to allow the programmer to improve the efficiency of common programming operations, such as programming loops. While the different types of absolute addressing operations are used generally, and are applied to most instructions, the techniques discussed here are usually applied to a smaller number of individual instructions. Thus, the different **addressing modes** available to a programmer are usually variations on direct addressing and its alternatives.

FIGURE S2.5

Fetch-Execute Cycle for Relative Addressing

```
PC -> MAR
MDR -> IR
IR[Address] + PC -> MAR
MDR + A -> A
PC + 1 -> PC
```

Immediate Addressing

On occasion, it would be acceptable and convenient to store the data within the instruction itself. This would be the case if the data is a constant. This technique is called **immediate addressing.**

Figure S2.6 is an example of a LOAD instruction with immediate addressing in a modified Little Man Computer. The modified computer uses a four-digit instruction; the additional digit is used to indicate the addressing mode being used. You could consider the addressing mode as part of the op code, but most computer vendors separate the addressing mode from the op code. In the figure, we have used addressing mode 1 to indicate immediate addressing. Notice that the size of the constant is limited to the size of the address field, in this case, two digits. In this example, the number 005 will be loaded into the calculator.

It is usually desirable to provide for negative numbers as well as positive numbers, so the range of values is necessarily limited even more. Complementary representation is used for this purpose.

Since the data is located in the address field of the instruction, the additional memory access for obtaining the data is not required. Thus, this instruction executes faster, which may be useful if the instruction is within a loop that will be executed many times in a program. The fetch-execute cycle is simplified to the steps shown in Figure S2.7. Compare these steps with the steps used for direct addressing, described in Section 7.4.

An instruction with immediate addressing is capable only of manipulating constant numbers unless the instruction itself is changed. Since it is usually undesirable to change an instruction during the execution of a program (if one forgets to change it back, the program will execute differently the next time it is executed), immediate addressing is of limited use. It could be used for adding a constant to an expression, however.

Notice that if the computer provides a variety of addressing modes, the instruction word must include extra bits so that the computer can identify the addressing mode to be performed. In some computers 1 or 2 additional bits is sufficient to indicate the addressing mode, but in other computers 3 or 4, or even more, bits are required for this purpose.

Indirect Addressing

As we previously indicated, direct addressing separates the location of the data from the location of the instruction. On many occasions it is desirable to go one step farther, to separate the *address* of the data from the instruction. This will be the case when the address of the data itself varies during the execution of the program. The most obvious example is the use of subscripts to describe a data table. Each subscript value points to a different data value. In this case, the address field of the instruction will contain the address of the address of the data. The address of the data can change to reflect the current subscript, without having to modify the address that is part of the instruction word.

Figure S2.8 shows a typical table of data as stored in memory. You can see that to address the various elements of the table, it will be necessary to change the address that loads the data.

FIGURE S2.6

Example of LMC Immediate Addressing

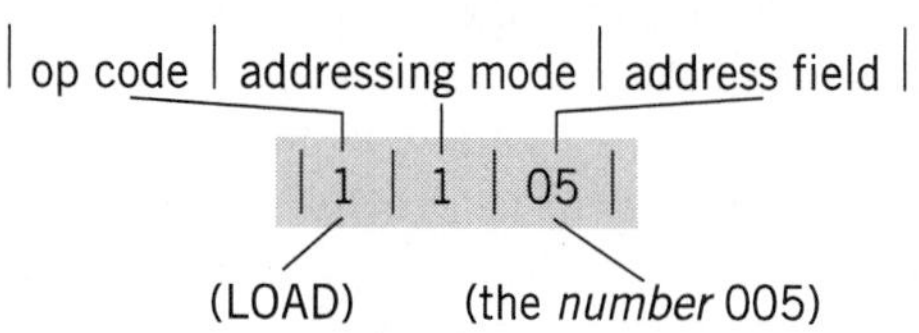

| op code | addressing mode | address field |

| 1 | 1 | 05 |

(LOAD) (the *number* 005)

FIGURE S2.7

Fetch-Execute Cycle with Immediate Addressing

PC -► MAR
MDR -► IR
IR[Address] -► A
PC + 1 -► PC

FIGURE S2.8

Storage of a Typical
Table of Data

Memory address	Data	Table subscript
77	136	TABLE(1)
78	554	TABLE(2)
79	302	TABLE(3)
.		

Figure S2.9 illustrates the steps used by the Little Man to find the address with **indirect addressing.** When the Little Man first reads the instruction (Figure S2.9a), he realizes that he must go to the address in the instruction to find the address of the data. Next (Figure S2.9b) he retrieves the address of the data. Had this been a direct addressing instruction, this location would have contained the data, but since it is an indirect instruction, the Little Man knows that he must go one more step removed. In Figure S2.9c, the Little Man has gone to the address indicated, and he can now retrieve the data.

Note that if we have the Little Man execute the exact same instruction, but change the address pointer in step (b), that he will retrieve a different set of data. This is shown in Figure S2.9d.

EXAMPLE

Suppose the modified Little Man is to execute the indirect ADD instruction

    3245

where the addressing mode digit value of "2" stands for indirect and 45 is the usual absolute Little Man address. Assume the following data prior to execution of the instruction. Which values will change and what will be the new values after the instruction is executed?

    A_{old} → 357
    mailbox 45 → 079
    mailbox 79 → 210

A normal, direct addressed instruction would expect to find the data in mailbox 45 as specified in the address field of the instruction. In this case, however, the instruction calls for an indirect address. Thus, the value in mailbox 45 is actually the *address* of the data, which is 79. Looking at mailbox 79, the data value is 210. Adding 210 to the previous value in A gives a new value

    A_{new} → 567

No other value is changed by this instruction.

As previously mentioned, one important application for indirect addressing is the indexing of subscripted tables. Observe from the previous example that incrementing the "data" value in mailbox 45 would mean that the next time the ADD instruction is executed, it would get its data from mailbox 80 instead of from mailbox 79. Can you see that this technique could be used easily to add a column of subscripted numbers?

It would be possible to address a table of values using direct addressing, but to do so would require modification of the address field in the instruction. Since the computer does not distinguish between an instruction and data, it is possible to treat the instruction as data, and thereby modify its address field. This is illustrated by the program segment with comments shown in Figure S2.10. This program segment adds 20 numbers, stored in mailboxes 60–79, and then outputs the result.

This segment is an example of the steps required to add the data in a table, using direct addressing. Trace this segment *carefully.* Notice in steps 09–11 that the *instruction* in location 07 is treated as data, incremented, and replaced to its original location.

FIGURE S2.9

Little Man Indirect Addressing

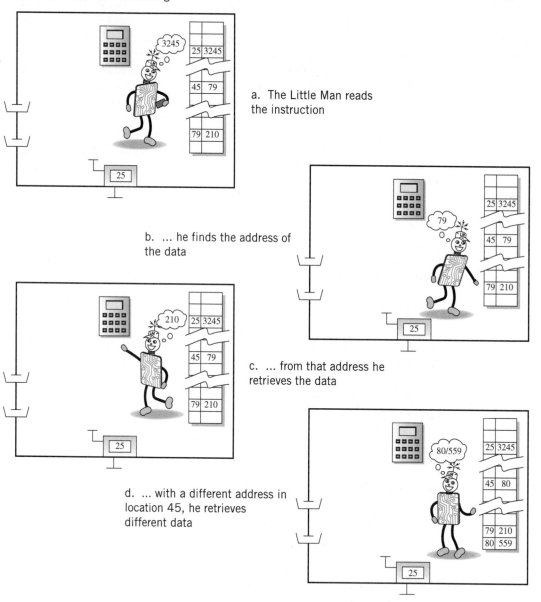

a. The Little Man reads the instruction

b. ... he finds the address of the data

c. ... from that address he retrieves the data

d. ... with a different address in location 45, he retrieves different data

We briefly mentioned the technique of modifying instructions "on the fly" when we discussed immediate addressing. This technique of programming is known as **impure coding.** It has two major disadvantages. First, since the instruction must be changed during execution of the program, it is not possible to store this program in read-only memory. Second, special care must be taken to assure that the instruction is restored to its original value before the program is executed again. This is a potential problem if the program might be interrupted in the midst

FIGURE S2.10

A Totalizer Loop with Direct Addressing

Mailbox	Instruction	Comments
00	LOAD 90	/this actually loads "ADD 60"..
01	STORE 07	/..into mailbox 07
02	LOAD 91	/initialize the totalizer
03	STORE 99	
04	LOAD 92	/initialize the counter to 19
05	STORE 98	
06	LOAD 99	/load the total
07	0	/ [ADD 60, ADD 61, etc.]
08	STORE 99	/and store the new total
09	LOAD 07	/modify the instruction in 07..
10	ADD 93	/..by adding 1 as though the..
11	STORE 07	/..instruction were data
12	LOAD 98	
13	SUB 93	/decrement the counter
14	BRP 05	/loop back if not done
15	LOAD 99	/done..
16	OUT	/..output the result
17	COFFEE BREAK	
90	ADD 60	/initial data for location 07
91	0	
92	19	
93	1	
98		/used to hold the current count
99		/used to hold the current total

of execution. Proper initialization is the purpose of instructions 00–01 in the figure. Programs that modify themselves during execution are considered risky. Pure code is defined as program code that does not modify itself during execution.

The same program segment is shown using indirect addressing with a modified Little Man instruction set in Figure S2.11. We have used an asterisk to indicate that the instruction code includes indirect addressing. No asterisk means that the instruction is a normal, direct addressing instruction. (Obviously, this is not a representation we could really use in an LMC.)

Notice that in this example, the instruction is never modified. The address, which is incremented each time, is stored in the separate data region. This has an important secondary advantage: the instructions for the program could, if desirable, be stored in ROM, with RAM used for the address of the data and for the data itself. You should study these examples carefully to understand how indirect addressing is used in this application.

FIGURE S2.11

The Same Totalizer Loop with Indirect Addressing

Mailbox	Instruction	Comments
00	LOAD 90	/this time just the initial
01	STORE 97	/..address is saved
02	LOAD 91	/as...
03	STORE 99	
04	LOAD 92	/ ...
05	STORE 98	
06	LOAD 99	/...before
07	ADD *97	/ this is the indirect instruction
08	STORE 99	
09	LOAD 97	/modify the address in 97 (this is direct)
10	ADD 93	/..by adding 1 to it ...
11	STORE 97	
12	LOAD 98	/as...
13	SUB 93	
14	BRP 05	/ ...
15	LOAD 99	
16	OUT	
17	COFFEE BREAK	/...before
90	60	/now this is the initial address
91	0	
92	19	
93	1	
97		/used to hold the address of the data
98		/used to hold the current count
99		/used to hold the current total

A parenthetical note: If you have been exposed to the concept of pointers in Pascal or C, you have probably recognized the fundamental similarity between indirect addressing and the use of pointers.

There is one other important application for indirect addressing that should be mentioned. When an instruction requires data from outside the current range of one of the absolute addressing methods, or when a long jump is required, the indirect addressing technique can be used to reach the desired address.

As an example, suppose the modified Little Man Computer uses a base register system to address 10 paragraphs of 100 locations each. A JUMP INDIRECT instruction would be able to jump to any location in any paragraph. To see this, suppose that the base register has the value 00, and the programmer wants the Little Man to jump to location 575 for the next instruction. The following two instructions will accomplish this:

```
        JUMP  *99
                      .
                      .
                      .
    99  575
         .
```

Register Indirect Addressing

Register deferred or **register indirect addressing** is a very powerful addressing technique used by the Intel X86 series CPUs, HP VAX CPUs, Motorola 680X0 CPUs, and others. (Some vendors call this addressing mode "register *deferred* addressing.") This addressing mode is similar to indirect addressing with one difference: instead of using a memory location as a pointer to the address of the data, that address pointer is stored in a general-purpose register. The instruction goes to the general-purpose register to find the address of the data. This is illustrated in Figure S2.12.

Register indirect addressing is very efficient. Once the pointer address has been loaded into the register (which of course requires a separate instruction), data can be accessed in the same number of fetch-execute steps as direct addressing, since the register may be reached immediately from its field in the instruction register. Yet, the size of the address field required is small: usually only 3 or 4 bits to specify the particular register, and some method of indicating the addressing mode. Thus, this is an excellent method for addressing a large memory space with a small instruction word.

A variation on this idea even increments or decrements the address pointer that is stored in the register. This method is known as **autoincrementing** or **autodecrementing.** If you are familiar with the "C" programming language, you might be interested to know that this addressing mode is a direct implementation of the "++" and "−−" operations. This feature is provided because indexing through an array is such a common programming operation. Typically these instructions increment or decrement the register each time the instruction is executed, in addition to the normal function of the instruction. The instruction itself might be a LOAD or a STORE or an ADD or some other similar operation. Thus, each execution of the instruction will access the subsequent memory location in the array. This feature simplifies the writing of program loops by combining two operations into a single instruction, replacing, for example, instructions 7, 9, 10, and 11 in Figure S2.11.

Some CPUs also provide an addressing mode that treats the memory location reached as another address pointer and thus provide true indirection from that point.

FIGURE S2.12

Obtaining the Data with Register Indirect Addressing

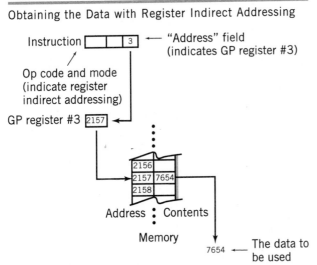

EXAMPLE

The Motorola 68000 CPU MOVE instruction demonstrates the efficiency possible using addressing based on registers. The 68000 CPU has 16 general-purpose registers, 8 intended for data and 8 for addresses. A single MOVE instruction fulfills both LOAD and STORE functions; it can move data from register to register, from register to memory, from memory to register, and even from memory to memory. The format for a move instruction is shown in Figure S2.13. There is a 4-bit op code for this instruction. Six bits are used for the source address, and 6 bits are used for the destination address. Thus, only 16 bits is required for the basic MOVE instruction. The two 6-bit addresses use 3 bits to specify a register; the other 3 bits are used to indicate an addressing mode. The addressing modes include register direct (i.e., the register itself), register indirect, register indirect with postincrement of the address, and register indirect with predecrement of the address. (There are also several other addressing modes that use the memory location following the instruction as an extension to the instruction to provide absolute addressing, immediate addressing, and memory indirect addressing.) Since the general-purpose registers hold 32 bits, a 16-bit move instruction is capable of reaching 4 billion different memory addresses.

Indexed Addressing

The example in Figure S2.11 shows that we can address a table of data by modifying the address of the data and using that address indirectly to obtain the data. An alternative approach uses the address in the instruction, as in direct addressing, but modifies this address by adding in a value from another register. The register used for this purpose can be another general-purpose register, or it may be a special index register. This technique is known as *indexing* the address. The technique is shown diagrammatically in Figure S2.14.

Indexing is similar conceptually to base offset addressing. Both offset the address by an amount stored in another register. The difference, philosophically, is that the base

FIGURE S2.13

68000 MOVE Instruction Format

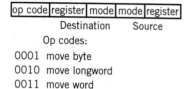

op code	register	mode	mode	register
	Destination			Source

Op codes:
0001 move byte
0010 move longword
0011 move word

FIGURE S2.14

Modifying an Address with an Index Register

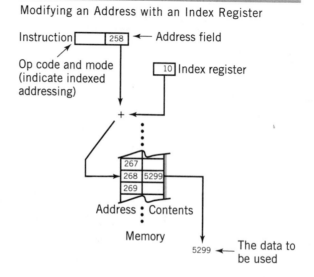

address is intended primarily to locate a block of addressing as a way of expanding the addressing range for a given address field size, whereas the index register is used primarily as a table offset for handling subscripting. Thus, the value in a base address register is likely to be large, and rarely changed during execution of a program; the value in an index register is most likely small, and frequently changing. The flow diagram in Figure S2.15 illustrates an example that uses both base offset and **indexed addressing.**

Some computers provide instructions that *autoindex.* Autoindexing is similar to autoincrementing, except that it is the index register that is incremented.

If the value in the index register is 0, indexed addressing reduces to direct addressing.

Figure S2.16 shows the totalizer loop program yet one final time, this time using indexed addressing. The "@" symbol is used to indicate that the instruction is indexed. The index register in this example is called the X register, and it is loaded in a manner similar to the LOAD X (mnemonic LDX) instruction. LDA is used as the mnemonic for the LOAD A instruction to distinguish the two different instructions. It is also common to provide a DECrement or INCrement instruction for the X register, since this is the most common use for the register, and also CONDITIONAL BRANCH instructions similar to those provided for the A register. This particular program adds in reverse order. In this way, X can be used both as an offset for addressing the table and as a counter, resulting in more efficient code. Notice how much shorter the program is this time.

It should be noted that some systems allow the index to be multiplied by a scaling factor of 2^n (i.e., 2, 4, 8, …) before it is added to the

FIGURE S2.15

Indexing a Base Offset Address

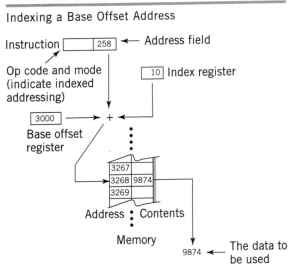

FIGURE S2.16

A Totalizer Loop with Indexed Addressing

Mailbox	Instruction	Comments
00	LDA 91	/total is kept in A. This sets A to 0. (not indexed)
01	LDX 92	/initialize the counter to 19
02	ADD @60	/ADD 79, ADD 78, etc. as X is decremented
03	DEC X	/Decrement the index—19, 18, etc.
04	BRPX 02	/text if done (when X decrements from 0 to –1)
05	OUT	/done, ..output the result from A
06	COFFEE BREAK	
91	0	
92	19	

address. (The index register is simply shifted left, of course!) This allows the index to work easily on arrays regardless of the number of bytes required for elements of the particular data type, as long as each element occupies a 2^n number of bytes.

Indirect Indexed and Indexed Indirect Addressing

It is possible in some computers to have both indirect and indexed addressing in use at the same time, although this ability is of limited use. (It could be used to find a row of data in a two-dimensional table stored by columns, for example). The order in which the two address modes are applied is significant. The resulting address will not be the same in both cases. The following example shows the application of both modes of addressing. We suggest careful study of this example. Understanding this example will clarify and differentiate for you the concepts of both indirect and indexed addressing.

EXAMPLE

Assume the following values for X and various memory locations:

Location	Contents
40	50
60	80
70	185
80	323
X	20

The instruction

    LDA @*40 (indexed, then indirect)

will proceed as follows.

Indexing 40 leaves an indexed address of 60. Since memory location 60 contains the final address (because indirection must still take place), the final address of the data is 80. Therefore, the value *323* is loaded into the accumulator.

Now assume instead that the instruction is

    LDA *@40 (indirect, then indexed)

Performing the indirect from address 40 yields the preindexed address 50. Indexing 50 by the value 20 in the index register results in the final address of 70. Therefore, the value *185* is loaded into the accumulator.

Obviously, there are many variations on addressing, and we can't (or wouldn't want to!) discuss them all. Hopefully, this brief introduction provided you with a flavor of the possibilities.

SUMMARY AND REVIEW

In this supplementary chapter we have considered different techniques for addressing memory. The Little Man Computer is limited to direct, absolute addressing. Register addressing is a fast alternative when the number of registers is sufficient to reduce the number of memory accesses required. Immediate addressing can also reduce the number of memory accesses. Alternatives to absolute addressing include base offset addressing and relative addressing. Alternatives to direct addressing include indirect addressing, indexed addressing, and combinations of the two. Register deferred addressing is particularly effective at reducing instruction size.

KEY CONCEPTS AND TERMS

absolute addressing
addressing modes
autodecrementing
autoincrementing
base register addressing
direct addressing

immediate addressing
impure coding
indexed addressing
indirect addressing
real mode addressing
register addressing

register deferred addressing
register indirect addressing
relative addressing
relocatability

EXERCISES

S2.1 Determine the fetch-execute cycle for a Little Man LOAD instruction in a machine that uses relative addressing.

S2.2 It is common in programming to write a single instruction infinite loop into the program, which simply sits and waits for some interruption to come into the computer from outside. An example of this is the ">" prompt in MS-DOS. After the prompt is printed, the program waits for the user to type something from the keyboard.

Such a loop can be created by using the jump instruction, and jumping to the current location, that is the instruction being executed. This will cause the JUMP instruction to be executed over and over again.

Assume that the JUMP instruction will be located at memory location 34.

  a. What instruction will be found in that location if the machine uses absolute addressing?

  b. What instruction will be found if the machine uses relative addressing?

  c. Suppose the JUMP instruction is to be located at memory location 77. How will your answer in (b) change?

S2.3 Immediate addressing cannot be applied to the store instruction. Why not?

S2.4 Show the fetch-execute cycle for a STORE instruction with indirect absolute addressing.

S2.5 Show the fetch-execute cycle for an ADD instruction with both indirect and indexed addressing modes in use. Assume that the indexed mode is applied first.

S2.6 To create a larger data space for an immediate instruction, some vendors use a variant known as *extended immediate addressing*. In this mode, the data to be used is stored at the memory location following the instruction. Thus, the immediate data can be the size of a full memory word. Show the fetch-execute cycle for a LOAD EXTENDED IMMEDIATE instruction.

S2.7 Assume a modified LMC that supports indexed addressing. Rewrite the program loader (see Exercise 6.14) with indexed addressing, and no impure code.

S2.8 The Little Man Computer Corporation has recently announced the new improved Little Woman Computer (LWC), which features a new, increased mailbox address space, plus indexed addressing for convenient table handling capability.

The new machine has an additional three-digit calculator, called the indexer. The machine also has a new instruction 0XX, to support the new index register. The 0XX instruction works as follows:

000 The Little Woman sets the indexer to 0.

00X The Little Woman adds, using immediate mode, the value X to whatever is already in the indexer.

0XX (where XX is in the range 10–99) The Little Woman adds the contents of mailbox XX, using direct addressing to whatever is already in the indexer.

The following instructions are modified to use indexed addressing. The address contents of the indexer are always added to XX to determine the final address:

```
LOAD (5XX)
STORE (3XX)
ADD (1XX)
SUBTRACT (2XX)
```

The HALT instruction is reassigned code 900. There is an additional BRANCH ON MATCH instruction, 9xx (excluding 900, 901, and 902) which causes a branch to location xx if the value in the index register matches that in the A register.

a. Describe the steps the Little Woman goes through to perform an ADD instruction.

b. Write an LWC program that accepts a series of input numbers and stores them, one to a mailbox. The number of values to be accepted is provided as the first input entry. Then, the program adds the stored numbers and prints out the total.

c. What is the total possible address space for the LWC? What are the means used to expand the space? (worded differently, how does one get data from outside the usual 0–99 range?)

d. Suppose we don't want to use indexed addressing. What can we do to make the four indexed instructions look just like they did in the original machine?

S2.9 The Little Prince Computer (introduced in Chapter 7, Exercise 7.12) MOVE instruction can be extended as follows. The MOVE instruction is a two-word instruction

```
0XX
NYY
```

stored in consecutive mailboxes. N will represent the addressing mode. If N is 0, addressing is direct, as before. If N is 1, *both* XX and YY are indexed, based on the value in the calculator (A).

a. Show the modified fetch-execute cycle for this instruction with indexing.

b. Use this instruction to write an LPC program that moves a group of data stored at 20–30 to location 60.

S2.10 The Obliter-8 Computer uses relative addressing. The machine has two registers, A, the accumulator, and X, the index register. The machine supports direct, indirect, and indexed relative addressing. Each instruction uses two consecutive memory locations, call them PC and PC+1. The first is the op code; the second contains an address relative to its location (i.e., relative to PC+1).

Given the data that follows, what will be the result of

a. an ADD indirect at location 1278? (Note: The indirect address is absolute, *not* relative.)

b. an ADD indexed at location 1278?

1278	ADD	1320	510
1279	10	1321	1322
.		1322	16
.		1323	8
1288	1323	1324	124
1289	1299		
1290	1322		
1291	1300	7	4
1292	10	8	1289
.		9	116
1298	1300	10	1298
1299	1320	11	1321
1300	1323	12	1324
1301	1322		
1302	1291	A	2111
1303	25	X	12

S2.11 Yet another modified LMC has come forth. This one extends the memory space of the machine by adding base register addressing. The LMC III has a three-digit base register. The value stored in this register is added to *all* addresses when addressing memory. The base register value is added to the final value of all addresses; that is, it is added *last* if multiple addressing modes are used. Note, too, that the value in the base register is added to everything, including the PC. Thus, if the PC says 55, and the BR contains 400, the next instruction is fetched from location 455. If that instruction is LOAD 99, the data is found in location 499.

a. For a fixed value in the base register, how much memory can a programmer access?

b. What is the *total* range of memory?

c. Show the fetch-execute cycle for an add instruction with indirect addressing in this machine.

d. Consider the following set of values for various registers and memory locations. What value ultimately ends up in A?

A → 60		85 → 92
BR → 220		92 → 333
PC → 40		166 → 77
40 → ADD (indirect) 85		305 → 166
260 → ADD (indirect) 85		386 → 4
		390 → 211

S2.12 As do other computer companies, the LMC Corporation has discovered it can be profitable to introduce a new machine every few months. This is known in the industry as "progress" or, sometimes, as "planned obsolescence." The latest product from the LMC Corporation, the LLC (Little Lulu Computer), uses direct relative addressing for the LOAD, STORE, ADD, SUBTRACT, and all BRANCH instructions. All other instructions are unchanged. The XX field in the relative instructions represents a 10's complement relative address (-50 to +49).

a.   Write a program in LLC code that inputs three numbers and outputs them, largest number first.

b.   Show the fetch-execute cycle for a STORE instruction in the LLC. You may assume that the sign handling for the relative address is handled automatically.

c.   Suppose the location counter reset button jammed, so that instead of resetting to 0 when pushed, it resets to 35. Rather than fix the button, we'll load the program starting at location 35 instead of at mailbox 0. (This technique, known as relocation, is required for systems where multiple programs must reside in memory simultaneously.)

What changes must be made to your program to make it work in this case?

S2.13   The Pomegranate Seedless instruction set supports several different addressing modes, including both indexed and indirect, either individually or together in either order.

The format for a store-in-memory instruction looks like this

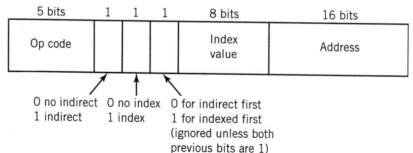

The following mnemonic example gives the idea:

```
SIM 1, 1, 0, 220, 1696
```

and says to store the accumulator at a location indirect from 1696 (decimal), then indexed by 220 (decimal).

For the following three cases, and the given data, show the *sequence* of values to be found in the memory address register. Your last value will obviously be the *location* where the data will be stored.

a.   `SIM 1, 0, 0, 125, 1623`

b.   `SIM 1, 1, 0, 125, 1623`

c.   `SIM 1, 1, 1, 125, 1623`

Memory data (values in decimal) is

1621	1628	1745	1539
1622	1745	1746	1628
1623	1749	1747	1849
1624	1748	1748	1776 (a good year!)
1625	1621	1749	1902 (not bad either!)
1626	1722		

S2.14 The text discusses one method of branching to subroutines, using stacks. An alternative method for a CALL instruction is to store the return address in the first location of the subroutine and then JUMP to the next location of the subroutine. To return, the program simply does an indirect jump through the first location of the subroutine.

    a. Can you see any disadvantage to this method as opposed to the stack method? (Hint: Consider the traditional recursive program that performs factorials or any other recursive program with which you are familiar.)

    b. Here is the fetch-execute cycle for a CALL instruction. Study it carefully.

```
PC → MAR
MDR → IR
IR[ADD] → MAR
PC +1 → MDR (write)
IR[ADD] + 1 → PC
```

    Write the equivalent fetch-execute cycle for the RETURN instruction.

    c. Location 20 has a CALL 40 instruction in it. What is stored in location 40? Where does the subroutine actually begin? Describe exactly the steps that take place when this instruction is executed, and when the subroutine RETURN is executed.

S2.15 Assume that you wish to build a stack on a Little Man Computer that is standard except for the addition of indirect addressing capability. The stack will be located starting at mailbox 70. A current stack pointer is stored in location 90.

    a. Write a Little Man code segment that will add a value to the stack. The value will come from the calculator. Make sure that your code leaves everything ready for the next push or pop action.

    b. Write a code segment that will pop a value from the stack to the calculator.

    c. Even without indirect addressing, it is possible to implement push and pop instructions using Little Man code, but the task is more difficult. Describe carefully the steps that you must take to simulate a PUSH instruction in this case.

SUPPLEMENTARY CHAPTER 3

COMMUNICATION CHANNEL TECHNOLOGY

S3.0 INTRODUCTION

Communication channels are fundamental to modern technology, whether we are discussing wired networks, wireless networks, the backbone of the Internet, cell phones, satellite television, or even your TV remote control. Chapter 11 introduces the fundamental concepts of loosely coupled computer systems and data communications technology. The discussion describes communication channels that connect the computers together into clusters or networks, along with the data signals and protocols that make communication possible. The channels may be point-to-point or multipoint, depending on the nature of the connection and the method of communication.

The discussion of channels in Chapter 11 is presented from the perspective of the computers only, without concern for the details of the technology of the channel itself. For those interested in a deeper understanding of the data communications process, Supplementary Chapter 3 provides an additional perspective, with an introduction to the technology of the communication channel.

First, in Section S3.1, we introduce the concept of a communication channel and discuss the technology of communication channels. The major topics of interest include the signaling methods, the choice of media, and the characteristics of channels. Fundamental signaling techniques and the general characteristics of channels are covered in Sections S3.3 In Section S3.4, we look at the nature of transmission media, identify specific media that are commonly used, and discuss the relationship between the selection of a communication channel medium and a signaling method. The chapter concludes with a short review that integrates all the technological components and factors that make up a communication channel.

Overall, our focus is on computer interconnectivity. Other types of communication channels are outside the scope of this discussion.

S3.1 COMMUNICATION CHANNEL TECHNOLOGY

Conceptually, communication between loosely coupled computers is provided by a communication channel. The conceptual connection between two computers is shown in Figure S3.1. A communication channel consists of a transmitter and a receiver, a transmission signaling method, and a medium to carry the signal. The transmission signaling method used depends not only on the channel medium but also on other factors such as the distance between end points, the application, and other technical, physical, and economic considerations. The transmitter and receiver act as an interface to the computer or other connecting device and may also be required at one or both ends to convert the data into a form suitable for the signaling method used, and for compatibility with the equipment at the other end of the channel. The channel may pass data in one direction only, or it may be used to transmit and receive data in both directions. We have already noted that a channel may be point-to-point or may be shared and that a channel carries data serially. At any given instant, the computers or other devices using the channel may be sending, receiving, or both.

All the transmitters and receivers connected to a channel must agree on the signaling method to be used on the channel. There must also be agreement between each of the computers as to the meaning of each communication. Discussion of the issues related to agreement between systems and system components takes place in Chapter 11.

We are being careful to note that the view of a communication channel from the perspective of the computer interface to the channel is conceptual. Physically, the digital signal coming from the computer may pass through a number of different media, signal converters, signaling methods, switches, multiplexers, repeaters, amplifiers, network routers, and other devices. For example, the channel may be a telephone channel, conceptually employing the electrical representation of audio produced by a modem as the transmission signaling method used to carry the digital signal from an office computer to another computer located in a salesperson's car. The telephone signal goes through one or more switching centers where it is combined with other telephone signals, amplified, and directed to a cellular phone center. Before arriving at the cellular phone center, it is converted into a digital signal, quite different from the original digital data but, instead, representing a mixture of the audio from the modem that the original data had been converted to, combined with the voice or data audio of other phone calls. The telephone office might be connected to the cellular phone center by fiber optic cable. In this case, the digital signal takes the form of light pulses. At the cellular phone center, the form of the signal is changed yet again. This time it is separated from the other calls and converted into a form suitable for transmission as a radio wave. It is then received via radio in the salesman's car, converted from radio wave back to audio representation, and then by another modem back to digital data for use in the computer connected to the cellular phone.

This example is illustrated in Figure S3.2. Although this is a complex example, it is not untypical of modern communication applications. We selected it to show you some of the different possible forms that the data might take as it passes from one end of the channel to the other. Conceptually, the channel is a phone line that carries the electrical representation of audio as a signaling method. Physically, the data passes through several different communication channel forms representing audio, digital, possibly light, and radio signals. Realistically, the conceptual channel is made up of a number of separate physical channels with converters between each channel, but the intermediate operations are invisible to the computers located at each end of the conceptual telephone channel.

A communication channel is characterized primarily by the signaling transmission method used; by its bandwidth or bit rate capacity; by the direction or directions in

FIGURE S3.1

A Communication Channel

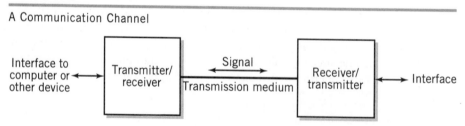

FIGURE S3.2

Physical Implementation of a Conceptual Channel

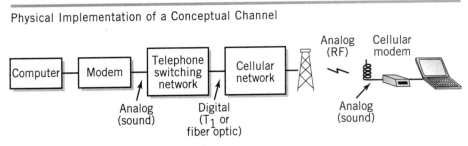

which signals can flow; by its noise, attenuation, and distortion characteristics; and by the medium used.

There are many different signaling methods in use, but the most important consideration is whether a signaling method is analog or digital. Analog transmission uses a continuously varying waveform to carry data. Digital transmission carries data in digital form, using two different values of electrical voltage or current or an on/off light source.[1] The choice of digital or analog transmission signaling depends upon a number of factors. Some media are only suitable for one or the other. Where either is suitable, the choice is made on the basis of other factors such as noise characteristics, the application, the bandwidth requirements, and other uses for which the channel is to be shared. Except where analog transmission is required by the medium, there is a strong tendency toward digital transmission in most circumstances. Digital transmission has the advantage that it is less susceptible to noise and interference, which means that the original data can be reproduced exactly at the receiving end of the channel. When a digital signal is to be transmitted on an analog channel, it is necessary to convert the digital signal into a form suitable for analog transmission. The converse is also true. The methods of conversion, and resulting limitations, are discussed in Section S3.2.

A point-to-point channel may pass data in one direction only, or may be used both to transmit and receive data. A unidirectional channel is called a **simplex** channel. A bidirectional channel may transmit data one direction at a time, in which case it is called a **half-duplex** channel, or in both directions simultaneously, known as **full-duplex** transmission. The concept of directionality is less important in multipoint channels, since any transmitter connected to the shared channel effectively **broadcasts** its message to all connected receivers. In this case the receiver will have built-in address capability to identify the messages intended for it.

It is also possible to carry multiple messages over a channel, using one of two **multiplexing** techniques. Digital channels use **time division multiplexing** (TDM). Analog channels can also use time division multiplexing, but most use **frequency division multiplexing** (FDM) instead. Multiplexing techniques are discussed briefly in Section S3.2.

---

[1] To be strictly accurate, technically, switched light is a digital signal superimposed on an analog waveform of extremely high frequency, using a modulation technique called analog shift keying (ASK). We will introduce modulation and analog shift keying later in this section. ASK imposes some technical conditions on the use of light as a transmission signaling method that are beyond the scope of our discussion. Practically speaking, we can treat light transmission as if it were digital.

S3.2 THE FUNDAMENTALS OF SIGNALING TECHNOLOGY

A signal is carried on a communication channel as an electrical voltage, an electromagnetic radio wave, or a switched light. Data is represented by changes in the signal as a function of time. The signal may take on a continuous range of values, in which case it is known as an **analog** signal, or it can take on only discrete values, in which case it is known as a **discrete** signal. A *binary* discrete signal is usually called a **digital** signal. We are primarily interested here in analog and digital signals, although we note in passing that the video signal going to a CRT from a computer video card takes on only specific values, 16 or 256 or some different number of values depending on the video adapter used, and is therefore considered to be discrete rather than digital. Figure S3.3 shows an analog signal and a digital signal. We shall not consider discrete signals further here. A representation of a signal shown as a function of time is called a **waveform.**

Computer data is fundamentally digital in nature. A digital waveform might represent a sequence of bits of data on a bus line, for example. Sound is analog. The loudness of sound coming from a stereo speaker would be represented by a continuously changing waveform. The electromagnetic waves used for radio transmission are also analog.

It is often necessary or desirable to be able to transform a digital signal into some analog equivalent representation or vice versa. For example, analog sound is stored digitally on a compact disk. Conversely, to transmit computer data on an ordinary voice-grade phone line requires that the computer data must be represented by an analog signal, since the phone line is designed to carry sound. (Actually, the phone line carries analog electrical voltage signals that *represent* the sound wave, which are converted back to actual sound at the earpiece of the phone receiving the signal.)

Ideally, the transformation between digital and analog should be reversible. That is to say, if we transform a digital waveform into an analog representation and then transform it back, the resulting digital waveform should be identical to the original. For digital waveforms, this is theoretically achievable. In practice, all systems, both digital and analog, are subject to noise, attenuation, and distortion, and it is often necessary to provide compensation in the form of error correction. Nonetheless, under most conditions, it is possible

FIGURE S3.3

Analog and Digital Waveforms

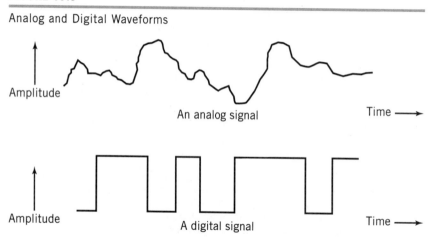

to recover the original digital data exactly. When analog data is converted into digital form, however, a small amount of information is lost during the transformation, and it is not possible to recover the original analog waveform exactly, although the error can be reduced to the point that it doesn't matter.

The medium itself may require transformation of a signal from analog to digital (A-to-D) or vice versa if that the signal is to be transmitted through a medium that can carry only one or the other. Wires can carry either digital or analog signals, but as we already noted, normal residential phone lines carry analog signal only. Radio signals, known as radio waves, require another type of analog signal, with the digital signal imbedded within.

Analog Signaling

Although digital transmission is favored for most use these days, analog transmission methods are required for wireless media, such as radio and sound, for wireless networking, and for most telephone communication. Radio transmission methods include satellite, cellular phone, wireless networking, and microwave communications. Radio waves can also be converted to equivalent electrical signals and used with wire media and may be preferred when a mixture of digital and analog data is being transmitted through the cable, such as cable TV with a digital Internet feed, though most cable TV is now digitally distributed and converted to analog at the customer's site.

The basic unit of analog transmission is a sine wave. A sine wave is shown in Figure S3.4. A sine wave has an **amplitude** A, or size, and a **frequency**, measured as the number of times the sine wave is repeated per second. The instantaneous value of the sine wave varies with time, ranging from 0 to amplitude A, back to 0, to value −A, and back to 0 again. The value may measure voltage, or loudness, or the mechanical movement of the metal in a bell, or some other quantity. The **period** of a sine wave is the amount of time it takes to trace out one complete cycle of the wave. Thus, the frequency, f, is defined as the number of periods per second, or mathematically,

$$f = 1/T$$

where T is the period, measured in seconds.

The amplitude and period are shown in the diagram. For this particular sine wave, the period is 1/4 second, and the frequency is 4 cycles per second, or more commonly, 4 Hertz.

FIGURE S3.4

A Sine Wave

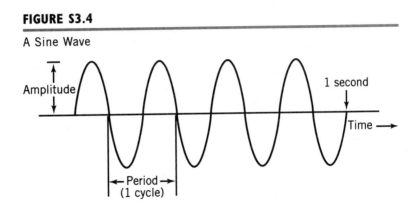

The Hertz, usually abbreviated Hz, is the unit used to measure frequency. One Hertz corresponds to one cycle per second. Note from the diagram, also, that since the sine wave is symmetric about the center axis, its amplitude is measured from the center axis to either peak, not from negative to positive peak.

Why a sine wave? Sine waves occur naturally throughout nature. Sound, radio waves, and light are all composed of sine waves. Even ripples on a pond are sinusoidal. Although the sine wave may seem an odd waveform to occur so commonly, the sine wave is related in a simple way to a circle. Picture a marble rolling around a circle at constant speed. If you view the circle edgewise, the marble will trace out a sine wave in time. This is illustrated in Figure S3.5. For this reason, points on the sine wave are often designated in degrees. The sine wave begins at 0° and ranges to 360° and then repeats from 0° again. At any given instant in time, the amplitude of the wave is given by the position of the marble for the specified angle. Mathematically, that value is represented by the equation

$$v = A \sin[\Theta]$$

where A is the maximum amplitude, corresponding to the radius of the circle, and [?] is the angle shown in the diagram.

To show you the practical aspect of this illustration, electricity is generated by the rotor of an electrical generator rotating in a circle at the rate of sixty revolutions per second. The electrical output is a standard 117-volt 60-cycle (more accurately Hertz) alternating current sine wave. The instantaneous output of the sine wave corresponds to the angular position of the rotor as it rotates. (Incidentally, the actual amplitude of a 117-volt sine wave is approximately 165 volts. The technique used to measure AC voltage is based on a special kind of averaging.)

In addition to the amplitude and frequency, it is possible to measure the position of a sine wave with respect to a reference sine wave. The difference, measured in degrees, is known as the **phase** of the sine wave. This measurement is shown in Figure S3.6.

An important characteristic of sine waves is that mathematically *all* waveforms, regardless of shape, both analog and digital, can be represented as the sum of sine waves of different frequencies, phase, and amplitudes. The constituent frequencies that make up a signal are known as the **spectrum** of the signal. The **bandwidth** of a channel is the range of frequencies that are passed by the channel with only a small amount of attenuation. Other frequencies are blocked by the channel. To reproduce a signal faithfully, the spectrum of the signal must fall within the bandwidth of the channel, and conversely the bandwidth of the

FIGURE S3.5

The Relationship Between a Circle and a Sine Wave

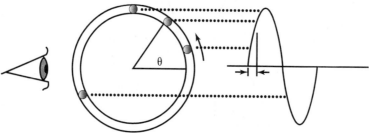

FIGURE S3.6

Phase-Shifted Sine Waves: (a) Reference Waveform, (b) Phase-Shifted 90°, (c) Phase-Shifted 180°

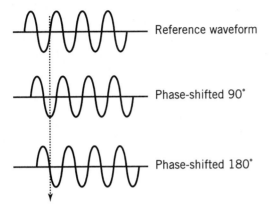

Reference waveform

Phase-shifted 90°

Phase-shifted 180°

channel must be wide enough to pass all the frequency components of desired signals. In many cases, it is appropriate to limit the bandwidth intentionally to prevent interference from other signals. There are electronic means to control the bandwidth of a channel, using a process called **filtering.**

Sound waves use frequencies between approximately 20 Hz and 20,000 Hz, although some animals can hear sounds outside this range. A dog whistle produces a wave of approximately 25,000 Hz. Most stereo systems have a bandwidth of at least 20–20,000 Hz, for the faithful reproduction of sound. Telephones have a bandwidth of only about 0–4000 Hz, which makes them unsuitable to carry high-fidelity sound but adequate for voice. The telephone bandwidth limits the speed that data can be transmitted through a conventional phone line. Sound waves are produced by vibrating molecules and require a medium such as air or water. A microphone converts sound to an identical analog electrical signal for transmission through the wires of a phone line, or stereo amplifier, or whatever.

Radio waves are electromagnetic in nature. Radio waves can be transmitted at frequencies as low as 60 Hz, although radio waves of frequencies this low are not useful for most purposes. Currently, radio waves can use frequencies up to about 300 GHz (pronounced gigahertz), or 300 billion Hertz. To give you some reference points, the standard AM radio band occupies the range between 550 KHz and 1.6 MHz, the standard FM band from 88 MHz to 108 MHz (what is the frequency of your favorite station?), television from 54 MHz to about 700 MHz, and cellular telephones and other devices around 900 MHz (K = kilo = thousands, and M = mega = millions). The bandwidth required for different types of signals depends on the application. AM radio stations, for example, use a bandwidth of about 20 KHz, centered about the dial frequency of the station. TV stations require a bandwidth in excess of 4.5 MHz. Each TV channel provides a 6-MHz bandwidth in a different part of the frequency spectrum. Channel 2 uses the frequency range 54–60 MHz, for example, and channel 3 uses 60–66 MHz. By limiting the bandwidth of the TV receiver, we are able to tune in separate stations. A general map of the useful frequency spectrum indicating various familiar sound and electromagnetic wave regions is shown in Figure S3.7.

FIGURE S3.7

The Frequency Spectrum

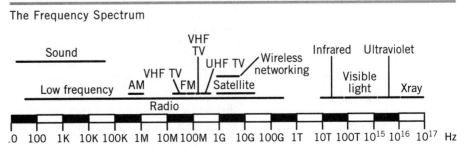

Electromagnetic waves use space as a medium, although many materials are nearly transparent to the wave, so that the wave passes right through the material with little or no attenuation. Air, for example, is transparent at all frequencies. Most other materials are more transparent at low frequencies than at high frequencies. AM radio band waves will pass through reasonable thicknesses of solid stone, for example, whereas FM radio band waves are attenuated more. The result is that your AM/FM car radio works better on AM when you're in a tunnel. Leaves and thick rain clouds can block a satellite TV signal. Light is also made up of electromagnetic waves, with frequencies in the region of 100 thousand billion Hz. There are only a few materials that are transparent to light.

In practice, the sine waves that we have discussed are of limited use by themselves. A sound made up of a sine wave produces a single, pure tone. A 440-Hz sine wave produces the tone called "A," for example. There is not much useful information value (or musical interest) in a pure sine wave tone. Instead, sine waves are used as **carriers** for the data that we wish to transmit. We **modulate**, or *change*, one or more of the three characteristics of the sine wave, amplitude, frequency, or phase, to represent the signal that is to be transmitted. Thus, an AM, or amplitude-modulated, radio station at 1100 KHz would use a sine wave carrier of 1100 KHz. The music broadcast on that station would modulate the amplitude of the carrier to correspond to the sound of the music. The AM station uses only one type of modulation. A standard TV signal uses all three types of modulation: amplitude modulation to represent the picture, frequency modulation to represent the sound, and phase modulation to represent the color. You should be able to guess what kind of modulation is used by an FM station! To restore the original waveform that was used to modulate the carrier, we use a **demodulator** or **detector**. An example of a carrier amplitude modulated by another analog signal is shown in Figure S3.8. Note that amplitude modulation is symmetric with respect to the center of the carrier sine wave.

For digital signals, the carrier signal is modulated with only two possible values, the value representing a "0" and the value representing a "1." In this case, the modulation technique is called **amplitude shift keying (ASK), frequency shift keying (FSK),** or **phase shift keying (PSK).** Examples of each are shown in Figure S3.9.

FIGURE S3.8

Amplitude Modulations:
(a) Data Waveform, (b) Carrier,
(c) Modulated Waveform

Data waveform   Carrier

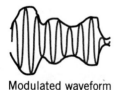

Modulated waveform

The spectrum of frequencies used for a modulated signal depend on the frequency of the carrier used and will include the carrier frequency itself. The bandwidth of the modulated signal depends on the type of modulation. The bandwidth of an amplitude-modulated wave is approximately double the highest frequency in the waveform being modulated. In other words, the 20-KHz bandwidth of an AM radio station is suitable for transmitting audio frequencies up to about 10 KHz; FM bandwidth requirements are somewhat larger. The 400-KHz bandwidth of an FM station can carry audio frequencies up to approximately 45 KHz.

Modulating the same signal with a sine wave carrier of different frequency will require the same amount of bandwidth but will move the spectrum by changing the basic frequency about which the bandwidth of the signal occurs. This means that, by modulating different data signals with different carrier frequencies, it is possible to carry multiple signals on the same

FIGURE S3.9

ASK, FSK, and PSK

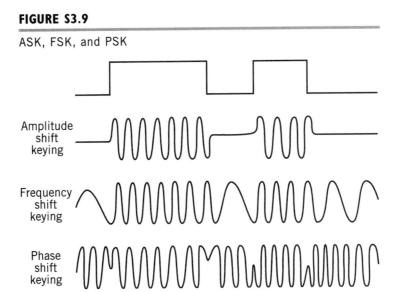

Amplitude shift keying

Frequency shift keying

Phase shift keying

channel, if the overall channel bandwidth is wide enough to include the spectra for each signal. Filtering can separate the different data signals at the receiving end. This technique is called **frequency division multiplexing.** It can be used to carry several phone conversations on long-distance phone lines, for example, or to carry multiple analog TV channels on a cable system.

Analog signals are particularly susceptible to noise and attenuation in a channel because the distortion created cannot be detected and reversed. **Attenuation,** or signal loss, is the reduction of a signal that occurs in a medium as a function of the physical length of the channel. Attenuation limits the possible length of a channel. Signal loss can also occur if there are taps or splitters along the channel. These are devices that remove some of the energy of the signal for use, for example, to implement multipoint connectivity. **Amplifiers** can be used to restore the original strength of the signal. All channels generate some noise internally, and as the signal gets weaker, the noise becomes more predominant with respect to the signal. In this case, amplification does not help, since the noise is amplified also. Maintaining a high signal-to-noise ratio is important in maintaining the integrity of an analog signal. Minimizing external noise, such as electrical noise from other devices and from such natural sources as lightning, is also important. External noise, of course, can change the basic shape of the signal, and may make it impossible to recover the original signal. If the noise falls within the same frequency range as the signal, there is no way to separate the noise from the signal.

In addition, analog signals are susceptible to variations in attenuation and phase shifts that occur across the channel spectrum. Consider the situation shown in Figure S3.10. If the signal is made up of sine waves of frequencies from different parts of the spectrum, say, at the points marked f_1 and f_2, then the composite signal at the output of the channel is distorted, since the different sine wave components have been attenuated by different amounts. The channel will also change the phase of some components more than others, which also contributes to the distortion. (Television ghosts are an example of phase-shifted signals distorting the original signal.) To some extent, filtering can compensate for these variations, but realistically, signal distortion is always present in a channel. The goal, then, when working with analog signaling, is to design a system in which noise, attenuation, and spectral distortion do not prevent recovery of the original data.

Digital Signaling Concepts

Digital data being carried by a digital communication channel is already in correct format, so no conversion is necessary. Since there is no carrier present on the channel, there may be no way to detect a string of bits at the receiving end of the channel for some signals. The signal in Figure S3.11, for example, consists of a string of twelve zeros, but there's no way to tell. A "0" is represented by a value of 0 volts, and the state of the line when no signal is present is also 0 volts. Obviously, there is no way to determine the presence of this signal.

This example shows one difficulty in coordinating digital data that is transmitted from one system to another. One obvious way to solve this problem is to use a different value for the "0" bit, say, −5 volts. This solution helps somewhat, but we still can't tell one bit from another in the data stream. Furthermore, with this approach, the channel is carrying three different values rather than two, which increases the channel's susceptibility to noise.

As another example, consider a related problem, a steady stream of bits across a communication channel from one computer to another. Suppose that each group of 8 bits forms a byte. If the stream is continuous, how does the receiving computer know how to group the bits into bytes?

FIGURE S3.10

A Realistic Channel Spectrum

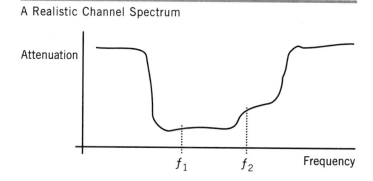

FIGURE S3.11

A Problematic Digital Signal

Some method of synchronizing digital signals between the sending computer and the receiving computer is always necessary, to be able to identify the position of each bit successfully at the receiver. The basic problem is that the sending computer may opt to transmit data at any time, and the receiving computer has no way of knowing when data will actually be sent. The difficulty of synchronization is compounded by likely slight differences in timing in each system, so that the receiver may sample the data at a slightly different rate. If the sequence of bits is long, the receiver may ultimately sample the wrong bit, creating an error. Figure S3.12 illustrates this situation. In this illustration the timing difference is somewhat exaggerated, for clarity.

There are a number of different ways of synchronizing the two systems. One solution is to convert the data into a signaling method that provides, say, a $0 \rightarrow 1$ transition whenever two consecutive bits are the same, and a $1 \rightarrow 0$ transition whenever they are different. This technique guarantees at least one transition per bit of data sent through the channel. The transitions can be used for synchronization.

Still another approach provides clear start and stop signals for the data and keeps the number of bits of data in a transmission short, usually a single byte. This method resynchronizes the timing between the transmitter and receiver for each byte of data, so that the receiver knows exactly when each bit is expected to occur. This approach is common with low-speed modems, for small amounts of data. It is somewhat inefficient, because two extra bits (the start and stop signals) must be sent for each byte of data. This technique is called **asynchronous transmission.**

An alternate approach is to send some sort of data signal continuously between the sender and receiver. This is called **synchronous transmission.** It is used by high-speed modems and in many other point-to-point methods. When there is no actual data available to send, the sending system simply sends a unique predetermined combination of bits over and over again. Thus, there is always a signal to be used for timing synchronization, and the unique pattern can be used to determine the starting point of actual data.

Digital signals can also be used to represent analog waveforms. We have already mentioned the compact disk as an example. Other examples include the digital signals that represent video in a direct satellite TV system and the digitization of sound that can be used to store telephone voice mail in a computer.

FIGURE S3.12

Reception Errors Resulting from Timing Mismatch Between Sending and Receiving Computers

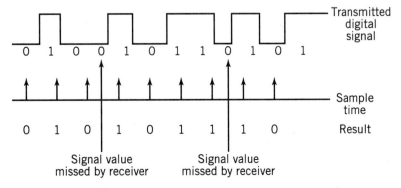

One way of converting analog data into digital form is shown in Figure S3.13. This method is called **pulse code modulation.** There are three steps in the process. In step 1, the analog waveform is sampled at regular time interval, as shown in Figure S3.13a. In Figure S3.13b the maximum possible amplitude of the waveform is divided into intervals corresponding to a range of binary numbers. This example uses 256 levels, which will result in 8 bits per sample. The sampled values are each converted into their corresponding number value. Incidentally, the information lost in converting data from analog to digital can be seen in this step: it consists of the difference between the actual value of the sample and the value corresponding to the nearest available number. Finally, in Figure S3.13c, the number is reduced to its binary equivalent. The device that performs this conversion is called an **A-to-D converter.**

FIGURE S3.13

The A-to-D Conversion Process

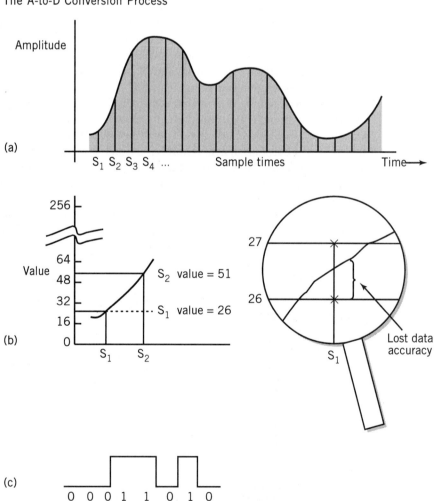

Digital signals are susceptible to noise, attenuation, and distortion, just as analog signals are. However, it is only necessary to distinguish between two levels, so much more distortion and noise in the channel can be tolerated. It is also possible to recreate the original signal at intervals along the channel, since the original shape is limited to ones and zeros. **Repeaters** are used for this purpose. Repeaters make it possible to transmit digital signals over long distances. Error correction techniques can also be used to repair data. Error correction can be particularly effective in the presence of bursts of noise.

Digital signals can also be multiplexed to allow different signals to share a channel. **Time division multiplexing (TDM)** is normally employed for this purpose. Figure S3.14 illustrates a time division multiplexer being used to share a communication channel among three digital signals. We've used the idea of a rotary switch to illustrate the operation of the multiplexer, although the switch is actually electronic. Each signal is sampled in turn, at a rate high enough to assure that no data is lost. The data is combined and transmitted over the channel. At the other end of the channel the process is reversed. Each sample is sent to its respective destination.

The bandwidth of a channel is also important for digital transmission. Remember that even digital signals can be represented as a sum of sine waves of different frequency. The higher the data rate, the higher the frequencies of the sine waves that make up the signal. Thus, a channel of wider bandwidth can carry data at a higher data rate, effectively increasing the data capacity of the channel.

Modems and Codecs

Home-to-service-provider network connections commonly rely on telephone or cable service to provide connectivity. **Modems (mo**dulator/**dem**odulators) convert the digital signals from the computer to analog signals for transmission over the phone line and vice versa. The devices providing **digital subscriber line (DSL)** service over the phone line and digital cable service are also called modems, but are actually **codecs (co**der/**dec**oders), which convert between DSL or cable service formats and Ethernet. Ethernet is used for the actual connection between the codec and the computer because Ethernet capability is generally provided on modern PCs. The signals on both sides of the codec are digital.

FIGURE S3.14

Time Division Multiplexing

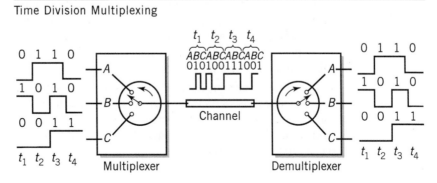

Speeds of 1 Mbps and more are possible with DSL and cable services. Modems are subject to traditional telephone line bandwidth limits. On a standard voice-grade phone line it is possible to transmit 2400 pieces of data per second, called the **baud rate.**

Combinations of ASK, FSK, and PSK are used to extend modem capability to 28.8 Kbps by embedding twelve values in each piece of data. Use of a wider bandwidth at the telephone switching office permits downloads at 56 Kbps.

S3.3 TRANSMISSION MEDIA AND CORRELATED SIGNALING METHODS

A transmission medium is defined as the means used to carry the signal being transmitted from one location to another. Data may be transmitted using electrical signals on wires, with optical signals on fiber optic cable, or without wires, using radio waves or, less commonly, light or sound. A transmission medium is characterized by its physical properties, by the signaling method(s) that it supports, by its **bandwidth,** and by its sensitivity to outside interference, or **noise.**

Transmission media that confine the signal physically to a cable of some kind are called **guided media.** Media that broadcast the signal openly using radio waves, light, or sound are called **unguided media.** Unguided media do not confine the signal to a particular area, but the signal may be focused in a particular direction.

You have already seen that the bandwidth and noise affect the capability of a channel to transmit data. Although the effect is more obvious with analog signaling, the same is true for both analog and digital signaling. Communication theory shows that the data capacity of a channel increases as the bandwidth of the channel increases. Noise in a channel is measured relative to the size of the signal. The measurement is called the **signal-to-noise ratio.** As you would expect, a higher signal-to-noise ratio for a given bandwidth increases the data capacity of a channel.

Consider the characteristics and general capabilities of each media type in turn:

- Electrically based media require a complete **circuit** consisting of two wires, one to carry the signal, the other as a return. This is perhaps most familiar to you from the electrical wiring in your house. (Some electrical wiring uses a third wire, which is connected to the ground to protect you from shocks, but the third wire is not actually part of the circuit.)

  Electrically based media are often referred to as *wired* media, or just *wire.* Wire carries the signals in the form of changing electrical voltage or current. Analog or digital signaling methods may be used. Wired media are the natural choices in many instances because the signals to be transmitted are already in electrical form and will be used in electrical form at the receiving end, so no conversions are necessary. Wire is inexpensive and easy to use. Wire channels are easily interconnected to extend a channel, to form networks, and to pass signals from one channel to another.

  The most common electrical transmission medium is coaxial cable. **Coaxial cable** consists of a wire surrounded by insulation. The second "wire" consists of a copper shield that surrounds the insulation. The shield acts as a signal return, but also prevents external noise signals from interfering with the signal carried by the inner wire.

Coaxial cable is capable of high bandwidths. It can be used for high-speed transmission of digital signals, at rates of up to 100 million bps, or even more. It can also carry wide-bandwidth analog signals. The cable used to carry cable TV is coaxial cable. Analog cable TV uses frequency-division multiplexing to carry dozens of channels of television at 6 MHz of bandwidth per channel. Coaxial cable bandwidths in excess of 500 MHz are possible. Similarly, the cable can also be used to carry a large number of data compressed time-division multiplexed digital TV signals.

A simpler wire medium, called **twisted pair,** is used with telephones and some networks. Twisted pair consists of two wires twisted together. This medium is not quite as effective a noise barrier as coaxial cable, but it is sufficient for shorter distances and slower signals. Groups of twisted pairs are frequently **bundled** together in a larger cable. Twisted pair wiring is far more susceptible to noise than coaxial cable.

■ Fiber optic cables carry signals in the form of light. Optical signals are produced by using the electrical data signal to turn a light on and off very rapidly. A laser or light-emitting diode is used as the light source. It is not possible to use a conventional light bulb, because a light bulb cannot be switched on and off rapidly enough. An optical detector at the other end of the cable converts the light signal back to electrical form. The cable itself consists of one or more strands of glass fiber specially designed to carry waves of light. Each strand is thinner than a human hair and may be tens or hundreds of miles long. The bundle of fibers is surrounded by a plastic sheath, called cladding, to protect the fibers. Fiber optic cables are often grouped together in bundles, which are further protected by an additional tough plastic jacket. Light is confined to the fibers, and attenuation is very low. Since light is an electromagnetic wave, turning a light on and off is technically a form of ASK. Most users tend to think of fiber optic transmission as a digital signaling method, for practical purposes. Since light waves are of such high frequency, fiber optic cable provides an extremely wide bandwidth. A single fiber can carry information at rates of hundreds of millions of bits per second. Fiber optic cable is nearly invulnerable to most forms of noise, since the signal is optical, not electrical.

The major shortcoming of fiber optic cable is that it is difficult to use. Signals must be converted from electrical form and back. It is difficult to tap into a fiber optic cable. While this provides security, it also makes it difficult to use fiber optic cable for any application that requires multipoint connections. Nonetheless, its huge data-carrying capacity makes fiber optic technology highly desirable in many situations. Entire communities are being "rewired" with fiber optic cables to provide improved communication capability for the future.

Electromagnetic wave transmissions do not require a specific physical medium, but simply propagate through space or through any material that is relatively transparent to the waves. The waves themselves are the medium. Electromagnetic waves having frequencies above 1 GHz but below the frequencies of light are generally referred to as microwaves. Microwaves are the most common form of wave transmission medium, although lower-frequency radio waves are also used. Microwaves are an unguided medium, but they can be tightly focused and used point-to-point between microwave antennas or between a microwave antenna and a satellite. Lower-frequency radio waves are less directional and harder to focus and require much larger antennas. (The size of an antenna is inversely proportional to its frequency.) They also provide less bandwidth. Conversely, higher-frequency waves are more susceptible to attenuation within the physical medium that the wave travels through. A heavy rainstorm can make microwave communication difficult, whereas low-frequency radio waves are sometimes used as a communication channel under water.

Microwave communication applications include large-scale Internet backbone channels, direct satellite-to-home television, and 802.11 ("WiFi") wireless networking.

It is usually necessary to convert between electrical and electromagnetic media formats. However, this technology is well developed and relatively inexpensive. One difficulty with the use of radio waves is interference between different communications using the same carrier frequencies. Although the frequency spectrum seems large, it is heavily used in most areas of the spectrum where communication is practical. (Consider the number of times that you have picked up your neighbor's conversation on a cordless phone, for example.) Higher frequencies are somewhat more available because of the ability to focus the wave in a particular direction. The highest usable frequencies are, of course, light waves. There are wireless networks and direct computer-to computer channels that use infrared light as a medium.

SUMMARY AND REVIEW

Communication between loosely coupled computers consists of messages passed over a communication channel. A communication channel is characterized by the transmission medium; the signaling transmission method; the channel capacity or bandwidth; the direction(s) of message flow; and the noise, attenuation, and distortion factors. Realistically, a channel may be made up of several subchannels, each with its own characteristics. The overall channel is defined primarily by the characteristics measured and observed at its access points.

The signaling method may be either analog or digital depending on the medium, the requirements of the sender and receiver stations, and a number of other factors. There are three primary types of medium in use: wires, fiber optics, and electromagnetic radiation. Wires can pass analog and digital signals. Fiber optics use light signals. Electromagnetic radiation media include radio and microwaves and require analog waveforms. Wire and fiber optics are guided media; electromagnetic radiation is unguided.

It is possible to transform data between analog and digital signaling methods; however, there is a small amount of unavoidable data loss in the analog-to-digital transformation process. Digital signals (and some analog signals) are transformed into electromagnetic waves by the process of modulation. Modulation works by varying the amplitude, frequency, or phase of the sine wave that acts as a carrier for the signal carrier.

KEY CONCEPTS AND TERMS

A-to-D converter	demodulation	multiplexing
amplifier	detector	noise
amplitude	digital signal	period
amplitude modulation	digital subscriber line (DSL)	phase
amplitude shift keying	discrete signal	phase shift keying (PSK)
(ASK)	electromagnetic radiation	pulse code modulation
analog	electromagnetic wave	repeaters
asynchronous transmission	fiber optic	signal distortion
attenuation	filtering	signal-to-noise ratio
bandwidth	frequency	simplex
baud rate	frequency division	sine wave
broadcast	multiplexing (FDM)	spectrum
bundled twisted pair	frequency shift keying (FSK)	synchronous transmission
carriers	full-duplex	terminal controller
channel	guided medium	time division multiplexing
circuit	half-duplex	(TDM)
coaxial cable	medium	twisted pair
codec	modem	unguided media
communication channel	modulation	waveform

FOR FURTHER READING

Data communication is an important topic of current interest in the field of information technology. There are numerous excellent books on data communication technology, and new ones appear every day. Of the recent books, Stallings and Van Slyke [STAL01] and Fitzgerald and Dennis [FITZ01] explain the technology clearly at a level appropriate for students of IT. Other books that are good include Stamper [STAM99] and Halsall [HALS96]. For more technical depth, Stallings [STAL00] is recommended.

EXERCISES

S3.1   Draw a pair of sine waves that are 45° out of phase.

S3.2   Consider a message that is made up of a sequence of bits as follows:

> 0111001011010110...

Suppose that we transmit this message using a combination of FSK and ASK. Draw waveforms that would represent each pair of bits, then use your representations to draw a complete waveform that represents the entire message.

S3.3   On a sheet of graph paper, draw an FSK waveform that represents the following waveform. The carrier frequency of a 0 is 1000 Hz, and that of a 1 is 2000 Hz. The data rate is 500 bps.

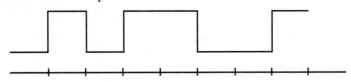

S3.4 Suppose you own a widespread chain of turkey tartare and sushi fast-food joints. Your stores are scattered all over the mainland United States and Canada. There are also a few stores in Western Europe. The computers in each store must communicate with the central operation in Texas on a regular basis, but not with each other. Describe a technology (medium and signaling method) that would be suited to this application.

S3.5 Many phone companies are replacing the wire in their phone systems with fiber optic cable. What do they expect to gain from doing so?

S3.6 The governments of Freedonia and Sylvania need to set up data communications to prevent the possibility of war. Discuss the security implications of fiber optic versus coaxial wire versus satellite as a means of communication.

S3.7 In recent years, much of the storage and communication of data has been in digital form, even if the source data is actually analog. Even television is being transmitted digitally. What benefits and advantages are gained by using digital storage and signaling?

S3.8 Consider a communication system that converts a digital signal to analog form for transmission, then recovers the digital signal at the receiving end. Another system starts with an analog signal, which it then converts to digital form for transmission, and recovers the analog signal at the receiving end. Both systems require both A-to-D and D-to-A conversion, yet one system is considered more reliable than the other. Which one? Why? Compare the A-to-D-to-A communication system with one that is entirely analog. What are the important factors affecting the performance of each system?

S3.9 Discuss the trade-offs between coaxial wire and fiber optics in a network made up of fifty computer stations all located within 1000 feet of each other.

S3.10 What effect does time division multiplexing have on the bandwidth requirements of a channel?

S3.11 Describe the advantages that repeaters have over amplifiers.

S3.12 Discuss the trade-offs between fiber optic and satellite communication in terms of costs, signal capacity, signaling method, interference, likelihood of failure and repair issues, multipoint capability, reconfiguration capability, and noise.

S3.13 What effect would you expect a wider bandwidth to have on the noise in a channel?

S3.14 A waveform travels in space at a rate of approximately 300 million meters per second. The *wavelength* of a sine wave is the actual distance in space that is used by one sine wave as it travels. What is the wavelength of a 100-MHz sine wave? What is the wavelength of a 500-MHz sine wave? Antennas to send and receive electromagnetic waves are often sized to be one-half of the wavelength for the particular wave being used. Compare your previous calculations to the size of VHF and UHF television antennas. How large would a 1/2 wavelength antenna have to be to transmit a 60-Hz wave?

S3.15 **a.** The *Doppler effect* is the varying frequency of the sound made by a train whistle as the train approaches and then moves away from you. The Doppler effect is also used to measure the speed of stars in space relative to the earth. Explain this effect on the basis of what you know about the relationship of wavelength (see Exercise S3.14), speed of light or sound, and frequency.

b. On a cold day, the speed of sound decreases. What effect would that have on the sound of the train whistle?

S3.16 a. A simple TV cable converter converts the TV signal of a channel on the cable to channel 3 for reception on the TV set. A clever viewer notices that she can pick up the adjacent channel that is normally blacked out by tuning her TV set to channel 4. What does this tell you about the way channels are carried on the cable?

b. The converter on a direct broadcast satellite also converts TV signals to channel 3 for reception. However, changing the TV set to channel 4 does not result in reception of the adjacent channel. Why not? How are the different TV signals carried on the channel?

S3.17 As indicated in the chapter text, any wave can be represented as a sum of sine waves of various frequencies, amplitudes, and phases. This problem explores the effects of channel bandwidth, shape of the spectrum, and phase distortion on the shape of a waveform.

A square wave is made up of sine waves according to the following equation:

$$S=\sin\ (2\pi ft) + \tfrac{1}{3} \sin\ (3 \times 2\pi ft) + \tfrac{1}{5} \sin\ (5 \times 2\pi ft) + \ldots$$

It is difficult to plot sine waves with any accuracy. Instead, we will use a triangular waveform shape as an approximation for the sine wave.

a. On a sheet of graph paper, carefully construct a triangular wave that starts at 0, rises to a maximum value of 15, falls to a minimum value of −15, then returns to 0. Your waveform should extend over 15 units on the time scale. Now construct a second triangle wave with an amplitude of 5 and a time span of 5. Your second waveform should start at 0. Add the amplitudes of the new waveform and the previous one to produce a new waveform which is the sum of the two. What do you observe?

b. Now create a third waveform of amplitude 3 and time span 3, and add it to the previous result. What do you observe? If the bandwidth is limited so that only the first two waves can pass through the channel, what is the effect on the waveform?

c. Next, start with a fresh sheet of graph paper. Draw the fundamental triangle wave. Draw the second triangle wave, but this time shift the phase 90°, so that the positive peak of the second wave coincides with the initial zero position of the fundamental. Add the two waveforms. What effect did the phase shift have on the summed waveform shape?

d. On another fresh sheet of graph paper, draw the fundamental waveform one more time. Draw the second waveform, this time with a height of 3 instead of 5. Also draw the third waveform with a height of 4 instead of 3. All waveforms start at 0, that is, with no phase shift distortion. Add the three waveforms. What effect did the altered spectrum shape have on the waveform?

e. Based on the original amplitudes of the waves and the modified amplitudes used in part (d), draw the spectrum of the channel.

BIBLIOGRAPHY

A

Abel, P. *IBM PC Assembly Language and Programming,* 5th ed. Englewood Cliffs, NJ: Prentice Hall, 2001.

Adobe Systems, Inc., Staff. *PostScript Language Program Design* ("The Green Book"). Reading, MA: Addison-Wesley, 1993.

——. *PostScript Language Reference Manual,* 3rd ed. ("The Red Book"). Reading, MA: Addison-Wesley, 1999.

——. *PostScript Language Tutorial and Cookbook* ("The Blue Book"). Reading, MA: Addison-Wesley, 1985.

Aho, A. V., R. Sethi, and J. D. Ullman. *Compilers, Principles, Techniques, and Tools.* Reading, MA: Addison-Wesley, 1986.

Aken, B. R., Jr. "Large Systems and Enterprise System Architecture," *IBM Systems Journal,* Vol. 28, no. 1 (1989), pp. 4–13.

Allison, B. R., and C. van Ingen. "Technical Description of the DEC 7000 and DEC 10000 AXP Family," *Digital Technical Journal,* Vol. 4, no. 4 (Special Issue 1992), pp. 100–110.

Alpert, D., and D. Avnon. "Architecture of the Pentium Microprocessor," *IEEE Micro,* Vol. 13, no. 3 (June 1993), pp. 11–21.

Anderson, D. *FireWire System Architecture: IEEE 1394,* 2nd Ed. Richardson, TX: Mindshare, Addison Wesley Longman, 1998.

Anderson, D. *Universal System Bus System Architecture,* 2nd Ed. Richardson, TX: Mindshare, Addison Wesley Longman, 2001.

Anderson, D., and T. Shanley. *PCI System Architecture,* 4th ed. PC Systems Architecture Series. Richardson, TX: Mindshare, Addison Wesley Longman, 1999.

Anderson, D., and T. Shanley. *Pentium Processor System Architecture,* PC System Architecture Series, Volume 5. Richardson, TX: Mindshare, 1995.

Atkinson, T. D., U. O. Gagliardi, G. Raviola, and H. S. Schwenk, Jr.," Modern Central Processor Architecture," *Proceedings of the IEEE,* Vol. 63, no. 6 (June 1975), pp. 863–870.

AT&T Bell Laboratories. *Unix System Readings and Applications,* Volumes I and II. Englewood Cliffs, NJ: Prentice Hall, 1987.

B

Bach, M. *The Design of the Unix Operating System.* Englewood Cliffs, NJ: PTR Prentice Hall, 1990.

Bacon, J. *Concurrent Systems, Operating Systems, Database and Distributed Systems: An Integrated Approach,* 2nd ed. Reading, MA: Addison Wesley Longman, 1998.

Bailes, G., and R. Riser. *The IBM 370, Computer Organization and Assembly Language.* St. Louis: West, 1987.

Bambara, R. J., and H. F. Cervone. *MVS and UNIX: A Survival Handbook for Users, Developers, and Managers.* New York: McGraw Hill, 1998.

Barfield, L. *The User Interface, Concepts and Design.* Reading, MA: Addison-Wesley, 1993.

Beck, M., H. Bohme, M. Dziadzka, U. Kunitz, R. Magnus, and D. Verworner. *Linux Kernel Programming,* 3rd ed. Reading. MA: Addison Wesley Longman, 2002.

Becker, M. C., M. S. Allen, C. R. Moore, J. S. Muhich, and D. P. Tuttle. "The PowerPC 601 Microprocessor," *IEEE Micro,* Vol. 13, no. 5 (October 1993), pp. 54–67.

——. *Beowulf Introduction & Overview.* http: //www. Beowulf. org/intro. html.

Biggerstaff, T. J. *Systems Software Tools.* Englewood Cliffs, NJ: Prentice Hall, 1986.

Borland International. *Turbo Assembler User's Guide.* Scotts Valley, CA: Borland, 1990.

Brewer, E. "Clusters: Multiply and Conquer," *Data Communications,* July, 1997.

Brey, B. *The Intel 32-Bit Microprocessors, 80386, 80486, and Pentium.* Englewood Cliffs, NJ: Prentice Hall, 1995.

——. *The Intel Microprocessors: Architecture, Programs and Interface.* New York: Macmillan, 1991.

Brockschmidt, K. *Inside OLE-2.* Redmond, WA: Microsoft Press, 1994.

Brookshear, J. G. *Computer Science, An Overview.* Menlo Park, CA: Benjamin/Cummings, 1985.

Brown, G. D. *System 390 JCL,* 4th ed. New York: John Wiley, 1998.

Brumbaugh, L. J. *VSAM, Architecture, Theory, and Applications.* New York: McGraw-Hill, 1993.

Brumm, P., and D. Brumm. *80386: A Programming and Design Handbook.* Blue Ridge Summit, PA: TAB Books, 1989.

Burgess, B., N. Ullah, P. Van Overen, and D. Ogden. "The PowerPC 603 Microprocessor," *Comm. of the ACM,* Vol. 37, no. 6 (June 1994), pp. 34–41.

Burke, P. H. "IBM ES/9000 Series: First Look. " In *Datapro,,* Computer System Series: Systems 3937. New York: McGraw-Hill, May 1993.

Buyya, R. *High Performance Cluster Computing: Architecture and Systems, Vol. 1.* Saddle River, NJ: Prentice Hall, 1999.

C

Calta, S. A., J. A. deVeer, E. Loizides, and R. N. Strangwayes. "Enterprise Systems Connection (ESCON)Architecture —System Overview," *IBM J. of Research and.*

Development, Vol. 36, no. 4 (July 1992), pp. 535–552.

Card, R., E. Dumas, and F. Mevel. *The Linux Kernel Book.* New York: John Wiley, 1998.

Caton, M. "High-End Printers Are Making Quality Output Affordable," *PC Week,* Vol. 11, no. 14 (April 11, 1994), p. 102.

Christian, K., and S. Richter. *The UNIX Operating System,* 3rd ed. New York: John Wiley, 1994.

Cluley, J. C. *Programming for Minicomputers.* Bristol, PA: Crane, Russak, 1978.

Cohen, A. M. *A Guide to Networking,* 2nd ed. Boston, MA: Boyd &Fraser, 1995.

Colwell, R. P., and R. L. Steck. "A 0.6 μm BiCMOS Processor with Dynamic Execution," *Digest of Technical Papers, IEEE International Solid State Circuits Conference,* Vol 38, February 1995, San Francisco, CA.

Comer, D. E. *Internetworking with TCP/IP,* Volume 1, *Principles, Protocols, and Architecture,* 4th ed. Englewood Cliffs, NJ: Prentice Hall, 2000.

——. "Special Issue on ATM Networking," *Comm. of the ACM,* Vol. 38, no. 2 (February 1995), pp. 28–109.

Cox, K., and D. Walker. *User Interface Design,* 2nd ed. New York: Simon &Schuster, 1993.

Cooper, D. *Standard Pascal User Reference Manual.* New York: W. W. Norton, 1983.

Cormier, R. L., R. J. Dugan, and R. R. Guyette. "System/370 Extended Architecture: The Channel Subsystem," *IBM J. of Research and Development,* Vol. 27, no. 3 (May 1983), pp. 206–217.

Cortada, J. W. *Historical Dictionary of Data Processing,* Volume 1, *Biographies,* Volume 2, *Organizations,* Volume 3, *Technology.* Westport, CT: Greenwood Press, 1987.

Cramer, W., and G. Kane. *68000 Microprocessor Handbook,* 2nd ed. New York: Osborne McGraw-Hill, 1986.

Crawford, J. "The i486 CPU: Executing Instructions in One Clock Cycle," *IEEE Micro,* Vol. 10, no. 1 (February 1990), pp. 27–36.

D

Davidson, J., and R. Vaughn. "The Effect of Instruction Set Complexity on Program Size and Performance," *Proceedings, Second International Conference on Architectural Support for Programming Languages and Operating Systems,* October 1987, Palo Alto, CA.

Davis, W., and T. M. Rajkumar. *Operating Systems, A Systematic View,* 5th ed. Redwood City, CA: Benjamin/Cummings, 2002.

Decker, R., and S. Hirshfield. *The Analytical Engine, An Introduction to Computer Science Using The Internet.* Boston: PWS, 1998.

Deitel, H. *Operating Systems,* 2nd ed. Reading, MA: Addison-Wesley, 1990.

Denning, P. J. "Virtual Memory," *Computer Surveys,* Vol. 2 (September 1970), pp. 153–189.

Dershem, H. L., and M. J. Jipping. *Programming Languages, Structures and Models.* Boston: PWS Publishing, 1993.

Diefendorff, K. "History of the PowerPC Architecture," *Comm. of the ACM,* Vol. 37, no. 6 (June 1994), pp. 28–33.

——, R. Oehler, and R. Hochsprung. "Evolution of the PowerPC Architecture," *IEEE Micro,* Vol. 14, no. 2 (April 1994), pp. 34–49.

Dijkstra, E. W. "The Structure of the T. H. E. Multiprogramming System," *Comm. of the ACM,* Vol. 11, no. 5 (May 1968), pp. 341–346.

Donovan, J. J. *Systems Programming.* New York: McGraw-Hill, 1972.

DuCharme, B. *The Operating Systems Handbook, UNIX, Open VMS, OS/400, VM, MVS.* New York: McGraw-Hill, 1994.

Duncan, R.," A Survey of Parallel Computer Architectures," *Computer,* Vol. 23, no. 2, 1990, pp. 5–16.

E

El-Ayat, K. A., and R. K. Agarwal. "The Intel 80386 —Architecture and Implementation," *IEEE Micro,* Vol. 5, no. 6 (December 1985), pp. 4–22.

Elliott, J. C., and M. W. Sachs. "The IBM Enterprise Systems Connection (ESCON) Architecture," *IBM J. of Research and Development,* Vol. 36, no. 4 (July 1992), pp. 577–592.

Ellzey, R. S. *Computer System Software, the Programmer/Machine Interface.* Chicago, IL: Science Research Associates, 1987.

Ethington, B. *Introducing Microsoft Windows 95.* Redmond, WA: Microsoft Press, 1995.

F

Feng, W., M. Warren, and E. Weigle. "The Bladed Beowulf: A Cost-Effective Alternative to Traditional Beowulfs". *Proceedings of the Int'l Conf. On Parallel Processing,* IEEE Press, 2002.

Fiedler, D. "The Unix Tutorial, Part 2: Unix as an Application-Programs Base," *Byte,* Vol. 8, no. 9 (September 1983), pp. 257–278.

———. "The Unix Tutorial, Part 1: An Introduction to Features and Facilities," *Byte*, Vol. 8, no. 8 (August 1983), pp. 188–219.

Fisher, C. N., and R. J. LeBlanc, Jr. *Crafting a Compiler.* Redwood City, CA: Benjamin/Cummings, 1988.

Fitzgerald, J., and A. Dennis. *Business Data Communications and Networking,* 7th ed. New York: John Wiley, 2001.

Flanagan, J. R., T. A. Gregg, and D. F. Casper. "The IBM Enterprise Systems Connection (ESCON)Channel —A Versatile Building Block," *IBM J. of Research and Development,* Vol. 36, no. 4 (July, 1992), pp. 617–632.

Flores, I. *The Logic of Computer Arithmetic.* Englewood Cliffs, NJ: Prentice Hall, 1963.

Flynn, I. M., and A. M. McHoes. *Understanding Operating Systems,* 3nd ed., Florence, KY: PWS Publishing, 2000.

Folk, M. J., and B. Zoellick. *File Structures,* 2nd ed. Reading, MA: Addison-Wesley, 1992.

Ford, W., and W. Topp. *MC68000 Assembly Language and Systems Programming.* Lexington, MA: D. C. Heath, 1988.

Fountain, D. "The Pentium: More RISC than CISC," *Byte,* Vol. 18, no. 10 (September 1993), p. 195.

Franklin, M. *Using the IBM PC: Organization and Assembly Language Programming.* New York: Holt, Rinehart and Winston, 1984.

G

Gagliardi, U. O. "Trends in Computing-System Architecture," *Proc. of the IEEE,* Vol. 63, no. 6 (June 1975), pp. 858–862.

Gentzsch, W. "DOT-COMing the Grid: Using Grids for Business," *Sun Microsystems,* WWW. sun. com.

Georgiou, C. J., T. A. Larsen, P. W. Oakhill, and B. Salimi. "The IBM Enterprise Systems Connection (ESCON)Director: A Dynamic Switch for 200 Mb/s Fiber Optic Links," *IBM J. of Research and Development,* Vol. 36, no. 4 (July 1992), pp. 593–616.

Gibson, D. H., and G. S. Rao. "Design of the IBM System/390 Computer Family for Numerically Intensive Applications: An Overview for Engineers and Scientists," *IBM J. of Research and Development,* Vol. 36, no. 4 (July 1992), pp. 695–712.

Gibson, G. A. *Computer Systems, Concepts and Design,* Englewood Cliffs, NJ: Prentice Hall, 1991.

Gifford, D., and A. Spector. "Case Study: IBM's System/360–370 Architecture," *Comm. of the ACM,* Vol. 30, no. 4 (April 1987), pp. 292–297ff.

Glass, G., and K. Ables. *UNIX for Programmers and Users, A Complete Guide,* 2nd ed. Englewood Cliffs, NJ: Prentice Hall, 1999.

Goldberg, D. "What Every Computer Scientist Should Know About Floating Point Arithmetic," *ACM Computing Surveys,* Vol. 23, no. 1 (March 1991), pp. 5–48.

Goodman, J., and K. Miller. *A Programmer's View of Computer Architecture, with Assembly Language Examples from the MIPS RISC Architecture.* Philadelphia: W. B. Saunders, 1993.

Graham, N. *Introduction to Computer Science,* 3rd ed. St. Louis: West, 1979.

Gries, D. *Compiler Construction for Digital Computers.* New York: John Wiley, 1971.

Grosch, H. R. J. "The Way It Was: 1957, A Vintage Year," *Datamation* (September 1977), pp. 75–78.

Grosshans, D. *Files Systems: Design and Implementation.* Englewood Cliffs, NJ: Prentice Hall, 1986.

Gustavson, D. "Computer Buses —A Tutorial," *IEEE Micro,* Vol. 4, no. 4 (August 1984), pp. 7–22.

H

Halfhill, T. R., "Inside the Mind of Microsoft," *Byte,* Vol. 20, no. 8 (August 1995), pp. 48–52.

——. "Intel 's P6," *Byte,* Vol. 20, no. 4 (April 1995), pp. 42–58.

——. "AMD vs. Superman," *Byte,* Vol. 19, no. 11 (November 1994), pp. 95–104.

——. "80X86 Wars," *Byte,* Vol. 19, no. 6 (June 1994), pp. 74–88.

Halsall, F. *Data Communications, Computer Networks, and OSI,* 4th ed. Reading, MA: Addison-Wesley, 1996.

Hatfield, D. J., and J. Gerald. "Program Restructuring for Virtual Memory," *IBM Systems Journal,* Vol. 10, no. 3 (1971), pp. 189ff.

Hayes, J. P. *Computer Architecture and Organization,* 2nd ed. New York: McGraw-Hill, 1988.

Heath, S. *PowerPC, A Practical Companion.* Oxford: Butterworth Heinemann, 1994.

Henle, R. A., and B. W. Kuvshinoff. *Desktop Computers.* Oxford: Oxford University Press, 1992.

Hennessy, J. L., and D. A. Patterson. *Computer Architecture, A Quantitative Approach,* 3nd ed. San Francisco: Morgan Kaufmann, 2002.

Hill, M. D. "A Case for Direct-Mapped Caches," *IEEE Computer,* Vol. 21, no. 12 (December 1988), pp. 25–40.

Honeycutt, J. *Inside Microsoft Windows 2000 Professional.* Indianapolis, IN: New Riders, 2000.

Hopkins, M. E. "A Perspective on the 801/Reduced Instruction Set Computer," *IBM Systems Journal,* Vol. 26, no. 1 (1987), pp. 107–121.

Horner, D. R. *Operating Systems, Concepts and Applications.* Glendale, IL: Scott Foresman, 1989.

Hoskins, J. *IBM System/390,* 3rd ed. New York: John Wiley, 1994.

Hoskins, J., and B. Frank. *Exploring Eserver zSeries and S/390 Servers,* 7th ed. Gulf Breeze, FL: Maximum Press, 2001.

Hummel, R. L. *PC Magazine Programmer's Technical Reference.* Emeryville, CA: Ziff-Davis Press, 1992.

Hunter, P. *Network Operating Systems, Making the Right Choice.* Reading, MA: Addison Wesley, 1995.

I

——. *IBM eServer zSeries 900 and z/OS Reference Guide,* Armonk, NY: IBM Corp., 2002.

——. *IBM System/370 Principles of Operation,* 9th ed. Armonk, NY: IBM Corp., 1981.

——. *IBM z/Architecture Principles of Operation,* Armonk, NY: IBM Corp., 2001.

IBM Corporation. *The PowerPC Architecture,* 2nd ed. San Francisco: Morgan Kaufmann, May 1994.

Intel Corporation. "Cache Subsystems." In *80386 Hardware Reference Manual.* Mt. Prospect, IL: Intel, 1987.

Intel Corporation. *IA-64 Architecture Manual, Vols. 1-4,* Mt. Prospect, IL, Intel, 2002.

Intel Corporation. *Microprocessors,* Volume II. Mt. Prospect, IL: Intel, 1991.

Irvine, K. R. *Assembly Language for the Intel-Based Computers* 4th Ed. Englewood Cliffs, NJ: Prentice Hall, 2000.

——. *ISA Bus Speci. cation and Application Notes.* Mt. Prospect, IL: Intel, January 30, 1990.

J

Jamsa, K. *DOS, the Complete Reference,* 4th ed. New York: Osborne McGraw-Hill, 1993.

Janossy, J. G., and S. Samuels. *CICS/ESA Primer.* New York: John Wiley, 1995.

Jensen, K., and N. Wirth. *Pascal User Manual and Report,* 4th Ed. Wien: Springer Verlag, 1991.

Johnson, R. H. *MVS, Concepts and Facilities.* New York: Intertext, McGraw-Hill, 1989.

Jones, O. *Introduction to the X Window System.* Englewood Cliffs, NJ: Prentice Hall, 2000.

K

Kane, G., and J. Heinrich. *MIPS RISC Architecture.* Englewood Cliffs, NJ: PTR Prentice Hall, 1992.

Kapps, C., and R. L. Stafford. *Vax Assembly Language and Architecture.* Boston, MA: Prindle, Weber, &Schmidt, 1985.

Katzan, H., Jr. *Operating Systems, A Pragmatic Approach.* New York: Van Nostrand Reinhold, 1973.

Kay, D. C., and J. R. Levine. *Graphics File Formats,* 2nd ed. New York: Windcrest/McGraw- Hill, 1995.

Kendall, G. W. "Inside the PCI Local Bus," *Byte,* Vol. 19, no. 2 (February 1994), pp. 177–180.

Kennedy, R. C. "The Elegant Kludge [Windows 95]," *Byte,* Vol. 20, no. 8 (August 1995), pp. 54–60.

Kim, B. G., and P. Wang. "ATM Network: Goals and Challenges," *Comm. of the ACM,* Vol. 38, no. 2, February 1995, pp. 39–44.

——. "Examining the Peer-to-Peer Connectivity and Multiple Network Support of Chicago," *Microsoft Systems Journal,* Vol. 9, no. 11 (November 1994), pp. 15–32.

King, G. M., D. M. Dias, and P. S. Yu. "Cluster Architectures and S/390 Parallel Sysplex Scalability," *IBM System J.,* Vol. 36, no. 2, 1997, pp. 221–241.

Kirk, D. S. *The MVS Primer.* Boston, MA: QED, 1992.

Knuth, D. *The Art of Computer Programming,* Volume 2, *Seminumerical Algorithms,* 3nd ed. Reading, MA: Addison-Wesley, 1997.

Korpela, E., et al. SETI@Home: Massively Distributed Computing for SETI, *www. computer. org/cise/articles/seti. htm,* 2001.

Kulisch, U., and W. Maranker. *Computer Arithmetic in Theory and Practice.* New York: Academic Press, 1981.

L

Lane, M. G., and J. D. Mooney. *A Practical Approach to Operating Systems.* Boston, MA: Boyd &Fraser, 1988.

Lehrer, T. *That Was the Year That Was* (recording). Originally released 1965, reissued on CD, Reprise 6179.

Levy, H. M., and R. H. Eckhouse, Jr. *Computer Programming and Architecture, The VAX 11.* Bedford, MA: Digital Press, 1980.

Lewin, M. H. *Logic Design and Computer Organization.* Reading, MA: Addison-Wesley, 1983.

Liaw, M. "Reading GIF Files," *Dr. Dobb's Journal,* Vol. 20, no. 2 (February 1995), pp. 56–60ff.

Lipschutz, S. *Essential Computer Mathematics,* Schaum 's Outline Series in Computers. New York: McGraw-Hill, 1982.

Liptay, J. S. "Design of the IBM Enterprises System/9000 High-End Processor," *IBM J. of Research and Development,* Vol. 36, no. 4 (July 1992), pp. 713–732.

Livadas, P. *File Structures: Theory and Practice.* Englewood Cliffs, NJ: Prentice Hall, 1990.

M

MacCabe, A. B. *Computer Systems, Architecture, Organization, and Programming.* Homewood, IL: Richard D. Irwin, 1993.

Mano, M. M. *Digital Design.* Englewood Cliffs, NJ: Prentice Hall, 1991.

Mansfield, N. *The Joy of X: An Overview of the X Window System.* Reading, MA: Addison- Wesley, 1994.

Marcellus, D. H. *Systems Programming for Small Computers.* Englewood Cliffs, NJ: Prentice Hall, 1984.

Marcus, A., N. Smilonich, and L. Thompson. *The Cross-GUI Handbook for Multiplatform User Interface Design.* Reading, MA: Addison-Wesley, 1995.

Markoff, J. "David Gelernter's Romance with Linda," *The New York Times,* Business Section, January 19, 1992, pp. 1ff.

Martin, J., and J. Leben. *TCP/IP Internetworking: Architecture, Administration, and Programming.* Englewood Cliffs, NJ: PTR Prentice Hall, 1994a.

——, K. K. Chapman, and J. Leben. *Local Area Networks,* 2nd ed. Englewood Cliffs, NJ: PTR Prentice Hall, 1994b.

Mayhew, D. J. *Principles and Guidelines in Software User Interface Design.* Englewood Cliffs, NJ: PTR Prentice Hall, 1992.

McDowell, S., and M. Seger. *USB Explained.* Englewood Cliffs, NJ: Prentice Hall, 1999.

McIlroy, M. D., E. N. Pinson, and B. A. Tague. "UNIX Time-Sharing System: Foreword," *Bell System Technical Journal,* Vol. 57, no. 6 (July–August 1978), pp. ix–xiv, reprinted in *UNIX System: Reading and Applications,* Volume 1. Englewood Cliffs, NJ: Prentice Hall, 1987.

Messmer, H. *The Indispensable PC Hardware Book,* 4th ed. Reading, MA: Addison Wesley Longman, 2001.

Methvin, D. "An Architecture Rede. ned," *PC Tech Journal,* Vol. 5, no. 8 (August 1987), pp. 58–70.

Meyer, J., and T. Downing *Java Virtual Machine,* Sebastopol, CA: O'Reilly &Assoc., 1997.

Microsoft Corporation. *Microsoft Windows 2000 Resource Kit.* Redmond WA: Microsoft Press, 2000.

Miller, M. A. *Internetworking: A Guide to Network Communications, LAN to LAN;LAN to WAN,* 2nd ed. New York, NY: M&T Books/MIS Press, 1995.

——. *The 68000 Family, Architecture Programming and Applications,* 2nd ed. Columbus, OH: Charles E. Merrill, 1992.

Miller, M. J. "Getting Ready for Windows 95," *PC Magazine,* Vol. 14, no. 9 (May 16, 1995), pp. 102–136.

Mollenhoff, C. R. *Atanasoff, Forgotten Father of the Computer.* Ames: Iowa State University Press, 1988.

Moore, C. R., and R. C. Stanphill. "The PowerPC Alliance," *Comm. of the ACM,* Vol. 37, no. 6 (June 1994), pp. 25–27.

Morgan, C. L. *Bluebook of Assembly Routines for the IBM PC &XT.* Corte Madera, CA: Waite Group, 1984.

Murray, J. D., and W. van Ryper. *Encyclopedia of Graphics File Formats,* 2nd ed. Sebastopol, CA: O'Reilly &Assoc., 1996.

N

Nich, J., C. Vaill, and H. Zhong. "Virtual-Time Round-Robins: An O(1) Proportional Share Scheduler," *Proc. Of the 2001 USENIX Annual Tech. Conf.* June, 2001.

Nick, J. M., B. B. Moore, J. -Y. Chung, and N. S. Bowen. "S/390 Cluster Technology: Parallel Sysplex," *IBM System J.,* Vol. 36, no. 2, 1997, pp. 172–201.

Nick, J. M., J. -Y. Chung, and N. S. Bowen, "Overview of IBM S/390 Parallel Sysplex—A Commercial Parallel Processing System," *Proc. of the IEEE International Parallel Processing Symposium,* Hawaii, 1996, pp. 488–495.

Niedermiller-Chaf. ns, D. *CNE Training Guide, Networking Technologies,* 3rd ed. Indianapolis, IN: New Riders, 1994.

Northrup, T. *Introducing Microsoft Windows 2000 Server.* Redmond, WA: Microsoft Press, 1999.

O

Oney, W. "Unconstrained Filenames on the PC!Introducing Chicago's Protected Mode Fat File System," *Microsoft Systems Journal,* Vol. 9, no. 8 (August 1994), pp. 13–24.

P

Paceley, L. "Intel P6 Technology." Mt. Prospect, IL: Intel, 1995.

Padega, A. "System /370 Extended Architecture: Design Considerations," *IBM J. of Research and Development,* Vol. 27, no. 3 (May 1983), pp. 193–202.

Panko, R. *Business Data Communications and Networking,* 2nd ed. Upper Saddle River NJ: Prentice Hall, 1999.

Parker, T. *Teach Yourself TCP/IP in 14 Days,* 2nd ed. Indianapolis, IN: Sams, 1996.

Patterson, D. A., and J. L. Hennessy. *Computer Organization and Design, The Hardware/Software Interface.* San Francisco: Morgan Kaufmann, 1994.

Patterson, D. A., and R. S. Piepho. "RISC Assessment: A High-Level Language Experiment," *Proc. 9th Annual Symp. on Comp. Arch,* Austin, 1982, pp. 3-8.

Patterson, D. A., and C. H. Sequin. "RISC I: A Reduced Instruction Set VLSI Computer," *Proc. 8th Annual Symp. on Comp. Arch,* Minneapolis, 1981, pp. 443–457.

——. *PCI to PCI Bridge Architecture Speci. cation,* Revision 1. 0, PCI Special Interest Group, April 5, 1994.

——. *PCI Local Bus Speci. cation,* Production Version, Version 2, PCI Special Interest Group, 1993.

——. *PC Magazine, Special Connectivity Issue,* Vol. 10, no. 15 (September 10, 1991).

Peek, J., T. O'Reilly, and M. Loukides. *UNIX Power Tools.* New York, NY: O'Reilly & Assoc. /Bantam, 1993.

Pfister, G. F., *In Search of Clusters,* 2nd ed. Saddle River, NJ: Prentice Hall 1998.

Pietrek, M. "Understanding Windows 95 Memory Management: Paging, Address Spaces, and Contexts," *Microsoft Systems Journal,* Vol. 10, no. 4 (April 1995), pp. 19–36.

——. "Stepping Up to 32 Bits: Chicago 's Process, Thread, and Memory Management," *Microsoft Systems Journal,* Vol. 9, no. 8 (August 1994), pp. 13–26.

Plambeck, K. E. *PowerPC Architecture.* Autin, TX: IBM, 1993.

——. *PowerPC 601, RISC Microprocessor User's Manual,* Item MPC601UM/AD, Revision 1. Phoenix, AZ : Motorola, 1993.

——. "Concepts of Enterprise Systems Architecture/370," *IBM Systems Journal,* Vol. 28, no. 1 (1989), pp. 39–57.

Pogue, D. *Mac OS X, The Missing Manual.* Sebastopol, CA: O'Reilly & Assoc., 2002.

Prasad, N. S., and J. Savit. *IBM Mainframes,* 2nd ed. New York: McGraw-Hill, 1994.

Preece, J., et al. *Human Computer Interaction.* Reading, MA: Addison-Wesley, 1994.

Proser, F. P., and D. E. Winkel. *The Art of Digital Design,* 2nd ed. Englewood Cliffs, NJ: Prentice Hall, 1987.

Prosise, J. "Under the Hood, Windows 95 and Its Competitors," *PC Magazine,* Vol. 14, no. 9 (May 16, 1995), pp. 139–157.

Q

Quercia, V., and T. O'Reilly. *X Windows System User's Guide,* Volume 3. Sebastopol, CA: O'Reilly &Assoc., 1993.

Quinlan, T. "Taligent Gives First PEEK to Users, ISVs," *InfoWorld,* Vol. 16, no. 23 (June 6, 1994), p. 1+.

R

Rains, A. L., and M. J. Palmer. *Local Area Networking with Novell Software,* 2nd ed. Danvers, MA: Boyd &Fraser, 1994.

Rao, G. S., T. A. Gregg, C. A. Price, C. L. Rao, and S. J. Repka. "IBM S/390 Parallel Enterprise Servers G3 and G4," *IBM J. of Research and Development,* Vol. 41, no. 4 &5, 1997, pp. 397–404.

Reiss, L., and J. Radin. *X Window Inside and Out.* New York: Osborne McGraw-Hill, 1992. Richter, J. *Advanced Windows,* 3rd ed. Redmond, WA: Microsoft Press, 1997.

Ridge, D., et al. "Beowulf: Harnessing the Power of Parallelism in a Pile of PCs,". *Proc. Of IEEE Aerospace,* 1997.

Ridge, P. M., D. M. Golden, I. Luk, and S. E. Sindorf. *Sound Blaster, The Of. cial Book,* 2nd ed. New York: Osborne McGraw-Hill, 1994.

Rimmer, S. *Bit Mapped Graphics,* 2nd ed. New York: Windcrest/McGraw-Hill, 1993.

Ritchie, D. M. "The Evolution of the UNIX Time-Sharing System," *AT&T Bell System Technical Journal,* Vol. 63, no. 8 (October 1984), pp. 1–17, reprinted in *UNIX System: Reading and Applications,* Volume II. Englewood Cliffs, NJ: Prentice Hall, 1987.

Rochester, J. B., and J. Gantz. *The Naked Computer: A Layperson 's Almanac of Computer Lore, Wizardry, Personalities, Memorabilia, World Records, Mindblowers, and Tomfoolery.* New York: William A. Morrow, 1983.

Rodrigues, D. E. "Architecture of the IBM Personal Computer" (term paper). Waltham, MA: Bentley College, 1984.

Rosch, W. *Hardware Bible,* 5th ed. Indianapolis, IN: Que, 2000.

Rosen, K. H., R. R. Rosinski, and J. M. Farber. *Unix System V Release 4: An Introduction for New and Experienced Users.* New York: Osborne McGraw-Hill, 1990.

Rosen, S. "Programming Systems and Languages, A Historical Survey," *Proc. of the Spring Joint Computer Conference,* Vol. 24, AFIPS, 1964, pp. 1–14.

Ryan, B. "Inside the Pentium," *Byte,* Vol. 18, no. 6 (May 1993), pp. 102–104.

——. "RISC Drives PowerPC," *Byte,* Vol. 18, no. 9 (August 1993), pp. 79–90.

S

Salomon, D. *Assemblers and Loaders.* Chichester, England: Ellis Horwood, 1992.

Samson, S. L. *MVS Performance Management: OS/390 Edition, SP Version 5.* New York: McGraw Hill 1997.

Sargent, M., III, and R. L. Shoemaker. *The Personal Computer from the Inside Out,* 3rd ed. Reading, MA: Addison-Wesley, 1995.

Scalzi, C. A., A. G. Ganek, and R. J. Schmalz. "Enterprise Systems Architecture/370: An Architecture for Multiple Virtual Space Access and Authorization," *IBM Systems Journal,* Vol. 28, no. 1 (1989), pp. 15–37.

Schulke, M. H., and L. J. Rose. "IBM ES/9000 Series," *Datapro,* Computer System Series: Systems 3938. New York: McGraw-Hill, January 1993.

Senturia, S., and B. Wedlock. *Electronic Circuits and Applications.* New York: John Wiley, 1975.

Shanley, T. *Pentium Pro and Pentium II,* 2nd ed. PC Systems Architecture Series. Richardson, TX: Mindshare, Addison Wesley Longman, 1998.

Shanley, T. *Power PC 601 System Architecture,* PC Systems Architecture Series, Volume 7. Richardson, TX: Mindshare, 1994.

Silberschatz, A., P. Galvin, and G. Gagne. *Operating System Concepts,* 6th ed. New York: John Wiley, 2001.

Smith, A. J. "Cache Memories," *Computing Surveys,* Vol. 14, no. 3 (September 1982), pp. 473–530.

Smith, R. *Learning Postscript, A Visual Approach.* Berkeley, CA: Peachpit Press, 1990.

Smith, R. M., and P. Yeh. "Integrated Cryptographic Facility of the Enterprise Systems Architecture/390: Design Considerations," *IBM J. of Research and Development,* Vol. 36, no. 4 (July 1992), pp. 683–694.

Sobell, M. G. *Unix System V, A Practical Guide,* 3rd ed. Redwood City, CA: Benjamin/Cummings, 1995.

Solomon, D. A. *Inside Windows NT,* 2nd ed. Redmond, WA: Microsoft Press, 1998.

Solomon, D. A. and M. Russinovich. *Inside Microsoft Windows 2000,* 3rd ed. Redmond, WA: Microsoft Press, 2000.

Soltis, F. G. and P. Conte, *Inside the AS/400,* 2nd ed. Loveland, CO: 29th Street Press, 1998.

Spaniol, O. *Computer Arithmetic.* New York: John Wiley, 1981.

Stallings, W. *Computer Organization and Architecture,* 6th ed. Indianapolis, IN: Macmillan, 2002.

——. *Operating Systems,* 4th ed. Indianapolis, IN: Macmillan, 2000.

——. *Data and Computer Communications,* 6th ed. Indianapolis, IN: Macmillan, 2000.

——. *Local and Metropolitan Networks,* 6th ed. Saddle River, NJ: Prentice Hall, 2000.

——, and R. Van Slyke. *Business Data Communications,* 4th ed. Saddle River, NJ: Prentice Hall, 2001.

Stamper, D. A. *Business Data Communications,* 5th ed. Redwood City, CA: Benjamin/Cummings, 1999.

Stoddard, S. D. *Principles of Assembler Language Programming for the IBM 370.* New York: McGraw-Hill, 1985.

Suko, R. W. "MVS, A History of IBM's Most Powerful and Reliable Operating System," unpublished document, IBM, Poughkeepsie, NY, April 26, 1993.

Sullivan, J. W., and S. W. Tyler, eds. *Intelligent User Interfaces.* New York, NY: ACM Press, 1991.

Swartzlander, E. E., ed. *Computer Arithmetic,* Volumes I and II. Piscataway, NJ: IEEE Computer Society Press, 1990.

——, ed. *Computer Design Development: Principal Papers.* Indianapolis, IN: Hayden, 1976.

T

Tabak, D. *Advanced Microprocessors,* 2nd ed. New York: McGraw-Hill, 1995.

Tanenbaum, A. S. *Distributed Operating Systems.* Englewood Cliffs, NJ: Prentice Hall, 1995.

——. *Modern Operating Systems.* Englewood Cliffs, NJ: Prentice Hall, 1992.

——. *Structured Computer Organization,* 4th ed. Englewood Cliffs, NJ: Prentice Hall, 1999.

——, and A. Woodhull. *Operating Systems, Design and Implementation,* 2nd ed. Englewood Cliffs, NJ: Prentice Hall, 1997.

Taylor, J., *DVD Demysti. ed,* New York: McGraw Hill, 1998.

Teufel, B. *Organization of Programming Languages.* Wien: Springer-Verlag, 1991.

Thompson, T. "Power PC Performs for Less," *Byte,* Vol. 18, no. 9 (August 1993), pp. 56–74.

——, and B. Ryan. "PowerPC 620 Soars," *Byte,* Vol. 19. no. 11 (November 1994), pp. 113– 120.

Thorne, M. *Computer Organization and Assembly Language Programming for IBM PCs and Compatibles,* 2nd ed. Redwood City, CA: Benjamin/Cummings, 1991.

——. "A Tour of the P6 Microacrchitecture, February 1995. " Mt. Prospect, IL: Intel, 1995.

Treu, S. *User Interface Design, A Structured Approach.* New York, NY: Plenum Press, 1994.

U

Ullman, J. D. *Fundamental Concepts of Programming Systems.* Reading, MA: Addison-Wesley, 1976.

Unicode Consortium, The. *The Unicode Standard, Version 3. 0.* Reading, MA: Addison-Wesley, 2000.

V

Vacca, J. R. "Taking the RISC out of Servers," *Computerworld,* Vol. 29, no. 25 (June 19, 1995), p. 99.

Vahalia, U. *Unix Internals: The New Frontier.* Englewood Cliffs, NJ: Prentice Hall, 1996.

Various authors. *X Window System,* set of volumes. Sebastopol, CA: O'Reilly &Assoc.

Vetter, R. J. "ATM Concepts, Architectures, and Protocols," *Comm. of the ACM,* Vol. 38, no. 2 (February 1995), pp. 30–38.

W

Wakerly, J. F. *Digital Design, Principles and Practices,* 3rd ed. Englewood Cliffs, NJ: Prentice Hall, 2000.

Warford, J. S. *Computer Systems.* Sudbury, MA: Jones and Bartlett, 1999.

Wayner, P. "SPARC Strikes Back," *Byte,* Vol. 19, no. 11 (November 1994), pp. 105–112.

Weiderhold, G. *File Organization for Data Base Design.* New York: McGraw-Hill, 1987.

Weizer, N. "A History of Operating Systems," *Datamation* (January 1961), pp. 118–126.

Wells, P. "The 80286 Microprocessor," *Byte,* Vol. 9, no. 11 (November 1984), pp. 231–241.

White, R. *How Computers Work.* 6th ed., Emeryville, CA: Que, 2001.

Wilkes, M. V. "The Best Way to Design an Automatic Calculating Machine," *Report of the Manchester University Inaugural Conference,* Manchester University Electrical Engineering Department, pp. 16–18, 1951, reprinted in [SWAR76, pp. 266–270].

Wray, W. C., and J. D. Green. ed. *Using Microprocessors and Microcomputers, the Motorola Family.* Englewood Cliffs, NJ: Prentice Hall Career and Technology, 1994.

Y

Yau, S. S. ed. "50 Years of Computing," *Computer,* Vol. 29, no. 10, 1996, pp. 24–111.

Young, J. L. *The Insider's Guide to Power PC Computing.* Indianapolis, IN: Que, 1994.

Z

Zaks, R., and A. Wolfe. *From Chips to Systems: An Introduction to Microcomputers.* Alameda, CA: Sybex, 1987.

PHOTO CREDITS

CHAPTER 1

Figure 1.9 and Figure 1.11: Courtesy International Business Machines Corporation. Unauthorized use not permitted.

Figure 1.10: Courtesy Hewlett-Packard Company. Reprinted with permission.

Figure 1.13: Courtesy Sperry Univac, Division of Sperry Corporation.

CHAPTER 3

Figure 3.10 (left and right): Irv Englander.

Figure 3.12: Dreamworks/PhotoFest

CHAPTER 7

Figure 7.10: Courtesy Intel Corporation.

CHAPTER 10

Figure 10.4: Courtesy Western Digital Corporation.

SUPPLEMENTARY CHAPTER 1

Figure S1.1 (left and right): Courtesy Motorola.

INDEX